GW00777351

A century remembered

Preface

Published by The Rural Heritage Society.

A catalogue record of this book is available from the British Library
ISBN 0-9542174-0-3

Publication edited by John Leonhardt,

managed by Anne Wooster

designed and produced by Peter Grainger

and printed by Pardy & Sons (Printers) Ltd Parkside, Ringwood, Hampshire, BH24 3SF

It was in the spring of 1999 that John Leonhardt first suggested that the Rural Heritage Society's contribution to the Millennium should be a retrospective book about life in the village over the last century, to capture people's memories before they were lost.

John presented his ideas to members of the society at the Annual General Meeting in 1999 and since then the project has snowballed as the result of the enthusiasm of contributors and the editorial and production teams. In fact, so enthusiastic has been the response that the book has more than doubled in size from that originally planned.

It has been a privilege to have been associated with the publication and those who have contributed to its success. These include the members of the committee of the Rural Heritage Society from the beginning of the project: Gerald Humphreys, Mary Fletcher, Shiamala Comer and John Palmer, and, in particular, those who have given up so much of their own time to bringing the project to fruition: John Leonhardt as Editor, Anne Wooster as Project Manager, Lyn Hyde as Assistant to the Editor and Peter Grainger as Designer and Producer. There has also been a team of other helpers whom we thank for proof reading and other tasks: Antony Hopkins, Hilary Catchpole, Michael Turner, Auriel Fielder, Nick Crispin, Jan Maclarty, Francis Cory-Wright, Margaret Crawford, Martin and Karen Hatt, Rus Westmacott, Dan Graham, Mike Walsham, Rosemary Williams and Nicola Darragh-Haddow.

And, of course, a special thank you to all the contributors, from those who have set out to research a subject in detail and write a literary article, to those who have passed on an odd remark or answered an apparently trivial question which has led to an added detail or correction, and those who have kindly lent us valuable pictures and documents. We hope their names have all been printed in their proper places in the book. The reader will see that they are far too numerous to list here, but without their entirely voluntary contributions this book could never have been written.

We also gratefully acknowledge the generous grants from the Heritage Lottery Fund and from Dacorum Borough Council's Millennium Fund without which this book could never have been printed.

We also acknowledge the support of Ashridge Management College in helping us to achieve a higher level of sales than we might otherwise have expected.

George Godar

Chairman
Rural Heritage Society of Little Gaddesden, Ringshall, Hudnall and Ashridge.

Cover pictures:

Main picture - William Bunting (Shep) and Border Leicesters from Home Farm on Pulridge Hill, circa 1950.

Inset - Sheep at Church Farm, 1999

A century remembered

THE VILLAGE MILLENNIUM BOOK
FOR LITTLE GADDESDEN, RINGSHALL, HUDNALL AND ASHRIDGE

Edited by
JOHN LEONHARDT

A Rural Heritage Society Publication

About this book

This book has come into being because people were invited to write it and because so many of them wanted to do so.

Its aims were ambitious from the start: to record every aspect of the village for the last hundred years and to give a complete account of the village in 1999. It had to be put together in a very short time, however, so that it could be published as a "Millenium book", and this was the first limitation. The comments which follow are intended to clarify things for the reader and for anyone who in the future might look at it as a book of reference.

As a work of history of our village, this book is only intended to add to and update the books already written on the subject, not to repeat or replace what they contain. At least five good books on the history of Little Gaddesden or Ashridge or both were written in the twentieth century. I recommend them to fill in the gaps in this book, in particular Canon Howard Senar's book "Little Gaddesden and Ashridge", published in 1983, much of whose material I have deliberately omitted because he has covered it. I only regret that some of these books are difficult to obtain. They are listed in the bibliography and some are referred to in the text.

THE PERIOD covered in this book begins a little before 1899 for reasons which will be noticed by the reader. It ends at the end of 1999, apart from some subsequent Millennium celebrations and a few late photographs.

THE AREA covered is the Civil Parish of Little Gaddesden, which came into being in 1894 when Hudnall, Ringshall and a large area of Ashridge were added to the old Little Gaddesden Parish. I have also overstepped this boundary here and there where neighbours have strong links with us.

THE EVENTS covered are concentrated in the village itself. The history of the wider world can easily be read elsewhere, and is only admitted where its relation to the village is essential to the story.

THE TOPICS covered are as many as I could think up and find people to tell about. Inevitably some are sketchy and others are very thorough.

THE PEOPLE covered will no doubt be the most contentious issue about the book. As part of the second aim, I have tried to mention at least the name of every adult living here in December 1999, and have indeed invited every such person (by hand-delivered note) to write something if they wished, though not promising to print every word submitted. Naturally some people do not want to write. The book could not contain the name of every person who lived here in the last hundred years and still have room for everything else.

The omissions which may upset people will be those of distinguished achievements or memorable lives in the village. The omissions which I know about are generally to be found in Canon Senar's book, so I am happy that they are on record there. Those that I do not know about can partly be blamed on the people who didn't write to me about them, but much is on record in those other village archives: the Gaddesden Diary, the Parish News and the Rural Heritage Society Newsletter. To see these lined up on a shelf is to realise that not everything could be repeated in this volume

THE ACCURACY can be judged on the kind of article that has been written. Some, such as the main items on the church, the school and Ashridge college have been carefully researched. Others have just been submitted straight from memory. I have cross-checked many of the dates and names against each other, and corrected such anomalies as I could find. Some dates have had to be left rather vague, though could probably have been improved by further research. In matters of property, businesses and farms there is always the danger of mistaking owners, tenants, managers, assistants and people using each other's resources by private agreements. I have sometimes used ambiguous phrases to avoid these traps.

CAN ERRORS AND OMISSIONS BE CORRECTED?

Yes, but probably not in a second edition. Articles which improve on any of the themes in this book will almost certainly be welcomed in one of the village journals mentioned above, whichever is most appropriate.

John Leonhardt - Editor, Spring 2000

Contents

1

The geography of Little Gaddesden

If the Chiltern Hills are taken to start at the Goring Gap where the Thames separates them from the Berkshire downs, and, end at Luton where the Lea Valley separates them from the East Anglian Heights, that is about 40 miles from south-west to north-east, then Little Gaddesden is about three-quarters of the way along.

There are two wind-gaps through the scarp at this point: the Tring Gap and the Dagnall Gap, their wide mouths leaving a narrow spur of scarp between them ending at Ivinghoe Beacon. Little Gaddesden lies on the plateau just south-east of this spur, between 2 miles and 5 miles from the beacon. Great Gaddesden lies further southeast, with its old village by the River Gade and most of its land on the plateau on the opposite side of the river. Little Gaddesden, as a Civil Parish, is now about two thirds the size of Great Gaddesden. Before 1885 (when Hudnall became the first piece to be transferred from Buckinghamshire), Little Gaddesden was only half it's present size. It was only joined to the rest of Hertfordshire through Studham, which has since been transferred to Bedfordshire.

The old Little Gaddesden parish contained the head of one dry valley, Nobody's Bottom, and the shallow combe off the Gade Valley at Lamsey which marks the south side of the hoo, or spur, where Hoo Wood is. The combe on the north side of the hoo crosses the parish boundary.

The enlarged parish brings in the dry valleys of Golden Valley and its branch, Witchcraft Bottom, two more Gade Valley combes at Hudnall, and one side of the top end of the dry valley which leads to Frithsden.

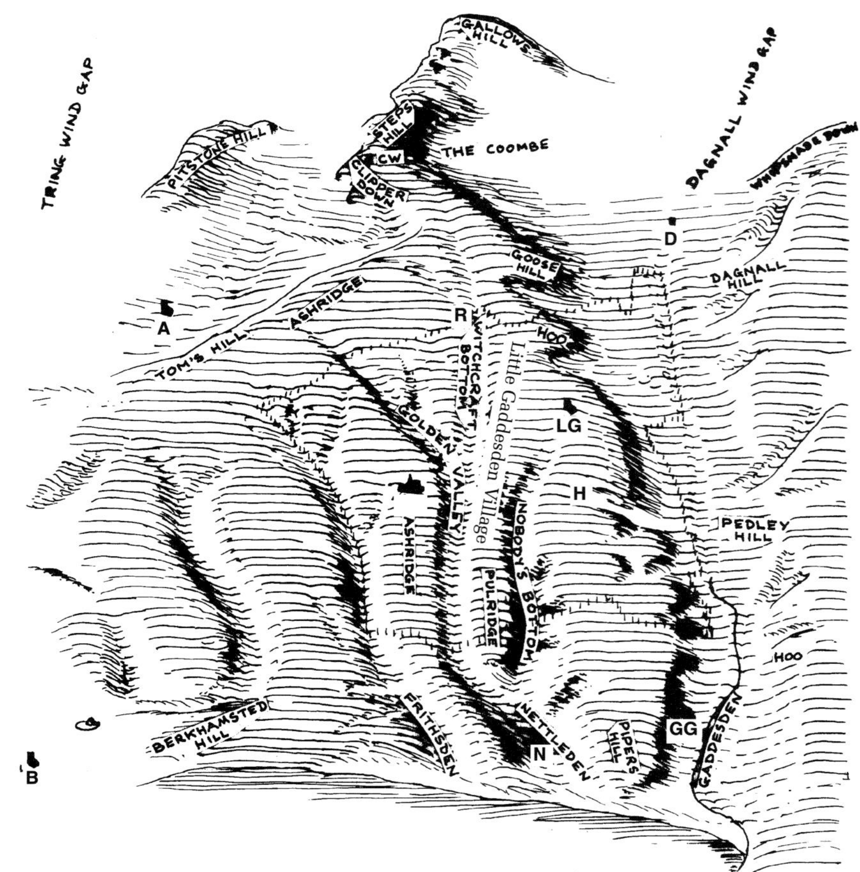

The land form around Little Gaddesden - a perspective view looking north-west.

Names indicating geomorphology have been added.

-DEN indicates a valley, so Gaddesden is marked appropriately in the Gade Valley. Little Gaddesden, perversely, is on the plateau. The Parish boundary (modern version) is picked out with an imaginary fence. Ashridge is more than a single ridge.

Other locations:

A - Aldbury Church
AH - Ashridge House
B - Berkhamsted Church
BC - Berkhamsted Castle
CW - Crawley Wood (the highest point shown)
D - Dagnall Church
GG - Great Gaddesden Church
H - Hudnall Hamlet
LG - Little Gaddesden Church
N - Nettleden Church
R - Ringshall Hamlet

The altitude of the parish is from 116 metres (381 feet) between Fourways Corner and Lower Gade Farm on the Leighton Buzzard Road, to 211 metres (692 feet) at The Bungalow, behind no.35 Ringshall Cottages. The Ringshall Reservoir is on the 215 metre contour, so it could provide sufficient water pressure for the whole village. The main sewage works, on the other hand, is only on the 145 metre contour, and cut off from certain areas, such as Hudnall, by intervening valleys, so cannot provide main drainage for every house.

The surface geology is Clay-with-Flints on the plateau and the uppermost parts of the slopes, thinning out to expose Upper Chalk, then a thin band of Chalk Rock, then Middle Chalk as you descend the valleys. Upper Chalk is much more flinty than Middle Chalk. Chalk Rock exposures form banks which are favoured by badgers. The solid geology is chalk under everything, down to well below the bottom of the Gade Valley, so over 100 metres thick, and it contains the water which can be reached by our deep wells and boreholes.

The soil is Brown Earth on the clay and Brown Calcareous Soil where the chalk is near the surface. The pH of the Brown Earth tends to be 4 to 5 in woods and 5 to 6 in grassland. That of the Brown Calcareous Soil is 6 to 7.

The agricultural classification of the land is all Grade 3. On a scale of 1 to 5, this is average, allowing mixed farming with livestock and field crops, but mostly heavy to work because of the clay and stones, which also make it difficult for root crops. Nevertheless, down in Dagnall there is an area which has long been very successful for potatoes.

People starting up gardens on new sites find they have to work hard to improve the soil for horticulture, but the old cottage gardens have often got a deep loam, the result of centuries of manuring and diligent toil.

Politically, the old Little Gaddesden has been in Hertfordshire for as far back as we can trace. The new area includes bits of old Buckinghamshire, including both Ringshall and Hudnall. The present parish borders onto both Bucks and Bedfordshire. The triple point where Herts, Bucks and Beds meet is on the Leighton Buzzard Road half way between Dagnall roundabout and Mile Barn, 290 yards south of the entrance to Well Farm. Little Gaddesden is currently in the Borough of Dacorum, which includes Hemel Hempstead, Berkhamsted and Tring.

Ecclesiastically, the civil parish contains one complete church parish, Little Gaddesden, and parts of three others, Studham, Nettleden-with-Potten End, and Great Berkhamsted. It used to contain part of Edlesborough as well, until Hudnall was transferred from that parish to Little Gaddesden in 1973, 79 years after it had been transferred to the civil parish. (See the map in the colour section).

2

A CENTURY REMEMBERED

A tour of the village on Saturday 12th August 1899

by the editor with help especially from George Stanbridge's diary and old maps

A HOT DAY WITH A NICE BREEZE.

Leaving Nettleden by pony and trap and trotting towards Pulridge Hill, with the last cottage behind you, the view on the right is chequered by small fields, hedges and tree belts, not the huge open field of a hundred years later. Here and there may be seen hay or corn ricks. At the foot of the hill where the road turns sharp right there is no smallholding, but a path leading to Peacock Lodge, later to be known as Nettleden Lodge.

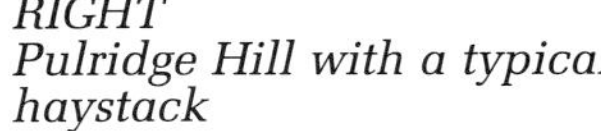

RIGHT
Pulridge Hill with a typical haystack

BELOW
Covetous Corner in 1999

Turning up the hill you enter an avenue of Beech trees which will still be much loved in 1963 when nearly all will be felled. Climbing slowly you reach Pulridge Wood which is continuous on both sides and contains no buildings. The left hand side has some old chalk pits and a pond and pheasant pens in it. Emerging from the wood onto the ridge, the meadow on the left has no houses in it.

On the right there are more fields divided by hedges, but perhaps you can see the Covetous Corner cottages on the far side. In about 70 years time the only hedge left will be the one at the roadside. Ahead on the left are some farm buildings called Cromer Farm containing steam-powered grinding mills. They will stand there many years yet before being replaced by a house, 'Ranch House', later to be known as 'Willow Wood'. This is followed by woodland on the left. A bit further a well-gravelled track joins you on the right, leading back behind you down into the fields and up the other side of the valley by a track called Birds Pightle to Covetous Corner. Continuing on the main road the woods on the left conceal the next houses which come into view round the bend. On the left is Cromer Wood Cottage. There is nothing in the woods you have just passed to suggest that one day they will be cleared to build Cromer Close and Ashridge Cottages.

The next building is Home Farm, on the right, a busy place whose long brick frontage incorporating four farmworkers cottages will still look much the same in a hundred years, though very different behind the facade. The first cottage is the lodge for the keeper of the gate opposite, which leads into Ashridge Park. Through the entrance in the middle of the row of cottages can be seen the farm house, barns, and other paraphernalia of farming. From Home Farm onwards the buildings of 1899 are very similar to what will be seen in 1999, though some will be rebuilt and some paddocks will be filled in.

Your drive will take you past Little Gaddesden House set well back from the road, where Lady Brownlow's brother, The Hon. Alfred Talbot, his wife Emily, and four children live. The future of the village will depend on them in ways they cannot yet foresee. There follows Robin Hood House (just a private house), and the numbered cottages from number 62 backwards.

There is a kerbed pavement here probably, as can be seen in a photograph of about this time. The principal roads are gravel, and seem to be well levelled in pictures. There is only light traffic, consisting of the occasional cart drawn by a pony or a couple of horses, some ridden horses, sometimes a bicycle, even a

Hudnall Corner and the house Kinghams Meadow with the Manor House in the distance early in the century

tandem, and just occasionally a steam traction engine. Petrol-engined vehicles have perhaps not yet been seen in the village. The speed limit is 14 miles per hour for all powered vehicles on all roads in town and country alike. In 1903 this will be raised to 20 mph. which will remain in force until 1930 when speed limits for cars in the village will be abolished until the 70 mph limit is introduced in the 1960s.

There is no Robin Hood Farm, but the house Kinghams Meadow stands on the corner of Hudnall Lane. If you turn right down Hudnall Lane you will find no houses until you get almost to Hudnall Common. In the dip in the road, Nursery Meadow on your left has turned green again since the hay cutting which finished a month ago. In a week's time there will be 24 heifers grazing there. The top of a hay rick can be seen over the hedge in Massey's meadow beyond, with its neat thatching of oat straw.

After the dip the first house in Hudnall is seen on the left. This is the Countess Brownlow Home for Boys which will still be recognisable a hundred years later as the private house "Upper Gade", and next to it numbers 5 and 6 Hudnall. There are two more cottages behind, and numbers 1 to 4 and Hudnall Farm are down a track to the right, the final building being a little Wesleyan chapel in the corner of the common. That's all there is to Hudnall hamlet, apart from two cottages at Covetous Corner half a mile away. By the end of the century this hamlet will have grown from 12 to 59 houses.

In Stony-hill, between Hudnall and Badger Wood, is the stubble from the oats, the last of which were carted off to the rick-yard at Church Farm on Tuesday, and a patch of ripening barley which will be cut at the end of August.

It's no use looking for buildings down the hill at Four Ways Corner as there are none there at all. The nearest building down there is Mile Barn.

Returning, therefore, to the corner of the Green and turning right, we may see the cows from Bridgewater Farm on the Green, with a boy to keep an eye on them. The Manor House, where Colonel and Mrs Wheatley live, is there with its coffin-shaped chimney, and other landmarks are the Red House (a very busy area where the Ashridge Estate Yard is situated and the big steam-powered village water pump), Marian Lodge (behind iron railings, not the long and high stone garden wall which will be built later with some controversy), the Village Shop and Post Office at number 42, with its porch right on the Green, and many of the other cottages which will still look superficially the same in a hundred years, ending with the Reading Room

The village shop and post office at no.42 about 1900

Left to right:

The Peck children around the pram, Mrs Tilly Pratt, Hubert Halsey (Dilys Hudson's uncle), Miss Evelyn Pratt, Mr Robert Pratt (Postmaster), Johnny Worral (Schoolmaster, retired 1896)

(John O'Gaddesden's), a smaller house than it would later become, and not yet hidden by the memorial to a war scarcely expected.

Opposite John O'Gaddesden's is the cross, water fountain and seat in memory of Lady Marian Alford, but there is no cross on the Green near the Manor House, as Adelaide, Lady Brownlow, is still very much alive. Ashridge House itself, the seat of Lord and Lady Brownlow, may be seen from some points on the Green. Opposite the Red House is a path to Ashridge House, but this will be closed eventually. Although Ashridge has dominated the village for centuries, it has only come within Little Gaddesden civil parish as recently as 1895, and even in 1999 will still not be in the church parish.

At the end of the Green, as in 1999, there is a gate leading into the Park on the left, but it is closed unless the gatekeeper opens it. His house, Gaddesden Lodge, which some now call Fountain Lodge because of the new memorial, will later be called Tudor Lodge. Numbers 26,27 and 28 face down the Green and will still look just the same in a hundred years.

ABOVE TOP
Fountain Lodge (now Tudor Lodge) in the 1920s and below it Tudor Lodge in 1999

BELOW TOP
Church Road corner after the 1903 rebuilding of 20 and 21. No. 26 is in the foreground

BOTTOM
No. 44 on the green

The entrance to Church Road is gated at this time because the road runs through a field where farmstock sometimes graze. There is also a gate into the fenced School area. There is no village hall or playing field here, as there will be in later times. Beyond the school are the Bede Houses for widows, but there are no other buildings until the church itself, and beyond that Church Farm house and farmyard overlooking the valley. Below it are the Lamsey Cottages and Lamsey Farm buildings which are also part of Church Farm.

The rickyard at Lamsey already has several ricks standing, including hay stacks, one of clover hay, a winter oat stack finished on Thursday and a wheat stack done yesterday. Today they are building a pea stack, bringing in the peas on a cart from Big Field, far away down to the left beside the road to Dagnall. The farmer, George Stanbridge, is short-handed, and is having to work at the pea rick himself. After the peas they will be bringing in some of the wheat which is already cut and dried, and adding it to the top of the pea stack. George is very experienced, but he is making a mistake here, because when he puts more wheat on top on Monday, the peas will give way on one side and they will have a rare job straightening it up. Also in Big Field is a reaper and binder drawn by two horses driven by Hucklesby, cutting a rather poor crop of barley. Several of the larger fields have been divided into areas for different crops, and in part of South Field, straight down the hill, is a flock of sheep in a fold made of hazel hurdles which were set up on Thursday by the new shepherd. There are some blocks of fodder turnips trying to grow, but they have been badly attacked by flies this year, and one block has recently been resown for the third time. The swedes are not so bad.

The farmer's wife, Pollie, with the two older children, is away on holiday at Leigh-on-Sea for a fortnight, having caught the train from Dunstable on the Wednesday before the bank holiday, which, as usual, was the first Monday in August. Some of the farm labourers were hoping to get at least a half day's holiday on the Monday, but with the

LEFT:
Witchcraft Bottom: Ringshall Drive and the house now called Witches Hollow early in the century

BELOW:
The Bede Houses

harvest needing so much work, and no extra labourers to be found, they were persuaded to stay on with the promise of a holiday after harvesting was finished.

Anyway, to continue our tour, we must go back to the end of Church Road and turn right. We pass the old cottages, numbers 24 to 20, but nos.20 and 21 are getting a bit dilapidated, and in about three years time Lord Brownlow will replace them with something much better. Adjoining the road are cottages 19 to 15 on the left, which will look very similar in a hundred years, as will the Bridgewater Arms Hotel on the right, though its function as a hotel will not last out the century. Number 15 will some time in the 1930's and 40's spend a few years as the village post office before it, in its turn, will be replaced by another.

Opposite the hotel is a path that leads down the hill into Ringshall Drive and Witchcraft Bottom, where some old cottages which until recently were part of Ivinghoe parish will still be seen a century later, under the names of Faerie Hollow, Witches Hollow, Cherry Tree Cottage and Witchcraft Hill. Cherry Tree cottage will in time be cut off from the Bridgewater Arms Path and joined to a new road to be known as Alderton Drive.

Back to the hotel, we find next to it a dairy, and the herd is in the fields behind. We continue along our original line through the village. There will be no village shop on the right until 1947. The houses on the right are numbered from 14 down to 1 where the village ends, and on the left is the large Rectory estate, later to be known as the private house Beaney, where the Reverend Francis Hodgson is just concluding his incumbency. He will preach his farewell sermon on October 22nd. His wife Odeyne has designed the new hymn board, created by

Nos 6 to 13 Little Gaddesden, early in the century

TOP:
Old Park Lodge, about 1930.

ABOVE
Old barn and deer larder at Thunderdell Lodge from a painting by Virginia Westmacott

RIGHT
Ringshall Lodge in 1889

David Clark, of Cromer Wood Cottage, which goes up in the church this year. Part of the Rectory land will become Gatesdene Close in 50 years time.

Many of the last cottages on the right will still look practically the same in a hundred years, and numbers 1 to 4 will still be called the "Town Houses" by some.

After the Rectory's outbuildings on the left, the straight road to Ringshall lies between farmland to the right and Ashridge Park on the left, and no houses interrupt this scene on either side. At the far end is the entrance to Hall Farm on the right, and on the left Ringshall Lodge controls the next park gate, which will be blocked off by a garage and a swimming pool some time in the future. Beyond Hall Farm, set back some distance on the left side of the road to Dagnall are the Reservoir cottage, Coppice Cottage and Meadow Farm as they will remain through the next century.

Turning towards Northchurch, we pass the old Ringshall Cottages on the right, including Fountain's shop and a laundry. These were only transferred from Ivinghoe, Bucks, into Little Gaddesden in 1895. The Ivinghoe road, on the right, does not pass any more buildings behind the row of cottages until Wards Hurst Farm.

Continuing in the Northchurch direction, here also we have to trot a mile along the park fence before we come to any more buildings, and then on the left is Thunderdell Lodge. Before reaching it, there may be a glimpse of Old Park Lodge, set well inside the park away from the road, and a distant view of Ashridge House a mile to the east down Prince's Riding, opposite the view of the Bridgewater Monument, just over half a mile to the west. In 1899, we are looking at a monument 67 years old. In 1899 the Bridgewaters are remembered only by the oldest inhabitants, just as in 1999 the Brownlows will be, but both have left permanent marks on Ashridge and Little Gaddesden.

How the Bridgewater line became extinguished in 1829 (and the last dowager Countess died in 1849) may be read in other histories, although there is a direct female blood line from the third Earl of Bridgewater, (who died in 1701) to the second and third Earls Brownlow (who held these titles from 1853 to 1921).

Lady Marian Alford

Christened Marianne, but nearly always written Marian, Viscountess Alford was the mother of both the 2nd and 3rd Earl Brownlow. She wasn't a Lady Brownlow because her husband, Viscount Alford, died without inheriting the Brownlow title. The reasons for this may be read in other histories, but Lady Marian is mentioned here because the memory of her good work for the village, including its water supply, was recent in 1899, and her memorial on the Green was still fresh. The garden behind the seat was kept in beautiful condition within living memory, consisting of bushes, paths and various flowers. It had a curved line of evergreen bushes behind the curve of the seat.

By the 1980's it was very overgrown, and the laurels behind the garden had blocked the footpath. The Scouts cut back the laurels in 1988 and planted some daffodils, but it has not been restored to a garden, though the front of it is kept attractive with flowers in the trough. In 1999 this is looked after by Pat Allen of John O'Gaddesden's. At the right hand end is a tall cypress tree, the overgrown survivor of the line of evergreen bushes, and in spring it is framed in cherry blossom from the cherry tree which has grown up behind it. The inscription on the back of the seat is now hard to read. The wording is shown below.

RIGHT: The Alford memorial fountain

The inscription on the seat appears in one line

+ IN+LOVING+MEMORY+OF+THE+LADY+MARIAN+ ALFORD+ERECTED+JUNE+2+1891+BY+HER+FRIENDS

The inscription on the fountain, from St John's Gospel, chapter 4, verse 14

"WHOSOEVER DRINKETH OF THE WATER THAT I SHALL GIVE HIM SHALL NEVER THIRST BUT THE WATER THAT I SHALL GIVE HIM SHALL BE IN HIM A WELL OF WATER SPRINGING UP INTO EVERLASTING LIFE"

RESIDENTS AND VISITORS PRESENT ON CENSUS NIGHT, APRIL 5TH 1891

Little Gaddesden, Hudnall, Ashridge Park, Woodyard, Coldharbour, Ringshall, Wards Hurst and Hog Hall
(Parts of Ringshall not in Ivinghoe Parish: Reservoir Meadow is included, but not Hall Farm, Meadow Farm or Coppice Cottage.)

NUMBER OF PEOPLE LISTED WITH EACH SURNAME

Allison 5
Andrews 9
Austin 9
Baldwin 1
Ballam 6
Batchelor 4
Bearton 2
Beauchamp 1
Bignall 1
Black 1
Boarder 5
Brodie 1
Brotherton 1
Buggey 7
Bunn 6
Burrows 7
Cains 9
Canham 4
Carlton 1
Carpenter 2
Carter 6
Chappell 2
Chennells 2
Clements 1
Clifton 7
Collier 4
Court 1
Crawley 1
Cutler 5
Davy 1
Denison 2
Dollimore 1
Double 1
Draper 15
Edwards 3
Else 1
Faulkner 1
Fenn 9
Flowers 1
Fordham 2
Fountain 23
Fowler 3
Gadbury 5
Galletly 1
Garnett 2
Garrett 15
Ghost 2
Ginger 6
Goodedge 4
Grant 1
Gray 3
Green 3
Groom 5
Guy 1
Hadley 1
Haines 1
Halsey 4
Harris 1
Harrowell 1
Hart 5
Henley 1
Herbert 3
Hoar 8
Hobbs 9
Holland 10
Horn 1
Hucklesby 7
Hughes 2
Impey 10
Janes 6
Jarvis 2
Johnson 9
Jones 14
Judkins 1
Key 1
Keyte 3
Killick 1
King 1
Kingswood 5
Kipping 1
Kirk 1
Lait 1
Lane 5
Lee 7
Liberty 7
Lissenden 1
Lock 1
Lowe 4
Lunnon 7
Makepeace 1
Maple 1
Maunders 9
May 4
Mayling 5
Melmouth 1
Munden 8
Nicholes 6
Nicholson 2
Noyes 1
Oakins 10
Okins 2
Orchard 1
Parsons 1
Pattison 4
Pinner 6
Potter 1
Pratt 3
Price 2
Puddefoot 1
Purton 12
Readding 1
Reeve 1
Robertson 1
Rogers 21
Rose 1
Ruffett 6
Saunders 7
Scott 8
Scrivener 4
Seabrook 2
Shackleton 1
Simmonds 19
Smart 3
Smith 2
Solerian 1
Stanley 2
Stanners 6
Stansfield 2
Stevens 1
Sutherland 3
Sutton 5
Symes 2
Temple 5
Thame 5
Thorn 4
Tomlin 2
Tompkins 1
Tripp 1
Underwood 6
Venus 1
Wardle 1
Warren 1
Wells 17
Wheatley 5
White 6
Whitman 21
Wibden 4
Wild 1
Wilson 1
Windmill 3
Winter 2
Worrall 2
Wright 5
Young 5

Information from the census

by Lyn Hyde and the Editor

We have to go back to 1891 for full census details, as the 1901 details will not be publicly available until 2001.

The following observations are obtained from the handwritten documents. To make a fair comparison with 1991 we have to add up not only Little Gaddesden, but some neighbouring areas which have been added to it since 1891.

On April 5th 1891, the enumerators of the areas we need recorded the following:

Little Gaddesden (Herts):	86 houses (2 being unoccupied)-	322 people
Hudnall (Bucks):	12 houses -	66 people
Part of Pitstone (Bucks):	2 houses -	11 people
(The Brownlows were away)		
Part of Berkhamsted (Herts):	5 houses -	14 people
Part of Ivinghoe (Bucks):	41 houses -	191 people
TOTAL:	146 houses -	604 people
(Average 4.1 people per house)		

The Little Gaddesden houses are all along the main road through the village except for the 11 Bede Houses, Church Farm and 2 Lamsey Cottages.
The two in Pitstone Parish were Ashridge House itself (but there were only staff in residence on census day), and "Ashridge Bothy".
The Berkhamsted houses were Berkhamsted Lodge, "Cottage in Firs", two at Woodyard (1 unoccupied) and Thunderdell Lodge.
The Ivinghoe ones were the 32 cottages at Ringshall and 9 in Ashridge Park.

There is a published population for Little Gaddesden in 1891 of 378. This is an adjusted figure which doesn't include Ringshall or Ashridge Park, but presumably includes Hudnall, which on the original documents is described as being in Little Gaddesden parish even though in the county of Bucks.

The identical area in 1991 contained about 440 houses and apartments and 1097 people, making 2.5 people per house.
In 1999 the number of houses has gone up to 461 by my reckoning, mainly due to building at Church Farm, The Lye and Pond Lane.

Although there are fewer people per house, the houses are mostly bigger now. In 1891, as now, there was rarely, if ever, more than one couple in a house, but each couple had more young singles living with them.

An odd finding is that although in Little Gaddesden females out-numbered males (as usual in populations) by 177 to 135, in Ringshall and the Park males out-numbered females by 107 to 84. As there was no place set up as a particular lodging for men, they were all families, there is no obvious explanation.

The 32 Ringshall Cottages make a convenient example:
No house had more than one married couple.
27 of them were occupied by a married couple, of which: 9 had from 5 to 9 children or other young relatives with them, 15 had from 1 to 4 children or other young relatives, 3 had no other relatives with them. Four of the cottages were headed by a man with no wife present (2 were widowers): all these had either 3 or 4 children or grandchildren with them. 1 cottage only was occupied by a single woman. There were only 3 occupants unrelated to the main family of the house they lived in.

For anyone studying these census sheets, they should note that the Ringshall Cottages were numbered in reverse order in 1891. The present-day no.35 was no.1.

The census also shows everyone's place of birth. Now only a small proportion of us were born here, but in 1891 about half of the population was born in Little Gaddesden, Hudnall or Ringshall. Some of the others came from quite surprising places.

LOCAL PLACES OF BIRTH:

Little Gaddesden, Ringshall and Hudnall:... 225
Ivinghoe (which may include more from Ringshall):.............................. 38
Eaton Bray & Edlesborough (which may include more from Hudnall):..34
Dagnall:.. 20
Berkhamsted & Northchurch:... 15
Nettleden, Great Gaddesden & St Margarets:..................................14
Studham:...9
Frithsden:..8
Aldbury:..6
Hemel Hempstead:...5
TOTAL OF THESE:...374

LOCAL COUNTIES:

Hertfordshire (district unspecified: 16, Harpenden: 2)..........................18
Buckinghamshire (district unspecified: 9, Wendover: 7)........................16
Bedfordshire (district unspecified: 9, Luton: 1).......................................10
TOTAL OF THESE:...44

NEXT RING OF COUNTIES:

Middlesex, Berkshire, Oxfordshire, Northamptonshire, Huntingdonshire, Cambridge and Essex:.. 17

UP TO 100 MILES AWAY:

London:..11
Surrey:...11
Suffolk, Kent, Sussex, Hampshire, Wiltshire, Leicester, Rutland, Norfolk, Worcester, Nottingham and Lincoln:.. 26

FURTHER ENGLISH COUNTIES:
Dorset, Somerset, Devon, Cheshire, Shropshire and Yorkshire:........... 19

OTHER COUNTRIES:
Scotland:.. 3
Ireland:...1
France:...2
Belgium:...1
Madeira:.. 1
India and Bengal:..2 (one a visitor)
Jamaica:...1

TOTAL OF ALL CHECKED:... 514

GENERAL INDEX

* = Main entry, # = Picture
Roman Numerals = Map and colour pages (following page 288)

continued on page 18

A CENTURY REMEMBERED

Occupations at the turn of the century

by Lyn Hyde and the Editor

We have a complete picture for 1891 from the census returns. The first thing we notice is the 116 school children, who are entered as "scholar". Then there are 76 wives who have nothing entered under occupation. Of the very few wives who have got a named occupation there is a sewing mistress (the schoolmaster's daughter, Fanny Worrall), an agricultural labourer (Eliza Hughes), a dairywoman at Home Farm (Elizabeth Draper), 2 laundresses at Ringshall (Eliza Whitman and Caroline Hobbs), 2 strawplaiters (Esther Ginger and Sarah Ruffett), the grocer at Ringshall (Susan Fountain), and an assistant at the post office at no.41 on the Green (Matilda Pratt, the postmaster's wife).

For widows and unmarried women, on the other hand, there is nearly always an occupation, except for the 11 annuitants (pensioners) aged from 59 to 84 in the Bede Houses. Domestic service is by far the commonest job for the women - 77 of them including cooks, housekeepers and all sorts of maids.

Other occupations of widows and unmarried women are: a few dressmakers and needlewomen, wool spinners and a flax spinner, the matron of the convalescent home at Hudnall (Ann Jarvis), 2 nurses, 2 governesses, the licensed victualler at the Bridgewater Arms (Mary Allison, widow) and her barmaid daughter (Georgina), the grocer at no. 41 (later to be no 42) on the Green (Arabella Pratt, widow) and a draper at no 14 (Marianne Fordham, aged 77).

The men almost always have a job, even if over 65 years old. These older ones are the farmer at Church Farm (George Underwood, 69), a clerk of works (Joseph Wright, 68), 4 general labourers (67,68,71,77), 2 agricultural labourers (69, 66), a gardener's labourer (Thomas Thame, 75), a woodman (James Whitman, 67), a road labourer (72), and 2 pensioners at lodge gates, of which one is specifically described as the gate keeper (George Scott, 78, at Berkhamsted Lodge; the other is Sylvester Rogers, 76, living at Home Farm Lodge.)

There are only two old ones without occupations: an army pensioner (74), and one living on his own means (the Scot, Alexander Nicholas, 68),

Of the younger men, 65 years old or under, about 50 are agricultural labourers, 28 gardeners and 18 general labourers. Then come a variety of more specific jobs and crafts: 13 carpenters, 5 plumbers, and one or two each of the following list:

farmer at Hudnall Farm (Edward Hoar), farmer's bailiff, herdsman, fowl breeder, machine fitter, stationary engine driver, horse keeper/groom, coachman, blacksmith, stone mason, bricklayer, painter, roadman, wheelwright, furnace stoker, forester, gamekeeper, tailor, soldier, grocer's assistant, a few domestic servants (usher, houseman, footman, butler), 3 apprentices, and a 12-year old telegraph boy (Henry Cains).

On the more professional and clerical side there are the rector (Charlton Lane), the schoolmaster (John Worrall) and his assistant (Samuel Green), the sub-postmaster (Robert Pratt), postman (Edward Garrett), 2 land agents (William Wheatley and Joseph Parsons), another clerk of works (John Sutherland), the estate bailiff (Joseph Stanley), a contractor (John Stanners) and an office clerk. William Wheatley's son was "reading for the army" (Philip Wheatley, 19).

By 1899 several of these entries will be out of date, of course, and two in particular are the farmer at Church Farm and the Rector. George Underwood died, though there was still an Underwood at Hudnall keeping lambs. George Stanbridge took over the rent of Church Farm and moved in in 1894. Rector Charlton Lane died in 1892 and was succeeded by the Reverend Francis Hodgson from 1893 to 1899, leaving an inter-regnum at the century's end.

For comparison, the occupations of the 1990's will be found on page 103.

GENERAL INDEX

continued from page 17

continued on page 19

Retrospect of 1899

by George Stanbridge, farmer at Church Farm

The past year has been a very trying one for me: the drought being disastrous to crops of all kinds. The Barley being quite a failure, although harvested well: this land does burn so being gravelly & very thin. The hay crop is the worst we have had, since here we have been! although we have had two or three droughts previous, but they did not affect us quite so much in the meadows.

The roots have been as great a failure before; but not worse! for we have practically nothing except 4 acres of Thousand-head which is good. Prices have been as bad as the weather & I have been unfortunate in not taking my corn on the market at the right time! or it would not have hit me so hard. The present War - in South Africa: which is attaining a gigantic form, & the end is not in sight either: has had a depressing effect on our produce; but nearly everything else has become dearer, & many things considerably. All kinds of machinery 20% iron work included, coal 10% & in some places much more. Labour during the year has been scarcer than ever, and consequently wages have had to be risen.

We have now arrived at a critical time, as the keep is very short, should the winter harden we should be driven to extremities later on: I trust it will hold open.

Introduction to 1900

(George Stanbridge rewrote some similar comments to the above on the next day, and added some other details)

..... The past year has been disastrous to many of us, myself in particular, as this happens to be a farm that cannot stand a drought. The stock did not pay a penny for grazing, & in fact would lose a lot of cash if they had been sold at Michaelmas.

..... We are now engaged in a most serious war with the Transvaal, & Orange Free State Republic. Our troops have already met with several severe Reverses with great losses of Officers and men. It was generally thought when the war began, in October: that we should soon settle the enemy! but it appears they are too much for us at present; our original army of 70,000 men was thought to be ample for the task! but now they are to be augmented to 200,000 & more if required. What a miscalculation on the part of our Government.

GENERAL INDEX

continued from page 18

continued on page 21

Lord Brownlow and the Talbot connection

by Barbara Cassell

Adelbert Cust, the young 3rd Earl Brownlow, married the Hon. Adelaide Talbot in 1868, the year after he inherited the title and the Ashridge Estate. She was the third and youngest daughter of Henry Talbot, 18th Earl of Shrewsbury, a family which came over with William the Conqueror and whose head is the premier Earl of England.

The Talbots were a fairly remarkable bunch of people - mostly tall and handsome and with a real feeling of concern for those who were not so wealthy as themselves. They did much to try to provide comfort and help and with it fun. The height has carried on; I was able to pick out the Talbot Mayor of Hemel Hempstead from the others in a photograph by his height. Soon after the war I was in London and saw a group of tall ladies in the distance, and I thought 'how wonderful', but as I drew closer I realised they were all Talbot cousins of mine.

LORD AND LADY BROWNLOW: ADELBERT AND ADELAIDE

Adelaide and her two sisters were an artistic family, and all entertained well-known writers and artists in their house parties. Then of course Lord Brownlow entertained politicians and royalty. There is a picture of him with Edward, Prince of Wales, at an Ashridge shoot, and Lady Brownlow was a personal friend of Alexandra, Princess of Wales. These two ladies were reckoned to be the most beautiful ladies in London.

There was gaiety at Ashridge. Conty (Constance) Sitwell was one of the Talbots, and here is a description by her of the Christmas play of 1911:

"... the rehearsals were held in a warm narrow theatre at one end of the orangery at Ashridge. The silly play was called 'The Wedding March' and I was to be the Bride ... Ginger (Humphrey Talbot) was a policeman, and at the last performance pranced on to the stage at the end of one of the scenes, while Granville Ram was singing 'Gingah, Gingah, Jolly Old Captain Ginger - Jolly Old Pot - O.K. What, what' ... we had a fine banquet in the dining room in between, having all collected in the ante-room with its crimson brocade walls and smelling of flowers, before dinner. There was cousin Adelaide Brownlow in all her dignity, a beautiful gold cloak over her dress, and her pearls; there was Cooie (Constance Lane) as a marchioness, K Talbot with ringlets like Mrs Browning, Granville Ram, quite charming, wearing a stock, and his hair brushed back; there was also cousin Emily and Alfred, the Wheatleys, the Custs, Roger Wodehouse, Aunt Adela ... The long table looked so splendid - all the silver vases out and all the silver sconces on the walls - the line of footmen behind with their cutaway coats and silk stockings against the panelled background ... Bridget and Ginger sat at the end of the table ... I could see Bridget grinning and Ginger laughing."

Bridget, Humphrey and Geoffrey Talbot with their father, Alfred, at Little Gaddesden House.

It shows that although they were grand, they knew how to enjoy life as well. Adelaide was very happily married and she was a success with everybody - her one great tragedy was that she never had any children. She and her husband were model landlords for their period and they did much in this village: a remarkably early provision of piped water and sewage treatment; a brass band and so on. One of her problems was that she felt it her duty to visit the cottagers after the birth of a child, and on occasions she had to congratulate a woman exhausted by bearing a large family, and not really wanting another baby - when she herself was desperately longing for a child. Some of her friends seemed to think that she worried far too much about tenants and relations less well off than herself.

Conty Sitwell describes her:

"When one looks back and thinks of all the servants ... it seems queer that we should have taken so much for granted, a magnificence which appears feudal - almost royal - now, and it is difficult to give an impression of such a mode of living, and of the earnest and humble Christianity which accompanied it day by day, without laying it open to the charge of insincerity ... or careless ease. Yet

ease there was not in the presence of Adelaide Brownlow ... her whole being was bent on helping others ... how often the half-eaten ham had disappeared and was found to have accompanied her on the afternoon drive, and been left at a lonely cottage. "Adelaide, you will leave me some of that ham, won't you, before you run away with it?" I remember Cousin Addie saying, with his loud laugh, after cutting off a slice for himself ... at her funeral the tear-stained faces of the cottage women were there in scores."
(She died on 16th March 1917.)

ALFRED AND EMILY TALBOT

Alfred was reputed to be Adelaide's favourite brother, a younger son of the 18th Earl of Shrewsbury. I believe he came to Little Gaddesden to be near her and proved to be a great help to both Lord and Lady Brownlow.
He came in 1880 because Little Gaddesden House was empty. It was built in the mid-nineteenth century as the agent's house and office for the Ashridge Estate. The main entrance led into a long and corridor-like hall; to the right was the private house, and to the left the agent's office with its walk-in safe and telephone to the rest of the house, and then there was the clerk's office with windows too high to see out of - above were guest bedrooms. It was vacant because the agent's wife wouldn't live there because she thought it was so ugly. She was a Cust from the Brownlow family and her husband was Colonel Wheatley. They lived in the Manor House instead.
Alfred married Emily de Grey of Norfolk in 1882. He was conscious of the many poor people who needed help and enjoyment in their lives, and there are many events and activities on record in the 1880's and 90's by which they helped both London and local people. One of the most useful locally was the Ladies' Sewing Guild. This was not for fancy work, but good useful clothes. Many were distributed in the villages of the Ashridge Estate. In 1891 there was a particularly severe and long winter, and Alfred and his wife organised a soup kitchen three times a week at Ivinghoe and Edlesborough, and they distributed sacks of coal to the tenants.

When Alfred took on Little Gaddesden House, the clerk's room was turned into the school room for the family, although of course the boys ultimately went to Eton. My father remembered the house as comfortable and well-run with banks of chrysanthemums in the long entrance hall in the autumn and winter seasons.

Alfred sometimes took church services at Edlesborough as a layman, and he was responsible for finding a rector for Little Gaddesden, the Revd. Edward Clark, in 1904. They also provided some fun and took part in the theatre at Ashridge; organised the Christmas tree and the tea.

Emily died suddenly in 1912, and it is said the whole village was stunned. Alfred died in 1913. They had four children: Bridget, Humphrey (Ginger), Geoffrey, and Kathleen (K).

Editor's note: All of these appear later on in this book. Geoffrey appears in the roll of honour of those who died in the 1914-18 war.

ADELA AND THE REVEREND CHARLTON GEORGE LANE

Adela Talbot was the daughter of one of Lady Brownlow's other brothers, The Hon. and Rev. George Gustavus Talbot, of Gloucestershire. Adela was invited to Ashridge on a number of occasions by Lady Brownlow, her aunt, and she had a

GENERAL INDEX
continued from page 19

continued on page 22

brother, Gustavus Arthur Talbot, who came to live in Marchmont House in Hemel Hempstead in 1897, and who was Mayor and Hemel's first member of parliament from 1918 to 1920, when he died. One of his daughters was Constance (Conty) who married William Sitwell - I have quoted from some of her books.

Adela married the Reverend Charlton Lane in 1888. He had been Rector of Little Gaddesden since 1870, and was a widower with two daughters. Charlton and Adela had two children of their own: my aunt Constance (known as Cooie to distinguish her from her cousin Conty) and my father, Charlton, who were both born in Little Gaddesden. Then tragedy struck, as my grandfather the Rector died of pneumonia in November 1892. After this my grandmother moved to Nettleden House.

I remember staying at Nettleden House as a child; and my grandmother was the person who spotted that I liked music and was trying to play the piano. She was a tall dignified old lady, but she had a good sense of humour and plenty of spirit. She insisted on learning to drive at the age of 70, telling the car to "whoa" down Nettleden Hill, and getting the policeman to turn the car round for her in Berkhamsted when she went shopping there. Mr Meredith of Potten End told me how he always got a ride back with her after choir practice to make sure she got home safely. He didn't seem to mind having to walk back to Potten End at all - the ride in her car was a rare treat and well worth it. She died in 1936, outliving her husband by 44 years.

CONSTANCE LANE (COOIE)

My aunt Cooie was a good artist. She was asked by the Brownlows to paint the frescoes at Ashridge in 1913, and she shared the commission with her friend from the Slade School of Art, Dora Carrington. Dora wrote:

"About six workmen are running about erecting scaffolding, and carrying buckets. Lane and me feel like great masters controlling this band of men and having a big wall to cover with our works of art" (A reproduction of one of these is in the colour section).

Cooie lived at St Margaret's after her mother died, but she died in her fifties in 1944, leaving her brother:

SIR CHARLTON ADELBERT GUSTAVUS LANE (TONY)

He suffered from his parents' choice of Christian names, and is the second Charlton, the second Adelbert and the third Gustavus to be mentioned in this account, so it is just as well he was generally known as Tony.

He spent most of his life in the Colonial Civil Service going to Africa in 1910. He married Millicent Newdigate from Coventry. They had a son, Richard, born in Mwanza in Tanganyika, and a daughter, myself, born in Zanzibar. This story is not drifting away from Little Gaddesden because I came here often visiting our relations, in later years with my husband Alfred, and we came back to live here in 1970, the year before Bridget Talbot died.

Editor's note: So the 18th Earl of Shrewsbury has had descendants in the village without a break since 1868.

GENERAL INDEX

continued from page 21

continued on page 23

The Boy Scouts

In 1907 Major-General Robert Baden-Powell wrote "Scouting for Boys" and organised an experimental camp for twenty boys on Brownsea Island, Poole Harbour. The book was published in fortnightly parts beginning in January 1908. The Scout Movement came into existence as a result of boys reading the book and forming themselves into patrols. It soon developed into an organisation, Baden-Powell becoming the leader. In 1910 there was a plan to start a Troop in Little Gaddesden, and the first event was a concert to raise funds for it. This was organised by Bridget Talbot and took place on December 15th. In 1911 there was a rummage sale and another concert, after which the Troop was officially started with Harry Temple as the Scoutmaster and Bernard Phillips as Assistant Scoutmaster.

The boys who joined the Little Gaddesden troup at the start, on October 26th 1911, were, (with age about the time of joining): Arthur Whitman (17), Frank Johnson (16), Arthur Halsey (15), A. Basford (15), Percy Hobbs (15), Archie Wells (14), Jim Whitman (14), George Pinnock (14), Gerald Green (13), Bernard Halsey (13), Francis Green (13), Edward Bunn (12), Denis Phillips (12), Arthur Pinnock (11) and Cecil Crack (10).

They formed two patrols, but with new members joining soon afterwards this became three, the Lions, Wolves and Peewits. Photographed in 1912, the Patrol Leaders were Frank Johnson, F. Whitman and Arthur Whitman respectively. The last two were both about 17 when they joined, and soon afterwards left and joined the Hertfordshire Territorials and were serving in France in 1914. The first meeting place in 1911 was the Reading Room at John O'Gaddesden's, but by the end of the year they had moved into the old Volunteer Armoury adjacent to no.27 where the Scoutmaster lived. Bridget Talbot was the President. The Treasurer was first Mr Pratt, and then Humphrey Talbot, Bridget's brother.

The Scouts quickly settled in to all kinds of training activities, including two first aid classes at the Ashridge private waiting room at Berkhamsted Station, run by Dr McBride. The boys were sent down by Lady Brownlow in the big motor. They were also soon practising numbers for another concert, amongst which was the Kirkby Malzeard Sword Dance, for six performers, which seems to have been a great hit on more than one occasion. Miss Cotsworth taught it to them at Ashridge. Harry Temple accompanied it on the violin.

The boys were soon joining activities with other Troops, including a rally with the Beacon Scouts at Ivinghoe, a performance at the Ivinghoe Scouts concert, and in June 1912 nineteen of them went to a one-day rally of about 700 Hertfordshire Scouts at Balls Park, Hertford. Later that month they went to a rally near Aldbury.

Their first camp was held in August 1912 for a week near the stream between Dagnall and Edlesborough, on Mr Ashby's farm. The activities included signalling and trail-following on the downs, and a field day involving attacking the Tring Scouts camp on Moneybury Hill, and another in which a Dunstable Troop joined in.

Cooking competitions were held in autumn. In one of these fourteen boys were each given a rabbit by Lord Brownlow and had to skin it and make a stew, including vegetables and dumplings. Arthur Pinnock's was the best.

In December 8th 1912, Baden-Powell himself came to Ashridge. First he inspected the Little Gaddesden Troop in their own headquarters, where there was a display of things they had made. Then there was a rally of 300 to 400 scouts who had walked or cycled from the surrounding district to Ashridge House. There was an inspection, a service, and a talk by the Chief Scout,

GENERAL INDEX
continued from page 22

continued on page 24

continued on page 35

followed by tea and buns provided by Lord and Lady Brownlow.
On Easter Bank Holiday Monday in 1913 another Field Day was held jointly with the Tring, Dunstable and Aldbury Troops in Ashridge Park. The account of this event, with a map, refers to various landmarks by contemporary names, thus: Thunderdale (known as Thunderdell both before that time and now), Tring Lodge (now Old Copse Lodge), Peacock Lodge (Nettleden Lodge), Bunn's Lodge (Home Farm Lodge), Cox's House (Old Park Lodge), Viner's Cottages (Woodyard).

The aim was to get a "convoy", consisting of about five ponies and donkeys ridden by various scouts and Bridget Talbot herself, from the Armoury to Thunderdale Lodge, which represented a fort under siege. The Tring Scouts and half the Dunstable ones formed an opposing force whose starting point was Tring Lodge. The rest were in support of the convoy. They included a bicycle corps and the besieged force of five (who were allowed to make sorties), under Bridget's sister K, at Thunderdale.

The Golden Valley and part of Princes Riding were designated a river which ran all the way from the Bridgewater Monument to Peacock Lodge, and which could only be crossed at four "bridges" marked by flags. Precise rules of engagement were laid down, and there were umpires. For instance: "Bridges may be held by half the number of Scouts attacking the bridge. That is to say 3 scouts holding the bridge need not retire till 6 of the enemy appear within 20 yards." "Anywhere else it will only require one more of the enemy within 20 yards - that is to say 2 Scouts may take one, 4 take 3,..." Captured Scouts had to hand over their arm badges. "The L.G. force wins if more than half the number of enemy are taken. The Tring force wins if the convoy is captured or is unable to get through to the fort before 2.45."

In the event, the Little Gaddesden force won, the convoy having taken a southerly route via the "bridge" near Bunn's Lodge, around the southern perimeter of Ashridge garden to near Coldharbour, where they had to lie low, as foot scouts ahead had spotted an enemy force. The bicycle corps, who had been decoying elsewhere, were sent for, and arrived in the nick of time to make up sufficient numbers to advance on the enemy, and the convoy was galloped through into safety. A larger force of the enemy had gone off to the Monument, expecting the convoy to come that way.

The next year, however, war was declared with Germany, and a very different sort of conflict was seen.

Continued in next chapter.

1914 - 1918: The Great War

In addition to this chapter, information about this wartime period will be found in the histories of the school (p. 152) and the church (p. 131).

At least three other histories of Little Gaddesden mention the fact that Field Marshall Lord Kitchener was summoned to the War Office, the day before war was declared, by a telegram delivered to him while having tea on the loggia at Ashridge with Lady Brownlow. It seems a good starting point for this chapter.

War with Germany had been feared for some years, however, and army training camps already existed on both of the main estates of the Brownlows: Belton (Lincolnshire) and Ashridge. Here Colonel Wheatley, the Ashridge Estate Manager, was in command of the Bedfordshire Volunteer Infantry Brigade. When they moved on, the Inns of Court Officers Training Corps came.

Ashridge became a hospital and convalescent home for soldiers, controlled by St Albans Hospital and mainly staffed by the Red Cross. (Ashridge would become a hospital again in the second world war.) Lady Brownlow was deeply involved in the welfare of the soldiers at Belton, as well as Ashridge. She and Lord Brownlow, who were both now aged about 70, spent time at both their country houses, as well as their London home. It was a great strain on her, and she died in London in 1917. She was buried at Belton.

Soldiers at Ashridge during the Great War

THE BOY SCOUTS

(continued from page 24)

In 1914 the oldest scouts who had joined the Troop when it began in 1911 were old enough for military service. By 1918 there were many more. George Pinnock, who was one of the original Troop, had already gone off to the Liscard Sea Training Home in November 1912 at the age of about 14, having just left school. Three years later, the entry "Helped to sink a German submarine in the North Sea" was entered against his name in the Scout Diary but, in 1916, he died in action.

Frank Johnson, Patrol Leader of the Lions in 1914, was killed in France in 1916. Arthur Whitman, Patrol Leader of the Peewits, was also killed in action. In the country as a whole the war deprived the Scouts of many of their leaders. In Little Gaddesden Bernard Phillips, the Assistant Scoutmaster, joined the Royal Navy. Countrywide, Boy Scouts started undertaking all kinds of non-military public service, as men went off to fight. The labour force of the country, as well as the town, was depleted. Little Gaddesden Scouts joined in helping to shock an 18 acre field of corn for Mr Ashby, on whose farm they once again camped. The Diary records that "since the opening of the Ashridge Hospital for sick recruits and wounded, the L. G. Scouts have never failed to go down to Berkhamsted in turn, whatever the weather, to fetch medicines for the hospital in the evening".

About Doris Fenn

Doris Fenn, Little Gaddesden's most detailed domestic chronicler of the twentieth century, arrived to live in the village in February 1915, and she had spent a long summer holiday here in 1914. She was only seven. She was sent from Mill Hill, Hendon, to live with her great uncle and aunt, Harry and Kitty Temple at 27 Little Gaddesden, away from the attacks of the German zeppelins, which had frightened her. She published her memories in 1996. Ninety pages of her book "The Ashridge Estate and Little Gaddesden, 1915 - 1955" are devoted to the period 1914-1919 (including some accounts of earlier history) which she remembers in every detail. Here you may read all about clothing - and who made it, home cooking, lighting, washing, washing-up - and in what order, making beds, furnishings, fuel and fire-lighting, spring cleaning, school discipline and lessons and exactly what the teachers were like, friends, children's games, keeping chickens, wildlife, transport, stone-picking, social customs, shops and roundsmen, and occasional mentions of the Boy Scouts, her uncle being the Scoutmaster, and the meeting room just outside the door. Her father was working in a munitions factory in Edgware, and her mother wrote to her regularly from their home in Mill Hill where her elder sister remained. Although there was another Fenn family in the village, one of whom, William Fenn, is named on the war memorial, she was not a known relation. The war did not impinge much on her own life, apart from living away from her parents, so her account is not unlike the village in peace-time.

Her book would, in fact, tell you all you want to know about our village, but can't find in this one. It is not for me to rewrite her accounts, though I have used it to check various details - you should try to get a copy.

I will quote, however, from her account of the death of Lady Brownlow in 1917:

The owners of the lands forgotten, but they and their tenants endured the sadness and humiliation of war. Lady Brownlow's visitors were the wounded, given hospitality at Ashridge House and Belton House. The sadness eventually made her ill, and she died on March 16 in 1917. Her death brought further sadness to the people of Little Gaddesden. She had been admired and loved for her care for the improvement in the standard of life for the villagers. Lord Brownlow had supported her leadership during their long years of happy marriage. Fear of the future without her was of great concern for everyone.

Doris continued to live at no.27 with the Temples until 1924, when she went off to start a teaching career. From 1924 to 1927 she came every weekend, and then moved further afield, after which her visits were during holidays. She kept in close touch with friends in the village well into the 1990's when she wrote her book.

Roll of Honour 1914 - 1918

by David Heard

In memory of those men from the village whose names appear on the Little Gaddesden War Memorial having served and died in the two World Wars of the 20th century

Roll of Honour: 1914-1918

12593 Private Charles BATCHELOR of the 6th Battalion, Bedfordshire Regiment died on 21.12.1915 killed in action, and is buried in the Bienvillers Cemetery, France.

Born in Little Gaddesden, he enlisted at Hertford and was living in Hemel Hempstead at the time.

1847 Private Vernon BATCHELOR of the 1st Battalion, Hertfordshire Regiment died of wounds on 25.07.1916 aged 22 and is buried in the St Sever Cemetery, Rouen, France.

Born in Studham, he entered Little Gaddesden School on 29.05.1899, but left the neighbourhood on 14.12.1900 and his name was removed from the register. He was readmitted on 26.10.1903 and left on 29.01.1908 at 14 yrs old.

He was living in Berkhamsted at the time and enrolled in Ashridge.

F/3278 Lance Corporal Albert BIERTON of the 1st Battalion, Middlesex Regiment was killed in action on 23.10.1918 aged 26 and is buried in the Cross Roads Fontaine-au-Bois Cemetery, France.

Born in Ivinghoe, he lived in Little Gaddesden and attended the village school. He was absent with mumps in November 1897.

He distinguished himself in exams in January 1903 and left school on 10.02.1905 with a Certificate of Proficiency.

22068 Private William Arthur COOK of the 8th Battalion, Bedfordshire Regiment died of wounds on 27.09.1916 aged 23 and is buried in Grove Town Cemetery, Meaulte, Somme, France.

He was born in Berkhamsted, the son of William George and Sarah Ann Cook, later resident in Little Gaddesden, attending the village school, which he left on 04.05.1908. He enlisted in Bedford.

2170 Gunner William COOPER of D Battery, 59th Brigade, Royal Field Artillery was killed in action on 23.09.1917 and is buried in Gwalia Cemetery, Poperingue, Belgium.

Born in Eastney, Portsmouth, he lived in Hudnall, enlisting in Fulham.

James DUNN served in the Machine Gun Corps. More information is required to trace this soldier. There are in excess of 100 James Dunns on record as dying in the 1st World War.

3531 Corporal Hamor William FENN of the 1st Battalion, Hertfordshire Regiment died on 22.03.1916 and is buried in the Longuenesse (St Omer) Souvenir Cemetery, France.

He lived at 18 Little Gaddesden and attended the village school. He distinguished himself in exams and a note in the school log dated 25.04.1892 shows, having gained a certificate of proficiency he "has gone stone picking on the Estate for an indefinite period."

20776 Private Arthur FOWLER of the 5th Battalion, King's Shropshire Light Infantry was killed in action on 22.08.1917 and is buried in the New Irish Farm Cemetery, St Jean-les-Ypres, Belgium.

Born in Ivinghoe, he enlisted in Berkhamsted whilst living in Aylesbury, Bucks.

7164 Private Alfred GARMENT of the 1st Battalion, Northamptonshire Regiment was killed in action on 09.05.1915. His name appears on Le Touret Memorial, France.

He was born in Potten End and enlisted in London.

R/13924 Rifleman Arthur Bertram GENTLE of A Company, 12th Battalion, King's Royal Rifle Corps was killed in action on 31.08.1916 and buried in Delville Wood Cemetery, Longueval, France.

Born in Abbotts Langley, he enlisted in Tonbridge whilst living in Colchester. However, his gravestone is inscribed "of Little Gaddesden".

The grave of Arthur Gentle at Delville Wood Cemetery

37096 Private Edward GROOM of the 1st Battalion, The Queens (Royal West Surrey) Regiment died of disease on 22.03.1917 and is buried in La Neuville Communal Cemetery, France.

Born in Hemel Hempstead, he enlisted in Luton whilst resident in Eaton Bray.

265166 Private George HOAR of the Hertfordshire Regiment was killed in action on 31.07.1917. His name appears on the Menin Gate, Ypres, Belgium.

He was born in Little Gaddesden and lived at 5 Hudnall. He attended the village school, entering on 26.04.1897. A note in the school log shows he had whooping cough in April 1898. He enlisted at Ashridge.

364 Lance Serjt Walter HOLLAND of the 2nd Battalion, The Rifle Brigade (The Prince Consort's Own) was killed in action on 14.03.1915 aged 29. His name appears on Le Touret Memorial, France.

He was born in Little Gaddesden and entered the village school on 14.04.1890. A note in the school log shows he re-entered school on 07.04.1891, having been absent for most of the winter through delicacy of health.

He had his name removed from the register as "they have moved to Tottenhoe". However, another note dated 22.02.1895 shows he was awarded a certificate for distinguishing himself in Religious Knowledge and then another that "little Walter of Ringshall splintered his arm through a fall when playing with another boy of his own size and age" in February 1895.

His residence is shown as Redbyn, P.O.Saskatchewan., Canada at the time of his death.

Cpl. Alexander Frederick JOHNSON of G Company, Royal Engineers died on 06.09.1915 and is buried in St. Peter and St. Paul's Church, Little Gaddesden.

He distinguished himself in examinations at the village school according to a note in the log on 27.01.1898.

15603 Private Frank JOHNSON of the 1st Battalion, Royal Berkshire Regiment was killed in action on 13.11.1916 aged 22. His name appears on the Thiepval Memorial, France.

He was born in Little Gaddesden and attended the village school from 18.04.1898 until 01.03.1911. He lived at 29 Ringshall but enlisted in Wokingham, Berks, whilst his residence is recorded as Berkhamsted.

Private William MAYLING of the Hertfordshire Regiment died on 03.09.1916 aged 20 and is buried in the churchyard of St. Peter and St. Paul's, Little Gaddesden.

He lived at 24 Ringshall and is first entered on the school register on 10.04.1899. He distinguished himself in diocesan exams according to a note in the school log dated 26.01.1903 and passed his Labour certificate on 25.11.1908.

3/7947 Private Alfred MEAD of the 7th Battalion, Bedfordshire Regiment was killed in action on 03.05.1917. His name appears on the Arras Memorial, Faubourg, D'Amiens Cemetery, France.

He was born in Great Gaddesden but later resident at 1 Little Gaddesden. He enlisted at Hertford.

A/203426 Rifleman Ernest NICHOLES of the 16th Battalion, the County of London Regiment, King's Royal Rifle Corps was killed in action on 24.10.1917 aged 31 and is buried in Louverval Military Cemetery, Doignes, France.

He was born in Ivinghoe and lived at Wards Hurst, Ringshall. He attended the village school and left to become an apprentice to a draper on 14.01.1901 in Aylesbury.

He enlisted in London but his name is on the memorial at Ivinghoe as Wards Hurst was in that parish.

177585 Sapper Samuel George OAKINS of the Depot, Royal Engineers was killed in action on 11.11.1917 aged 33 and is buried in Ypres Reservoir Cemetery Belgium.

Born on 02.12.1883, he entered school on 18.04.1887 and lived at 36 Little Gaddesden. He was awarded a certificate, having distinguished himself in Religious Knowledge examinations as noted in the school log of 22.02.1895.

He left school in 1895 with a certificate of proficiency and enlisted in Berkhamsted.

Sam Oakins

J/31811 Ordinary Seaman George PINNOCK of H.M.S. Black Prince, R.N. was killed in action on 31.05.1916. His name appears on the memorial in the Chatham Naval Cemetery, Kent.

He lived in Little Gaddesden and was entered on the school register on 25.09.1903, leaving on 21.10.1912 aged 14.

147225 Pnr. Frederick PURTON of the Corps of Engineers, formerly in the 5th Battalion, Special Brigade, Royal Engineers died of accident injuries aged 21 on 25.04.1916 and is buried in Calais Southern Cemetery, France.

He lived at 1 Little Gaddesden, having been born in Berkhamsted. He entered the school on 18.04.1898 He failed his Labour Certificate according to a note in the school log of 25.11.1908. He broke his collarbone badly, tobogganing on Hudnall Common, and left school on 23.03.1909 aged 14.

Flt. Lt. Geoffrey Richard Henry TALBOT of the Royal Naval Air Service died in an aircraft accident over Dover together with his mechanic on 29.06.1916 aged 28.

Born on 29.03.1888 in Little Gaddesden House, he was the son of the Hon. Alfred Chetwynd and Emily Augusta Louise Talbot. He was baptised in the church on 10.05.1888. He first went to boarding school at Westgate and subsequently to Eton. There was a burial service at the parish Church of St. Peter and St. Paul for him on 04.07.1916 as reported in the local paper. There is a marginal note in the Burial Register: "After Coroner's Inquest".

Geoffrey Talbot in flying kit

91895 William Henry WHITE of the 15th Bn. Durham Light Infantry was killed in action on Monday, 09.09.1918 aged 38 and is buried in the Gouzeaucourt New British Cemetery, Nord, France.

He was the son of Samuel and Mary White of Little Gaddesden and the husband of Elizabeth Ann White of Thunderdell Lodge, Ashridge Park.

265227 Lance Sergt. Arthur WHITMAN of the Hertfordshire Regiment was killed in action aged 22 on 31.07.1917. His name appears on the Menin Gate, Ypres, Belgium

Born in Little Gaddesden he lived at 40 Little Gaddesden. He attended the village school and received Standard 2nd prize of 1s 6d plus a good attendance prize of 2s 0d for attending school the maximum number of 422 times in 1903. He left school on 16.06.1908.

The War Memorials

> *The central inscriptions are:*
>
> IN MEMORY OF THE GLORIOUS DEAD
>
> *and*
>
> THANKS BE TO GOD WHICH GIVETH US THE VICTORY

War memorials showing a list of all those who gave their lives were not a custom. The building of war memorials after the Great War was an idea which, once started, quickly spread to every parish in the nation. The designs took many forms, and the one on Little Gaddesden's Green is unusual. It consists of a wall built by the estate bricklayers, incorporating various decorative features, inscriptions and a central roof. It was designed by Mrs Wheatley to incorporate 24 Italian moulded stone medallions of three designs, which are set in the flanking walls, perhaps intentionally representing the number of the fallen. Another 25 of these same medallions can be seen in the balustrade around the Fernery at Ashridge House. Nearer the centre are the two stones with the main inscriptions, and in the centre is the tallest part of the structure bearing two smaller inscriptions, shelves, and the tiled sloping roof. The timber work supporting the roof was made by Harry Temple, the carpenter who lived across the road at no. 27, and just under the ridge are bottles which contain, according to his niece, Doris Fenn, the names of villagers of importance before and during the war. At the foot, containers of earth are used for the miniature wooden crosses, replaced every year.

The large stone on the right bears the roll of honour: the names of 23 of those listed on the previous page, Ernest Nicholes being the exception because he is commemorated at Ivinghoe.

The war memorial in front of the unextended John O'Gaddesden's House in the 1920s

+
THIS MEMORIAL
IS ERECTED
IN HONOUR
OF
THE ONE HUNDRED
AND THIRTY SIX MEN
WHO WENT FROM
THE VILLAGES OF
LITTLE GADDESDEN
HUDNALL
AND RINGSHALL
AND SERVED IN THE
WAR
OF 1914 = 1918
THE NAMES OF THOSE
WHO GAVE THEIR LIVES
FOR THEIR COUNTRY
ARE CUT
ON THE STONES HERE
THE NAMES OF THOSE
WHO RETURNED
TO ENGLAND
ARE PRESERVED
IN THE CHURCH

The large stone on the left was altered after the second world war. (See page 73) The original inscription is shown on the right:

At the dedication of this memorial, in 1921, the service sheet displayed the following three quotations:
"Live thou for England - we for England died"
"Yesterday returneth not, perchance tomorrow cometh not"
"This is thine hour - misuse it not"

The Little Gaddesden branch of the Royal British Legion now looks after this memorial. (See the article on page 242)

The names referred to as "preserved in the church" are found on a framed illuminated printed sheet with a manuscript list of the people of the village who served in the 1914-18 war, regardless of whether they died. This actually has 119 names on it in alphabetical order of surnames, with the units in which they served. These include the full 24 who died, their names being marked R.I.P. It is headed:

The Roll of Honour

Men who have answered their Country's call in defence of a "Scrap of Paper"
FROM LITTLE GADDESDEN, RINGSHALL, & HUDNALL.

The "scrap of paper" referred to was the treaty of 1839 by which the great nations of Europe agreed to recognise Belgium as an independent and perpetually neutral state, and which was broken by Germany at the outset of the war.

Also in the church there is a third war memorial. This is a decoratively carved wooden panel, on which the names of 22 of the fallen are carved, this time in alphabetical order of their Christian names. Ernest Nicholes is again omitted, and so is William White.

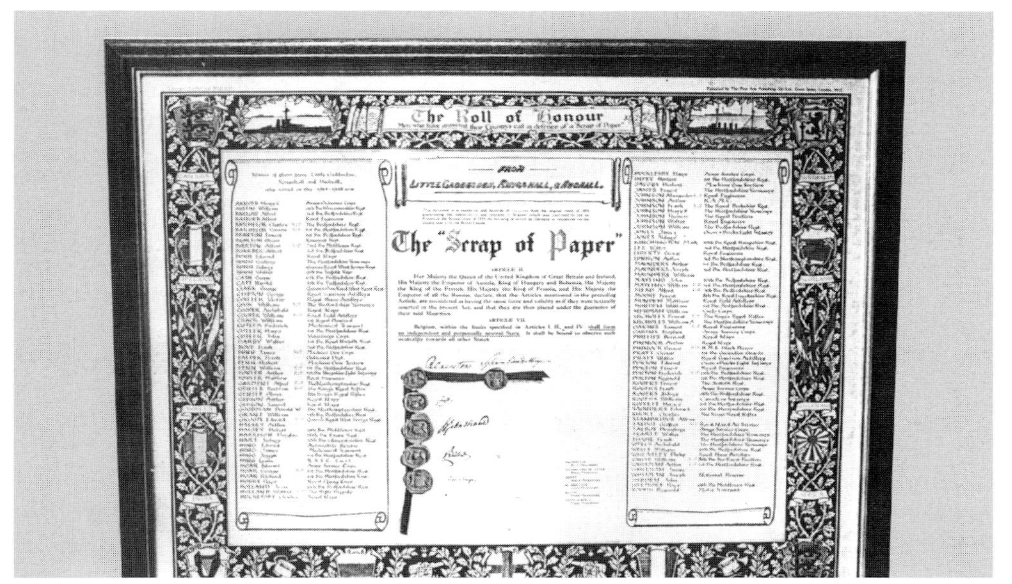

The Roll of Honour which may be seen in the church

A CENTURY REMEMBERED

1917 - 1939

The main events of this period are summarised below. The 1920's were particularly turbulent years for the village.

1917 Lady Adelaide Brownlow died
1918 The Armistice signed: end of the Great War
1921 War Memorial dedicated (See previous chapter.)
1921 Adelbert, third (and last) Earl Brownlow, died
1923 Furnishings of Ashridge House began to be sold
1925 Estate lands offered for sale
1926 The National Trust bought its first part of the Ashridge lands
1927 Ashridge House and lands bought by Mr Edgar Creyke Fairweather
1928 Ashridge House and much land resold: bought by Thomas Place
1928 Ashridge House resold to Urban Hanlon Broughton who donated it to the Conservative Party
1928 Many acres of land, including the Green, bought from E.C. Fairweather by Major Munro Cuthbertson
1928 Many tenants bought their own cottages
1929 Ashridge House opened as the Bonar Law College

An important section of Kay Sanecki's chapter on Ashridge College covers this period. See pages 145 - 146

Until this period there had only been one memorial on the village green, Lady Marian Alford's Cross. Soon there were to be two more because, as well as the war memorial, a cross in memory of Adelaide, Lady Brownlow, was to be erected. A clearing through the trees makes this the only point on the green from which Ashridge House can be seen, and likewise the cross can be easily seen from the house as there is no building in the background from this angle.

The Adelaide Memorial

The inscription is on panels making the four faces of the memorial, with a quotation from Psalm 85 around the octagonal step below

**IN REMEMBRANCE
OF
ADELAIDE**

**WIFE OF
ADELBERT
3RD EARL BROWNLOW**

**BORN 1844
MARRIED 1869
DIED 1917**

**DAUGHTER OF
HENRY 18TH EARL OF
SHREWSBURY AND TALBOT**

**MERCY AND TRUTH HAVE MET TOGETHER
RIGHTEOUSNESS AND PEACE HAVE KISSED EACH OTHER**

The Brownlow Estate in its final years

In 1918, Lord Brownlow, now being a widower and aged 74, was no longer the active man he used to be. He spent perhaps more of his time at his other property, Belton House in Lincolnshire. The estate, however, continued to run efficiently, managed by Colonel Wheatley, who had been his agent since 1882 and lived in the Manor House.

The two following accounts, both by John Oakins, (1910 - 1985) give some idea of this period.

Rose and John Oakins, about 1919

MEMORIES OF MY GRANDFATHER JOHN T. OAKINS

by John Oakins

(Editor's note: The Berkhamsted Deanery Magazine in 1925 reports the death of John Thomas Oakins in July, aged 80, but this is an error as he was 85. It notes that he was born in Ashridge Park, lived in Dagnall for a while, returned to Little Gaddesden in 1880, and was Sexton and Parish Clerk from 1892 until he was 74 years of age. In 1891 he lived at no.1, but some time after 1913 he moved to no.36. His grandson John Oakins was born in 1910, so these memories, which he put down in the 1980's, refer to the very end of the Brownlow era.)

The Friday night ritual in winter was walking to church holding a candle lantern to show my grandfather the way. The first job was to heat the chimney which ran up one corner of the tower, setting light to shavings and bavins (small bundles of waste birch-wood from the besom-makers on the Ashridge estate) from a small metal fire-place. Once the chimney was warm the procedure was to light the furnace in the stoke-hole, ten feet underground. This then heated ducts under the floor. The fuel was coke: unfortunately when the wind was in the west fumes erupted making the congregation cough and splutter and at times the fire had to be put out altogether.

On Sundays grandfather rang the two bells.. Lord and Lady Brownlow and the village gentry sat on pews in the belfry, and the staff from Ashridge and the big houses sat in allocated seats either side of the main aisle.

(Editor's note: 'Belfry', usually meaning the bell chamber, in this instance meant the bottom of the tower, of course. It cannot be used for seating now because all the space is needed for the ringers of the six bells we now have.)

The youth of the village sat in a block of pews where the font now stands and occasional frivolity in that corner during a long sermon resulted in grandfather removing the culprits with some commotion, while the rector held up the sermon.

Grandfather was an expert with the scythe keeping the churchyard tidy. My cousin and I should have raked up the grass but we liked running on the walls which made him very wroth. We were never quite right as we were either too near the scythe or too far away, but he knew if he sent us home he would have to rake the grass himself.

Another task I had was to help him fill the brass double-burner oil lamps - there were ten of these and the wicks had to be trimmed and the lamp glasses cleaned.

The church silver was placed in a large wicker basket covered with a green baize cover after the Sunday services and taken to the rectory (which is now known as Beaney), the servants there keeping it bright and clean, the staff consisting of a cook, house-parlourmaid, nanny and a gardener.

On Sunday evenings in the winter three storm lanterns hanging from posts up Church Road guided the congregation to church.

MORE OF THE LATE BROWNLOW ERA

by John Oakins

The Ashridge Estate was self contained with Ashridge House the centre and Lord and Lady Brownlow living there most of the time. The house in the midst of the Park had 365 rooms all lit by oil lamps. It was two men's work to keep them filled and trimmed. The house was supplied by the garden and farms for meat and vegetables. It also had extensive pleasure grounds with ornamental pools and fountains.

The Park had a perimeter fence nine miles round it with six lodges to house the gate-keepers. The gates were kept locked, the gatekeepers holding the keys. It was just a case of letting through the carts, broughams, coal-carts and horses; the only cars in the village were a black Daimler limousine belonging to Lord Brownlow and a green Napier two-seater with a soft hood and dicky seat belonging to Colonel Wheatley the estate agent. Near what is now called Tudor Lodge is the memorial to Lady Marian Alford, mother of the second and third Earls Brownlow. It included a drinking fountain for people to refresh themselves, with a trough for horses and a lower one for dogs. The water flowed from a bronze fish's mouth which has disappeared. The half circle seat had wooden slats kept clean by the lodge-keeper.

There were herds of red deer and fallow deer providing skins and venison, and the Park was alive with rabbits.

The Head Keeper's house known as Old Park Lodge, and eight cottages, were the only buildings actually in the Park (apart from Ashridge House itself). Almost all the inhabitants of Ringshall, Hudnall and Little Gaddesden worked on the Estate, and a lot from Studham, Nettleden and Aldbury came in, as horsemen, labourers, treefellers, carters, blacksmiths, wheelwrights, carpenters, bricklayers, painters and plumbers. Little Gaddesden was the model village with piped water and flush lavatories. It had its own pumping station with covered reservoir, but only in the big houses was water piped inside the house, such as the Manor House where the Estate Agent, Colonel Wheatley, lived.

The Estate Office was run by a chief clerk, Joey Parsons, and three other clerks. It was joined to what is now known as The Red House. Colonel Wheatley attended here daily, and up this drive was the Ashridge Water Works. Also here was the timber mill where Ashridge oaks were cut for gates, posts and fencing, while on the opposite side were the workshops for plumbers, painters, carpenters and wheelwrights. This work-yard was the hub of the village.

The foremen rode around in pony carts, a few workmen had cycles, but most walked. That is why there are so many footpaths on the Ashridge Estate, the workmen making for the nearest way to their place of work.

One old building labourer, name of Owen Impey, who lived next door to us,

GENERAL INDEX
continued from page 24

continued on page 36

The now derelict and overgrown bridge overlooking Golden Valley, 2000

got up at 5 am and started off to work at 6 am to walk to Slapton (that's about five miles) to get the mortar mixed by 7 am for the bricklayers. At 5 pm he had the same walk home. I can still remember the smell of suet dumpling coming from that house, bacon and onion one end and jam the other, but it must have done him good as after all that walking and labour he then had his own garden to dig!

The school then was enclosed by a wall and two gates to keep out the sheep as the surrounding meadows were not fenced, and at the village end of the Church Road was a white gate which was kept locked with a small side gate for children to get to school and village folk to get to church. The key was held by the keeper of the park gate across the road.

My grandfather (John T. Oakins) and father (Stephen J. Oakins) were born in Little Gaddesden. Father was a son of a normal family: he had four brothers and six sisters. He left school at the age of twelve and was a telegraph boy and then a postman. He was one of the few in the village who did not work on the estate.

The mail came up to the village by pony cart. A postman, Johnny Garrett, who lived in a cottage in the castle grounds at Berkhamsted, delivered in the village on foot while my father walked by the footpath to Dagnall and delivered there and came back via Wards Hurst Farm, a round trip of seven miles. Then for the evening collection he cycled to Dagnall and collected from the box and the Post Office and then collected from the box at Ringshall, blowing a whistle to let the inhabitants know the box was being cleared, and on many occasions someone coming out called "Hang on a minute, Steve!" For the use of his cycle he was paid 3d a week. Father did the Dagnall round for 29 years and then the round was taken over by motor cycle and sidecar and he was transferred to Berkhamsted. The parishioners of Dagnall presented him with a clock for his services, which is still striking and keeping good time.

The youth of the village met at the Reading Room to play darts, billiards and bagatelle. This was at John O'Gaddesden's before its present alteration. The village had its first Village Hall soon after the 1914-18 war. It was a wooden army hut that came from Gadebridge Park, taken down and rebuilt in the village by two local tradesmen in what is now the playing field. Up to that time the school had been used for concerts etc. This hall was well used. Miss Kathleen Talbot founded the West Herts Musical Festival and the first competitions were held in it. Afterwards the competition got so big it was held in Dean's Hall, Berkhamsted School.

My father in his later years was the night watchman at Ashridge House. He had two Airedale dogs to patrol with. He had to pull a telltale wire to indicate he was doing his job and not sleeping! He took turns with John Saunders, and they kept the gravel round the house tidy, with John Saunders also keeping Duncombe Terrace swept. (This is also known as Rainbow Ride.) The Brownlow carriage used this, and a wooden tea house was used for picnics, still standing until burnt down in the 1980's. (Now rebuilt - Ed).

Before I left school I used to deliver milk from a can with a gill measure and also on Saturdays and school holidays from Easter to August look after fourteen cows on the village green for Uncle Bert. The Green was yellow with buttercups and sorrel all summer. I remember on one occasion as I was about to eat my bread and cheese a silly moo wandered on to the road just as Ralph Patterson was coming home on his bike. He went over the handlebars. He was grazed and bruised. I picked up his bike which was somewhat bent and took it on to his house just behind the green. No sympathy from his wife: "You shouldn't have been going so fast" says she. I then got back to my pitch on the green and my

Stephen Oakins, the postman

GENERAL INDEX

continued from page 35

continued on page 37

lunch-bag and found the silly moos had finished off my sandwiches. These particular cows, when taken back to the cow barns just went in their own stalls which had the usual names over the top, of Buttercup, Daisy, Bluebell, Rosebud etc.

No.42 was the village shop and Post Office run by Matilda and Robert Pratt. Tilly would cut an acid drop in half to get the correct weight. The telephone kiosk was inside the Post Office - no smoking allowed in this or damage to the directories.

When I was a lad we had a good football team. Teams from the villages around came to play. The referee used to change in the harness room behind the Bridgewater Arms and the teams changed in the hay and straw barns next to the cows. Frequently one or other went home with a mouse in his pocket. No shower or washing facilities were thought of then. On one occasion after a cup match when the ref had caused a lot of controversy he had to be escorted back to his changing room as the angry crowd were going to put him in the horse trough, and who should that ref be but the future chairman of the Football Association, Sir Stanley Rous.

In 1928 the estate was sold in lots and the cottagers were given the chance to buy their own home. My father, never having earned more than £3 a week, managed to buy no 11, the house we lived in, and no 10, the one next door occupied by Joseph Buggey who didn't want to buy. The pair of houses cost £240. In 1928 I knew everyone in the village.

(Editor's note: John and Win Oakins moved to no.10. John died in 1985 and Win continued living there until 1996 when she moved into Bede Court. Stephen Oakins the younger, John's brother, moved into no.11 when his mother Frances Oakins died around 1970.)

Nos. 10 and 11 Little Gaddesden

GENERAL INDEX

continued from page 36

continued on page 43

Lord Brownlow's heirs

Adelbert, third Earl Brownlow, died on March 17th 1921 aged 77. The circumstances are described on page 142. In Little Gaddesden you get the impression that he was the last Lord Brownlow. He didn't have any sons or daughters, it is true, but he certainly had an heir, a second cousin aged 54, a great-grandson of his great grandfather Brownlow Cust, with the same name as his own: Adelbert Cust (though with different middle names). This Adelbert was the next Lord Brownlow but, as he did not inherit the Earldom, his title was fifth Baron Brownlow. (An Earl is two ranks above a Baron in the peerage.)

It has already been mentioned that Earl and Lady Brownlow divided their time between their two big estates: Ashridge and Belton. In fact the Cust and Brownlow family had held the Belton estate since the early 17th century, and only inherited the Ashridge estate in the 19th century through marriage to an heiress of the Egertons. In Earl Brownlow's will he stipulated that Ashridge would be sold and Belton kept. The fifth Baron therefore inherited Belton in Lincolnshire where he and his heirs lived on, disappearing from the Little Gaddesden scene although involved in national affairs. In 1999 the title is held by Peregrine Cust, 7th Baron Brownlow.

Little Gaddesden church is full of memorials to the Egertons, holders of the Bridgewater title, the last of whom died in 1849. It is at Belton church that you will find the Cust and Brownlow memorials, and that is where Adelbert and Adelaide are buried.

1925 - NOTES FROM THE BERKHAMSTED DEANERY MAGAZINE

A garden fête in the Rectory on July 18th 1925 raised £60, a substantial sum. The event included an entertainment, and dancing on the lawn in the evening to the Silver Star Band. The article gives the receipts from every sideshow, including "Guess the weight of the choir ladies", which raised 10 shillings. The most exciting was "Bowling for the pig" (£5 raised), which seems to have been a regular attraction in this parish, as it was a main feature of the fêtes in the late 1940's. The main concern for fund-raising was the furnishing of the "memorial chapel to the fallen". Although there is no chapel with this dedication now, we have the carved wooden war memorial at the entrance to the Bridgewater Chapel, which is a focus for the annual Royal British Legion service on Remembrance Sunday.

The Batchelor family

By May Sears

My father was Thomas Sidney Batchelor. He came from Chequers End, Gaddesden Row. My mother was Lucy Richardson from Cambridgeshire. She was housekeeper to farmer brothers named Finch in Gaddesden Row, where they met and married.

My father obtained employment with the Hertfordshire County Council as a road sweeper in the Little Gaddesden area, where he worked for more than 40 years. He rented no.23 Little Gaddesden from the Ashridge Estate, and lived there for many years. I was born there in May 1915, and named May Elizabeth. My sisters were twins Pearl and Ruby, born in September 1916.

During the first world war my father was also a Special Constable. After doing his usual day's work he would have his tea, then put on his peaked hat and pick up his truncheon and whistle and go on duty. There was a "lock-up" at no.23, a large barn at the back (incorporated in the house) and below the third bedroom (looking into the school) there was a polished wooden seat all along the back wall. There were rings in the wall also, and a drain in the middle of the barn floor. I believe one suspect was caught near Goose Hill and detained here. The local policeman was George Williams who lived at no.21.

My father started a paper delivery when we were teenagers and able to help. He would start off very early on Sunday mornings, and cycle to the Gazette office in Lower Kings Road, Berkhamsted. He arrived home again about 8 o'clock, had his breakfast, and was off again delivering papers. I had a bicycle, and delivered papers in the Ringshall and Park areas. My sisters each helped nearer to home. The customers paid $2^1/_2$d for delivery.

A few years later, when I had left school, Mr Harold Ward started a paper delivery - he cycled from Hemel Hempstead. He then took over my father's Sunday round, and I am sure my father would have been pleased. Both of my parents were buried in Little Gaddesden church yard: Lucy Batchelor 1947, Thomas Sidney Batchelor 1969.

May, Ruby and Pearl Batchelor with their mother and father (Lucy and Thomas)

The Sears family

By May Sears, who was May Batchelor at the time in which this account is set.

Thomas George and Frederick Charles Sear came to Little Gaddesden in 1920 when Tom was eight years old and Fred five.
They were born in Berkhamsted. Their father was Alfred Sear and their mother Florence Proctor, both from Marsworth.
Their parents died during the first world war: their father was a regular soldier and their mother a straw plaiter who became ill and died. No members of their family came forward to look after them and they were sent to Dr Barnardo's home in Essex. They didn't like being there as the bigger boys used to bully them. Luckily they weren't there very long. Mr Francis Rogers and his wife decided to foster them. They already had a young son, Edward (Ted) Rogers. They lived in the park. Next door was Mr William Munden and his wife. It was the second pair of cottages from Ringshall, and many years later became Cherry Tree Cottage, the pair now being one house.

They settled down very well with the Rogers family and loved living in the park. Somehow their name got changed from Sear to Sears, and Thomas was always called Tim. Tim helped Frankie (as Francis was known) with the garden and the chickens, and Fred helped Mrs Rogers in the house with cleaning the fender and spoons etc. on Saturdays. Tim used to run all the errands. He fetched the milk every morning from Mr Bert Andrews' farm behind the Bridgewater Arms. He also brought Munden's, Hart's and Halsey's milk. The latter were living in Witches Hollow. They had milk cans with lids. Once the snow was so deep he fell and dropped a can which was lost until some weeks later when the snow thawed.

Frankie Rogers

Tim was often sent to Pratt's shop to get groceries for Mrs Rogers, who was a very good cook. She had worked for McDougall's, the flour people, before she was married. Frankie was a gardener at Ashridge House, and also verger at the village church. Tim was sent to the shop to get candles for the church. He was very small for his age and found a bundle of the large candles very heavy.

Frankie used to walk through the park to the Bridgewater Arms, cross the road to continue across Bridgewater Meadow to the Bede Houses and on to the church on Friday nights to light the boiler furnace under the church, and Tim would go with him for company. They would go again on Saturday nights, often in a blizzard, to try to get the church warm for Sunday. Mrs Pratt always grumbled that the church was cold. We children used to like to stand over the gratings where the warm air came through from below. Of course there were oil lamps to fill too, and candles to replace. It was never warm all over, being such a large place. Thank goodness for central heating and the new radiators.

The three boys got on well together, and went to the village school. I was there also with my twin sisters Ruby and Pearl. We all started at 5 years of age and continued until we were 14 years. Our head teachers were Mr Harrison, Mr Parker and Mr Jones. Miss F. Wright was infant teacher, Mrs Drewitt taught the

The school garden in 1926/27 with the Bede Houses behind.

Schoolboys, L to R:

Frank Welling, Bob Austin, George Wright, Bill Clifton, Alec Andrews (sitting), Albert Clark, Frank White, Pelham Oakins, Tim Sears and Gordon Pocock.

middle class and played the piano, and taught the senior girls cookery.

As it was a Church of England School we started the day with a hymn and prayers and half an hour's religious instruction. The rector came once a week to test us on what we had been learning. We finished the day also with a hymn.

Before school the seniors had to go into the school garden to read the thermometer and the rainfall and check the barometer which was on the wall in the senior class, and report on the weather.

The older boys had carpentry in one of the Bede Houses. The table tops, which had a vice attached, were turned over for the girls on cookery day. Both boys and girls learned gardening in my day. I shared a plot with Gordon Welling. We grew vegetables and flowers, and experimented with artificial manures. The boys made a theodolite for measuring height, and we went into the park to measure the tallest beech tree, the Queen Beech, which was in Golden Valley. We also went to Church Farm fields to measure hay stacks and find out how much hay was in them. We girls wondered what use this would be to us when we left school, but we enjoyed going into the meadows instead of being in school.

Tim always loved growing things, and went to Denison House where Mr Blake and Dickie Wells taught him everything they knew about growing grapes, tomatoes, cucumbers, melons etc. He also worked in the Ashridge gardens where he mainly did the clipping of the yew trees. When a boy he went to Ashridge with Frankie Rogers on Saturday mornings, and led the horse which pulled the mowing machine on the big lawn. It wore leather shoes so it didn't damage the turf.

Tim and I were married in 1935, and in 1938 we went to High Firs, Hemel Hempstead, where he was chauffeur-gardener.

Faerie Hollow in 1930

How the land was saved for the National Trust

Editor's notes:
The National Trust was founded in 1895.
Many of the characters in the following account, and the author of it, are related to Lady Brownlow as shown in the Talbot family tree on page 313 and described on pages 20 - 22.

by Barbara Cassell

Perhaps the main cause for gratitude to the memory of Bridget Talbot is the part she played in enabling the National Trust to buy Ashridge Park. Her brother

The Golden Valley 1930

Humphrey was concerned as a trustee of the Brownlow Estate; however, he was prey to long periods of depression - hence the "family joke" that he would not have achieved what he did without Bridget behind him. Of course he was a man and so was listened to more readily than Bridget, and he certainly had the entrée to important places. Another member of the group to save Ashridge was Sir James Craufurd of Aldbury - he was a barrister/civil servant.

Conty Sitwell wrote in 'Bounteous Days' :

"October 11th 1925
I went to stay at Little Gaddesden with Bridget. The next day history was made, as far as saving the park at Ashridge was concerned; a plot was hatched to preserve it. For it was to be sold, we knew, and all the marvellous beeches were to be cut down and sold... In the afternoon we two walked up to Ashridge by the familiar little paths. It really looked marvellous - the green slopes lying so peacefully in the sun - more beautiful than ever, now we thought it might perish with all its memories and what it meant to us and to many others.

When we got home again and were beginning tea Jim Craufurd appeared. A plan to save the park was discussed and our talks continued until 10 p.m. We went to church in

Bridget Talbot and her dog Paddy in 1901

above: Some of the Ashridge beeches in 1930.

below: Witches Hollow in 1930.

the middle of it all and the choir sang 'Jerusalem' and the words "England's green and pleasant land" spurred us on still further. So we rang Humphrey, who was a trustee for the estate, and asked him to meet us in London the next day to discuss a joint campaign. Jim and I composed a letter which we hoped would be signed by the Prime Minister, Mr Baldwin, and Lord Balfour, to be sent to The Times.

"October 12th
The next day was most exciting, in one way or another. Bridget and I set off early from Berkhamsted, just catching the train, and were met by Humphrey at Euston as planned. I did respect him, for he looked quite ill with worry and unhappiness over Ashridge. I felt how deeply he loved beauty and realised its tremendous importance. We held a long discussion, feeling like conspirators, and then launched Bridget off to Downing Street to do what she could.
I went back to Marchmont in the evening and Bridget rang up to say that she had caught Mr Baldwin, who was most anxious to help and had wired Lord Balfour to this effect. I did admire her determination and felt she ought to have a statue put up to her as the saviour of Ashridge.

"October 13th
The next morning I had a letter from an unknown gentleman thanking me with great feeling for my letter in The Times. I thought a great deal about the matter and wondered what was happening at the Trustees' meeting. It had really become a painful subject. The Times could really almost be called an Ashridge number, for there were a leading article, appeals, letters and comments about Mr Baldwin's interview. Indeed the first item of the news was that Lord Balfour had called on Mr Baldwin yesterday....

"October 14th
A light-hearted luncheon the next day with Jim Craufurd and Cooie. Bridget arrived in the middle. We all laughed a great deal, especially Jim, about how his letter had been 'put before' the Cabinet. He was in tremendous spirits and I felt had reached the zenith of his career!
There were still columns in The Times about it all; but it was rather a painful subject really with so little time to act and so much beauty threatened. We were very much amused by the leading article, appealing to Humphrey (as one of the Trustees) who, having been something of a family joke for years, was now the centre of so much attention."

Editor's comment: The campaign was very successful. Enough money was raised to purchase in 1926 the first two and a half square miles of land for the National Trust Ashridge Estate. Two areas were within the park: Thunderdell Wood and part of the adjoining "Old Park". Outside the park the acquisitions consisted of Berkhamsted Common, Northchurch Common, Aldbury Common, Pitstone Common, Ivinghoe Common, Duncombe Terrace, Flat Isleys, Steps Hill, The Coombe and Ivinghoe Beacon. This area was considerably increased in later years.
See the chapter on the National Trust on page 190

The school in the 1920s

by Min Catchpole

I write as one of three living generations to have had the privilege of being educated at Little Gaddesden School. My father, and possibly also my grandfather, attended the village school.

My earliest memories are of Miss Wright, who taught all subjects, including needlework, and was very strict. I remember being taught to count with small seashells which were kept in pastille tins.

Mrs Drewitt, my aunt, was my teacher in the Intermediate Class. I loved her handicraft lessons, where we were taught leatherwork, basket-making and seating of stools. Our classroom was separated from that of the top class by a very heavy curtain. The rooms were kept warm in winter by a donkey stove in the centre of an outer wall.

Shortly after I moved to the top class Vicars Bell arrived to take up the post of Headmaster following the death at an early age of Mr Jones. One of his first "reforms" was to place the cane on the top of a cupboard and it was never used again! I have so many wonderful memories of Vicars Bell, as do Hilary, Ian and Pat (the generation after me).

Music was a very important element of life at Little Gaddesden School, both choral and orchestral. We were so lucky to have the opportunity to learn a musical instrument. Music festivals were held in Deans Hall, Berkhamsted School, and we competed always in those.

Finally I must say how much we enjoyed our Christmas parties, provided by Mr and Mrs Rawdon Smith of John O'Gaddesden's House; they were very memorable occasions held in the old Village Hall which was so sadly destroyed by fire.

continued by Hilary, Ian and Pat on page 84

The Countess Brownlow Home for Boys

By Sam Richards. (Abridged)

Editor's note: The author had suffered two bouts of pneumonia at the age of six, leading to endless bronchitis problems. His father and his little brother both died of tuberculosis. He was an outpatient at St Thomas's Hospital, London, with which Countess Brownlow (Adelaide, wife of the third Earl) had strong links, which is how he came to be sent to the Countess Brownlow convalescent home for boys.

The building is now a private house, "Upper Gade".

This story is about another such boy called Billy, presumably fictitious, but based upon Sam's own experience. Hilda and Grace are undoubtedly the Welling girls, so the other people mentioned are probably equally real.

"Poor little blighter," was the thought of the only other occupant of the carriage. He'd been witness to the little drama played out on Euston Station a few moments ago... The open carriage door, Billy sitting just inside, holding onto his mother's hand so tightly - obviously dreading the inevitable.

Billy's dad - a tall, extremely thin man with black, curly hair - standing so still,

GENERAL INDEX

continued from page 37

continued on page 44

GENERAL INDEX
continued from page 43

continued on page 45

his deep-set eyes expressionless. The last words from Billy's mum (called out as the guard slammed the door shut), "I'll write you a letter, you'll get it tomorrow," found the man wondering, "What is all this about? Whatever it is, it's bloody sad."

Billy sat in his corner seat, looking out of the window; not seeing the soot-encrusted backs of the drab houses huddled alongside the rail tracks gradually giving way to green fields, to grazing cattle. He was aware only of his own sadness and of the train, as its wheels clackety-clacked over the rails, saying to him, 'going-away' - 'going away' - 'going-away'...

The matron, watching the handful of people emerging from the afternoon train at Berkhampstead, spotted Billy immediately, this eight-year-old, pathetically thin, lost-looking little boy, clutching his string-bound, brown paper parcel. With care she wrapped the thick travelling rug around Billy as the taxi trundled out of the station yard.

After tea he was taken over by 'nurse'. Nurse was a war widow; a living victim (ten years on) of that 1914 to 1918 war-to-end-wars. But perhaps the twelve boys in her care filled the need for the children she was herself denied. She knew the weakness, the debilitation, the aftermath of bronchitis, and helping Billy out of his evening bath wrapped him gently, snugly, into the huge, soft, white towel.

"So, you're back Billy," she said softly. "It's nice to see you again, and you know, don't you? - like last year, you're going to get better."

'The Countess Brownlow Home for Boys' at the tiny hamlet of Hudnall, was a large brick-built, red-tiled house with two lawns, a large kitchen garden, a chicken-run and several small outhouses containing tools, sacks of corn and discarded items from the house. The house itself was L-shaped, with a large conservatory which housed the boys' outdoor clothes. Each boy had his own cape, wellington boots and a wide-brimmed felt hat and, with such snug protection, they felt capable of coping with the wildest of weather.

Leading off from the conservatory were doors to the house, to the wash-room (with its two long, zinc baths), and to the kitchen. The kitchen contained the equivalent of a present-day Aga, an equally large gas cooker and a row of

BELOW LEFT
The Countess Brownlow Home in 1935 - 36

BELOW RIGHT
The Nurse and Matron in 1935 - 36

cooking rings, heated by paraffin. Always it was a busy, bustling place; a merry place where the cook, the nurse and Hilda would be endlessly preparing meals and (with the assistance of the boys), clearing away after them. Meal-times were a joy, with the food cooked to perfection and served in the games-cum-dining room, its large sash windows framing country scenes; trees, flowers, changing skies and - occasionally - the ancient gardener.

But the boys were not concerned with views. They - like all young things - adapted quickly to new surroundings, finding Hudnall Common - with its tall ferns, its copses and trees made for climbing - a perfect playground. (It was the night time which brought thoughts of home crowding into each boy's mind; bringing sadness for each one of them.)

But the light of day always heralded the return of cheerfulness - for the matron, whose personality set the tone - not only radiated warmth and contagious good humour; she had that wonderful gift of making important the things she wanted done: showing the boys personally how to make a bed, how to fold the corners, how to clean and polish her husband's large, brown walking shoes.

Occasionally - accompanied by matron - the boys visited Ashridge House, the former home of the Countess Brownlow. This elegant mansion - built of stone and complemented with delightful gardens of flowers and shrubs - was set in landscaped grounds, where beeches - surely the noblest of trees - stood in peaceful splendour, bluebells carpeting the sloping ground beneath the trees. The whole scene was breathtakingly beautiful to Billy's eyes.

He found himself wondering about Countess Brownlow - whose portrait hung above the fireplace in the dining room. To Billy, this beautiful, young, dark-haired lady was far removed from humanity. A goddess - at the very least!

In later years, Billy wished he could have known this remarkable lady, for he saw then a woman of kindness. A woman who, in creating a 'shared-environment' with boys from a totally different background, did so with no hint of patronization. Had there been, the atmosphere at the Home most surely would have reflected it.

The two, perpetually smiling, lady teachers at Little Gaddesden's village school, greeted Billy with warmth and pleasure, their soft Hertfordshire dialect enhancing their gentle natures. Once again Billy found himself (together with the other children at the pretty little school), bringing flowers and hedgerow plants to draw and paint on the coarse grey paper provided, and - as last year - the wooden rails attached to the classroom walls saw Billy's efforts reflecting the seasons, as winter gave way to spring and summer.

To get to school meant crossing two fields. In the

GENERAL INDEX
continued from page 44

continued on page 46

The clump of pines and pit in Nursery Field, still there in 1999

middle of one stood a clump of pine trees; and beneath those trees - half-hidden in the soft, sweetly smelling earth - the boys had discovered the remnants of an ancient rubbish dump, and only too often a frantic last-minute dash would save them from being late to school, due to the excitement of unearthing yet more fascinating relics from that treasure house.

And then there was Hilda.

Hilda lived with her mum and dad and sister Grace, in a house close by the Home, and dad - when sitting in his garden - was always surrounded by admiring boys from the Home. His face wore a continuous smile and he was forever making things out of wood for those boys. Bows and arrows were his speciality, and the matron didn't have the normal fear, that of impending catastrophe regarding those weapons; and for their part, the boys never had an accident resulting from their furious 'Cowboys and Indians'.

Hilda would be around fourteen or fifteen and Billy - who was now nine - knew that his heart was hers for ever and ever. She was the general dogsbody at the Home, and was a sparkling, pretty girl with long auburn-coloured hair. A laughing, full-of-fun, full-of-life girl, who captivated all the boys with her charm and vitality. Billy was privileged, beyond his wildest dreams when, upon her obtaining permission from the matron, he went with Hilda and Grace to the Tin-Hut on the edge of Hudnall Common, for Evening Service.

Billy had been pronounced fit!

The day had arrived at last - He was going home!

He held in his hand six newly-laid eggs in a brown paper bag. They were a present from a little old lady who lived all by herself in a small thatched cottage on the edge of Hudnall Common. (Each boy, leaving for home, took with him six new-laid eggs for his mum.) To collect his eggs meant walking from the garden gate to the old lady's front door. Her garden was one huge blanket of orange. Those marigolds - basking in the morning sunshine - were, to Billy, so beautiful. They became - together with the foxgloves, which grew, with their serene majesty at the base of the 'seven-beeches' on the common - easily his favourite flowers for all time.

Matron gave Billy a quick hug before he clambered into the London train. She saw another of her little boys returning to face another winter of thick, poisonous yellow fog which, hand-in-hand with poverty and overcrowding, would inflict further damage to his lungs. She did learn eventually that all was not doom-and-gloom because, unknown at the time was the effect that 'barrage of beauty' would have on a lad whose whole life-style - before the Countess Brownlow experience - had been devoid of beauty. The matron would learn also that, among the many young chest-sufferers to pass through her hands, there would be survivors, some of whom - including Billy - would return. Return to re-live their memories and - in their own way - to say 'thank you'

'Going-back-home' - 'Going-back-home' - 'Going-back-home' sang the train wheels ... That it was back to the foulness of life at the Elephant and Castle in the 1920's with its crudity, its squalor, the fearful swearing and bullying, back to dad's continuous coughing and his own yearly bronchitis mattered not one jot. The train had hardly stopped before Billy was running along the platform at Euston - his hands full of parcel and country eggs.

"Mum! - Dad!" ..... He just couldn't get to them fast enough.

Editor's note: Sam and his wife returned to visit the former Home in 1993, and kept in touch with Sarah Gall regularly thereafter, making a yearly visit until he died in January 1999.

GENERAL INDEX

continued from page 45

continued on page 48

An era of new building begins on the old Brownlow Estate

Land was sold and re-sold as larger tracts were split into smaller, and housing plots planned and sold. Various architects and builders were employed. The reasearch done by Canon Senar for his book on Little Gaddesden has provided most of the dates which I have used for this summary, and some of those would have been approximate. It was in about 1929 that new houses started to appear in the village, Kaim End at Hudnall and Ringshall End on the Beacon Road being two mentioned for this date, and the Ashridge Cottages commissioned by Sir John and Lady Davidson from the same architect, Clough Williams-Ellis, who converted Ashridge House.

Further building at Hudnall followed in the early 1930's, and the first 10 houses in Chapel Close were built in 1936-38, (though it was not called Chapel Close at first, as the The Methodist Church was not built until 1939).

In the park, the southeast side of Ringshall Road saw some building in the late 1930's, along with a few sites in Golf Club Road and Alderton Drive, though many of the houses seen there now were not built until after 1950. Some of the houses towards Pulridge and in that part of the wood called Park Pulridge also date from that time.

The builder who built the most houses prior to 1939 was probably Fred Whitman, who employed other village craftsmen and workmen, many of whom had formerly worked on the Brownlow estate. His father George had been a builder, but they both turned to farming for a while at Hudnall Common Farm, (p. 210)

above:
"Hedges", now "Chastleton", one of F.G.Whitman's first buildings in Hudnall Lane. The lady is Rhoda Miller who was active in village life and ran a prayer group.

below:
No.18 Little Gaddesden was set up as an estate office by Thomas Place for the sale of building plots

Frederick George Whitman

By his daughter Freda Morris

(See also her article about the rest of the Whitman family in chapter 19).

My father, F.G. Whitman, was the tenant at Hudnall Common Farm. He bought it in 1928 when the Ashridge Estate was sold and continued farming until 1929.

In 1929 he began building speculatively. His first house was Bury Orchard, Hudnall. He sketched many of his own plans and was always thoughtful for the effect of each house on its surroundings. Many of his houses were built with reclaimed bricks for this reason. He built Herkomer House for my brother, George Whitman junior, visiting Watford where a large house was being demolished, and buying materials and also the wonderful carved front door (mentioned in Canon Senar's book "Little Gaddesden and Ashridge").

Examples of his building skills are found in Gatesdene Close and the Crovells Estate, Hudnall, which were all built by him. When he did the alterations to John O' Gaddesden's House, the architect highly commended my father for his building expertise in matching the existing part of the house.

Some building craftsmen came from the surrounding area: from Little Gaddesden carpenters Steve Oakins and Bob Willmore, bricklayer Richard Fountain, painters Bob Jones and Jubal Jones. Also employed were George Purple and William Green. Electrical work was done by Stanley Ives, then of Hemel Hempstead, who lived for many years at Crovells, Hudnall.

Frederick G Whitman

Editor's notes: Some of the examples given: Gatesdene Close, the Crovells estate and work at John O'Gaddesden's, actually date from 1948 onwards, though the Crovells land was bought by Whitman in 1938. Examples of Whitman's work in

the 1930s however are recorded in Canon Senar's book, including at least nine houses in "Hudnall Common", ten in Hudnall Lane and two in Chapel Close. Earlier still, in the late 1920s, are the two Beany Cottages and Kaim End. The drive to Kaim End was extended to give access to the Crovells and now the whole road is referred to as (The) Grovells, (C has become G) though no road sign with this name has been seen. Other men who worked with F.G.Whitman are mentioned in the article on John O'Gaddesden's, (page 263). He died in 1961 at the age of 72 or 73.

Frederick Whitman's team building Hudnall Park in 1933

More from the 1930's

This was a period of both opening up and enclosing. As Bill White recalls: "I do remember some Shakespeare plays in the Golden Valley about 1936 when they saved that part of Ashridge Park from building, and being chased off the village green after it had been bought by Colonel Cuthbertson."

It was in 1930 that the National Trust acquired a really large part of the Park, including the Golden Valley and much of the land for the Ashridge Golf Course. The broad part of the Green, however, was privately owned until 1946 and the part on the opposite side of the road until 1986. The former now belongs to the Hertfordshire County Council and the latter to the National Trust.

Memories of the Red Lodge, Ashridge, 1930 - 1940

By Margaret Fox and Jean Strutt, daughters of Viscount and Lady Davidson

Although our memories of Ashridge differ, our shared impressions are of idyllic holidays spent amidst beauty and peace, and of the freedom and companionship which we joyfully embraced.

Our father was given the use of the Red Lodge (part of Ashridge House) which had been converted into a simple family holiday home. As Chairman of the Conservative Party he played a significant role in bringing into being Mr Urban Broughton's vision of the historic buildings of Ashridge becoming an educational centre, as well as being responsible for raising funds for the Bonar Law Memorial Trust.

Students from those days will recall the charm and humour of Major General Sir Reginald Hoskins, the first Principal of the College, under whose careful and compassionate leadership it was established; but we remember him as the rather daunting father of Ann Hoskins, our close friend and confederate. It was she who, together with Antony Hopkins, shared so many of our adventures and entertainments.

We enjoyed uninhibited freedom; countless games of cockie-olly and sardines

GENERAL INDEX

continued from page 46

continued on page 51

in the gardens and woods, tennis and swimming during warm days, musical evenings to delight and enchant, seemingly endless rides on our ponies through the natural splendour of the Golden Valley; and every morning, as we joined the College students in the Chapel for Morning Prayer, we gave thanks for it all to our Creator.

The ephemeral spirit of those pre-war years is lucidly captured in the pages of The Ashridge Journal, which was edited by Arthur Bryant. As Educational Adviser, his task was to provide academic depth to the College syllabus, but he also sought to inculcate a breadth of vision in the students by introducing a leaven of cultural and historical self-awareness into every course.

left to right: Margaret Davidson, Lady Davidson, Lord Davidson, Lady Hoskins and Ann Hoskins

For the first year after war was declared we were there more than ever, and were able to join the Little Gaddesden Choral Society. Rehearsals took place at the Manor where K Talbot provided the piano accompaniment. There, under the direction of Dorothy Erhart, we prepared to join other choral societies from all over Hertfordshire in a performance of Messiah in Berkhamsted Town Hall under the baton of Dr Reginald Jacques.

The ordeal of the homeward journey after those evening rehearsals remains a shared memory. Perhaps it was our first experience of the discomfort of war, finding our way home without torches, in darkness made blacker by the blackout and darker still by the impenetrable whispering blackness of the Ashridge trees, our feet frozen in the deep snow of that first winter of the war. It is a memory of such marked contrast with earlier impressions of Ashridge summers, green and warm and peaceful, of the Pony Club, the laughter of the fancy-dress parties and treasure hunts, and the timeless childhood joy of family and friendships.

Memories of a a childhood in Ashridge

by Antony Hopkins (born Antony Reynolds)

Back in 1930, my adoptive father Major T H C Hopkins (at that time housemaster at Incent's, Berkhamsted School) bought two derelict semi-detached cottages surrounded by two acres of weeds. They were situated on the border between Berkhamsted Common and Ashridge Park, and the name 'Woodyard' referred to a small sawmill in the open barn in the paddock opposite. I have dim memories of the house in a chaotic state as builders worked on the subsequent conversion to a single dwelling, but I was in hospital at the time of the move and so have no recollection of it. I was only 10 years old but, once there, I helped in what ways I could, chopping away at undergrowth and nettles and helping a little Irish labourer called Billy Mahon dig out terraces where the surrounding earth had been allowed to encroach directly against the southern wall of the house. My contribution may have been puny, but I enjoyed the work immensely and

Woodyard Cottages about 1930

shovelled away barrow-loads of clay with a will.

Soon we were settled in, and a more beautiful place in which to spend one's childhood can scarcely be imagined. Most blissful was my twelfth year, in which, owing to another operation, I was excused school. I had a tutor for 3 hours a day and spent the rest of the time with my beloved pony 'Dancing Girl', exploring the thousands of acres of National Trust land which surrounded us.

The Pony Club flourished under Mrs Gibbs at 'Beaney' and many happy events took place there including games of mock polo where, instead of a ball, a loofah would be tucked under the arm; opponents were supposed to grab it and carry it goal-wards.

Although being brought up as an only child, I had close friends at Ashridge, the Davidson Family, the Gordons and Ann Hoskins, all of whom lived at the big house. The gardens were our playground and, to this day, I delight in showing visitors from abroad the secret places that we knew so well as children. We used to swim in the concrete water tank in the courtyard.

My main contact with the village was through a little choir, enthusiastically conducted at the Manor House by Dorothy Erhart. I think Vicars Bell, the village schoolmaster, and I were the only two tenors and, sometimes, I doubted the worth of rehearsing Handel's 'Messiah' with such a tiny group. It all became worthwhile when we became part of a much bigger choir made up of all the local choral societies; suddenly we had grown from a dozen or so singers to become members of a 250-strong group conducted for the occasion by Dr Reginald Jacques. (I could not have dreamed that only a few years later I would become pianist to his famous Bach Choir in London.)

above:
Antony Hopkins at the piano at Woodyard Cottage

below:
as the Pied Piper at an Ashridge fancy dress party

When the prospect of war loomed and Ashridge was to become a hospital, it provided me with an opportunity to contribute to the war effort. Owing to a groggy left knee I was spared the call-up; instead I became 'salvage officer' at Ashridge. Camped out in the stables under the archway I would spend the day sorting huge piles of rubbish into separate heaps of rags, paper and fat. Once a week we would take bits of rather smelly waste to the local sewage farm. It was on these journeys that I learned to drive under the tuition of an engineer called Mac. Never to be forgotten is the occasion when I practised an emergency stop so effectively that the bins in the back of the van slid forward and emptied their contents over us!

I had enrolled at the Royal College of Music the very month that war broke out and my voluntary work at Ashridge soon became too much of a burden to combine with studies in London. From then on I would play the organ on Sundays in the hospital chapel or give occasional little concerts for the nurses. In time, even that became too much and I settled into 'digs' in London, my idyllic teenage years put behind me for ever.

CHAPTER 5 - *World War II*

1939 - 1945
The second World War

As 1939 came in, the Reverend Charles Wager was in his fifth year as Rector, Vicars Bell was in his tenth year as Schoolmaster, and Ashridge House was in its tenth year as the Bonar Law Memorial College.

German troops were already active establishing Hitler's dominance in Austria and threatening other neighbouring countries. In Britain contingency plans of many kinds were made, but there was one which would soon challenge village life all over the country: the evacuation of children from target areas. The evacuees were already on the move two days before war was declared. You will find them mentioned in many places in this book, but this chapter starts with two personal accounts. The first is by the late Vi Hughes, introduced by Betty Lait, and the second is by Betty Rogers. They tell the two sides of the same story.

Apart from this chapter, there are references to the war in the articles on the Church (page 132), the School (pages 155, 164) and Ashridge College (page 145).

Reminiscences of Vi Hughes

Vi Hughes was a much-respected resident who lived at one time at 'The Spinney'. Many will remember her; she was a woman of spirit and determination. The following account is taken from a tape of a talk she gave to the village school children in 1968. I have tried to keep as near as possible to her words.
Betty Lait

"Try to picture how things were. I shall start in 1938. At that time the old Post Office was on the other side of the road opposite the Bridgewater Arms. There was no house where Miss Crawford lives (No. 24 Little Gaddesden). The school was still the Victorian brick building; the entrance on the corner. The girls came in this way and the boys had to go round to the back. There were only two rooms. One room, on the left, for the infants and the big room. This was divided into two by a curtain hung on a rod. There were no lavatories inside the school; if you wanted to spend a penny you had to dash across the playground, never mind if it was pouring with rain or snowing. There were no plugs to pull, six lavatories all in a row. At the end of the day the headmaster, Mr Bell, had to swill down the trough. A nice job!

In 1938, most people knew a war was coming. In the village we formed a committee. One of our jobs was to go round the village measuring people for gas masks. We also asked who would be prepared to take into their homes children from London. Most wanted mothers and babies - you know how everyone loves babies. Well, in the end, as you know, war came.

I remember it was the Friday before war was declared; without warning a huge red London double-decker bus arrived in the middle of the village; fifty evacuees came off, boys and girls. We were all alerted; I took a gang of children to Ringshall. I remember one little boy; his name was Francis Bacon. On our way walking, we had no cars, we stopped at the village shop; all the children had a penny in their pocket. This little boy, Francis, thought I was rather important. He came up to me with his ice-cream and said, "Would you like first suck, Miss?"

GENERAL INDEX
continued from page 48

Finally, we got all the children to their foster homes. The next day, another bus arrived. We thought mothers and babies, not a bit of it, another forty boys and girls. The next day, Sunday, was the day war broke out. I was in Ringshall taking children from the last lot who had arrived and seeing how the ones I had placed were getting on. It was a lovely sunny September day; somebody had their window open. I heard the Prime Minister, Neville Chamberlain, say "As from now England is at war with Germany". I think I was outside the Laundry on the Ringshall Road.

We never had our mothers and babies; all we had were little boys and girls. The last lot arrived that very Sunday. We were desperate; all our homes were full and we had children to spare. I can't think why, but most people wanted little girls - nobody wanted little boys. We found ourselves with twenty spare little boys with nowhere to go. The large house, 'Beany', in those days was called 'Benhay'; Major Gibbs lived there and he was going to war. Mrs Gibbs and their children were going to Canada. We had an empty house and into this house went twenty grubby and tired little boys at the end of a very long day. Not enough beds, some had to sleep on the floor but, the next day, we had camp beds, blankets and plenty of people to help.

Before the evacuees came the village school had fifty pupils. Now there were one hundred and forty more. One night the village hall, a wooden building, was burnt to the ground. This was where all the dinners were cooked and served to the children - two hundred dinners to be cooked. Somehow we managed. Army camp cookers arrived and on that day everyone sat down to a hot meal.

The London children became part of the village and we became one large family.

Vi Hughes is in the Women's Institute picture on page 249

Little Gaddesden lst September 1939

by Betty Rogers, who was then Betty Humphreys

I was 14 when war was declared and went to a grammar school in Hampstead. I was the eldest of four children, having three brothers younger than me. When war seemed imminent, arrangements were made for evacuation of school children. My parents decided that I should leave my school and join my brothers so that I could keep a motherly eye on them. Incidentally. my own school went to Rutland, so I really think destiny took a hand in deciding that I should be a 'Little Gaddesdenite'.

We left London on Friday lst September, boarding a train at Gospel Oak station. We were told to carry a change of clothes, our gas masks and enough food for 24 hours. We also had a label attached to our clothing. My parents came to wave us off not knowing where our destination was to be. It seemed a very long journey to us children but eventually the train stopped and we all trooped out of the station at Berkhamsted, where a fleet of buses was waiting to take us to our respective places of safety. They were double-decker buses and had great

LITTLE GADDESDEN CIVIL PARISH

Residents at 31 December 1999

(This list has been compiled from the Electoral Roll (age 18 and over), and further information from residents. If any information is incorrect, we apologise most sincerely)

The names are presented as follows:
Surname, date first member of the family arrived in the village, husband and wife, child l, & child 2 etc.

Abraham: (1980) Richard and June: Jonathan, Caroline & Daniel:
Adams: Douglas and Teri: (1998) Rupert, Philippa & Sophie
Akery: Frank
Akery: Stephen and Lynn: (1986) Elliott, Laura & Alexander
Alderson: Gary and Shirley
Alexander: (1955) John and Helena
Allen: Peter and Patricia
Allen: Simon
Allen: Tracey
Allen: (1972)Trafford
Amos: Jennifer
Anderson: Sally
Anstee: (1987) Neil and Patricia
Archer: (1988) Anthony and Louise: Annabel, James & Lucinda
Ashman: (1998) Antony and Blanche
Askert: (1978) Bjorn and Marit: Per & Patrik
Atkins: Dennis and Jill
Aylwin: (1948) David and Enid

Bacon: Patricia
Bagshawe: Richard
Bailey: Norman and Bé
Banerji: Arnab and Susan: Arun & Robin
Banks: (Pre 1900) Wilf
Barnes: Kenneth and Caroline: Matthew, Abbie & Emma
Barnett: John: Charlotte & Emma
Baron: (1950) Clifford and Marjory
Barrington: Ross and Dorreen: Glenn
Beazley: James and Ann
Bell: (1999) Colin and Jeanette: Christopher, Nicholas & Emily
Berry: (1978) Arthur and Geraldine
Bexon: William and Sheena: Henry, Gabriella
Billen: (1982) Ralph and Jutta: Nicola & Michael:
Birdseye: Wilfred and Dele
Birks: (1978) Ken and Jenny
Birks: Alison
Blackborough: (1986) Diane & Michael
Bland: (1992) Michael
Bleackley: Dr and Mrs Pat
Bolton: Roger and Julia: Olivia & Jessica
Box: (1983) Eddis and Dora
Bradfield: (1951) Elizabeth
Brooks: Michael and Jill and Carly
Broughton: (1970) Stanley
Brown: (1999) Downie and Moya: Matthew & Kirsty
Brown: (1994) Peter and Sarah: Amelia & Flora
Browne: (1999) Robert and Maria: Oliver
Browne: Simon
Buesst: (1946) Adrian and Ursula: Miles
Buck: Graham
Buckingham: Claire
Bullock: Mireille
Bunting: (1928) Alan and Jane: Daniel
Bunting: Kenneth and Rebecca: Emma & Gary
Bunting: (1928) Peter and Janet: Philip
Burch: Joan
Burdess: (1973) Paul and Vicki
Burrell: William and Christine
Burnell: (1995) Julie
Byrne: (1983) Harry and Patricia:

Cade: Susan
Cameron: Dr Marjorie: Richard, Sally, Winifred
Camfield: (1999) James
Continued on page 53

difficulty, I remember, coming along the Ringshall Road because of the overhanging trees.

We arrived at the old wooden village hall that stood behind John O'Gaddesden's. Our party, from Fleet Road and Hogarth School in Chiswick, was met by a reception committee and a fleet of cars which were to take us to our billets. We were told that the place we had come to was Little Gaddesden in Hertfordshire. It could have been High Street, China for all we knew; it seemed as though we had been travelling for hours. I remember several people well on the first day, Mrs Hughes and Miss Moore among them. They all worked so hard trying to find suitable homes for us all and trying to keep families together.

My younger brother and I were taken by car to Hudnall along the village green, which had white posts and chain fencing all round it - soon to be removed for war metal. This was the first car ride many of the children had ever had. I was billeted at Hudnall Farm Cottages with Mrs Geater, who had a son and daughter about the same age as my brother and me and we all soon became firm friends.

I must confess I came to the country prepared to be condescending towards the natives but I was in for a shock as I soon discovered that, mostly, they were better housed and better educated for living than us 'Townies'. We were told to report to the school on Saturday morning, where we were first introduced to Mr Bell, the Headmaster. I couldn't believe my eyes. Could this man, dressed in red shorts, orange shirt and sandals be a headmaster. Those I had known had always been so formal but here was a man who sat on the lid of his desk, smoking his pipe, to talk to us. We were told that the school would be held on Monday as usual, but for only half-a-day, as the school could not accommodate us all. We weren't segregated but mixed with the village children and had classes according to ages.

War was declared on Sunday 3rd September, with a trial of air-raid sirens. Church bells tolled as a warning of invasion and we realised that war was with us.

We quickly settled down in school and learnt a lot of new things. We had handwork with Mrs Drewitt - I made a basket which I had until a few years ago, also leather work, danced round the Maypole and went for glorious walks in Ashridge and Hoo Wood.

Hudnall Common became a favourite playground, with its chalk pit with sides that seemed to us as steep as the Matterhorn. Also it was a good source of wood to help out the fuel situation.

Everyone was encouraged to do their bit towards the war effort and school was no exception. After the first winter it was decided to form a Young Farmers Club, so pig sties were built, rabbit hutches made, hen runs erected and livestock purchased. We all took turns in feeding and cleaning out. Maths became fun working out the cost of food etc. and profit made. Whenever pigs were fattened and killed, the pork was shared among members and we drew lots for the prime cuts. The gardens were planted with vegetables and we learnt that potatoes, beans, etc. were not things we bought for so much a pound from the street markets, but things that had to be looked after to be at their best. I remember when we dug our first potato crop a boy from London told Mr Bell that he thought it a good idea to hide the 'spuds' so that Hitler wouldn't find them. I also learnt a lot about growing apples; at the time Hudnall Farm was a flourishing apple farm. Mr Geater worked there for Mrs Heathcote, and the first autumn I was there I picked, graded and packed Cox's Orange Pippins. I didn't know so much went into apple growing; how they had to be pruned, sprayed and generally nursed for 12 months of the year.

1999 Residents list continued from page 52

Cannon: (1986) Graeme and Louise: Jennifer & Katherine
Case: Hubert and Pauline
Cassell: (Pre 1900) Alfred and Barbara
Cassidy: James
Catchpole: (Pre 1900)) Ian and Pat: Emma & Deborah
Catchpole: (Pre 1900) Min and Hilary
Catesby: (1993) Brian and Beryl
Catling: Kevin and Shirley: Katie & Dean
Cattell: Roger and Jayne: Gemma & Nathan
Chapman: (1995) John and Susanne: Sadie & Cassie
Chilton: (1979) David and Sigrid: Joe
Christian: (1927) Jane: Daisy-Jane
Christofferson: (1973) Torgeir and Anamargrethe
Clark: (1998) Robert
Clifford: Elizabeth
Coates: Reginald and Shelia
Cohn: (Mid 1980s) Ronald and Barbara
Collier: (1937) Clive and Penny: Ryan & Wayne:
Collier: (1937) Percy
Collier: (1937) Stanley
Comer: (1993) Philip and Shiamala: Jeremy
Cook: Carol
Cooper: (1998) Andrew and Heather: Aisha
Cooper: (1988) Tim and Glenda
Coombs: (1999) Robert and Paula: Andrew, Michael, William & Nicola
Corby: Robert (Bill) and Brenda
Cornwall: Phillip and Eunice
Cory-Wright: (1925) Francis
Cowlard: George and Edith
Cox: Mark and Sarah
Crack: (Pre 1900) Kathleen
Crawford: (1965) Margaret
Crawford: (1965) Patrick
Creed: (pre-1900) Pat
Cripps: (1929) Graham and Fiona: Hannah & Harry
Crispin: (mid-1940s) Nicolas
Crowhurst: John and Patricia
Cullimore: Philip and Tracey
Cunningham: Peggy
Cusdin: (1953) Sidney (Teddy)

Dahl: (1971) Per and Margaretha
Dalton: (1989) John and Shelia:
Daly: Renee
Danbury: John and Yvonne
Darragh-Haddow: William and Gail: Nicola
Davies: Claire
Davies: Joan
Davies: Jean
Davis: (1980) David and Carol: Justin & Nicola
Davis: (1986) John and Janet
Davis: Michael
Davis: (1965) William and Jane
Day: (1971) Jeremy and Barbara
Dibley: Gary
Dickens: Philip and Pamela
Dickinson: Melvyn and Diana: Elizabeth & Phillip
Dickson: (1957) Kenneth
Dilks: (1987) James and Julie: Sam
Dilks: (1987) John and Susan: Ben & Amy
Dixon: Margaret
Dobson: Diane
Docherty: (1998) Mark and Fiona McWilliams: Isabelle
Docker: Christopher
Dover: (1978) Carla and son Willum
Drinkwater: (1989) Dr David and Janet: Anna
Duncan: (1987) Thomas and Kathleen: Robert & Sarah
Dunham: Howard
Dyson: Peter and Pamela: Clare

Eames: Leonard and Elizabeth
Eccles: (1984) Geoffrey and Marjorie
Ehrlich: Geoffrey and Susan
Ehrlich: Josef and Anne
Elkes: Stephen and Lorna
Elliott: Paul and Joanna
Ephgrave: Martin and Patricia: Matthew, Oliver, Sarah & Michael
Erlick: Arnold and Elise
Evans: Heather

Continued on page 54

The winter of 1939-40 was very severe; we had never seen such snow in our lives before. Hudnall Lane had drifts over the hedges and transport came to a halt. We trudged to school through the fields; it was easier than trying to go through the roads. We took sandwiches as there were no school meals then. The snow drifts looked beautiful and we spent hours tobogganing. A lot of children returned to London during this winter, some with tragic results - one family being killed within days of returning.

I loved life in the village, with the friendliness of everyone; neighbours you really knew chatted away in the evenings whilst working in their gardens. Then there was that mysterious 'grapevine' that gets news from Ringshall to Hudnall in no time at all. I had a good example of this on my first day at Little Gaddesden; my two brothers were whisked away to a different billet to me but, before an hour had passed, we learnt that they were at Covetous Corner with Mrs Leggett.

The trades people also held a fascination for me. I had never seen food delivered before, except milk, but everything was brought to the door. The Co-op came every week by horse and cart from Berkhamsted with groceries, milk by pony and trap, not in bottles but with a churn and measured into a jug at the door. During the winter, when roads were impassable, the dairy came round with a sledge. There was also a butcher's boy, who delivered meat on a cycle; he was always whistling and shared his chocolate with me.

I thought that living in the country would be boring but how wrong I was. There was always so much going on; the usual organisations were still meeting in spite of war. I joined the Guides and we built fires and cooked in the open air. Miss Moore was the Guider and, under her leadership, we did our bit by knitting squares for blankets and collecting rose hips for syrup. Later I joined the Women's Institute; Mrs Hughes was President and we were kept busy knitting for the Forces and making jam.

Ashridge has always played a big part in Gaddesden affairs and wartime was no exception. Prefab huts were soon erected to receive wounded from the war. Doctors and nurses came to look after them. Some of the nurses I remember well as quite a number attended services held at the Methodist Chapel that used to stand in the wood behind Hudnall Farm. The mid-week service there was very enjoyable; all the congregation took part in singing hymns and prayers. One particular nurse had a beautiful voice and always sang Crimond to us. There were also dances organised for the troops in Ashridge.

Our first Christmas away from home was a happy one; everyone did their utmost to make us feel at home. My brothers and I were invited to spend Christmas at Hudnall Farm with Mrs Heathcote. There was quite a party and, although it was wartime, we had a wonderful Christmas turkey and a Christmas pudding that was flamed with brandy. I had never seen this before and I must admit I was a little scared. We all had presents from a large tree and played games and sang carols round the lovely fireplace with a huge log blazing. Mr Ellen also lived at Hudnall Farm Cottages and rounded all the children up and took us carol singing, accompanied by him on his mouth organ. That evening was the first time I had been in the Manor House, where Miss Talbot entertained us with hot chocolate and biscuits.

Once when the army were on manoeuvres the King visited Hudnall Farm and had lunch with his officers in the apple sheds. It was all very hush-hush and nobody knew about his visit except us living on the farm. He gave us a friendly wave as he left.

After I left school I went to live and work at Janes' butcher's shop (now no

1999 Residents list continued from page 53

Evans: (1999) Michael and Jackie
Evans: Robin and Susan
Evans: Richard and Barbara: Alex & James

Faulconer: (1978) Derek and Tessa
Fay: (1994) Anthony and Mary
Fielder: (1977) Auriel: Ian
Filby: Michael
Fishenden: (1997)Neil and Melanie: David & Nicholas:
Fleckney: Clive and Gillian: Rebecca & Elizabeth
Fisher: Vivien
Fletcher: (1985) David and Mary: Stephen & Victoria
Foord-Kelcey: (1939) Nicholas and Vivien: Guy & Luke
Forster: (pre 1900) Geoffrey and Wendy: Adrian
Fotsch: Robert
Fountain: Reginald
Fountain: Paul
Foxall: (1948) Peter and Enid
Francis: (1966) Christine
Fraser: Colin and Susanna
Filipedes: (1999) Chistopher and Katherine:
Fraser-Beck: (1962) Stuart and Patricia:
Freake: George and Hilda: Mark
Frostick: (1989) Nigel and Gillian: Thomas

Gadbury: (1990) George and Betty: Iain, Halina-Joy
Gall: (1984) Francois and Sarah: Nicholas, Tamara, Saskia & Edward
Gascoigne: Victor
Geater: Keith and Daphne
Gibson: David and Bessie
Gilbert: Malcolm and Lynda
Gillespie: (1976) William and Doreen
Godar: George and Susan: Sarah & Rebecca
Godwin: (1956) John and Jean
Goldberg: Matilda
Gomez: Denise
Good: (1999) James and Rachael
Gould: (1979) John and Susan
Graham: (1986) Dan and Jenny: Simon
Grainger: Andrew
Grant: Nicholas and Belinda
Gray: (1956) Syd and Stella
Green: (1996) Stuart and Sally: Oliver & Alexander
Green: Leslie and Margaret
Green: Roland
Green: (1935)William and Roma: Derek
Greenall: Mark and Wendy
Greenleas: (1995) Mark and Gillian: Alastair & Charlotte
Gregory: Brian and Sylvia
Griffiths: Darren

Hackett: David and Penny: Ben & Jennifer
Haldane: Roy
Halsey: Philip and Patricia
Hamilton: Nelson and Victoria
Hancock: Michael and Gillian
Harris: Peter and Caryl
Harris: (1996) Warren and Helen: James, Oliver & Tobias
Hart: (1963) Thomas and Rosamunde
Harvey: Lloyd and Eileen: Josh, Liam & Colm
Hatt: (1994) Martin and Karen: Sam & Ben
Hawkridge: David and Jean
Hayes: (1983) Richard and Ellen: Charlotte & Emily
Hayes: (1996) Amanda
Haynes: Mandy
Heard: (1981) David and Anne
Hedges: Mary
Heeps: Jenny
Hemley: Adam
Hepburn: (1968) David and Lois
Heron: Peggy
Hewitt: David and Irene
Hill: Doris
Hill: Simon and Sara
Hill: William
Hinchliff: (1994) Stephen and Anne: Josephine
Hind: Patricia
Hobbs: Sarah
Hockings: Timothy and Helene

Continued on page 55

longer a shop, but converted into a residence). Mrs Janes was a lovely person and I was very happy there. I helped with the accounts and, when their help went into the Air Force, I did a lot in the shop and also delivered meat to Little Gaddesden and other surrounding villages. Mrs Janes was very nervous of air-raids and, when she heard the German planes going over and heard gun-fire, she often put on her fur coat and went into the fridge with the meat. All the time I was there she never overcame this fear and, I must say, it was justified in some ways - several bombs fell on the village and one about two hundred yards from the shop.

The London balloon barrage could be seen on clear days and, on one particularly clear morning after the sirens had sounded, one very old-timer, living in Hudnall Lane at the time, pointed at the distant balloon specks and was heard to say, "Here they come in their thousands", thinking the sky to be full of enemy planes.

There is so much I could tell you about my impressions; the more I think about my first years in Little Gaddesden, the more I seem to remember, like cooking lessons we had at Beaney. The poor boys living there were fed on the results. They all survived though. Ronnie Waters was one of them.

The things that stick in my mind most are the things I now take for granted, like the brilliant moonlight we get in the country, the spotless snow and everyone knowing each other, not from inquisitiveness but genuine friendliness. For those that remained, country life soon became preferable to town life. Firm friendships grew up between town and country children and 'Old Wardy's' and Miss Pratt's shop soon became as familiar to us as to any Gaddesdenites (as the locals were referred to by us Townies).

Little was it thought in the early days that the village would be the growing-up place for many of the children who remained to pass from childhood to adults during the six years of war. Six years when the village saw the development of the big military hospital at Ashridge and the even larger army camps on Ringshall Common when, during the preparation for the invasion of Europe, it was not uncommon to see army vehicles up to the largest tanks and guns rumbling through the streets and fields alike.

There must be many children who arrived, quite out of depth, in bewilderment, on lst September 1939, who now remember Little Gaddesden wasn't such a bad phase in their lives after all and, to some, it was not just a phase but a permanent home.

The Home Guard - its early days in Little Gaddesden

by Michael McCaul

This note does not pretend to provide a full account of the Little Gaddesden Home Guard's activities for 1940-44 but contains the personal recollections of a 17 year old recruit, who served until leaving for military service early in 1941.

In a broadcast at 9 pm on 14 May 1940, Anthony Eden, Secretary of State for War, called for the establishment of a part-time volunteer force of men between

1999 Residents list continued from page 54

Hodge: Rex and Heather (1965)
Hodgson: Peter and Jacqueline: Maxine
Holden: (1980s) John and Tracy: Oliver, Rebeka, Oscar & Luke
Hollings: Mark
Honour: Jill: Leon, Luke and Laura
Hook: (1999) Peter and Karen: Isaac & Penny
Hooper: Neal
Hope: Jeanne: (1970)
Hopkins: Christopher and Patricia
Hopkins: Len and Margaret: (1963)
Hopkins: Antony
Hornsey: Lee and Karen Potts: Daniel & Jack???
Hughes: Gwyneth (1989)
Hughes: (1971) James and Dilla
Hughes: Matthew
Hughes: (1971) Peter and Georgina: James, Emma, Richard, Abbi & Peter
Hughes: (1971) Richard and Susan:
Humphreys: (1962) Gerald and Rita
Hunn: (1980) Peter and Nicky: Pippa and Lucy
Hunt: Ken
Hunt: Tony
Hurrell: (1991) Jack and Jennifer: Simon & Daniel
Hutton: (1995) Olive and Stanley
Hyde: Arnold and Lyn: Victoria & Robert:

Isherwood: (1984) Patrick and Anne: Caroline & Joe
Ives: (1954) Joan

James: (1980) Philip and Heidi
Jefferson: Peter:
Jefferson: (1996) Tracy
Jefferson-Perry: (1996) Alice
Jefferson-Perry: (1996) Harry
Jenkins: Graham and Margaret: Nicholas, Jonathan, Edward & William (1997)
Jones: (1977) Paul and Jean

Kelly: Paul
Keohame: Paul
Kibble: (1988) Ian and Deborah: Emma & Aaron
King: Carol
King: Ralph and Valerie
Kirkpatrick: (1979) Anne
Knight: Suzanne:
Kruger: Lorna

Lait: (1989) Betty
Lane: Mark and Lynne
Laver: Janet
Lee: Stephen
Leonhardt: (1977) John and Julie: Peter
Lishman: (1984) Mary
Littlejohn: Mike
Lloyd: James and Louise
Lord: Martin
Love: William

Magson: Andrew and Julie
Mahapatra: Diptimay and Ruth: Robert
Maioni: Silvia
Malkin: Kevin
Maniloffe: Edmund and Denise: Kaliff, Bhrak & Jamahl
Mann: Bob and Jane: Josephine
Mann: (1974) Peter
Marks: (pre 1900) Rose: Peter
Marshall: Marjorie
Marshall: (1977) Julian and Philippa
Martin: (1973) Mollie
Martin: Patricia
Martin: Maurice and Elaine
Martin: Steve
Masters: Neill and Ellen
Masters: (1992) Jeffrey and Fiona
Mawhood: (1993) Piers and Christine: Robin, Richard & Ben
Mayling: George
McCann: Paul
McCarthy: (1985) Shaun and Julie: Georgina, Emma & Michael
McCarthy: (1992) Scarlet & Edward

Continued on page 56

1999 Residents list continued from page 55

Maclarty: Janet
McCracken: (1975)James and Angela: James
McGarvey: Janice
McGee: Adam
McGill: Helen
Mac Ginnis: Shelia
Mead: Megan
Mecklenburgh: Howard and Michelle
Memszak: Caroline
Miller: Michael and Liza
Miller: (1993) Stewart & Kathy: Neil
Mitchell: (1984) John and Wendy
Mocatta: (1926) John and Naomi
Mogg: (Pre 1900) Colin and Barbara
Mogg: (Pre 1900) Andrew
Moody: (1975) Tony and and Vanessa: Anna & Kate
Mooring: Tony: David
Moran: Michael and Sandra: Sarah Jane
Moreton: Jeremy and Vanessa
Morgan: Phillip and Teresa
Moriarty: (1995) Jacqueline: Sophie
Morris: Anna
Moulster: Ronald and Kathleen
Mountfort: (1950) Victor and Phyllis
Muddiman: (1975) Stella
Mundella: Anthony and Hilary
Muir: Ian and Shona: Jonathan & James
Musgrave: (1985) Isobel: James, Alex, Jennie & Heather
Musgrave: Marjorie
Musk: Leonard

Nash: (1998) Barry and Sue: Lucinda & Charles
Nash: (1954)Dot:
Nash: (1939) Kenneth and Cherry
Nash: (1998) Nan
Nation: Katie
Neale: Deborah
Newman: (1998) Raymond and Mollie
Newman: Robin and Brenda
Noble: (1992) Peter and Susan: Katherine:
Nolan: Thomas and Anne
Norton: Damian and Susan
Nowell-Withers: (1989) David and Margaret: Stephanie
Nunn: (1980) Peter and Carol: Michelle & Nicola

O'Connor: (1991) Tom and Tracy
O'Neill: Elizabeth: Karoline
Oakins: (Pre 1900) Win
Odedra: Naresh and Gigi: Amit & Santock
Orwin: Douglas and Jean: Neil
Orsborn: Charles and Shirley
Osborn-Jones: (1975) Christopher and Carolyn: Timothy, Jennifer, Adam & Rosie
Oswald: (1995) Stuart and Debra: Daniel
Ouseley: (1949) Eve

Palmer: Gordon and Vera
Palmer: John and Gillian: Dominic & Martine
Page: Deborah
Parmar: Pratibha
Parker: Kelly
Parker: Nicholas and Margaret
Paterson: (1976) Bill and Fiona
Pearce: Peter and Kay
Pearse: Michael and Pamela
Perrott: (1999) Jeremy and Amanda: Lucy & Lilly
Peters: (1979) Prof Wallace (Peter) and Ruth
Pickrell: Donna
Pike: Anthony and Anne: Lucy & Robert
Plumley: Mary
Pollard: Roger
Pollard: Natasha
Potts: (1999) Robert and Maureen
Power: Steve and Ann: Clare & Tom
Price: (1975) Geoffrey and Marilyn Price
Pritchard: Alan and Susan
Pulver: Alan and Leila: Dominic & Tristan
Purple: (Circa 1926) Elsie

Rabbetts: Richard (Bunny) and Jan
Radford: William and Jean

Continued on page 60

17 and 65, for the purpose of supporting the main field force. Volunteers were advised simply to report to their local Police Station. This broadcast was made less than a week after the German 'blitzkrieg' began on the continent in which airborne forces and parachutists were said to have played an important part, as in Norway in April.

In Little Gaddesden, the first volunteer called at the local Police House at 7 am on Wednesday 15 May. He arrived on horseback and dismounted outside the house itself, while his horse cast longing eyes on PC Parker's well-tended roses. PC Parker was not at all pleased by this early visit, because he had heard nothing of the broadcast during a period of night duty at Berkhamsted. In the event, this volunteer proved to be over-age and was not recruited!

Between Wednesday and Saturday (18th), PC Parker had 'logged on' some 50 recruits, who received orders to attend a meeting at the Red House, residence of Major J N Gray, on Saturday afternoon, who had been appointed local commander. They would be visited by the Company Commander of Berkhamsted, Col R H Haslam. Unfortunately the Colonel was late on parade, to the displeasure of those volunteers who had urgent duties to perform, including the afternoon milking. Nevertheless the Colonel had some interesting things to say. The Little Gaddesden Platoon (No. 5) was part of the Berkhamsted Company (No 7, later B) and formed part of a County Force. It would be from Berkhamsted that the Platoon would receive its call-out instructions; a telephone point was established in the Old Armoury (behind No. 27 Little Gaddesden) which, at night, would be manned by John Oakins and George Wright. It was recognised that telephones were few and far between, so the call-out would involve cars speeding through the village, backed-up by youths on bicycles making some house-to-house calls.

The Platoon Commander established four sections, based on the Golf Club, Hudnall Four Ways Garage, Ringshall Deer Leap Garage and one at Great Gaddesden. Their role initially was to mount night and dawn patrols in these areas. Each section had two rifles. Some patrols included enforcement of the 'black-out' in their briefs and there were some very heated exchanges with delinquent householders, particularly in the Park.

The dawn patrols were regarded as particularly important but, on one morning, the Golf House patrol not only failed to wake up in time but even to hear the telephone!

Meanwhile, there were drill sessions at the week-ends and some rifle practice at Piccotts End. The platoon was also introduced to the Mills bomb or '35' grenade, with which veteran members were only too familiar. For some reason it was decided that the Local Defence Volunteers could not be issued with these grenades but instead they were introduced to the 'Petrol Bomb' (Molotov Cocktail) and the 'sticky bomb'. Some petrol bombs also included phosphorus. At the Deer Leap, a bombing platform was built to the side of a barn overlooking the roadblock. It was not possible to employ a roadblock at the Village Green end of Hudnall Lane, but a wire hawser across the Lane was supported by a remote-controlled roadblock, operated from a concealed point from what is now the garden of Treetops.

An antique farm wagon was also found to be placed across the Ivinghoe Road. It was to be supported from a firing point concealed below ground level, manned by a sub-section of Ringshall-based veterans, led by Bill Harmon, a retired Metropolitan Police Sergeant.

In early July, the Platoon was delighted to receive a delivery of '303' rifles, recently imported from the USA, where they had been taken from depot and where they had been stored in grease. Grease removal was a tedious business. These rifles came with rimless ammunition, as opposed to the 'rimmed' rounds used by the British Army since the First World War. Some veteran volunteers had anxious moments when the rimless rounds sometimes were not extracted before the next round being loaded actually caused the rifle to be fired.

These US rifles (P.40s) arrived only a few days before the Platoon was called out on the afternoon of 16th July. The siren sounded in Berkhamsted and in Little Gaddesden the roadblocks were put in position. Volunteers were instructed to stop all vehicles and detain those who could not produce identification and place their vehicles under guard in the car park which, in the event, was to contain many vehicles. There were, of course, complaints about such treatment and one complainant was the Mayor of Dunstable, who had been looking forward to picnicking on Ringshall Common with his family. Quite reasonably he pointed out that the alarm was not in force at Dagnall (Bucks) or Dunstable (Beds).

It was not until the evening that the alarm was called off by Company Headquarters, but not before questions being asked about what had caused the alarm to be activated. The explanation heard in Little Gaddesden was that earlier in the day someone saw numerous white blobs in the sky high over Hemel Hempstead, identified them as parachutes, and reported this to Company Headquarters, where the Duty Officer, wakened from a post-prandial nap, panicked and decided on the call-out! Not long before the alarm was called off, a Fleet Air Arm officer, accompanied by an attractive young lady and driving an MG sports car, was stopped at the Deer Leap on his way to Dunstable, after an afternoon on Ringshall Common. He had no means of identification. He was offered the use of the telephone to secure confirmation of his identity from someone who knew him but he reacted strongly to the suggestion that we might wish to contact his home address! Since no-one had any doubt that he was whom he said he was, he was allowed to go and left expressing warm thanks and appreciation as to the tactful handling of his case!

Little Gaddesden saw little of the daytime Battle of Britain but, on August night patrols, heard a number of single German aircraft overflying the area. No bombs were dropped but, on 24 August (the date on which the Luftwaffe began bombing London by night), an aircraft dropped a large number of incendiaries which fell in fields at Dagnall, in which the bombs seemed to fall uncannily between the stooks of corn waiting to be carted, and did little damage. The entire platoon was called out during the evening but there were no further incidents.

Meanwhile the LDV had been renamed the 'Home Guard', at Winston Churchill's insistence, and khaki battledress began to replace the ill-fitting clothing issued in June. Training went on and there were one or two inconclusive 'mock'

BELOW TOP
Betty Bunting, Molly Austin, Lottie Liberty, Mrs Thame, Ivy Fleckney and another of the wives at a garage which was used as an ARP or Home Guard base.

BOTTOM
Concrete road blocks, now outside Beaney.

attacks by the Hudnall Platoon on the Deer Leap Ringshall Platoon.

September had always seemed to be the most likely month in which the Germans might invade by land and air and the air attacks on London's East End on 7/8th September were seen as a possible preliminary. As is now known, on the afternoon of 7th September, Whitehall had decided the invasion was imminent and, at 8.07 pm, Home Forces' Headquarters issued an order, "All troops to battle stations" which led, among other things, to the Home Guard being called out and, in many places (but not here), the church bells were rung. At 8.30 pm the call reached Little Gaddesden, where roadblocks were quickly established. It seemed to some that this call was no rehearsal but rather the 'real thing' when the roadblocks having been mounted, a column of Dorset Regt bren-carriers and trucks arrived and required the roadblock at Deer Leap to be moved so that the column could take up their 'battle station' on Goosehill, overlooking a secret RAF establishment at Edlesborough. The order to stand down at about 10 pm came as a sort of anti-climax.

As far as is known, no German agent landed by parachute in the village but various small deception devices were dropped by the Luftwaffe to suggest that landings had been made. While the Germans did not abandon their plan to invade until February 1941, the aerial bombardment of towns and cities went on until May 1941. During this campaign over 100 bombs fell within the parish but only two caused real damage. In late September, one of a stick of twelve small bombs (two of which virtually straddled the Church) hit the water main in Ringshall Road; clearly the bomb had passed between the telephone wires and the hedge before hitting the water main. Earlier, on 9 September, a land mine landed only a few hundred yards from Ashridge Hospital but did no lasting damage.

There was, in fact, little for the Home Guard to do in the winter of 1940/1 but to continue to train and mount night patrols, absorbing a good deal of time and effort, often on the part of hard-working middle-aged volunteers. But the Home

Guard went from strength to strength in the field of training, which involved access to advanced weaponry and a good deal of exercising with locally-based Field Forces. Its strength was improved in 1941 when Government decided on a measure of conscription. The Home Guard continued to develop its resources until 1944; in some parts of the country Home Guards were employed as auxiliaries in AA Batteries, but the Little Gaddesden Platoon remained as a part of the local Defence plan until being part of the national stand down in December 1944. According to a message from King George VI, in May 1941, " the Home Guard stands in the direct line of the various bodies of Militia, trained bands, fencibles and volunteers, the records of whose fine spirit and military aptitude adorn many a page of our history".

During four years, the Platoon had earned small sums of money by way of subsistence allowances, the scales of which were meagre indeed. A sum of about £90 was due but, as the individual sums involved were difficult to calculate, there was consensus that the 'ration money' be used to assist in the formation of The Gaddesden Society, still very much a feature of village life today.

The Home Guard in 1942

Members identified in the photograph are numbered from left to right:

BACK ROW:
3rd Sam Geater
4th Jack Mayling
5th Reg Purton
7th Harry Clifton
11th Francis Cobb
12th Seth Janes
13th Fred Andrews
14th Alec Andrews
18th Arthur Whitman
19th Harold Ward
21st William McCaul
23rd Herbert Duncan

THIRD ROW
1st Arthur Collett
2nd Harry Hucklesby
3rd Billy Clifton
6th Ken Page
7th George Wright
10th Gordon Stock
11th Cyril Wright
14th Goodman

SECOND ROW
1st Jubal Jones
3rd Selby Hughes
4th Vicars Bell
5th Tyler
6th Col. Gray
7th Horace Halsey
8th Bunn
9th Jo Hing

FRONT ROW
1st Billy Moor
2nd Stanley Bunting
3rd Dick Orange
10th George Purple
12th Arthur Maunders

Blitz over Gaddesden

by Lyn Hyde

When I was a little girl there were several patches of stinging nettles growing in the meadow behind No 10 which marked the places where bombs fell during the War. I, of course, imagined it had been the blitz and that Gaddesden was as badly hit as London, Coventry, etc. In fact they were from a stray German bomber which had lost its way and was jettisoning its bombs before heading home. They fell up near the Church, in the back meadow and more up the Ringshall Road near 'Saxons', which broke the water main and flooded the road. This was in September 1940. My mother had taken three evacuee children, the Bacon family, two boys (yes, one was called Francis) and a girl. Their family in Clapham sent frequent letters complaining that they hadn't been to bed for nights because of the bombing, so mother suggested a week's rest in the country. Mum, Granny and baby Bacon duly arrived. The bombs, of course, fell during their first couple of days - the nearest they had been to an explosion and they nearly took the first train back to Clapham but managed to overcome their fears and stayed until after Christmas.

This sounds like quite a house full and I can't imagine where they all slept, in a house with three small bedrooms and an attic room. When I queried this, Mother said "Oh that wasn't all we had - Mrs Birch was staying too". Mrs Birch,

1999 Residents list continued from page 56

Rafferty: (Pre 1911) Gwen: Gillian
Rait-Kerr: (1968) Diana
Ray: Jennifer
Rayner: William and Barbara
Read: (1993) Frances
Reed: Paulette
Refsum: Harry
Refsum: George
Reid: (1993) Warwick and Melodie
Reinecke: (1993) Shirley
Reynolds: (1997)Mark and Kéké: Oliver, Georgina, Elliott & Gregory
Reynolds: Peter
Reynolds: Sarah
Richards: Linda
Richardson: Philip
Rickaby: Barbara
Rigby: John and Margery
Roe: (1970) Eric and Hilda
Rogers: (pre 1900) Betty
Rogers: (pre 1900) Geoff and Mary
Rogers: (pre 1900) Mary
Rogers: (pre 1900) Neil and Cathy: James
Rogers: Tony
Rose: Adrian and Samantha
Rusling: Graham

Saner: John and Annie: Nick and Victoria
Saunders: Kenneth and Loveday
Saunders: (1994) Steve and Nicola; Amelia & Paul
Schaverien: (1974) Bernard and Adele
Scott: (1993) Caroline
Scott: Michael, Amanda & Alan
Sears: May
Sears: (1969) Tony and Sue: Mark
Seddon: Roger and Dasa
Serby: Anne
Sexton: (1998) David and Josephine: Paul & Caroline
Shaw: (1981) Tina: Jennifer, Debbie, Miriam, Amy, Tim & Nigel
Sheaf: (1998) Andrew and Mary: Alexander & Nicolas
Sheard: (1994) Andrew and Barbara: Elizabeth
Sheridan: (1982) Chris and Sylvia: Victoria
Sherratt: (1997) David and Sona:Jessica
Sherringham: (1949) Alf
Shuttleworth: (1992) Sally: Bethany
Simkin: Graham and Sue: Lizzie, Sarah, Rachel & Matthew
Simon: (1970) Anthony and Marjorie
Simpson: (1989) David and Liz: Nigel, Darren, Adam & Caroline
Slone-Murphy: Michael
Smith: Claire
Smith: (1998) Geoff and Christina
Smith: Harry and Pearl
Soria: Juan and Martha
Sozzo: Salvatore
Spencer: Christopher and Susan
Squires: (1987) Alan and Sue: Tom
Stanners: Helen
Stanton-Kipping: Anthony and Elizabeth
Starck: Edward and Yvonne
Stevens: (1987) David and Pauline
Stewart-Hunter: Mary
Stinton: (Pre 1900) Mike and Janet
Stupples: Janet
Street: Elizabeth
Strike: Tracy
Sullivan: Peter
Sutton: David and Alison
Swift: Roger and Pat

Tankel: (1972) Susan
Tannett: (1983) William (Wim) and Jackie: Simon, Jennie and Tom
Targett: Colin and Brenda
Thomas: John and Patricia
Thomas: (1996) Nicholas amd Jeanette: Katie, Jenny, Charlotte, Joshua, Harrison & Joseph
Thompson: Ian
Thompson: Irving and Meryl

Continued on page 61

it appears, was the wife of a Dunkirk evacuee who had lost a leg and was in hospital at Ashridge. Captain Birch was frequently collected in his wheel chair and entertained to tea. It must have been very cosy with six Bacons, my parents and sister and Mrs Birch, but in wartime you made the best of, and shared, everything you had. To help with the sleeping arrangements, two narrow iron bedsteads, with very lumpy mattresses, were supplied by the authorities, returnable of course. Wash days were a major task - no washing machines - the whites were boiled in the copper, the rest done by hand. Then it was all put through the mangle and hung out to dry. Ironing was no better (this was before polyester). Mother can't remember when she got her first electric iron but the old flat irons were hard work - one to heat on the stove, the other in use, very hot to start with, but cooling all the time.

Mother had a selection of people staying during the war years - evacuee children, their parents and school teachers, relatives of patients at Ashridge, plus the arrival of my sister and brother. In 1941 my father was called up, just before the birth of my brother. Dad was sent for training in Lincolnshire. So, when my brother was six weeks old, the family went up to visit before Father was sent abroad for two years. I hadn't realised that families did not know which country their relatives were in until I came across a series of notes and countries in the front of the dictionary at home, ie: "Love to all the family - Italy", "Thinking of you always - Egypt" etc. This was to be the wording of the telegram to let them know which news to look out for. However, the telegram never arrived, appropriate perhaps - just as well they didn't know he was at Anzio and Tripoli, and, of course, they were kept busy with the day-to-day tasks.

Childhood memories of the second World War

by Geoff Rogers

EVERYDAY VILLAGE SERVICES

I was born in the early thirties at Ringshall, the youngest of seven children. Mother used to have the Co-op call once a week. She would order one week and it would be delivered the next week in a four wheeled covered wagon. Mr Sears with his hard hat, breeches and gaiters would call on Wednesdays. He would stop at our house to have his lunch. He always fed the horse first before having his own. He would be at our house a good half hour and, needless to say, what goes in must come out in a big pile on the road. Mother was up there when the horse moved off with her bucket and little shovel - around the roses it went. She had the best roses in Ringshall!

There were three bakers who called at houses in Ringshall and Little Gaddesden - the Co-op, Mr Groom from Potten End, and the Gadsden brothers from Dagnall. We also had a butcher who lived in Hudnall - Mr Janes. My brother John was working there until he was called up in the Air Force. There was also a shop at Ringshall - Fountain Stores.

Mr Ward had a paper shop and post office. The shop used to be in a house next to the Bridgewater Arms car park. There was also Miss Pratt's shop down the middle of the Green. Number 14 Ringshall was a laundry - seven or eight ladies worked there. And, of course, there was the Deer Leap garage. Mr Savage ran the garage for Mr Bedford from Potten End.

Mr Janes owned Hall Farm. My father worked for him for many years. By the laundry at the Ivinghoe Road junction there used to be an island with a sign post in the middle. On Sunday afternoons in summer, a Walls' icecream tricycle stood on that island selling ice creams. Mr Bedford also owned the swimming pool. My father told me that there was going to be a hotel built there but the war stopped that.

I remember teams of horses (six) pulling timber wagons up the hill towards Berkhamsted. They had huge trunks on the wagons. Then there was Mr Thame who worked for Easts in Berkhamsted. He had a two-wheeled wagon with huge butts hanging between the wheels - it was called a long shaft. They also felled a lot of oak trees in Hoo Wood. There were huge piles of butts in the field opposite the Spinney. Fensome of Markyate carted them to Luton.

Mr Maunders was a painter and decorator. He lived at number 18 Ringshall. He had a motor bike and side-car. I can see him now with his ladders sticking out front and rear of the wooden side-car. Milk was delivered daily, measured out with a ladle on your door step. There were three sizes of ladle - half pint, one pint and two pints. They hung on the side of an oval can which must have held at least four gallons. Miss Moore delivered that for Mr Andrews from the farm behind the Bridgewater Arms Hotel. Any surplus milk he sold to the Hygienic dairies, later to be taken over by the Express Dairies.

Mr Janes , the "shoeman" as Mum called him, used to bring the shoes and boots to your house on order - you ordered them one Wednesday and he would bring them the following Wednesday. He would bring about a dozen pairs for you to try from his shop in Edlesborough. There was always a pair to suit you. Mr Moore used to come from Dunstable. He used to bring ladies' clothes etc to your door - you name it, he brought it.

Mr Gower came once a fortnight with paraffin oil and candles - some used oil for lamps, some cooked with it and some used it for heating - it was a bit smelly though! Mr Gower used to fill five stone beer jars which hold about a gallon each. I still have two of them today. That would see us through the dark, winter nights for a fortnight with a bit to spare in case we got snowed up, which happened quite a lot in those days. Mother didn't have electric until the late 50s.

There was also Mr Saunders who lived at number 35 Ringshall. He had a lorry and a man working for him. He delivered coal and wood. His yard was where Ashridge farm is now. He also had a contract to collect the rubbish in the village for the Council. All in bins - there were no plastic bags in those days.

WAR AND THE VILLAGE

There were a lot of soldiers stationed on the common at Ringshall. Army lorries would fill up all day at the Deer Leap Garage. Big tankers would fill up the pumps three or four times a day. The lorries would queue up all day to fill up - queues were as far as the Golf Course Drive. There was never a shortage of petrol. The main base was the Monument Drive. The parade grounds you can still see today. When they were on manoeuvres, they were all over the place - over the golf course, through gardens with their tanks and bren-gun carriers. You could not do much about it. I remember that the postman left his bike by a wall down by the laundry. A tank came along and flattened it. You should have seen his face when he came back!

1999 Residents list continued from page 60

Thompson: (1994) Michael and Christina: Andrew & Alexander
Thompson: Peter and Lesley
Thorburn: Wilson and Anna
Thorne: Susan
Thornhill: (1983) Geoffrey and Beryl
Tilley: Richard and Jane: Robert and Helen
Tillotston: Gillian
Timms: (1964) Joyce
Toop: (1995) Geoffrey and Elizabeth: Louise
Townsend: James and Alison: Lara and Sarah
Tucker: (1990): David (Tommy) and Annette
Turner: (1999): Ann
Turner: (1959) Mike and Maggie: Kate
Turner: Paul and Vivienne: James & Katy

Ulf-Hansen: Christian

Vest: Richard and Sarah
Viney: Mark and Carol

Walker: Janine
Walker: Jean
Walker: Karen
Walker: (1986) Ian and Jane: Ross & Lewis
Walsham: Michael and Sandra: James
Warburton: (1985) Mike: Fiona and Ben
Ward: (1976) Bob
Warman: (1993) Keith
Waters: (1939) Ron and Jennie
Watkins: Peter and Marilyn: Jackson & Johanna
Watson: (1999) Simon and Philippa: Angus
Webster: Nicholas and Anne: Rachel, Sarah & Catriona
Webster: David and Gail: Michael & Nicholas
Westmacott: (1969) Rus and Virginia
Whaley: (1971) Christopher and Helen: James & Samantha
Whittall: Graham and Deborah: Laura
Whitby: Phyllis
White: (1985) Colin and Sue: Sophie & Charlie
Wicks: Geoffrey and Maureen
Wiggins: David and Linda
Williams: (1986) John and Ann
Williams: Rosemary
Williamson: (1991) David and June
Willis: (1999) Hilary
Wilson: John
Wilson: (1975) Kenneth and Betty
Wood: Ian
Wood: Ian J
Woodmansee: (1996) Carl and Kate: Alice
Woods: Paul and Sarah
Wooster: (1967): Arthur and Anne

Young: Eilidh

On the golf course fairways, big posts were sunk in the ground. They were like small trees some 20 to 30 feet tall. I was told that it was so that planes and gliders could not land. An army cookhouse was opposite the house with the blue tiles. I remember a refrigerated lorry standing there with back door open, sides of meat hanging up with a large date stamp on it. The year was 1931, the year I was born. It must have been past its sell by date as I can remember it - it would not be allowed today! I also remember when they were on manoeuvres. There were anti-aircraft guns in the field next to 3 Ringshall. They were of course on Army rations. One of the gun crew was just over the hedge from our house. Mother gave them eggs and bread and in return they gave her tins of corned beef. My sister married a soldier after the war. He was stationed at the Monument.

At Beaney there were a lot of Land Army girls. They worked on farms around the district. One or two of them married village lads (they were a little too old for me!!). At Ashridge House there was a hospital which later became part of the Public Records Office. The buildings have since been knocked down. There were a lot of wounded from Dunkirk. All the walking wounded had blue uniforms with white shirts and red ties. It was terrible to see some of the more seriously wounded.

Sunday evenings were spent sitting as a family whilst my father played the organ. I remember one Sunday sitting around the table at home when the air raid warning went off. The siren was on the garage just up the road from 3 Ringshall. Then we heard aircraft overhead. Dad said, "That's them damn Germans again". Mother replied "They are all somebody's boys". Well there was then a huge bang. Cups and saucers rocked on the table. Dad remarked how close the noise was. The next day we learned that it was a land mine which fell near the Woodyard Drive. I went up there to see where it dropped. There was a huge hole, many trees were blown away and bits of parachute were all over the place. *(At Woodyard Cottage windows and a door were blown in - Antony Hopkins).*

A few bombs fell around the village. A string of bombs fell one Friday night from Hudnall to Ringshall. The last one fell just behind the swimming pool. The one before that fell in the road by the Spinney and burst the water main. I think that they were all meant for the hospital, but they did not succeed. A buzz bomb fell in the woods by Aldbury Turn. Later in the war a rocket fell in a field at Dagnall, shattering all the windows in Church Farm on the hill above.

SCHOOL DAYS

My school days were for a start happy. I remember my first day at school - brother George took me. At the bottom of the road were big iron gates about six or seven feet tall. These gates were later taken down to "help the war effort". Mrs Drewitt was my first teacher. She was always very kind to me. She lived at 44 Little Gaddesden on the Green. When the evacuees from London arrived, we only went to school for half a day. There was not enough room for us all. Later we went to school in Denison House (half way down the Green) which was used as extra space. A teacher named David Foster came down with the evacuees. I did not like him at first. When I got to know him better, I realised what a very nice man he actually was.

My mother had two evacuees to stay with us. They came on Sunday lunchtime. She sorted them out, and it was my job to take them to school on the Monday. We got down to the Bridgewater Arms. Mr Andrews' surplus milk was stacked in crates. The evacuees had never seen anything like this - one said that he had just found a cow's nest!

When I was about ten years old, I joined the Young Farmers' Club at school. We had one day a week working with the animals. We kept pigs, chickens and rabbits, and grew vegetables for the school kitchen. Our one day a week duty extended to Saturdays, Sundays and the school holidays as well - the animals still needed to be fed. We built three pig sties under the guidance of Mr Foster and Mr Bell, the headmaster. We built them with breeze blocks, and in fact one is still standing today. One particular day, I was rendering a wall inside one of the sties when a buzz bomb fell in Aldbury. When I went back to work after lunch, all the plaster had fallen off because of the vibration. We used to collect the swill (waste food) from the Bridgewater Arms Hotel - I must say that the pigs lived very well!! We would put the swill in a 50 gallon boiler where it would boil for a good half hour. We would then tip it into an old galvanised bath to cool. Meal and bran were mixed with it and the mixture would last about three days. One day I was emptying the boiler when my foot slipped off the edge of the bath into the boiling hot swill. My foot was scalded badly and I was taken up to Ashridge hospital. My foot was very blistered and sore, but minor in comparison with other injuries I saw at the hospital. One day I was planting potatoes in the school garden - one of the tasks for the day - with an evacuee. He said that he thought it was a good place to hide the potatoes from the Germans! We used to have a pig killed for Christmas. Each member used to go home with a joint which was cut up by Mr Foster. I know that Mother was always pleased! The other pigs were sold to butchers to help the war effort.

My mother went to the Village School. So did I and my two children and my grandson, Toby, and grand daughter, Kate, today. Four generations to date! My grandson was even christened in the school hall when the church was closed for repairs in 1990 - a record I think!!

The Balloon

By Bill White, who now lives at Bathealton in Somerset

In 1939, I went to Hemel Hempstead Grammar School by bicycle. One unique experience was some time in the middle of the war, when I cycled home through the fog one evening to find the area full of RAF and police. It seemed that a Polish gentlemen who was living at no 62 had that evening in the gloom seen a broken wire rope trailing through the clouds and rain, which had passed between nos 61 and 62. Bravely he had seized the rope and tied it to our clothes line post which was also anchored to our chicken houses. The RAF had arrived with winches and somehow winched it down, though the line post and the chicken house went up in the air some six feet during the process. It was a balloon. Once it was down I was told to hold the vent open whilst they emptied it of hydrogen. I did not do my homework, was sick the next day, and no one at school believed a word.

We'll eat again

by Lyn Hyde

This is the title of a book of World War II recipes given to my mother-in-law this Christmas and, of course, it started the reminiscences - dried egg, spam, how they served tripe in the canteen she helped to run and there were 'significant left-overs', to which they added gravy browning next day and had people coming back for more!

When I got home to Gaddesden, I went to ask my mother, "What did you eat in the war, Mum?"

It wasn't only what they ate but how they cooked and shopped that was so different 50 years ago. My parents married in 1935 and moved into No 10, next door to my grandparents. In fact the war made fewer changes to their lives in the early years than it did to those living in towns, until they housed first evacuees, then relatives of wounded soldiers who were being nursed at Ashridge and then, of course, my father was called up in 1942.

Even when I was a child (in the 50s) there was no freezer, or even a refrigerator, and my mother was not keen on salted or pickled vegetables. We would, however, occasionally buy a pack of frozen peas and a sack of potatoes when our own ran out. Other than that, we ate what was ready in the garden at the time. This could mean weeks of brussel sprouts or runner beans, but they all tasted so good! During the war my father and grandfather, who were both excellent gardeners, kept our families, plus evacuees and town relatives, who came for weekends for some sleep away from the bombing, in fresh fruit and vegetables. It was all organic too. Chicken and pig bedding was dug into the garden and, as for insecticide, I remember being paid for sand castle buckets of caterpillars off the cabbages.

Little Gaddesden, with its gardens, had ample space not only for vegetable plots but for chicken pens as well and most people kept a few hens. So the dreaded dried egg had to be resorted to only when the hens went off the lay. Most of the cottages still had pig sties from the Brownlow days and my parents kept three pigs at a time to fatten up and send off to market. The pigs were collected in my dad's car, tied in sacks and loaded into the back. Mother remembers collecting some from Bovingdon once, when the door flew open and the little piglet went sack-racing up the road with her and Dad in hot pursuit.

Milk was still collected daily from the farm run by Fred and Alec Andrews behind the Bridgewater Arms. Bread was delivered in the village by Wessell Gadsden from Dagnall and by Fred the Bread from Potten End.

As far as groceries were concerned, Mr Reading's Stores delivered from Berkhamsted as usual. In the early days he came round with his horse and cart; Mother can't remember when he changed to a van. He would collect your basket with its shopping list (and, during the war, your coupons) and deliver your order back to your door. The 'Little Man' came round on a Wednesday with his mobile shop and, as I remember (not during the war), we went up the steps and made our own selection from his shelves.

Meat was certainly more difficult to come by and one family story I had got muddled over the years was that a neighbour was shooting pigeons down the garden and accidentally shot my sister's rabbit, which my mother then skinned and cooked and no one could face eating. What actually happened was that the neighbour shot my grandmother's cat by accident, which they didn't eat, but when my sister lost interest in the rabbit it was served up. A cautionary tale to all children who neglect their pets! More generally, meat was delivered around the village by Seth Janes from Hudnall.

Once all the ingredients were assembled, they were cooked on the 'cook and heat' rather like a coal-fired Aga, but the fire part had no door. It brings a whole new concept to 'toiling over a hot stove' - nice in winter but not so good in the summer. Lastly, the washing up. Fortunately the stove also heated the water but there was no squirt of washing-up liquid, but soda crystals to leave your plates clean and your hands like sandpaper.

Five land girls
TOP ROW:
Unknown, Joyce Lillicrop, unknown.
FRONT ROW:
Maureen Mathias, Jean Inscough

The Land Girls

Editor's note:
In this war many women took over jobs previously done by men. There was an organised recruitment of town girls to work in agriculture, as had already been successfully tried in the first world war. These were the Women's Land Army, or Land Girls. Phyl Mountfort, who has lived in the village since 1950, had been a land girl in Toddington. Mary Barnes, who now lives in Dorking, and Jean Ponder, now in Kew, were land girls in Little Gaddesden. Benhay, in the following account, is the earlier name for Beaney. You will see from another

The Benhay Hostel in the late 40s

article that it also provided accommodation for twenty evacuee boys. Up to 1928 it had been the Rectory: an extensive building with servant accommodation, outhouses and a parish room.

by Mary Barnes, formerly Mary Hopkinson

The five years I was in Little Gaddesden were the happiest of my life. I was a Land Girl from 1941 to 1946. We arrived at Benhay on October 1st 1941, thirty-five of us from Yorkshire. I became a tractor driver and was taught to plough by Mr King (Bill) who worked at Home Farm. He was a wonderful ploughman and won many trophies, especially for horse ploughing. I loved every minute. You can imagine the joy of working in the fields after mill chimneys and smoke from the factories. The swimming pool at Ringshall: what a luxury during the war. We did change some things: cleared Northchurch Common for potatoes, and part of the Park. I made friends in the village with Mrs Crack and her family. It was like a second home to me and I still visit her.

from a conversation with Jean Ponder, formerly Jean Inscough

Jean joined the Women's Land Army in 1950, as she had been too young during the war, and the organisation was still needed for several years afterwards. She remained until it was disbanded in about 1952. When she joined there were still about 40 of them at Benhay, and many were still from northern England. Their domestic arrangements included several to each bedroom and a communal room in which they sometimes had dances to a gramophone. There was a matron in charge, and a cook and other staff. They were provided with bicycles which they used a lot on Saturdays and Sundays, which were always days off.

To get to work they were taken in a van, singing as they went, and dropped off at various farms. Jean drove a tractor, which sometimes meant ploughing, sometimes potato lifting, and various other processes of cultivation. Some of the tilling was still done by horses which often meant someone to lead and someone to go behind. Leading the horse was one of the duller jobs. Other jobs included hedging and ditching, hoeing, rick-building, mucking-out and calving. Milking was done by machine, but the milk was still sent out from the farms in churns at that time. Jean remembers there were a lot of Friesian cows and some Ayrshires. She also remembers planting gladioli in fields, but cannot remember clearly whereabouts.

After leaving she went into nursing, but the fellowship of the land girls was very strong and the annual week-long reunion in Birmingham was very popular.

The children still had fun

By Madeleine Gilpin, who was Madeleine Gallo, and now lives at Ardley-with-Fewcott in Oxfordshire

My father and mother were Ange and Eleanor Gallo.

After suffering a terrible night of bombing in London where we lived, when I was five years old, and my brothers Jim and Michael were 8 and nearly 2, father set about looking for a "safe" place for us all to live in the country. He found this wonderful site and had the house built. It cost him £2,000, and at the end of the war he sold it for exactly the same sum. So in 1946, much to the dismay of us children, we returned to London.

It was a real pleasure in recent times to meet Pat and Roger Swift of Oak Tree Cottage, named after the huge oak tree which used to stand outside. While we were living next door in Le Logis, now Gade Lodge, the people in Oak Tree Cottage were the Ibisons. They had a baby son called John. Mr Ibison was the owner of Four Ways Garage, and he had a thrillingly exciting old car yard at the back, in which he allowed us to play. We spent many, many happy hours "driving" those stationary old cars. If the rubber bulbs were not perished we got a splendid throaty "honk" out of the old horns, and sometimes even managed to get the semaphore signals to come out.

TOP
Ange Gallo with Mike and Madeleine

BOTTOM
Jim, Madeleine, Mike and their mother Eleanor Gallo

(Editor's note: There was nothing between Le Logis and the garage at that time, White Rails not having been built.)

One of the earliest incidents which occurred was when my mother woke one morning to a most dreadful smell which filled the house. Fearing the worst (a gas attack) she hurriedly made us children don our gas masks and this was the sight that greeted the milkman when he called at our door. He fell about laughing as he explained to my mother that "the dreadful smell" came from the chicken farm and the wind was blowing in our direction. My mother never forgot how foolish she felt!

We used to have a dear lady, called Mrs Johnson, who used to come and help my mother with her "endless chores" (or so they seemed to me). She was a smashing person who lived at Great Gaddesden in the row of cottages, on the left going towards Hemel, near the middle of the row and the well.

The wood at the side of the field at the back of our house was an adventure playground for us and we knew every inch of it. In the Springtime the floor was carpeted with bluebells and the banks were covered with primroses and violets. When I look back on how we used to pick armfuls of these wonderful wild flowers I feel a deep sense of shame, but of course conservation and the ban on picking wild flowers was not in force then or I feel sure we'd have been more considerate.

At the top of the field, but still in the wood, was a magnificent glade of beech trees. These were on an open embankment and of course we used to use the branches as an anchor for our rope and would swing wildly out into the field. Oh, those were the days! Quite fearless we were!

(Editor's note: Those beech trees are still there in the south of Hudnall Common, but surrounded by thicket.)

My father, who was confined to London doing fire-watching duty, occasionally was able to join us and then it would be "all hands to the saw". He would march us children into the beeches and search the undergrowth for fallen branches. Then with a huge (for us) log balanced on one shoulder we would trudge back down to the house where he'd saw them up for our fires.

Facing our wood, on the other side of the road going up Hudnall hill, there was a lot of open ground well grazed by rabbits which had huge craters in it. A great deal of extraordinary rubbish, and even barbed wire, had been dumped in the bottom of some, and I can recall retrieving masses of staples as a "treasure" which we used to hoard secretly until our mother discovered our hiding place.

Another very exciting moment for us was on one occasion when the army had been holding manoeuvres in "our" wood. My mother had forbidden us children to go anywhere near the wood whilst the soldiers were using it, but of course we watched their every move like hawks. Their tanks and jeeps had no sooner moved out of the wood than we three were there doing our own manoeuvres - wriggling about on our stomachs with sticks across our forearms (pretend rifles) and thoroughly enjoying ourselves when, suddenly, my elder brother, Jim, spotted three "stick-like" objects on the ground. They appeared to have a sort of "egg-shaped" clay end with something metal implanted in it. Being the eldest, my brother immediately told us to leave them alone and rushed back to tell our mother. She came quickly back to the spot, saw what they were, and jumping on to her bicycle, tore down the road after the soldiers. A captain returned with her (her bike in his jeep) and taking these three hand grenades (for that is what they were) he tossed them over the hedge in front of our house into the field beyond. There was a terrific explosion, much to our delight and excitement.

At one time, beside the haystacks we loved so much to play on, a caravan was parked. A man lived in it and I suppose he worked for the farmer. Now he had a shot gun and I suppose he would shoot rabbits for the pot. We children were fascinated by this gun and I remember one day he showed it to Jim and myself. We were inside his caravan and he pointed the gun out and fired it. Unfortunately my younger brother, Michael, ran across his line of fire and received the shot in his face. Luckily it surrounded his left eye and did not touch the eye itself. My mother was frantic, as you can imagine, and we were rushed up to Ashridge hospital

Top:
Jim, Mike and Madeleine with their mother at Le Logis

Bottom:
Jennifer Willie, Jim Gallo and Richard Willie at Le Logis

by Mr Ibison. An American doctor managed to pick out most of the pellets, but to this day he has little scars.

You can imagine with what excitement we awoke one day to learn that a plane had crashed in a nearby field. It was as much as we could do to eat our breakfast before jumping onto our bikes to cycle over to see it. Of course, it had already been attended to by the Authorities, but I remember Jim searching for souvenirs which he kept in secret on top of his cupboard in his bedroom for ages.

We younger children went to school (my elder brother was sent to boarding school) at the top of the hill, to a school evacuated from London run by teachers who used the Froebel system of education. Miss O.B.Priestman was the Headteacher there, and one of my favourite teachers, who was a magnificent artist, was Miss Duncan, who taught us pottery. I spent some time, during one summer holiday when my mother was ill, boarding there. I hated that. The school was located in Denison House which had the most exquisite grounds. We used to look for fossils in the high limestone wall whilst we waited for the bus to take us home.

There was a group of boys at the school who had a “club”. Being a real tomboy, I was desperate to join them. However, they kept making conditions for me to join, which grew harder and harder. I climbed a pile of coke on the barn with bare feet, and I climbed first one, and then another, cedar tree (a much more difficult task). The last achievement was not witnessed and I couldn’t face it a second time. I never did get to join the club of Michael Dew and Anthony Gammie.

My elder brother was friends with some children who lived along the road from the Manor House. Their names were Jennifer and Richard Willie (who were twins) and Philip Wade. Jennifer and Richard brought their pony down to our garden and we were allowed to have a ride.

For the adults, my mother especially, it was a troublesome and worrying time. My bedroom window faced towards London and I can recall waking up in the dark one night to see her silhouette outlined against the night sky, staring out of the window towards Town. I asked her what she was doing and she said she was watching London burn - it was the height of the Blitz. When I looked out with her I could see the sky reddened by the flames.

But for us children, those were wonderful, carefree and happy times and I consider I was most fortunate to have the opportunity to spend my early life in these glorious and unforgettable surroundings.

Bridget Talbot and the War

by Barbara Cassell

Early in the 1939 War Bridget Talbot realised that many sailors were losing their lives after being torpedoed, despite wearing life jackets. The trouble was that they could not be seen in the dark. She asked - or more likely, told - the Admiralty to fit automatic waterproof lights to the jackets but the Navy closed ranks against attack from a civilian, with mysterious statements about ‘technical reasons’. Bridget found a local workshop to make a working example of a light and then she sallied forth again, but she relied on being related to one of the Sea Lords, and went to see him at the Admiralty. Her forcefulness, and his rank, led

NAMES INDEX

continued on page 69

to a sea change, with the adoption of the automatic light and to the saving of the lives of countless sailors and airmen.

As far as many in Little Gaddesden were concerned, she sat in her big house and became quite eccentric and, of course, there are many stories about her to justify her reputation. The following story is one she told with a chuckle, as well as with indignation.

"I arrived at Glasgow Railway Station during the war to see thousands of soldiers settling down for the night on the hard platforms. Naturally I asked what was going on and, eventually, was told that they were due to embark in a convoy to fight abroad but that, owing to the possibility of air raids, they had to stay on land until the last moment. I asked the officer why he didn't find proper billets for the men but he shrugged his shoulders. So the next day I booked a room in the best hotel and told the Red Cross the Press was coming and told the Press that the Red Cross was coming. We had the meeting and they appointed me to go to the Lord Provost of Glasgow. He was a very bad tempered man who didn't like being told what to do by a Sassenach woman. I told him he could accommodate lots of soldiers in his corridors alone. I said it was monstrous that these men were going abroad to fight for us, where some would die, and we were letting them spend their last nights in this country on hard platforms. He gave in and billets were arranged for the men."

She chuckled after telling this story when she said the Provost had a heart attack in the next couple of days - and it probably served him right. These stories show just what courageous determination she had when official indifference led

Ashridge EMS Hospital

by Jim Harries

Jim Harries was an RAF surgeon at Ashridge when it was used as a hospital.

Ashridge House was taken over in the early years of the Second World War to become an Emergency Medical Services hospital for Charing Cross Hospital patients. These were expected bombing casualties for further treatment and convalescence.

The wards initially were in the main building, on the ground floor, whilst awaiting the building of a thousand-bed hospital in the grounds on the Little Gaddesden side of the house. Each ward was housed in a single storey brick-walled building with corrugated asbestos roof, and connected to each other by covered ways. Each ward contained roughly 30 beds.

There were two operating theatres, two maternity wards, three wards for tuberculosis patients, as well as Medical Surgical and Orthopaedic wards.

Many local mothers had their babies at this hospital.

Nurses were provided from Charing Cross, University College and St John's and St Elizabeth's Hospitals. Many retired Charing Cross Consultants returned to 'active' service at Ashridge to work throughout the war and medical students were trained, gaining experience at Ashridge and Charing Cross hospitals. For a time, students were housed in accommodation at Chaulden House, Boxmoor and bussed to Ashridge each day. Some lodged in the changing rooms at Berkhamsted Golf Club.

NAMES INDEX

continued from page 68

continued on page 70

Green Line single-decker buses were converted into ambulances and conveyed stretcher patients from London, and later, after D-Day, air-evacuated casualties from Europe, via RAF Bovingdon. When Allied Forces over-ran Walcharen Island in Holland, numerous German wounded, from the German Hospital there, were evacuated to Ashridge and treated in two wards.

In the crypt beneath the main building there was a bar which Sam Dornan, Henry Cotton's assistant, frequently visited!

About the hospital

by Dorothea Patterson

My father, Norman Patterson, was a consultant at the Royal Bucks Hospital, Aylesbury, and in 1937 he built a house, Nob's Crook, on the Golf Course Road in Ashridge to be near Aylesbury. My brother Ian Patterson was called up immediately on the outbreak of war and went to France with the expeditionary force. After Dunkirk he went to India and later fought in Greece where he died in an air crash at the war's end. I, Dorothea, having had some experience of photography, worked as a technician in the X-ray department at Ashridge, then a hospital with staff from Charing Cross Hospital and University College Hospital.

After the evacuation from Dunkirk we received many both English and French wounded. At the beginning some of them were housed in the house itself, then in the newly erected huts. The X-ray department was in one of these huts. Many local residents entertained the soldiers in their homes, and sometimes impromptu dancing took place in the wards. From time to time we were required to stay overnight in the house on fire-watching duty.

We also entertained some of the servicemen camped in the park. I remember some of a Guards regiment (the Cherry Pickers) coming to tea. They said, "Can we bring our dog?" - OUR dog, Mars, who it seemed spent his time ensconced in the most comfortable chair in the mess. We made good friends with two Dutch soldiers from South Africa. Many of these men had been conscripted to provide "other ranks" for the Dutch officers who had escaped from Holland without any troops.

We had a number of people living with us during the war years:
Dr Thatcher, assistant to Adrian Boult at the B.B.C. He came complete with equipment to monitor the music programmes from Germany.
Two Danes who considered that we, the British, could fight their war for them!
Two West Indian nurses from Canada on leave, and a number of service men also on leave.

Despite the war, it was an interesting life in a very friendly village where one knew everyone and the social barriers were down. We soon knew many of the old village families - the Rogers and Oranges, the Oakins family, the Johnsons, the Maylings, the Andrews family, the Harmons and the Rector Ted Wager and Nellie Wager, the schoolmaster Vicars Bell and Dorothy Bell, and Canon and Mrs Meyer (the great gardeners, who lived in the back part of the Manor House) and many more. After a while I left the hospital and went to work in London.

(For a post-war continuation, see page 76)

NAMES INDEX

continued from page 69

continued on page 73

General de Gaulle at Rodinghead

by Gail Webster

Donald Lockhart built Rodinghead in 1936-7 for Mr and Mrs Watson, paper merchants from Johnstone, near Glasgow.

During the War, Mrs Watson returned to Glasgow and the house was let; between autumn 1941 and Autumn 1942 General de Gaulle used Rodinghead as a retreat from his London office, and his wife Yvonne and their Down's Syndrome daughter Anne were in permanent residence. Mme de Gaulle subsequently referred, in a letter to her niece, to a stay of "puis un an à Berkhamsted - une jolie villa moderne agréable."

Ciné film and photographs were taken during this period of the General and his wife in the house and garden, apparently at the suggestion of Churchill, to promote de Gaulle and the Free French. These remain some of the few photos taken of de Gaulle whilst he was in England, and Rodinghead regularly appears in biographies, with Madame de Gaulle in a spotted dress.

Pictures taken during the war of General de Gaulle and his wife Yvonne at Rodinghead

Roll of Honour - 1939 - 1945

by David Heard

189553 Lt. Henry GORDON
of the Gloucestershire Regiment, attached to The Gordon Highlanders, died on 18.11.1944. He is remembered on the Rangoon Memorial, Burmah. He attended Berkhamsted School, leaving in 1939, and joined the army in September 1940. He had twin sisters who became air hostesses for BOAC in the 1950's.

He was the son of Captain Gordon who fought in World War I, winning the MC and losing an arm and an eye. Captain Gordon was Bursar at Ashridge College before World War II and Secretary of the hospital on conversion in 1939.

265751 Lt. Duncan James GRAY
of the 10th (2nd Bn. The Tower Hamlets Rifles) Battalion, The Rifle Brigade, died on 01.09.1944 aged 22 and is buried in the Florence War Cemetery. He was the son of James Neville and Hildegard Gray of Little Gaddesden.

Leonard Hing

1142066 Lance Bombardier Leonard HING
of the 59th (6th Battalion,The Hampshire Regiment) Anti-Tank Regiment, Royal Artillery, died on 23.09.1944 aged 24 and is buried in St. Peter and St. Paul's churchyard, Little Gaddesden.

He was born on 27.08.1920 the son of Lewis and Annie Elizabeth Hing of 17 Little Gaddesden. He attended the village school (see picture on page 156) and was called up in 1942, doing his training at Shoeburyness. He went to France two days after D-day and was wounded in the head. He returned to Ratcliffe Infirmary where he died of wounds.

1396485 Flight Sergeant William Searl NEWMAN
of the R.A.F. (V.R.) died as a result of a flying accident, crashing on take-off on 15.10.1944. He is buried in the churchyard of St. Peter and St. Paul's, Little Gaddesden.

He was the only son of William and Alice Elizabeth Newman of 61 Robin Hood Cottages, Little Gaddesden, who both died during the war. Billy stayed with the Purtons of 5 Chapel Close when on leave. He attended the local school (see picture on page 156) followed by Hemel Hempstead School.

115033 Major W. O'KELLY M.C.
of the Royal Army Service Corps died in Ashridge Hospital on 19.06.1941 and is buried in the churchyard of St. Peter and St. Paul, Little Gaddesden.

He was the son of William Henry and Frances Josephine Peart O'Kelly and husband of Gladys Winifred. He was a Reserve Officer in the Home Guard, having possibly fought in the 1st World War.

69411 Major Ian PATTERSON MC.
of "L" Squadron, Special Boat Service, A.A.C. died aged 30 in a plane crash when flying into Bari on 21.12.44 in a Dakota full of wounded, which hit an olive tree and crashed on a hillside. He is buried in Bari War Cemetery, Italy. Born on 02.04.1914 he was the only son of Norman and Winifred Dorothea Patterson of Nobs Crook, Ashridge Park and sister of Dorothea Patterson.

He gained his commission in 1936 in the 20/76th Field Battalion, 9th Field Regiment. He went to France on being called up having been in the reserve, being evacuated from Dunkirk. In 1941 he volunteered for service in India where he became a parachutist with the 151 Parachute Battalion, training Gurkhas. In 1943 he joined the Special Boat Service as detachment commander campaigning amongst the Greek Islands. On 21.07.1944 he was awarded the Military Cross for outstanding services behind enemy lines and on 04.01.1945 he was mentioned in dispatches in the London Gazette for distinguished service .

5950504 Private Edward ROGERS
of the 5th Battalion, The Suffolk Regiment died aged 23 on 25.07.1943 and his name appears on the Singapore Memorial. Son of Francis and Lilly Rogers of Little Gaddesden, (see pages 39 and 255) he left school at 14 but couldn't get a job. In 1938 he got a part time job, later full time, at Sainsbury's in Berkhamsted, but joined the army in 1939.

The War Memorial updated

After the Second World War, the inscription on the left hand stone of the memorial on the Green was altered and shortened to make room for six new names, mainly by omitting the reference to those who returned alive. (See page 31) Also the First World War ending date was changed from 1918 to 1919. The dates 1914 and 1919 were added to the top of the right hand stone, which was otherwise unchanged. The new left hand inscription is:

+
IN HONOUR
OF THE
MEN AND WOMEN
WHO WENT FROM THE
VILLAGES OF
LITTLE GADDESDEN
HUDNALL
AND RINGSHALL
AND SERVED IN THE
WARS OF
1914=1919 AND 1939=1945
THE
NAMES OF THOSE
WHO GAVE THEIR LIVES
FOR THEIR COUNTRY
ARE CUT
ON THE STONES HERE.
1939=1945

Then follow the names of six of the fallen of the 1939-45 War, as listed above, omitting Major W. O'Kelly. It may be that he was not a local man, as he died in Ashridge hospital.
The same six names were added to the wooden memorial in the church, but without putting them in order of Christian names as had been done for the First World War.

NAMES INDEX
continued from page 70

continued on page 82

The second half of the century - 1945 to 1989

This half of the century did not have the great upheavals of the first half. The changes were more gradual, yet cumulative. A movement developed and gradually increased in strength, to preserve the appearance of the village, but there was no way of preserving the way of life. Nevertheless we have retained many geographical meeting points which so many other villages have lost in this period: a general store with post office, a primary school, a church with regular services, a sports pavilion and bowls pavilion, a scout hut, a VPA members' shop, a pub, a golf club, and a village hall in which many village societies hold their meetings and events. We even have that rare commodity nowadays, a village policeman who lives here.

So the village can still socialise in leisure and shopping. What it can hardly do now is socialise in work. Most people of working age who want jobs have jobs, but few are working alongside their village neighbours. The one exception is the school children, who work together, as well as play together, until they are moved on to another school, sometimes at quite a young age. (In the first quarter of the century the village school provided education up to the age of 14 for most pupils).

After the war was over there was more than a return to the social life of pre-war days, because the war itself had strengthened ties, and people were full of energy to recover from war-time restrictions (which took some years) and to enjoy life.

It may seem strange (though the older members of the village will understand) but it was the fellowship of the Home Guard which sprang the village into its new life.

May 8th was 'V.E.' Day, Victory in Europe. The 1945 poster, below, is headed: To Commemorate The Formation Of The L.D.V. in May, 1940 THE GADDESDEN SOCIETY (founded by the Home Guard) will hold it's first GARDEN FETE

The Gaddesden Society

by Mary Lishman

THE GADDESDEN SOCIETY

GARDEN FÊTE

ON CHURCH MEADOW, LITTLE GADDESDEN

2.30 TO 11

SATURDAY, 26TH MAY

SIDE SHOWS
- Bowling for the Pig
- Darts
- Hoop-la
- Shooting
- Pillow Fights
- Penny Rolling
- Hidden Treasure
- Many other Side Shows
- Competitions

MUSICAL DAY

ATTRACTIONS
- Flower Show (Open to All)
- Fortune Teller
- Slide
- Pony Rides
- Treasure Hunt

CONCERT PARTY 7.0

ICE CREAMS — SOFT DRINKS — TEAS 4.0

DANCING 8.30-11.0

ADMISSION FREE TO FÊTE GROUND

The Gaddesden Society was founded in 1945 when No 5 Platoon, 76 Company, Hertfordshire Home Guard was disbanded. Its aims were to encourage the spirit of voluntary service, to promote a sense of community and good fellowship and to preserve the natural amenities of the area.

It was also dedicated to getting a Village Hall, and a great deal of correspondence went on between the Society and the various authorities on this subject. It was even suggested that a library should be built in the Village - but, of course, that was before television arrived!

Former members of No 5 Platoon automatically qualified for membership of the Society - other residents of Little Gaddesden and surrounding villages were invited to join and, from early replies, it is clear that this was considered an honour and the invitations were accepted without hesitation.

There was an elected President and five elected Chairmen of committees - comprising Education, Entertainment, Golfing, Rifle Shooting and Football. The Society organised educational lectures, art exhibitions, concerts, sports and whist drives, and each year there was a Grand Fête to raise funds for the proposed Village Hall. These fêtes really were grand, as the posters which have survived show. They were officially opened at 2.30 pm and went on till 11 pm, with supper and dancing. A high-ranking officer performed the opening ceremony and, in 1955, records show this was Major Harry Rogers Junior, Commander of USAF Bovingdon, accompanied by his wife "who gave a very generous cheque". There was also a torchlight procession through the Village, followed by a pig roast and fireworks, on November 5th.

By degrees the various groups formed their own Clubs and most continue to this day. They were referred to as 'our siblings' when they first went independent! It is clear that before the Village Hall was completed in 1957 there were activities taking place all over the Village, catering for all interests. The Art Club was holding exhibitions still under the 'umbrella' of the Society, and the Rifle Club used a range at the Red House, but this only survived for about a year, as the range did not come up to War Office standards of safety and it had to be abandoned. The Golfing Club later became the Artisans Club at Ashridge, and all the others are alive and well.

In order to keep the Village informed of all the activities on offer, the Society started the Gaddesden Diary in 1955 and this delightful publication is still going strong. (see page 85). The Gaddesden Society Village Sports were originally part of the Annual Fête and are still very popular in their own right. It is very exciting and gratifying to see 'young and old' athletes competing so enthusiastically each year. It is wonderful that we still have so much support from the whole Village for this simple but enjoyable tradition.

Happily, the Gaddesden Society still survives and we hold meetings every month, on the third Wednesday, from September to May. We try to have local speakers and our subjects are wide and varied. It would not be possible to list them all; suffice to say in the first half of the year 2000 the subjects will be television production, crime writing, travelling the waterways of Russia, the

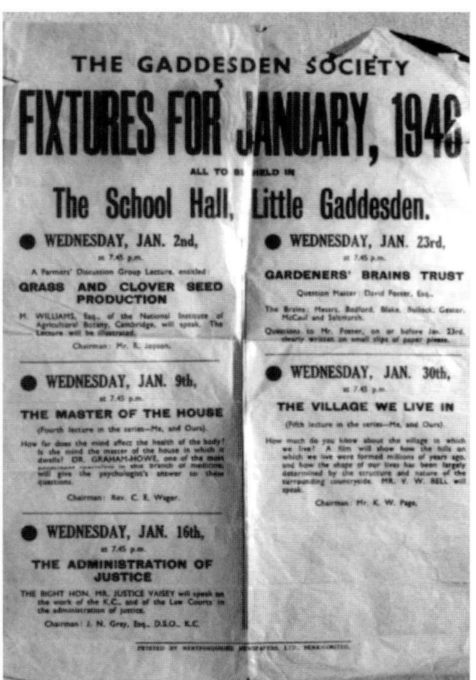

BELOW LEFT
a poster from 1946:

Signs of an intellectual village? The five talks in a single month in the village hall would not have looked out of place at Ashridge College. The second one is subtitled "How far does the mind affect the health of the body?" and is the fourth of a series. The speaker, Dr Graham-Howe, is billed as "one of the most prominent specialists in this branch of medicine". The speaker at the third event is the Rt. Hon. Mr Justice Vasey. The meeting on Jan 30th is, again, one of a series, and the speaker, introducing a film on the effect geology has had on our countryside, is the headmaster, Vicars Bell.

BELOW RIGHT
another poster from 1946:

'V.J.'Day (victory in Japan) was 9th August 1945. World War II was now really over, and this Victory Celebration was held in the village in June 1946.

This is the 1947 fête of the Gaddesden Society, jointly with the British Legion this time. The flower show has been dropped - probably held on another day - and the sports events have been given prominence, including the races for over 30s and over 50s in which a handicap of 1 yard per year of age is allowed. We still have races with this allowance (maybe the slightly more generous metre) in our village sports.

House of Lords and a wartime journey home from India! - and all by people who either lived or live in the Village.

For my part it is an honour to be the President of a small society which has survived for 54 years, and I sincerely hope that with all the changes to come in the new Millennium there will still be residents who will give some time to continue this tradition and keep the spirit of the Gaddesden Society alive.

Editors Note: Mary tells me that she and her husband, David Lishman, came to Little Gaddesden House from Berkhamsted in 1984 and immediately began to take part in many of the village activities. Mary joined the Gaddesden Society Committee in 1985 when Len Hopkins was President. On his retirement in 1989, Geoffrey Moore was elected but, sadly, he died before the first meeting in September. Mary was asked to become Acting President and was elected President at the next A G M and has been happy to 'carry on the good work'.

A blossoming of the Arts

by Dorothea Patterson

(A continuation of her war-time account from page 70)

After the war new societies sprang up under the umbrella of the Gaddesden Society: the Drama Club, the Music Society, the Village Produce Association, the Art Club and others. I was one of the original members of the Art Club with Mrs Wager, Mrs Irene Foord-Kelcey, Mrs Patterson (my mother), Mrs Bell, Geoffrey Drewitt (who painted the murals in the School Hall), Bill Woods, John Wynn-Morgan etc. We met on Saturdays in the School Hall with a tutor, Bernard Adams, introduced by Mrs Foord-Kelcey.

The first Drama Club productions took place in the School Hall. I was responsible for the scenery with the help of Les Ouseley, our skilled set-builder. It had to be carefully built around the stove at the back of the stage, on one occasion diguised as a mummy-case. Mr Bell liked to add his touch with a paint-loaded brush. During one production a romance was seen to develop between Louise Dunne and David Hughes, both teachers at the school, who soon became Mr and Mrs Hughes.

An American girl, Beth Taylor from Virginia, soon joined the school staff, and she lodged with us for some eight years. For many years at bonfire night there was a celebration with a bonfire just inside the park gates opposite Church Road. Torchlight processions came from all parts of the village. Beth Taylor and I led from the Deer Leap. Hot drinks were supplied. All these activities moved when the new village hall was built in 1957. The Drama Club expanded with the arrival of David Wray who proved a powerful influence, and memorable productions took place, including several Shakespeare plays, with performances from Enid Foxall, Patsy Blackmore, Jeffery Ede, Geoffrey Tandy, Elizabeth Russell and others. Beards sprouted. Could this nation-wide fashion have been inaugurated in Little Gaddesden?

Some time during these years I remember taking part in an archaeological dig, directed by Geoffrey Tandy, exploring the foundations of the early village in a field near the church.

After my mother died I remained in the village. During that time I had several young lodgers, including two golf assistants to Alex Hay, the professional at Ashridge Golf Club. For the annual Golf Club Dance Alex and I used our large attic to create murals on a different theme every year. Alex was a very clever painter, full of ideas.

In 1974 I sold the house and moved to Berkhamsted.

Part of an excavation at Little Gaddesden in the early 1950s.

Buildings after 1945

Two of the big residences in 1945 were occupied by the Talbot sisters: Bridget, the older, in Little Gaddesden House, and K (Kathleen) in the Manor House. (Pages 269 and 266)

The Reverend Charles Wager was at the Rectory opposite no. 20, and the much larger previous rectory, Benhay or Beaney, was soon to return to private use after the departure of its wartime evacuees and landgirls.

Over the years, Little Gaddesden House, the Manor House and Beaney became divided into smaller residences, as did also the Red House on the Green; but some of the small cottages were joined to make larger ones. Almost every house, it seems, has had some kind of extension added. Planning regulations have varied over the years, not only in their statements, but in their interpretation. During the 40s, 50s and 60s it was much easier to build on open sites than it was in the 70s, 80s and 90s when it was almost, but not quite, impossible.

At the south end of Cromer Wood a second council estate was built in 1949: Cromer Close. The first one, Chapel Close, had been built before the war. Little by little, other houses sprang up in odd spaces and on the vacant plots in Alderton Drive and Golf Club Road. Church Road was still a wide open space until 1953, the only buildings being the school and the Bede Houses, the old village hall having been burnt down in 1943 and not replaced until 1957. There were only fields along the rest of the road to the church. Then in 1953 Coronation Villas were built, otherwise known as numbers 1 to 6 Church Road, filling in part of the space between the Bede Houses and the School. The other houses in Church Road went up from 1960 to 1967, and lastly, in 1969, the 21 new bungalows of Bede Court were built to replace the Bede Houses which were then 104 years old. Their purpose was the

At the opening of Bede Court: Canon Senar, PeterHaydon, unknown and Win and John Oakins.

Bede Court with residents May Sears and Reg Fountain

same, to provide simple housing for pensioners, with a warden on hand in one of them in case of need. The old building originally consisted of eleven residences (as at the 1891 census, when the resident help had consisted of two young relations of the pensioners, and all were female), but these had been reduced in number by amalgamation.

At Ashridge College new uses were found for the hospital "huts", as explained in the chapter on the college. They became a teacher training college for three years from 1946, for ex-service personnel. One of those trainees was Les Ouseley, who subsequently came to live in the village and became in due course the Parish Clerk. Footpath number 25 is named "The Ouseley Path" because he collected the statements from older residents which established that it had been in regular use as a right of way. Times were hard for him and his family when they moved here, as can be read in the next article.

Living with Miss Talbot

by Eve Ouseley

It was on October 31st 1949 that we arrived at Little Gaddesden House. A cold, wet foggy day, we had travelled up from Portsmouth, my two little boys Graham 6 and Mervyn 3, in the furniture van with our few pieces of furniture and belongings. My husband Les had not returned from school, so the housekeeper Mrs MacAdam welcomed us, but was a little perturbed about the furniture - we were supposedly coming to a furnished apartment. However, Miss Talbot being away, we were able to find inconspicuous spaces among the other things. This was not my first visit to L.G House. Miss T had summoned me for inspection a week previously. I had left Graham at school and with a neighbour and made, at that time a long and arduous journey from Portsmouth to St.Albans, where Les met us and brought us the rest of the way on the motor bike. Miss Talbot was not there - she was at a cocktail party in Ashridge and did not arrive until quite late. This meant we had to travel back to Portsmouth on the motor bike, during the night and a thunderstorm. Mind you, she had regaled us with coffee and sherry, but many of you will know that this was not the luxury it was meant to be.

Our apartment was rather spread out. The kitchen and main door was entered from the court yard, then we proceeded down a long corridor to our lavatory on the left, which was also a long narrow room, the loo being at the very far end. A little further on on the right was our sitting room. We were never able to use this as we could not afford the extra fuel, Les only then starting his teaching career. My mother and sister came to stay once and they sat in there with their fur coats on. Up the spacious stairway to our bedrooms, ours had a rather elaborate Italian ironwork bed, and the bathroom as big as a ballroom and very cold, and difficult to get hot water for bathing. Miss T had been glad to let us rent these rooms for the sum of £2.10s. to keep it aired, but the arrangement was that when she was able to rent the place for double we should be offered alternative accommodation.

The morning after we arrived, Les took us down the park and I saw for the first time the Golden Valley, and indeed Golden Valley it truly was. The rain and fog had cleared, and the sun shone through the mist and autumn leaves and golden bracken. We were invited to take part in the torchlight procession to the firework display, where apart from fireworks we were given Oxo or cocoa to drink, and music and singing added extra fun and enjoyment. The week after we arrived was the start of the Olde Tyme Dance Club and I was glad to go along as one of their first and most enthusiastic members.

As most of you will remember, the recently demolished Public Records Office was for three years an Emergency Teacher Training College where Les had done his training, and the year we came there were several young men from the Portsmouth area attending, and at half term and holidays they hired a coach to take them home and for 10/- took the boys and myself with them.

In January the inevitable happened. Miss T found her wealthy tenant, Col. Chris Harrison with wife Jane and three children, two boys and a girl, so we quite cheerfully moved rooms as agreed. To the Blue Room, quite a large pleasant room, but so packed with furniture and books, and difficult to clean, we had to invest in a vacuum cleaner. Across the passage way from here was a large pantry, which we converted into a kitchen, but then we had to journey down a passage through Miss Talbot's kitchen, out through the garden room, into a passage in the yard, up a wooden staircase and into two rooms over the stable and garage. How I managed to rest evenings after the children were in bed, I cannot imagine, they were further away from us than a detached house.

One weekend while Miss Talbot was away, we moved out of the big house into the stable rooms, which were unfurnished, although she said otherwise - indeed there was a wardrobe made of wooden boxes covered in wallpaper and an old table. Conditions here were pretty grim - we had no water and I had to cross the courtyard for every drop of water I used and boil it on the small cooker. In order to dispose of the waste water I had to repeat the process in reverse, our lav was a chemical affair under the building, with the coal. However this is just to explain the setup, and as I look back there were so many amusing incidents connected with the years we were connected with Miss Talbot, and we are only too well aware that had it not been for Miss T we probably would never have known the happiness of becoming villagers of Little Gaddesden.

The maypole on the Green in about the 1940s

During our first few months at Little Gaddesden House, Miss T took me with her to a political meeting at the Village School. She provided me with a list of questions I was to put to Lord and Lady Davidson. She first introduced me to them both with, "May I introduce Mrs Ouseley, my little Socialist friend". This was not quite true, but everybody was polite. I cannot remember that I asked any of these questions, I was far too shy, and yet I feel I was probably too scared of Miss T not to. At the end of the meeting she backed her little Austin into a ditch of sorts in the dark, and sent me to ask Lord Davidson to get her out, and sure enough Lord D and his Chauffeur did just that. Then when she stood as prospective

Entertaining at Little Gaddesden House in the 60s

Back row:
Mrs and Mr Green from Dagnall, Rose Hing, Bridget Talbot, Dora Drewitt, Marion Leggett, Mrs Ruby Barrett, Miss May Whitman.

Front row:
Jubal Jones, Nell Munden, Mr Chapman from Studham, Sid Batchelor, unknown, Mrs M Bail, Arthur and Mrs Maunders.

Liberal candidate for Bermondsey we helped her blow up balloons and Les painted the logo on them. My greatest involvement with her was the May Day activities. She worked so hard to make the event enjoyable for the children. My boys in turn were parts of the dragon, or St George, and Lorna much later was May Queen. We sliced and buttered the buns for the children, and served tea and orange juice. I can see her now scattering toffees in the garden at the back of the house. One year she decided that a quartet would sing The Gaddesden May Song and The Spotted Cow, but she did not tell me till the morning of the event that I was to sing the soprano line, together with the headmaster of Ashlyns and two other people. We rehearsed in the morning and endeavoured to render it in the afternoon with all the excited noises off from children etc. The event from year to year wandered off the actual May Day, and usually was a bit of a shambles, but the children seemed to enjoy it and her enthusiasm and effort never faltered.

In August 1951, we thankfully moved into our council house, very sparse and under-furnished, but the space was lovely. This time we moved on a tractor. After our departure from L.G.House Miss Talbot was always asking for little jobs to be done, for which we did not have a lot of time or inclination. On one occasion she invited me to be a fellow guest when she entertained some blind gentlemen from St Dunstan's to lunch. She assured me that I was only required to chat and entertain then, and I was quite happy to do this. In the afternoon, we all went to Ashridge for afternoon tea, and I went with Jim Whitman to take a couple of them home to Sandy.

Kathleen Talbot

by Barbara Cassell

Whereas Bridget Talbot's story has come in varous parts, K's is best left in one piece, and this seems a good place to tell it, even though it begins in the time of an earlier chapter.

The Talbot family in 1900: back row:
Bridget, Alfred and Emily with Kathleen in the middle. The couple in front are not known

Always known as K (she refused to be called Kathleen), she was the youngest of the family and about ten years younger than Bridget. She was quite the opposite of her sister, and I remember Sir Granville Ram saying to me that one could see K deciding she would not be vague and unpunctual like Bridget and Humphrey. K also received the O.B.E. for public services, and also saved an old house, when she bought the Manor House after the Ashridge sale. I do not believe the Alfred Talbots were very rich, but they had rich, grand, aunts and cousins who had no children, and so both the sisters inherited quite a lot of money and jewellery.

K was very musical: she probably did not have much formal music education in the modern sense - she never went to school, but had lessons in piano playing, singing and languages, and she must have acquired a knowledge of harmony and such technical matters. She certainly would have sought advice

about conducting. She produced performances of Arne's setting of the Masque of Comus, conducted by Susan Lushington. The first was at Little Gaddesden House in 1922. There was a grander performance at Eton College on 11th December that year with John Gielgud as the 'Younger brother'. Elizabeth Mitchell-Innes was 'The Lady'. The latter married Sir Granville Ram. (She is buried in Little Gaddesden churchyard.) The Masque of Comus was repeated in the Middle Temple, and there were notices in all the main newspapers.

K started a music festival in Berkhamsted in the 1920's, and this kept going until 1939. She conducted Little Gaddesden Choir; my aunt Cooie Lane was extremely unpunctual and she was always nervous of being late for K's rehearsals.

After the war K became involved in the Rural Music Schools movement, and from this realised two things: (1) the need for County Music Advisers, with attendant local support - the growth of some excellent Youth Orchestras stems from this; and (2) there should be some training available for amateur conductors of choirs and orchestras. She helped to start the Talbot-Lampton Music School.

K's other great interest was in her garden, and the production of fruit and vegetables, not just flowers. She carried on the Little Gaddesden House tradition of flower shows and was a founder of the Village Produce Association. Her war job was spreading the word about food production via the V.P.A. and similar societies all over the country. This was not a 'cushy' job for a middle aged lady, when one remembers the lack of petrol, black-out, and no signposts in most areas, and she really did go all over the country.

K's friend, Dorothy Erhart, came to live in the Manor House with her mother; and in fact stayed there until her own death in 1971. Dorothy was a professional harpsichordist (and there weren't many of them in those days), and she gave concerts and taught music in London. There were concerts at the Manor House at regular intervals - some of them in conjunction with the Music Club, and some of them of their own arranging. I remember a piano recital given by the young Antony Hopkins. The Manor House was opened regularly to the public after K received a government grant for the repair of the roof.

K was not very demonstrative, and one has only discovered all these accomplishments after her death, but I was always fond of her - the music was our link, I suppose. K and my mother trained as Voluntary Aid Detachment nurses during the 1914-18 war, and in fact K introduced my parents to each other. She died, much too young, of a cerebral haemorrhage in Austria in 1958, and poor Bridget was devastated. She had been concerned with Bridget's problems during the previous year, as Bridget had been in hospital with a broken leg, causing despair to nurses, doctors, and anyone else within reach.

Humphrey had died earlier of a heart attack; he was due to marry his sweetheart from his youth, who had become widowed, and he collapsed early on his wedding day in the 1950's. As their other brother, Geoffrey, had died in the Royal Naval Air Service in 1916, Bridget was now the sole survivor of the family, and lived until 1971. None of the four had married or had children.

The Masque of Comus in the grounds of Little Gaddesden House. Principals (left to right):
Elizabeth Mitchell-Innes as Attendant Spirit, Barbara Druce as Elder Brother, Christabel Liddell as The Lady, Peter Quennell (sitting on the ground) as Younger Brother, Mrs Gerald Bevan as Sabrina, spirit of the River Severn. Chorus: Local girls.

The lower picture shows L. Granville Ram as the enchanter Comus, and Christabel Liddell

Memories of a village policeman

Extracts from a talk given by Alf Sherringham in about 1994

I suppose I should begin my thoughts at the beginning when, in 1949, I was at Bishops Stortford and whilst on night duty I was told I had been posted to Little Gaddesden. Now in those days certain country villages, known as bus stations, were used by the powers that be as punishment stations, which meant outside toilets etc and oil lamps. Naturally I wondered what I had done wrong but, after discussions with my wife, I decided to leave the decision to her and, after her first visit, we decided to give it a go.

We arrived at number 21 in September 1949, all turning up on a furniture van. My wife was in front with my youngest, aged 2 years, on her lap, myself with my son, aged 9 years, and other daughter, aged 6 years, sitting on the settee which was on the tailboard of the van; that was how one moved in those days. The furniture men were very pleased with the house as the staircase was very wide, which made the furniture so much easier to get upstairs - lovely house. I was informed later that it was the last house to be built on the Brownlow Estate; one can see the monogram on the south side.

Editor's Note: it was built about 1903.

The next day an old gentleman came into the garden dressed in an army greatcoat pinned at the neck, deerstalker hat (rather well-worn), wellington boots, and in his hand was a cabbage. He introduced himself as the local vicar (Rev Charles Wager) from across the road, and offered me the cabbage as he thought it would do for lunch as I had just arrived - a grand man.

Later that day, on looking over the fence at the rear of the house, I saw a man dressed in a khaki coloured shirt, shorts and a red scarf around his neck, sitting on a chair with his bare feet in a bowl of water. On seeing me he called and introduced himself as the village schoolmaster (Mr Vicars Bell). I had rather misgivings about Little Gaddesden which were soon allayed as time went on.

My colleague in the force (PC Parker), who was due to retire, arranged for me to be taken around my patch. I then began my most enjoyable fifteen years in the Herts Police. My patch consisted of the village, Hudnall Common, St Margarets, Ringshall, Ashridge Park, Berkhamsted Common, Nettleden and Frithsden, which I duly patrolled on my trusty cycle.

On week-ends cycle racing was seen in the village. A large number of cyclists would come racing from Ringshall but, unfortunately, rains would cause a large amount of gravel to gather in the road at the end of Church Road, and without fail the leading cyclist would skid and take a tumble. This would cause the following racers to come off their bikes as well, much to the delight of my children who sat on the garden wall waiting for it to happen (wicked children!).

There was also motor car racing. These vehicles came from the direction of Pulridge and would turn into Hudnall Lane. Unfortunately this happened in the early hours of the morning and the drivers would change gear to turn the corner, much to the disgust of the resident of Kinghams Meadow on the corner, who would summon me, and I would find him in the road in his pyjamas being very rude to the motorists whom he had stopped.

Duties included serving summonses, executing warrants, posting public notices and other police matters, but being part of the village was the most important part. In those days if Tommy or Johnny misbehaved, their mothers would consult me and ask me to have a few words with the youngster.

Certain things I do remember - standing by the Deer Leap and hearing the

NAMES INDEX

continued from page 73

continued on page 83

nightingales singing over by the reservoir, or seeing the glow-worms on the banks down the side of Hudnall Lane.

My thoughts of Ashridge, from the first time of visiting, were very pleasant; the times of the bursar's twins trying on my helmet and forever hiding my cycle; these are memories I hold dear.

When the House of Citizenship (see page 147) was in residence, some of the girls were doing a thesis on the village. They spent most of their time in the police cottage being entertained by my wife with tea and cakes. No doubt they learnt more about the village there than they would outside. One afternoon I was sitting in a hut at the end of Lime Walk, feeling rather sore after playing football. There were students resident in Lime Walk at that time. I heard footsteps and saw a young man heading towards the sleeping quarters. I asked him who he was and, as he was rather vague, I detained him. It later transpired that he was on the run from some prison. He was very unlucky for, had he chosen to, he could have run away from me - being so sore at that time I would never has chased him.

At Coldharbour Farm one of the cottages was occupied by three potters. One hot summer afternoon we had reports of a fire. On arrival we found one of the potters inside a cottage from which blue smoke was pouring out of the doorway. There he was, stripped to the waist, busy making blackberry jam, some of which had caught fire.

On Sunday mornings folks employed in restaurants would be busy collecting mushrooms and other fungi for eating places in London.

The Gypsies and Travellers were numerous but were never a great problem to me. I got to know several of the families very well and always admired how they managed to keep so clean in all sorts of weather, especially the children. I was fortunate to meet a real Romany couple who resided in a wonderful horse-drawn caravan, the contents of which were a joy to behold.

A curious things about the Bridgewater Arms hotel was that, for a short time, prisoners on parole were employed there in menial tasks and had to report to my house every day.

I must mention Fred the golf caddie who, after a good day, would usually end up at the local and would want to fight everyone. We would settle him down in one of the huts on the golf course for the night. However one night in the dead of winter, I found him on the Green near the War Memorial covered in snow and nearly frozen. I suppose he had got drunk, lost his way back to the hut and fallen down. Fortunately I found him in time.

Both my wife and I got involved with the youngsters in the village, especially the footballers. My wife would heat up the stone copper in the barn so that hot water could be taken to the bath to enable the lads to wash themselves after the match.

I remember an occasion when standing at Hudnall crossroads.

NAMES INDEX

continued from page 82

continued on page 84

No 21 Little Gaddesden, initially a private residence, then the police house, then the schoolmaster's house and now lived in by the Leonhardt family

The hunt was in full cry and a rather enthusiastic follower came to me and asked if I had seen the hunt. I informed him that the dogs were towards Mile Barn. He promptly told me they were not dogs but hounds. Soon after that, the fox came down Pedley Hill with what appeared to be a very satisfied grin on his face.

At the furthest part of Ashridge grounds in the south was a building which was known as the Ancient Britons Hut. Unfortunately it was in a state of decay and I have never been able to trace its origin. Perhaps it was a playhouse for the children of Ashridge.

No 21, the Police House, was a lovely house with its black and red tiled floor, its huge dresser, the long pantry with its marble top cupboards and the large cupboard under the stairs where the children played. Outside was the lovely garden with the mistletoe growing up the apple tree and, near the front door, the Victoria plum tree which, when full of plums, the tradesmen would sample.

Editor's note: This house was the police house from 1928 to 1983, then the schoolmaster's house until 1991. It has been my house since 1995. I am afraid most of the tiled floor is hidden under a carpet but the huge dresser has been rescued from the outhouse and restored. The pantry and marble top cupboards have gone. All the old fruit trees had gone but we have planted nine new ones of assorted varieties, including a Victoria plum.

The village school in the 1950s

by Hilary, Ian and Pat Catchpole
Continued from page 43 (Min Catchpole)

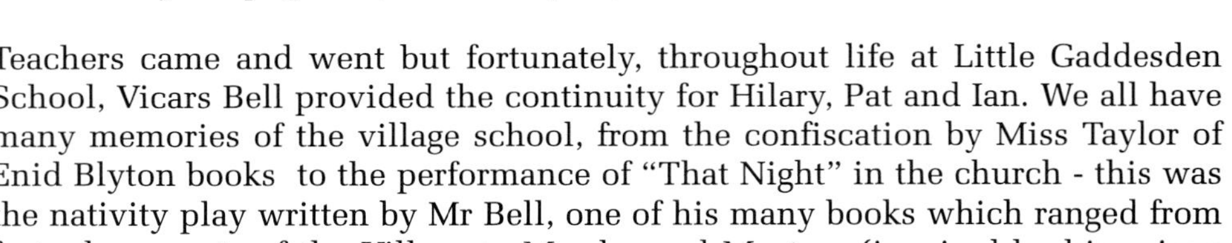

Teachers came and went but fortunately, throughout life at Little Gaddesden School, Vicars Bell provided the continuity for Hilary, Pat and Ian. We all have many memories of the village school, from the confiscation by Miss Taylor of Enid Blyton books to the performance of "That Night" in the church - this was the nativity play written by Mr Bell, one of his many books which ranged from factual accounts of the Village to Murder and Mystery (inspired by his prison visits, for which he was awarded an MBE).

Memories of Vicars Bell and the village school would themselves fill several books but maybe the one thing we all remember is Vicars Bell's ability to bring any story to life. For the youngest children in the school it was "Monkey" the hand puppet that kept them enthralled, whereas for the older children it was Bilbo Baggins, Gandalf, Thorin, and the other characters from The Hobbit, who carried them off into fantasy land.

The teaching methods adopted by the staff at Little Gaddesden School

The school with the 1953 classroom extension - taken about 1980.

NAMES INDEX
continued from page 83

continued on page 87

during the 1950's drew attention from teachers around the world and it was a common occurrence for lessons to be observed by men and women of other nationalities.

Ex pupils from Little Gaddesden will themselves undoubtedly be spread around the world, and one likes to think that some elements of our formative education have been imparted to others and have given as much pleasure to subsequent generations as they did to us. We did, of course, gain a sound education in maths, history, geography, music, art, religious instruction, natural history and physical education, but many will agree that the introduction to literature underpinned everything.

Vicars Bell left in the same year as Pat and Ian, so here there was a break in the continuity from generation to generation. However, Vicars Bell's influence still lingers on within our school in the form of the Library which is dedicated to his memory in response to the very generous legacy he bequeathed. It was indeed fitting that the library created by a later Headmaster - Stanley Spencer - should be opened by Genista McIntosh, a former pupil of the school who was awarded a baronial title for her work in the Arts and Theatre world. . . . . .

Continued by the next generation on page 102

The Gaddesden Diary

by Margaret Crawford

The first issue of the Gaddesden Diary was published by the Gaddesden Society in the Spring of 1955. It was printed on octavo paper, sold at 6d, and covered the months April, May and June. The cover, as now, was designed by Dorothea Patterson, who was the sub-editor, and showed a rather fierce-looking owl. I believe one of the many 'forms' into which Rosina Massey, the supposed witch who lived in Witchcraft Bottom, could turn herself was an owl. The cover changed to the 'Tree of All Seasons' design, which we still use, in 1959. Major Dundas Heenan, the then Chairman of the Society, wrote in the Foreword that it would be published quarterly, distributed to the members, and sold at the Post Office. Irene Foord-Kelcey, whose brain-child this was, was helped in every way by Mr Ken Thorn who lived at no. 43 and whose firm Swift's in Luton printed the Diary and took care of the advertising. She said in her first editorial that it aimed to give an account of what had been happening in the previous quarter and to publish a programme of forthcoming events. It still does!

One of the first copies of the Gaddesden Diary

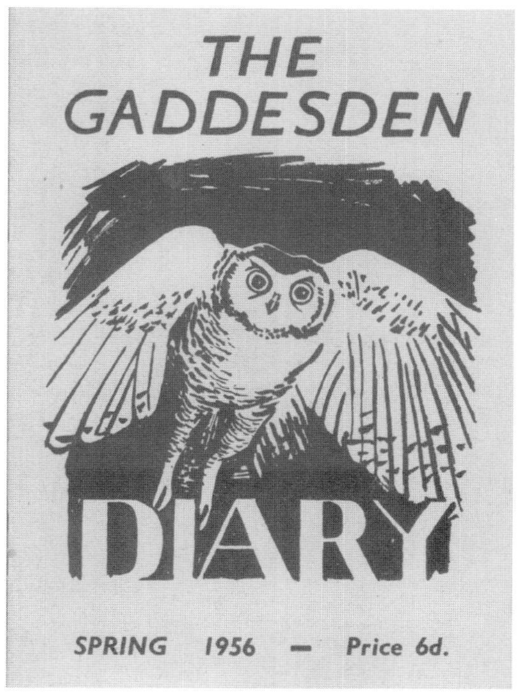

The first issue gave a full account of the meeting on November 15th 1954 convened by the Parish Council in the School Hall to discuss and approve proposals for a new Village Hall. Of the advertisers, H.H. Dickman (the chemist in Berkhamsted) and the Village Store and Post Office (then run by Mr H.V. Ward) are the only ones still in existence and still advertising.

Most of the societies who contribute now to the Diary were already in existence, although some were in a different form: e.g. the Drama Club, which as well as putting on plays also met once a month in members' houses for play reading; the Cricket Club was the Ashridge Cricket Club, and there was a Flower Show organised

THE
GADDESDEN
DIARY
AUTUMN 1999 — Price 75p
PUBLISHED QUARTERLY BY THE GADDESDEN SOCIETY

A current Gaddesden Diary

jointly by the Women's Institute, British Legion and Village Produce Association. Ashridge House, which was then a College of Citizenship, invited members of the Gaddesden Society to some of their weekend lectures (organised by Miss Hilda Blake who lived at no.46), and encouraged them to stay to lunch and take part in discussion groups and question time. Some of the lectures were: The British Colonies Outside Africa, The British in Africa, The Aims of Education, and (in June 1956) Germany and the West. I think the residents of Little Gaddesden were lucky to have the opportunity of attending these courses - I wonder what the take-up would be nowadays when, despite all the modern labour-saving gadgets, people seem to have so little leisure time.

When reading the varied activities of the varous clubs it becomes very obvious that people then had time to organise all kinds of activities. One of the clubs no longer with us was the Old Time Dancing Club which in 1955 had a membership of 60. When I arrived in 1965 Albert Williams was still running old time dancing in the school hall with a membership of about 14.

However, many things haven't changed. In Winter 1955 there was an anti-litter campaign. There were endless problems over the new village hall: "The Management Committee have been facing a three-cornered attack; from the planning authorities upon the question of exterior design, from a Government department on the question of the registration of their Title Deeds, and from another Government Department on the question of the formulation of a Charitable Trust Deed."

I was fascinated to read in the Spring 1956 Diary of the discovery by Dr Goddard, in a box in the bank, of a flagon so tarnished that it was thought to be pewter, but when cleaned turned out to be a fine piece of Carolean plate belonging to Little Gaddesden church and dated 1635. I noted with interest in the Winter 1956 issue that our branch of the British Legion in nearly twenty years had collected £2000 from Poppy Day sales - a considerable sum in those days. In the 1957 issue 14 members of the W.I. Choir, conducted by Daisy Thorn, won a Gold Star at the W.I. Choir Festival at Hatfield. I was 'shocked' to see an advertisement in the Autumn 1957 Diary asking people to place their bets with L.R.B. Commissions Turf Accountants in Lower Kings Road, Berkhamsted.

In the Summer 1956 Diary the death in May of its founder Mrs Irene Foord-Kelcey was reported and tribute paid to her work and the standard she set. In the next Winter issue a welcome was given to the new editor Mrs Rawdon Smith. Editorial grumbles about copy not received and some of the 'silent societies' were much as now.

The Mobile Library started in 1958, and the place and time of stopping places were given. In Spring 1958 the Bee-keepers Association under the guidance of Miss J. Moore, who lived at Greenacre, made its first appearance. Its last was in Spring 1967.

In Summer 1961 the Diary reported on the formation of the Little Gaddesden Preservation Society whose chairman was Captain David Magnay, and Captain Ashby was both Secretary and Treasurer. It seems to have folded in Autumn 1969.

(Continued on page 90)

Recollections from Elizabeth Bradfield

by Jan Maclarty

Elizabeth had a nursery school in her house in 1956-57 (see page 173).

She had two children at the village school. She transported them in her donkey cart, stopping on the way home to buy sweets from Miss Pratt. In her shop on the green the sweets were always weighed out. There were egg baskets hanging on hooks in the ceiling and the cat always sat on the counter.

It was the same donkey and trap that used to carry the May Queen for Bridget Talbot's May Day celebrations. Six boys formed the dragon, slain by St George on his horse. Children were garlanded and danced with ribbons. The same donkey gave rides for 6d. at the annual Conservative fete on the green.

Mr Williams in the Post Office was a hero. He was held at gun-point, but refused to hand over any money, and the robber left empty handed.

The Women's Institute was very active, meeting in the new village hall built in 1956 for £3,000. Ten shillings was donated towards it by each household. The W.I. had its own flourishing drama group. The president, Vi Hughes, acted and produced, and many other members were "naturals" on the stage, winning many competitions. Elizabeth was secretary at that time and was later president herself.

The Good Neighbours Group of the W.I. regularly visited the Cheshire Home and mended linen and clothes. This group also worked at Lagley Hall Old People's Club (Berkhamsted), laying tables and washing up, until Dacorum employed paid staff in the 70s.

Yve Dickson in the 1950s organised the 'adoption' of a Polish family, sending parcels, and later their children came to stay in the village.

Any sick person in the village received a card.

The Rev R.C.Paterson was Rector. All were made welcome at the Rectory, including the Ladies Sewing Circle on Thursday afternoons stitching articles for an annual sale. The proceeds were for the church. Use of the rectory for such purposes ended when the next Rector had the church vestry built.

When one of Elizabeth's children was ill she could not get to the chemist to collect the prescription - hence the idea of the prescription service. Those with cars volunteered, and the service was organised by Vi Hughes from her home for eleven years, helping those with transport difficulties.

And was there really a spy during the last war in a house in Witchcraft Hill? Equipment used by spies was allegedly found in the loft.

Life in the park

from a conversation with Willy Hill

In 1962 Willy and Lucy Hill had been managing the village shop at Toddington, and finding that the work was becoming too much for them. When they saw an advertisement for a live-in chauffeur in Little Gaddesden, Willy applied for, and obtained, the job. His employer was Mr Arthur Robert Oldcorn-Slater, more simply referred to as Mr Slater, senior partner in the firm of West, Wake and Price, City accountants. He lived at what is now Bridgewater House on the Ringshall-Northchurch road, though at that time it was Bridgewater Lodge. The Slaters had lived there from about 1958. It was originally built for Henry Cotton, the golf professional.

The Hills' accommodation was a flat above three garages, and it was essential that Kuki the poodle was compatible with their Scotty, Max. Fortunately the

NAMES INDEX

continued from page 84

continued on page 88

NAMES INDEX
continued from page 87

continued on page 89

two dogs got on well. The car that Willy was to drive was a Bentley, registration number WOF 600, and later a Rolls Royce. Appearance was as important as competence in this job. Willy describing Mr Slater said, "He would be about five foot seven, always immaculately turned out. One year he was voted Best Dressed Man of the Year by the 'Tailor and Cutter'. I had to appear the same. My suit and uniform were made to measure by Gieves of Bond Street, and no one could have made a finer turn-out when they went out in the Rolls Royce."

Mr Slater's decision to acquire this Rolls Royce came about like this. "One day he said, 'I want you to drive the Bentley to such-and-such garage in Golders Green. Here's a cheque in an envelope. A test drive is being arranged.' I drove it up the M1. I got back after fifty miles and said, 'You have a deal' and gave him the cheque. He was taking the Bentley in part exchange." The Rolls Royce was a second hand Silver Cloud of about 1955, first model of the eight-cylinder series, with a silver body and coral black roof line, registered 4681 PE.

"I've never had an accident in my life. I've learnt my lesson from the hairy moments and experiences I've had." Willy drove the Bentley, and later the Rolls, a lot, as Mr Slater would be away ten to twelve nights per month on business, and wherever they went Willy would be booked in to a hotel of at least three star grading. One of his regular visits was to a gravel pit at Bishops Lydiard near Taunton.

Mr Slater and his wife, Barbara, were both in their second marriages. It was because of her arthritis that they had a bungalow built in their grounds, which were on the corner of the main road and Golf Club Road. The old house opened on to the main road, and its name was changed to Bridgewater House. The new bungalow opened on to Golf Club Road, and took its name from the old house, Bridgewater Lodge. The old house was sold to Dr Ehrlich in about 1965, "one of the best engineers of two-stroke engines."

Barbara Slater's brother was Trevor Huddleston C.R., the monk who famously campaigned against apartheid in South Africa, and became successively Bishop of Masasi, Bishop of Stepney and Archbishop of the Indian Ocean. He used to visit his sister, and he gave Willy's daughter Sandra an "uncut" copy of "Naught for your Comfort".

Arthur and Barbara each had one son and one daughter from their previous marriages. Arthur's son Alan kept all the back numbers of the Financial Times in the loft, and one of Willy's jobs was to keep them in order and find the right one when it was needed for reference. Alan was in due course taken on as a partner in his father's firm.

Willy Hill with Mr Smalley's Rolls Royce Silver Cloud

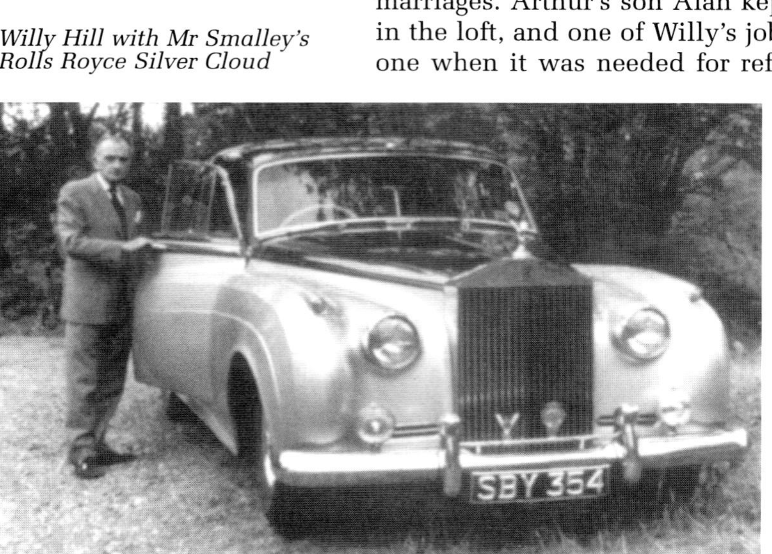

One of the garages contained Willy's own Mini, in which he taught his daughter to drive. When they first arrived at Bridgewater Lodge, Sandra had just left school and, having got a job in Luton, stayed there with her god-parents during the week. The Slaters took a great interest in her, and Arthur was delighted when she passed her driving test. She came over on the next Sunday, and Mr Slater said "Hill, will you get the Rolls out". I heard it move off, and in the passenger seat was Mr Slater, and Sandra was driving. They drove around a bit - up to the Monument at first - and eventually went via St Albans to Flamstead and called in at Cecil Parkinson's for a chat. Cecil Parkinson, the well-known politician, was their son-in-law, married to Barbara's daughter, Ann. When they got back, Barbara protested that her husband should not have put Sandra in such a position when she had only just passed her test and never driven so big, or so valuable, a car, but it was typical of his generous nature to do something like that.

Willy recalls some of the social circle of that neighbourhood in the 1960s. Some of these jottings may be of interest. Some of the names crop up elsewhere in this book, or were notable for their connection with a village organisation. Some are still here, so I hope they do not find anything wrong in these notes. The area from Blue Cottage to Thunderdell Lodge was known as Millionaire's Row.

Bridge was a favourite pastime with the Slaters and friends such as the Napiers, Turneys and Smalleys, the ladies often playing in the afternoon and the whole family after dinner, (another of Willy's jobs being to wait at table). Mr Napier, an American at Journeys End, was British President of Nielson Research Marketing at Headington. Mr and Mrs Smalley had lived in Hong Kong where he was an import/export merchant, and they had been prisoners of the Japanese for three years (not the only Little Gaddesden people who had experienced this). They also had a Rolls Royce, and used to ask Willy to give it a run and check it when they were away, which would be for about three months at a time. The photograph shows Willy with this one, which was a six-cylinder Silver Cloud with automatic gear-box, registered SBY 354.

At Wynford (now Windyridge) in Hudnall Lane were Cecil and Sheila Ford. Cecil was a film producer, one of his films being "The Guns of Navarone". One of their great friends was Roy Blackmore, a local businessman. His wife, Patsy Blackmore, has been one of our most active drama club members and producers. So also has been Enid Foxall. She and her husband Peter lived at Ringshall Rise. Her father had Stag Wood built. Her brother, Sir Donald Hawley, lived at West Pulridge, and was British ambassador in Kuala Lumpur. Mr George Macnab of Princes Riding, a Scot as his name suggests, was a surgeon at Westminster Hospital, and his wife Crystal was a concert pianist and often hosted the Music Club at their house. Mr Verrells at Witchwood was the owner of a Silver Spur Bentley, another of the cars which Willy was sometimes asked to drive, as, for instance, when they went to the airport to take a plane. This car was maintained by Jack Rogers. At Blue Cottage were Ernest and Iris Clayton. Ernest, working on the Stock Exchange, used to ring Willy up with useful investment tips. Iris ran a nursery school for many years, and was also a much loved Sunday School teacher in her later years.

The garden of the new Bridgewater Lodge was landscaped by Bill Moore of Ringshall. He put in a dog-bone shaped flower bed with up to 150 floribunda roses and six large standard roses. These were so beautiful that a party was held in the garden to enjoy them, and it became an annual event with guests from London. Willy Hill himself, with John Fitzpatrick, Mr Slater's boy golf caddy, planted one and a half hundredweight of daffodils round the perimeter of the lawn, and they are still there.

When Mr Slater retired he moved to Harpenden. Willy bought no. 12 Ringshall and was still employed by Mr Slater, but also by Mr Napier and Mr Foxall for various days each.

Not long after that, in 1969, Willy and Lucy moved into 12 Bede Court, the second bungalow to be occupied there after they were built. The first resident was Miss Rene Wells at no. 11, who lived there until about 1988. Lucy died in 1997, and Willy sadly passed on in 2000.

NAMES INDEX
continued from page 88

continued on page 90

More from the Gaddesden Diary 1963 to 1966

by Margaret Crawford

The beech trees on Pulridge Hill as they were about 1950.

I was interested to note in the Summer 1963 Diary a report from the Little Gaddesden Preservation Society about the felling of the beech trees on Pulridge Hill, doubts as to whether it was really necessary, and promises of replanting. I can remember these beeches well as on occasion my family drove out to Little Gaddesden from Chandler's Cross where we then lived. They met forming an arch all the way up the hill and were lovely. I see in the Autumn Diary that the Preservation Society did arrange with Mr Green, the new owner of the land on the side of the road, for replanting 36 trees at the cost of £1 per tree. I seem to recall that at a later date a fire destroyed most of them.

In Summer 1964 the Diary pays tribute to the retiring policeman, Alf Sherringham, and comments on the foundations being laid for the new police house in Church Road.

In Autumn 1964 the Village Hall was nearly paid for and at last they had a proper car park built in the summer. Horror of horrors, the Preservation Society reported that there was talk of Hudnall Farm being developed as a housing estate.

I learn from the Autumn 1965 Diary that Mr Joe Hing, a founder member of the Gaddesden Society, who was described as 'part of the old village' had died. To commemorate their Golden Jubilee the Women's Institute had given the seat at Hudnall Corner, and the Parish Council had erected one on the Post Office forecourt - both still appreciated by many people. *(continued on page 95)*

Some final tales of Bridget Talbot

by Barbara Cassell

My personal memories of the Little Gaddesden Talbots date from about 1938. The family consisted of Bridget, who continued at Little Gaddesden House after the death of her parents, K at the Manor House, and Humphrey who owned Swakeleys near Uxbridge. None of them was married and all owned large houses to 'save' them. I remember going to a Christmas party at Little Gaddesden House where we performed energetic charades. My parents were abroad and so my brother and I stayed with our aunt Cooie at St Margarets for the holidays.

When I visited Little Gaddesden House it was already divided, but it did still have the appearance and atmosphere of a big house - if somewhat untidy.

Tales of Bridget are legion, and perhaps one can say that she enjoyed being a 'character' in her old age. I think relations of her generation found her fun but not to be relied upon - one cousin said she wouldn't even buy a bale of hay from her! However, she was pretty when young and she was always popular with children - who perhaps were encouraged to be slightly naughty, although she did start a scout group at the house in 1912.

There were many tales of quite grand people being invited to lunch or tea, who arrived to find no Bridget and no food. Then there were the occasions when she travelled on a train without a ticket, and she was twice prosecuted for this. Dorothy Erhart, who lived at the Manor House with K, had a lovely story of going to Euston when both had rail tickets; however, when she was asked for a ticket at Euston, she flatly refused to find one - so the inspector was called. After all the fuss was over Dorothy asked her: "Why did you make this fuss when I

NAMES INDEX
continued on page 91

continued on page 91

saw you buy a ticket?" Bridget's answer was that it was in her raincoat pocket, but underneath some extremely useful lavatory paper labelled 'British Rail', and she was not going to turn her pocket out in front of an inspector.

On the other hand Bridget was awarded the O.B.E. for public services, and these stem from her great interest in St Dunstan's Training for the Blind where she was active in the Summer Camps, and in the welfare of the Merchant Navy - apart from her concern with the village of Little Gaddesden.

by Alfred Cassell

On my last visit to Edlesborough church I saw a fine piece of ornamental ironwork set behind glass over a doorway: it was described in the guide as an example of ninteenth century French work. Which church Bridget Talbot worshipped at depended upon which vicar she was currently agreeing with. When we stayed with her we slept in her Italian bed, which had a magnificent head-piece but no foot-piece. She told us the missing piece was behind the altar in Edlesborough church 'to brighten it up'. You may still be able to see it.

EDITOR'S NOTE

There is a memorial to Bridget Talbot beside the footpath from Edlesborough Church to Ivinghoe. It is just over half a mile southwest of the church, beside the tributary of the Whistle Brook where it emerges from Coombe Bottom. It is a horizontal stone supported at each end like a stool. The inscription is:

IN MEMORY OF
BRIDGET ELIZABETH TALBOT O.B.E.
OF LITTLE GADDESDEN & KIPLIN HALL
SEAMAN'S FRIEND AND DEFENDER OF HUMAN RIGHTS.
SHE HELPED TO PRESERVE THESE DOWNS FOR YOU WHO READ THIS.

DIED 29th NOV. 1971.

INVENTOR OF LIFE SAVING WATER TIGHT TORCH FOR MARINERS.

Cromer Close in the early sixties

by Catherine Camfield, daughter of Geoff and Mary Rogers

I was born in 1955 and, from eight months old, lived in Cromer Close until I got married twenty-two years later. As most people looking back on their childhood will say, life seemed so simple then.

The Co-op shop visited the village every Monday - Mum would religiously prepare her list which she kept in a small notebook. Mr McIntyre from Berkhamsted came in his van on Wednesday afternoons. It was he who introduced me and my brother to the new flavour in crisps - Oxo. Until that time, we only knew plain crisps. Mr Janes from Edlesborough would call each week to sell shoes and electrical goods. All my school shoes came from him.

NAMES INDEX
continued from page 90

continued on page 92

Mum said that I needed brown shoes with a buckle, and he always bought a good selection the following week for me to try on. Doris Cocks brought groceries on a Friday night, and Wessel Gadsden regularly delivered freshly made loaves. I remember my Uncle John, a butcher, delivering meat to us on a Tuesday. A far cry from the services on offer today in the village where I now live!

My brother and I would regularly visit Mrs Peachey's sweet shop which was near to Little Gaddesden House. Before that, Mum tells me that there used to be a general store nearby, owned by Mr and Mrs Quennel, but I cannot remember that. I do not know how Mrs Peachey ever made a profit! I recall her selling only sweets and little else. My friends and I from Cromer Close would often make visits to her to buy sweets to eat "down the park". She would always make us very welcome. When I started learning French at school, the visits were made more of a chore for me. Mrs Peachey could speak fluent French and insisted on testing me before I could buy anything!

Summer holidays were spent "down the park" from early morning to dusk. We were safe and secure at that time. We made camps, and had "excursions" to the Monument and to Poplar pond on the golf course. We would also look for missing golf balls which we could then sell back to the golfers for pocket money. Spring meant bluebells which grew in the park near to Cromer Close. Summer meant playing in the road down Cromer Close - there were very few people with cars. Autumn meant a return to Little Gaddesden School - a place which I loved - Mum never had to drag me there! Winter meant snow and lots of it, and Dad taking us down the park sledging.

I was very sad to leave Little Gaddesden School. I went to Ashlyns School, which I learned very quickly to enjoy, and had to travel there on the school bus - girls upstairs and boys downstairs. This I did for seven years. The journey there has changed very little in thirty years - the views from the bus would still be the same now, but the amount of traffic has increased enormously. My fear was to miss the school bus home - Mum and Dad did not have a car and buses to Gaddesden from Berkhamsted were infrequent.

When I got married, I moved away from the village. Like so many, we found house prices were too expensive in the village for a newly married couple. My parents still live in the same house in Cromer Close. I consider myself very fortunate to have been born and raised in the village. When I visit my parents, I can still clearly see the village where I grew up. Many faces of my childhood are still there. Many of the village services and shops have disappeared, but Little Gaddesden has changed a lot less than most places. Long may it continue like that!

Village School Life - 1968 to 1974

by Sarah Walters, daughter of John and Betty Rogers

I started school in January 1968 and I remember being very disappointed as snow prevented me from attending on my first day. We used to walk (or cycle in later years) along the village green from Chapel Close every day to the School and met with many families from Hudnall Lane and Cromer Close doing the same thing.

My years at the Village School were very happy ones and I have very fond memories of my time there. As a new girl in the School I remember being

NAMES INDEX

continued from page 91

continued on page 93

particularly daunted by lunchtimes and morning assemblies as all the School was present and the older children all seemed so much bigger than us. We each had to sit with an older pupil whose job it was to look after us in the morning assembly, and at lunchtime there were two prefects per table, who were supposed to pour the water, make sure we ate up and did not misbehave too much. Morning assembly was very important as it was the focal point of worship each day. The members of staff at the time, Mr Williams, Mrs Bishop and Mrs Hendy, took it in turns to do assembly each day, sometimes with their classes and sometimes alone, and Canon Senar always came on a Friday.

Thursdays were a special treat as we had a service of worship on the radio to which we had to listen and sing along. As you progressed through the School there was the opportunity to do your own assembly, and many of us were entertained by different sketches and interpretations of bible stories or famous other stories. (Does anyone remember me as Winnie the Pooh stuck in Rabbit's hole?)

The best way to talk about the School is to describe the school year. In this way it might appear that the School was nothing but special events. However, a great deal of teaching and learning went on there, and I am sure that countless village children who went through the School owe a lot to those early years of their education in Little Gaddesden School. I am very grateful for the good start that I had there and feel sure that I would not have become a teacher myself had it not been for the excellent experience that I had there.

The School year began in September and this was accompanied by the long winter term with its build-up to Christmas. The first thing in the calendar was Harvest Festival and we would go to church, as we did each term for a special mid-week service, and we would bring our gifts and sing our favourite harvest hymns. This was followed by the Sausage and Mash Supper, when a hearty meal of sausages, beans and mash, with cider for the adults, would be followed by community singing and country dancing. The next big event in the school year was the School Bazaar, when funds were raised for the School. The village was split into areas and roads and the children of the top class (now known as national curriculum years 5 & 6) would do a house-to-house collection for goods to sell. This resulted in a fun Friday evening at the end of November selling our pottery, goods, cakes, etc and playing fête-type games in order to raise money for the School.

The highlight of the school year was always Christmas, with class parties and the Nativity Play. I remember the excitement of being an angel and having to creep outside the school hall in the dark to make a secret entrance through the kitchen door singing the final verse of 'While Shepherds watched their flocks by night'. There were always two performances of this - one in the evening for the parents and then one on the following afternoon for the other people in the village, including those in Bede Court. There was a close link between the members of the top class and the residents in Bede Court and we were encouraged to regularly visit our partners, write cards to them and invite them to school functions. I spent many a happy afternoon chatting to my partner, Mrs Geater, at her home in Bede Court.

The spring term always seemed the shortest, as Easter determined when the holidays would be. The highlight of this term was the Valentine's Social when there were games and country dancing for all, with a light supper. My favourite game at this was called 'winking', which involved attracting the opposite sex with a wink and trying to get them to sit on your chair without their partner noticing and preventing them from doing so. We would also be training hard for

NAMES INDEX
continued from page 92

continued on page 94

football and netball games, which we played against the other village school teams in the area. Aldbury were our greatest rivals and I know from my brothers that the football pitch was well-liked as it sloped down the hill and this was ideal if shooting that way in the second half!

The summer term was, perhaps, in many ways the busiest. It started with the Maypole in early May. My first Maypole at the School was danced on the village green in front of the Manor House. The procession started from Little Gaddesden House, the home of Miss Talbot, where we enjoyed refreshments of currant buns and tea, and then processed to the village green for the crowning of the May Queen and then the fight of St George and the Dragon. There must be many a boy from the School who remembers being inside the green dragon suit and having to re-enact the fight of St George and the Dragon. The victor was duly knighted and then the dancing began. In later years the venue swapped to the School and the procession went around Bede Court, following a band playing recorders and other musical instruments. The actual Maypole Dances had been regularly practised in our country-dancing lessons over the previous few weeks. The most difficult was the single plaiting which had an unforgettable tune and rhythm and involved all the ribbons being plaited over and under as we danced around. Other morris-type dances followed for the lower school.

The next event was the Singing Festival, originally in Hitchin and then, later, at the Hemel Hempstead Pavilion. Singing was a major part of our timetable with Singing Together and Time and Tune from the radio once a week, hymn practice every Wednesday afternoon and regular class singing lessons with Daisy Thorn. She drilled us passionately in scales, rounds (Who can remember 'Gaily sings the Donkey'?) and songs for the Singing Festival. Some of us were never the most tuneful of singers, but we sang with enthusiasm and commitment.

Sport featured in the summer term, with regular swimming lessons at the Deer Leap Pool. We had to walk from the School, leaving at playtime and being back in time for lunch. When it got very hot, we would hang our swimming things along the hedge around the orchard to dry out so that we could return again after school. We also had our school sports to train for, as well as the Inter-Village School Sports. Everyone was encouraged to take part, even those who were not so sporty. My forte was the egg and spoon. I did not (and still do not) have the build for running, but I could keep a steady hand, and I always represented the School at that. In fact I have not lost the touch after 25 years, as I won the Mums' race at my son's School Sports Day this year.

We also had the Educational Visit in June, and I remember trips to the Tower of London, Warwick Castle, the Cutty Sark, Coventry Cathedral and Windsor Castle. These were always great fun and resulted in project work for weeks before and after the trip.

The end of the year was marked by Open Evening when all our work was on display and our exam results were published. Swimming certificates were presented and the cups were awarded for sport and effort. There was then the Summer Concert which was characterised by singing and sketches which were performed to parents and villagers alike, and this was followed by refreshments.

Of course, all this had to come to an end, and in July 1974 I was a 'leaver' from Little Gaddesden School and destined to go to the Cavendish School in Hemel Hempstead. This end of an era was marked by a Leavers' Service at the Church and the presentation of a Book of Common Prayer to each leaver. The final send-off was to be given the bumps by the rest of the class at the end of the day.

People say that your school days are the happiest ones of your life, and I think

NAMES INDEX

continued from page 93

continued on page 95

that those lucky enough to have been at Little Gaddesden School during those years 1968 to 1974 would certainly have had an experience which would allow them to say that.

The Gaddesden Diary continued

by Margaret Crawford

PRICES AND PRINTING

The Summer 1959 issue was the last one at the price of 6d. It went up to 1/- from the next issue, and in Summer 1963 was raised to 1/6. In Spring 1967 the editor announced that alas this would be the last issue in that form. Rising printing costs and the effects of the 'squeeze' on some of the advertisers had defeated her, so that in future the Diary would be run off on a duplicator, but the price would be the same, i.e. 1/6. The page size changed from octavo to quarto, and the calendar pages were in the centre, the layout and format being much the same as it is now, but with the club secretaries page at the back, not the front. It stayed at the same price when decimal currency was introduced with the Summer 1970 issue, being quoted in both currencies on the next four issues, i.e. 1/6 and $7^{1}/_{2}$p, after which it was evidently considered that Little Gaddesden had mastered the new coinage!
Subsequent editors have worked hard to keep the price down, but in 1975 it went up to $12^{1}/_{2}$p after 12 years unchanged; in 1977 to 15p; and in 1980 to 25p.

We went back to having it printed in Summer 1993 when Sylvan Services took over the typesetting from Maylands. We stayed with Ken Thorn's printing firm Swift's until the retirement of his partner, Mrs Unwin, to whom he left the business. In 1999 the price is 75p, thirty times its original 1955 price.

EVENTS REPORTED FROM 1967 TO 1982

1967: This year was the start of Christian Stewardship in the parish. The Youth Club was added to the list of clubs, and the Football Club started to write a quarterly report.

1968: The village lost its 'roadman', Mr Price, and he was long lamented until recently, when Dacorum decreed that we should appoint a Village Warden. In Summer the Diary started making a little money and supplementing the income of the Gaddesden Society instead of vice versa.

1969: The Winter Diary, although compiled by Mrs Rawdon Smith also, alas, announced her death which must have occurred just as they were going to press. Albert Williams, the then headmaster of the village school, wrote the appreciation and paid tribute to her work as editor for twelve years, and her work with so many other village activities, including the church and the school. The completion and Opening of Bede Court was also mentioned in this Diary.

1970: In the Spring issue Miss Sheila Ladner was welcomed as editor, but in the next issue Mrs Vi Hughes was listed as editor. Miss Ladner was a teacher at the school, but left at the end of the spring term that year; history does not relate

NAMES INDEX

continued from page 94

continued on page 96

whether producing one edition of the Diary was the cause.

1971: Annette Revell took over from Vi Hughes in Spring. She managed to give her editorials a much more modern and political slant and I much admired the way she handled things. I note we were having one of our frequent fights against the withdrawal of the bus service and raising money for the Sports Club Pavilion. The bus time table was published in the Diary for the first time.

It was a 'bad' year for the village as it saw the deaths of two redoubtable characters who had done much for the village - Miss Dorothy Erhart, the notable harpsichordist and musician who lived at the Manor House, in April, and Bridget Talbot from Little Gaddesden House at the end of the year.

1972: Summer saw the addition of two charitable societies - Shelter and the Arthritis and Rheumatism Council - alas neither of them with us any more, though the latter lasted until a short while ago.

1974: In Spring the editorial broke the dire news that as from 1st April the control of our local affairs, hitherto exercised by the Berkhamsted Rural District Council, would now be in the hands of Dacorum District Council (later to become the Borough Council). The Parish Council report noted that the County Council were negotiating the purchase of the strip of land opposite, and running parallel to, the Green. I also see that I started writing the Music Club reports, a job I only relinquished in 1998.

The Parish Church gave details of the Book of Remembrance which was dedicated and presented in its cabinet on Sunday May 26th. This was given by Commander Pain in remembrance of his wife Elsie. It was sad that their marriage had been of such short duration, Elsie having fallen seriously ill - we had all been so happy for both of them. It may not be known that there are two sections to this book. The first contains the names of former parishioners against the date when they died. The second is a list of benefactions to the church, like the names of those who contributed to the building of the vestry.

1975: Spring reported the formation of the new Rural Heritage Society, with John Campbell (of no. 22/23 Little Gaddesden) as the first Chairman.

The Music Club report mentioned the recording at Ashridge College on December 15th of the Radio 3 programme 'Music in Question' of which Antony Hopkins was chairman. The contestants were Susan Drake, harpist, Yuval Zaliouk, conductor of the Israeli State Orchestra and Martin Ronchetti, a clarinettist with the B.B.C. Welsh Orchestra. The programme was broadcast on February 20th.

The Summer issue reported on the official opening of the Sports Pavilion on the Spring Bank Holiday.

1977: The Spring Diary was much taken up with plans for the Queen's Silver Jubilee which Little Gaddesden was celebrating on the specially moved Bank Holiday weekend, 4th to 7th June, plus a mention of the two rustic seats for the Green - we still have one of them.

In the Summer issue Canon Senar took over as editor, with Vi Hughes continuing to round up material, helped by Ann Griffiths and Christine Francis. Annette Revell was thanked for her six years in office, and Albert Williams for his help with distribution.

NAMES INDEX

continued from page 95

continued on page 97

1980: In the Summer Vanessa Moody joined the editorial team, replacing Ann Griffiths.
1982: In the Winter issue was the reopening of the Brownie Pack under the aegis of Anne Webster and Julie Leonhardt. The Summer Diary contained the bombshell of Canon Senar's moving to the Diocese of Exeter in the early Autumn after 20 years as Rector.

At this point my name appears on the editorial team with Vanessa, just the two of us seeming to be in charge, but this is not quite how I remember it: for several issues Enid Foxall held my hand and gave me wise guidance, bowing out in Spring 1984 when Mollie Martin joined the team. Vanessa, Mollie and I look like being the longest editors since the Diary started, still here in 1999.

EDITOR'S NOTE: For the purposes of this book the Gaddesden Diary features conclude here.

Parish Fairs - 1979 and 1980

Under Canon Senar the parish church organised a Country Craft Fair in 1979 and, finding it a great success, followed it up by a similar event in 1980 called Rural Living in the 80's, which had special displays for the benefit of the disabled.

The Chairman of the Organising Committee was Professor Richard Edwards of Chailey Cottage, who wrote of the first one: "The Craft Fair is not primarily a Fund Raising event but proceeds over and above those necessary to cover expenses will help the Church to do its work in Little Gaddesden and ..... outside our Parish. ..... Many of these [rural skills, arts and handicrafts] have to be kept alive or they may be lost for ever..... We would like to feel that our church is giving these activities a helping hand."

The Rector's message was very apt:

"Traditionally the Christian Church has encouraged craftsmanship. Today's exercise is a modest attempt to continue this in Little Gaddesden. We inherit here a tradition of craftsmanship, encouraged by the proximity of Ashridge House and continued today in the Ashridge Gardens and National Trust lands for our daily admiration.

Our inheritance goes back to the early 14th century to John O'Gaddesden whose skill as a physician was recognised nationally and throughout Europe. Our Chairman today is of the same profession!

In the 18th century William Ellis, Churchwarden here, was known beyond our shores for his agricultural implements and farming. In the 19th Century, Wyatville and G.E. Street in architecture, Richard Westmacott in sculpture and C.E. Kempe in stained glass contributed the work of men of renown. In our day John Webb silversmith

NAMES INDEX
continued from page 96

continued on page 98

The Village Bygones display with (left to right) Ray Light (in striped shirt), Peter Bunting, Geoff Rogers and Alan Bunting.

has added to our treasures, and Taylor's of Loughborough cast our new parish church bells.

There has been too the Little Gaddesden school of embroidery and kindred arts, linked probably with the founders of the Royal School of Needlework, and the Wood Carving tradition of the David Clark/Harry Temple School, not forgetting the examples of the work of the 'Mouse Man' of Yorkshire and the 'Acorn Man' of Little Gaddesden.

All these have one thing in common. They produced excellent work because they were prepared for hard work, fatiguing hours, patience, persistence in the face of frustration and disappointment, and continual thinking. This inspired their lives.

Perhaps this Craft Fair will give a new impetus to a similar devotion to produce work of lasting worth and beauty."

In his reference to the Mouse Man and the Acorn Man it seems the Rector assumed people would know he meant Robert Thompson of Kilburn, Yorks, and John Oakins (churchwarden 1955 - 1980) who both made furnishings which can be seen in the church. A carved mouse or acorn was incorporated as a signature.

The events took place on the village playing field with stalls and a marquee, and in the village hall, school hall and scout hut.

The list of exhibitors and stallholders which follows is drawn from both the 1979 and 1980 events. It shows the names of those participants who lived in the village, and lists the subjects of the remainder.

Bonsai trees; Patchwork: Diana Ashby of Starswood, Hudnall
Cakes: Minnie Catchpole, Kath Banks, Eileen Clift, Dolly Hill, Winnie Oakins, Molly Williams
Children's Pets Corner: Val Janes of no.36 and Jennie Waters
Cleaving: Jim Wiggins of 3 Trust Cottages, Ringshall (The subject of the brochure cover picture)
Furniture miniatures and restoration: Nigel Ashby of Starswood, Hudnall
Herbs, dried flowers, plants and produce: Hilary Catchpole of no.13
Horticultural Equipment: Ken Wilson of Deer Leap Horticulture
Land Utilisation Survey: John Leonhardt of Hudnall Park Field Centre
Local Bird Populations: Ernie Janes of no.36 and Chris Mead
Little Gaddesden Art Class: Doris Hill-Smith of Farthings
Little Gaddesden Art Club
Little Gaddesden Bellringers: Roger Turner of 5 Church Road
Little Gaddesden Women's Institute: Joan Humphreys of 28 Ringshall
Model Making: David Wray of Little Coldharbour Farm
National Trust
Pressed Flower Art: Suzanne Brooker of The Cottage, Hudnall Lane
Spinning and Weaving: Virginia Westmacott of 2 Hudnall and Katharine Smith
Spinning and Weaving: West Herts Guild of Weavers, Little Coldharbour Farm
Upholstery: Doris Wiggins of 3 Trust Cottages, Ringshall
Village Bygones: Alan Bunting of 15 Cromer Close
Village Produce Association: Alan Bunting of 15 Cromer Close
Wildlife Photographs: Ernie Janes of no.36

NAMES INDEX
continued from page 97

continued on page 100

Displays from outside the village included bread demonstrating, canal art, cane and rush seating, corn dollies, embroidery, handmade jewellery, illuminated lettering, fabric painting, lampshades, macramé, pottery, stained glass, Victorian rag dolls, wood engraving, wood sculpture, wood turning, aids for the handicapped, craft work by the severely disabled, toy library for handicapped children, countryside in the 80's, Frithsden wines, R.S.P.B., whole food, books, solid fuel stoves, baskets, dolls and glove puppets, and saddlery.

LEFT:
David Wray working on one of his models

TOP:
Nigel Ashby displays his miniature furniture

ABOVE:
The brochure cover shows Jim Wiggins' hands cleaving hazel with a froe.

Little Gaddesden - and how we came to be here

by Richard Abraham

Little Gaddesden? Where's that? These questions formed part of a conversation in late August 1980 between a Watford Police Superintendent and one of his officers. The latter, having had enough of town policing, was seeking pastures new, and felt that a return to a rural way of life was long overdue. Having been born and brought up in a small village in Somerset, where I embraced all of the country pursuits and loved the way of life, it still surprises me that I had lived and worked in towns for about eight years.

I had married earlier in the month, and with the full support of my new wife, I felt that now was the time to move on. How to achieve it and where to move were the questions that Superintendent Geoff Smith was being asked; his answer prompting my question as to the location of this small, idyllic, edge-of-Chilterns village, which he had described in such glowing terms. Geoff explained that if I wanted the post, and the final decision did not rest with him, there was a snag! The current incumbent was taking early retirement on medical grounds and the job had not been advertised as available. But first of all, he suggested, go and look at the place. He added that the village policeman's job at Wigginton was also vacant and that had been advertised.

So it was that on the evening of 1 September June and I found out where both villages were, and drove out to take a look at them. However, as it was dark, the visits were less than satisfactory, though we dismissed Wigginton as the main road location of the house did not appeal. Though it was difficult to judge, Little Gaddesden seemed more to our liking and, as we sat in the Bridgewater Arms for the very first time, we decided that a second look here would be worthwhile. On a Saturday afternoon five days later, we parked in the pub car park and walked around the village, falling in love there and then with a place of which we had been blissfully unaware a little over a week before. This trip included our first visit to the Village Stores where we met Janet Stinton, who had her very small, tousle-haired son, Barry, with her. Later, walking along the Green, I picked up a penny - 1977, but still shiny - and we decided that it would bring us luck in our endeavour to come and live here. There turned out to be something of an obstacle to that, one which had to be overcome with a degree of subterfuge!

The next time I spoke to Geoff Smith the news was not good. The Little Gaddesden job had still not been advertised and the Wigginton one, which we did not want anyway, was as good as promised to someone from Tring Police Station, who had been covering the area from there. To enable Geoff to 'pull a few strings', I was advised to apply for Wigginton and risk my credentials being preferred to the one who was already in line for it. Geoff would then make enquiries to establish facts he already knew through the grapevine and endorse my application recommending that I be considered for Little Gaddesden when that post was advertised. A bit risky, we felt, but it paid off and my application was taken further.

June and I came back on Saturday 13 September for a Village Fair when we met a lot of locals, though the only one I clearly remember was the late Canon

NAMES INDEX

continued from page 98

continued on page 101

Howard Senar, who had then been Rector for a good many years.

Everything we saw, and everyone we met that day, only enhanced our view that we desperately wanted to come and live in Little Gaddesden, but there was still the interview to get through! That took place at Hemel Hempstead Police Station on 3 October - and I blew it! Going back home to June, I felt very depressed. Questions concerning the geographical area covered by the Little Gaddesden Beat, the current crime rate and trends, local villains and other relevant information required of the Village Policeman, I was unable to answer. Looking back, I cannot believe how little prepared I had been for that interview. It is also difficult to understand how someone so ill-prepared could be informed just three days later that the job was his! Moreover, I was also told that I was far and away the best of the short-listed candidates for such a sought-after post. The penny's magic was working well .

We moved into the Police House, Church Road, Little Gaddesden on a very wet Tuesday 11 November 1980, pausing only to borrow a saw from a neighbour with which to cut off the gate post, thus enabling the furniture van to get nearer to the house.

Whilst we unloaded, someone who I knew professionally, but who lived in Ringshall, Derek Craib, came striding over the front lawn with an outstretched hand of welcome. From Berkhamsted Police, a bearded Sergeant came ambling up the drive to reveal himself as someone I had last seen seventeen years earlier, when we had shared a double desk at our Somerset Grammar School. Our next visitors were the then School Headmaster's wife, Molly Williams, and Canon Senar's wife, Felicity, both of whom bore home-made cakes. They were closely followed by Barbara Day, Alan Bunting and Audrey Allen and many others in those first few weeks. The following Sunday Howard Senar introduced us from the pulpit to the congregation at our first family service.

At that time, part of our garden was, and continued to be until he could no longer cope with it, cultivated by a marvellous ex-miner from Durham, Bede Court resident, Chris Dawson. Thus it began, and in that way it has continued, being surrounded by warm and friendly people. We have had, and still have, the most delightful next-door neighbours and our involvement in this wonderful community has always given us the greatest pleasure. In those times of personal crisis and bereavement, and there have been a few of those, we have always been supported and have been able to draw strength from those around us.

The rest is history. We still have the 1977 lucky penny, no longer shiny but much treasured, and there has never been a moment in the past nineteen-plus years when we have regretted coming to live in this village. Phillippa and James, my children from my first marriage, came to live with us in the late eighties and loved it here. They remained until adulthood when they left to 'seek their fortunes' as far afield as Hemel Hempstead. Our own children came along in 1987 and 1990, with young Daniel bringing up the rear two years ago. Jonathan and Caroline enjoy living here as much as we always have and cannot envisage being anywhere else.

My Police career must come to an end at Christmas 2002 and, as at the start of this account, I have to ask a question. I now know very definitely where Little Gaddesden is but, given that the house we moved into in November 1980 belongs to the Police Authority, the question I must ask is, "How do I stay here for the rest of my life?" Perhaps my lucky penny will help us again - we do hope so.

NAMES INDEX

continued from page 100

Y/Z

Little Gaddesden school in the 1980s and 90s

by Emma and Debbie Catchpole

Continued from page 85 (Hilary, Ian and Pat Catchpole)

Emma and Debbie are the last of the three living generations of Catchpoles, with Debbie the youngest in the family. Debbie was the last one to attend Little Gaddesden School and both she and Emma saw many changes during their time there.

Emma started there in 1986 and Debbie in 1989, leaving in 1992 and 1995 respectively. Throughout this time the number of people attending the school grew in number greatly. Within the years that they were there three different head teachers worked tirelessly for the benefit of the pupils: firstly Mr Williams; secondly Mr Spencer, who increased the number of children at the school greatly and who was known to everyone as Mr Happy.

We were all very upset to see him leave to take up a teaching post in Yorkshire where he tragically died in a car crash. We saw this as a very sad coincidence as Mr Bell had also died in his car.

Lastly, Mrs Iveson, who took over when Mr Spencer left. Having a head mistress rather than a head master meant that there was an all-female teaching staff for the first time in many years. During our time, we began to see pupils coming to the school from outside the village and also many children leaving to attend the various private schools in the surrounding area.

When Mrs Iveson was head teacher, there was much emphasis put on the importance of music and we had a small choir which participated in several concerts, including in the village for the elderly and larger concerts in the Royal Albert Hall and the Barbican Centre. We had the chance to learn the recorder, the violin or the cello, and these lessons proved to be very popular. We had a gardening club on Wednesday lunch times and years 4, 5 and 6 went swimming every Friday morning in Hemel Hempstead. A link with the village church was still maintained by end of term services being held at the church, and Mr Roger Turner visiting us in assemblies to talk to us about God and the church of St. Peter and St. Paul.

We had both a netball and football team who played matches against teams from the surrounding village schools. It was perhaps particularly significant of the 1990's that at one stage Debbie had to make a decision whether she wanted to play in the netball team like all of the other girls or whether she wanted to play football. She chose the football team, and was thus the only girl in the team and had to have a changing room all to herself when playing matches. The look on the opposing players' faces when they realised they were to be marking a girl made her proud to be making even the smallest of changes towards sexual equality in sport.

Both Emma and Debbie will always remember their time at Little Gaddesden School with happy memories, as will their parents, aunts, uncle, great uncle, second cousins and grandmother!

Employment at the turn of another century

In the 1990s the occupations of the village are totally different from the 1890s. Although the first half of the century had some big upheavals, the impression we get is that the change in occupation has taken place in many small steps, proceeding much further in the second half of the century than the first.

In this chapter we have three views of employment: first a brief census summary, secondly some subjective impressions, and thirdly part of an investigation carried out by Sarah Godar.

FROM THE 1991 CENSUS

Women aged 16 to 59 were described as being 57% in employment, a lower figure than most Hertfordshire parishes, 61% to 66% being typical. The number of households consisting of pensioners only was a high figure, 28.6%.

In order to find the proportion of the residents aged 18 or over who had qualifications to diploma or degree level, we have to refer to a wider area, Ashridge Ward, which includes Great Gaddesden and Potten End. The figure was 34%, the eighth highest in the county, not far below the top ranking Harpenden, where it was 39.8%. (The ten lowest ranking wards in the county had 6%or under.) In Ashridge ward there is also a figure for the employment of men, 94%.

GENERAL IMPRESSIONS

That figure of 57% employment for women is unlikely to include nearly so much domestic service as it did in 1891, though that occupation still exists. So much of the daily work in a household has been simplified by electricity, which was totally absent in the village in 1891, or even 1911, that even well-off householders manage with little or no help in that direction. This kind of employment is still needed in places like the residential home for the elderly, Ashridge, the public house, and so on, but many of the employees do not live in the village.

Second to universal electricity probably comes personal transport as a cause of change. Long journeys to and from work mean that the place of work and the place of employment are often not the same. Nursing and school teaching are known to be quite common occupations for women who live in the village but do their work in Hemel Hempstead or Berkhamsted, for instance. Women in other professions are travelling further afield.

Thirdly, new methods of communication have multiplied in the last decade of the century, making it possible to pursue more kinds of employment at home involving, for instance, trading, writing, designing and negotiating.

For men, the figure of 94% employment (presumably referring only to those of employable age and health) certainly does not include much labouring as it did a hundred years ago. Some of the changes are similar to those mentioned for women. We are particularly aware of many in the financial and legal professions, some of whom travel regularly abroad to do their work. Our village has also been home to architects, engineers, surgeons, physicians and academics, often with professorial chairs.

The labouring jobs have changed, like the domestic jobs, through mechanisation. Just as many fields are ploughed, sown, weeded and harvested as before, and there is just as much tree-felling and planting, hedge-cutting and fencing. There is building - and although new building is restricted (there was not much in 1891 either), there are always extensions and repairs being done, and there are road repairs. The tractor and mechanical digger, with all their attachments, the combine harvester, the chain saw and all the other power tools, and the road-laying machines have all extended the mechanisation which began with the steam-powered traction engines with their thrashing machines and elevators, and the steam ploughs with which the century began. Not only are there very few men now needed to do all this work, but many of them are more mobile, and do not have to live near their work.

As for the horses, well, there are still a lot about, and therefore there are people looking after them. I've only seen one horse, though, in the last twenty years, that looked as though it had a job to do. People have given up using them to get from one place to another, or to carry goods about. Like the people, their employment has changed. They now provide recreation and exercise and opportunity for competitive skills. There are some working horses about, but not here.

Lastly, what about that figure of 28% of households consisting of pensioners only? Remember that in 1891 only the elderly widows and one man were pensioners. All the old men continued to put down the jobs they did. Many of these 1991 pensioners must also be part of the 34% of the population with degrees or diplomas, as many professional people stay here after retiring or come here to retire.

A Study of Little Gaddesden in 1997

In 1997 an investigation was carried out by Sarah Godar for part of the assessment for her Advanced Level Geography Examination. The main question was "Does Little Gaddesden still display traditional village characteristics today?"

A significant part of the study was a questionnaire sent to a sample of 135 households, of which 115 were returned, a proportion which in itself shows the interest local people have in this kind of question, or the feeling of solidarity with one of their own number doing an exam!

The questionnnaire put simple questions to establish the number in the household, the age structure, their occupation in classified groups, place of work, means of getting there, length of residence, and previous generations in the village.

Old records were used for comparison, including some data from 1850, which goes back a bit further than the scope of the present book because it takes us back into the days of the straw-plaiting village industry, which had almost died out by 1890.

This article is a selection of the findings from Sarah's 60-page work.

Little Gaddesden in 1997

by Sarah Godar

OCCUPATIONS IN 1850 AND 1997

"The occupational structure has altered from an agricultural to a professional base"

The split pie chart of occupations in 1850 and 1997 shows the expected decrease in agricultural work, straw plaiting and domestic service, and increase in professional work. The comparatively unchanged proportion of dependent people conceals a change from married women dependent on their husbands (1850) to elderly people dependent on pensions (1997).

In 1997 more women are independent than in 1850.

In 1850 there were very few older residents due to a lack of health care and state benefits but in 1997 there are many pensioners.

PLACES OF EMPLOYMENT OF THE POPULATION OF LITTLE GADDESDEN

"Little Gaddesden has become a commuter village"

In the figure below, the circle for each town is proportional to the number of people from Little Gaddesden employed there.

The unexpectedly high proportion of employment within Little Gaddesden itself is accounted for by the ability of professionals to work from home, using telecommunications, which gives a false picture of employment within the village.

Berkhamsted and Hemel Hempstead are both within a 10km radius and so are not defined as commuter destinations.

St Albans and Watford are both within a 25km radius of Little Gaddesden and are commuted to by either car or train. Both of these towns lie south-east of Little Gaddesden towards London where there is an efficient transport network.

Firms in London employ over half of the population surveyed, despite Little Gaddesden being situated 50km from the city. Therefore it can be concluded that Little Gaddesden has become commuter-orientated, with many residents working outside the village. Contrastingly, in 1850 most of the population were employed in agricultural activities, as shown in the previous figure.

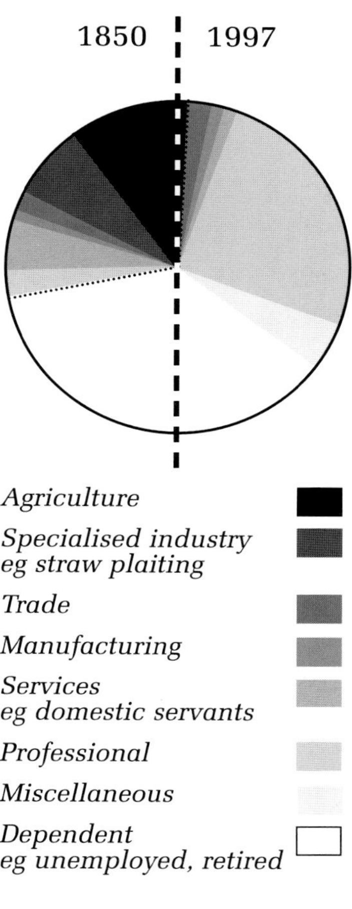

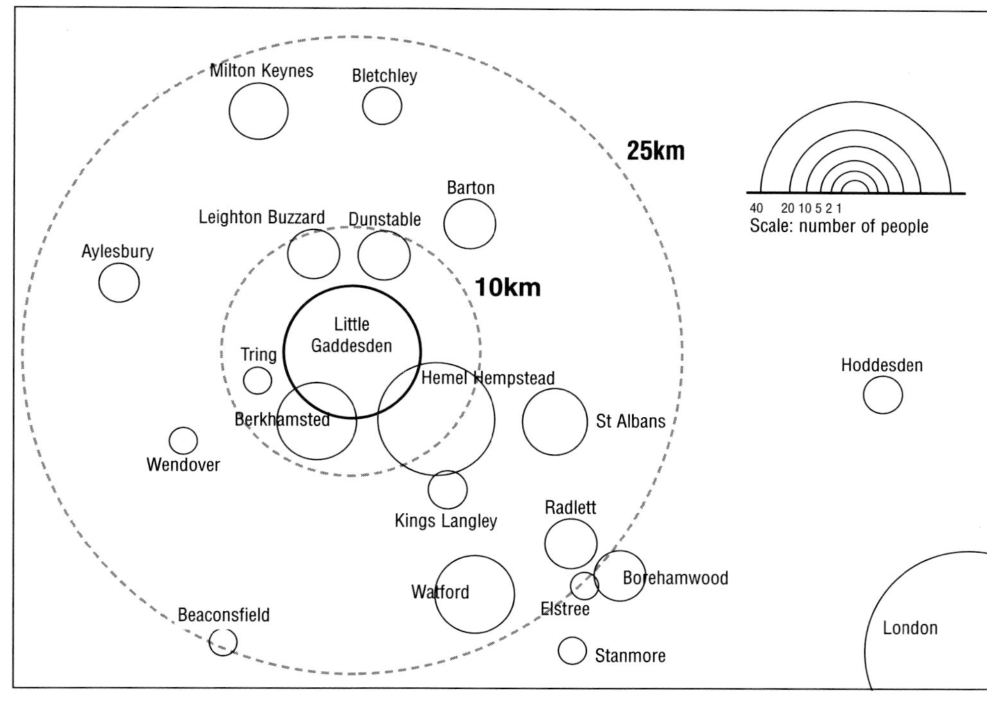

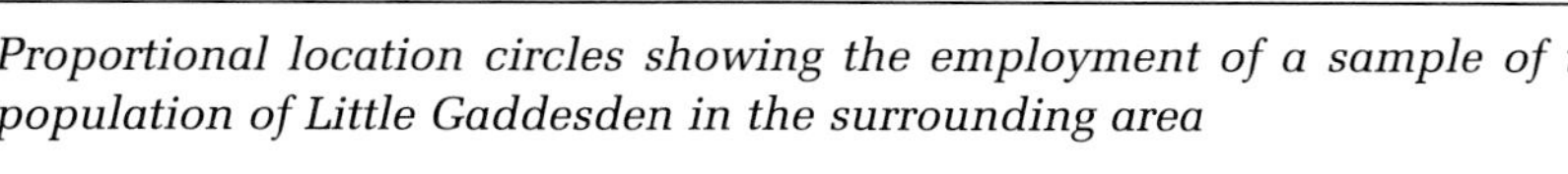

Proportional location circles showing the employment of a sample of the population of Little Gaddesden in the surrounding area

MIGRATION INTO LITTLE GADDESDEN

"The population has become more affluent"

The proportional bar chart below shows migration into the village. Newcomers are residents who have moved into the village in the past five years: a third of the sample population. The sample itself is about a quarter of the households in the village.

The pie charts represent the occupational structure of the newcomers as compared to the established residents. Two thirds of the the newcomers are professionals and are therefore in a high income bracket, suggesting that they are more affluent. The established residents incorporate a higher proportion of

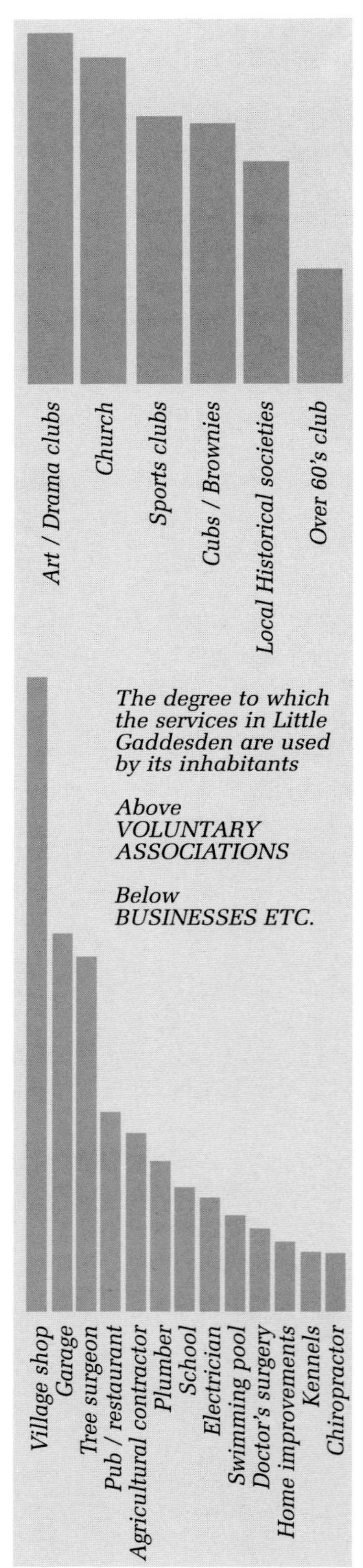

The degree to which the services in Little Gaddesden are used by its inhabitants

Above VOLUNTARY ASSOCIATIONS

Below BUSINESSES ETC.

pensioners, suggesting that couples have remained in the village throughout their retirement.

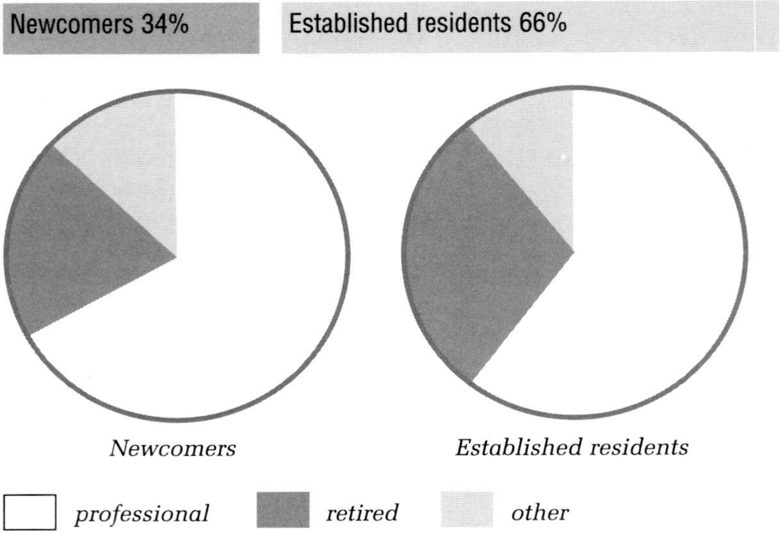

ANALYSIS OF THE THE USE OF SERVICES IN LITTLE GADDESDEN

"The use of services by village residents has decreased"

The figure on the left represents the frequency with which each service is used by residents, who were asked to rate them from 0 to 4.

There were a surprising number of businesses in the village catering for traditional needs: the electrician, plumber and tree surgeon are all family businesses.

Because of its convenience, the village shop is used to the greatest extent by the villagers. With this exception, many village businesses are falling into disuse and this will continue because residents are prepared to hire superior services, leaving traditional village businesses lacking demand.

The upper histogram shows services provided by the village community itself. Many clubs, eg the Youth Club, depend on interaction between the younger generations in the village. Because of the affluence of the area, children are sent to private schools, reducing the likelihood of their making local friends and diminishing their involvement in the community.

The services which are run voluntarily mainly attract older established residents, eg the bowls club, or newcomers to the village who wish to join the community life, eg the tennis club. Even these services are not well-used by village residents.

These results are taken from a sample population and perhaps give an uneven view of the overall use of these services. Some of these clubs target certain generations and if the sample population did not include residents of a certain age the service appears to be used less than it actually is, eg the over-60s club.

Therefore, it can be seen that both businesses and voluntary services are declining in the village, due to the present lack of community involvement.

A boy's life at Little Gaddesden

by Ryan Collier

STARTING OUT

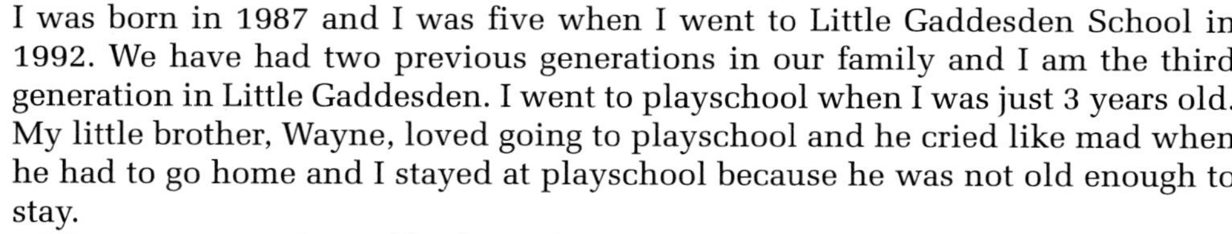

I was born in 1987 and I was five when I went to Little Gaddesden School in 1992. We have had two previous generations in our family and I am the third generation in Little Gaddesden. I went to playschool when I was just 3 years old. My little brother, Wayne, loved going to playschool and he cried like mad when he had to go home and I stayed at playschool because he was not old enough to stay.

I first went to Little Gaddesden School in 1992. Like every 5 year old who went to Little Gaddesden School I was put in Reception. In Reception we just listened to stories, drew pictures and learnt how to use scissors. In Year 1 things got a bit more difficult. We had to print and do 'dots to dots'.

THE NEXT STAGE

In Class 2 things got a lot harder. We had to learn how to do joined up writing and learn tens and units. Up to Year 3 now where the maths was hard. We had to do the Romans which was one of my worst subjects I had ever done. The PE got harder and I also joined the chess club. I finished 5th best when I left school. On to Class 4 now where the work got incredibly harder. The best part of being in Class 4 was doing art and PE.

THE FUTURE

I am hoping to get on well at Tring School and make loads of new friends. I hope to get some merits at Tring so I will get a certificate.

This is Ryan Collier going off to Tring School
Bye Little Gaddesden.

What it was like at my old school

by Daniel Oswald (Little Gaddesden School 1996 - 1999)

It all started when I first came to Little Gaddesden School in Year 4 with my first teacher Mrs Griffin. I had walked through the doors of my new school; it was quite weird coming into a school so small with only 100 pupils from a school so big with 250 pupils in it.

I liked the scenery around me - all the trees and the birds; it was a lot different from all the cars and buildings close together at my old house. I enjoyed having all the space on the field outside in front of the school with a cricket pitch, football pitch, bowls, rounders and tennis, not to mention a playground.

On the second day I had settled in fine. I knew all the people in my class and I had met my new head mistress in my first assembly in the school. The food was lovely and so were the teachers.

To start with the work was easy because it was just add and take maths, drawing a big poster in English and in art we were doing rockets with loo rolls and shoe boxes. As time passed the work got slightly harder; in art we started to do masks and in maths we did prime numbers and factors.

By then I was year 5 and we had a new head teacher called Mr Tim Bowen. He had this strange idea to knock down the old school hall and build a brand new school hall attached to the school building. He had said we needed to raise £40,000 to build the new school hall. So that's what happened. We had sponsored fêtes and a sponsored walk along the whole Ridgeway. On the day that the old year 6 left, when I was year 5 they had collected all the money that they needed at that stage. It was unfair to all the year 6 after they had walked part of the Ridgeway. Even the year 5s had walked some or the whole Ridgeway.

It was nearly the end of the school year; the old year 6s had left and we were now year 6. We had just enough time to visit the Isle of Wight for a week; it was the best time of that school year.

I had really enjoyed my time at that school and wish I could go again.

A year in the life of a Little Gaddesden schoolboy

1999 to 2000 by Phillip Dickinson

JANUARY

Mum, Dad, my sister and I go off for a walk with our dog, Kes on New Years Day. It is so cold; the trees are stripped bare of their leaves. Robins stand out on the trees with their bright red breasts. We come back with icicles hanging down from our noses and our ears feel like blocks of ice cream. We come into the house to find a batch of homemade mince pies keeping warm on the Rayburn cooker.

It's only three days till we are back at school, and it starts to snow so we go tobogganing in Golden Valley. All my friends are there. There's never much snow here so we all make the most of it whilst we can.

Back at school.

FEBRUARY

I'm still going to football club on Saturday mornings; it's cold and muddy but good fun. Iain Horner, our coach, comes every weekend, and is getting a good squad together.

Half term is here and Grandma visits us. She comes down by train from Lancaster and we collect her from Watford station. It's my birthday this month and a group of my friends came with me to Rollers – the roller-skating rink at Milton Keynes - and then they came back to my house for a sleepover. I get a new GT red bicycle with 21 gears from my Mum and Dad. With the bike we go into

Ashridge woods to find a half pipe bike track and its really good even if I get really muddy.

MARCH

The days are much lighter and longer now. All the leaves are beginning to come out, and the daffodils and tulips are rising up to show their beauty. We walk through the fields from home, to see the newborn lambs. It's only one more field, that's full of ponies, before we reach the Village shop. I grab a paper bag and fill it up with penny sweets; my favourite is the red liquorice. At school Mrs. Birks, our Art teacher is helping us make pop-out Easter cards. I am learning my words, which I have to read out for the Easter Church service.

APRIL

Every year at Easter the Easter Bunny comes and gives us Easter eggs. My favourites are the Dairy Milk and the Celebration Eggs.

MAY

The top year are taking their SAT Exams (School Assessment Tests) – it looks like hard work!

I've just received my Photographer's Badge at Cubs, which I go to every Tuesday at 6.30pm. to 8pm. It is held in the Scout Hut behind the Village Hall. For this Badge I made up an album of photographs, which I took, of my sister feeding her pony, grooming her pony, tacking up and riding. I've also got the following Badges: Athletes 3, Sportsman, Computers, First Aid, Cook, and Camper. One evening at Cubs we walk down into Ashridge and make dens out of fallen branches and bracken. We are all put in teams to see who has used the best strategy for building dens.

JUNE

One day in June Class 4 has a school trip to Hudnall Outdoor Centre to study the River Gade. We take a minibus to the river, which is in a field off Lady's Mile at Water End. We have to find out the speed of the river, the width of the river, and the temperature. To find the temperature the teacher gives us a little machine with a cord on the end. We put the cord into the river and a panel on the machine tells us the temperature in Centigrade. We also have to fish out river creatures using nets. We put them into polythene bags and take them to the centre to find out what lives at the source of this river.

Now it is getting much warmer and whenever I walk home from school, I see lots of people playing Bowls, on the Bowling Green

JULY

Every year Little Gaddesden School holds a Sports Day. I'm in the Blue team and we come second this year. We do a variety of different sports such as Skipping, Sprinting, Obstacle Race, Potato race, Sack race, Egg & Spoon race. The winning team this year are the Yellow Team and they win a Cup, which is on show in the School.

The School's Summer Fête is held in July and the theme is 'Bygone Days'. It

Cottages through trees

Pale winter sunlight
on old apricot bricks,
a string of cottages
on the edge of the wood
looking as if they grew
out of the earth.

No sound, the air still,
the gardens silent,
brown wands of foxgloves
stand as tattered
prayer flags, fluttering
and forlorn.

These are the last days
of the old year, bleak
lonely, the dead season
the turning of the year.
Last beams of sunlight
cast shadows on old walls.

Mary Blake

More poems by Mary can be found on pages 119, 129, 157, 199, 229, 241, 273 and 285.

is held on the Village playing fields with lots of stalls set up. It is fun, despite the fact that I split my finger open on the 'Smash the Crockery' stall. The best part is when I soak Mr. Bowen, our Head teacher, on 'Drown the Clown'. I bet our Head regrets volunteering after I throw a big wet sponge right at his nose, - but he was a good sport.

After the Fête there is a Children's Disco in the village hall, which a lot of the young children attend. There is a sad magician there. In the evening there is a Hog Roast and Dance in a marquee on the playing field. It is really fun because all my friends are there and we are playing football in the dark, so we can't see if we have scored a goal or not.

We break up for summer holidays at the end of July for a six week break.

AUGUST

I always look forward to a sunny day and going up to Deer Leap Outdoor Swimming Pool. The water is really cold but you get used to it after a while. Sometimes we play Frisbee in the gardens there; it often gets stuck in the hedge. The best part of going to Deer Leap is jumping off the top board and diving off the springboard. I normally buy some chips, which are wrapped in a paper cone and taste delicious.

Another place I like to visit is Badger Wood, close to our house. We make dens there and there is a rope swing, but you have to cling on tight or you fall into nettles.

SEPTEMBER

Back to School! I find I am sitting at a back row desk, which is a top year privilege. We're doing the Tudor period in History, studying Mountains in Geography, the Human Body in Science, Compass and Protractor work in Maths, Direct Speech and Reported speech in English, sewing angels in Art, studying Hinduism in R.E., singing David Copperfield in Music, and playing Hockey in P.E. In Technology we work with the Reception and Year 1 helping them make things like – candle holders, robots, musical instruments. I'm also in the choir and in a French club at school.

By the end of September my friends and I walk along the Green to search for conkers and sweet chestnuts. After stringing up our prize conkers we have conker fights in the School playground until the teachers confiscate them.

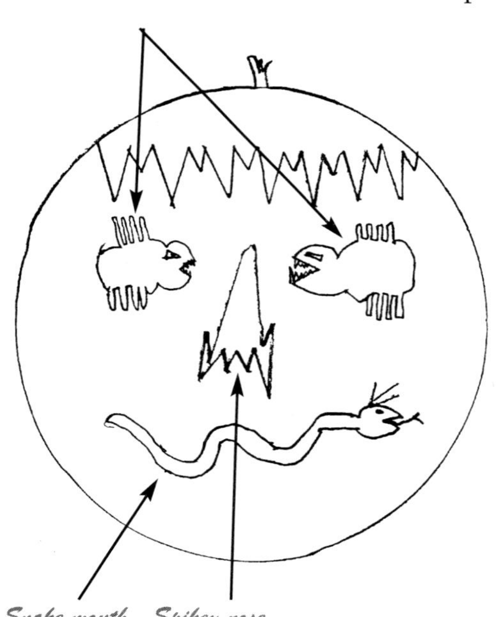

OCTOBER

At Hallowe'en I dress up as a Ghost and go to a party. We all go Trick or Treating in the area and get bags of sweets, including a £2 coin. I carve an evil pumpkin and I put the pumpkin outside for the night.

One day very early in the morning when my Mum takes our dog for her walk through the fields it is quite scary, because it is still dark. She hears deer hooves pounding towards her. She runs out of the way behind a tree otherwise the deer will knock her down. This is the rutting season and we can often hear stags nearby from our house.

NOVEMBER

I'm starting to learn my music that we will sing in the choir at the Christingle Service next month. The new School Hall is being built. The workmen have brought in diggers and have removed most of our playground. We can't even play Football now and the girls can't play Netball!

The 5th November is the Ashridge Fireworks display, which we always go to watch. There are a variety of fireworks - cracklers, rockets, and bangers. My favourite is probably the ones that go very high into the sky, and then luminous colours fill the sky. One firework lands just in front of the barrier, not far from me. I was playing with a Sparkler and when it has finished I accidentally touch the hot end so when I get home I have to put some baking powder on it to cool it down.

DECEMBER

Everyone is busy in School practising for our Christmas plays. December never moves along quickly enough as we are so looking forward to Christmas and all the presents and seeing cousins and Aunts and Uncles. My Grandma is coming to stay this Christmas and we will have the traditional roast turkey, roast potatoes, bread sauce and stuffing with lots of vegetables, then a Christmas pudding flamed with brandy. Hopefully Mum will make my favourite pudding Lemon Meringue Pie.

At the end of term the Christingle service in the local church takes place where we sing Away In a Manger, The lights are dimmed. We are given a christingle orange with lots of sweets on. We have to walk around the church trying not to burn each other's hair because it is really crowded.

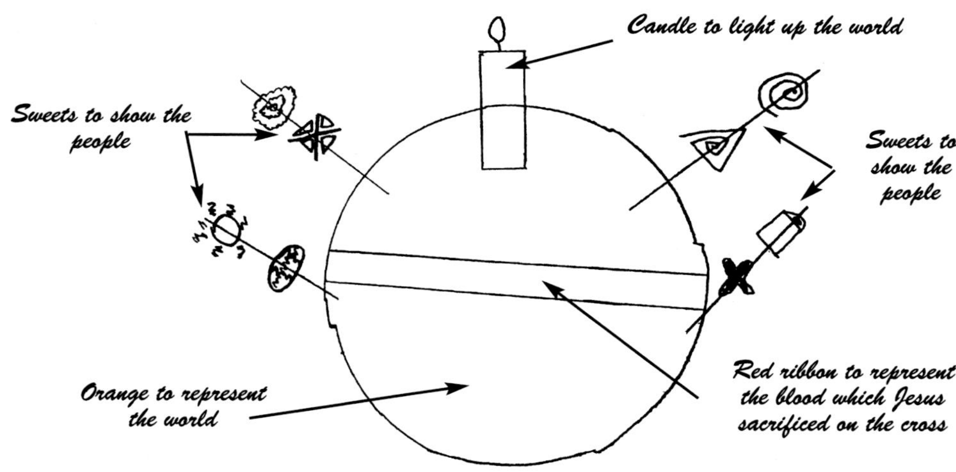

I then have a two week holiday; this holiday is going to be particularly special because it is the Millennium and I will be joining a party in the village hall: It's going to be a Barn Dance with a Sausage & Mash supper. Then on the stroke of midnight there is going to be a big firework display.
It SHOULD BE REALLY AMAZING. – COOL

I wonder how Little Gaddesden will change during the next Millennium?

THE LYE

by Andrew Sheaf

We are a mid-Atlantic family who 'escaped' from Hampstead during 1997 after living previously in Japan and U.S.A. I am British, my wife Mary is Canadian, our first son Alexander was born in Hampstead and our second son Nicholas was born in 1999 in Little Gaddesden and christened here.

We were the first purchasers of the houses in the redevelopment of the Hudnall Lane Expotechnik site during 1998: The Lye. Berkeley Homes has built 11 houses on the site, mostly family houses of 4 to 5 bedrooms. This development won first place in the Evening Standard New Homes Awards in the category for developers of more than 100 homes a year. We secured No.3, the largest plot, with about one acre of garden. Since moving in, the garden has been steadily developed from absolutely nothing and now includes a fruit orchard.

We are both former investment bankers, still with involvement in the financial industry. We have joined the Rural Heritage Society and the Music Club.

Events of 1999

With the number of social organisations there are in the village, there is always something going on, from weekly meetings to annual big events with all their preparations. Talks, demonstrations, recitals, parties, entertainments, sales, matches, walks, visits, camps, have followed their usual cycle. The accounts of the various organisations will give some idea of the general background. Here are just some of the more noticeable or more public events of the year:

February 6th: The Village Produce Association's Winter Show in the Village Hall.

June 4th to 5th: The Art Club's annual exhibition in the Village Hall.

June 5th: The annual Village Sports Day on the Playing Field.

above:
Geoff Price's pictures of the eclipse as seen from the village.

below:
Roger Turner presents Bob Ward with the Women's Institute cup

August 11th: The big astronomical event of the year, a total eclipse of the sun in Great Britain, the first one since 1928 and the last one until 2090. All three of these events missed or will miss Little Gaddesden, however. It was a very cloudy day in 1999, but the partial eclipse was seen through the clouds and photographed by Geoff Price. Many people from the village travelled south for the real event. Those in the south of Cornwall or Alderney mostly missed getting a direct view of the two minutes totality, but experienced the developing event in tantalising glimpses and strange effects of the darkness of totality. People who went further abroad had good views, and in fact one may go abroad to see a total eclipse in almost any year, though often in quite inconvenient places.

August 28th: The Village produce Association's Summer Show in the Village Hall. Bob Ward has been challenging the ladies of the village by making items for numerous cookery categories in the show. On this occasion he won the Women's Institute Cup for the exhibitor gaining the most points in the cookery section.

November 5th: The annual Ashridge fireworks display, but without the bonfire this year. It was as spectacular as we have come to expect, and located as usual on the open ground in front of Ashridge House beyond the car park. It is a village affair, not advertised but just known about, free of charge but usually with a collection for a local charity and a barbecue stall. It is the brilliance of the fireworks that makes these events popular. Any interest in Guy Fawkes and his thwarted plot would be rather academic now if it weren't for this relic of an old celebration.

November 14th: The annual Remembrance Day Service at the War Memorial on the Village Green, accompanied by the Atlas Copco Band.

Naresh and Gigi's daughter Toral at the Orissa Event

November 19th: An "Indian Evening" in the Village Hall was held to raise funds for the Orissa cyclone disaster in eastern India. In some ways this was the most outstanding event of the year, combining an extremely short preparation period with a packed turn-out. Mr Diptimay Mahapatra of no.42 on the Green has relations in the afflicted area, and when Naresh and Gigi Odedra at the village shop heard about it they planned and organised the event at two weeks notice, or less, advertising it in the shop, and recruiting the help of members of their family from miles away. The tickets, allowing for the maximum number the hall could hold, were sold out.

A huge table at the entrance was laden with tureens and dishes of the most tempting Indian foods, and the Indian families were turned out in their best clothes, the ladies and girls wearing the most beautifully coloured saris. The walls were decorated with coloured Indian motifs and drapes. Mr Mahapatra gave a short talk describing the destruction of buildings and crops in Orissa. Then followed the meal, and Indian dancing on stage. The atmosphere encouraged generosity, and additional funds were raised by a raffle, an appeal, the sale of Indian spices, and at the end, the sale of the floral table decorations which had been made by Janet Stinton. £2,935 was raised by the end of the day, which became £3,500 finally.

November 26th to December 4th: Four showings of the Drama Club's Revue in the village hall, their second event since they re-formed after a few years closure. Both this and the first event, Peter Pan at the end of 1998, had opportunities for children to perform, a key point in the revival of the Club, as well as scope for first-rate adult talent.

From 1999 into 2000

"MILLENNIUM" EVENTS

December 31st: First there was a party in the Village Hall, with a barn dance. At midnight Old Lang Syne was sung and everyone went outside.

At the church the bell-ringers were ringing in the new year, new century and new millennium on the six bells at midnight: The six bells rang a few rounds, then one by one a bell ceased ringing until just before midnight only one bell was left. Then a pause, and on the stroke of midnight all six came in again and rang rounds for a few more minutes.

Meanwhile, as midnight came there was the sound of fireworks from all around the countryside at once, with flashes lighting up the sky. This had never been experienced before, as the usual displays on November 5th have never been at any united time.

Our village fireworks display was on the playing field.

Planting the millennium yew: John Leonhardt, Elizabeth Sheard, William Morgan, Alexander Sheaf and Ben Hatt.

Rose Marks, whose residence in the village, although not continuous, dates back to her birth here in 1913, also assisted in the ceremony

January 1st 2000: Millennium church service.

March 4th 2000: The Church Millennium Pageant. Over fifty banners representing saints, martyrs and other heroes of the church had been prepared by children and adults, and were carried in procession from the village hall to the church. A pageant of the history of the church was then performed, with verses read by four narrators while the actions were mimed by children to a background of music and changing lights.

March 12th 2000: A Yew tree was planted in the church yard at a ceremonial service. This "Millennium Yew" is a rooted cutting from the veteran male yew tree in the churchyard of Hambledon, near Godalming in Surrey. The Hambledon Yew is itself estimated to be 2000 years old, with a massive hollow trunk you can stand up in. The cutting was one of thousands from similar veterans prepared by the Conservation Foundation. It was 36 cm tall when we planted it, and had just come into flower.

August 24th to 25th 2000: A bank holiday weekend to complete the millennium festivities. The events were:

A flower festival in the church, with flower arrangements all representing events and services of the church.

An extra exhibition by the Art Club in the village hall.

An exhibition of historic photographs of the village in the village hall.

A pig roast and Barn Dance, organised by the VPA, on Friday evening on the playing field, preceded by a children's fancy dress procession through the village.

Village sports, mostly for children, transferred from Saturday to Monday morning because of rain.

Cricket matches on Saturday and Sunday afternoon on the playing field (Little Gaddesden versus Booker and Great Gaddesden respectively) and on Sunday afternoon at Ashridge (Ashridge versus Bellingdon).

A fête on the village green on Saturday afternoon.

A garden party in the gardens of Ashridge House on Sunday, with a treasure hunt, music by the Pan Harmony steel combo in the afternoon and a concert by the Dacorum Symphony Orchestra in the evening, followed by fireworks in front of the house.

The Parish Council

by Eric Roe, Chairman

Present day Parish Councils were instituted under the terms of the Local Government Act 1894. Prior to this, local administration was carried out by some early civil authorities but primarily by the Church through the Church Wardens, Overseers and the vestry (a form of meeting, not the building).

The incumbent was thus both the spiritual and secular leader of the village. His secular duties were transferred to the new Councils, but strong links were maintained between the Church and the Council.

In our case, the incumbent for the time being was chairman of the Parish Council for all but four years between 1894 and 1928. At various periods during the past century, the Rector and Churchwardens have served as elected Parish Councillors.

A journey through 100 years of minutes of Parish Council meetings is an interesting exercise. The same topics for attention appear regularly, and still do today. Traffic, condition of roads and footpaths, damage to the green and cycling on footpaths are but a few examples.

There have been changes, of course, and these are chronicled in the Minutes. It is strange now to learn that in 1899 the Council decided to exclude the public from future meetings. It is not clear for what period that continued and public participation is now a matter of course.

Special matters of interest have occurred. Until 1914 there was no public telephone box in the village. The Council had negotiated for two years to achieve this despite refusals by the Post Office. One was eventually installed on the basis that we guaranteed the income. In its first year, the Council made up a £10 shortfall, a large sum then.

Potato blight in 1918 was a widespread problem. This was met by the Council by the purchase of a "knapsack-sprayer" for general village use. We had no V.P.A. then!

The first Village Hall was built in 1921 upon land at the rear of John O'Gaddesden's House, initially leased from Lord Brownlow. This fell victim to an arsonist in 1943, ten years after the land had been conveyed to the Parish Council.

Difficulties were encountered at the time that the Ashridge Estate was broken up and sold. The most serious of these was notification that the Estate could no longer supply water to the village. The Council took the matter up with the Rural District Council and supplies were assured.

During the period 1929 – 1933 the Council were concerned that there was inadequate provision for 'cottage and council houses', many of the Estate houses having been sold to occupiers and private owners. Search was made for suitable sites, and Mr. M. Cuthbertson sold land in Hudnall Lane for this purpose. The first tenants took possession in 1934.

Mr. Cuthbertson appeared again in 1933, when steps were initiated to acquire the Village Green. This approach did not succeed and it was not until 1946 that the Green was presented to the County Council by the owners. The Green is now leased by, and administered by the Parish Council.

Again, in late 1938, Mr. Cuthbertson responded to a Parish Council search for a 'recreation ground'. Terms were agreed to buy 5 acres adjoining the village Hall for £1,150. The Council had obtained a promise of a grant of 50% and put the matter to the 1939 Parish Assembly. The Assembly voted against the scheme, and the Council decided to postpone the matter until after the war. The field was eventually acquired in 1949, the price for approximately 6 acres being £750.

The 1950's saw achievement of the replacement of the Village Hall. In October 1949 Basil Phillips offered the land to the village as a gift and in February 1952 a Deed of Gift transferred land to the Parish for the Hall, and to the British Legion for a club house. Land exchanges created the present site and the Parish Council has acquired an additional parcel at the rear recently.

A Committee was set up to raise the necessary finance for the building. This was chaired by Mr P A Block, the co-opted chairman of the Parish Council from 1952 to 1963. The funds were raised by grants and loans from official bodies and by subscription from residents and societies, and the Hall was completed in 1957. It is managed by an autonomous Committee set up under the Deed of Gift consisting of representatives from the village organisations and one Parish Council member.

The question of speeding traffic and a request for a speed limit, first arose in the early 1930's. It appeared at regular intervals, and was the subject of constant badgering of the Highway Authority until 1993 when a 40 mph limit was obtained at last.

The late 1960's saw the replacement of the original Bede Houses by the present Bede Court. These houses were originally built by the Alford family to house widows and were sold when the Estate was broken up. The Mead family Trustees made the land available for warden controlled housing and Bede Court now provides twenty units of accommodation plus the warden's house. They were completed in 1969.

The Cricket and Football Clubs initiated a drive for the provision of a pavilion at the sports ground in 1970. Supported by the Council, by grants and by public subscription, the pavilion was opened in 1975.

Further additions to the sports ground were the provision of hard courts by the Tennis Club in 1977, and the Bowling Green in 1983.

The accumulation of many years of problems with the Village Green led to the adoption of Bylaws in 1984. These regulate the use of the Green, and are provided to all residents adjoining the Green from time to time.

Open discussions on main drainage were instigated in 1981. The Council obtained the agreement of the drainage authority to the installation and, after the usual postponements, the main drainage system became operational in 1987.

Thus to the year 2000. Bus services have been a cause of complaint since 1930, and remain so today. Planning decisions by the Planning Authority have been a cause for complaint since 1950, they remain so today. Cycling on footpaths has been a cause for complaint since 1906, it remains so today.

Despite the sameness, residents are still prepared to serve in local administration. It is apparent from the records, that Parish Councillors and the committees of the various village societies have been, over many years, drawn from a relatively small group of people. With the demands of modern life the numbers appear to be on a downward trend. In 1925 there were 18 candidates for 6 seats on the Parish Council. In 1999 there were 6 candidates for 7 seats!

Charities in Little Gaddesden

UP TO THE YEAR 2000

by Jeremy Day and Michael McCaul

THE ANCIENT CHARITIES

Between 1597 and 1849 seven charities were created by bequests for the relief of the poor in the Parish of Little Gaddesden. Three of these bequests were made by members of the Bridgewater family of Ashridge. In 1687 the Second Earl of Bridgewater purchased an annuity worth £4.10s. on Marsh meadow near Goosehill. In 1792, Lady Caroline Egerton, in her Will, gave £50 to the poor. In 1848, the Countess of Bridgewater left £10,000 in her Will for the relief of the poor of the Ashridge Estates and a similar large sum for educational purposes in several local village schools, which is the subject of the next article.

In 1707, one of the seven bequests was made by the Rector of the day in the form of a bread charity. Three were made by ordinary parishioners: in 1597 Mrs Elizabeth Winchester of Ringshall left money (in 1860 worth £2.10s.) for the education of fatherless children, while one former resident in Aldbury bequeathed £420 and Phillip Power, who was Churchwarden at the time of his death in 1616, bequeathed all his land and house for the village poor. His charitable actions may well have been influenced by his experiences in administering, as Churchwarden, the Poor Law of 1603.

In 1894, all seven charities were consolidated under the title *The Lady Caroline Egerton and other Charities* and ceased to be ecclesiastical charities. At that time the annual income was about £75 but was sufficient to distribute more than one ton of coal to all villagers having an income of not more than £1 per week. There were also distributions of blankets and bread as required. By 1960, it had ceased to be possible to distribute even small quantities of coal and, since that time, with an income that had increased to about £760 a year, augmented by generous donations, the Trustees have distributed small cash payments at Christmas each year to those considered to be in need.

The assets of the seven *Lady Caroline Egerton and other Charities* were merged with those of *The Turney Trust* as a capital endowment of £2,055 when these two previously separate charities were combined under the title of *The Little Gaddesden Charities* on 27 June1997.

THE TURNEY TRUST

In 1979, Mrs Margaret Turney of 42 Little Gaddesden informed the then Rector of the Parish, The Revd Canon Howard Senar, that she wished, in her Will, to leave a sum of money to be held by the Rector, for the time being, to be used for the assistance of persons in Little Gaddesden in times of need, irrespective of their religious or political views. Mrs Turney died in January 1985 and her Will contained a bequest "To the Rector for the time being of the Parish Church of St Peter and St Paul,Little Gaddesden in the sum of ten thousand pounds to be used by him at his unfettered discretion in accordance with her wishes already communicated to him". Mrs Turney's wishes were further confirmed in a separate letter in which she stated that there was no requirement to distinguish between any capital or income of the bequest.

The Trusteeship body of the Ancient Charities at the time of their merger with The Turney Trust consisted of:

Chairman of the Parish Council:
Mr Eric Roe

Incumbent of the Parish Church:
Rev Robert Hollinghurst

Parish Council Representative:
Mrs Anne Wooster

Churchwarden Representative:
Mr Michael McCaul

Representative from Ashridge Management College:
Mr Michael Blackborough

Co-opted Trustee:
Colonel Jeremy Day

The Little Gaddesden Charities Trusteeship body consists of:

Two ex-officio Trustees:
The incumbent of the Parish Church:
Rev Robert Hollinghurst

Chairman of the Parish Council:
Mr Eric Roe

Two co-opted Trustees:
Mr Michael McCaul
Colonel Jeremy Day

A Trustee nominated by Ashridge Management College:
Mr Michael Blackborough

By the time Mrs Turney had died, the Revd Howard Senar had left the parish and the Incumbency had been suspended, with a Priest-in-Charge carrying out the duties formerly carried out by the Rector. In these changed circumstances it became necessary to seek an amendment to Mrs Turney's Will so that her executor could be given a legal discharge of his responsibilities in progressing the bequest for the benefit of the people of Little Gaddesden, otherwise the legacy would have lapsed. The executor accordingly approached the residual beneficiaries who agreed that the Will should be amended so that the bequest could be made to 'The Priest-in-Charge and the Churchwardens for the time being'. These three officials, then the Revd Canon Christopher Newton, Mr George Catchpole and Colonel Jeremy Day, agreed in a signed document dated 20 December 1985 to accept the legacy and to discharge Mrs Turney's wishes as Trustees of the legacy.

The Trustees decided that the legacy should be given the title *The Turney Trust.* Subsequently, on 16 June 1989, by which time Mr Trafford Allen and Mr Michael McCaul had succeeded Mr Catchpole and Colonel Day as Churchwardens and Trustees, Mr Leonard Hopkins, a close friend of Mrs Turney for many years, and Colonel Day were invited to act as additional Trustees for the time being.

The Trust was entered in the Charity Commissioners' central register of charities on 8 March 1992. Having established the Trust as a registered charity, the Trustees next step was to apply to the Charity Commissioners for the making of a 'Scheme' to regulate the conduct of the Trust and to provide for Trustees broadly representative of parishioners of the Parish Church and others in the village.

In the course of discussion on the production of a 'Scheme' for the Trust it occurred to Mr McCaul, one of the existing Trustees, who also happened to be the Churchwarden Trustee of the *Lady Caroline Egerton and Other Charities* that, as the objects of both charities were broadly similar, it would be sensible for the two charities to be merged. This suggestion was endorsed by both sets of Trustees in mid 1993 and negotiations began with the Charity Commissioners on the composition of a Trusteeship body and terms of reference for the conduct of such a charity. Throughout their discussions the Trustees of both charities felt strongly that the links over past centuries between Ashridge and the inhabitants of Little Gaddesden should be preserved by having one Trustee nominated by the Ashridge Management College. After difficult and protracted correspondence between the two sets of Trustees and the Charity Commissioners a 'Scheme' for a new single charity with the title of *The Little Gaddesden Charities* was finally sealed on 27 June 1997.

Throughout the discussions on the creation of *The Turney Trust* and its subsequent merger with the *Lady Caroline and other Charities* both sets of Trustees were guided by, and received wonderful support during the period 1985 to 1997 from, Mr David Cheetham, Solicitor of Messrs Claytons of St Albans, who also held the post of Legal Secretary to the Bishop of St Albans.

The Countess of Bridgewater Trust

by Ken Dickson

(Charity No 3074612)

When Charlotte Catherine Anne, Countess of Bridgewater, died in 1849 she left, in addition to the charity mentioned in the previous article, a bequest of £6,000 of which the annual interest was to be used for the religious and secular education of the children on the Ashridge estate.

She was the widow of General John William Egerton, 7th Earl, who died in 1823. They were both enlightened land-owners and cared for the welfare and living conditions of their people on the estate. At one time 800 men were employed on it. On becoming a widow, the Countess ran the estate herself right up to her end and commanded the absolute respect and loyalty of her tenants.

After her death the Countess of Bridgewater Trust was established to handle the investment and to distribute the income. The Trust still continues though, after the break-up of the estate in the 1920s, there have been changes in the make-up of the Trustees and the operation of the Trust.

The situation is now that there are 3 ex-officio Trustees:

The Chief Executive of the Ashridge (Bonar Law Memorial) Trust
The incumbents of Little Gaddesden, and of Eaton Bray with Edlesborough

There are also two co-opted Trustees currently:

Col R A Corby OBE TD DL
Mr Stanley Broughton

The Secretary is Mr K A M Dickson,

Past restrictions on the investment of charitable funds resulted, over the years, in a halving of the Trust's capital. There is now more freedom for the Trustees to invest in approved funds, which bring both capital appreciation as well as income. Accordingly, the Trust's capital is now approximately £8,500.

The Trustees' distribution for 1999 was £300. The annual distribution to schools and Sunday schools in the old Ashridge estate area continues in the proportions set by the Countess.

The Trustees aim to maintain a moderate rate of capital growth and, it is hoped, some continuing increase in the annual distribution.

After Rain

the smell of it
planting out seedlings
the feel of it
as a child in the west country
the colour of it
as though the blood
of our ancestors
flowed in it,
here in the east
in this flint country
it is the homely colour
of the wren,
on our hills
where the plough has been
it is speckled as
skylark's eggs,
best
is the digging of it
the warmth of the sun
as it shines bright on it
the silky fat worm
that wriggles
and wriggles from out of it
but after rain
oh, the smell of it
earth...

Mary Blake

Village medical services

Doctors

Visiting doctors have held surgeries in the village as long as anyone living here now can remember. The places used have included the following:

No. 5 L.G. (later known as October House) in the 1920s and 30s
No. 36 L.G.
No. 27 L.G.
Behind Yew Tree Cottage (Nos. 39-40 L.G.) in 1946
The new Village Hall. A room here has been used by Dr Colin Andrews' practice for many years, either weekly or fortnightly. Dr Andrews, although not now living here himself, was born in the village and is one of the same Andrews family who have had members living here continuously since the 19th century.

There were also many doctors at Ashridge Hospital, 1939 to 1945

THE MOBILE LIBRARY

A mobile library has been provided by the County Library Service for many years. In the 1970s it used to come on Thursdays. The van now comes on alternate Wednesdays and calls at Ringshall, the Village Hall, Hudnall and Cromer Close, making a total of 2 hours stopping time in the village. The librarians are Reg Appleby and Daphne Whitehorn (pictured below in 1999). Reg does the driving.

Nurses and health visitors

Resident nurses have included:

Nurse Pearson in 1921 at the Bede Houses
Nurse Morris in the 1930s - 40s at Ashridge Cottages
Nurse Hobbs in the 1930s - 40s at no. 35 L.G.
Nurse Mayling for many years up to the 1970s at 24 Ringshall

An infant welfare clinic was held from the late 1940s until the mid 1980s. In the latter part of this period it was held in the village hall on the second Tuesday of every month.

A Health Visitor or Nurse attended, sometimes with a doctor. Babies were weighed and examined, advice given, and immunisations carried out. Volunteers from the village (for many years Gwen Purton (also secretary) and latterly Yve Dickson for instance) assisted in preparing the room, helping with the weighing and making tea.

Hospital visiting service

In 1962 the Hospital Visiting Service was formed to help villagers who did not have cars to visit close relations in hospital. The service is still in operation, and now includes transport of patients to hospital and consultants' appointments. The demand is such that the supply of volunteer drivers is sometimes inadequate. The organiser for many years was Anne Webster. In 1999 Beryl Catesby took over.

Buses

Julie Leonhardt catching the bus to Berkhamsted in 1999

A Green Line Coach map of 1938 shows two linking bus routes through the village. The 352 goes from Dunstable to Northchurch through Ringshall. The 317 comes from Watford through Sarratt, Chipperfield and Bovingdon to Boxmoor and Hemel Hempstead and then through Great Gaddesden to Hudnall, Little Gaddesden and Ringshall and on to Northchurch. The connection with coach route F at Northchurch makes it impossible to see if it went further. The 1939 edition shows an extra route, 319, taking the Nettleden route from Water End.

The 1959 and 1962 London Transport Country Bus maps show the same route 352 through Ringshall, but make it clear that it continues from Northchurch to Berkhamsted. The 317 still takes the same route from Hemel Hempstead through the village to Northchurch and on to Berkhamsted, but starts at Boxmoor station, not coming through Bovingdon and the villages further south as in 1939. The Nettleden route has become the 317A, and starts at Two Waters and terminates at Ringshall.

By 1972 the 352 route has been withdrawn but the 317 and 317A continue and are run by London Country Bus Services, no longer London Transport. The 317A now continues from Ringshall to Berkhamsted

Coming through a period of bus privatisation, nearer to the present day, the old 317 and 317A persist as routes 30 and 31. Around 1990 the operator was Little Jim's. The present operator is Arriva. A new route, 327, on Summer Sundays Only, links the village with Hemel Hempstead, Berkhamsted, Tring, Aldbury, Whipsnade and Dunstable. This is run by Seamarks and is called the Chiltern Ramblers Bus, calling at Ringshall six times in the day.

In 1999 the 30 and 31 buses run from Monday to Saturday. There are four a day from Berkhamsted through the village to Hemel Hempstead (three via Hudnall and one via Nettleden). There are three buses in the reverse direction (one via Hudnall and two via Nettleden). In addition the last bus of the day comes from Hemel Hempstead through Hudnall and turns back to Hemel Hempstead at Hudnall Corner (at 6.04 pm) via Nettleden. Some of the buses after reaching Berkhamsted now add a trip to Aldbury and back. The first bus into Hemel reaches the town centre before 8.25 am and can therefore be used for work or school. The first one to Berkhamsted doesn't arrive there until 11.12 am.

Roads and paths

by the Editor

There are fewer through roads in the parish now than there were in 1899, but more no-through roads. The latter have been built to serve the extra housing.

Hubert Case, the village warden in 1999 who, in his couple of years in office, quickly gained a reputation for keeping our roadside verges tidy.

BLOCKED ROADS

1. The road from opposite Beaney to the Bottom Road via Church Farm and Lamsey Farm. This has remained a public right of way, being first classified as a "road used as a public path", no.19, and now a public bridleway. The loop through Church Farm has been bypassed by a shorter and steeper short-cut. Although always gated, it was originally used by four-wheeled vehicles, but that is now a physical impossibility.

2. Ringshall Drive. This was the road through the park from Ringshall Lodge, joining the drive from Little Gaddesden Lodge (Tudor Lodge) to Ashridge House. It was blocked at the Ringshall end when the swimming pool was built, but a public footpath still exists into Ringshall, skirting the swimmimg pool area on the downhill side, and emerging 200 yards from Ringshall Lodge.

3. The road from Ashridge House to Water End via Peacock Lodge (Nettleden Lodge) and by-passing Nettleden by the south. This was gated at Peacock Lodge, and was used by vehicles visiting Ashridge House before the estate was sold. A mile short of Water End it joined the public road known as "Ladies Mile" locally, which can mean a short mile - it is about a furlong short of a mile, though it might refer to its use by the Lady of the House. Unlike the other two roads mentioned above, there is no way through on this route now, even for walkers.

Many of the new housing estate cul-de-sacs are not public rights of way, neither is the route through the park from Tudor Lodge to Berkhamsted Lodge, on which tolls are collected by Ashridge College.

PUBLIC RIGHTS OF WAY (*see map on page Vll in the maps section*)

Public rights of way on footpaths and bridleways became defined legally as local authority surveys were completed from 1947 onwards. Hertfordshire's first definitive map was completed before 1974. In 1978 these were copied onto a map published by the Rural Heritage Society of this village, at which time 18 public footpaths, 3 public bridleways and 2 roads used as public paths (RUPP) were marked in the parish. Since then the last category has ceased to exist, RUPP no.9, St Margaret's Lane, being upgraded to a Byway Open to All Traffic (BOAT) and the other one, no.19 mentioned above, becoming a diverted bridleway plus a branch bridleway linking it to Church Farm and the church. This branch is expected to be given the number 26.

Two new footpaths have been defined since 1978: no.24, the path along the front of the houses on the Green, and in 1988 no.25, the "Ouseley Path" from Cromer Close to Ashridge House. Both of these were unopposed.

Footpath no.7 from near Home Farm to Rodinghead was the subject of a heated dispute in the village in 1988. Equally convinced witnesses gave evidence that it should or should not be reclassified as a bridleway. The legal decision was that it was already correctly classified as a footpath.

There are also "permissive" paths and bridleways which are not rights of way but used by the public by permission of the owner. The National Trust have a network of permissive bridleways, some of which are in the parish. Jackie Wilson is the Riding Warden who patrols the horse tracks of Ashridge to ensure they are properly used. The National Trust have recently also designated a boundary trail (for walkers) which includes a new permissive footpath in the parish linking footpath 7 to Nettleden's footpath 14 via Webb's Copse.

1999 - 2000 car sticker for the toll road (red)

Village water supply

by the children of the village school in about 1930

Regarding the pre-Brownlow water supplies, the children's account states:

"There were three ponds of which we know. They were Poplar, Blue Pot, and Rectory Pond. The most important of these three ponds was Blue Pot; it was important because it is near the Manor House in the centre of the village. We think this was used by the Saxons. Poplar Pond is in Ashridge Park, not far from Ashridge House. Rectory Pond was at the beginning of the village coming from Ringshall. It was filled in toward the end of the 19th century and Benhay stables were built over it"

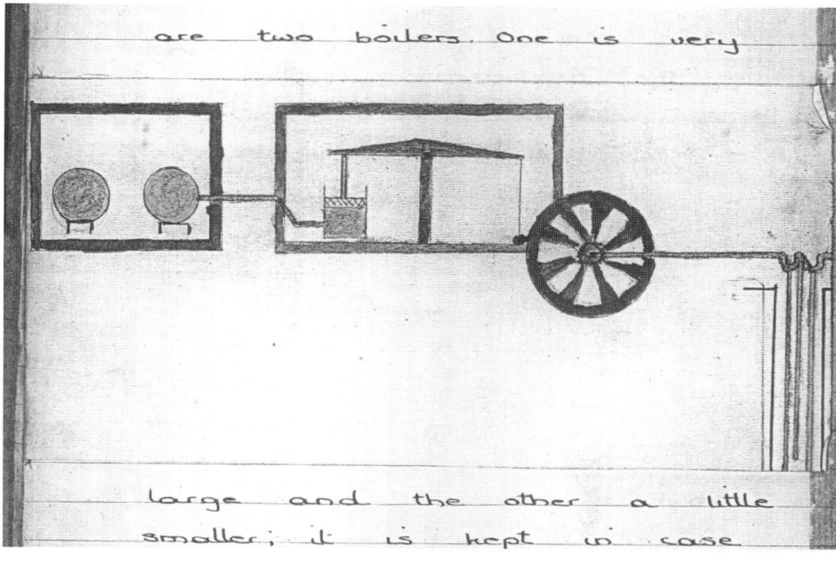

Drawing of the steam water pump in the school book of the village, c.1932

Vicars Bell, who was the teacher responsible for the children's work, wrote in his own book, published in 1949, that Blue Pot Pond was "immediately in front of the manor house, and now used as a dump for hard-core." There is a depression fairly near the manor house, though not immediately in front of it, in 1999, bisected by the park fence. It was larger and shown as a pond on the 1876 "25-inch" ordnance survey map. The pond restored in 1991-92 is 100 yards further from the house. There are in fact lots of ponds shown on the 25-inch maps, scattered all over the woods and fields.

The children's book then goes on to wells, with the scale diagram shown, and then the following account of the pumping station. Vicars Bell only came to the village in 1929, and the book was compiled from 1930 to 1937. He speaks in his own book of the steam engine working until about 1930, and Canon Senar mentions the date of demolition of the chimney as the early 1930's. The following account must have been written between these two dates:

"In 1858 Lord Brownlow provided a proper water supply. A well was sunk at the back of the work yard and an engine and pumps installed. The tall chimney stack, surrounded by a screen of poplar trees, still stands. And the engine, after seventy-five years in use, is still in working condition, although it is now superseded by an electric motor. In the boiler room there are two boilers. One is very large and the other a little smaller; it is kept in case the large one breaks down. The smaller one is kept nearest the engine. A pipe leads from the boiler room to the pumps and this pipe is full of steam. When the pressure of the steam reached 20 lb per sq inch the engine started. A large beam, balanced on a tall pillar, was slowly driven up and down by the piston. The further end of the beam is attached to a large 10 ft fly wheel with wooden gearing. The rotation of this wheel is transmitted to a crank shaft at the head of the well. Here the rotation of the shaft was changed to the vertical movement of steel rods which reached to the pumps, 200 feet below the ground. The water which was used in the condenser flowed into a small reservoir where it cooled and ran back again. The pumps forced water from the well into a very large tank which holds 10,000 gallons of water. Another one pumped the water from the 10,000 gallon tank into the Reservoir at Ringshall, where the water is stored. This has a capacity of 275,000 gallons."

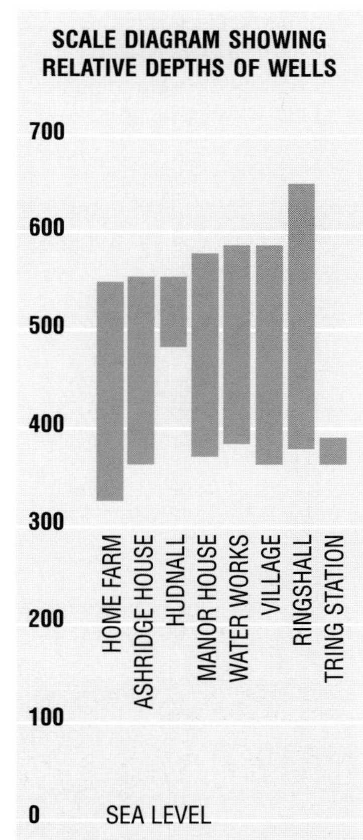

Wells shown in the 1930 school book of the village. Height in feet

Other pipelines and cables

Water was the only system laid under the ground here before 1900. Other systems, both underground and overhead, follow:

TELEGRAPH AND TELEPHONE

In 1899 the village post office at no.42 was probably the only place from which a message could be sent "by wire". It was a very expensive service (priced by the word) compared with the post, and therefore only used for very urgent messages. George Stanbridge used it when needing urgent spare parts for his farm machinery, enabling him to collect the part from the railway station sometimes on the same day. For incoming messages a telegraph boy was employed to take the messages, written out on a form and sealed in an envelope, immediately to the address required, usually by bicycle. This telegram service continued for three-quarters of a century, the bicycle, however, being replaced with something quicker. Letters were also very quick in 1899, and if the receiver replied "by return", an answer could often be received the day after a letter was sent. This is now virtually impossible, but the arrival of the public telephone box in 1914 and the house telephone made it less important, and the fax machines, mobile phones and e-mail services which have multiplied in the 1980's and 1990's have improved rapid communication still further.

Private telephones appear to have started in the village in the 1930's (see Freda Morris's reminiscences on page 300), an early telephone exchange having been installed at Kingham's Meadow. The present exchange is next to the playing field by the tennis courts, and the modern equipment only takes a small fraction of the space provided for the old mechanical relays. The wired telephone links in 1999 are a mixture of overhead and underground lines.

A point of contention in the village now is the need for more aerials to make radio links for the telephone system. Conspicuous objects are resented as spoiling the village just as much now as in 1929.

WATER SUPPLY UPDATE TO THE PRESENT

Our water supply, via the same well and reservoir, had become the responsibility of the Rickmansworth and Uxbridge Valley Water Company at some stage subsequent to the Brownlow era. In 1981 they demolished the building which had housed the old steam engine, in spite of protests.

Later they were taken over by Three Rivers Water plc which is part of the Générale des Eaux Group. In the mid 1990s a new pipeline was laid linking our system to the other mains of the company, but our water still comes from the well behind the Red House via the electric pump to the covered reservoir at Ringshall.

Another old well was recently discovered in the grounds of Nos 29-30 Little Gaddesden.

RIGHT
Nos.26 to 28 and the War Memorial showing cable and poles, mid century

BELOW
The telephone exchange near the tennis courts.

ELECTRICITY

In 1929 plans to bring electricity mains to the village were being opposed by some, Bridget Talbot included. One of her reasons was that overhead cables would spoil the village. Electricity must have arrived early in the 1930's. In 1999 most of the supply is still by overhead line.

SEWERS

All sewage in the village was treated or disposed of near to its point of origin until 1987. Houses, or small groups of them, had cesspits and septic tanks requiring pumping out at intervals which had to be determined by the owner. Many of them were quite ancient and often a bit of a mystery. One or two notorious damp or smelly areas were positioned where people could disagree about who was to blame, or whereabouts in the ground the faulty system was located. Ashridge had quite a large system of its own just north-east of the house.

A feasibility study in 1983 revealed that if a main drainage system were built, out of 209 households asked, 134 households would like to be connected and 18 would not (leaving 57 undecided or unanswered).

As it was difficult to design, and as some of the plans looked like causing problems such as permanent heavy tanker traffic in the Golden Valley, it didn't get started until 1987. The irregular lie of the land meant that in some places the pipes had to be laid in extremely deep trenches to maintain an adequate gradient to keep the flow going. Along the Green the excavation did not block the road because it was done on the Green itself, which with all the links to the adjoining properties made a terrible mess. Where the road itself had to be dug up the situation was worse, needing such prolonged road closures that the Bridgewater Arms went out of business. The main route was from Ringshall (where a pump was needed) along the main road through the village, and down into Golden Valley opposite Home Farm. Branches were laid from such side roads as could drain into it without additional pumps, and from the Cromer Close end of the village. Hudnall Lane was included as far as Field End. Hudnall itself was out of reach. It took getting on for a year to complete.

The unconnected parts of the parish still have their various pits and tanks. Hudnall Park had a new electrically powered mixing and aerating system installed in 1998, serving three houses.

OIL

In 1982 a long distance fuel oil pipeline was laid through Well Farm in the northernmost corner of the parish. It is connected to the Buncefield Oil Terminal in Hemel Hempstead, where pipelines from other parts of the country also converge.

Now that it is used widely as a heating fuel, the oil delivered to your house by a road tanker will first have come through one of these pipelines.

GAS

There has been no gas main in the village. People with gas fired heating systems or cookers make use of large storage tanks or smaller gas cylinders, either of which require road deliveries.

TELEVISION CABLES - None

Aircraft

by the Editor

Unknown in 1900, powered aircraft have become part of the village environment, and balloons also, in spite of their much longer history, have only in recent years become familiar sights here. I have not discovered an account of when the first aeroplane passed over Little Gaddesden, but the area must have attracted some early fliers even if it did not lie on a regular route. On page 309 a 1920s plane passes over, but it is not until the second World War that this book records any others, particularly those that dropped bombs or crashed.

Our nearest aerodromes (that I know of) have been Cheddington (5 miles), Bovingdon (6 miles), neither of them with a functional runway now, Halton (7 miles) and the gliding club at Dunstable Downs (4 miles). The aircraft from Dunstable Downs, and the gliders which they tow up, are rarely seen in the village, but can sometimes be glimpsed catching the sun over in the Whipsnade direction from a viewpoint in the east, such as the churchyard.

Bovingdon airfield retains one important feature, the VHF omnidirectional navigation beacon. Around this point circle the airliners in the holding stack waiting their turn to approach Heathrow. On a clear evening they can be seen from Church Road. Although tiny, and too far off for any sound to be heard, they sometimes gleam in the low sunlight as they bank to the right, and then become grey as their angle changes. There are often four in sight at once, sometimes you can make out five or six. You have to watch one intently to see it complete its slow wide circle. The lowest one, on its transit from right to left, no longer turns, but continues out of sight on the Heathrow approach as those above it all come down a little. In other weather conditions, often in the early morning, the vapour trails of high altitude aircraft remain behind long enough to alter the look of the sky, many accumulating in long tracks from horizon to horizon.

Halton continues as an R.A.F. station, and holds an annual air show. You know something of this kind is going on when you hear an unfamiliar engine noise, and looking up you see a Spitfire or Lancaster pass over the village, or a pair of biplanes. The airfield there is only suitable for light aircraft and gliders. Most of the planes for the show have to come from other airfields at the right time for their display.

Hot air balloon over Hudnall in 1994

Private planes and helicopters often fly over, the slower ones occasionally making a turn or two to view the scene below. Every so often we get callers at the door offering prints of the aerial photographs taken by some of these planes, which position themselves to get an excellent view of each house in turn. Most of the planes just keep on their straight course, but the helicopters, having no need of runways, are sometimes stopping at the village itself, often at Ashridge House.

Hot air balloons are often seen, usually in the late afternoon or evening. As they cannot fly any closer to Luton airport than Little Gaddesden, they never come from the Luton direction, and if the wind is taking them towards Luton, our area is where they are making preparations to land, so they often come over very low and sometimes land in one of our larger fields such as Hudnall Common. Local children then gather to watch, and sometimes help to fold the balloon. Soon the support vehicle arrives to load up the balloon and pick up the passengers. Although both wild and domestic animals take no notice of aeroplanes, many of them are very sensitive to balloons, particularly as they intermittently give out a roar from their burners, which sets the dogs barking or the cows and sheep running. This especially happens as they come low, adjusting their buoyancy for an accurate landing.

If large aircraft are near enough to make out their colours and markings they are usually coming from or going to Luton Airport, ten miles away. In the late 1970's and 1980's most of these were from Monarch or Britannia Airlines. At Hudnall, after dark, planes on a long approach used to be first seen as a bright light somewhere in the east-south-east. As each plane was on a straight course for Hudnall Park, children staying there were very puzzled, as the light would not seem to move for more than a minute. If a bright planet such as Jupiter or Venus were also in the sky, there could be quite a resemblance. Then it would be noticed that the light drifted just slightly to one side, or went a little higher, and the talk would be of U.F.O.s. It seemed ages before the gain in altitude and brightness were enough for them to realise that it was approaching, and it was an anticlimax if they watched long enough for it to resolve into the two landing lights of a plane passing overhead. Just after that it would start its bank to the right as it started a big turn of about 150 degrees to line up with Luton's runway. In daylight, it looked as though the planes were actually using Hudnall Park as a landmark, as it is a white house standing alone in a field, unscreened by any trees, but it is unlikely that they needed one. This line is not used now, at least by large aircraft. If an airliner approached from the north-east, however, it would be climbing up from Luton, and if it were a BAC 111 it would be very noisy, and if it were in the small hours it would be very unwelcome, and that is the subject of another article.

AN AIRSHIP REMEMBERED

by George Rogers

Although I was only five at the time, I can clearly remember seeing the R101 airship flying up the valley from Hemel Hempstead on its way to Cardington - or was it the R100?

It was in 1929. It was the unusual sound of the engine that made people in Ringshall come out to see what it was.

After passing by it seemed to bank slightly as it changed direction.

(Both R100 and R101 were built in 1929. In 1930 R101 crashed in France and R100 was scrapped - Ed)

Airspace over Little Gaddesden

by Stuart Green - Easyjet pilot

Little Gaddesden is situated within the Luton Airport air traffic control zone which is a roughly rectangular shaped section of airspace centred upon Luton encompassing Tring and Berkhamsted to the west, Stevenage and Hitchin to the east and Harpenden to the south. The vertical extent of the zone is to 3,500 feet above sea level. Above this, air traffic control is undertaken by the London Air Traffic Control Centre (LATCC) at West Drayton, which is reponsible for traffic both in the Lower UK airspace from 3,500 feet to approximately 24,500 feet (flight level 245, that's 4.6 miles up) and the Upper UK airspace above flight level 245. In this airspace are two parallel airways above Little Gaddesden, one above the other. They are aligned between Honiley, near Birmingham, and Biggin Hill, south-east of London, and most of their traffic is south-east-bound into northern Europe and

An easyJet Boeing 737 at Luton Airport in July 1999

beyond. The lower one extends up to about 17,000 feet (flight level 170: 3 miles up) and is airway B71. The upper one, UB71, extends right up to 66,000 feet (flight level 660: 12.5 miles up)

The closest navigational beacons to Little Gaddesden are at Henton near Stoke Mandeville and the disused Bovingdon airfield, both of which are used for certain Luton departures. Aircraft bound for Northern Ireland and Scotland, approach Little Gaddesden on a bearing of 259 (about WSW) and turn right over Ashridge at a minimum height of 3000 feet on to route Olney 1B to the north. Those bound for France, Spain, Switzerland, other parts of Europe and North Africa continue without turning at Ashridge, reaching 6000 feet or more at Henton beacon where they turn southwest for Compton (near Reading) and on to cross the south coast near Worthing. North-bound aircraft from Heathrow also join the Olney 1B route, though at higher altitude. The Bovingdon beacon is also widely used by London Heathrow both for some departure routes and as a holding facility when traffic flow is being restricted.

The Easyjet fleet consists of about 19 Boeing 737-300s, of which only four are over 2 years old. They have quieter engines than the 737-200 which is still used by some airlines. The next ones to be obtained will be 737-700s and 800s which are more fuel-efficient. The familiar livery with a huge orange telephone number painted on the fuselage will be replaced with a web-site address.

Aircraft noise

by Francis Cory-Wright

Once upon a time Little Gaddesden and its surrounding hamlets was a quiet place to live. Not any more. Since the late 1960's - allowing for intermittent respites - the village has had to suffer periodical bouts of aircraft frenzy, culminating in the operations of Court Line until this fly-by-night airline went bust, to everyone's relief.

The factors that brought this about were the introduction of jet aircraft and cheap package holidays to Spain, along with charter flights, from Luton Airport, originally designed as a small municipal airfield catering for general aviation to serve local industry. Then, as now, airline operators were immune from legislation which has been progressively tightened in respect of all other forms of noise nuisance. The law in this country does not permit suing airlines on the ground of unmitigated noise, nor the airports that they operate from, nor the Civil Aviation Authority which has the ultimate responsibility for air traffic.

Air transport is regarded as vital to the national economy, such that few restrictions were allowed to stand in the way of its expansion to meet the cut-throat competition with our continental rivals, particularly in France, Germany and Holland. Little Gaddesden found itself in the eye of the storm during the 1960's and 70's in particular, reaching a climax of sorts in 1984, to be followed by a relative lull lasting fourteen years.

Village residents haven't taken this lying down; indeed not. We banded together to form an action group styled GADDACAN, under the umbrella of LADACAN: Luton and District Association for the Control of Aircraft Noise, with members in three counties. Stratagems included a rota of members to telephone Luton Borough Councillors at their homes to complain whenever they were awoken by planes in the small hours, since it was the council that owned and operated the airport. It seemed fair that they should be woken when we were. There were no answering machines to intercept the calls in those days. Several councillors went ex-directory as battle was joined. With communities up in arms about the disturbance at other airports, especially in the south-east, a combined action group for Heathrow, Gatwick, Stansted and Luton was formed: FLAG: the Four London Airports Group. The powers-that-be then became seriously alarmed once aircraft noise became a political hot-potato nationally, and of such magnitude that the government could not ignore it.

Planning legislation soon followed as a matter of expediency. Environmental studies were undertaken and aircraft noise was well and truly on the national agenda, so public clamour had its long overdue reward. Airport authorities began to take noise seriously, as did the manufacturers of jet engines, body frames and "hush kits". So much did noise become an imperative, both nationally and internationally, that the World Health Authority made it an issue. GADDACAN and LADACAN played an important role in this reassessment by the authorities of the impact of air travel on the environment, and bringing in pollution as well as noise, the phrase "environmental assessment" entered the vocabulary.

Nowadays international airports are obliged to meet specified targets and quotas reflecting times, heights, preferential routes and minimum noise indicators, with penalties on airlines which infringe these regulations. These regulations are limited to the Designated London Airports, however, which means the other three, not Luton. As Luton airport grows in size this anomaly will need to be addressed. The airport has now styled itself London Luton Airport Ltd even though it is not a Designated London Airport.

Meanwhile, up to 1998, our village was not unduly disturbed by aircraft noise to the extent that we had been 16 or more years ago. Then a flight path was changed and a new route called Olney 1B was tried out, and another known as FMS. These had an immediate impact on the village which led to the resurrection of GADDACAN, and also an alliance of Councils in the areas affected, (parts of Herts, Beds and Bucks, including Dacorum) known as LLATVCC: London Luton Airport Towns and Villages Consultative Committee, of which the Chairman is our own Parish Council Chairman Eric Roe, and the Hon Secretary David Heard is also from our village. This organisation applied to join the Airport Consultative Committee, but was turned down in December 1999 on the grounds that local environmental interests were already adequately represented and there was no vacancy for another seat. LLATVCC disputes the adequate representation of our interests.

In 1999 a new passenger terminal was opened and a new railway station constructed, though the latter is not yet operational, and the passenger traffic has increased. At present the airport caters for a throughput of about 5 million passengers per year (MPPA) and a fast-growing cargo traffic. Beds County Structure Plan countenances a doubling of this, but the airport authority itself envisages that it could in theory handle a 6-fold increase, up to 30 MPPA in the long term, placing it on a par with Gatwick. However, it is unlikely to reach these dimensions due to the constraints of the terrain, apart from planning and environmental constraints imposed on it.

Finally, if the airport's ambitions can be kept in check, it will continue to serve our neighbourhood quite well to have a well-managed local airport, provided night flights are prohibited. So far there is no sign of this happening, especially for landing flights anyway.

How else...

Soft rain falls on the garden
enamels the leaves
faint wash of green
shadows the bare apple tree,

what does God look like?
the small boy asks,
difficult question
the woman replies

rain as sea mist
enfolds them, cobwebs
their hair, as through wet
grass
they walk to the wood,

I think I know
the boy says quickly
unaware, as angels
tumble from the skies

God is enormous
cloud of ears.

Puddles sparkle, ripple
in the breeze of wings,
rain falls softly on the garden
enamels the leaves.

Mary Blake

St Peter and St Paul's Church Little Gaddesden

by Michael McCaul

When the 20th century dawned, the parish of Little Gaddesden was in interregnum. But on 6th February 1900, Dr G Woods was inducted as Rector in succession to Rev F H Hodgson. Woods was a Doctor of Divinity who had served as Master of Trinity College, Oxford, before coming to the parish which, since 1895, had included Ringshall.

On 20th January, Queen Victoria died; the chancel was draped in black and the bell was tolled 100 times in memory of this remarkable lady.

Dr Woods found the Parish church in fine order and good repair thanks to the generosity of the Brownlows towards the end of the previous century. Lord Brownlow, himself a Church Commissioner, actually served as a Churchwarden in 1907.

Woods took a close interest in the Village School, which he admitted to having been surprised by its high standard. Since 1884, the Head Teacher had been 'Sammy' Green who, like his predecessor and father-in-law, John Worral, also served as choirmaster. In 1903 a presentation was made to Sammy Green to mark his thirty years connection with the school. Dr Woods was well connected in the church hierarchy and brought some distinguished preachers to the parish church, where the Book of Common Prayer (1662) and Hymns Ancient and Modern were in use. Evensong on Sundays was held in the afternoon in the winter months, except when there was moonlight enough to light the way to the church at 6.30 pm. Additionally, lanterns were placed in trees on the route.

In 1904 Dr Woods resigned the living here, apparently on account of his wife having found the Gaddesden climate detrimental to her health. He left to become Master of the Inner Temple, then a Crown appointment. His wife did not completely sever links with the village as she took with her, from the village, a maid who served the Woods for many years thereafter.

One of Dr Wood's disappointments was that the Parish Magazine which the Rev Hodgson had started soon after his arrival in 1892 ceased publication, although this did indeed relieve him of financing the annual deficit. Prior to the death of the previous Rector, the Rev Charlton Lane, in 1892, and since 1878, the parish had depended on contributions made to the monthly Ivinghoe Deanery magazine, which itself folded in 1893. Presumably Lane made contributions, some of particular historical interest, on the basis that, notwithstanding Little Gaddesden's membership of the Berkhamsted Deanery, he was also Chaplain of Ashridge, which was itself part of Pitstone and in the Ivinghoe Deanery. There is nothing in Church papers to show what happened thereafter until 1923-24, when cuttings were made of two reports from the Berkhamsted Deanery magazine regretting the death of John Oakins, who had been Parish Clerk for many years up to 1914, and on a village fête. In any event, there seems to have been no initiative to revive

Print by Dorothea Patterson

the Parish magazine here until the Rev Howard Senar's arrival in 1962.

The successor to Dr Woods was the Rev E Clark. He retired in 1919 and his ministry had lasted longer than perhaps he would have wished due to the Great War (1914-1918) which in so many ways disrupted life in the parish and in the homes of those mourning their losses. Some 23 young men from the village were killed in the war.

Ashridge House was turned into a military hospital for convalescent soldiers.The wounded at Ashridge added to the Rev Clark's pastoral work in the village itself. He personally had written movingly about the death in action in 1915 of William Fenn, a young officer from the village whom Clark had found to be an exemplary member of the congregation pre-war. In 1917 soldiers from Ashridge were amongst a confirmation class held by Clark.

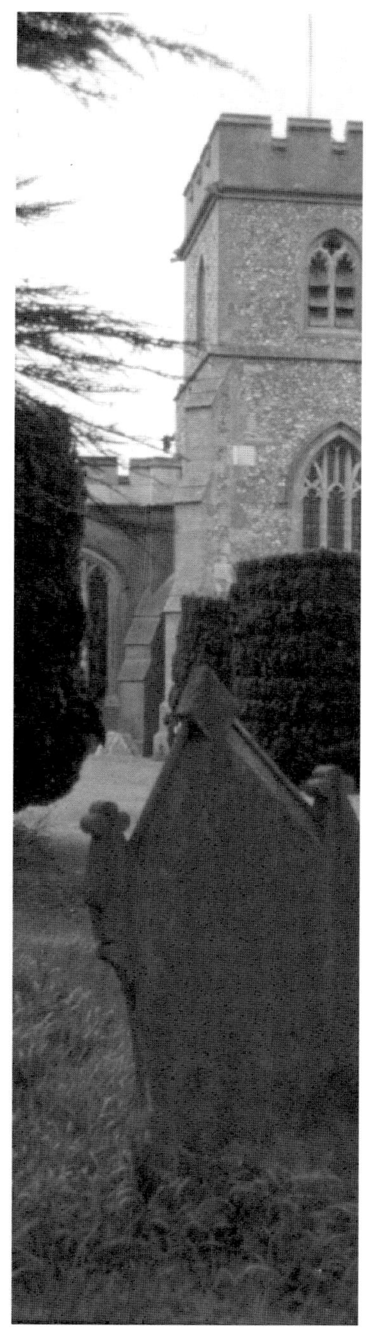

The Village School, which had maintained a high standard pre-war, lost its Head Teacher, Sammy Green, to retirement (after 51 years employment at the school) in July 1914. His successor, Douglas Harrison, had made an outstanding impression not only at the school but also as choir master and organist before being called up for military service in 1916. His temporary replacement at the school was Miss Winifred Sapsford, while a thirteen-year-old village boy, Ralph Kibby, took over as organist, a position which he filled until 1934, when he moved to Great Gaddesden.

During the Great War a roll was kept, and exhibited in the porch, of all those in the parish called up for some form of national service. This piece of paper was overlooked for many years but, at the behest of the Royal British Legion, it was restored recently and is shown on a wall in the Baptistry. A memorial to those in the parish who fell in both world wars hangs on the wall close to the pulpit.

Harrison returned in 1919 as a lieutenant who had been wounded in action, and found a new clergyman in office; the Rev Thomas Goudge had been inducted in January 1919, after military service as a Chaplain, and was to achieve the rare distinction of a chaplain being awarded the DSO. Some of the returning soldiers (who in effect became the nucleus of the local branch of the British Legion formed in 1921) encouraged by the Parish Council, of which Goudge was Chairman, and greatly facilitated by the Estate's Agent, Col W Wheatley, acting with Lord Brownlow's approval, purchased two redundant army huts and rebuilt them on a small piece of land in Church Road, to become the Village Hall. The War Memorial on the Green was designed by Mrs Wheatley.

The parish had its share of resettlement problems arising from the war, but it received a really heavy blow when Lord Brownlow himself died in March 1921 at the age of 77. Worse was to follow when it became known that the entire Ashridge Estate was to be sold to defray death duties. All employees received a year's pay and, in the parish, some eighty cottagers were enabled to purchase their houses. But many were left without jobs or prospects in the village.

In 1924, the Rev Arthur Bidlake succeeded Rev Goudge. He resigned in 1928 not long after the Trustees of the Ashridge Estate, thanks to the efforts of Miss Bridget Talbot and many others, were able to sell the House to the Bonar Law Memorial Trust and large parts of the estate to the National Trust, leaving some land free for private development, including farmland which surrounded the church, which was, of course, not part of the sale.

Without its patron, and most generous supporter, the Parish and its Parochial Church Council (introduced after the War) faced a difficult time. It was at this time that, as a sort of forerunner to the existing Covenant Scheme, a Free Will Offering scheme to strengthen the finances was introduced; envelopes were not used but the contributions of its members were carefully noted in a large Cash Book.

In 1929, Vicars Bell took over as Village Schoolmaster. An account of his illustrious career until 1963 is recorded elsewhere but it should be noted that through no fault of his own, the School itself became impoverished in 1938, only to be rescued, at the behest of the Bishop of St Albans, by a large donation from a lady parishioner who, in 1929, had purchased the Rectory and renamed it 'Beaney'.

On 12 April 1934, Rev Charles E Wager was inducted by the Bishop of St Albans as Rector. Both men had earlier represented the Church in Africa - Michael Furse had been Bishop of Pretoria and Wager had done a tour there as a missionary. He was also a former Prison Chaplain.

The Rev Wager's rectorship lasted until 1953 and thus spanned the years of World War II, as well as the accession of Queen Elizabeth II in 1952. He was a quiet and unassuming man, held in high regard for his preaching, as well as for the short essays on spiritual matters which he contributed to the Berkhamsted Deanery magazine from time to time. He maintained close and fruitful relations with Vicars Bell at the School which, in 1939, absorbed a large number of evacuees and their teachers from North London. Mrs Wager herself held, for many years, her own class for the pre-school children of the parish and was held in high regard. Soon after her arrival in the parish in 1934, she had produced on the lawn at Beaney a memorable amateur performance of 'A Midsummer Night's Dream' which testified to her skill as a producer.

Unlike the situation in World War 1 Ashridge Hospital, with its hundreds of both military and civilian patients, fell outside the Rector of Little Gaddesden's remit and his offer to assist with pastoral work there, for which he was so well qualified, was rejected by the Vicar of Nettleden and Potten End, who took his own duties so seriously there that he installed himself in a caravan. Conflicts over parish boundaries had been apparent also in 1938 when the Ministry of Health called for the reservation of 50 grave spaces for the members of H M Forces who might die at the wartime hospital planned for Ashridge but Rev Wager pointed out that Ashridge was not part of his parish.

Following Rev Wager's retirement in 1953, the new incumbent was Rev R C Paterson, a retired senior bank official, then but recently ordained. He remained at his post until 1959 when he decided to accept the offer of a living in his native

St Peter and St Paul's at sunset

Scotland. Daily he walked to the Church to ring the bell at 8 am, and said Evensong often without a congregation. His wife provided transport for elderly parishioners to attend Sunday services and much other assistance was provided for those in need. During Rev Paterson's ministry, negotiations were completed to enable the acceptance of an offer by Mr Basil Phillips of a piece of land adjoining the west wall of the Churchyard in exchange for 'Church Acre', a one acre plot situated in the middle of large fields at Church Farm, which the Parish had owned (and for which rent had been exacted) since probably the fifteenth century. This was to be the new burial ground, subsequently consecrated and first used in 1957.

It was in the fifties also that a supply of electricity was provided (its installation had been delayed for fifteen years by the War and its aftermath); in the early sixties a 'main' water supply to the churchyard was installed. Furthermore, in the fifties, and following a theft of lead from the Church roof, a number of repairs to the roof and fabric were made, including the underpinning of the exterior wall of the chancel at the East End; this wall had been extended by about three feet in the 1870s and its subsidence was thought to have been partly attributable to 'bomb blast' during the War. Bearing in mind its rural location, a relatively large number of German bombs fell in the Parish during the Blitz of 1940, including a stick which virtually straddled the Church, while a V2 rocket landed in nearby Hoo Wood in early 1945.

Rev David Bickerton was Rector between 1959 and 1961. He was followed by Rev (later Canon) Howard Senar, who retired in 1982, after twenty years of distinguished service to the Parish.

In the middle sixties a new vestry block (architect John Brandon Jones RIBA) was erected on the north side of the Church; the 'old' vestry, since at least 1878, had been concealed behind a curtained-off space at the East End of the South aisle, which was later dedicated as a chapel. At much the same time a major refurbishment of the Church's interior, and of its furniture and fittings, was embarked upon and completed under the tireless direction of the Rector, who even found time to serve for a few years on the Parish Council. He was also the inspiration for the introduction of a Stewardship campaign, as well as for a young persons' club known as the 'Sword and Keys'. Both were most successful. Following tradition, once a year the Rector even sat in his robes at the top of the Village Green to solicit financial contributions from passers-by, while members of the Church worked hard to arrange Craft Fairs, which attracted large numbers of visitors. Canon Senar abandoned this tradition after the Stewardship campaign.

In 1973 the hamlet of Hudnall was transferred from the parish of Edlesborough (diocese of Oxford) to Little Gaddesden; Dagnall was also tentatively offered to the parish but the plan did not mature. But Ashridge House, where successive Rectors of this parish had officiated as Chaplain to the Bridgwater and Brownlow families, remained with the parish of Nettleden, included for centuries in the Oxford diocese as part of the parish of Pitstone. Nevertheless, the owners of Ashridge (now the Ashridge Management College), invited Rev Senar to be their Chaplain.

In 1977 a new ring of six bells was installed in the belfry in memory of Miss Margaret Griffiths, a parishioner, formerly senior History Mistress at Berkhamsted School for Girls, who had died in 1976 and had made a bequest for this purpose. Two of the bells installed in 1831 remained, with one having been recast, but all of the four larger bells (one recast) had come from Chellington Church in Bedfordshire. The contractor concerned was 'Taylor of

The Rev Canon Howard Senar

Loughborough' while George Catchpole, himself a keen ringer, assisted a great deal with the actual installation in the belfry. (see page 138)

In the early seventies Rev Senar introduced the liturgies of the Alternative Service Book of 1970 to the Parish but not without some resistance from a minority of worshippers favouring the 1662 version of the Book of Common Prayer. He also favoured the use of the English Hymnal in lieu of Hymns Ancient and Modern. The Series III marriage service was introduced in 1978.

Busy as he was with both parochial and some Deanery business, Rev Senar found time to write a pamphlet on Little Gaddesden Church; the many photos it contained were the work of a parishioner, Ernest Janes. In effect, this pamphlet became a trial run for a more extensive book on the parish, as well as on Ashridge which, with considerable assistance from many members of the parish, including Ernest Janes, he began to prepare in the late seventies and which he was able to produce as a 'hard cover' book in 1982, entitled 'Little Gaddesden and Ashridge'. In its preface he wrote "The Rector of a parish is uniquely placed to became a repository of stories of people and events of years gone by both in his parish church and its parish". In September 1982, the time had come for Rev Senar and his wife (Felicity) to retire to Devon. But he was not to be replaced; the Benefice of Little Gaddesden was suspended and the Diocesan

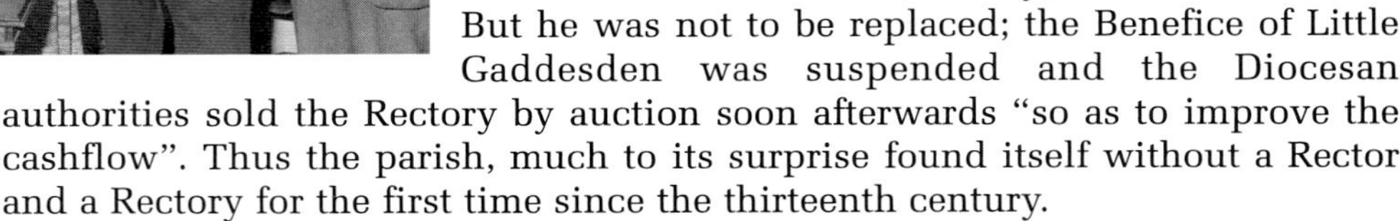

authorities sold the Rectory by auction soon afterwards "so as to improve the cashflow". Thus the parish, much to its surprise found itself without a Rector and a Rectory for the first time since the thirteenth century.

Presentation to Howard and Felicity Senar when they left the village in 1982.

LEFT TO RIGHT
John Lewis, George Catchpole, Howard Senar. Felicity Senar, Chris Osborn-Jones (behind Felicity), John Oakins, Len Hopkins (behind John), Jeremy Day.

The interregnums lasted until 1997. It would have been a difficult task even for a full-time Rector to take the place of Howard Senar but the four non-resident Priests-in-Charge, who were appointed to fill the gap between 1982 and 1997, all of whom worked very hard, bearing in mind that all had parochial duties elsewhere, were Alan Naylor-Smith, Christopher Newton (Canon of Oxford), Brian Saunders and Neil Roscrow, assisted by his wife Pamela, (ordained in 1994). The Parish was grateful not only to them but to others who came to take services, especially Rev 'Jim' Lawrenson, Harry Hall (Canon of St David's) and Rev A G Ogilvie. The Parish also benefited from the services of our two resident Readers, Trafford Allen and Roger Turner and particularly the former, who served also as Churchwarden from 1988 onwards.

From October 1990 to May 1991, during the ministry of Rev Brian Saunders, the Church was closed for all purposes and weekly services were held in the School Hall. Vacation of the Church was necessary

BELOW RIGHT
At the confirmation of Glynis Blake and Rita Humphreys by the Archbishop of Tanzania August 1988

LEFT TO RIGHT
George Catchpole, Gerald Humphreys, James Blake, Rev Brian Saunders, Glynis Blake, Archbishop John Ramadhani, Rita Humphreys, Nicola Hancock, Jeremy Day

BELOW
Rev Brian Saunders

to enable the contractor, who had been at work since September 1989, in effecting major repairs to the roof timbers of the South Aisle, including the chapel. This work was called for by the discovery, in July 1989, of some dry rot in the roof over the South Aisle, including the vaulted roof in the chapel, which was soon found to be extensive. In particular, it was found that the thirty foot horizontal wooden beam, erected by Jeffry Wyatt in the 1820s and which had been bricked in when the two arches in the South Aisle were erected under it in the 1870s, was replete with dry rot and likely to collapse at any time. This beam had to be removed while leaving the two arches standing and was replaced by a reinforced concrete beam which was cast in situ!

The total cost of this repair work was just less than £150,000 and the fact that all of this sum was found within the village spoke well of the generosity of parishioners and the fund-raising ability of the Restoration Appeal Committee, as well as the financial shrewdness of successive Parish Treasurers. In September 1991, Dr Robert Runcie, formerly Archbishop of Canterbury, came to preach at the service of thanksgiving, which was held prior to a memorable Church Flower Festival and a week-end of fund-raising activities, totalling more than £8,000.

Outside the church at the start of the annual pilgrimage to St Albans Abbey in 1996.

L to R:
Tim, Miriam and Debbie Shaw with their father Gerry, and Emma and Debbie Catchpole.

Down the years, the Parochial Church Council has continued to support the School Governors of the Village School and their plans to provide increased accommodation and improved facilities. Additions to the School were made in 1973 and 1995 and a major plan to increase space and facilities has just been put in train; this includes the demolition of the School Dining Hall, built in 1940 to cope with the flow of children evacuees to the village.

During the nineties, Parish funds were found to pay for a number of repairs and improvements, including improvement of the central heating and of the Church's somewhat eccentric electricity supply, the provision in the graveyard of a hard-surface path (to obviate the need for straw to be laid in bad weather), repairs to the Church Tower and Belfry and much needed attention to the paths around the Church. Furthermore the Church received from the Mead Trust, a gift of land adjoining the graveyard for use as a car-park. The necessary work was under the direction of Ralph King, whose services were invaluable and enabled costs to be reduced appreciably.

While undeniably missing the presence of an active resident incumbent living in the Parish, it may be thought that in all the circumstances the various Parish Officers and the Parochial Church Council did remarkably well during the interregnum, not only to remain afloat but even to advance. The interregnum came to an end in 1997 when, after protracted and sometimes heated discussion, the Diocese decided that the Parishes of Great and Little Gaddesden should become a United Benefice and that this would involve the appointment of a priest who would share his time between Little Gaddesden, where he would be known as the Rector, and Great Gaddesden, where he would be known as the Vicar and live in the Vicarage. In October 1997, the Rev Robert Hollingshurst was inducted as Rector at Little Gaddesden and remains en poste. He, and his wife Enid, have worked diligently to bring the two parishes closer together and at Little Gaddesden he has seen a revival of the Sunday School, which meets regularly in the Church and makes use of

Easter Monday 1998 - Josephine Mann, Debbie Catchpole, Peter Leonhardt and Willum Dover with a banner for a new era made by the youth of both parishes.

the space in the South Aisle formerly occupied by the Old Vestry. The parochial electoral roll for 1999 bears 169 names.

The local government reforms of the 1970s led to the creation of the Borough of Dacorum, of which Great and Little Gaddesden (previously administered by different rural district councils) found themselves a part. In 1994 both ecclesiastical parishes became part of the newly formed Berkhamsted Deanery. What the future holds for these two ancient parishes remains to be seen but there is no doubt that they stand closer in 1999 than at any time since the Domesday Book of 1086.

TOP:
The Sword and Keys Society at St Albans, 1968.
Standing:
L to R: Rose Haldane (later Montfort), Pat Griffiths (now Catchpole), Philip Mountfort, Ann Griffiths (now Anderton), Ian Catchpole behind Ann, Robert Pannell.
In front: Jonathan Williams, Ian Williams

ABOVE:
The Sword and Keys in 1966: L to R: Ian Catchpole, Gillian Bagshawe, Philip Mountfort, Nicola Tandy, Mary Carrington, Jane Dickson, Hilary Catchpole, Vivienne Banks (below Hilary), Ann Griffiths.

The Sword and Keys Society

by Pat and Ian Catchpole

The Sword and Keys, named after the emblems associated with our church's patron saints, was formed in 1962 following the departure of the Reverend David Bickerton to the Parishes of Sandford Courtenay and Honeychurch in Devon. Prior to his resigning the living of Little Gaddesden, David Bickerton had prepared a large group of teenagers for confirmation and, rather than abandon them so soon after their confirmation, he invited them all to visit his new parishes and stay as 'guests' in the Church Hall.

Under the guidance and supervision of Beth Taylor, a teacher at the school, initially and then the Rector, Canon Senar, the Sword and Keys Society met in the School Hall every Friday evening; a group of young people, confirmed in the Anglican faith, having fun whilst raising money for a range of worthy causes.

Being a church youth group the Sword and Keys Society clearly required approval of, and support from, the Rector and Parochial Church Council: this was never lacking, although for the members of the society the religious principles on which the society was founded were sometimes hard to accept! We ran a yearly sale, this included the usual stalls and handicraft made throughout the year. The funds were always given away in their entirety, but we were never allowed to have a raffle or even guess the weight of a cake, as this was considered to be gambling and not suitable for a church youth group.

It is impossible here to cover every event in the history of the society but perhaps some of the most notable are: the bicycle and radio given to the Leighton Buzzard Children's home, the Ciborium donated to the church, the sword and keys hassocks, the Easter Gardens, help with the maintenance of the old churchyard and of course the annual pilgrimages to St Albans Abbey. We certainly remember one Easter Garden, which we had made outside on the approach to the main entrance of the church. It was a great success but eventually the time came for it to be removed. We met on the Friday evening, (we had constructed it with large stones and flints) so to help the removal process we borrowed the church wheelbarrow which was an old wooden one. Unfortunately, we did not realise just how heavy the stones were and the old wheelbarrow fell apart under the strain. As you can imagine we also fell about laughing. The Rector, however, was trying to conduct a confirmation class in the Bridgewater Chapel. It so happened that the following Sunday the sermon was on quietness in the churchyard. This was not the only time the Rector found inspiration for a sermon from us.

We continued to meet as friends for many years, eventually six members resulted in three marriages.

We all respected the Rector's views, even if we did not always agree with them. He will always hold a very special place in our hearts.

At Grantchester in 1968: Sword and Keys members Ian Williams and Derry Franklin

The church stewardship campaign of 1967

Every so often a community of the church somewhere experiences an awakening. Some aspect of the faith becomes vividly more real to someone or some few, and they find the power which makes it spread into the community in a way that strengthens all and is seen to be good.

Each of these movements seems to be different from the last one, and some people are caught up in it and some are passed by, yet all can be seen as parts of the same divine plan. They satisfy the same test set by our Lord to distinguish true from false prophets: You shall know them by their fruits.

One of these movements locally gave the Methodist Church its vigour in Hudnall in the mid-19th century.

In recent years the most powerful of these movements to affect Little Gaddesden is judged by many to be the Christian Stewardship campaign, a national movement which reached our Parish Church in 1967.

A small team of village people was enthused with the idea, and communicated it through the village with the effect of richly enlivening the church for a generation. The message was put across by Ken Dickson, who was chairman of stewardship, a position which he found himself, with some surprise, undertaking on the instigation of the Rector, Howard Senar, and in which he soon became passionately involved.

EXTRACTS FROM KEN DICKSON'S EXPOSITION OF STEWARDSHIP

We are seeking to tap the very real inner strength of our Parish, so that its spirit may be released to transform our lives here, and, through our Church, to transform our contribution to God's work in the world outside.

........Each of us, we suggest, should reconsider what is the proportion of our Time, and our Abilities, and our Money, we should give back to God to help the needs of others.

.....in our Christian Stewardship Brochure .... we have set out the Parish Programme of work that we should like to undertake. ...(including) two causes outside the Parish that we are particularly keen to support.

In our Brochure is a Questionnaire. It covers a variety of simple but worthwhile ways in which you can give practical help in the Parish. Please complete this with careful thought, perhaps treating it as a starting point for further service.

Church Stewardship brochure cover designed by Dorothea Patterson in 1967

Our feelings are that the use of ALL our money, and ALL our resources of time and abilities should reflect conscious thought and prayer, directed towards using the means at our disposal as God himself would have us use them. Surely, that is the path towards real contentment and personal fulfilment.

.... Our hope is that as a result of our Campaign there will be a greater realisation of the responsibilities as well as the privileges of being a Christian. We hope that a new and deeper spirit may be developed and fostered; also that even today, when man's technological achievement produces a mirage of self sufficiency, we may bear witness to a true and living Faith.

The campaign did in truth transform the lives of many, and brought new life to the church. It was the starting point of many of the activities which continue in the church today. There have been a number of lesser campaigns for more specific needs since, with successes of their own kind, but none with such breadth or far-reaching consequences in terms of lasting personal commitment.

Bell-ringing

by Roger Turner

The story of bell-ringing in Little Gaddesden begins in 1976. Some money had become available for a project which the then rector Canon Howard Senar had been advocating since he came to the parish in 1962. In March 1976 he asked me to form a ringing band and we practised at Great Gaddesden during the summer and in the autumn began an association with Langleybury Church ringers which was to last for eighteen months while Taylors of Loughborough put together a ring of six bells.

No.1, the treble, was a new bell cast in 1977 the year of the Queen's Silver Jubilee; No 2 was the larger of the two bells already hanging in the tower, re-cast; nos. 3 – 6 were a ring of four from St. Nicholas' Chellington, a redundant Bedfordshire church transformed into a Diocesan Residential Youth Centre. Nos. 4 and 5 were re-cast but 3, cast in 1654 and 6, the tenor, cast in about 1450, didn't need re-casting, making our tenor one of the oldest ringing bells in the country. The chiming bell is the smaller of the two bells already in the tower which were cast by John Briant of Hertford in 1820. The bells weigh between three and six hundredweight each (150 to 300 Kg) and sound in the key of B flat. They were given in memory of Margaret Elizabeth Griffiths, one time senior history mistress at Berkhamsted Girls' School, who lived at No 25 on the Green.

Before the bells were brought from Loughborough to Little Gaddesden a frame to receive them had to be constructed within the tower, the whole task taking Ged Flatters from Taylors and George Catchpole, Little Gaddesden Church Warden, a fortnight, with help on the day the bells were hauled into the frame (March 6th 1978) from Jack Pannell and Vic Mountfort. The latter is still one of our ringers.

The bells were tried out on March 9th, less than three weeks before Easter where they would be officially rung for the first time by the unaided local band. I have to say that the new light and easy ring caused problems as we had become used to a heavier and less easy ring at Langleybury. But this is all history and a photo in the Ringing World of August 18th 1978 shows 18 ringers (aged 10 –90) and names a further six not in the photo. Six of those 24 still ring at Little Gaddesden twenty-one years later, including George Catchpole's son Ian, joined now by Ian's daughter Debbie.

During those early years we rang twice on Sunday as well as early on Easter Day, Ascension Day and the Patronal Festival; we would go on outings and attend District Meetings. The attraction of a new ring brought many visitors. Over the years ringers have come and gone. Douglas Ball moved to Aldbury and in no time at all Aldbury had a new ring of six, though of course their tone is not as good as Little Gaddesden's. The attraction to outsiders of a bright new ring has fallen away somewhat; in the 80s we would host over 60 to tea when the District Meeting came to us; now the number is nearer 30. One unbroken tradition is ringing in the New Year as we shall in 2000.

It was a sad day when George died during a ringing practice in September 1988. He took over as Tower Captain (remaining Steeple Keeper) when I left the village in 1983, but I took over again in 1988 and Vic Mountfort took over as Steeple Keeper. I handed over the Tower Captaincy to Virginia Westmacott, one of the original new band, in 1996.

In preparation for the millennium she energetically sent out a call for new ringers; four have responded and are making excellent progress. We still ring every Sunday morning when there is a service and, on Tuesdays, are greatly helped at practice by ringers from outside the village, some of whom have been sharing their expertise with us for many years.

The ringers remain a lively group within the church community and we hope that whoever writes this article in the 2100 Little Gaddesden book will be able to tell a similar story.

The recast bell number 4. Its note is D and it weighs 5cwt 1qr 23lb

Hudnall Methodist Church

by David Williamson

(Summarised from 'The Dunstable Methodist *Grail*' 1843 - 1993 with the permission of Rev David Jenkins, Superintendent Minister of the Dunstable Circuit)

A Methodist congregation worshipped in Hudnall Village continuously from 1838 to 1989 although there is a record of services being held as far back as 1813. The early congregations worshipped in barns, farm kitchens, cart sheds, a limehouse, a bake house and a butcher's shop at the back of Mr Purton's house. For a period of nearly 2 years, (around 1874) after the Lord of the Manor of Ashridge (Adelbert, 3rd Earl Brownlow) acquired the farm where they met and turned them out of the barn on his land, the small flock met in the open on Hudnall Common in all weathers.

Eventually, in 1888, Lord Brownlow was persuaded, in the face of opposition from the Established Church, to allow the Methodists to rent a piece of land and build a wooden chapel. It was to be erected as much out of sight as possible

The "Chapel in the Wood" at Hudnall Common

ABOVE LEFT
At the opening of the new Hudnall Methodist Church-

BACK ROW
Emily Whitman, (wife of Frederick - builder of the church), Annie Jones, Ann Munden, another Jones, May Whitman, Nell Munden, Reg Purton (nephew of Sarah Purton), Kit Purton (Reg's wife)

FRONT ROW
Sarah Purton, Jubal Jones, Mrs Wells.

ABOVE RIGHT
The Methodist Church in Hudnall Lane, opened 1940, closed 1989

BELOW
Leslie Boarder in 1989

and it became known as 'The Chapel in the Wood', sited along Hudnall Common. There was seating for 60 adults and 40 children, with an allowance of 18 inches per sitting (bottoms were smaller in those days!). Mrs Sarah Purton ensured that oil lamps and a fire were lit well before the services began, to provide an atmosphere of cozy warmth on cold dark days, when many walked from Little Gaddesden and Ringshall to the services. Many took their tea and stayed between services. When the kettle boiled, it was time to finish the afternoon service. (Services were held at 2 pm, 6 pm and, on Tuesday, 7 pm.) Loyal service was given over many years by families - the Boarders, Hoars, Jones, Mundens, Purtons, Wells and the Whitmans.

The Chapel in the Wood was the centre of Methodist worship for 50 years. After the Ashridge estate was broken up land was acquired in Hudnall Lane, and valiant efforts were made to raise funds for a new brick-built chapel and school hall. Many events were held in the Tithe Barn on Mr Hoar's farm near the old chapel. Much support came from other churches in the Dunstable circuit.

Eventually work was started. The foundation stone laying ceremony took place on Whit Monday 1939. The building was erected by Mr Fred Whitman from a long established local Methodist family. The new church was formally opened on Good Friday 1940 and the school room in 1947.

The new location had brought the church across the boundary out of Hudnall into Little Gaddesden. The sign outside, at any rate in later years, announced 'Hudnall and Little Gaddesden Methodist Church'. In the early years congregations were large and new families, like the Dawsons, kept the light of faith burning. But, as the old members died and families moved away, new members did not come to take their place. Membership declined in later years and, sadly, it had to be decided to close the church which had opened with such high hopes and so much sacrifice. 50 years after the stone laying, the closing service took place on 19 March 1989. This service was conducted by Mr Les Boarder, a Methodist local (lay) preacher from one of the founder families.

It is fitting that a lay preacher should have conducted this service. The whole history of Methodism in Hudnall is a witness to the power of the spirit among folk lacking in money, power and influence, and who had to struggle against those who had all three. Perhaps the Holy Spirit works best in people facing adversity. (Les Boarder died in November 1999.)

Ashridge House and College

by Kay Sanecki

10

Ashridge can look back over its 700 year history with a certain amount of accuracy but no period has been as active as the last century. A hundred years ago the house and estate were revelling in a heyday of splendour and liveliness providing employment for many local families and entertainment for royalty and the aristocracy. Cottages and schools were maintained in good repair and the Earl and Countess Brownlow took a benevolent interest in all their tenants. The lofty halls of the house and extensive gardens provided the venue for innumerable social events. The woods and commons were rich in game and both H.M. King Edward VII and H.M. King George V joined regularly in shooting parties. Ashridge was famous for well-known herds of both red and fallow deer and a variety of game birds was maintained for sport.

Hosts and visitors had just reason to expect the imperialistic splendour of England and the British Empire to continue unimpeded, and the measured roll of the seasons to sustain country life. Lord and Lady Brownlow divided their time between Ashridge, their London home and Belton, their estate in Lincolnshire, so it was not surprising that when war broke out in 1914 Lady Brownlow devoted much time to the newly formed Red Cross, turning part of Ashridge into a convalescent home for troops and Belton into a Red Cross Hospital. It is generally accepted that her concern and anxieties over that work led to her death in 1917, following which the Earl lost much of his interest in his estate. Col. Wheatley, his agent, continued to work on the estate and farms and managed the business affairs.

Locally, the account of the Earl's unexpected death (1921) is well known. It followed his investiture by King George V as a Knight Grand Cross of the Royal Victorian Order for his wartime services. He suffered a heart attack on his return to Belton from Buckingham Palace. There followed for the Ashridge estate a period of inactivity and decline, and for the local residents an acute sense of loss and insecurity. Lord Brownlow's executors organised a series of sales and the estate was put on the market. Local residents led by Miss Bridget Talbot, niece to the Countess Brownlow, launched a campaign, supported by the Prime Minister and his Cabinet, to raise funds sufficient to enable the National Trust to purchase part of the estate to maintain in perpetuity and to prevent it from being broken up and developed. The Ashridge woodland was the first established timber to be bought by the National Trust. To this day the Trust continues a policy of buying back parts of the original estate as they come onto the market. Herein lies the core of the overwhelmingly lovely surrounding area – so close to London - that we all enjoy today. Several local residents own properties with deeds dating back to the 1920s where areas of the estate were sold piecemeal.

An excellent neighbour relationship has since been maintained between the National Trust and the College (as the house became). One of their Regional Land Agents, Richard Wheeler has served on our Grounds Committee since its inception seventeen years ago, and the Ashridge Gardens Manager, Michael Thompson has, for some time, been a member of the National Trust Ashridge Estate Committee. When the National Trust celebrated the centenary of its foundation in 1995 the local members of the Thames and Chiltern Region attended a gala dinner at Ashridge. In the same year the College and the Trust joined to inaugurate a Summer School for garden historians at Ashridge, which continues to be run annually.

In the 1920s the house itself was stripped of almost everything that could be removed. Sothebys organised a series of sales, and today many local families have artefacts

ABOVE
The library in 1900 - 1910

RIGHT
Lord and Lady Brownlow in 1914. Next to Lady Brownlow are Mrs Wheatley, Colonel Wheatley and their two daughters.

acquired from the estate at that time. Undoubtedly the greatest loss to the building was the sale of the stained glass windows from the chapel. They had consisted of 109 panels of sixteenth century German glass brought to England by Wyatville from the Bavarian monastery of Steinfeld for this chapel in 1817. Rich in colour the panels represented biblical scenes. At the auction they were bought entirely by a Mr. Crook who donated them immediately to the Victoria & Albert Museum. For many years they have lain in store, unexamined and undervalued, but local interest has been stimulated during the last decade principally due to the enthusiasm of Mr Francis Cory-Wright of Little Gaddesden. The panels are now beautifully displayed in Galleries 116 and 117 of the Museum.

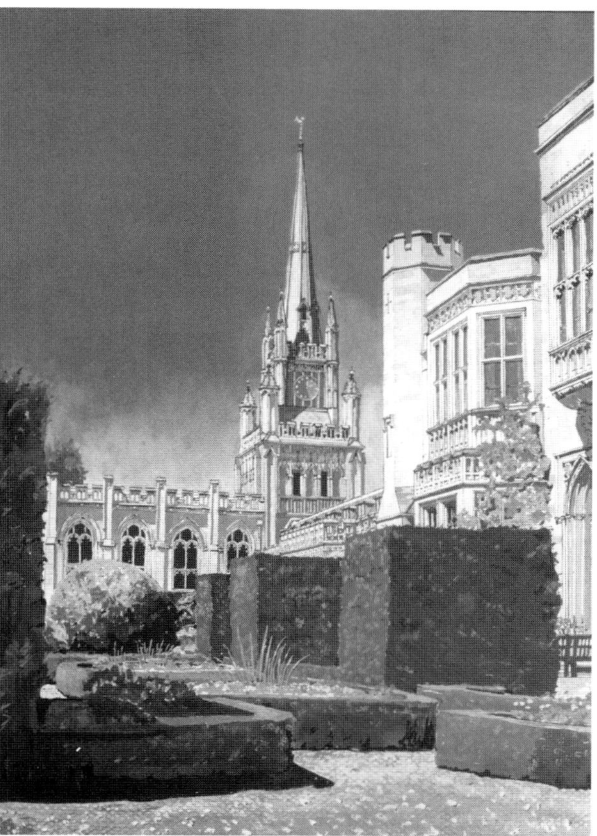

A painting by Teddy Cusdin

In the Ashridge Chapel, a place of great beauty and craftsmanship, the remaining treasure is the organ, a two-manual instrument set into Wyatville's lovely oak casing. Built by Thomas Elliott of Tottenham Court, London and installed about 1818 it now remains of considerable historic importance. Mr Arthur Kibby who joined the College in the 1920s was the College organist for some fifty years and has been followed by Mr. Alan Johnson. Recitals are arranged by visiting organists and a fair number of organ enthusiasts come to appreciate its period value. During a recent restoration of the organ (1990) a Brother from the Steinfeld monastery visited Ashridge. He was in England to trace the whereabouts of all the glass that had been sold in the early nineteenth century. His interest in the window glass fled when he saw the organ. It transpired that he is an organist who gives recitals all over Europe and his enthusiasm for the Ashridge organ knew no bounds. He spent some hours with the organ restorers as they worked.

The story of the purchase of the building and garden in 1928 by Mr Urban Hanlon Broughton is well known locally. His donation of it to the Conservative Party, together with the setting up of the Bonar Law Memorial Trust forged the foundation of the College. From 1928 until the outbreak of war in 1939 the Conservative Party inhabited a somewhat threadbare building to train prospective Conservative Parliamentary candidates and Party workers and run general courses. To adapt a building that was without electricity and had only two basic bathrooms, the architect Clough Williams-Ellis was called in. He updated the kitchens and laundry, converted the conservatory that ran between the house and the chapel to be a dining hall, installed telephone boxes in the front hall and lit the main tower hall adding lamp shades of which Miss Bridget Talbot disapproved strongly. Her account of some of the work (which is in the Ashridge Archives) expresses horror at the 'cocktail bar lamp shades'. They remain to this day!

Miss Talbot was affronted by the way the purchase of the house had been negotiated but whatever the facts, the setting up of the Bonar Law Memorial Trust was an astute move and while the Trust itself has been augmented during the intervening years, Ashridge is still guided by the administration of this fund set up in the 1920s. The stated intention of the Deed of Trust was to 'preserve the building and grounds for England'. Thus, over the years, mainly since the 1960s, repair and restoration has been a responsible on-going programme. In a building of this kind, faced with a soft chalk-based Totternhoe stone, there is a constant need for restoration work to the fabric of the building and to the roof. Over the years the outward profile has changed in that almost every tall chimney has been dismantled. In 1922 immediately following Earl Brownlow's death, the stone chapel spire was removed; it was considered to be unsafe. A fibreglass replica spire was put into place on 6th June 1969, positioned by a Wessex helicopter, that for a couple of days beforehand had practised the operation on Dunstable Downs. (Recently the pilot of the helicopter, John Tighe has written to Ashridge to say that although today it is unremarkable to see equipment being transported in this way, the operation for the Ashridge spire represented one of the first exercises in which a helicopter was used to lift and move a large object).

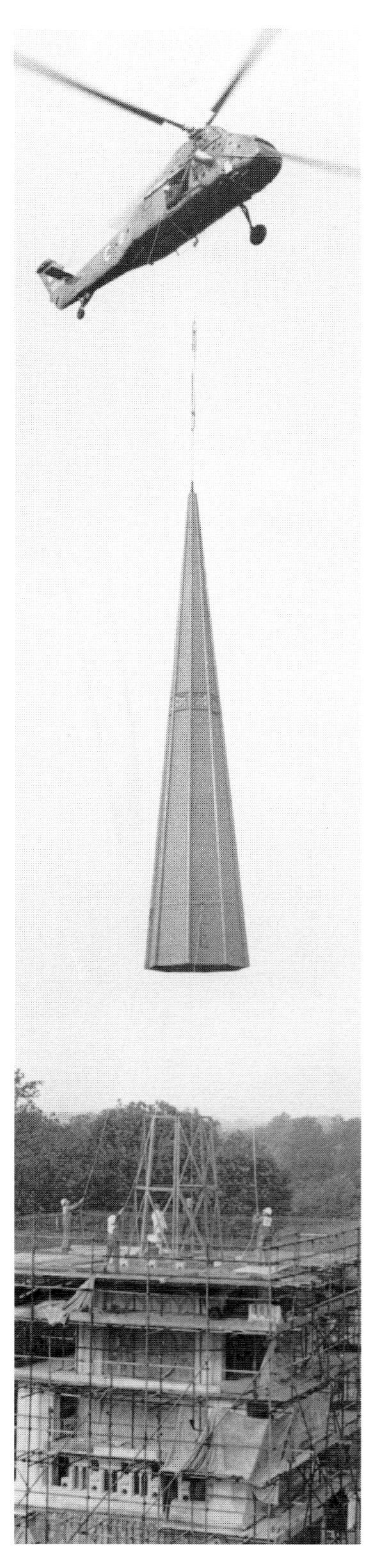

The new fibreglass spire being guided on to the steel frame.

THE BONAR LAW COLLEGE

The Bonar Law College opened its doors formally on lst July 1929 when the title deeds were handed over to Mr Stanley Baldwin, the Prime Minister, by Lord Fairhaven in the presence of more than a thousand people. (Lord Fairhaven was the son of Urban Hanlon Broughton and remained a College governor for many years.) A month later the first course was run. Behind the thinking was the intent to widen horizons not only for the Conservative Party workers, but for the general public – a further education initiative as it might be regarded today. It was Mr. J. C. C. Davidson, M.P. for Hemel Hempstead, (later Viscount Davidson) whose visionary ideas and tireless work behind the scenes infused the drive and will to establish the College. It soon became evident that the idea of residential short courses appealed and by the early 1930s 2-3000 people attended the Ashridge programmes during the course of a year. Generally accepted to have been run on a shoestring the weekend courses cost 3 guineas and the full week £7. There was a skeleton administrative staff (and three typewriters) and both the Principal, Major General Sir Reginald Hoskins and his wife worked hard. Guest speakers were brought in, and the Ashridge tradition of working beyond the doors in a wider world was started.

Founded in 1930 by General Hoskins the Principal, Arthur Bryant and Captain Henry Gordon, the Bursar, the Ashridge Fellowship came into being. It enabled visiting lecturers and students to maintain contact by occasional meetings and the Ashridge Journal. Tours were organised, one to Canada and another to the West Indies, while a third to the Baltic was cancelled prior to the outbreak of war in 1939. The Fellowship continued until 1959 when it ceased to exist, but the idea, modernised in intent, was re-established as the Ashridge Association in 1972. Delegates and tutors confer from time to time in

Major-General Sir William Hoskins, Principal, with a group of delegates including Enoch Powell, (back right) in 1932.

workshops and seminars at Ashridge, and maintain contact by an on-going series of meetings and social events.

It is thought-provoking to look back to the early days of the Bonar Law College when a Pensions Scheme for which 17 members of staff were eligible was set up whereby full-time male employees (21-57 years) in receipt of salaries in excess of £350 per annum were eligible and female employees (25-53 years) who had completed three years continuous service were included. The changes in administrative staff, together with the encumbrance of the large building and the gathering clouds of war prompted the Trustees to offer Ashridge to the Ministry of Health for use as a hospital.

ABOVE
The 1940 hospital buildings, used after the war for education and then as part of the Public Records Office until 1982

BELOW LEFT
General Eisenhower reviewing the Eleventh Hussars in woods at Ashridge in 1944.

ASHRIDGE HOSPITAL

In the autumn of 1939 the house was accepted for use as an emergency hospital. The majority of the 20,000 patients that passed through were civilians transferred through the London hospitals – Charing Cross, University College and Queen Elizabeth. At first beds were taken into the main rooms of the house, but very quickly 29 concrete huts were built on the open parkland to the north of the house and the first patients there were 500 of the wounded from the beaches of Dunkirk in May 1940.

Upwards of 2000 people claim to have been born at Ashridge between 1940 and 1946 and as many as 12,000 operations were performed. The main house served as residential quarters for doctors and nurses and to this end, the beautiful orangery by Sir Jeffry Wyatville (1821) was gutted and rebuilt to provide single rooms. The main hall, suitably blacked out, served as a reception area and canteen, and the cellars and crypt served as stores – and air raid shelters. All the catering was in the capable hands of the Jarvis family who served Ashridge from the first days of the Bonar Law College until the late 1980s. Captain Gordon,

The road through the Public Record Office huts and Dan, the Boxer dog of the Assistant Keeper of Records - Jeffery Ede - in 1951

who was the College Bursar, stayed on during the War to guard the interests of the College and gradually to serve as hospital administrator. After the war he was asked to go back to London with Charing Cross Hospital, but elected to stay at the College.

The deep woodland of the Ashridge estate provided cover for several army camps, and the Home Guard during the course of hostilities and certainly during the build up to the 'second front' in 1944. For example the XIth Hussars and a Highland Division left there on 3rd June 1944 and landed at Juno beach in Normandy six days later. Local stories surface from time to time about the leaders, General de Gaulle, General Montgomery and General Eisenhower meeting at the house, but there seems little substantial evidence. The generals and others visited the camps and General de Gaulle certainly came to the hospital on several occasions to speak to the French wounded.

A huge water tank filled the area of kitchen court, and was used as a swimming pool during the 1940s and early 50s. Its true purpose was as a reserve water supply in the event of incendiary bombs falling on the roof.

In 1946 the house was returned to the Bonar Law Memorial Trust, once again in need of refurbishment and funds and the grid of concrete wards stood to the north of the building until 1982. Despite appeals to the appropriate government department, somehow funds were not available for them to uphold the terms of the contract whereby the land was to be returned in the condition in which it had been commandeered; that is parkland. In the days immediately following the war the Ministry of Education used some of the huts for a teacher training establishment named the Gaddesden Training College and under the supervision of the Hertfordshire Education Authority.

So for three years men and women demobilized from H.M. Forces were trained there, and subsequently the same buildings formed part of the Public Records Offices prior to its re-establishment at Kew. In the late 1960s and early 1970s a research Department for the College itself was originally housed in huts, first under Philip Sadler and then Dr. Bernard Barry.

Increasingly disadvantageous and an eyesore for the developing College – the huts were screened by trees planted in the 1950s – the retention of the huts as Crown Property meant that the through road from Little Gaddesden to Berkhamsted was closed. Traffic - such as it was in the mid-century – cars, horses and carts, motor bikes, emergency vehicles, all had to pass beneath the windows of the house and past the main entrance. In 1982 the huts were demolished and the through right-of-way was restored and a private College car park made and the College pitch and putt course laid out by Malcolm Lingard, the Head Gardener. Alongside is the cricket pitch which has served Little Gaddesden for many years.

THE GARDEN

One considerable advantage of garden neglect such as was evident during the first half of the century is that existing features do not get swept away. Today the garden is of considerable historic value and clearing and replanting operations of the 1960s and 70s here opened the way for genuine restoration in the last decade. To celebrate the Coronation of H.M. King George VI in 1937 an avenue of Liquidambar trees were planted, now mature and splendid, and limes replaced the ancient lime trees felled in 1952 to celebrate the Coronation of the present Queen. The famous circular rosarie (1821) has been totally restored in 1999 to celebrate the Millennium, now with its central fountain it is a magical place. The public are welcomed to the garden on weekend afternoons during the summer or by special arrangement.

THE STRUGGLE TO RE-ESTABLISH THE COLLEGE

The Governors' Minutes for the period 1947-1957 record the broad outline of the financial problems that beset the post war era. Under the Chairmanship of Lord Davidson, whose determination and foresight carried it through the Ashridge Management College was ultimately established with the first course running in April 1959. The property was in 1952 offered to the National Trust with the idea that the College would be the tenant. When the response was received that the National Trust would be interested and would require an endowment of £80,000, the College Governors decided that if the National Trust considered that to be sufficient, then they could manage on that sum and the offer of the property was withdrawn. How different the subsequent history of the College and of the site would have been and while the present Trustees and Governors would be the first to admit the enormous responsibility of the maintenance of the building, now 190 years old, the development of the site would have been restricted.

Direct appeals were made for financial help to some of the larger companies in 1949. Letting was discussed, or closing during the winter months and various fund-raising schemes. Miss Dorothy Neville-Rolfe was invited by the Governors to bring her establishment The House of Citizenship here. This was a superior finishing school for young ladies – subsequently housed at Hartwell House, near Aylesbury. So from January 1950 paying the rent and running alongside Ashridge business management courses the House of Citizenship helped to allow the College to assemble both funds and personnel to establish what was to become a world leader in its field forty years later.

The 1821 Rosarie in Ashridge garden, restored in 1999

ASHRIDGE TODAY

Ashridge differs from most business schools and management colleges in that it no longer adheres to the 'talk and chalk' or case study approaches to teaching. Long ago the introduction of a somewhat hilarious and even formidable business game stamped an individuality upon the Ashridge approach. 'Exercise Command' for example devised by a senior tutor, Fred Keay, in the late 1960s brought staff and delegates together in frenzied competition. Today, the College has crossed the lawns to undertake outdoor learning activities far removed from the business environment, to clear away inhibitions and disconnect thought channels, as it were. Recently a group of managers were given the task of coaching the West Indies cricket team, and others were persuaded to sing duets with a pop group – there is a need to relate and to see the other point of view!

But, of more serious intent, while the radical thinking remains to be executive education in the broadest sense, untold avenues have been opened up by consultancy activities. Some £4 million per annum is generated from this source. Research, as might be expected, is a continuous commitment with three Centres working individually and accruing something in the order of £1 million per annum, while tailored and open courses account for about £16 million. Herein lies the daily bread, as it were, but for the past ten years Ashridge has provided its own MBA degree (Master of Business Administration) and is actively seeking degree awarding status. This may take some time, but it is indicative of the ever-widening prospects and the ever-consolidating achievements Ashridge works towards. Maintaining its individuality is an important ingredient and this does not necessarily rely upon the attractive house and unrivalled surroundings (all of which have to be maintained). Its uniqueness has been demonstrated for example in its pioneering of a consultancy project as a core part of the MBA Programme – an idea more recently copied by some of the US business schools.

Recently (1998) Ashridge was accredited by EQUIS – The European Quality Improvement Scheme, organized by the European Foundation for Management Development. Further, an independent survey of executive education devised by the Financial Times in May 1999 rated Ashridge into the top place in the UK tied with Cranfield Management School. The same survey listed it as third in Europe and seventh in the world. On the international stage Ashridge is a recognized player and is at present actively seeking to strengthen this position. For many years it has been working in Europe with a strong involvement in Germany and has done pioneering work in Eastern Europe, notably the Czech Republic. For this latter assignment Edgar Wille was awarded the Order of the British Empire in 1999. Joint programmes exist with other Colleges of cognate aims in USA (Duke, Michigan and Cornell), with Monash Mount Eliza in Australia and more recently with Stellenbosch in South Africa. Undoubtedly the future is being designed to work away from the home base with the avowed intent of becoming a leading world player. Such ever-widening involvements stem from a point in 1982 when the charter for the Deed of Trust was amended to allow Ashridge tutors, consultants and administrators to work internationally rather than all the delegates having to travel to Berkhamsted. This favoured multi-national companies and reduced the strain on the already seam-splitting building.

The Learning Resource Centre constructed in 1989. The 1913 frescoes were conserved. (See page 22, and page XV in the colour section)

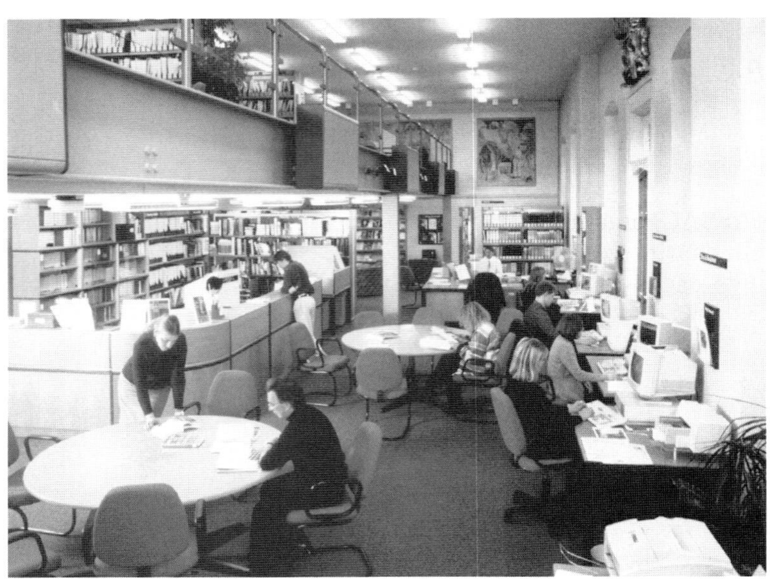

Building development began in 1970 and continued for twenty years. With such a proud Grade I listed building tampering is taboo, and extensions and renovations have to be approached particularly sensitively and mindful of local planning policies. Almost all the work is undertaken by Ashridge's own maintenance teams led by Buildings Manager, Mick Blackborough. Local residents frequently express surprise when they realize the extent of the development because from passing along the road through Ashridge Park it is judiciously screened by National Trust woodland. Coach houses, stables, servants' hall, workshops and gardeners' sheds have all been transformed with particular attention to the retention of outward characteristics under the careful eye of the College architect, Derek Rogers of Tring.

Central to the development is the Learning Resource Centre – (far too technical to be referred to as a Library!) – built in 1989 within the shell of the old servants' hall. As the century turns that is to be developed and expanded again at a projected cost of £1 million into the shell of what was the original monastic barn built in 1480, and in spite of changes over the years still retaining the majority of the structural internal beams. Ashridge can claim justifiably to work at the forefront of learning technology based on the substantial traditions of its surroundings.

Tommy Forrester's Christmas card design

The Learning Resource Centre – 'State of the Art Centre' – supports the information and learning requirements of the Ashridge staff and delegates. It houses a range of external and internal databases, books and audio-visual collections to the extent of 80 thousand items. Acknowledged as one of the primary business information centres in the UK it is managed by Andrew Ettinger, Director of Learning Resources. In 1998 he was voted European Business Librarian of the Year by the European Business Schools Librarians Group. The award is sponsored by Information Access, a British company.

Other business awards have come to Ashridge recently such as Investors in People in 1995 renewed in 1998. Then in the same year the Booker Prize for Excellence for the best specialist caterer was collected by Graham Rusling, Food Production Manager.

LINKS WITH LITTLE GADDESDEN

Ashridge does not only receive awards, it makes them from time to time. In the summer of 1999 four local Junior Schools were invited to enter a competition to design a Christmas card for Ashridge. Thousands of our cards go out to many parts of the world, and it was felt that we should recognize the children whose lives are on the threshold of a new century. Many designs of high quality came in and were judged by professional people from outside. The winner was Tommy Forrester from Little Gaddesden Church of England Primary School. He received his award and the school gained a computer of their choice. It is a matter of some delight that this link with the village has emerged from the competition.

The Ashridge Sports and Social Activities Club (ASSAC) organises a very wide variety of events for staff and their families, all charity based. So through sponsorship and fund raising thousands of pounds each year are donated to various charities.

ASPIRING ARCHES

During the past three and a half years a strong link of friendship and common purpose between Little Gaddesden and Ashridge has been forged among embroiderers who have helped to create a mighty fabric wall-hanging. In celebration of the Millennium, coupled with the 40th anniversary of the Management College – from those shaky beginnings in 1959 – a wall hanging was hung and unveiled on 15th November 1999. It was designed and created by Wendy Dolan and Jae Maries, professional fabric artists. It measures 8.5m by 3.5m and represents many elements of the building in a lively design and stunningly rich colours. Its purpose is to celebrate the beauty of the building and the vibrancy of the life within it, but moreover to create something for the year 2000 that we can leave for the generations that will follow. It is impossible to know the interior of this building without marvelling at some of the rich craftsmanship and we felt, humble embroiderers as we might be, that we ought to provide something of our time. The handworked 76 elements of the border of the hanging and much of the hand stitching embellishment on the panel was done by ladies from Little Gaddesden, Ashridge staff and retired staff. It was due to Mrs Pat Catchpole of Ringshall, who lived at Ashridge as a child, that the Little Gaddesden embroiderers took part. Without their enthusiasm and loyal attendance at workshops over three years we would have been struggling to complete the work. They and their guests joined us for the unveiling ceremony and a champagne celebration when Michael Osbaldeston, the Chief Executive, unveiled the work. Many other members of the Ashridge staff contributed a few stitches so that about 80 people in all have the satisfaction of leaving something for posterity in recognition of the stimulating and rewarding ambience in which we live and work.

Ashridge once again houses a lively society, as it did a century ago, a society and organisation that looks to the future but acknowledges the labour and skills of the past.

The embroiderers with their completed work "Aspiring Arches"

LEFT TO RIGHT

LEFT HAND SIDE

BACK:
Ann Wallis, Elizabeth Draiden, Carol Long, Virginia Westmacott, Margrit Bennet, Jackie Hodgson

MIDDLE:
Judi Hartley, Rosemary Gardham, Una Covernton, Margaret Spavins, Kay Sanecki, Jae Maries

FRONT:
Mavis Blofield, Albertine Shaw, Marilyn Blenkins, Jen Roberts, Jenny Birks, Christina Thompson

RIGHT HAND SIDE

BACK:
Margaret Green, Irene Dell, Ann Hunt, Christine Brown, Ina Smith

MIDDLE:
Wendy Dolan, Barbara Madgwick, Dorothea Patterson, Margaret Jones, Sheelah Wray, Dorothy Reed

FRONT:
Pat Catchpole, Anita Johnson, Jill Monger, Lynn Cox, Cherry Nash, Jill Waghorn

CHAPTER 11 - *Educational establishments*

Our Church of England School

A GEM IN LITTLE GADDESDEN'S CROWN

by Ken and Jane Dickson

THE ETHOS OF THE SCHOOL

The school prayer makes this clear:

O Lord, bless our school;
That, working together and playing together
We may learn to serve you
And to help one another.

There has been a constant spiritual presence in the school assisted not only by a succession of Rectors and Priests, but also by Headteachers, Staff and Governors appointed not only on merit but as practising Christians. Two of our Heads, Vicars Bell and John Prior, were subsequently ordained to the Ministry. A succession of former pupils have gone on to serve others in many ways and places. All involved in the day to day running of the school have sought to help the children develop in mind, body and spirit. In addition there is spiritual and practical support from the Diocesan Director of Education and his Team.

BELOW
A school class in 1898

BOTTOM
Samuel Green, teacher at the village school from 1863 and Head from 1896, retired 1914

THE EARLY BACKGROUND

At the beginning of the 20th Century, the school was under the patronage of the Brownlow family of Ashridge. They were dedicated to the enrichment of life of all on the estate. Under the supervision of the School Managers, the Headmaster Samuel Green and his staff ran the school with the Rector much involved. It is surprising that the number of children in the school – which occupied the church-like buildings – was roughly the same as now with all our facilities – 100!

Log Book entries are revealing: Saturday 19 January 1907: "Lord and Lady Brownlow kindly gave the children a school treat. The children and the teachers met at the school at 3 o'clock and reached Ashridge at 3.15. A tea was awaiting them, and after tea a conjuring performance. All then went into the Grand Entrance where a ship was made to sail in with presents for all. Lord and Lady Brownlow were most kind in personally seeing that the children enjoyed themselves."

29 May 1907: "As a tribute to Empire Day, the Rector and Mr Whitely, a School Manager, spoke to the children on the duty of patriotism, and respect and loyalty for the flag, and all then sang the National Anthem. Each child was given a medal, and there was a half holiday."

Children stayed at school until they were 14 and then started work. The curriculum was aimed at giving an understanding of what was required to live in a rural community. Lessons were designed to develop practical skills and to help children gain an understanding of nature and the locality.

In 1908, the syllabus contained lessons in:

1 Hygiene
2 Conversation and the correct addressing of people by Speech and Letter.
3 History – The Houses of Parliament, King, Lords and Commons.

4 Patriotism – The King's Army and the King's Navy
5 A Loaf of Bread – Sowing, Reaping and Baking.
6 Milk – Animals from which we obtain it – Butter and Cheese.
7 Bees.
8 Cultivating Vegetables.
9 Growth of Plants from Seeds – Rooting, Grafting etc.
10 Easy Flowers and Fruits to grow in a Cottage Garden.
11 Insects and Birds useful to us.
12 The Countryside – Seasonal Walks through Lanes, Fields and Woods.
13 Noxious Animals and Vermin.

The school in about 1920

In addition there were practical lessons in handwork and gardening and, for girls, needlework and cookery.

The teaching of the Christian Faith, under the guidance of the Rector, had a high priority. Diocesan Inspectors regularly tested the children on the Bible and the Prayer Book. Learning of poems and songs and reciting and singing them were important teaching methods. When harvest came the children were required to provide extra labour. The local farmer advised the Head when the children were wanted and the summer holiday was then taken. The children could also be called on to pick fruit and to collect fallen wood after gales.

They walked to school in all weathers and some walked miles each way. In severe winters, snow prevented some from reaching school. Attendance could also be much reduced by childhood illnesses such as whooping cough, measles, chicken pox, mumps and scarlet fever. In hard winters it was a battle to keep the school warm. In March 1928 the temperature in the large room once dropped to an all-time low of 31·0°F. The children must have been a tough lot, because it is only in September 1935 that an entry appears: "Adequate heating at last!"

THE 1914 – 18 WAR

On 31 July 1914, Samuel Green retired after 50 years teaching at the school, the last 18 as Headmaster. He had also been church organist, choirmaster, and Sunday school teacher. He had married, in 1883, Fanny Worall, daughter of John Worall, the previous and first Headmaster. Douglas Harrison succeeded Samuel Green. At first there was little sign of the war impacting on the school. There are occasional references in the Log Book: "Two of the staff Miss Wright and Miss Andrews (later Mrs Drewitt) attended an exam in ambulance work and nursing." In October 1915, the County Council asked the school to make economies. The Head took advantage of October 21st that year –Trafalgar Day – to address the whole school. Then on 5 June 1916 the Headmaster, Douglas Harrison, went off to join the army. There is a later reference to him coming back to see the children as Lieutenant D. Harrison of the 14th Battalion Essex Regiment.

The Head who took over from Douglas Harrison,

Pictured below - the school group from 1920

TOP ROW
Florence White, Unnamed boy, Les Mead, Pelham Oakins, Alec Saunders, George Wright, Albert Clark, John Phillips

MIDDLE ROW, SEATED
Doris Fountain(later Cocks), Frances Thame, Cicely Mead, unnamed girl, unnamed girl, Rose Oakins, Mrs Dora Drewitt, Robert Hobbs (standing)

BOTTOM ROW
unnamed boy, George Halsey, unnamed boy, unnamed boy, Alec Andrews

until he returned after the war, was Miss Winifred Sapsford. There is no doubt that she was excellent. Among other things she developed a good relationship with the "V.A.D. Hospital at Ashridge" to which gifts from the children of eggs, carrots and beetroot were given. The last H.M.I. report on her work at the school dated 11 November 1918 noted that: "The Mistress temporarily in charge during the absence of the Headmaster on war service has filled the post with conspicuous success." She stayed on until the end of January 1919 to give Mr Harrison a chance to recover from his wounds.

In her fascinating book "The Ashridge Estate and Little Gaddesden", Doris Fenn (a former pupil and later pupil teacher at our school) tells of Douglas Harrison's return to school: "We were assembled in the large classroom and there was excitement in the senior class as we waited, and we kept standing up to look out of the windows. Mr Harrison was a tall sturdy man, and we were all very subdued as we saw him limping up the road.......There was some fear that he would be rather severe, but after a short talk the usual routine was followed. He chose a hymn and played the piano, as he had done a few years before. He was a good teacher......The highlight of his headship was the production of a musical comedy – "Golden Hair and the Three Bears".

It is obvious from the Log Book that his abdominal wound still troubled him, and could be why he left on 29 July 1921. He had been poorly during the month. His last comment was: "We close for Midsummer holidays. I finish my work with this entry as Headmaster of this school."

FIVE MORE HEADS IN THE NEXT SEVEN YEARS

Mr James Woolfall became Head on 6 September 1921 for two terms. The Diocesan Inspector's report November 1921 mentioned that under him the same good work was continuing. "A good and reverent tone prevailed in the school, and the whole atmosphere was refined".

Mr Albert Parker came on 1 May 1922. He changed the curriculum giving less time to Arithmetic and more to PT, Music and general information. The extra time for Music seemed to pay off as the children were first in the Little Gaddesden Music Festival. When examined on Religious Knowledge their work was "at a high level, and their best subject the New Testament."

When Mr Parker left on 31 August 1924, Mr William Jones took charge. An HMI report two months later stated: "The present Headmaster had taken action to improve weak points in mental arithmetic, spelling and handwriting, but there is good practical instruction in cookery, gardening and handicraft." There was great excitement when the film "Boadicea" was being "shot" at Ivinghoe in July 1926. The children paid several visits to watch it, and some were able to take part as "extras"! There was a good HMI report in July 1928 with praise for making use of the rural environment for teaching, and for the well-developed teaching of Cookery, Gardening and Woodwork. The good spirit between staff and pupils was noted. An application was made to the Herts County Council for a grant towards a hut for Woodwork and Cookery, which was in use by April 1929. The number on the roll, which had been steadily falling, was then just 50. Unfortunately, at

A school group from 1922

TOP ROW
Marion Hobbs, Pelham Oakins, Bill Clifton, Violet Oakins

MIDDLE ROW
Reggie ?, Nora Hobbs, Edna Saunders, Dolly Pinnock, Hilda Welling, Frank Welling, May Batchelor, Cissie Rogers

BOTTOM ROW
Harry Clifton, Olive Hoar, Ruby Batchelor, Nora Purton, Grace Welling, Pearl Batchelor, Madeline Thame, Arthur Clifton

the end of June 1929, Mr Jones died.

Mrs E.M. Jones was then appointed as a Supply Headteacher. During her 3 month stay there was an inspection by the Hertfordshire Agricultural Institute. Complete satisfaction was expressed at finding "the whole garden in such a clean and excellent condition with the crops healthy and promising in spite of the dry season."

THE VICARS BELL PERIOD 1929 – 1963

Everyone who knew Vicars Bell will agree he was different. He had original ideas – the log book for December 1 1930 entry reads: "started serving hot Horlicks milk to children during playtime, and attendance improved!" He dressed unconventionally, sometimes in shorts and an open neck shirt. Under his care the children blossomed and the school acquired more than a local reputation.

He had a gift for teaching English Literature and the English Language, enthralling the children with his own stories and his reading of prose and poetry and developing in them a rare knowledge and love of literature. He would sell his "old" books for a copper or two to encourage the reading of good stories. He was not in favour of the children "doing subjects". A lesson on English could easily slip into History or Geography. He would let the discussion evolve thus maintaining the interest and participation of the children. There was no set timetable, but each week included singing – mainly traditional English folksongs – and country dancing, for which his wife Dorothy played the piano. The children also enjoyed painting, pottery, crafts and mixed hockey.

Time was found during the school day for Drama. In August 1933, the school put on a potted version of "A Midsummer Night's Dream" in the Manor House garden, followed by a display of maypole and country dancing. About 200 parents and friends attended, enjoying "the loudest voiced Nick Bottom who ever appeared on any stage." When the play was performed again, in July 1962, the children concerned provided a never-to-be-forgotten performance of the play within a play, the tale of Pyramus and Thisbe.

The Nativity Play "That Night," which Vicars Bell wrote himself, was performed by the children year after year. It had a profound effect on them and the audience. Some words from the Foreword will show why: "This play is designed to move the hearts of men...The characters have been so conceived and created so that each member of the cast and the audience must be driven to see himself, and his own attitude to life, somewhere portrayed, and his own difficulties of belief and behaviour somewhere enacted......The purpose of the play is to convey not so much the Message of Christmas, but the Truth of Christmas. The plain, bare, awful truth of the incarnation, of the divine invasion of History. The play must be unstagey.....There is no room for prettiness....The players must feel that they are at home in that place where God is homeless, and all men are at home.... And finally, as far as the players are concerned, the right kind of piety will come, not from pious exhortation, but from the long discipline of detailed and painstaking rehearsal."

Uneasy with traditional ideas of strict, teacher-

The school in 1926/7

TOP ROW
Bill Clifton, Lynda Whitman, Nora Hobbs, Violet Oakins, Rose Oakins (later Marks), Marion Hobbs, Cicely Rogers (later Orange), Bob Austin, Alec Andrews, Frank Cleal

MIDDLE ROW
Irene Whitman, Lena Whitman, Ivy Thame, Min Andrews (later Catchpole), Pearl Batchelor (later Smith), Madeline Thame, Joyce Cleal, Ada Rogers (later Eginton), Grace Welling, Ruby Batchelor (later Barrett), May Batchelor (later Sears)

BOTTOM ROW
Gordon Welling, Ted Rogers, Harry Clifton, Jack? Austin, Tom Sear (Tim Sears), Sam Oakins, Frederick Sear (Sears), Steve Oakins, Bert Rogers.

imposed class discipline, Vicars Bell had his own ideas on helping the children develop their individual talents and potential and encouraging them to take a pride in working for themselves. As an early experiment, he left his class on their own for a whole morning; they were told that they were free to do what they liked - discipline was withdrawn! On that first occasion, out of a class of 29 only 9 seemed to have enjoyed it and as there was a great deal of noise and throwing of pellets, 11 left the classroom altogether and worked quietly in the cookery hut. In the afternoon the children eagerly discussed and analysed their behaviour and as a result Vicars Bell felt that they had drawn valuable conclusions about the nature of anti-social behaviour and authority. Subsequently, children benefited greatly from his unconventional methods, leaving our school able to learn independently and to approach new work with confidence. He started the practice of holding Open Days for the parents to come in and see their children's work. He also started the Annual Sports Day.

Vicars Bell

THE 1939 – 1945 WAR AND AFTER

Vicars Bell's biggest challenge came on Saturday 2 September 1939. With war imminent, 54 children and 4 teachers arrived, evacuated from Fleet Road School, Hampstead. This was supposed to be our full quota. Then on Sunday 3 September 1939, the day war was declared, he was phoned at 8.30am and advised a further 100 children and 7 teachers from Hogarth Road School, Chiswick were on the way. They arrived at 9.30am with no rations. With this influx of 193 children and 14 teachers, the local response was wonderful: "By 5.30pm we had requisitioned and obtained loans of food for 24 hours, converted the Boys' Convalescent Home at Hudnall and Benhay (Beaney) into hostels, and borrowed beds and bedding. The local helpers returned home for lunch at 6.00pm!"

Trenches were dug by British Legion volunteers to provide protection for the children against bombing. The school was then permitted to open again on Monday 11 September 1939. It was decided to divide the children into two groups, A and B, and to run the school on a two shift system. Group A under Vicars Bell operated from 9.00am to 12.30pm and Group B under Mr. Leo Kitchen, Head of Hogarth Road School, from 1.30 to

School group in 1930

BACK ROW
Bert Rogers, unnamed boy, Ken Page, unnamed boy, John Rogers

FIFTH ROW
Ray Hing, Ted Rogers, Steve Oakins, Geoffrey Drewitt, Gordon Welling, unnamed boy, Vincent Parham, Jack Austin

FOURTH ROW
Gordon Purton, Len Hing, Freda Whitman, Minnie Andrews, Ivy Thame, Nancy Jones, Ethyl Rogers, Ada Rogers, Amy Bristow, Betty King, Phyllis Whitman, Cyril Thame, George Purple, Jack Aylott

THIRD ROW
Arthur Whitman, Bill Duncan, Gilbert Stone, Billy Newman, unnamed boy, Ralph Parker, George Rogers

SECOND ROW
unnamed boy, unnamed boy, Irene Richardson, Phyllis Munden, Ruth Goodman, Valerie Hitchman, Beryl Abrahams, Joan Hing, Phyllis Gadsden, unnamed boy, Stan Purple

FRONT ROW
Billy White, Maurice Purton, Billy Duncombe, 3 unnamed boys, Jack Duncombe

4.30pm. Vicars Bell retained a lightly held and undefined control of the whole system. By November 1939, the use of three rooms at Denison House had been obtained, which enabled the school to be open all day as one school. The log book entry on 13 November 1939 states: "The school is running smoothly now, largely due to the spirit of co-operation of the London teachers. There are great gains on both sides both for country and town children. It should be recorded that many of the London children were verminous on arrival." It was some weeks before the school was given a clean bill of health. In December they had to vacate the rooms at Denison House but, by using two rooms at Benhay as classrooms, and with two classes in the (old) Village Hall and three in the school, things continued.

In April 1940 there were 184 on the roll. Vicars Bell and Mr. Foster (from Fleet Road) founded a Young Farmers' Club for senior children. They started with two does, a buck rabbit, a hen and chicks. In May, logbook entries mentioned: "Farmers' Club in full swing. Pig sty being built. Mr. Cuppage (Fleet Road) and V.B. joined the L.D.V". (Local Defence Volunteers later renamed the Home Guard). Also: "France fell. Six weaners bought for pig sty." In September 1940 Mr. Cuppage left to join the Royal Navy, numbers were up to 194 and bombs fell in the parish.

In March 1941 Vicars Bell was elected a Governor of the National Froebel Foundation, a highly regarded teacher training establishment. In April he noted: "string of bombs dropped on the line Kaim End – The Spinney, two too near the school to be pleasant!"

In January 1942, as the Young Farmers' Club had been so successful in every way including social, it was decided to form a Music Club meeting fortnightly. Miss Dorothy Erhart (piano) and other local professional players gave their services.

At 2.00am on 3 May 1943, the Village Hall was burnt down by a young arsonist. The Tool Shed was used as a kitchen and, with some food and utensils salvaged, 100 meals were served in school at 12 noon. Blitz cooking equipment arrived the next day but it was 12 months before the 'new', pre-fab school hall was finished. This was not only used for school dinners but also provided a facility for country dancing and the showing of films.

It is not surprising that by June 1944, Vicars Bell was showing the strain. It was aggravated by the unexpected recall to London of David Foster of Fleet Road School who had been his "right and left hands since 2 Sept 1939." Vicars Bell wrote in the Log: "No one could have had a more faithful and courageous colleague. I take a dim view of the London County Council who gave him 3 days notice and me none. I have cared for hundreds of L.C.C. children, lost two stones and gained some grey hairs. I think that they might have allowed me to get someone to replace him."

Entries in the Log became fewer. He was, though, able to record in March 1945: "The Music Club has had a successful start. One of the few encouraging things in life!" On 10 September 1945, because of staff illness, he had to cope with the whole school of 85, ages 5 – 14 plus. Then in January 1946, he lost the teaching services of Mrs. Drewitt (née Andrews) who had reached the retirement age of 60 years. A former pupil at the school, she had been a much respected, dedicated and loyal teacher. Fortunately things then began to look up. He engaged two first rate assistants: David Hughes, just demobilised from the army, and Miss A Macdonald to take charge of the infants. Numbers had fallen to 46 but he was confident that he could now build up the "educationally derelict school."

A poignant entry on 28 October 1946: "I am appealing to old scholars for a small memorial to William Newman (Flight Sergeant R.A.F.), Len Hing (Bombardier R.A.) and Ted Rogers (Beds & Herts Regt.) The former was killed in a crash at home, after completing many attacks over enemy territory. Len died of wounds received at Caen. Both these are buried in our churchyard. Ted died on the Burma Railway. They were good lads." There is no record of the outcome of this appeal.

February 1947 saw the country in the grip of frost and snow; there were 10 days of bitter weather. On one day we had 22 degrees of frost. Heavy snows and cold winds caused drifts on the roads, brought influenza and colds, and reduced attendance at school by 30%. Vicars Bell noted that "the children were showing the strain, and few looked well." He kept fires going at weekends. One day there was no one to cook school dinner. Vicars Bell and a few boys and girls started to do so. "Then two mothers arrived, and offers of help poured in." With Spring things improved; by April 1947 there were 54 on the roll. The 17th Annual Open Day on 23 July was a very successful and enjoyable day with 150 visitors, including mothers who had been children in the top class in the 1930's. In September the roll had increased to 63. Miss Louise Dunne joined the staff, later to become Mrs David Hughes.

Things continued uneventfully until June 1952. Then the builders arrived to add the existing flat roofed section providing a further two classrooms. A September 1952 entry: "Building goes on apace. We have curtains across the middle of the Hall. Mr Hughes has a class at one end, Miss Weetman a class at the other. Mud everywhere. A tough beginning for a new teacher. Miss Weetman shows great courage and determination. I continue in my old room, with builders all around me." The Bishop dedicated the new buildings on 11 June 1953.

When the Autumn Term started in September 1953 there were 89 on the roll. The staff then was Vicars Bell, David Hughes, and an Infant teacher, Miss Elizabeth (Beth) Taylor who restarted the teaching of weaving and basketry. Numbers peaked at 102 in January 1955, and seating became a problem. An indication of the success of the school, and its reputation nationally, was that during the 1950s both the London University Institute of Education and the Froebel Education Foundation sent parties of students to see our school. During the 1950s the school expanded to four classes and benefited from the use of the "new" village hall for Music, Drama and PE.

In his last log book entry, Vicars Bell wrote: "The staff and the children gave me a wrist watch when I left on 27 July 1963. This is my last entry, my first being in 1929. I leave with many regrets, and with grateful feelings towards the Hertfordshire Education Committee, who have always used me well. The only people I have consistently failed to please are H.M.Inspectors. They do not think I know what schooling is for. And the feeling is mutual."

In November 1999 Baroness McIntosh (née Genista Tandy), paid fitting tribute to Vicars Bell in her maiden speech in the House of Lords. "I was fortunate to attend a small village school...which was run by a head teacher of quite

I hardly noticed

until the flowers came
then field edges
hedgerows
banks, eiderdowned,

soft humps some white
some barely pink, as if
the palest flamingo butterfly

had trailed her wings
across their open petals
leaving only a promise
of colour;

leaves small pointed spears
disgorging largesse
wreathing it tight,

quilting the countryside.
Convolvulus, devils garters
bindweed...

Mary Blake

Baroness McIntosh of Hudnall

remarkable gifts. His name was Vicars Bell and in his day he was recognised as a significant contributor to educational thinking. I suspect that his methods, which were a bit chaotic, and perhaps did not always include sufficient attention to the 'Rithmetic bit of the 'Three Rs', would find little favour in today's bracing environment. But his greatness lay in his conviction that children could learn through exposure to the arts.

"Our young lives were filled with music...with dance and, above all, with books and poems that he read aloud to us and plays which we performed. He introduced us to Dickens, Shakespeare, Tennyson, Keats, Shelley and the Bible...If he were alive now he would doubtless be sharing...Harry Potter with an audience of rapt seven year-olds. He did not make much concession to 'suitability' believing...that children are capable of understanding far more than we usually give them credit for...All of us (were) given a gift - the confidence to speak for ourselves."

In 1963, the year he retired, Vicars Bell was appointed M.B.E. for his services to education.

MR D.J. PRIOR 1963 - 1966

It was no easy thing for John Prior to take over as Headmaster from someone who had held that position for 34 Years. Vicars Bell was unorthodox and successful, John Prior was orthodox but also successful. In his stay of 3 years, he did excellent work. He set out to bring parents into the school and a number accepted his invitation to talk to the children on their own subject. His Open Days were well organised. His programme of visits to outside places, such as the Science Museum, the Victoria and Albert and London Airport, broadened the children's knowledge. He was much supported by Mrs Prior, who was also a teacher. She was always ready to cover when staff were away or unwell.

John Prior encouraged dancing, singing and sports. He also successfully helped the children to do well in swimming. On his last day at the school 39 swimming certificates were presented: 14 for 25 yards, 8 for 100 yards, 7 for 440 yards, 6 for half a mile, and 4 for Life Preservation. That must have been a very satisfactory note on which to leave.

MR A.J. WILLIAMS 1966 – 1988

When Albert and Molly Williams and their children Jon and Ian moved into School House in August 1966, the school gained another dedicated Headmaster and for the next 22 years, Albert and Molly initiated and supported all sorts of activities in school, the Church, and in our community.

He always had the highest standards for himself; he also set the highest standards for the children. He had the ability to help them do their best in whatever they did, working at the three R's day by day, or playing games, swimming, running, singing, dancing or whatever. The children always knew where they stood with him; what he said was obeyed!

He believed in giving the children the chance to test themselves against others.

The school played Football and Netball matches and competed in Athletics and Swimming events and Music Festivals. Often we were the smallest, or one of the smallest, schools taking part. Whatever the result there was always benefit and sometimes the results were surprisingly good; from 1979 – 1985, 7 years running, we won the Inter-Village School Sports against 5 other schools, two of which were much larger.

Albert Williams' Christian approach was of untold benefit to the children, a comfort to the parents, a support to the staff, and a boon to the community. He worked closely with Canon Howard Senar (our Rector from 1962 – 1982) who regularly came into the school each Friday and took assembly. There was a tradition of school services in church. Together the Rector and Albert organised school services in Church three times a term. The children were completely at home there and with the service, and made their own contributions. They were sidesmen, rang the bells, read the lessons, chose the hymns, accompanied the organ with their recorders and composed prayers of intercession. The Leavers' Service in July at the end of the school year was – and still is – very special.

Molly and Albert Williams

He was assisted by caring and dedicated staff, and had great teaching support from Muriel Bishop, Barbara Smith, Sally Ellis (later Stephenson) and Carol Vloothuis. It is good the latter is still there. Many villagers and parents helped in the school in a variety of ways, which added an additional homely touch. He fostered a two-way involvement between school and village and the village always turned out in force to support school events. Much enjoyed were the May Day celebrations with the crowning of the May Queen, the fight between St George and the Dragon and Morris and Maypole dancing afterwards. All the children took part in the Nativity plays when the school hall was invariably filled to over-flowing.

Parents meetings were held and Albert always endeavoured to ensure that parents came in regularly to discuss their child's progress. The Annual Fund Raising Bazaar was highly organised. The whole school building as well as the school hall was given over to the Bazaar. Many parents and former parents helped, the staff worked like beavers and the money raised for the school was invaluable. A most popular event was the annual Sausage and Mash Supper in the school hall at which around 100 parents, staff, and children sat down to a candle-lit meal. Afterwards the children entertained and a sing-song was followed by dancing and games. The Village Produce Association shows were always enlivened by numerous entries from the children in the different show categories.

Albert had a wonderful way of creating a

Class III in 1983

BACK ROW
Mrs Barbara Smith, Samantha Birks, Mark Sears, Denise Halsey, Anna Moody, Giles Grainger, Mr Albert Williams

MIDDLE ROW
Spencer King, Phillip Bunting, Caroline Heard, Kate Moody, Fergus Heron, Stephen Ballad

FRONT ROW
Victoria Sheridan, Miriam Shaw, Tina Mooring, Helen Morris, Alison Birks, Elizabeth Walsham

happy mix of generations. In November 1969 when the new Bede Court houses were opened, he discussed that with the children who decided that they would each like to "adopt" a resident, write a letter of welcome, deliver it personally, and keep in touch. Each year the children would put on a Christmas show and sing carols to the Over 60's, after which they would take round refreshments and talk to them. In addition there was an annual concert for the Over 60's and parents at the end of the Summer Term.

The school was extended in 1978 to provide a Staff Room and a Head's Room, and the existing office was converted into a Secretary's Office/Medical Room. Mrs Enid Foxall successfully organised a special appeal to raise the Governors' share of the costs.

During Albert Williams' period as Headmaster many changes in education policy took place. As an example: when he was appointed, there was a small group of School Managers whose main responsibilities were the maintenance of buildings and the appointment of staff. At the end of each Managers' meeting, the Headmaster would say: "Would you like to know what is happening in school?" The Managers with delight would say "Yes, please!" By the time he retired there was a large, democratically elected, body of Governors with legal responsibilities concerning the running of the school. Albert appeared to take these changes in his stride.

Unit 1 in 1989

BACK ROW
Mrs Sally Stephenson, Alex Musgrave, Christopher Dare, Robert Hyde, Dale Fisher, Amit Odedra, David Mooring, Mrs Jenny Birks, Miss Laura Bunting

THIRD ROW
Debbie Catchpole, Toral Odedra, David Gillings, Becky-May Godar, Nicky Gregory, Jemma Tompkins, Catherine Gregory

SECOND ROW
Vicky Wiggins, Dominic Moriarty, Samantha Whaley, Robert Duncan, Josephine Mann, Elliott Akery, Jenny Musgrave

FRONT ROW
Dale Gent, Alex Traherne, Tim Dare, Tom Tannett, Andrew Allen, Chris O'Brien

Albert would be the first to say that he could not have achieved what he did without Molly's wonderful support. When the School Secretary resigned in December 1968, Molly took over that responsibility, and carried it out for the next 20 years until Albert's retirement. It was a bonus to have her in School where she showed kindness and concern for the children and developed helpful relationships with the parents. Truly there was a void when Albert and Molly left the village at the end of the Summer Term 1988 to live in the home they had prepared for themselves in York.

MR S.E. SPENCER 1988 – 1991

When Albert Williams left the Governors were concerned. Would our small school of only 50 children attract the calibre of Head we were used to? Almost unbelievably a highly experienced Headteacher, Mr Stanley Spencer, was seeking to re-establish himself and his family in this country. He liked School House, took to the school and applied for the post. Following the customary selection interviews, he was offered the job and accepted. So once again School House was inhabited by a family: Stan, his wife Cynthia, daughter Claire, then 12, and son Philip, aged 10. Claire went to Cavendish School, and Philip had his final year in Stan's class here.

We soon discovered that in Stan we had the ultimate perfectionist! Everything had to meet his standards. Immediately on arrival he re-decorated his classroom, replaced the blackboard with a white board, altered shelving, installed cupboards and set up his own computer in his classroom. One of his early recommendations was that we should establish a "Parents and Friends of the School Association". He felt adding "Friends" would bring in those who might like to help the school in some way. The organisation could assist fund-raising and help relationships by arranging social events. Parents were consulted and welcomed the idea. Ever since, the Friends have worked tirelessly in the interest of the school and have organised many imaginative and successful events.

Stan – as his predecessor – worked all hours, days, week-ends and holidays. The Governors were able to offer his wife Cynthia, also a gifted teacher, one day's teaching a week and she too made herself available to help in the school in any way she could. Stan and his staff, at great personal effort, kept on top of steadily increasing directives from above, including the introduction of the National Curriculum. As he had a good knowledge of Science (one of the new educational priorities) he was able to cope with that too. Parents were pleased, visitors were impressed and applications for admission increased. Under his headship the number on the roll increased from 50 to 69. The staff did wonderfully well coping with the pressures brought by the increased numbers.

Unit 2 in 1989

TOP ROW
James Musgrave, Sarah Duncan, Dean Fisher, Maxine Hodgson, Collette Francis, Simon Stone Mrs Muriel Bishop

MIDDLE ROW
Victoria Hyde, Emma Stebbings, Rebecca Fleckney, Sarah Godar, Elizabeth Simkin, Elizabeth Fleckney, Sonal Odedra

FRONT ROW
Emily King, Katy Turner, Sarah Simkin, Emma Catchpole, Beth Ryall, Josie Wright, Charlotte O'Brien

SITTING ON THE FLOOR
Martin Beddall, Tim Shaw

The school received an unexpected gift; in his Will Vicars Bell made a bequest of £10,000, the interest on which was to be used to purchase books for the School Library. Stan said: "Pity we have not a proper Library!" The Governors responded, initiating a project to build an extension to house a Library (named, at Stan's suggestion, 'the Vicars Bell Library'). The maximum grant of £ 4,000 was obtained, whilst the Governors, the Friends and the local community raised the further £10,000 required. In March 1991 the library was officially opened by Mrs Genista McIntosh, formerly Planning Controller at the Royal Shakespeare Company and, at the time of the opening, Executive Director of the National Theatre. (In 1999, a Life Barony was conferred on her for her services to the Arts. She chose for her style and title Baroness McIntosh of Hudnall - to local delight.) Her visit was a great success and she much enjoyed the children performing a scene from "A Midsummer Night's Dream" in her honour.

There was, however, a pressing matter to cope with: the resignation of Stan Spencer. In his letter of resignation Stan regretted having to go, but had become increasingly concerned at the uncertainty of ever being able to provide his family with a secure future in this area. He had obtained a Headship in Yorkshire, his native county, where he could purchase a house. The regret at the parting after eight successful terms was mutual and none felt it more than our children. Stan had the gift of relating to children of all ages; as far as they were concerned he was a real Pied Piper. They would have followed him and his guitar anywhere! He had been the right man at the right time and had set the School on a sound footing for the future.

MRS MARY IVESON 1991 - 1996

Mary Iveson became Headteacher in April 1991. Her resilience was an asset as she had to cope with continual educational and administrative changes and a major remodelling of the school. Her first challenge was the introduction of Local Management of Schools. For the first time the Headteacher and Governors had control of the annual budget – based on the number of children in school at

Unit 3 in 1989

BACK ROW
Scott Haslehurst, James Turner, Philip Spencer, Martin Halsey, Michael Billen, Sam Fisher, Mr Stanley Spencer

MIDDLE ROW
Amy Shaw, Samantha Gillings, Emma Humphrey, Holly Chilton, Kelly Hodgson

FRONT ROW
Annabel Browne, Teresa Gent, Sophie Burdess, Lucy Pike, Amy Beddall, Lindsey Spooner

the beginning of each financial year – and could decide how best to use it. This was probably the most helpful of all the educational changes.

Mary Iveson was the first Headteacher to live outside the village but her commitment to the school and her strong Christian faith made our adjustment to this change easier. She achieved an instant rapport with the staff and parents. In addition to her management skills, we benefited from her desire to develop music and her skilled conducting. In this connection it should be noted that later the school was specially invited to sing at the Barbican, as well as singing at the Albert Hall with other Hertfordshire schools.

Numbers on the roll continued to increase and reached 79 in January 1992. This, whilst encouraging, brought increased pressure on teachers and on classroom space. An expansion plan, incorporating suggestions from the Headteacher and Governors, was produced by our Architect, Mr. Paul Burdess. This plan included building a fourth classroom in the high roof of the Victorian building, relocating toilets, providing a teaching area for Science and Technology, and creating a larger staff room. The plans were officially submitted to the Diocese for the approval and allocation of funds in June 1992.

In September 1992, Mary learnt that the Department of Education and Science still had funds available for school building projects in the current 1992/3 financial year. The Chairman of Governors (Ken Dickson) enquired if we could obtain an allocation from those funds. He was advised: "Yes if planning authorisation was obtained, Local Education Authority and DES approval given, and the building work completed and invoiced by the end of February 1993 (i.e. in $4^1/_2$ months)." In addition, the Governors would need to meet 7.5% of the total cost plus any shortfall in Diocesan or LEA contributions. In other words the Governors' financial commitment would be open-ended and could be £10,000 or more! The financial risk was accepted; it was an act of faith. Action was put in hand and Iver Cooley, a Berkhamsted builder, was awarded the contract. All the officials concerned: Planning Officer, Buildings Inspector, Fire Officer, Historic Buildings Officer, the LEA and the DES required the inclusion of additional work. However, with wonderful co-operation between Architect, builder and school the remodelling was completed in time. The total cost of the work had steadily increased finally reaching £164,000. Of this the Governors had to find £17,000. With the magnificent support of the Friends Association, the local community and all associated with the school and good work by our then Vice Chairman and Treasurer, Mr Paul Jones, the Governors' share was found plus an additional £3000 for other items - £20,000 in all. Special mention must be made of the role of Mr Alan Bradfield, the governor with the responsibility for buildings. He did invaluable work liaising between Architect, builders and Governors. The official opening of our re-modelled school was performed by Bishop Robin Smith of Hertford on 6 July 1993, a great event well-supported by parents and our local community.

Two other events of Mary Iveson's period as Headteacher should be noted: the Thanksgiving Service for Stanley Spencer and the Ofsted Inspection. All who knew Stan were distressed when he died as a result of a motor accident and there was a great desire for a service in our church to thank God for his life and

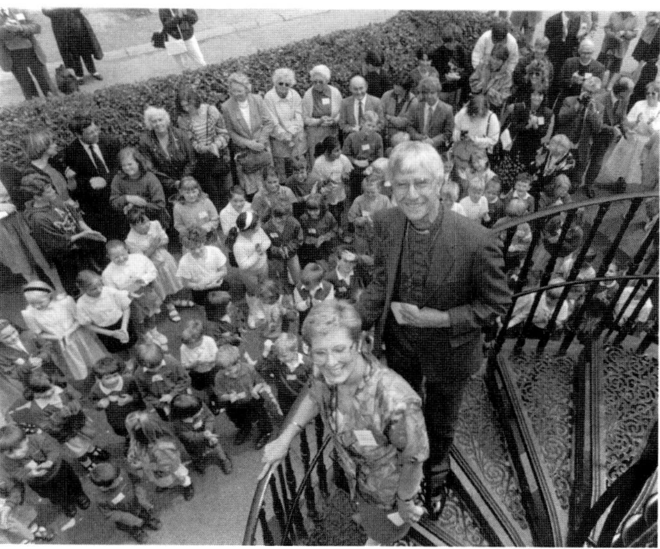

ABOVE LEFT:
In the new classroom, built in the roof space above the old one.

LEFT TO RIGHT
BACK ROW
Joan Penrose (violin teacher), Mary Iveson, Rt Rev Robin Smith (Bishop of Hertford), Ken Dickson (Chairman of Governors)

FRONT ROW
Jemma Tompkins, Debbie Catchpole, Jenny Musgrave, Vicki Wiggins, Joseph Merritt

ABOVE RIGHT
Mary Iveson and Bishop Robin Smith at the opening of the remodelled building

work and to express sympathy with his wife Cynthia and their children. This was held on Saturday 26 Sept 1992; the church was packed. Cynthia, Claire and Philip came and the school attended in force. Also present were those whom Stan had taught and who had moved to other schools. The service included hymns Stan used to play on his guitar and sing with the children: 'Who put the colours in the rainbow?'; 'Give me oil in my lamp'; 'I danced in the morning'; 'One more step along the road I go' and 'Colours of day'. The memorable service was conducted by the Revd. Brian Saunders, Parish Priest and Vice Chairman of School Governors.

Ofsted inspections are most demanding to prepare for, and can be exacting whilst they take place; ours was no exception. Our status as a Voluntary Aided Church School required not only the customary full inspection but also a separate Religious Education and Collective Worship inspection. The inspection report contained much praise for the school and how it was run, including a special commendation for Mary Iveson for her management of the school and the development of music. When Mary moved to the Lake District in Jan 1997, she could take great satisfaction from having made a real contribution to the school's continuing success and expansion.

MR.TIMOTHY BOWEN 1997- 2000

There is no doubt that under Tim Bowen the school is running excellently and that he is receiving great support from our very competent staff. There are now over 100 on the roll, with pressure for more children to be accepted. Once again we have a gifted musician as our Head, and music continues to go from strength to strength. The 1999 Nativity Plays for Infants and Juniors were well-performed and enjoyed by players and audiences alike.

The commitment of the Governors, under the chairmanship of Mr David Stevens, and wonderful parent support, has made it possible to proceed with the marvellous project of building a proper school hall. A further extension of the school building is also planned.

Throughout the century the school has been a happy and progressive place and a centre of village life. It still is - we are very fortunate.

Evacuees' farm is homesick cure

FROM A NEWSPAPER COLUMN - DATE - 1940s

by Iris Carpenter

TOP
Sharing out the pork. David Foster and Vicars Bell with the young farmers group in the village hall. The boy at the front is an evacuee - Jack Jackson.

ABOVE
One of the school pigs. The children marked E are evacuees, and those marked L are from local families.

LEFT to RIGHT:

Anne Munden L, Barbara Jones (later Mrs Colin Mogg) L, Valerie Haig (Ashridge House), Pat Penn E, Eileen Miles, unknown girl half hidden, Elsie Purple L half hidden, Betty Maunders L, Geoff Rogers L, Cliff Stebbins (Gaddesden Row), unknown E in front of C Stebbins, another unknown E, Jack Jackson E in foreground with pig, Tom Humphreys E, Ron Waters E, Bert Stratton E in front of R. Waters, Brian Burrows E, Keith Geater L, Bill Goodman L, David Webb E, Robin ...L behind D.Webb, Unknown. Note the Bridgewater Arms in the background.

LITTLE GADDESDEN, Herts, Tuesday

This village has found the way to stop London evacuee children being taken home by their parents. Twelve pigs, 41 chickens, three rabbits, a goat and a school run as a farmer's club have done what Government appeals and an army of welfare workers could not do. Mr. Vicars Bell, schoolmaster and club organiser, told me: "Parents have given up asking their children to go back home, they are so happy in their life here."

LEARNING BIOLOGY

The children are learning biology from breeding their own animals, sums from buying and selling their own produce.

The club's success can be judged from its balance sheet: Cash in hand, £8 10s.; stock worth £80. The club started on a £12 Government grant.

Dividends are a joint of pork when pigs are killed, fresh eggs and half-price vegetables. Members work in teams of four. Snags are duty on holidays and at week-ends - but the children do not do lessons on their "team" days.

The club has produced seven tons of potatoes, and has more customers for fresh vegetables than it can supply.

"We want a cow, then we can be really self-supporting," the chairman, 14-year-old Ralph Park, said to me.

If the chickens lay well, and the next litter of pigs is as bonny as the last, they'll have the cow by Christmas.

Vicars and Dorothy Bell

After leaving Little Gaddesden Vicars and Dorothy Bell lived in Cornwall and then Devon. They died together in a motor accident in Devon in1988.

EXTRACTS FROM THE ADDRESS BY JEFFERY EDE AT THEIR MEMORIAL SERVICE IN LITTLE GADDESDEN PARISH CHURCH

It is especially appropriate that Vicars and Dorothy should be remembered in the parish church in which they both sang in the choir and worshipped, and which was the keystone of their existence.

For Vicars and Dorothy, the 'parish' - the village - was the focus of their lives. The community contained within a parish boundary was for them a living organism, a family made up of a diversity of individuals, sometimes quarrelsome and fractious, but ultimately forced by necessity to find a common centre of interest without which healthy community life was impossible. This is a central theme running through all Vicars' books and underlay his belief that the lack of this sense of common identity was the source of many of the ills which today afflict our towns and cities.

Paradoxically, Vicars did not grow up in a village. Although of Scottish Presbyterian farming stock his parents were townsfolk. As a boy he went to

Reigate Grammar School. After leaving school he went to a Teachers Training College in London, where he met Dorothy. They married soon after he qualified as a teacher.

In 1927, aged 22, Vicars, with Dorothy at his side, began his career as a country schoolmaster at Spaldham Magna near Huntingdon. Eighteen months later he decided that his true vocaton was the priesthood. He entered King's College London to read theology, but left after 6 months having developed a T.B. spot on a lung. During his convalescence he experienced a crisis of conscience (sensitively described in 'The Dodo') and in September 1929 resumed his teaching career and successfully applied for the headship of Little Gaddesden village school. While Vicars was making a complete recovery from the spectre of tuberculosis (in those pre-antibiotic days a serious disease) Dorothy tragically had also become infected. Although she recovered the disease took its toll; her health suffered and she and Vicars sadly remained childless......

By the time I came to live in the village in 1951 they had both been totally accepted in the village. My wife and I remember vividly our first meeting with Vicars. On a hot July afternoon we walked down to the village school to enquire into the possibility of registering our four year old son as a pupil. We were greeted by the great man himself, unconventionally dressed in shorts and an open-necked shirt. We were introduced to his two assistants, David Hughes (also similarly clad) and an attractive young American from Richmond, Virginia, Beth Taylor, who had charge of the youngest children. Clearly this was no ordinary school.

Katharine Ede with her brother Martyn in 1952 at the Public Record Office huts where they lived. Their father was in charge of the records.

During the next few years we really began to appreciate the breadth of education provided and the principles underlying it.

The headmaster and staff shared a common conviction that each child had in him or her something to contribute to the community, if only the spark could be ignited. Their concern was not with pushing the bright pupils to pass the 11+ (although many did in fact win places at grammar and independent schools), but in stimulating each child to achieve its potential in whatever direction this might lie. A few parents disapproved of this concept, which they misunderstood as an absence of competition, but most appreciated the philosophy and were grateful for the end result, surely demonstrated by the overwhelming majority of boys and girls who achieved happiness and success in their subsequent careers.

Parents were encouraged to visit the school. On entering one found it bursting with vitality. The children looked at you with frank and lively friendliness and were not afraid to talk to you and the many distinguished visitors from home and overseas, educationalists of all creeds and colours, who came to see and learn.

There was a relaxed atmosphere of naturalness and companionship between teacher and pupil. Some parents felt that this resulted in a lack of discipline and failed to notice that discipline was exercised in more subtle ways. 'Sir' looking over the top of his glasses was the ultimate and most effective deterrent. I remember our daughter, aged about seven, who was consistently late for school dilly dallying on her way through the park. Realising one day that she had overstepped the mark, she hastily grabbed a handful of grasses. When asked "Katharine why are you late again?", her ingenious reply was that she had been collecting grasses. Whereupon Vicars asked if she could identify them all and suggested that she should spend playtime doing so with the aid of reference books in the library. Thus typically the punishment fitted the crime. The point was made.

Virtue was rewarded by the winner of a spelling test on a hot afternoon being sent to Mr Ward's shop to buy ice creams for the whole class. Another accolade for academic success was being allowed to go to Mr Ward's and buy 20 Senior Service for 'Sir' and be rewarded with a toffee.

Every day the last lesson was devoted to story telling or reading aloud - Dickens, Tolkien, poetry of all kinds - the only author banned was Enid Blyton (the Bard of Buxton). As for stories - best of all was Uncle George (an invention of Vicars') who kept spiders with wooden legs among other fantastic doings and happenings. One day Uncle George came to visit the school. He turned out to be Vicars' brother, but the children all believed he was Uncle George.

Vicars' and Dorothy's interest in music, art, drama and literature was not confined to school activities but played a large part in their ordinary lives. Rummaging through some papers a year ago I came across the programme of David Wray's production for the Gaddesden Society Drama Club of 'Twelfth Night'. Vicars played Feste, Orsino's clever, sardonic and very intelligent 'fool', a part which allowed full scope for his many talents. I shall always remember that lovely voice of his singing 'O Mistress Mine' to the accompaniment of Dorothy Erhart's harpsichord. Thinking about this production it occurred to me that Vicars had something of Feste in his make-up. Like Feste he was an elusive observer of life who could mock with wit and adroitness the follies of others, especially those committed by the arrogant fools of this world (the Malvolios and Sir Anthony Aguecheeks). But in deflating pretentiousness and exposing humbug, he was without malice: he enjoyed the eccentricities and foibles of his fellow men. Some of us who played village cricket with Vicars will remember with amusement his laconic but audible asides from first slip or silly mid-on....

In his 59th year he resigned his headmastership and went to Mirfield to train for the priesthood under the Community of the Resurrection, his long and distinguished service to education having been recognised by an M.B.E. He was ordained in the diocese of Exeter, spent some time as a curate in Tavistock, then held a living in Cornwall, and after ten happy years there retired to Tavistock again, where Vicars helped out in local churches. About 18 months ago when their old car had expired an anonymous parishioner gave them a brand new Metro, so that Vicars could continue his locum service in neighbouring parishes. It was in this car that they set out one spring morning, driving into the countryside to enjoy the cherry trees in full blossom. They died together that same day, their last act being to see at Eastertide the rebirth of the countryside which they both loved so much and which, I am sure, symbolised for them Christ's victory over death.

Little Gaddesden C of E School 1966 to 1988

by Albert Williams

When I took over the School in 1966 there were three classrooms and a tiny office which held a table and a chair. The office was used as a Staff Room, Medical Room and Secretary's Room. We shared a secretary with Northchurch School and she worked two mornings a week. The toilets were by the main door;

one for girls and another for boys but neither had doors and the first impression when entering the School was rather peculiar! Next to the boys' toilet was the Boiler Room. There was a sandpit at the front of the School and, at the back, a Hall. This was a pre-fab, put up during the second world war after the original had burnt down, and was meant as a temporary building. As I write, this Hall is still operating, although soon to be replaced. In 1966 there were murals at each end depicting scenes of wartime in the village and the evacuees; some inhabitants could recognise themselves. We saved the murals but they were tatty and we made enquiries of the painter who, by then, was Art Director of Northumberland Education Authority but he thought the pictures could not be 'touched-up'. The back section of the Hall had been partly shelved to take stock and partly converted into a library.

The school hall 1944 to 1999

The heating throughout was by coke and piles were dumped in the boiler house and in the outhouse by the School Canteen. Hods were used to fill the main boiler and the fires in the Hall. This was a messy and dusty operation. Later we arranged for oil heating and had a couple of marvellous Hall heaters, upon which we could heat food as well, if necessary; and we did when electricity supplies failed or there were strikes during the Heath Government.

There were no curtains or pinboards. Artwork had been put up with Copydex. We had no goal posts or netball posts. I put up as many pinboards as possible until I was fed up hammering holes for raw plugs. Groundsmen from the LEA marked out pitches on the playing field once we had permission from the Parish Council to use the land, and a local carpenter made the goal posts.

I found that during the first winter snow drifted through the roof tiles above the Infant Room and the ceiling was in danger. I remember getting my ladder and climbing into the loft, putting snow into a bucket and lowering the bucket by rope to those below. The local handyman (no names) covered inside the roof with hardboard to avoid a repetition. I got used to the loft because the water cisterns were there and the 'header tank' in particular - if this ball-cock doesn't function, the radiators won't heat - and this happened now and again, especially after a summer's rest. Living as we did six miles from the nearest town, many jobs came under the heading of DIY. One Christmas morning, after midnight service, I found an overflow from the girls' toilets and mended the ballcock at two in the morning. Regularly the gutters needed clearing and the sewage pipes rodded through.

Geoffrey Drewitt's murals on the end walls of the old hall

Eventually the annual School Bazaars brought us in a welcome income and amenities improved. Our Bazaars were in late November. The whole village was divided into sections and children volunteered to be responsible for each section (in pairs). Every house was notified of the impending Bazaar and the community was extremely supportive and generous. A week or so prior to the Bazaar, the children collected from the houses and brought the gifts to School, where they were sorted the next evening into the relevant items on separate tables. By the time of the Friday (evening) Bazaar there was little room in the Hall. In the evening, every available space was used, classrooms, hall, entrance and Village Hall and Scout Hut. One endearing legend lived on year after year, and the older pupils were splendid in pretence. We had 'Mother Hubbard's Cupboard' which started off bare until one morning in Assembly a kitten was

heard crying. When found, Sammy (his name) tearfully said he was hungry and from then on, each morning, tins of food appeared and Sammy inspected what he had. Each morn an infant came out to find what Sammy had eaten; usually he was hidden behind tins on one of the shelves. On the Bazaar morning, when Sammy was found, he was a BIG Sammy, bloated with all his food. Molly and I still have her knitted 'little and large' Sammys. Many anecdotes could be recounted of Bazaar adventures. It is sad that the safety of children precludes such dark-night adventures in the present climate.

The Sausage and Mash Suppers gave an opportunity for the children to learn how to serve meals, lay tables, give entertainment, have a singsong and all followed by a Barn Dance. We could seat approximately 100 and every year the tickets were sold out. Another annual event was the Maypole. Kind people loaned us a pony and the chosen Queen led a procession round Bede Court where children gave posies of flowers to those watching, and back to School. The dragon was in the procession with St George - the fun we had trying to get the dragon to walk properly! Twelve legs can get quite muddled up. The Queen was crowned by the previous year's Queen but the naughty dragon appeared. St George came to the rescue and, when the dragon was defeated (inevitably!), he was knighted and dancing began in honour of the Queen; usually Morris Dancing by the 7-9 year olds and then the Maypole.

TOP
Maypole dancing in 1988: Peter Leonhardt and Teresa Gent on the left.

ABOVE
The Queen of the May, Sarah Jane Moran, handing out sweets in 1988

We had end-of-year entertainment and Nativity Plays to which the village was invited. There were annual outings for parents as well as children. One year when we had a double-decker bus, the bus company went along the route by the Deer Leap Garage and down the lower road, cutting tree branches allowing the bus room to manoeuvre. We ran the Village Sports for the Gaddesden Society. We joined the larger schools in Hemel Hempstead for the annual Choir Festival.

We had a link with a school in Tower Hamlets, West Ham. Little Gaddesden children travelled by rail to Euston and then by Underground; a new experience for most; and then found what it was like to be in an inner-city school. For instance, the gates were locked, not to keep the children in but strangers out (unusual then but, sadly, common now) and if children wanted toilet paper they had to ask at the staff room. When West Ham visited us, they were picked up at Berkhamsted station by a fleet of cars supplied by parents and experienced the joys of the countryside. They saw lambs being born, were given 'lucky' horseshoes and realised gooseberries grew on bushes and not tins. It was a beneficial link for all.

As the years passed we were able to give all the children a taste of many sports during their seven years at primary level. Football, netball, hockey, cricket, cross-country (along Ashridge woods), volley ball and Padder tennis, as well as athletics in the form of hurdles, high and long jump, relays, etc. We had some years swimming at Deer Leap but in the latter years a kind parent offered her private pool. We inherited a few climbing frames and bought others. For variety a homemade see-saw was made out of a tree trunk and stout chestnut branch. When electricity lines were laid underground, a telegraph pole was begged from the contractor and made into a balancing pole. Little of this is now extant but we had lots of fun.

TOP
Betty Rogers in the school kitchen

ABOVE
The school staff in 1974

LEFT TO RIGHT
BACK ROW
Molly Williams, Kate Hendy, Albert Williams, Muriel Bishop, Gwen Rafferty

FRONT ROW
Jennie Waters, Dot Nash, Betty Rogers, Wyn Oakins

The kitchen staff were very patient. On good summer days we discussed having the midday meal outside and a salad was produced. The children lined up, collected their selection of food and had a free choice of where to sit in the climbing frame area. On Shrove Tuesdays the Staff had a Pancake Race. Each brought a frying-pan, the cook made the pancakes, and at mid-morning break we held the race round the playground, stopping at three places to toss the pancakes and enabling the children to cheer us on. The cooks made piles of pancakes, enough for everyone at lunch-time. The last day before Easter, the Kitchen Staff made meringue nests and put small sugar eggs inside, enough for all. Frequently we had gingerbread men - and once a gingerbread woman but she was too 'curvaceous' so we stopped that! How lucky we were with our staff.

Many of our staff, teaching and ancillary, stayed for years, in some cases up to eighteen. This could be construed as good or bad but it certainly made for security for the children and comradeship for the staff. One year, counting the absences, only eight days were noted for the whole staff of a dozen.

Like most schools, we had Morning Assembly. As a Church School this was important to us. In keeping with the Parish Church we used the English Hymnal and the 1662 Prayer Book, when occasion needed it. The School Governors gave a Prayer Book to every school leaver at eleven years old. From 1980 onwards the leavers received the Alternative Service Book. Morning Assemblies varied during the week. The Head took one, children another, the teacher on duty a third, a whole class the fourth and the Rector always came in on Fridays. Last thing on a Friday afternoon, the older children met in the Hall for a final prayer. Once a month the whole School, and any adults who wished, went for a service at St Peter and St Paul's. On Ascension Days, the whole School went to Church and then had the rest of the day as an occasional holiday. This custom dropped as the years passed and occasional holidays were no more. We brought in the tradition of the Christingle Service, and it was lovely to see the inside of the Church circled by young and old holding the candles and singing 'Away in a Manger'.

Which reminds me of the Christmas period. Our cook always prepared the Christmas pudding ingredients at the 'Stir-up Sunday' time. So on the Friday before 'Stir-up', after the Rector finished his homily, the large bowl of pudding ingredients was brought into the Assembly and everyone had a stir and, at the same time, a WISH (secret, of course). The infants began and it was fun to see the faces as the effort of stirring the mixture proved difficult; then, as the older children had a go, the mixture became easier and, by the time the adults stirred, the puddings were ready to cook! The cooked puddings, complete with holly and accompanied with the carol 'We all want some figgy pudding', were presented at the Christmas Dinner on the last day of term. It was then we had crackers and sat at 'long' tables with a top table for staff and Governors.

The old Bede Alms houses were demolished and the present Bede Court established in the 1970s. We wrote to each inhabitant and invited them to use the School playground and through the School House garden (now No 21) as a short cut to the shop and pub, etc. The toll was to pick a weed as they passed through! Many entered into the spirit and did so and over the years the short cut was used by people in general - and was not abused. Someone eventually said we could not stop them using the School House path as it was a right of way. Wrong! To avoid this we closed the path one day a year!

Bede Court inhabitants were asked if they would like partners with the children. Many did and, over several years, children popped up the road after school to see the senior citizens and friendships flourished. Christmas and Easter cards were made for Bede Court. Both young and old gained from the contacts. For a time the School supplied dinners during the weekdays and children delivered them. This stopped when the County supplied lunches from Hemel Hempstead.

During the 70s the School buildings were decorated, the toilets improved, new playground surfaces laid and an extension by the orchard was made. This comprised a staff room, a toilet and an office, plus a wider entrance opposite the Hall. Every classroom and the Hall had curtains. A village resident, whose house overlooked the playing field, was apparently impressed by the children and gave a sum of money with which we bought a lawn mower and curtains for the infant room. After her death, it was found she had left a further sum to the School. In return she wished a tree to be planted in the School orchard. This was done and narcissi planted around it. The other trees in the orchard have daffodils.

The teaching was always traditional. Reading was phonics, although Look and Say and other methods might be used when appropriate. We learnt our Tables. The fashion afflicting many places of teaching wholly by Projects, with children in small groups, was only used sparingly. By and large we continued to face the blackboard in the top class and use text books. The Timetable had subjects, Geography, History, Music, etc and Maths and English were taught every day in one form or another. Decimals, fractions and even pi, and practical work using triangular areas measuring the playing field and height of the trees were part of the curriculum. We had weekly tests and annual exams for the older ones. All children had reports and nearly 100% of parents came on Open Days.

Around 1970 an Inspector visited and called the staff together after school for a chat. He astonished us by declaring we should not use books to teach reading. Questioned, he said that every infant should draw a picture, the teacher would write on the picture what it was about, for example - 'Mummy hanging out the washing' for the child and then the picture should be put up. The child would be so pleased with this that he/she would gaze at the picture - and learn the words. After many pictures he/she would have an extensive vocabulary! Thirty children to a class? What time would be left for other lessons? What should we do with the (then) Janet and John books? Make a pile and burn them was his reply. Needless to say we ignored his advice but it shows how stupid practices crept in during the 70s.

By the 80s computers were showing. We had an early Sinclair computer and then the Government gave BBC computers to schools. In the past decade we all know the giant strides made and the importance of computers in the modern world. More important perhaps for secondary education than in the primary sector but maybe this is an old-fashioned thought!

My Safe Cycling Teaching Badge enabled us to have biennial cycling sessions with Highway Code exams with other schools. The local 'bobby' tested the children and awarded badges and certificates. Due to the heavy road traffic along the Green we were fortunate to have permission for the children to cycle on the footpath. This was with the proviso that when a child met a pedestrian, he/she dismounted, walked round and got on again. If coming from behind, the cycle bell should be rung as warning. We understood that children were good about this; at least there were few complaints. Gradually over the years to 1988, more and more children were brought to School by car. Church Road became a nightmare early morning and in the afternoon. The Village Hall car park saw much shunting and manoeuvres. In recent months, entry to School is via a new path from the Bridgewater Arms in an effort to solve the problem.

The School has always been well-supported by the Governors, who do a lot of work, all voluntary, and not everyone is aware of this. In the past decade, the work, red tape and bureaucracy have increased tremendously. Inspections, National Curricula, and Appraisals have all added to the strain that Staff and Governors face. When I take school groups round York Minster, I hear harrowing tales. In my career I was always responsible for a class, ie at the coal-face. I should think it is now impossible to be a Head and a class teacher as well.

Over the period of time - 1966 to 1988 - there are many more anecdotes, sad and happy incidents, that could be told but enough is enough.

Little Gaddesden C of E School has gone from strength to strength and with its new additions and projected School Hall, it will be better and better. We wish all concerned every happiness and success.

Little Gaddesden School from 1997

by Timothy Bowen

I was appointed as the Head Teacher of Little Gaddesden Church of England Primary School in January 1997 succeeding Mrs Mary Iveson.

The school usually has between 90 and 100 pupils on roll. There are four classes (two Infants and two Juniors) organised as follows:

Class 1 Reception and Year One pupils (4 to 6 years old). Mrs Kate Duncan is the class teacher, with Mrs Anne McCarthy as the Learning Support Assistant.
Class 2 Year Two pupils (6 and 7 years old). Mrs Veronica O'Donohoe and Mrs

Governors and staff in 1998

LEFT TO RIGHT

Jenny Birks, June Abraham, Vanessa Moody, Caty Allen, Tim Bowen, Jackie Tannett, Ann Tompkins, Veronica O'Donohoe, Carol Vloothuis, Paul Jones, Kate Duncan, Jean Jones, Liz Griffin, Ken Dickson, David Stevens (behind), Barbara Cassell, Anne Heard, Anne McCarthy, Diana Dickinson, Paul Hocking, Peter Brown

ABOVE
A group prepared for the Ridgeway Walk, 1998.

LEFT TO RIGHT
Jonathan Abraham, Tim Wilson, Gary Bunting, Tom Frostick, Stephanie Forrester, Catherine Reynolds, Elizabeth Dickinson, and Tommy Barthorp (seated)

BELOW
Construction of the new hall in 1999

BOTTOM
One of the elevation drawings by Paul Burdess, the architect for the project

Charis Georghegan are the class teachers, each teaching for half the week. Mrs O'Donohoe also teaches some extra P E lessons for all the classes.

Class 3 Years Three and Four (7 to 9 years old). Mrs Rosemarie Taylor is the class teacher, and I also teach these Years.

Class 4 Years Five and Six (9 to 11 years old). Mrs Carol Vloothuis is the class teacher, with Mrs Jenny Birks as the Learning Support Assistant.

Many extra-curricular activities take place, including football and netball clubs and a French club. The school has a strong musical tradition. Many children are members of the choir, which performs in church services and at larger events (for example concerts in The Royal Albert Hall) and a number of children receive musical instrument tuition.

For some time we have had an excellent after-school chess club run by Mr Ken Dickson and Mr David Heard. Chess is not only good for developing thought and concentration but is great fun. Since 1985, eight of our players have played for Hertfordshire Junior teams: Fleur Horner, Catherine Pearce, Helen Pearce, Robert Pearce, Thomas Whiddett, Alex Macintyre, James York and Sam Reynolds. Our players have also had success in chess competitions both in individual and team events.

In my three years as Head Teacher, the school has undergone major improvements to its premises. The upstairs classroom has been extended to provide more space for our older pupils. Class 1 has also been extended and modernised to provide a greatly improved learning environment for our youngest pupils.

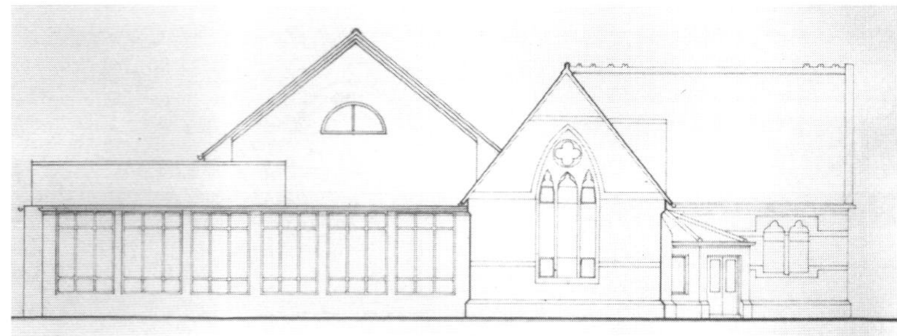

But, most ambitious of all, we are currently having a new school hall built. This will join the existing school building and replace the 'old' hall, which was constructed in World War Two to accommodate the evacuee children who came to the village. This should be opened in time for the start of the new school academic year in September 2000.

The building of the hall is the result of a tremendous fund-raising effort by both the Governors and Friends Association., who have raised nearly forty thousand pounds to support the work. In 1998, for example, the school took part in a Sponsored Walk of the entire Ridgeway Path to raise funds for our hall. The event culminated, one afternoon in May, with most of the children and their parents climbing the final section of the walk to the top of Ivinghoe Beacon. Looking to the future, we are hoping to extend the size of our downstairs classrooms to provide more spacious classrooms for our oldest pupils.

As a school we place great emphasis on the part we play in the life of the village. Examples of our activities are holding termly services in the Church, inviting residents of

Bede Court into school for lunch each half-term, holding an annual summer fair at which some of the other village organisations are represented and being represented at the Remembrance Day Parade. We value the support and loyalty of the village community and the genuine feeling of pride that many villagers have for our school.

The educational world is currently one of constant change and development. The National Curriculum is shortly due to be revised; we have implemented the Literacy and Numeracy strategies and Information and Communications Technology (the use of computers) will have an increasingly important and exciting role to play in educating the children for the next century.

Yet, despite all the change and development, the staff will aim to ensure that the school retains its special 'caring family' environment and its Christian ethos. As teachers we have a very privileged position, educating the young people of this village to take their place as responsible citizens in the next millennium. I hope that, in the future, many of our current pupils will look back at their time at our school, the friendships they made and the education they received with both pleasure and pride.

Educational premises in the village

by the Editor

The Bridgewater Arms: Although legendary in the village, because the children had to enter by a window, the use of a room here as a school only occurred from 1854 to 1858.
The present School in Church Road: In use since 1858.
Building previous to the house Tree Tops at the corner of Hudnall Lane and the Green: A school room for Ashridge apprentices, date uncertain.
Ashridge House: (Including boarding accommodation at all times.)
1. The Bonar Law College: a Conservative Party training college in citizenship from 1929 to 1939. Re-opening from 1947, merging into non-political and industrial courses in 1950, becoming totally non-political in 1954.
2. The Gaddesden Training College for teachers, from 1947 to about 1950, using the ex-hospital huts.
3. The House of Citizenship, a finishing school for young ladies from 1950 to 1957.
4. Ashridge Management College from 1959 to the present day.
Denison House (the whole of the old Marian Lodge, which was not divided as it is now):
1. An overflow for the village school briefly in 1939.
2. The Froebel School from Barons Court, London, during their evacuation from 1939 or 1940 to 1946. Included boarding accommodation.
Old Village Hall (near the site of the present sports pavilion): An overflow for the village school from the end of 1939 until burnt down in 1943.
Beaney (Benhay): An overflow for the village school from the end of 1939 until the evacuees dispersed by about 1945. Included boarding accommodation.
West Tower in Hudnall Lane: In 1956 a nursery school organised by Mrs

Elizabeth Bradfield and run by qualified teachers, 3 days a week. Alan Bradfield made a swing, see-saw and sandpit in the garden. Transferred after 1957 to the next location:

Blue Cottage at Ringshall: Mrs Iris Clayton ran the nursery school from 1958 to 1970. Transferred to the next location:

"New" Village Hall (the 1957 one): Continuation of the nursery school, also known as play school, now known as Pre-school Group, by Iris Clayton's daughter Val Janes from about 1970 until 1999. Then by Jacqui Moriarty assisted by five staff. Currently about 30 children aged from $2^1/_2$ to 5.

Hudnall Park: An Environmental Studies Centre for visiting pupils and students from other schools from 1972 onwards. Name changed to Field Studies Centre and then Outdoor Centre, but still the same establishment. Includes short-stay boarding accommodation.

The Froebel school at Denison House

FROM CONVERSATIONS WITH CELIA HENSMAN AND MICHAEL DEW

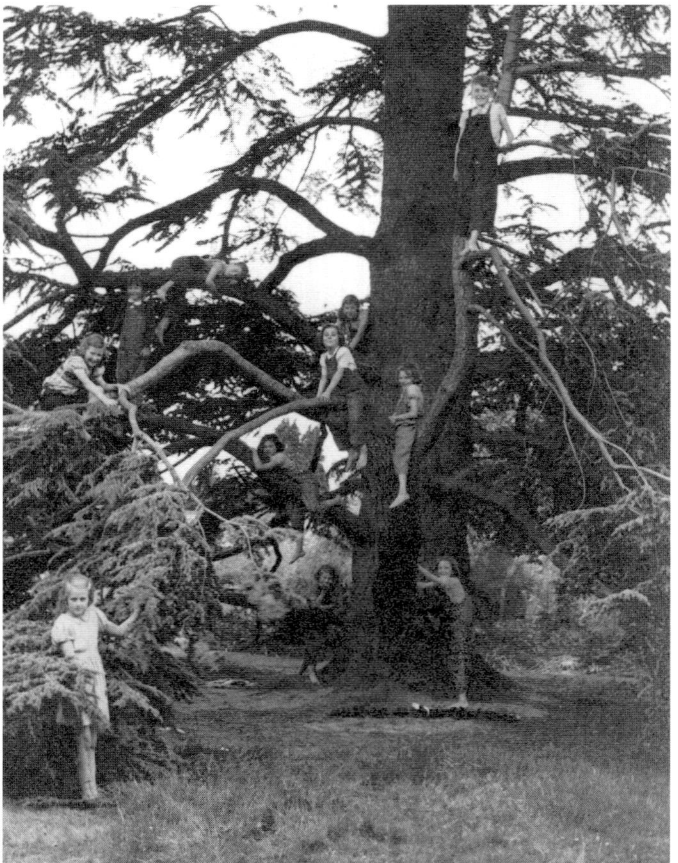

The cedar tree in Denison House when it was a Froebel School from 1940 to 1946. Celia Hensman, in dark clothes, is almost invisible, standing on a limb out on the left, just to the right of the girl with the outstretched arm. The girl in the foreground is Bridget Brown (now Smith) and the girl sitting on the lowest branch, seen against the trunk, is Jennifer Seebohm.

Michael Dew is now a Governor of the Froebel School in Roehampton, but he and Celia Hensman were boarding pupils here during the evacuation.

The Froebel School was at Barons Court when the second world war broke out, and for the evacuation moved briefly to Oxfordshire and then to Denison House, which the resident and owner, Mr Cuthbertson, made available by moving out. It had room for about 50 London pupils and their staff as boarders and also took day pupils from nearby, including Madeleine and Michael Gallo from Le Logis, Fourways Corner. See Madeleine's article on page 66.

The Headmistress was Miss Barbara Priestman. Other teachers included Miss Joyce Caiger-Smith (later the girls' Housemistress at Bedales School) and Miss Duncan.

The pupils were aged 5 to 12. Madeleine Gilpin (née Gallo) remembers:

"It was a wonderful place and I was so happy there. It had large lawns on which, one summer, we once did a 'pageant of history through the ages'. I remember I was one of a group of Roman children and wore a beautiful blue Roman tunic and danced around in bare feet on that lovely soft grass, after having had to recite a Roman verb in the Roman school. There were also two fabulous cedar trees." Eleanor Dunphy, another former pupil, now living in Berkhamsted, adds that these were called the girls' cedar and the boys' cedar, and she climbed both of them. These cedars are now in the grounds of the house Lutèce.

Some other pupils who lived in the village were the daughters of James Crooks, the distinguished surgeon, who lived at Meadow Farm, Ringshall, and Anthony Bridgewater who lived near the Deer Leap Swimming Pool. Many of the boarding pupils stayed on during the holidays.

Michael Dew remembers that there was a popular tea room at Four Ways Garage. In 1944 his parents moved into the area, taking a house at Water End, and he became a day pupil. At the age of ten he rode to school on his bike, preferring Pulridge Hill to Hudnall Lane hill when coming up in the morning. The school moved back to London in 1946.

Hudnall Park Field Studies Centre

Originally known as "Environmental Studies Centre" and recently changed again to "Outdoor Centre".

by John Leonhardt

When Hudnall Park came on the market in 1971 the Hertfordshire County Council were looking for a site for a residential centre for field studies for school parties. They already had some centres for day visits. Hudnall Park was chosen because of a fortunate combination of features: size (a bit small, but manageable), access to ideal surroundings, absence of any nearby distraction for students, and two annexed houses which could provide staff accommodation.

When the plans were known there was well-organised opposition from the village, especially the Hudnall residents, to what they saw as a threat to their peaceful existence and quiet cul-de-sac. Peaceful co-existence has since been the norm, however, with undesirable incidents very rare.

The first Warden was Peter Payne, a biology teacher, who combined the job with being the secretary of the Hertfordshire and Middlesex Trust for Nature Conservation. (This organisation is now known as the Herts and Middlesex Wildlife Trust, and has its own premises in Grebe House, St Albans.) The resident domestic staff were Frank and Phyllis Parkhurst. The former, as a skilled chef, soon established a reputation for the centre for the high quality of catering. I took over from Peter Payne in 1977, but without taking on the HMTNC secretarial work. By this time, Jane Baldwin had become the Assistant Warden, and the two of us worked together as a very effective partnership until the early 1990's when the financial problems of the County Council led to many redundancies which fragmented the organisation. By then there were about eight very successful field centres in Hertfordshire, all but Hudnall Park being for day visits only. Jane and I came to know all kinds of features of the surrounding area that could be used for the outdoor teaching of biology and geography, and worked out how to use them to fulfil the aims of the visiting class teachers. When there was a large class outdoors, say over 15 on a farm visit or a long walk, we would split them between us, which made for much more effective teaching. This is too expensive to do nowadays.

Students abroad

In recent years, students going on to further education have often chosen to spend a year taking a break from their usual studies. Some of them have spent most of their gap year in an activity of useful service abroad through the agency of one of the organisations specialising in this work, including the following examples from Little Gaddesden:

Elizabeth Simkin: In Northern Province, South Africa, teaching English at a very remote rural farm school. There were 120 pupils aged 6 to 19. Mostly bare-footed, they walked daily to school, some of them up to three hours each way.

Victoria Hyde: Also in Northern Province, South Africa, at first, teaching History and English to children aged 12 to 14 in a rural area. Then she was moved to Johannesburg and worked in child care at Cotlands Baby Sanctuary for abused, abandoned and AIDS babies and toddlers. This included helping look after a group of 3 to 6-year olds, some of whom were sick and one blind, on a week at the seaside.

Ian Fielder: In Nepal, teaching English to young monks in a Buddhist monastery.

We were very well served by various local organisations from Hemel Hempstead to Kensworth and Tring, including Home Farm, Great Gaddesden, where Nicholas Halsey let us show pupils and students every detail of the working of a large family-run commercial farm, and have access to the River Gade for aquatic studies. Until some time in the 1980's all the visiting schools were secondary. We had increased the working space by obtaining a "mobile classroom" in 1979, as the indoor room was not really big enough for a normal sized class.

Various changes in the legal obligations of schools, the national curriculum and funding policies made it increasingly difficult for schools with large year-groups to use our residential services. We started providing residential courses for primary schools, and also simultaneous day bookings. The facilities sometimes get overcrowded now, and the smaller children have to cope with some over-large furniture, but the courses are still very popular with those who can afford them. There are plans to provide more space by extra building, but there seems little hope of their being funded at present.

The high tradition of catering is carried on by Sally Shuttleworth who lives in the Bungalow (unfortunately leaving in 2000). The Head of Centre is Stuart Oswald, living in the Lodge. Stuart has introduced some popular team-building courses with physical activities.

Little Gaddesden School uses our facilities for an occasional visit, usually on a wild-life theme involving woodland, meadow or water life. Primary schools can also enjoy the broad delights of a country ramble with map-reading, hoping to see the deer, scrambling over huge fallen trees, and insisting on climbing up the side of Incombe Hole the steepest way. Many children, both from town and country, are astonishingly unaware of what a primrose, violet and foxglove look like, the difference between wheat and barley, the voice of the jackdaw, how to avoid disturbing sheep (and why), the direction of the sun at mid-day, and that a mile is a distance which they can easily walk. It is good to have the chance to bring children (and their accompanying adults very often) down to walking pace and get them to use their own eyes and ears. It is better still when they start to ask questions. Small children have sharp eyes and often spot obscure things which leave us with questions rather than answers, like a strange mark on a leaf or an odd-shaped stone. It was when asked to count the petals on Blackthorn flowers that the children revealed to me the odd fact that in a Hudnall hedge most of the flowers had six or seven instead of five petals.

Looking at the stars with visiting children

In the Advanced Level biology groups, the current demand from teachers is for investigations that lead to some statistical analysis. This can be very artificial, so we try to include some other more realistic or varied studies. We have recently been monitoring improvements in the invertebrate life in the Box Moor Trust's waters in Hemel Hempstead.

At Hudnall Park itself, the greatest delight to me is the wild flower meadow in the butterfly season, especially at the flying time of the Burnet Moths and the Marbled White Butterfly colony that has become established there since my first arrival.

The village shops and trades over the last century

by Mollie Martin with research by Lyn Hyde and others

In 1973, when our family came to Ringshall, there were only two neighbourhood shops - the Post Office and Shop in Little Gaddesden and Fountain's Stores, six doors away from where we lived. Listening to people who had been in the villages all their lives, it was a shock to learn just how many shops and delivery services there had been in the "old days". Now we have just the Post Office and Shop run by Naresh and Gigi - and how lucky we are to have them. This change in the structure of village life has probably been repeated to a greater or lesser degree in almost every sizeable village in England.

It is odd to realise that 50 years ago elderly people living in the villages were better provided for, in one respect at least, than they are now. In extreme old age they could still do their own shopping, even if they were housebound. (More of this later.)

The list of shops in Little Gaddesden and its associated hamlets is impressive. Well within living memory there were five shops in Little Gaddesden, one in Hudnall and one in Ringshall:

TOP:
No. 42 the old village shop, as it is today.

ABOVE:
Gigi and Naresh Odedra

BELOW:
The village shop in 1999 with (l to r) Rachel Kitchen, Lewis Walker, Tom Kitchen and Ross Walker

Fountain's Stores, Ringshall, the earliest shop on our records. Started by the Fountain family and run by them and their direct descendants, Doris Cocks (with her husband Frank) and Janet Stinton. Known in 1873. Closed in 1980.

Mr and Mrs Robert and Tilly Pratt's Post Office and General Stores, no. 42 LG on the Green. Established 1867. Miss Evelyn Pratt took over the management. In later years the shop operated without the post office. Closed in mid 1960's.

The Post Office and General Stores at no.15 LG, Mr and Mrs Cobb (née Miss Bevan), then Mr and Mrs Ward: Pre-1934 to 1947. Continuation in new premises between no.13 and 14: 1947 - 1969. Successive new managements under Mrs Ward's ownership: 1969 -1984. Now Naresh and Gigi Odedra run the shop; postmasters have changed from time to time: 1984 onwards.

Butcher's Shop at no.9 Hudnall, run by Fred Janes from before 1900. Seth Janes: 1930's to 1946. Mr Stringer: 1946-1962. Mr L. Cheshire: 1962 - mid 1980's.

Quennel's General and Hardware Shop, to the right of the entrance to the driveway to Little Gaddesden House. The site is now in the grounds of The Bothy. Known in 1949. Closed in 1960's.

Peachey's Sweets and General Store, also in the grounds of Little Gaddesden House. (The site is now Garden House): 1960's-1970's.

Fred Janes the butcher

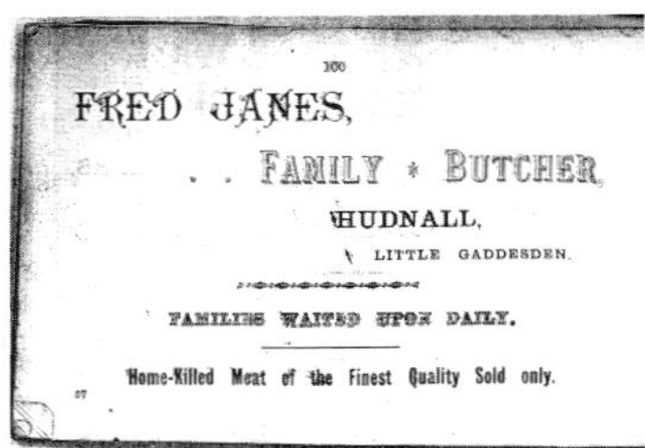

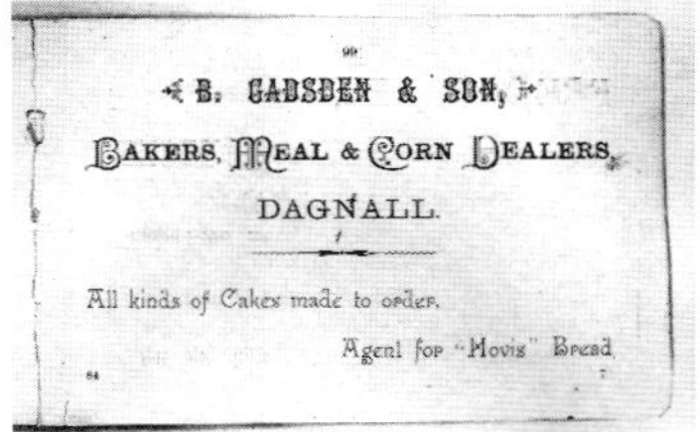

Advertisments for local services dating from 1903

Catchpole's Hardware Shop at no.13 LG -1950's-1960's

VPA Store for gardening requirements (Sunday mornings). From 1980 onwards.

And both the Deer Leap and Fourways Garages have sold sweets in recent years.

One could also buy milk, other dairy products, and fruit and vegetables direct from several village producers, and these may be read about in the section on farms and smallholdings.

When Miss Bevan was serving at the post office a customer took her horse right inside the shop.

In view of the current trend in village banking facilities, an entry in Canon Senar's book "Little Gaddesden and Ashridge" makes painful reading. This mentions a branch of Barclay's Bank (opening once a week) at no.18 Little Gaddesden in the 1930's. Let's just hope that the end-of-century passion for transforming "small and helpful" into "big and computerised" doesn't hit our villages too hard.

Car ownership started to increase in the 1960's but before that - even after the village bus service had started - there had been a different type of village mobility! Customers, particularly the elderly, could stay put, while the tradesmen came to them. Even people who were housebound could thus exercise their right of choice. Some deliveries came from the shops within the village, for example the Butcher and Fountain's Stores. From further off these delivery vans called regularly:

Co-op travelling shop. (Mr Sears at one time). Groceries once a week. 1930's? 1940's - 1960's

Mr MacIntyre. In a Trojan van from Berkhamsted. 1950s. Confectionery and preserves including 7lb stoneware jars of jam and marmalade.

Reading of Berkhamsted. Groceries and paraffin. 1930's - 1960's

Mr Gower. Fortnightly delivery of paraffin. 1940's

Others delivered to order: Sainsbury's, Kingham's Grocers, Home and Colonial and the International Stores, all in Berkhamsted, were still delivering orders in 1949, while Cook's of Northchurch and Horton's of Totternhoe delivered meat to Little Gaddesden and Ringshall customers, the latter from the 1940's to 1998.

Three bakers delivered:

The Co-op

Mr Wessel Gadsden and his brother of Gadsden Bakers, Dagnall. 1930's? 40's to 1960's

Mr Groom, and later Fred Taylor, of Groom's Bakery, Potten End. 1930's? 40's to 1989. Fred's delivery round only disappeared when Fred himself retired. It would have been a hard act to follow: Fred started his working day at 5 am.

Roy Haldane drives the Express Dairy float near the National Trust Estate yard

Milk was delivered from dairies in the village: In the 1940's Fred and Alec Andrews, or their assistant Miss Jean Moore, were delivering from the Bridgewater farm. Mr Underwood also had a milk round in 1949.
In 1999 milk is still being delivered to the village customers by the Express Dairy from their depot in Hemel Hempstead (since 1949 or earlier) and Mr Chris James of Tring (started 1990).

In the 1940's to 1960's women could still shop for new clothes without leaving their homes, from stock brought by Mr Fred Moore of Dunstable. Mr Janes of Edlesborough (or was it Dunstable?) delivered shoes and, later, electrical equipment ordered by customers from the the 1940's until his retirement in the 1980's. Until about the 1960's, when new materials for shoes were being introduced, soles and heels were made of either rubber or leather and needed regular repairing. Many people had the equipment to repair their own, but Mr Janes would take shoes away to repair. Earlier one little girl (now in her eighties) used to go to Berkhamsted only twice a year! "and that was when my mother marched all us children there and back, to buy shoes".

Little Gaddesden and Ringshall seem to have been astonishingly well provided with laundries - especially as almost every cottage would have its own copper and many of the wives would have "taken in" other people's washing to augment their housekeeping money. The principal laundry was at Ringshall in what is now Pear Tree House. Originally a public house called The Egerton Arms, it became a laundry in the nineteenth century. The last two owners were Don Wight Goodman and his son Bill. Old photographs still exist, taken long before mechanisation crept in, of the little field next to the building, with dozens of sheets hung out to dry in the sun. After the laundry closed in 1981 it first became a furniture shop and showroom, and then offices. In 1999 the business part of the premises were demolished to make way for a new bungalow.

There was also a laundry at 37 Little Gaddesden, run by Nellie and Nance Munden, while the sisters Alice, Emmie and Edie Garrett ran a small hand laundry at no.13 Ringshall for many years, the last of the sisters dying in the 1950's.

Jim Whitman's laundry, originally at no.40 Little Gaddesden (Yew Tree Cottage) moved to new premises in Hudnall Lane but soon closed. The vacant site was later occupied by the Van der Vieren's factory, Vanguard Staples and from 1980 Expotechnik. The site is now The Lye.

Nance and Nell Munden

A sad and more homely washday memory from the 1930's is of the toddler who sat down in a "great pan of boiling water when my granny was boiling up the washing". He survived but "I had to go into hospital. A poor little chap I was - I couldn't sleep on my back for months". It didn't put him off washday - when he recovered he used to stoke the copper fire, augmenting the precious wood with old brussels sprout stalks! The copper and the mangle and dolly board make our automatics seem shamefully self-indulgent. Nevertheless a lot safer.

For visitors to the village there was, and still is, the Bridgewater Arms, at one time a hotel, and there were three tea gardens, one run by Mrs Liberty at no.5 Little Gaddesden (now October House, another run by Mrs Hing at 28 Ringshall, and one by the Ibisons at Oak Tree Cottage, Fourways.

Little Gaddesden, Hudnall and Ringshall have been exceptionally lucky to have so many tradesmen living in the villages, most of them with considerable knowledge about the vagaries of village plumbing. There are still manhole covers in 3 cottage yards with the name of "S.Jones, Builder, Ringshall" on them. Stanley Jones of no.30 was a builder and decorator, and also made coffins, from 1928 until 1940. The Maunders family (no.18 Ringshall) were also painters and decorators from the 1930's to 1950's. One of them (Billy) worked with Janet Stinton's grandfather, Richard Fountain, and with young Arthur Clifton in building the extra wing to John O'Gaddesden's House. This was one of the many constructions of Fred Whitman, the Hudnall builder mentioned frequently in this book.

Another man of infinite resource and kindness was George Catchpole of no.13 Little Gaddesden, who worked as a builder and plumber from after the war until 1988.

Coming closer to the present, we have:

Recent:
Gordon Cripps, who lived and worked in the village for many years. There are many beautiful local examples of his carpentry and joinery.
Brian Freake, building trades
George Mayling, building trades

Alec Saunders and, below, the signboard for his business at 35 Ringshall, around 1930

Current:
Tony Sears of White Rails, building trades
Mark Gent of Ward's Hurst, building trades
Tony Mooring of 2 Little Gaddesden, electrical contractor
Ken Birks of 12 Cromer Close, plumber
Steve Akery of Paddocks, Hudnall Lane, glazing and property maintenance

There are also many who undertake gardening work.

One household emergency produced the lovely remark "Don't worry about buying a spare part - I've got one kicking about the field somewhere" - an embodiment of all that is best about a village crisis. Family solidarity, too, is strong. Colin Mogg of Ringshall specialised in electrical work, heating and plumbing from 1960 to 1994, with his son Andrew joining him and continuing in the family tradition - doubly so, since Andrew is the grandson of Stanley Jones.

The old methods of heating and lighting in the the villages were candles, oil lamps and coal, with wooding as an every-day activity, gathering sticks and logs of fallen wood for the fires. Coal was often sold on a highly individual basis, a sack at a time brought by a small dealer - you had to pay for that sack before you could order another. Mr Edward Saunders of 35 Ringshall delivered coal and wood from a yard at Hall Farm in his lorry from the 1930's to 1940's - a far cry from the giant oil tankers of today - and indeed some cottages were without electricity in the 1930's. Although oil, gas (from big fixed cylinders refilled from tankers) and electricity are the main sources of heat now, many houses still keep a coal or wood-burning fire, and need the attention of the chimney sweep: the Wellings of Tring, father and son, have served the village for many years in this capacity.

In the 1940's the timber industry, with the added impetus given by the war, was thriving. Two firms, East's of Berkhamsted and Fensome's of Markyate were employed in carting timber from Ashridge. In 1999 there are two local tree surgeons to deal with the more individual aspects of timber management, Patrick Faulconer of Meadow House, Hudnall, who also supplies logs, and Rod Wilson of Lower Gade Farm who is also a general forestry contractor.

We also have a health and beauty therapist and a health and beauty masseuse and reflexologist in the village these days: Alison Birks and Diana Dickinson.

It's nice to be able to end this list of trades and occupations with Min Catchpole's memory of her mother saving rabbit skins for the rag-and-bone man (he also swapped crockery for rags) - and with the mysteriously nomadic haberdasher. And of course the gypsies, including that wonderful couple, the Drapers.

BELOW:
Doris Cocks on the last day of trading in the shop in 1980.

BOTTOM:
Fountain's Store in 1980.
The old village pump is under the arch

Fountain's Stores

NUMBERS 5 AND 6 RINGSHALL

by Janet Stinton (née Cocks)

Although we are not sure of the exact date when the shop was started it is mentioned in the 1878 rent agreement with Ashridge, when it was run by my great-grandmother (called Grocer's Wife in the 1881 census). My great-grandfather, Alfred Fountain, had got permission to build the 8 ft x 8 ft extension between the house and the pumphouse from Lord Brownlow and did the work himself. The stock came by a horse-drawn cart from Tring, bringing bacon, tea, flour, sugar, rice, etc. Other stock came from local sources - dripping and lard from the kitchens at Ashridge and milk and butter from nearby farms. Vinegar came in a barrel and biscuits loose in large tins. Nothing was pre-packed and everything had to be weighed or measured out: blue bags for sugar and paper cones for smaller quantities. In 1910 my grandfather married Everelda Winter from Berkhamsted and she then ran the shop after my great-grandmother died. You could also buy cups and saucers, kettles, buttons, ribbons and lace, etc.

When my mother Doris married in

1939, having me a year later and my sister a year later still, she helped in the shop as well. A few years after returning from the War my father (who, in the intervening years, worked for Harold Ward in the Post Office) took over the shop and made the premises larger by taking in the larder from the house. He also started deliveries.

In 1973 Mike and I came back to live at No 5 with Mark and Barry, and Dad and I extended the shop again to take in the sittingroom. We also added greengrocery to the stock, obtained an alcohol licence and Dad started to cook his own hams. Dad died in 1976, having been in hospital for over 2 years and, in 1980, I very reluctantly closed the door for the last time and transferred the business to Little Gaddesden Post Office to go into partnership with Phyl Mountfort, and Fountain's Stores is now a sitting room again.

Fountain's stores 1st March 1980

The Little Gaddesden village shop

by Gill Fleckney

Some time before 1934 there was a General Stores at 15 Little Gaddesden in the front room of the home of Mr and Mrs Cobb (née Bevan) and the Sub Post Office had been moved there from 42 Little Gaddesden. No.42, on the Green, continued as a grocer's which sold cut ham, bacon and cheese, run by Miss Evelyn Pratt and assisted by Miss Louie Cheeseman. Another General Stores was at no.5 Ringshall.

My father, Harold Ward, was apprenticed to Shaw's, the Grocer's in Hemel Hempstead but it is never quite clear in family history if he completed that apprenticeship or left suddenly after singing a rather derogatory song in the cold store about his manager, when he thought he was out of earshot. Anyway, the outcome was my father pedalling his delivery bike from 20 George Street, Hemel Hempstead, where he lived with his family, around the Gaddesdens, Dagnall and Whipsnade daily, selling newspapers, matches, tobacco and cigarettes. Another way of training and keeping fit as he was also goalie for St Albans Football Club. He started renting the shop at no. 15 in 1934.

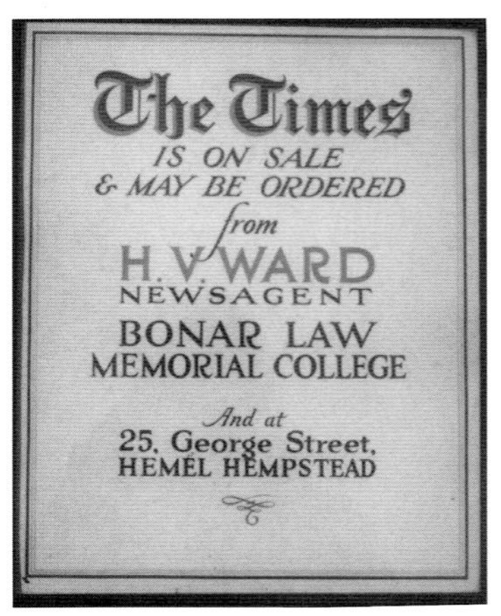

The sign used by Harold Ward when he sold newspapers at Ashridge House

He and my mother, Boxmoor born and bred, married in 1935 and moved into rented rooms at 47 Little Gaddesden and then into part of 14 Little Gaddesden. They bought that in 1940 when a branch of the Whitman family moved out. They were thus almost opposite the one room shop and Sub Post Office at no.15 where Mr and Mrs Cobb still lived in the house. They eventually moved business to the present village shop, which they had built for them by Mr Whitman and opened on 10th November 1947. The architect was Louis Moore of Theccans, later of Greenacre, who sent Harold Ward a receipt for his fees worded as follows:

20/3/48
Dear Mr Ward,
Many thanks for your cheque for Fifty Pounds in payment of my account. This by the way was fifty Guineas but I presume you are so used to deducting discounts that it becomes quite automatic. I shall have to have strictly nett printed on my billheads.
Yours faithfully
Louis Moore

An attached postage stamp for 2d endorsed with the date made this a legal receipt, as was required in those days. (A guinea was one pound and one shilling.)

The shop stayed in my family's hands until my father's death in 1969 after which my mother leased it to Mr Barlow, then Mrs Battell, and then to Mrs Phyl Mountfort and Mrs Janet Stinton. Before buying the business with Janet, Phyl Mountfort had worked there under Mr Barlow and Mrs Battel. Phyl became postmistress. Her sister, Mrs Fountain, also worked there. She was the wife of Reg Fountain who is no relation of the Fountain family of Fountain's Stores. The premises were finally sold on Mrs Ward's death in 1984 to Naresh and Gigi Odedra, who also bought the business.

Mr and Mrs Draper - the scissor grinders

by John Leonhardt

Josiah and Amy Draper used to come to the village twice a year, calling at their regular customers in particular, and looking for new ones. I used to ask them to grind garden shears, axes, a sickle, bill-hooks, the rotary lawn-mower blade and a carving knife - not all at the same visit.

Amy was born at Potten End in a tent, as Amy Parker. Her parents were travellers. Josiah was born in Staffordshire. His parents were also travellers. He started scissor-grinding with his father, with a pedalled machine.

Amy and Josiah in winter clothing, and with the grindstone running directly off the battery of the yellow car - January 1985

When first married they travelled only with a pram, then later with a horse and cart. (The horse, cart and harness cost them £2.10s.). They bought their first motor vehicle, an 'O' type Bedford lorry in 1953 from a coal merchant in Stratford-on-Avon. They did some scrap-dealing for a while, but found scissor-grinding more profitable. When they first began coming to Little Gaddesden I do not know, but I knew them from the late 1970's. In 1984 they had a Bedford van, no. HYM 467N, and came to the village in April and August.

During the year they travelled out to Worcester, Banbury, Oxford, Surrey, Hampshire and Bedfordshire. They were living in a caravan in Milton Keynes while on the Little Gaddesden round in 1984. Their next vehicle was a yellow van, NEG 410M.

It was always Josiah who did the grinding, using, in the days that I knew him, a small electric grindstone which he placed on the ground, connected to a spare car battery in the back of the van. He sat on the ground to work. He would take the shears apart to grind each blade, and oil them well. His grinding was always excellent. Amy would call at the door and collect the items to sharpen, and would collect the money.

They were an old couple in the 1980's, with wrinkled weather-beaten round faces, quite short in stature, he dressed in grey trousers and a jacket or waistcoat, and she in a longish coloured dress of some darkish hue as I recall. You could get them into conversation, but they would not talk much otherwise.

One day Josiah came without his wife. Amy had died of heart failure, it seemed. Using a motoring idiom of his period, Josiah said she had simply "conked out". He expressed his worry to me that the minister at her funeral had got her name wrong, and I tried to say that it was not such a terrible thing as everyone knew who she really was, God included. He sharpened my tools as usual, but he only came once or twice more. He left no calling card.

Bridgewater Arms

by Vivien Foord-Kelcey

Brewing took place at the Bridgewater Arms until the end of the 19th century.

From 1870 until 1878 Mr. Norris brewed the beer here and was followed by George Allison from 1882 to 1895. A licensee in the 1920's, a Mr. Geer, was also an engineer and he had electricity installed at the inn.

In later years extensive improvements were carried out on the taproom, the stables, and the outhouses, and the garden was enlarged and enclosed.

The bar at one end of the pub is called Shep's Bar. This had a separate entrance with a request for walkers or workmen with muddy boots to use this door. The floor is flagstone with no carpet and there used to be a door between the two bars, but now the pub is open plan. There is a text hanging in the bar explaining the name.

"Shep's Bar dedicated to William George Bunting, 1873-1956, a renowned local countryman known to all as Old Shep. He figured prominently in Cooper advertisements from 1935 onwards, his face familiar to farmers throughout the land. This colourful character regularly graced this bar where, over a jug of his favourite ale, he would offer advice and a friendly tale. He lived at Cromer Cottage."

According to Old Shep's grandson,

Alan Bunting, the last comment in this text is incorrect – Shep lived at 1 Home Farm Cottages.

The Trust House Forte Group bought the Bridgewater Arms and ran it for several years as an hotel. It was sold in 1977 to Mr. A.J Simon for £53,000.00. Tony Simon, who still lives in Little Gaddesden, did many renovations. He refurbished the ground floor to run it as a pub and restaurant without accommodation, and divided the residential areas into six new flats. He ran the business with a variety of managers, lasting only about six months each. According to Tony, they were all colourful characters. One kept a donkey in the garden but he had to be told to move it as it made such a noise that it was impossible to sell the flats when they were ready. When a woman customer complained that the publican had kicked the dog that he had with him behind the bar, he poured a pint of beer over her head. This all proved too much for Tony, and in 1979 he sold the Bridgewater Arms to Mr. W.W.Woods for £149,000.00.

William Bunting talking to Billy Batchelor at the Bridgewater Arms

Bill Woods ran the pub, with his son Paul, and they started brewing on the premises in 1981. A series of storage sheds were converted into a brewery and Bill took a course in brewing. Two types of bitter were produced and sold on the premises and to other outlets. Paul Woods is certain that the Bridgewater Arms has a ghost - apparently a lady who fell down the steps to the cellar and broke her neck. Her presence has often been felt around the inn, especially in the cellar, where she has also been seen, he didn't say when or by whom! Paul tells the story that once when he had been left to lock up the pub, he carefully slid the bolts and locked the big front door, witnessed by others, and left by the back door, leaving the building secure. To his surprise, when he arrived the next morning, the front door was standing open! Paul recalls that there is a large well partially under and behind the building, and believes it was used for watering the horses when the Bridgewater Arms was a coaching inn.

By 1987 Leonard Walker was the tenant and licensee, having been a manager of the Bridgewater Arms for the Trust House Forte Group in 1976. Sadly the pub was closed for business in March 1988, "owing to illness and lack of trade."

At this time the road through the village was closed for the laying of main drains making it almost impossible to reach the pub, and so it was hardly surprising that there was "lack of trade." Bill Woods put the Bridgewater Arms up for sale and in September 1988 William Goodman bought it for £325,000.00. William Goodman owned the laundry at Ringshall (in 1999 the building called The Coach House) which he sold when he bought the Bridgewater Arms. He also owned The Chequers at Pitstone.

Another local character at about this time was " Old Jim". This was Jim Fleckney, the Forester. He had his own special chair in the corner, which he used to reserve. He would telephone when he wanted to go to the pub and ask for a reserve sign to be put on the chair. As he used to walk across the fields, he also used to request that if he didn't arrive in a quarter of an hour someone would go to look for him, in case he was stuck in the mud and needed pulling out.

The property was purchased by Sunglint Ltd. in 1989, followed by Country Style Inns in 1991, who applied for planning permission for internal alterations which was approved in December of that year.

In 1996, the six part BBC 1 television series, Ivanhoe, was filming in the Golden Valley. There were hundreds of extras playing the hordes of Normans and Saxons, some being played by full-time Scottish Clansmen who also appeared in "Braveheart" and "Rob Roy". There were whole families camping in the valley. Apparently, they went into the Bridgewater Arms dressed in their kilts and playing their bagpipes.

When the film "First Knight" was filming near Ivinghoe Beacon, (also with the Clansmen) It is said that Richard Gere and Sean Connery also used to frequent the Bridgewater Arms. Unfortunately, I didn't hear of this at the time!

The present owners are The Old English Inns and Hotels Company and the current managers are Paul and Susan Graham. Paul is from Liverpool, but lived in New Zealand for twelve years and Susan is a New Zealander. They ran a restaurant in Christchurch. They have a little daughter and chose to come to the Bridgewater Arms because they liked the idea that she could walk to the Village School across the fields, so maintaining the historic link between the pub and the school.

Information obtained from:
"Little Gaddesden and Ashridge" by Howard Senar
"Here for the Beer – a gazetteer of the brewers of Hertfordshire" compiled by Helen Poole
"A Hertfordshire Valley" by Scott Hastie and David Spain
"The English Pub" by Andy Whipple and Rob Anderson
"Little Gaddesden" by Vicars Bell
The Dacorum Licence Records

Also from conversation with:
Alan Bunting, Paul Graham, Tony Simon, Ben Walsh and Paul Woods.

More Haunting

by Alice Leonhardt

While working as a part-time waitress at the Bridgewater Arms in 1991, I used to hear many stories from Rob, Sam and Nanny who were running the pub at the time.

They would tell of strange, ghostly occurrences such as doors being locked that had been open, items going missing and appearing again in strange places and the time when Rob got stuck in the cellar because a keg propping the door open fell over and rolled away so that the door slammed shut.

I was interested in these stories but sceptical until one lunchtime when I felt there may have been more to them. It had been a busy day in the pub, and after lunchtime closing all the staff sat down for a meal as we did every Sunday. Towards the end of the meal there was a strange chinking noise and suddenly a glass shot across the room and smashed on the far wall.

It happened so quickly we were unsure as to what had happened and where it had come from. The room felt cold and the atmosphere intense.

Rob got up to investigate and he found one single pint glass was missing from the high level shelf above the bar that had a ridge across the front for safety. The glass must have 'jumped' over the ridge and travelled across the room before hitting the wall, as if someone had thrown it. Rob got the dustpan and swept up the shattered glass. There was so much of it, it seemed much more than one glass.

To me there seemed to be a very strange presence in the room, but Rob, Sam and Nanny were quite blasé about the whole thing.

"That'll be the ghost again ... I wonder what's upset it this time."

I was surprised by their reaction but to them it was just another mysterious occurrence.

Editor's Note: Rob and Sam were husband and wife. Nanny, real name Gwen, was Rob's mother.

Deer Leap Horticulture

RON BROOKS GARDEN MACHINERY AND DEER LEAP HORTICULTURE

from a conversation with Ron Brooks

Ron Brooks, who had been working with farm machinery in the Tring area, came to Cromer Close in 1949 with his wife Maysie. After doing agricultural work with George Whitman and Jim Whitman, garage mechanic's work at Deer Leap Garage at two different periods, and a bit of construction work with George Catchpole in between, he discovered a niche for reconditioning garden machinery, starting with a lawn mower which someone in Alderton Drive was throwing out. It was a J.P. mower, a quality brand, and he resold it to Mr Haydon of Coneygarth who was satisfied with it for many years.

Having found a source of second hand mowers from a garden machinery showroom in Harpenden, he gradually developed a business. As it became viable he bought a second hand van from Fred Taylor the Potten End baker, and then managed to rent a barn at Home Farm from Mr Muddiman from about 1963. By now this had become his full-time self-employed business. Ron's son Derek eventually joined him.

When Mr Muddiman sold the property Ron took out a mortgage on the barn, did a lot of restoration work and built a workshop adjoining it. Most of this was done by his own hand. Brian Freake did the roofing. Ron also built the adjacent bungalow, which he moved into.

BELOW:
Ron Brooks's son Derek, and Arthur Hutchings

BOTTOM:
Ron Brooks at the Home Farm workshop.

After two years in the bungalow, however, he had to move out and sell the business, being unable to find (until just too late) financial backing to keep up his bank repayments.

continued by Peter Wilson and Marilyn Price

The business and the bungalow were purchased by Ken Wilson in September 1975. Renamed Deer Leap Horticulture, it has continued to be run as a family business since that date, so it is proud to be celebrating 25 years in the garden machinery business in the year 2000. The original family members were Ken and Betty Wilson and their son Peter. When permission was granted to extend the bungalow in 1991, their daughter Marilyn moved in with her husband Geoff and two sons, and the senior Wilsons were able to take late retirement and pass on the running of the business to Peter and Marilyn, thus maintaining the family element.

The barn showroom under the Wilsons' management

Deer Leap Horticulture has made a steady but deliberately constrained growth throughout its 25 years, and with the introduction of the two younger members, the intention is for it to remain a family concern giving personal service within the rural environment of Little Gaddesden.

Varying reports have been made from a number of sources about the origins of the barn from which the company operates, but it has proved difficult to establish the true history. It formed part of the original Home Farm complex - lending itself admirably to its use as a showroom for the sale of horticultural equipment, with the service and repair section operating from the adjacent workshop.

Deer Leap Garage

A Deer Leep Garage van and Ron Brooks's son Colin.

The garage originated in the 1930's or possibly earlier. The Ringshall Lodge has always been part of the site. It is a gatekeeper's lodge dating back to about 1817. It was still being used as the entrance to the park up to the sale of the Brownlow estate. Leslie Bedford, who may have been the first owner, added the swimming pool in the 1930's. He continued to own the garage through the 1940's and 50's. Mr Savage was the manager in the 1940's.

In 1952 it was a wooden garage and did car repairs as well as sell petrol. Les Bedford at that time also had a yard of builder's machinery at Potten End and trained race horses in that area. Ray Hing, Roger Goodman and Ron Brooks all worked for him at Deer Leap.

The Deer Leap garage on the last day of petrol sales

The wooden garage was burnt down in about 1958 and George Catchpole was employed to rebuild it. Hollings and Giltrow were the next owners. During their time, which included the 1960's, they were selling agents for the Rootes Group of vehicles, which were Humbers and Hillmans.

The next owner was Gordon Huxtable who took over in 1964 and later built up the agency for Subaru and Isuzu cars, all of which were four-wheel-drive vehicles, popular in rural areas such as this. He was one of their most successful agents, and many local people bought his cars and used his garage for servicing. There was great consternation when they learnt that Gordon was retiring and closing down the garage. The last day of petrol sales was July 25th 1997. The rest of the business closed down the following year.

1999 saw the gradual demolition of the garage until all that is left is the Ringshall Lodge, a listed building. The site has been approved for housing. The county boundary divides it into two parts, with Ringshall Lodge and the big oak tree on the Buckingham side, so planning permission has to be sought separately for each side of it.

Fourways Garage

Like Deer Leap Garage, this dates back to the 1930s. It was built by Fred Whitman using bricks from a demolished brewery at Dagnall. During the second world war Mr Ibison was the owner and there was a tea room there.

In 1955 it was O'Shea's and Eve Ouseley started working there. During the 1980's and 90's the petrol brand sold there was Murco. There were second-hand cars for sale and repair workshops.

In about 1996 the garage was unable to withstand a loss of business caused by a major road works which closed the main road for several weeks, and it closed down. The workshops of several small mechanical and engineering firms now occupy the rear of the premises, including Manual and Automatic Gearboxes and Woodside Body Shop. These are entered from Hudnall Lane. The main buildings and front yard are now the sales area of Turner Groundscare who sell John Deere and other agricultural and horticultural machinery.

The National Trust

ASHRIDGE ESTATE

with information provided by Graeme Cannon, Estate Manager and John Wilson, retired Head Ranger

Growth of the National Trust

DATE ACQUIRED

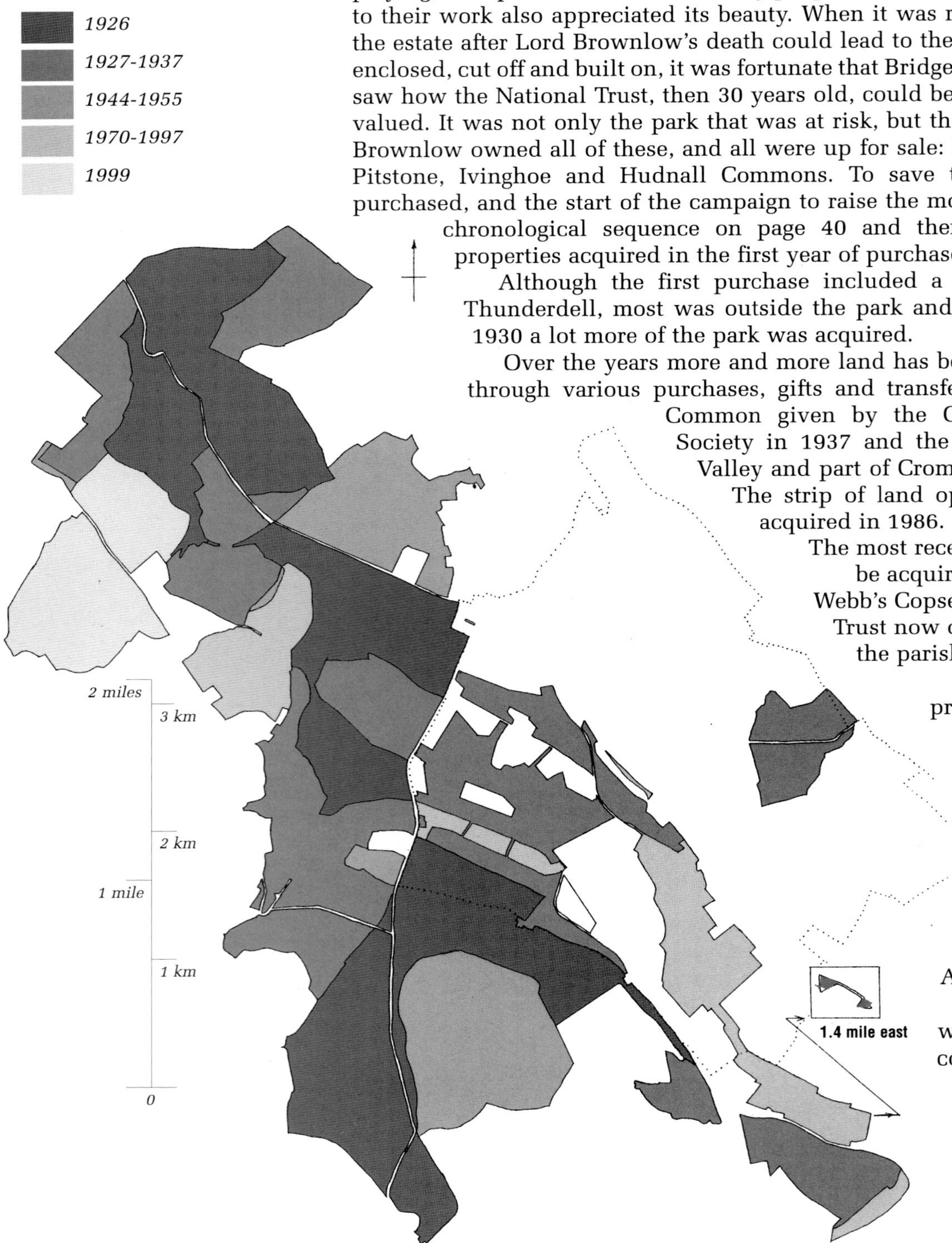

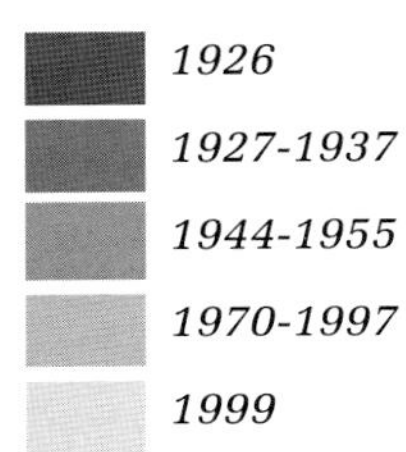

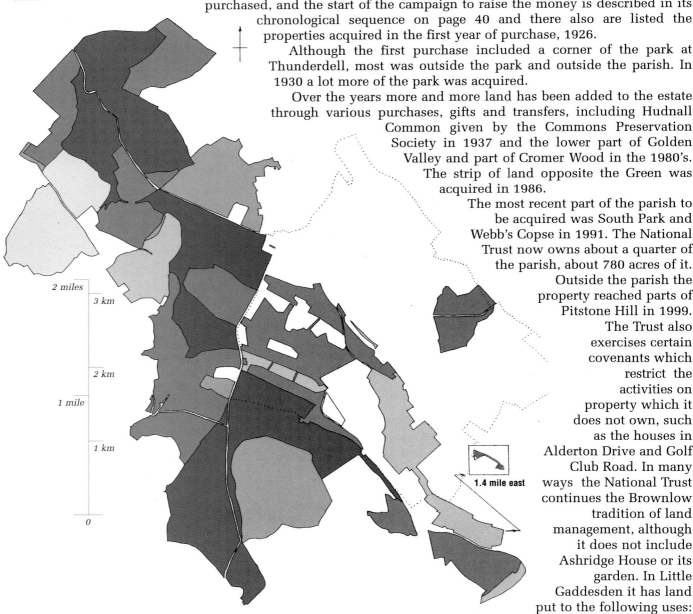

The Ashridge Estate under the Brownlows had been a great amenity to local people although privately owned. Some of the contributions to this book show how the park was not just used by the Brownlows' friends and relations. Many activities, both organised (like cricket matches) and casual (like children playing) took place there, and the many people who went through the park daily to their work also appreciated its beauty. When it was realised that the sale of the estate after Lord Brownlow's death could lead to the land being deforested, enclosed, cut off and built on, it was fortunate that Bridget Talbot and her friends saw how the National Trust, then 30 years old, could be the saviour of all they valued. It was not only the park that was at risk, but the local commons. Lord Brownlow owned all of these, and all were up for sale: Berkhamsted, Aldbury, Pitstone, Ivinghoe and Hudnall Commons. To save them, they had to be purchased, and the start of the campaign to raise the money is described in its chronological sequence on page 40 and there also are listed the properties acquired in the first year of purchase, 1926.

Although the first purchase included a corner of the park at Thunderdell, most was outside the park and outside the parish. In 1930 a lot more of the park was acquired.

Over the years more and more land has been added to the estate through various purchases, gifts and transfers, including Hudnall Common given by the Commons Preservation Society in 1937 and the lower part of Golden Valley and part of Cromer Wood in the 1980's. The strip of land opposite the Green was acquired in 1986.

The most recent part of the parish to be acquired was South Park and Webb's Copse in 1991. The National Trust now owns about a quarter of the parish, about 780 acres of it. Outside the parish the property reached parts of Pitstone Hill in 1999.

The Trust also exercises certain covenants which restrict the activities on property which it does not own, such as the houses in Alderton Drive and Golf Club Road. In many ways the National Trust continues the Brownlow tradition of land management, although it does not include Ashridge House or its garden. In Little Gaddesden it has land put to the following uses:

2 miles
3 km
2 km
1 mile
1 km
0
1.4 mile east

OPEN SPACES FOR THE RECREATION AND ENJOYMENT OF THE PUBLIC

Hudnall Common is one of these. No commoners' rights have been registered on this and some of the other commons mentioned above, though on Aldbury Common certain parishioners have negotiated rights of estover (allowing them to collect certain categories of fallen wood).

The final date for registering commoners' rights was January 1970. The public access is subject to the National Trust's byelaws. Horses must keep to the public bridleways and permissive horse tracks.

LAND MANAGED TO CONSERVE WILD PLANT AND ANIMAL LIFE

Parts of Hudnall Common fall into this category also. The scalloped verges of Hudnall Lane on the left going down the hill have become rich in wild flowers, and many butterflies enjoy these south-facing sun-traps in their season. Up to the early 1980's the thicket grew right down to the edge of the road, but John Wilson started a process of gradually clearing it back, and this has been continued under Graeme Cannon. Wild-life conservation is nowadays one of the most valuable functions of the Trust over the estate generally.

GRASSLAND MOWN FOR HAY OR SILAGE

Once again Hudnall Common provides an example. Although open for recreation, most of the grassland is cut once a year by arrangement with one of the farmers.

For many years the Blains of St Margaret's Farm made hay bales there, but St Margaret's is now only an arable farm, and in 1999 the grass was cut by Peter Stone of Park Farm for silage stored in black plastic wrapping.

GOLF COURSE

Most of Ashridge Golf Course (but not the Club House) is on Trust land. The public only have right of access over the public footpaths which cross the course, numbers 3,4,5 and 6.

GRAZING LAND

Old Park, acquired mostly in 1926, has been used for grazing cattle since 1957. South Park, acquired in 1991 as arable land, has been converted to grazing. Both are now rented to Peter Stone.

ARABLE LAND

Most of the Trust's arable farmland is now outside the parish, but North Park was an arable field until recently, farmed by Don Cox, and before him by John Mead.

The top of Hudnall Common was ploughed for food production during the second world war, along with other commons outside the parish. Old Park was arable before 1957 and Hudnall Common remained arable until 1960. Cereals were the main crops.

Roderick Wilson at a Royal Forestry Society meeting discussing the management of Hardings Rookery. Graeme Cannon is on the left.

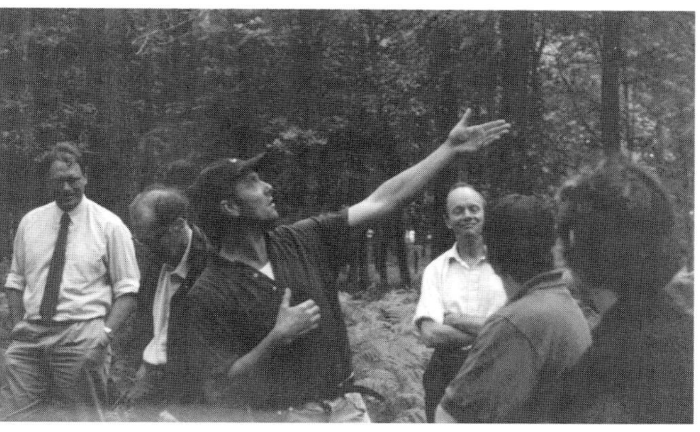

COMMERCIAL FORESTRY

The National Trust woodlands are of such a large area that it is possible to keep up rotations of felling and re-planting so that there is always a mixture of different ages. This makes for a successful combination of commercial forestry and woodland conservation. Both broad-leaved and conifer plantations are grown. Within the parish, timber is growing at Harding's Rookery (Beech), Thunderdell Wood (Sweet Chestnut) and other plots.

OTHER WOODLAND

There are quite extensive non-commercial areas of trees and scrub which have amenity, landscape and wildlife value. One very ancient Ash tree is still looked after by the National Trust even though its huge trunk has gone. In 1949 it was described by Henry (Harry) Gordon as follows:
"Shorn of most of its big branches, its majestic height now reduced to twenty feet by the collapse and disappearance of its top, completely hollow inside and

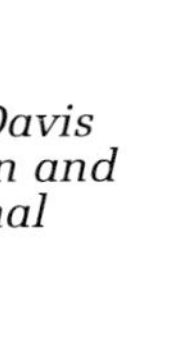

ABOVE
Harding's Rookery: Bob Davis - forester, Graeme Cannon and Richard Wheeler - Regional Land Agent.

RIGHT AND BELOW LEFT
Timber from Thunderdell Wood

BELOW RIGHT
The oldest Ash in Ashridge

resembling a great tube, this old warrior still contrives to live. Twice it has been in flames, due to visitors to the park lighting fires inside. I saw the veteran recently; its trunk still bore traces of the fires, but the remaining branches carried leaves. ... It seemed so wise and yet so lonely, like some giant of the past who had outlived his day and slipped silently into inarticulate old age. I patted its trunk to let it feel that someone still cared, because this is the only survivor of the original ashes of Asserugge."

Yes, this tree is still with us in 1999, now a circle of vigorous but crooked young trunks, in the middle of which can still be seen a few craggy lumps of the original and the hollow place in the centre. It is hidden, unrecognised, in the woods outside the college garden fence near the Golden Valley. The other ancient Ash, the King Ash, was in Park Pulridge Wood but is now lost. (see page 279)

The village pond opposite the green

PONDS

The Trust has several good wild ponds in the golf course and woods of the parish. The one opposite the Green was restored in 1991-92, which required sealing the brick retaining wall on the down-hill side and making a new lining of clay. A good selection of native plants was introduced and the pond was soon colonised by all kinds of invertebrates and frogs. Mallard and Moorhen are often seen there.

Forestry work with the National Trust

from conversations with Tom and Alethea Thame and John Wilson

Jim Fleckney receiving his award

The longest serving forester the National Trust Ashridge Estate had was Jim Fleckney, who was presented with a medal by the Queen Mother when he had completed forty years service in 1970. His forestry service was only interrupted by army service during the war. In 1946 or 1947 Tom Thame joined the team, his brother Cyril having joined a bit earlier. They lived at Dagnall at that time. The Head Ranger then was Bertie Marks who lived at Thunderdell Lodge adjoining the estate yard. Other foresters were Wally Dell and Arthur Moorcraft from Aldbury, and Ernie Saunders who walked every day from New Mill in Tring. Some years later Bertie Marks retired and Bill Scott took over. Jim Wiggins, who had worked under Bill Scott in Sussex, then joined the team.

In 1957 the Head Ranger's post again became vacant

John Wilson at Thunderdell Lodge in 1993

and John Wilson from Fountains Abbey, Studley Royal in Yorkshire, took over. John retired in 1991 but is still a well-known resident, now living in Ringshall. His son Roderick is a tree surgeon and forester who does contract work for the Trust. Of the other retired foresters, Tom Thame still lives opposite the estate yard with his wife Alethea, Jim Fleckney died in 1998, and Jim Wiggins was still living in Ringshall in 1999, though in failing health and often staying away with his family. He died early in 2000.

In Bertie Marks's day, and on into John Wilson's early years here, the forestry work was carried out through the agency of Brown and Merry of Tring. The work had to earn enough money to pay the foresters' wages at least. A lot of it was cutting and selling firewood, the foresters making deliveries by tractor and trailer as well as felling and logging. Most of it was sold to local members of the National Trust, who were entitled to a discount. Some of these were in Berkhamsted and Tring. The firewood was sold in various states at different prices, a cheap load consisting of a cord which the customer would cut up himself later. A cord is 128 cubic feet of logs about 4 feet long. The workers got two loads a year for their personal use and were able to supplement this with wood collected in their own time. They did, however, also buy coal for their fires, which warmed their homes, heated their water and fired their ovens. In 1948, when Thunderdell Cottages were newly built and Tom and Alethea moved into no.2, they had no electricity.

In Bill Scott's time acres of land were replanted, including Great Frithsden Copse. It first had to be cleared of old trees and scrub, and this was still in the days of hand tools. In John Wilson's time they replanted Little Frithsden Copse and Sallow Copse and cleared acres of bracken from the commons. The tools used for most of the timber work were the axe and the cross-cut saw. The most popular weight of axe for falling a tree was the seven pound.

I asked Tom Thame how they felled the trees, but round here they don't fell them, they fall them. "At the bottom of the tree it spreads out, it doesn't come straight down to the ground. Well, you had to cut all that off first."

I asked if it had to be made straight-sided right on down to the ground: "That's right. Well you had to, you see, because of the handles of the saw. It might only go back and forward about two inches because of the spread at the bottom. You could get a tree with a hell of a spur on - that's what we used to call them. They'd come down so far, then when they get "that" far from the ground they spread - you'd get three or four spurs. You had to chop them right down. There was sometimes half a day's axe work round one of those trees."

"Then you'd cut your tree; look and see which way the tree was leaning and which way you wanted it to fall. The throat was cut at the front. This was axe work. Then you went behind there and sawed the tree down. You left, say, a piece like that" (indicating a couple of inches) "and when you've got the tool about half way through you stick an iron wedge in."

When Jim Wiggins explained tree-falling to scouts he always called the V-shaped cut the "bird's mouth", but Tom always called it the "throat". The saw had, in fact, only been used for making one horizontal cut when falling the tree, but it was used a lot more afterwards for removing the boughs and logging. I asked about the length of the saws: "Well, you had a four foot, a six foot - well you did have a seven foot but they was mostly six foot."

These long cross-cut saws have a handle at each end and the two operators have to be perfectly harmonised to each other's motion. The blade is not rigid, so the most important rule is that you don't push while your partner is pulling, yet you must still guide the saw and take up the pull at the right moment on the return stroke. When someone new to it partnered an experienced man it could be weeks before he got it right. "Some of them didn't stay very long" said Tom.

Improvements in tools came in gradually. The first petrol-driven saw, in about 1957, required two men to work it, and was only good for the horizontal cut. The bow saw with a steel bow and replaceable blade with hardened teeth was good, but they do not come four feet long. The work really speeded up with the one-man petrol chain saw which could handle the old axe work, and does not have to have such a long blade because it has a free end. This saw still has one thing in common with the old cross-cut saw: the teeth need frequent sharpening. With the old cross-cut: "If you were out in the woods you might come against anything - sometimes in the middle of these trees or just at the outside you'd catch a bit of metal or a nail. And if you did you'd cut two small trees growing there, just cut the tops off, make two notches in the top, then lodge the saw upside down on these two pieces and then you've got a sharpening horse."

"How often did you find two trees at just the right distance?" - "There was so much wood on the go that it was no trouble at all." - "And then did you sharpen them with a file or a stone?" - "Oh a file."

Jim Wiggins was skilled in the craft of hurdle-making. He probably learnt that in Sussex before he came to Ashridge. It involves splitting hazel and weaving it into lengths of portable fencing, which used to be the standard way of dividing sheep fields so that the sheep could only graze off a portion at a time. He kept this skill up, making them from time to time and demonstrating at shows, at which he would appear wearing a traditional smock made by his wife Doris. This was a very practical garment made of very strong cloth, gathered into many tight folds in front by means of the smocking stitches which were sewn in fancy patterns. The smock would stand up to a lot of wear and pressure, as it would get when working with stout springy hazel or, in the case of a shepherd, when handling sheep.

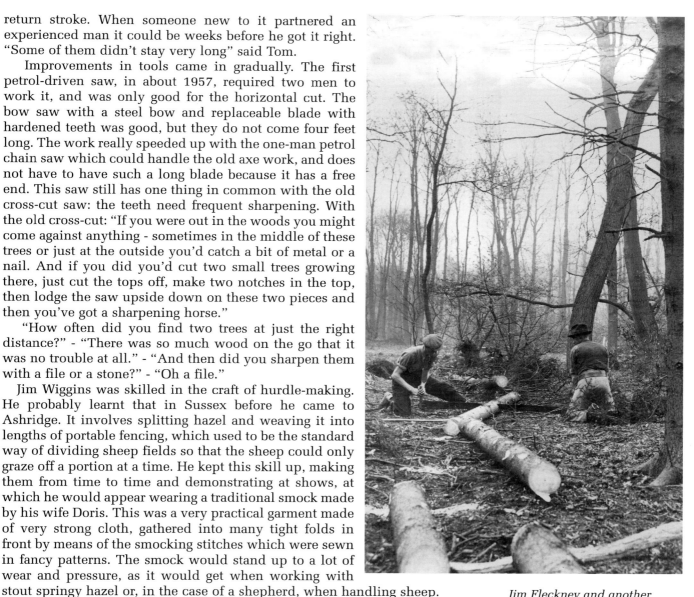

Jim Fleckney and another woodman with cross cut saw in 1936

Back in the 1940's, heavy timber was still moved by heavy horses. Ward's at Berkhamsted would take beech trees with horse-drawn limbers. Ken Ward was the buyer who came to measure up, and his uncle owned the business. They took timber for making veneers, various species but especially oak. By coincidence, when the Wards sold their business it was bought by Dennis Ward, who was no relation of theirs at all. Their sawmill was at Bourne End. Brown's at Luton also took good oak, and they were the first local firm to change from horses to lorries.

The job of the foresters included cutting the rides with hand scythes, and later on with petrol-driven Allen Scythes. "It's all right until you cut into a wasps' nest. Then you run like hell." They also had to be on call at all times in case of emergencies such as fallen trees across roads or, in the summer time, fires.

After John Wilson retired in 1991, Graeme Cannon took over. His title is now Estate Manager.

Farms and smallholdings

by the Editor

In this chapter the farms and smallholdings are taken in alphabetical order. There are also maps showing land use, farm boundaries and field names in the map section.

At the beginning of the century most of the farms were rented from the Brownlow Estate. The buildings and yards were near the farm house and the fields were close by. Over the years fields have changed hands piecemeal and holdings have expanded or contracted or become fragmented. In the last twenty or thirty years many of the farm houses have become occupied by residents who have no business with the farm, while farmers have moved into other properties. Farm buildings, becoming redundant, have been converted into housing. Nevertheless, there is still a very large proportion of the farmland that was there a hundred years ago if you include the grazing of horses used for recreational riding.

Nearly all our farms are still family units, which is contrary to the trend in other parts where the owners are big companies and the farmers are employees. Many of the farming families own their land, some rent it and some have a mixture of owned and rented land, the biggest landlord being the National Trust. The larger farms all run across our boundary into neighbouring parishes.

A lot of the seasonal work on farms, if it involves expensive machinery, is now done by contractors, who may also have farms of their own. If they are outside the parish they are likely to be missed in this book.

In the 1930s, the village school started a survey of the farms as part of their book of the village. I have quoted from it wherever possible.

Mowing hay at Cadding, Ashridge Farm in 1999

Ashridge Farm and Hall Farm

mainly from a conversation with Elizabeth Craib

Ashridge Farm is the name of the present-day farm and land. An early 19th century name is Ringshall Hall Farm. This is naturally shortened to Hall Farm when spoken of, but the Ordnance Survey in their 1897 and 1922 surveys call it Ringshall Farm. The Janes family lived here in 1899 (See page 302). The school children's survey of local farms in the 1930's lists Hall Farm but gives no information about it. Mrs Potton, wife of a Berkhamsted coal merchant, was the owner later on, when the house became separated from the land, as she sold the land to the Ellisons of Beaney Farm, but continued to live in the house. The land, now Ashridge Farm, was sold again in 1969 to the Craib family, and the original house, which is still called Hall Farm, was sold to the Cullen family in 1976.

Derek and Elizabeth Craib moved to Ashridge Farm from Bushey in 1969 in order to have enough room for their horses. Elizabeth and her two daughters, Janet and Margie, were keen riders. Derek was a solicitor. Elizabeth was not a stranger to the area, as she had been brought here on picnics from childhood in the 1920s, but she did not know the local people. There were riding stables, and there was planning permission to build another house. The Craibs had the present house built with a perfect view down the valley from the upstairs sitting room. They have about 60 to 65 acres of land, part of which is the wood known as Levi Spring.

Other horse owners, who had used the stables or grazing under the previous ownership, requested continuation of these arrangements, and the Craibs soon became closely involved with the local community. The daughters started to ride as escorts to less experienced riders, and staff were needed for the stables. Before long it became apparent that with qualified instructors a professional equestrian centre could be set up. A British Horse Society Instructor was in due course taken on, and stable hands. Additional buildings included more stables, a barn, tack rooms, a staff room, teaching room, rest room and a bungalow for resident staff. Then came students for the British Horse Society's examinations, some of whom were also in residence.

This professional centre ran from 1973 to 1991, with Margie Craib taking over the management from her mother in 1982. The instructor for the first three years was Tricia Elliot, who was followed by Simon Scott. At its peak the centre housed 35 horses and was training 12 students for B.H.S. exams. In the meadows 50 jumps were set out covering all levels of training, and

Ashridge Farm 1999

everything was strictly checked by the B.H.S. to conform with national standards.

On one occasion there was a phone call from the police, who asked if they could turn out as many riders and horses as possible to hunt for a missing girl. All the riders rose to the occasion and searched enthusiastically, but the girl was found to have gone off to a friend's house without telling her family.

The Craibs deliberately started reducing their activities in 1988, taking on fewer students, as Derek and Elizabeth wanted a quieter life and Margie wanted to work as a chiropractor, in which profession she had just qualified.

After 1991 the stables went back to something like the pre-1969 days, as a livery stable run by Jean Bruce-Smith under lease. In 1984 Derek Craib retired from his solicitor's practice and in 1994 he died. In 1999 Elizabeth Craib and her daughter Margie still live at the house.

Beaney Farm

mainly from Janet Stinton

In 1899 the house, Benhay, was the Rectory and the land that went with it would presumably have been used productively. It passed into private hands in 1928, and in due course was owned by Mr and Mrs Ellison. In their time, which included the 1950's and 60's, it was a very busy and thriving smallholding. Mr V. Ellison was the managing director of Blue Circle Cement, but Mrs Mary Ellison managed Beaney Farm and worked as hard at it as any of her employees. Amongst the girls who worked for her were Margaret Bruton (now Mrs Carver), Janet Cocks (now Mrs Stinton) and Wendy Janes (now Mrs Forster), all of whom still live in the village (or only just outside in the case of the Carvers).

As a market garden it produced all kinds of vegetables. Some of their produce was sold at a Village Produce Association stall at Hemel Hempstead's Thursday market, which they started. Besides their home grown produce they also sold pork brawn and cracked eggs. The brawn they made themselves from pigs' heads and trotters which they bought. The cracked eggs were got from Bunkers near Dunstable, and were so popular that people queued for them.

They also fattened Hereford cattle for beef and kept two or three house cows for milk. Cream and butter made from their own milk were sold. There were also sheep, chickens and geese, and for Christmas there were turkeys. There were also stables.

They also undertook catering, using, of course, their own produce. In the summer season this included running the tea shop at Deer Leap Swimming Pool, and they also catered for Hunt Balls at Ashridge.

At its peak the holding also included the field opposite the swimming pool, where brussels sprouts, potatoes, carrots and strawberries were amongst the produce grown; and some land at Stanbridge, out towards Leighton Buzzard. Janet Stinton remembers hand-picking peas there.

The Ellisons also bought the land which became Ashridge Farm and started the riding stables there. (See the previous article).

After they sold Beaney, and left, it soon became divided, farm buildings being converted into residences. The market garden no longer exists. There are still some paddocks and stables.

A COW'S TAIL

by Wendy Forster

When I left school in 1958 I decided I would have a go at hairdressing. I stuck it for four years and then decided on a career change! My mother saw Mrs Ellison, who lived at Beaney, on her horse one morning and said, "Have you a job for my daughter?" "Tell her to come on Monday at 8 o'clock and I'll find her something."

My first job on this Monday morning was to be introduced to Gladys the Jersey cow, and the chickens in their deep litter. The next suggestion was to learn to milk Gladys by hand. Well, after a few times I managed very well - until one day all was to go wrong! As usual she was waiting by the gate, she came in to the stable, I did the milking and was about to put her back into the field - but she thought "Oh no! Not today!" - and to my horror she went down the drive and on to the road, and even began to run. I had hold of her tail and I wrapped my other arm round the telegraph poles as we flew past to try and stop her. I imagined we would end up in Dagnall. The school bus came past and all the children yelled. My face was so red anyway they couldn't see my embarrassment. The yelling seemed to do the trick. We were as far as The Spinney when she decided to turn round and went meekly back. Janet Cocks (Stinton) and Margaret Bruton were standing in the road roaring with laughter. They had been watching!

When I got home my Mum said, "Wendy, what ever have you been doing today?" My face was still so red, but in the morning I had been creosoting and loads of it had splashed on my jumper and the hair from Gladys's back side had rubbed off. It looked like an Afghan coat!

Sloe-hatching

How is it possible
in so short a time
I could forget?

each year the same
shock, gasp of wonder
when unaware, I turn

and there, flowers
dense as a swarm
of bees, thick

as custard, leafless
hang on black arms
there against the sky

the blackthorn soars...

Mary Blake

Bridgewater Farm

Some time around the First World War the management of the Bridgewater Farm was taken on by the Andrews family. At various times it was run by Min Catchpole's father Leonard Andrews and her uncle Bert (Herbert) Andrews. Then her brothers Fred and Alec Andrews worked there, and took over when Leonard died. This family also ran the market garden at the Manor House.

Bridgewater Farm was a dairy farm around and behind the Bridgewater Arms and was owned by the hotel owners. In the 1930's, the village school children recorded that it consisted of 3 (or 4) fields of grass, totalling 26 acres, and there were 4 (or 3) hands. There were 45 cattle, 3 horses and 29 pigs. They also wrote a short article when the numbers had changed a bit, including the following extracts:

Some of the cows are light brown and dark brown. ... There are seven milking cows which are milked twice a day. Each of the cows gives about eleven gallons a week. All the pigs are kept in stys until they are big enough to be turned out. They are fed with bran and maize mixed with water.
There are three horses, one black and two brown ones which pull the carts and other things which horses have to pull.
There are four bullocks and four calves which Mr Andrews is fattening up to sell. Round at the back of the farm there are two ricks, one bracken and one hay.

Next to the hotel there were early 19th century stables with 18-inch solid brick walls (which were converted into the house Bridgewater Mews in about 1979-80 and bought by the present owners - Phil and Heidi James). The dairy and the cowsheds were just behind them. People could go there to buy milk or have it delivered. In time bottled milk was available.

After the farm and dairy closed, the land was rented to Church Farm. Most of the land now belongs to John Chapman and is used for horse and sheep grazing and hay or silage.

Church Farm

from George Stanbridge's diaries, a conversation with John and Megan Mead, and other sources

Cattle at Church Farm July 1983

Church Farm started the 20th century as one of the largest farms in the parish, Lamsey Farm being included in it. It must have been somewhere about 400 or 500 acres, but it has gradually been reduced as land has been transferred to other farms and holdings. Most of the original area is still open land, either farming or horse paddocks, but a small part has been used for a few houses.

It was owned by the Brownlows and the tenant was George Stanbridge, who had taken it on in 1893 and moved into the farmhouse from Kensworth in 1894. In 1900 it was a mixed farm but did not include a dairy herd. Beef cattle were bought, fattened and sold. From his diaries it seems that cows suckling their own calves were only occasionally kept. There was a flock of ewes producing lambs and wool. Pigs were bought and sold occasionally. There is no mention of any trade in poultry or eggs. The horses were the main source of power, though there was a steam engine, shared with his brother William at Green End and Isle of Wight Farms, Kensworth, and with Mr Ashby of Ivinghoe Aston and Studham, used for driving the thrashing machine. (The Ashby family still have the same Ivinghoe Aston Farm today. None of Little Gaddesden's farming families have held their farms through the whole century.) Naturally there was a lot of grazing land, and hay-making. Fodder crops included turnips, swedes, mangolds, thousand-head, rape, mustard, kale, clover and tares. Peas were grown. Cereal crops were wheat, barley and oats. Barley was sold to brewers, and oats were grown for the horses.

The brothers William and George married two sisters, Hattie and Pollie Lee in 1890 and 1895 respectively, and hardly a week went by without someone in the one family making a trip to see the other. Both men were farmers. Being from Kensworth, George did his banking and most of his shopping in Dunstable, but travelled around the livestock markets in other towns, particularly Leighton Buzzard.

His heavy purchases such as coal, sacks, extra fodder (linseed cake, cotton cake), fertiliser ('nitrate') and machine parts were brought in by horse and cart, often from the railway stations at Dunstable, Berkhamsted or Hemel Hempstead if not bought locally, and wheat was sent to Hemel Hempstead station.

George Stanbridge kept his diaries up to 1916, at which time his two sons, George (Sonnie) and Alban were working on the farm. Alban married Seth Janes's sister, and was therefore uncle to Wendy Janes, now Forster, and Ernie Janes, who are the custodians of the diaries. The sons eventually moved away from Little Gaddesden, as did Sonnie's twin sister Linda.

Later the ownership of the farm passed from the Brownlow Estate to the Bonar Law Memorial Trust. This could not have been before 1928. The trust leased it to tenant farmers until 1953. However, it is also recorded that Major Munro Cuthbertson owned the farm when Jim Whitman was farm manager, so we have not got the whole story here.

In the 1930's the village schoolchildren's survey of local farms recorded that Church Farm was 190 acres, divided into 2 arable fields and 3 of grass, and had three hands. The livestock was 83 cattle, 38 sheep, 3 horses and 109 poultry. In the mid 1940's George Mayling, as a lad about to leave school, worked there in holidays and weekends for Mr Pool. In the later 1940's or early 50's Ron Brooks worked there for Jim Whitman, who was farm manager. The last tenant was Mr Pike, and then in 1953 the farm was sold by the Bonar Law Trust to George Mead. It was managed by his son John Mead.

Lamsey Farm was not part of this holding. John built up a herd of Dairy Shorthorns from scratch, and also kept pigs, sheep and hens. In 1960 he married Megan and they moved into Field House, leaving the old Church Farm house for John's parents. An account of the farm in early 1972 shows an area of about 270 acres, including 25 rented from the Bridgewater Arms. About 70 acres were permanent grass and 200 acres were arable and grass leys. In that year the arable crop was barley alone, consisting of 128 acres. The break crops were the grass leys which sometimes included lucerne or, for a 2-year ley, early-flowering red clover. Other crops had been fodder kale and roots, and potatoes. The livestock

ABOVE
Sheep at Church farm 1999

BELOW
Autumn Leaf and Summer Breeze, two of Megan Mead's Gade Ponies by Church Road

BELOW LEFT
Sheep at Church Farm in August 1983

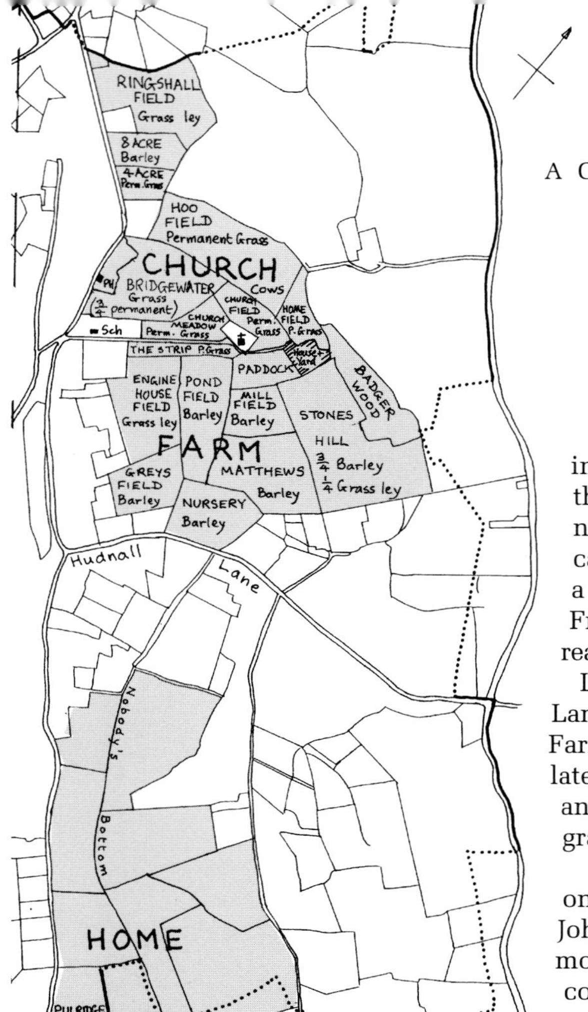

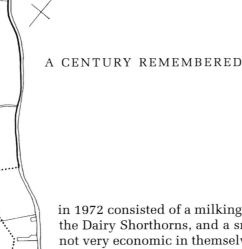

in 1972 consisted of a milking herd of Friesians, which had just replaced the Dairy Shorthorns, and a small flock of Clun Forest sheep. Although not very economic in themselves, the sheep improved the pasture for the cattle. Calves from the milking herd included both beef calves (sired by a kept Hereford bull, and suckled naturally) and dairy followers (pure Friesians by artificial insemination, and only suckled briefly before being reared 'artificially').

Later in 1972, however, several fields were sold, some to Don Cox (see Lamsey Farm), some to Douglas and Pat Creed for her sheep (see Moss Hall Farm), some to the O'Neills (see Red House Farm), some to Tom Thorne, later resold, and now leased to the Rogers family (see Goose Hill Farm), and some to Jack Overhill who sold it on to Martin Ephgrave for horse grazing.

Eventually cattle were given up altogether, and the farm concentrated on breeding ponies instead, though still keeping sheep. After the death of John Mead's mother Margaret in 1990, the Church Farm house and a few more fields close to it were sold, and the church farm buildings were converted into housing and sold.

In 1994 Church Farm became the property of Martin and Karen Hatt, and it now consists of the old house and some grassland leased out to various people for grazing horses and sheep. The sheep are from a farm in Boxmoor.

Meanwhile the Meads' holding became Field House with roughly a hundred acres of grassland for ponies and sheep.

It was a great shock to those who knew him when John Mead died in spring 1999. His wife Megan had to sell off the sheep almost immmediately, as the daily care of the animals had been by John and Megan alone. Megan has continued keeping the ponies.

Church Farm (Mr Mead) and Home Farm (Mr Muddiman) in 1972 before they were divided up and Home Farm hedges were removed.

The Coldharbour Farms and Hill Farm

Coldharbour is outside the parish boundary, but it is at the end of a road that can only be reached by passing close to Ashridge House, and so has a natural link to Little Gaddesden.

Great and Little Coldharbour were originally two farms, the former having a house probably dating back to the 17th century. The farmland lies entirely to the south of them and now belongs to neither. It amounts to about 300 acres of arable land belonging to the National Trust and farmed by Don Cox of Hill Farm, Northchurch, who also has Lamsey Farm, q.v. There is a small exception in a paddock or two close to the houses, used for grazing horses.

In 1979 Charlie and Barbara Wray kept a small dairy herd of Jerseys and some Gloucester Old Spot pigs at Little Coldharbour. Not long after this date the family moved to Wayside Farm, Kings Langley, taking the herd with them.

The Gloucester Old Spot sow "Nettie" (Caldwell Star's Antoinette V), 1980

Denison House Farm

(SUNMAN'S FARM)

When the village school children wrote their book about the village in the 1930's, this was the farm that they described in detail. The Nettleden fields that they mention must be, I think, the continuation of Golden Valley down to Nettleden Lodge (Peacock Lodge), part of the old Park, and therefore now the South Park of Park Farm (q.v.) and the lower part of Golden Valley Farm.

The 8 acres of Pulridge Wood mentioned would account for about half of that part of the wood which is on the Golden Valley side of the village road. A summary table shows that hay is the only crop, and also shows 74 cattle on the farm, which have been forgotten in the description, though the farm is big enough for them.

BY LITTLE GADDESDEN SCHOOL CHILDREN, ABOUT 1930-1935

Denison House Farm is a small one which consists of about 100 acres in which stock only is raised. The farm itself lies on clay-with-flints and the rest of the land is on the slope into Nettleden which is on a thin cap of clay-with-flints. The farm consists of five fields, two at the back of the House and three at Nettleden: Pulridge Wood also belongs to Denison House it consists of about 8 acres, the land is all grass.

The Nettleden fields are very poor pasture. The stock consists of twenty-five pigs, thirty-nine sheep, ten geese, fifty poultry and two horses. The pigs are fed on bran, wheatings and barley meal which are mixed together with water and given to them twice daily. The stys are cleaned out three or four times a week, and clean bracken and hay is placed in them. When the small pigs grow up they are sometimes let out with the sow. Twenty-five pigs are kept in four stys. When they are big pigs they are sold at Hockliffe.

The free range fowls are kept at the top of the big paddock; there are about thirty fowls; these are fed twice daily with wheat and maize mixed. Chicks are hatched out in incubators. Two are kept warm by lamps and one by electricity. The sheep are at Nettleden. Their pasture is two grass fields, they number thirty-nine and are fed once a day on flaked maize, beet pulp and hay. Geese number ten, they are left outside all day. Most of their time is spent on the pond. They are fed on wheat and maize mixed twice a day.

One horse and pony are kept in the park. They are fed three times a day on Oats, Chaff and Hay.

FLEUR DE LYS

The wooden cottage "Fleur de Lys" belongs to Well Farm. It was built by two sisters. Later, from 1955 onwards, it was occupied by successive members of the Cripps family. Nina Winterbottom (who had previously worked on Well Farm) married Gordon Cripps in 1969. Nina ran a smallholding here. She kept poultry and goats, and sold goat's milk and cheese. This business closed down in the 1990's because of the expense that would have been needed to convert her equipment to conform with the latest regulations. (Further details of the Cripps family are on page 292)

Four Acres Nursery

by Vivien Foord-Kelcey

Four Acres Nursery was started by Mr. and Mrs. Kateley in the early 1960's. Before then it was an open field owned by the O'Shea family who also owned Four Ways Garage. Ernie Hand, who lived at Pedley Farm for 56 years, farmed the land for a while. The field had gone wild by the time Mr. and Mrs. Kateley bought the land. They got planning permission to put a nursery there and bought second-hand greenhouses from Wallis' nursery, a carnation-growing nursery at Eaton Bray, which was closing down. Ernie Hand carted the greenhouses from Eaton Bray for them. He helped put them up and ploughed up the land. Bedding plants, flowers for cutting, and vegetables were grown. Tomatoes and runner beans were specialities.

The shop was built and in the 1970's planning permission was given to build a bungalow. Before this the Kateleys had been commuting from Hemel Hempstead. Mr. Kateley did the building work himself, even making the bricks using a mould and cement. When trade was low in the winter months, Mr. Kateley took a job delivering fuel for a Hemel Hempstead company and Mrs. Kateley dried flowers for sale. For a while, after Mr. Kateley died, Mrs. Kateley ran the business on her own.

Four Acres Nursery then became derelict for a few years. In 1988 Mr. and Mrs. Richard Horsman bought it and traded until 1995. Alan Bunting was the first manager. He restored the greenhouses and built the entrance gates himself. The business was built up, growing shrubs and bedding plants, supplying planted hanging baskets and pots and also cut flowers and floral arrangements.

Alan's daughter, Laura, helped out for about three years. Janet Stinton worked there for seven years and developed her interest in floristry while Julie Copcutt, a talented florist, also worked there. John Willan, who appears on television on the National Lottery programme, was also a manager for a while. Apparently he used to lecture at Oaklands College, the Agricultural College at St. Albans. He got his job with the Lottery through a contact he made at the Rotary Club whilst helping with the St. Albans carnival.

In 1990, during the big storm, sheets of glass from the greenhouses were flying around the car park and the roof was blown off the shop. Once there was a field fire and on another occasion Laura Bunting thwarted an attempted robbery, when she confronted the thieves and made them put back the petty cash that they were trying to steal.

In 1997, Mrs. Wendy Harvy took over the business, helped by her husband, Andy. That summer, the Beverly Sisters, a 1950's singing trio, called in, on their way from opening a supermarket in Leighton Buzzard. Mr. and Mrs. Harvy thought that they were members of a bowling team, as they were dressed in white and wore white hats!

The bungalow is now separate from Four Acres Nursery. Lynne van Brakel (formerly Horsman) still lives there.

GAYWOODS AND SILVER BIRCHES

The house Gaywoods was built in 1954, and with 6 acres of former Ashridge Park land it became a pig and poultry farm run by Mr Mitchell for a year before it was taken over by Eddie and Madge Nightall. They made it into a large poultry farm, with Rhode Island Red and Light Sussex breeds.

A bungalow, Silver Birches, was built in the grounds in 1966, which became the Nightalls' retirement home in 1972 when they sold off Gaywoods and its large garden. Another part of the land was sold to build Cedar House.

The Nightalls were very active members of the Village Produce Association long after their retirement, Eddie taking on the job of treasurer.

The poultry business was closed down, but re-started when Stephen and Nicky Saunders bought Silver Birches in 1994. With much less land it was naturally a smaller business. Some of the old pig sties were converted into hen houses. Nicky keeps fifty free range Rhode Island Reds and sells eggs at the door and to a few regular customers in Berkhamsted.

Golden Valley Farm

from a conversation with Neil Masters

Golden Valley Farm lies on the borders of Little Gaddesden, Nettleden and Frithsden. About 65 acres is in Little Gaddesden, including the farm buildings and bungalow, and about $3^1/_2$ acres of woodland, but this is less than half the farm. The fields at Frithsden are rented from the National Trust and the rest is owned by Neil Masters, who has been farming since 1979. The Masters family

have also farmed Binghams Park in Potten End since about 1960, when it was obtained by his father Doug Masters. There are two bungalow farm houses associated with Golden Valley farm. The one now called "Golden Valley Farm House", on the Frithsden ridge, is where the previous owner, Charlie Weir, lived. Neil used to have a herd of suckler cows, but now only has arable crops at Golden Valley. In 1999 these were oilseed rape: variety Apex; and wheat: variety Consort (a soft or biscuit wheat). Elsewhere on the farm was some winter linseed: variety Oliver, and on Binghams Park, wheat: variety Riband.

Off-the-cuff, Neil picked out two significant events in his time of farming. One was the banning of stubble-burning, which was a widespread practice until some time around 1990. The main benefit of this practice was destroying pests which might carry over into next year's crop, while at the same time making the subsequent ploughing easier. The disadvantage was the cloud of smoke and smuts drifting across other people's property and roads, and occasional damage to hedges. There was, however, a code of practice which was intended to keep the nuisance to a minimum and prevent damage.

The other change was the latest stage in modernisation of farm machinery. He bought his first new combine harvester in 1983 or 84 to replace two smaller ones. The controls for combines and other machinery are now electrified and computerised, including meters which register and display the area covered, quantities harvested, and so on, or programme the amount of water added to sprays.

TOP
Golden Valley Farm

ABOVE
Oilseed rape in flower

Goose Hill and Kilclooney Farms

from a conversation with George, Rene and Neil Rogers

Goose Hill is at Ringshall outside the Little Gaddesden boundary. The land belonged at one time to Walter Janes of Hall Farm. The Jones family of 30 Ringshall rented it for farming in the 1930's. George Rogers, still in his teens, worked for them and remembers taking Daisy, their cow, to graze some rough grass on the slope near Ringshall Coppice. Stanley Jones died in 1940. The ownership of the Goose Hill land was passed on some time thereabouts by Walter Janes to his son-in-law. *(Nora's husband - see the Andrews family tree)*

In George Rogers' words:

"Mr Parkins, that was the son-in-law of Mr Walter Janes - he had to do something after the war - he took his ground on from his father-in-law and then afterwards

he went back into the building trade, Dunstable, and he came and asked my father if he'd like to take it on. Well, my father said 'Well, no, I don't want it, but I guess George would'. I started up in 1945. My mother had said, 'You'd better soon start saving', so I saved up. I saved up just over £500 and that's how I started up. I could have bought a four-bedroom house for that."

When George started farming on Goose Hill there was no house there. George was born at no.3 Ringshall (which his father Alfred had bought when the Ashridge estate was sold in 1928) but moved to no.4 Pound Bank, Dagnall, when he married Rene, and then to 62 Little Gaddesden, which belonged to Mrs Shepherd of Robin Hood Farm. The Shepherds then needed 62 for their daughter and son-in-law, and George and Rene needed a house closer to Goose Hill. In 1954 they were able to buy a plot beside the Beacon road just beyond the Ringshall Cottages, and got Fred Whitman to build the house "Yeomans" for them. They moved in in 1955 and lived there for thirty years. Then they had the present bungalow built at Goose Hill itself. Besides Goose Hill, George has farmed various other plots of land and done contract work for other farmers. He farmed Robin Hood for Mrs Shepherd for some time, and then bought land there for himself in 1980. George's son Neil built a farmhouse there and it became Kilclooney Farm. This includes the field which used to be Hudnall Farm's orchard, and is now called the Apple Field. They farm one field "Gaddesden Field" which they rent from Mr Howitt of Coppice Cottage. This is one of the fields sold off from Church Farm in 1972, and lies between Moss Hall Farm and Ashridge Farm. It used to be called "Ringshall Field" as it was at the Ringshall end of Church Farm's land. They also farm at Gutteridge between Potten End and Berkhamsted. The various farms are

TOP
Rene Rogers in early days at Goose Hill

ABOVE
Rex Dean, Robert Batchelor, George Rogers at the wheel and Bill Moore, around 1950

BELOW
Neil Rogers clearing for replanting woodland at Goose Hill Farm

RIGHT
The Bucks side of the old county boundary at Kilclooney Farm

TOP RIGHT
George, James, Cathy and Neil Rogers - three generations at Kilclooney Farm

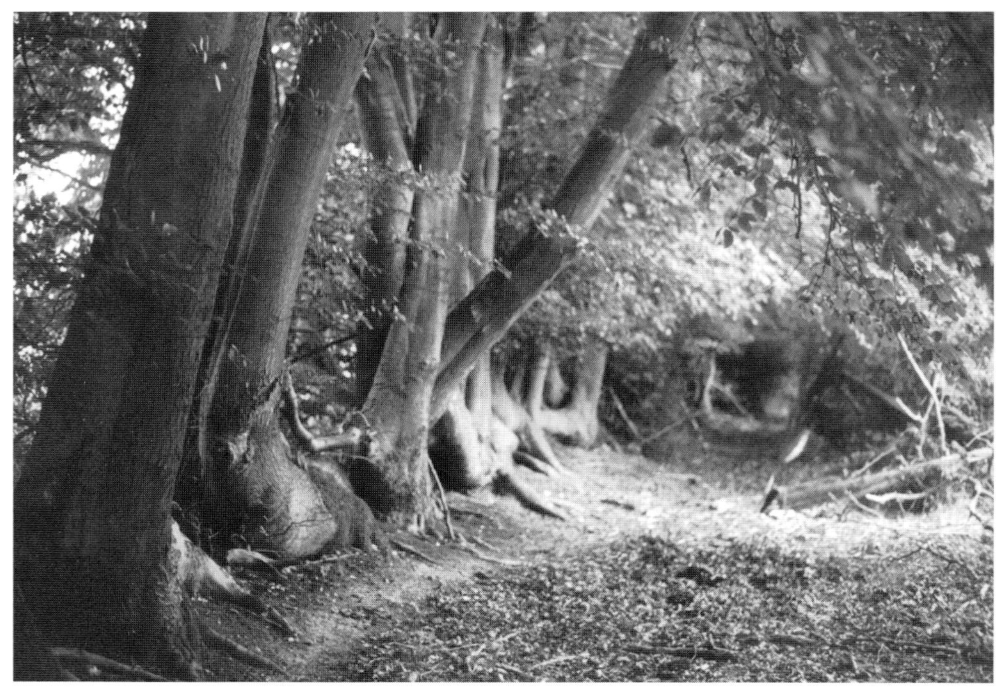

managed by George and Neil together, father and son.

Kilclooney is used for arable rotations, being in 1999 the Consort and Hereward varieties of wheat, the former on the Apple Field and the latter by the house. The Hereward was grown for seed. Gaddesden Field and part of Goose Hill were also Consort wheat, a soft milling variety. They keep sheep on the Goose Hill grassland: a flock of North Country Mule ewes and Charolais rams.

On the steeper slopes of Goose Hill they have about 20 acres of trees, including a plantation of Norway Spruce Christmas trees which are sold at the farm every December. The top of Oakley Wood was replanted about 1985 with Oak and Sweet Chestnut. Another 5 acres were planted up in 1996 under the Woodland Grant Scheme with Beech, Wild Cherry, Ash, Holly, Yew and Field Maple, with 10% Hazel and Hawthorn. The lower edge of the Apple Field at Hudnall is an ancient tree belt which is the old boundary between Hertfordshire and Buckinghamshire, from when Hudnall was in Bucks. This continues between Kilclooney and Kent House.

ABOVE
Derek Faulconer's Sussex cattle at Holly Tree Farm

Home Farm

From Canon Senar's history of the village George Underwood, and later his son, is recorded as tenant here in the late 19th century. In 1875, however, George was tenant of Hudnall Farm - if it was the same George. From the 1891 census, George Underwood, aged 69, was the farmer at Church Farm (he was a churchwarden and he died in 1893), and Roland Underwood, aged 34, was a farmer's bailiff at Hudnall, and no other Underwoods of working age are mentioned. The occupiers at the Home Farm houses in 1891 are agricultural labourers and a dairy woman - no farmer, manager or bailiff is recorded on those premises.

In 1899 and 1900 Underwood is mentioned rarely in George Stanbridge's diaries: he has lambs and he has ricks to thatch, but it is not clear where.

On October 2nd 1899 the "annual sheep sale" at Home Farm is mentioned. They were going for high prices. Since all the farms in the village were rented from the Brownlow estate, they would have shared a number of common services provided by the landlord. This included blacksmiths' work shoeing horses and other iron work, and building maintenance such as bricklaying and carpentry. The Cromer Farm Buildings (where Willow Wood now stands) are shown on maps of 1897 and 1922. They contained steam powered corn grinding mills and sheep-shearing machinery which would have been used by Home Farm and possibly other estate farms.

When the estate was sold, or soon after, Home Farm was bought by Cooper, McDougall and Robertsons, the firm with the big chemical factory in Berkhamsted whose most famous product was Cooper's Sheep Dip.

In about 1928 William Bunting, with his wife Martha, came to Home Farm to be the shepherd. He was known as Shep, eventually "Old Shep". Shep was a picturesque character who was depicted in many advertisements for agricultural veterinary products. His three sons, who were in their teens when they arrived, all followed their father's trade. George Bunting became the farm Foreman, Tom the Commercial Shepherd, and Stanley the Show Shepherd. Stanley was known as Nippy because of his agility in the football team. George's son Alan, and Alan's son Daniel have also kept sheep in the village.

HOLLY TREE FARM

This small strip of fields alongside Hudnall Lane was acquired by the Whitman family, no doubt with a view to building more houses. It was probably part of the Manor House nursery or Church Farm before that. It was purchased later by John Swaffield. Barns and a stable have been there for many years. In the 1990's it was used for free range hens, eggs being sold direct to calling customers as well as other outlets, but this business closed down some time before 1999.

At the end of 1999, Derek Faulconer bought it from John Swaffield and moved his Sussex cattle there. (See Meadow House.)

Old Shep (William Bunting), with his sheep

In the 1930's village school survey, Home Farm is described as having 360 acres and 18 farm hands. The crops grown are oats, wheat, kale, clover, hay, turnips, mangels, swedes, cabbage and barley. The livestock are only listed as 2000 poultry and 6 horses, but it seems that the list was never completed. They didn't write a number in unless they had found out what number to write. Those crops included plenty of forage which would be used for sheep.

In 1941 the Berkhamsted flock of pedigree Southdowns was founded by the purchase of ewe lambs from the Luton Hoo flock. This was strengthened by the purchase, in 1954, of most of the Hatch Gate breeding flock. The Southdowns were entered in shows from 1947 onwards and some of their best awards were: Reserve Supreme Champion at the Royal Show 1954 for a pen of shearling ewes; Male Champion at the Royal Show 1957; Supreme Championship of the Southdown Society's competition from 1954 to 1956.

Alf Sherringham, retired village policeman, included the following reminiscences in a talk he gave in about 1994. He is speaking of a period around the 1950's:

"The Home Farm played a large part in the village. As far as I was aware there were about seven veterinary surgeons at the large experimental place, plus a number of farm workers. There was a show shepherd, whose sheep won countless prizes. He was assisted by the working shepherd... during show time the sheep travelled all over the country.

In my capacity as local bobby it was necessary to supervise the dipping of the sheep at certain times of the year, plus the signing of livestock registers, which had to be done on all the farms on my patch. Every morning, Joan, the dog girl from Home Farm, could be seen exercising the dogs. As the farm was so well known, numerous visitors would be there, including film units. In those days the local bobby had to deal with all the diseases that the animals contracted, so if some unfortunate farmer or smallholder reported Swine Fever, Fowl Pest, or, even worse, Foot and Mouth Disease, there would be great consternation in the farming world. Then the poor old bobby would have to send numerous forms to the Ministry of Agriculture, plus making sure that conditions were complied with".

BELOW: The team at Home Farm, 1938-1939

*STANDING:
Bill Clifton, Farm Secretary, Ken Page, Tom Bunting, Charlie (Harry) Clifton, Stanley Bunting, Harry Abrahams.*

*SEATED:
The veterinary staff with Walter Downing (centre).*

In 1955 Cooper McDougall & Robertson started to build up the Berkhamsted Herd of pedigree Herefords importing high quality cattle with "no expense spared". The first were from New Zealand: a bull, Toko Excelsior and 3 heifers, followed by more from New Zealand, the USA and Canada. Both cows and bulls were entered in shows. Many first, second and third prizes were won. The cow, Berkhamsted Stardom, was Reserve

Breed Champion at Smithfield in 1959, and the bull, Star Way 37K, was first at Thame Show and first reserve Male Champion at the Royal Norfolk in the same year.

In 1960 Cooper, McDougall and Robertson withdrew from farming and sold up the farm. Mr R Jopson was farm manager at that time. When the pedigree Southdown sheep were sold in April, 98 ewes with lambs, 40 shearling ewes, 40 shearling rams and 4 stud rams were listed in the auction book, including the 5-year-old ram Ford Dreadnought 79, which they were particularly proud of.

In May the pedigree Hereford herd was sold, the auction book listing: 30 horned cows with calves or in calf, 29 poll cows with calves or in calf, 15 poll heifers (unserved), 12 poll yearling bulls, and the stock bull Star Way 37K. He was prized for siring poll calves (hornless) from horned cows. At the sale the herd was dispersed all over England, Scotland and Wales, the cattle fetching £67,515 in total.

The farm was sold, first to Mr Palmer, then on to Mr Green, and then to Mr Muddiman, within about a year. Mr Muddiman's holding extended from Home Farm buildings down the valley to Nettleden (incorporating the old Pulridge Farm, q.v.) and across to the boundary of St Margaret's Farm. It was about this time that the hedges were removed and about 16 old fields were united into one, though they have been divided up a bit since. Mr and Mrs Muddiman converted the old dovecot into Gade House and moved into it in the mid-1970's. They sold up the land in about 1973, to National Car Parks, but bought most of it back a couple of years later. The old farm buildings were mainly converted into a residential area, some of them already being cottages and a house. Woodhill Farm, which was built on the edge of Pulridge Wood, included a house for the farm manager and some barns. One very ancient barn at the old Home Farm was used from about 1962 for the horticultural machinery business started by Ron Brooks. (See page 187)

TOP LEFT
Home farm in 1999

TOP RIGHT
Stanley Bunting, the Show Shepherd

ABOVE
An Aberdeen Angus bull with Gordon Lobban.

BELOW
Home Farm from Nobody's Bottom in 1979, looking towards Hudnall Common

The land that Mr Muddiman did not buy back from National Car Parks was sold to Mr Blain of St Margaret's Farm (q.v.) and Sue Tankel and Jackie Fenton.

Sue and Jackie, with John Dixon, had the top end of the valley and a stable block. They replanted the arable field with grass, divided it into paddocks, and planted some trees. They started keeping horses and sheep. They installed a mobile home, now a bungalow, behind the old Home Farm House. From 1996 to 1998 the sheep on their paddocks belonged to Ian Orchard of Studham. In 1999 they only had horses, but plan to have sheep again. This is the Home Farm as it exists in 1999, about 45 or so acres.

Hudnall Park - Six Tunnels Farm

by John Leonhardt

John Wilson speculates that Hudnall Park may have long ago been a deer park, separated from Ashridge Park for keeping a different species of deer, a custom known in other areas, probably Red Deer in one and Fallow Deer in the other.

By 1875 Hudnall Park was just the name for one square field of 16 acres, but in the 1930's it became the name of a new house and several fields around it, bought to prevent anyone else building too close. It was owned originally by Kate Duncanson. Upper Tem Field was where the house was built, and the estate included about 7.5 acres of the old "Hudnall Park" Field. About 70 acres were farm land, and this was leased at one time to Mr Hurst of Nettleden Farm. In the late 1950's the lease was taken over from Mr Hurst by the Elding family of Six Tunnels Farm, Gaddesden Row. They still farm most of it, which is now owned by the Hertfordshire County Council. The Council acquired it when they bought the house as an Environmental Studies Centre in 1971, and now retain about 10 acres of meadow and 15 acres of woodland for wildlife. In the 1970's the agricultural area was all arable, being used for wheat and barley. In the 1980's the Eldings replanted it with a mixture of grass and clover which has now become permanent pasture. They have kept beef cattle of mixed breeds on it most of the time, laying them off every winter, and generally use a few acres for hay. For a short while they provided grazing for a few shire horses and small ponies. In 1999 their lease amounted to about 50 acres and they used it all for cattle.

Top picture, baling hay at Little Russells Piece, Hudnall Park, in 1979. and, below, the beef cattle at Hudnall Park in 1999 with Kilbracken in the background

Hudnall Common Farm

EARLY 20TH CENTURY

by Freda Morris - Frederick Whitman's daughter

After leaving school (in about 1900) Frederick George Whitman worked with his father George Whitman for a few years in the building trade. Then with his father he started farming and both lived at Hudnall Common Farm. Frederick married in 1911 and continued to farm, living at Mile Barn Farm. Sadly George died that same year at the age of 49 and as eldest son my father gave up the tenancy of Mile Barn Farm and moved back to Hudnall Common Farm as tenant there to run it. He continued farming until 1929, buying the farm from Francis Edward Fisher when the estate was sold in 1928. On the farm I remember ricks being built with the help of an elevator pony who went around and around all day. A thrashing machine was hired at harvest time.

His son, George Whitman, continued farming and did contract work for other farmers. Ron Brooks worked with him for a time.

Hudnall Farm

In 1875 this was a large farm, containing more than three-quarters of the land in Hudnall, and including all of Hudnall Common, which was pasture. About two-thirds of the farm was arable. It was all owned by Lord Brownlow, including the common, and the tenant was George Underwood. In 1891 the tenant was Edward Hoar, and George Underwood and his wife Sarah had moved to Church Farm, where he was tenant until he died in 1893. There was, however, a Roland Underwood at no.4 Hudnall as farmer's bailiff in 1891, who could have been the son of George and Sarah. In 1899 he was calling at Church Farm for some linseed cake for his lambs, and his children Arthur, Daisy and May went to play with the Stanbridge children at Church Farm.

Edward Hoar worked at the butcher's shop in Hudnall - before taking the Hudnall Farm tenancy if my information is correct. His wife Sophia was one of the Whitmans, born in Hudnall in about 1857. In 1899 Edward Hoar is mentioned in George Stanbridge's diary as having sold some calves to Charlie Allison of Well Farm at £5 each. In the 1900's he went bankrupt and moved into one of the Hudnall cottages. He had ten children. One of his sons, George, was killed in the First World War and is listed on the Roll of Honour. Another son, William, had a daughter Nellie who still lives in Berkhamsted.

Later in the century most of this large farm had been divided up among other holdings and part of its land was sold for houses. Hudnall Common was purchased by the Commons Preservation Society, and the National Trust acquired it in 1937. The remaining part of Hudnall Farm, to the west of the farm house, became a large commercial orchard with thousands of trees, including 7 acres of cordon apples. The Heathcotes ran this orchard. There is some more about it in wartime in Betty Rogers' article on page 55.

Phyl Mountfort worked there from 1954 to 1969, and George Parsons had taken over the ownership from the Heathcotes.

The orchard must have ceased business about 1969. It is now arable land and part of Kilclooney Farm. The Hudnall Farm House is now a private residence.

Lamsey Farm

with information from a conversation with Don Cox

In 1899 Lamsey Farm was part of Church Farm. It had a farmyard, some farm buildings and a farm workers cottage. In 1999 it has some newer larger buildings and some of the older parts are disused, but the cottage is still there. A house has been added to the site, and subsequently extended.

HUDNALL COMMON FARM

late 20th century

(There is a paddock of a bit less than an acre in front of the house where horses, ponies or sheep graze. Other paddocks are nearby. There is a block of stables.)

by Bill Paterson

We have lived in the village for 23 years after moving to Hudnall Common Farm from Radlett. Fiona and I both knew it long before we came to live here. Apart from the beauty of the village, we were keen to have more land and to be in an area suitable for horse riding. Both of our daughters, Claire and Katie, were keen riders, and my wife, who rode a lot at one time, now examines for the British Horse Society. Katie rode for England in the junior dressage and eventing teams. Claire and Katie were both married in the village church and Claire, who now lives in California, has had her two daughters christened here. Katie and her husband Nigel have bought a house in the village and hope to live here.

I retired from full time work some 12 years ago and devote a lot of my time to sculpture, principally stone carving.

There is a gap in the history of Lamsey Farm, but it was separate from Church Farm by 1954. Mr Muddiman of Home Farm had it for a time before 1973, when it changed hands twice, and became the property of Don Cox who farms it still. Don Cox and his father Victor had already, since about 1955, been farming Hill Farm this side of Northchurch, and Don still does. The Hill Farm land is all rented from the National Trust and comes up to Coldharbour, but none of it is in Little Gaddesden. As Don lives at Hill Farm, the house at Lamsey is rented out. An avenue of Large-leaved Lime has been planted leading up to the farm from the main road.

In 1972 the fields of Lamsey Farm made a strip running alongside the Leighton Buzzard Road for a length of one mile and, averaging about a third of a mile broad, would have been roughly 200 acres. Part of Church Farm was soon added to this, making about 310 to 320 acres in all at the present day. About 28 acres are outside the parish boundary. Don Cox and Keith Blain are the next largest landowners within the parish boundary after the National Trust, their acreages being so similar that it would be a rather academic point which of the two owned the most.

Lamsey and Hill Farm are both entirely arable these days. In 1999 the crops on Lamsey were barley (Regina), linseed (Barbara) and wheat (Abbot). The rotation here in its simplest form is two years of cereals followed by one of oilseed rape. The cereals are wheat and barley, usually in that order, or two successive years of the same one. Ploughing takes place very soon after harvest, and the next crop is planted in the autumn. If it is rape it is planted in September. This year spring linseed was planted instead of rape, on March 19th. It was harvested on September 3rd. Linseed "straw" is a wiry stuff not subject to the prohibition imposed on burning cereal straw, so was burnt on the field.

In an off-the cuff answer to the question of what was the most significant recent development in farming, Don replied, "The mobile phone".

TOP
From this angle, a corner of Lamsey Farmyard still looks as it did in George Stanbridge's time.

ABOVE
Don Cox in 1999

BELOW
Linseed ready for harvest, Barn Field at Lamsey Farm

RIGHT
Lamsey Farm with view towards Whipsnade downs

A COMPARISON OF THE BARLEY CROP OF 1899 AND 1999

GEORGE STANBRIDGE, 1899:

In January and February the last year's barley was being sold.
"February 8th: Dunstable: Went & saw Mr Bennett & persuaded him to have the remainder of Barley @ 32/- about 30 quarters: he had 30 in a week ago. But he sat on me a bit! said he would not have it, unless I had 10 barrels of beer between now & harvest! which of course I agreed to, as I know we should want it, & it is certainly the best beer we get anywhere now."
The last load of 1898 barley was sent to Bennett's malting on Feb.13th.
For the next planting he brought barley over from his brother's at the Isle of Wight Farm, Kensworth.
The fields to be sown were parts of Big Field, Mile Barn Field and Stony-hill. Other parts of all these fields were used for various other crops.

PREPARATION:
Big Field (up the main road towards Well Farm): Sowing superphosphate March 23rd-25th.
Mile Barn Field (by the main road opposite Mile Barn): Sheep were feeding on swedes, and were moved on to a fresh strip day by day, by moving the hurdles.
Stony-hill (south-east of Badger Wood): Ploughing finished March 21st. Drag-harrowed with three horses, March 30th - April 1st.

DRILLING BARLEY:
March 29th-31st: BIG FIELD DRILLED. Harrow behind the drill.
April 1st,3rd: Big Field harrowed over again.
April 3rd to 26th: MILE BARN FIELD DRILLED a bit at a time as the sheep were moved on and the remains of the swedes ploughed in and harrowed. 2 horses rolled down in front of the drill and they or others harrowed in behind. Within a day or two each bit was usually cross-harrowed.
April 5th-6th: Bottom part of STONY-HILL DRILLED.
April 6th: A small area in LAMSEY BARN FIELD DRILLED, called Little Chitty Piece.

FURTHER TREATMENT:
April 20th-21st: Big Field: Harrowed barley over to knock up charlock etc which was coming on thick.
April 27th-29th, May 13th: NITRATE sown on barley in Big Field, and on 19th in Stony-hill (5 cwt).
May 2nd,6th,8th: Horse-hoeing in Big Field and Lamsey Barn Field.
May 8th-12th,17th-19th: Rolling and crushing barley in Lamsey Barn Field and Mile Barn Field (and others?).
May 13th: "Harrowing grass seeds in Big Field on the barley". Presumably under-sowing.
Then nothing done until harvest.

HARVEST:
August 12th-15th: CUTTING IN BIG FIELD. Setting-up, carting, raking, final clearing to Aug.21st.
August 17th: CUTTING IN LAMSEY BARN FIELD. Carting etc to final clearing Aug 28th.

August 22nd-24th: CUTTING IN MILE BARN FIELD. Carting etc to final clearing Sept 4th.
August 28th-31st: CUTTING IN STONY-HILL. Carting etc to final clearing Sept 9th. The barley in this field was badly damaged. It was a bad place to dry. In fact all the barley was poor this year.

RICK-BUILDING:
Started soon after getting the barley to the rickyards. Some was put in a barn at first.
September 1st: Rough-thatched one barley stack and smooth-thatched another.
September 6th: Rick from Stony-hill barley, part sheaves, part loose, topped up.

THRASHING:
One rick was thrashed September 12th-13th. The barley was dressed (cleaned) on 21st and 23rd. The straw would have been kept and could have been used for cattle bedding or chopped small for fodder. The stubble in the fields was eventually ploughed in, e.g. October 3rd for some of Mile Barn Field.

SALE:
The barley, when sold, was mostly taken to Hemel Hempstead station. It would be in sacks which could be man-handled. The money was collected from Dixon at Dunstable. William Simmons sent a cart for 3 quarters for grinding.
It took 3 horses, with a van and a cart, to take 10 or 11 quarters of barley to the station. This happened on Sept. 23rd,25th & 26th. On 27th, Dixon paid for 36 quarters @ 30/- a quarter, making £54. (A quarter is 8 bushels or 64 gallons. A quarter of barley grain could weigh about 380 pounds, so it would take a bit less than 6 quarters to weigh a ton.)

TOP
Ron Fensome, driver of the combine harvester at Lamsey Farm

ABOVE
Loading barley for Burton-on-Trent in 1999

DON COX, 1999:

The field in which the barley was to be grown was Lamsey House Field, which includes the 1899 Lamsey Barn Field and Big Field as well as Little Barrels, Great Barrels, Step Furlong and Whites Close. The previous crop had also been barley. Both were winter barley.

PREPARATION:
August 20th 1998: Field ploughed and furrow-pressed. (By contractors, 6-furrow reversible plough.)
September 23rd: Cultivated.

DRILLING:
September 26th: Ring-rolled, then CULTIVATOR-DRILLED with 170 kilograms

per hectare of "Regina" winter barley.
September 27th: Harrowed, then ring-rolled.

FURTHER TREATMENT:
October 2nd: Slug pellets applied, 7 Kgs per Ha.
November 1st: Sprayed with herbicide and aphicide.
February 23rd 1999: Broadcast 160 Kgs/Ha of Ammonium Nitrate.
March 22nd: Broadcast 200 Kgs/Ha of Ammonium Nitrate.
April 8th: Sprayed with fungicide and growth regulator.
April 30th: Sprayed headland only with herbicide.
May 19th: Sprayed with fungicide.

HARVEST:
July 16th: COMBINED. (All of the 1899 processes from cutting through to thrashing in one go with one machine.)
July 18th: Straw baled for cattle.
The barley was stored in the barn at Lamsey, where it can be dried by blowing air warm or cold.

SALE:
Sold to Sidney C. Banks of Sandy, Bedfordshire, who collected 26 tons with a lorry on October 7th to take to the Bass Brewery in Burton-on-Trent.

Lower Gade Farm, Hudnall

by Nicholas Crispin

In the mid-1940s, Lower Gade, the poultry farm on the main road at Hudnall, was acquired by my father and his brother. My earliest memories of the farm, from just after the war, are inevitably hazy, but my brother and sister, with the advantage of age, have been able to provide additional detail.

By 1950, there were some 1500 hens in batteries, with additional houses for Christmas turkeys, two fertilizer factories (the only original buildings still standing) where chicken dung was dried to produce 'Avis - the 100% organic fertilizer', ideal for lawns and cricket pitches. There were also some highly productive apple trees, two cows (whose milk was carried home to Abbots Langley in small churns), a cold store (where I liked to hide until my teeth chattered), and a horse called Nutty. There was a guard dog, too: Boxer Bill, part boxer, part labrador. He barked only for strangers, as he could identify the cars of regular visitors. He also had a less pleasant reputation for worrying sheep up at St Margarets, which resulted in substantial curtailment to his liberty. Over the years, pigsties were built, and the stock reached 400 or so, the prime specimen being the boar, Watford Dreadnought. In the early days, the pigs were fed on a dark grey substance, some form of compressed pigswill, known to us as Luton Pudding.

The farm (Hertfordshire Egg Producers Ltd and Avis Fertilizer Ltd) was managed by my uncle, Max Crispin, who lived in Berkhamsted, and by Pip Phillips. Pip (properly Vera) lived at 'Le Logis' (now 'Gade Lodge') with her sister Nance, their father, and their dog Hurry. There were three other sisters: Phyl, Blue (short for Bluebell) and Nell, as well as a brother, Robert. Their elderly father, also Robert, had been gamekeeper to the Marquess of Northampton at Castle Ashby, and he still dressed accordingly every day, in waistcoat and gaiters. He would sit by a blazing fire, drinking tea noisily through his luxuriant moustache, happy to accept my father's bottle of whisky at Christmas. After his death, Pip and Nance lived on at 'Le Logis' until they too died, weeks apart, in the early 1980s.

There were other more shadowy figures involved in running the farm. Fred was in charge of the fertilizer factories, Mr Bescoby kept the accounts, and Jesse was a farm-hand from Great Gaddesden. Then there was a Polish refugee, Czeslaw Loseiwicz (possibly the correct spelling), who occupied one of the farm buildings. Like other 'displaced persons', he was required to work on the land for a year or two to earn permanent residence in Britain.

But the real characters were the Finnegan sisters (first names long forgotten), who lived in two huts in the field above the farm, just below Hill Wood. They always seemed old to me, swathed in layers of well worn dresses and darned woollen sweaters, with wisps of grey hair peeping from under their knitted hats, surrounded by their collection of chickens and cats. Milk they were rumoured to get from our cows, though they did have at least one goat of their own.

The neater hut was the bedroom, with curtains made from old sacks, panes of glass that did not quite fit, and a patched felt roof. Outside, a border of bright flowers lined a tidy footpath. By comparison, the larger hut seemed to sprawl, a noticeably more rickety structure. In the centre was a tall black stove, with a chimney pipe snaking up to the roof. It was a dark, gloomy room, and your eyes took time to get used to the twilight. You'd eventually make out some easy chairs, stuffing bursting from tears in the fabric. If you wanted to sit down, cats had to be moved.

As I remember it, I never did sit down. I'd just stand, wide-eyed, staring into the murky interior, amazed that this was actually anyone's home. I'd be offered a cup of hot milk: a blackened saucepan would be produced and placed on the stove. The cats knew what was happening: they'd all be watching keenly, hoping there'd be a saucerful for them. I'd always refuse the milk, because of my dislike for warm milk, not because of worries about hygiene. The sisters never struck me as dirty, just quaint, despite the overpowering smell of cat.

The farm also had office buildings, where Boxer would sleep in front of the coke stove, where the eggs were graded and packed, and where Pip plucked the warm poultry (some of it probably destined for Wally Tompkins, a butcher in Marlowes from whom we had a regular weekend joint, but who never seemed to want coupons from our ration books). There was also the largely disused office, with an aged typewriter, accounts books and, from earlier days, a record of how many eggs had been laid by each hen, so that the unproductive ones could be eliminated.

The farm was sold at the end of the 1950s, but the Finnegans remained very firmly in place. In the mid-1960s, however, the sisters were 'discovered', and their story and photograph were featured in the Gazette. This was the beginning of the end: officials visited them and decided thay could no longer stay where they were.

They were parted for the first time in many years: one transferred to an old people's home, the other admitted to St Paul's Hospital with a chest infection. Before long, both had died - an inevitable end, surely accelerated by enforced separation.

Manor House nursery

This nursery or market garden was between the Manor House and Hudnall Lane. The site included an orchard and greenhouses. People went there to buy their vegetables and fruit. Min Catchpole's father Leonard Andrews and her brother Alec Andrews both worked there at some time, and her uncle Bert Andrews took charge of it about the time that Leonard died. This was also when Alec and his brother Fred took charge of the Bridgewater Farm.

The site is now mainly the garden of the private house "Tree Tops" which was made by converting an earlier building.

Meadow Farm - Hudnall

There is another Meadow Farm: a house at Ringshall; and there is a smallholding in Hudnall called Meadow House. The one at Ringshall is the senior holder of the name.

Meadow Farm occupies most of a field that used to be called Godfreys. In 1875 it was grassland which was a part of Hudnall farm. By 1899 it was probably worked by Fred Janes, as it adjoined the house where his butcher's shop became established, and George Stanbridge commented on his haymaking while doing his own in the adjoining Nursery Meadow and Masseys Meadow. The Janes family had started their butcher's business by then, as he sold meat to Stanbridge in February and was over at Kensworth buying tegs (sheep) two days later. In those days a butcher would slaughter his own sheep as needed. The butcher's shop at Hudnall behind Plum Tree Cottage continued to trade until after 1980 or so, but "Godfreys" field had changed hands some years earlier. Meadow Farm was bought in 1977 by Julian and Philippa Marshall from Mr Inskip, who had bought it from Miss Lowe who kept hens. They came there from Wigginton because the land was what they needed for their horses. They kept two mares and bred competition horses. Their daughter was keen on eventing, and now lives with her husband and children nearby.

Besides the horses they also kept the Hudnall Herd of Aberdeen Angus cattle from 1978 to about 1985. These originally came from George Hurst of Nettleden. They now let out the grazing to sheep for the benefit of the pasture. They also keep Call Ducks, Sebastopol Geese and bantams, and have sold 200 ducks a year.

They have been trying to restore a wild flower meadow and have planted an attractive spinney in the middle of the property.

MEADOW FARM, RINGSHALL

Joseph Hing, born 1859, married Sarah Jane Ginger. They came to Little Gaddesden in 1893. He was to take up employment as a night watchman at Ashridge House. They also lived at Meadow Farm, Ringshall, farming an estate holding for 36 years. It was during this period that they had their family of 5 sons and 3 daughters, born from 1881 to 1895. The estate was sold in 1928, and the historic house and its neighbour Coppice Cottage passed through various distinguished owners. The farmland on the north side is now part of Goose Hill Farm, and on the south side is grazing land belonging to Mr Howitt of Coppice Cottage, used both for pony events and for the grazing of Goose Hill Farm sheep.

(There is more about the Hing Family in chapter19)

The picture on the left shows Julian and Philippa Marshall at Meadow Farm, Hudnall, with their Sebastopol geese

MEADOW HOUSE

This smallholding in Hudnall, formerly known as Covetous Meadow, is notable for the small breeding herd of pedigree Sussex cattle kept there by Derek Faulconer. They are a deep red-brown breed and the bull has long horns. At the end of 1999 the cows were moved to Holly Tree Farm in Hudnall Lane. (see page 207)

Bales of wheat straw on Mile Barn's "Valley Farm" field, with Hudnall Common top left

Mile Barn

Mile Barn is a large farm almost entirely on the Studham side of the main road from Hudnall to Dagnall, owned by Hugh Wynn Jones since the 1940's. Nowadays it is entirely arable, growing wheat and oilseed rape. Only one half of one field is in Little Gaddesden parish. This is called Valley Farm Field. It is on the Hudnall side of the main road alongside Hudnall Common Plantation. In 1875 this field was part of Hudnall Farm and known as The Beckings. It may have become part of Church Farm or Lamsey Farm at one time. The top end of it became the Crovells estate from 1948 onwards. In 1999 the field was used for a crop of wheat of the variety Riband.

Moss Hall Farm

Pat Creed is one of the Oakins family on her mother's side, and has written about her family and reminiscences on page 307.
Moss Hall Farm is on about 13 acres sold off from Church Farm by John Mead in 1972, and is currently used purely for sheep.

by Pat Creed

BELOW
Pat Creed shows off her Suffolks

BOTTOM
Pat's Suffolk lambs

In 1975 my husband Douglas and I bought a flock of pedigree Suffolk Sheep. Unfortunately Douglas died later that year. It eventually became very difficult tending the sheep, living on my own and having to travel half a mile to see them. Being pedigree sheep they must lamb early as the rams are used in the current year. This means winter lambing, and often in the middle of the night icy conditions made it virtually impossible to get the car out and it is not easy to walk the distance on an icy path. After abortive attempts at planning permission and two appeals to the Minister he eventually gave me permission for a mobile home in which I have lived ever since.

The sheep increased, multiplied and flourished together with my Old English Sheepdogs which I have kept for over forty years. We had parties of children to see the animals and the countryside. They came from as far afield as London and it was good to be able to show town children a glimpse of rural life. They enjoyed everything, especially helping to feed the lambs which were on bottles. Once we had a double decker bus which just managed to get into our drive!

The dogs did school visits and at one Hemel Hempstead school the children made a circle round us and sang "All Things Bright and Beautiful".

I find it reassuring to remember that my mother and her brothers and sisters used to play on the land when they were children, for they lived only a stone's throw away. I like to think that my forbears would be pleased that I have tried to keep their little corner of England rural.

Park Farm

from a conversation with Peter Stone

Peter Stone is the son of Gilbert Stone of the Old Dairy, an old cottage just outside the village on the Aldbury side, which has been divided and has had a bungalow added, so now provides three residences backing on to three fields. The smaller fields are owned by Gilbert. The remainder of the farm is run on fields leased from the National Trust, including the largest field adjoining the cottage and parts of Ashridge Park known as Old Park, North Park and South Park.

BELOW
Peter Stone at the Old Dairy

BOTTOM
Peter Stone's beef herd in South Park, 1999

The Stones, father and son, have been livestock farmers who have used various fields in the area in the past. Most of Old Park was bought by the National Trust in 1926, and the remainder of it in 1930. Various local farmers had grazing agreements with the National Trust at various times, and Gilbert Stone, who was already farming at Old Dairy, took on the grazing of Old Park from Keith Blain in about 1981. Three years later he took on Monument Meadow, also under the National Trust. Peter Stone, who now does all the farming, started up in 1987 or 88, with Old Park, Monument Meadow and other odd bits, adding the Old Dairy fields in about 1991, South Park in 1993 and North Park in early 1998. All his fields became actual tenancies of the National Trust in 1997 except the one which is still his father's property.

North Park is unfenced, so not used for grazing, but for hay or silage. South Park is one of the National Trust's more recent acquisitions, coming in two parts in 1988 and 1991. Before that it had been arable land for many years, divided into five or six fields. Now it has been made into one big pasture of 115 acres, one of the most scenic areas of grassland, lying in the lower end of Golden Valley, with its slopes and brow and scattered trees. The hundred-strong herd can appear over the hill, and spread out over the slope as they graze their way along the valley towards Cromer Wood. There is

The herd in Old Park

public access to this pasture.

Peter Stone's enterprise is entirely beef production. He buys steers which are about a year old or a bit over. They spend the winter in a large cowshed and yard, with silage as their main feed, and then go out to graze on the park for the summer. They must be sold before they are $29^1/_2$ months old to conform with the regulations on beef production which were introduced to ensure safety from B.S.E. They are sold at Thame, which is now the nearest available market and slaughterhouse.

Pulridge Farm

from a conversation with Vic and Phyl Mountfort

This farm extended from Pulridge Wood to Nettleden on the left side of the road as you go down. Ron Fleckney of Egginton, close to Leighton Buzzard, was the owner in 1950. He was also Best Man at Vic and Phyl Mountfort's wedding. Vic and Phyl came to Little Gaddesden in February 1950 for Vic to run the farm as bailiff. They moved into 14 Cromer Close which was "tied" to Pulridge Farm at that time. After a few years the owner died and the farm was bought by the same Mr Green who bought Home Farm from Mr Palmer. The purchase of Home Farm took place in 1960 or very soon after, so Pulridge Farm had become part of Home

Elizabeth O'Neill's field opposite the green and Christine Planton's Polish horses. On the right is the mare, Papaja.

Farm (q.v.) by the time Mr Muddiman bought it.
Meanwhile Phyl went to work at Hudnall Farm orchard (q.v.)in 1954, Vic went back into engineering in Dunstable, and they moved to Church Road in 1956.

Red House estate

During the Brownlow era and a few years afterwards Red House was the centre of the management of the Ashridge estate as described elsewhere, and then became a private residence. In 1972 it was bought from Mr and Mrs Block by Mr and Mrs Grieff and Elizabeth O'Neill, together with 15 adjoining acres from Church Farm known as Greys Field. They also own the field parallel to the Green on the opposite side from the houses. These fields have been used for grazing horses and beef cattle and haymaking. In 1999 the grazing parallel to the Green was used by Christine Planton of Edlesborough for her Polish mares.
Mr O'Neill died some years ago and Mrs O'Neill and her daughter Karoline moved into converted estate buildings behind Red House. Elizabeth O'Neill showed me the old estate workshop plans and the site of the old water works house where the steam pumping engine used to be. We were sorry when we learnt that Elizabeth had died, early in 2000.

POPPETS FARM

from a conversation with Bill Moore

This is a 2 acre site at Ringshall. Bill Moore built the farm for himself in 1950 and ran it as a smallholding until it no longer paid. He now treats it as a wildlife sanctuary. He also did a lot of garden designing over a wide area of south-east England.

Number 30 Ringshall

This Ringshall Cottage was linked to the small field which lay behind the cottages and backed onto Ivinghoe Common. In 1891 this cottage was recorded as number 6 because the census enumerator took the cottages in the reverse order, starting with what we now call number 35. Our no.30 was occupied by George and Isabella Jones, the grandparents of Barbara Mogg, who lives now with her husband Colin in a bungalow in that same field.

by Barbara Mogg

My Great Grandfather James Jones came to Ashridge around 1849 when Lady Marian Alford came with her son, the 3rd Earl Brownlow. He lived with his wife Eliza and a young family at the Woodyard for a time. They later became tenants of 30 Ringshall: the house, carpenter's shop and around 3 acres of meadow land with two large cartsheds. They ran a smallholding. James Jones was a carpenter, builder and contractor to the estate, employed on many properties in the village, namely the school and the outbuildings of the Ringshall Cottages of which I have old plans. On his death his widow became the tenant and carried on the smallholding with her family. In 1885 my Grandfather George Jones served an apprenticeship as a carpenter-joiner with Honour and Son of Tring. He continued the business as builder and undertaker, extending the farming, renting more land in the village and part of the Old Dairy meadow. From a small dairy at the house he sold milk, butter etc. He married Isabella Hobbs and they had five children: James, Adelaide, Harold, Kathleen and Stanley. Isabella had a reputation as the sharpest dealer in pigs.
My father, Stanley Jones, purchased 30 Ringshall and land when the Ashridge

Estate was sold. He was a carpenter and builder and continued with the business. He married Phyllis Waters of Studham and they had two children: myself and my brother Anthony Jones (Tony). During this time he enlarged the farm, renting arable land at Goose Hill. A young George Rogers was employed to help with the cows and pigs. He built the Haven, now called Badgers Wood, in Beacon Road for my grandmother. Unfortunately in 1940 my father died leaving a young family. We continued to live at Ringshall but the business came to an end. George Rogers took over Goose Hill where he now lives and farms.
Editor's note: The meadow at Ringshall was gradually reduced as parts of it were sold for family member housing, but a small part is still used for a few sheep. The subsequent history of Goose Hill is dealt with under that heading. Further details of the Jones and Mogg families can be found on page 306 in Chapter 20

St Margaret's Farm

from a conversation with Keith Blain

Keith Blain holds St Margaret's Farm, which includes 260 acres of farmland in our parish, and three-quarters of Hill Wood and half of Pulridge Wood. This makes him, with Don Cox, joint second largest landowner of Little Gaddesden, most of the acreage being in Hudnall. The farm house and buildings are in Great Gaddesden, as well as an even larger area of land.

Keith's father, Ernest Blain, came over from Wheathampstead in 1926, bringing with him (quite literally, as they walked all the way) his herd of Dairy Shorthorns. He came as a tenant of Mr Fairweather, who had acquired it as part of the Brownlow estate.

In 1928 he bought it from him. At that time the farmland amounted to about 130 acres, of which only Hill Wood and Wood Field were in Little Gaddesden. Like most local farms it was mixed, keeping pigs and sheep as well as the dairy herd, and growing cereals and fodder crops.

In 1933 Keith was born,and in the same year his father gave up the dairy herd but continued beef rearing. Keith grew up to take over the farm. Some land was lost when it was compulsorily purchased for a special school, the buildings and grounds of which eventually became the Amaravati Buddhist Centre which is there now - but that is Great Gaddesden's story. The farm grew, however, by purchases from adjoining farms, mostly from the former land of Little Gaddesden's Home Farm, although these fields had passed through other owners before becoming Mr Blain's. He managed to buy Wood Meadow and Four Ways Field in about 1960, at the time when Mr Muddiman bought the rest of the valley from Home Farm down to Nettleden.

In 1973 Mr Muddiman put his land up for sale again. Keith went to the auction at the Heath Park Hotel in Hemel Hempstead and sat at the front. The auctioneer, John Hodson, was just beginning to sell it when a man came in, asked for details and started bidding at once. His name was Hobson, and he was buying land for the business enterprise National Car Parks as an investment. Keith reckons he didn't even look at the land until after he had bought it, and recalls, "He paid £650 an acre for it, which doesn't sound much now. Of course it all went wrong for him then - land prices dropped rapidly."

So two years later the land was all sold again: Mr Muddiman bought nearly all of it back at much less than he had sold it for, and Mr Blain bought 80 acres of the fairly level bit, mostly in Hudnall, adjoining his farm. Across this field runs the public footpath "Bird's Pightle" which leads from Covetous Corner down into Nobody's Bottom, following some, now invisible, hedge-lines. At the opposite side of the valley used to be Bird's Field. The whole width of the valley now bears the name of Birds Pickle, as Keith was able to buy the rest of it from Mr Muddiman's estate just after the latter's death in 1995, along with all the lower part of the valley down to Nettleden. The upper and lower valley are now divided by a broad belt of setaside from beside the St Margaret's nunnery site to the middle of Pulridge Wood. This contains an old dell, and the old pond where a sheep enclosure stood, and clumps of trees and new-springing bushes. Most of it is just over the boundary, in Great Gaddesden.

Recently Keith sold off a strip of approximately 8 acres at the Cromer End of Birds Pickle to the Simkins of Hither Coppice. In 1999 this was fallow, but they have plans for paddocks here.

There were still sheep on the farm until 1997 but there is no livestock production at St Margaret's Farm now. It is all arable, the most profitable crop at present being wheat, but even that is low priced at present. Oilseed rape, linseed and field beans have been used as break crops. I asked what had been the most significant event to affect the running of the farm over the years and Keith replied that it was the current depression of the markets:

"I would say it was this last year or two years, definitely, since I've been farming. I started at fifteen and it's never been everything bad [as it is now]. We've had bad times but there's always something else that was all right ... Beef is one of the first things that is showing signs of coming back."

Harvesting wheat at St Margaret's Farm near Covetous Corner 1999

As for the 1999 harvest of Hereward bread wheat, Keith said he had learnt a lesson from it because it had only made a profit by mischance. The ground had been muddy for so long in the winter that he had been unable to drill the seed. Eventually a cold spell in February had frozen the ground solid so he broke it up with a shaker: a deep cultivator with a vibrating action produced by a heavy eccentric flywheel. Then he drilled the wheat into that surface and harrowed it later when the conditions allowed it. The crop came through much later than usual and the "spray man" said it wasn't advanced enough to apply the usual pesticides at the recommended time. In consequence the only treatment it had was fertilizer and, later, a spray against wild oats which were troublesome. The profit on the crop was due to the saving of expense on pesticides - and being able to harvest it all in one hot weekend in August so that its quality was up to bread wheat standard although the yield was low. He was also lucky to sell his Chablis as bread wheat. This variety does not usually make that grade.

The Spinney

THE WITCHCRAFT HERD OF DEXTER CATTLE

by Shiamala Comer

A small herd of pedigree Dexter Cattle live in the village, at The Spinney. We bought our first cow in September 1994, a year after we moved to the house. Dexters are a unique minority breed of cow in Britain. They are smaller, stockier, friskier and more intelligent than the modern breeds. Mostly shiny black, with a thick curly coat in winter; there is also a glowing red, as well as a dun variety. They make excellent mothers and are fantastic foragers; Dexters need nothing more than grass and hay to make excellent beef and delicious milk.

The origins of Dexters are lost in Celtic mists, with stories of descent from Spanish fighting bulls brought to Ireland in the 16th century. Whatever the truth of this, they are certainly closely related to the Kerry cow and similar small Celtic cattle found throughout Europe in the past.

The Witchcraft herd of Dexters at The Spinney

In 1998 when our herd got too big for our small acres, Norman and Bé Bailey came to our rescue and now Dexters graze the fields on both sides of Ringshall Drive and provide interest and pleasure to many walkers.

The prefix 'Witchcraft' is because of the historic links of the area to witches and magic. It is also an echo of my first cow's old and well-regarded bloodline of Woodmagic. Finally it is wonderful and magical to bring a breed back from near extinction to a thriving small scale commercial animal. Twenty-five years ago the Dexter was a rare breed with just 50 cows and 3 bulls. The national herd is now about 3,000, and, while BSE raged, they held their own without a single case.

Wards Hurst Farm

from a conversation with Paul Gent

Although outside the parish boundary, Wards Hurst has often been more connected with Little Gaddesden than with its own parish of Ivinghoe. It is also now our closest dairy farm, there being none left in Little Gaddesden. The fields

ABOVE
The Ward's Hurst Holstein Friesian dairy herd.

extend from Wards Hurst right down to Ringshall reservoir and the Trust Cottages. In 1891 the farmer was Charles Nicholes, married, with four young children. (One of these, Ernest, was killed in action in 1917.) A farm labourer, William Scott, lived in a tenement there with his family, including two sons, William G. and Frederick, who also worked on the farm.

In 1916 this farm is mentioned in Doris Fenn's book as "Mrs Underwood's Farm". It was renowned for her butter, which used to win prizes at the Tring Show. In 1928 the National Trust acquired the fields on the Crawley Wood side of the farm, and in 1944 the rest of the farm, with all the fields, except Ringshall End, down to Ringshall. Since then the farm has been a National Trust tenancy.

In about 1955 Paul Gent came to Wards Hurst with a herd of Dairy Shorthorns from his father's farm, Haresfoot, on the far side of Berkhamsted. His father was a dairy farmer before him, having come from Norfolk in 1932 when it was more profitable to produce milk nearer to London. Over the years he started breeding with a Friesian bull to increase milk yields, and then changed over to a registered herd of British Friesians, large-bodied black and white cattle, whereas the Shorthorns were red and white. Like many other Friesian owners he has in recent years interbred them with the very similar Holstein bulls, and now has, with his son Mark, the Wards Hurst herd of Holstein Friesians. There are 80 milking cows in the herd, and they win many prizes in agricultural shows such as the annual Hertfordshire Show at Redbourn.

The usual by-product of a dairy herd is beef calves, but in the present depressed state of the home-grown meat market the male calves offer no prospect of profit, only loss. They are shot at birth, much to the grief of the farmer, and only the dairy heifers are reared as replacements to the herd. Dave Ballad is the dairy-man.

The fields nearest to the farm are used for grazing, and a herd of wild Fallow Deer are regularly seen taking a share. There is an arable rotation including grass leys, cereals, and in 1999 linseed.

Well Farm

from a conversation with Pat Bleackley

The house at Well Farm is just outside our boundary, but some of the fields are within it, including the most northerly fields of the parish. Charlie Allison was farming here in 1899 but after that there is a big gap in my records but the drive

BELOW
Pat Bleackley, with Well Farm behind

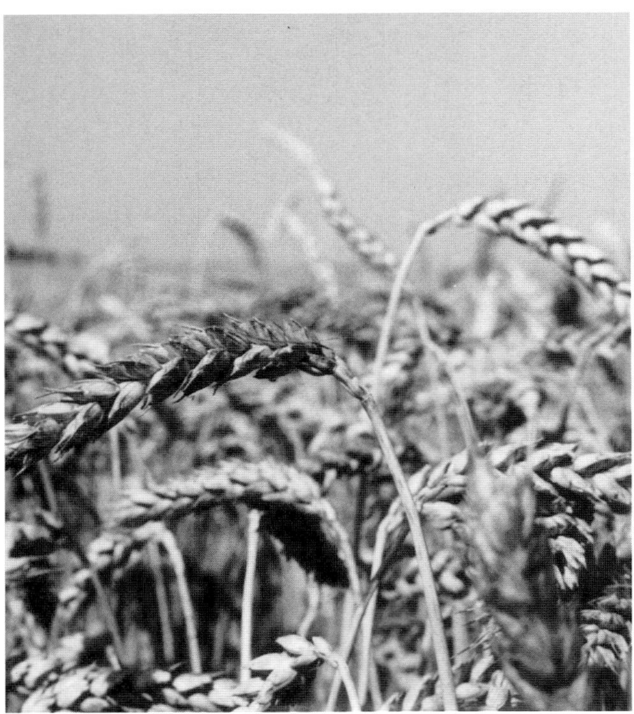

is said to have been built by Italian prisoners of war. George Strakosch took Well Farm in 1947 and married Pat a few years later. They bred race horses and polo ponies and also had arable land.

When George died the horse breeding came to an end and Pat Strakosch sold most of the farmland in 1978 to Tom Thorne of Rosebury Farm, Eaton Bray, retaining some fields adjoining the house. Pat later married David Bleackley and they still live in Well Farm house.

In 1999 the much reduced Well Farm is kept as grassland for horses.

Tom Thorne's land is used for arable crops and pigs. In 1999 he grew Riband wheat on each side of Well Farm drive. The pigs are just outside our parish. They can be seen beside the road down to Dagnall in the open, as they are reared in arks. They are hybrids, known simply as "PMC" - Pig Marketing Company.

The land here includes a rectangular bite out of the parish and county boundary which is the same size and shape as an old 6 acre field once called Parish Piece, but they don't quite fit each other. Parish Piece is now part of a larger field, but the county boundary still follows its old crooked course.

TOP
Wheat at Well Farm 1999

ABOVE
One of Tom Thorne's pigs 1999

Miscellaneous paddocks

In 1999 there could easily be a dozen meadows and paddocks not mentioned under their own headings. Typically these are used for grazing horses and ponies, sometimes in rotation with sheep. The grazing may be rented or permitted by some agreement or used by the owner. Hay or silage may be taken. A stable may be built.

An example is the paddock at Little Gaddesden House where Eddis and Dora Box keep Shetland Ponies.

Bee keepers

Just for the record, the following people have been mentioned as keeping bees:

Jean Moore who lived first at Theccans, then at Greenacre, "an expert".
Norman Patterson of Nob's Crook.
Mr Purton, gardener at Denison House.
Clifford Bingham, biology teacher at the Gaddesden Training College for Teachers, Ashridge, 1947-1950.
Chris Osborn-Jones at Hudnall House.
Ken Gorman of Milton Keynes kept bees at Hudnall Park in the 1980's.

CHAPTER 15 - *Sport and outdoor pusuits*

Country sports in Little Gaddesden

by Robert A Corby

Little Gaddesden Parish includes much of Ashridge Park, which is mainly a wooded area. Fox hunters, beaglers, harriers, shooters, rough and organised, and maybe hawkers, all, no doubt, operated here at times. Ashridge, in the Brownlow era, was highly organised for shooting and King George V honoured Ashridge and Little Gaddesden by coming to shoot here in the early part of the century. For this to happen, the organisation must have been of the highest order, with keepering, game quantity, and arrangements generally, being superb. Traces still remain of this organisation.

Shooting of game stopped in Ashridge soon after the National Trust took over because Miss Courtauld of Potten End, in her will, left a large sum of money to the Trust on condition that shooting of game ceased. But in the large area of the Park, keepering and control of vermin was essential and allowed, as now, the control of deer numbers. John Wilson, Head Ranger of the National Trust here after the 1939-45 war, therefore, arranged with suitable locals with guns, and dogs where needed, to clear vermin, rabbits, pigeons, magpies etc on arranged mornings and in selected areas and vermin was kept to an acceptable level.

It is also known that in the Brownlow days a pack of harriers was kept at Thunderdell Lodge by Lord Brownlow. These were, earlier, also kept at Brick Kiln Cottage nearer Berkhamsted. They were known as stag hounds when there. I, however, remember personally foxhunting in Ashridge and area in the 1920's and 30's with the then Hertfordshire Hunt.

In those days it was a celebrated hunt. It was started in 1775 by the second Marchioness of Salisbury possibly on the basis of the Hatfield Hunt. The Marchioness remained Master until her 70th birthday in 1819. She is immortalised in the "Lays of the Hertfordshire Hunt" written by Captain Robins, East Yorks Regiment (killed in action in 1915 by gas poisoning) as follows:

A lady holds the pride of place
In the roll of honour's front.
'Tis the grand old dame of the Cecil house
Who founded the Hatfield Hunt.
A health to the gallant Marchioness!
The noble name she bore
Still heads the toast we honour most -
'The men who have gone before'.

I recall meets at Ashridge House well. The garden then always held a fox and he was usually holloaed away at the Nettleden end and set sail for either Pulridge Wood or Frithsden Copse. If to Frithsden he usually ran to Berkhamsted Common, on to Sallow Copse, Aldbury, and possibly Combe Wood. If he chose Pulridge Wood and on to Hill Wood at Hudnall he was usually lost there. Living in Hudnall now, I know why. The woods are riddled with badger setts, and foxes well know where to get lost.

Meets were also held at the Bridgewater Arms Hotel. The first draw then was often Ringshall Copse, a certain "find", and on to Combe Wood and Ivinghoe Beacon or Incombe Hole and Duncombe Terrace. On one day in 1927 hounds met at the Bridgewater Arms and soon found a fox in Sallow Copse. He ran fast along Duncombe Terrace, crossed Ivinghoe Common to Wards Coombe. He then ran on to the Brook near Edlesborough, then right-handed up the downs, through Whipsnade Wood and on to Studham, where he was caught at Mansgrove after a brilliant hunt of 40 minutes, and the first 35 minutes covered seven and a half miles of country! Who would have guessed that in a few years

A reproduction of The Hertfordshire Hunt at Whipsnade, painted by Lionel Edwards.

this area would have been encircled with wire fencing and would be the home of wild animals - Whipsnade Zoo?

Also on the same day Lionel Edwards painted his famous picture of the Hertfordshire Hunt at Whipsnade. The field in that picture is led by Jack Molyneux, the Huntsman, originator of these hunting notes. Behind him on a grey horse is Miss Acland, later Mrs Cecily Wykeham-Musgrave and wife of Major Aubrey Wykeham-Musgrave, the last Agent of the Ashridge Estate. They lived, first, in Robin Hood House and later in Kilbracken, Hudnall Common until 1952, when the present writer moved in there.

I particularly recall one day hunting when I was on the Northchurch Road near Monument Drive with hounds running in Sallow Copse on my right, when a buck with great antlers emerged from the woods onto the road fifty yards in front of me. He then jumped from the middle of the road over the Park palings into the Park. Those palings stood on a little bank beside the road and must have been 6 feet high, yet the buck leapt over them in an enormous leap and disappeared.

In those days the Hertfordshire was a well-known hunt. The list of subscribers notes many distinguished people such as Earl Brownlow, the Marquis of Salisbury, Field Marshall the Earl of Cavan, the Earl of Strathmore (the Queen Mother's father) and more. The kennels at Kinsbourne Green were palatial, with a corridor down the middle through which a large motor coach could have been driven.

Ashridge and Little Gaddesden was a wooded part of the Herts Hunt country, which was enormous. It stretched from nearly Bedford in the north to, in the south, Watford, Bricket Wood, North Mymms and London Colney, in the west over to Leighton Buzzard along the Euston railway line and in the east over beyond Luton and Hitchin. In 1970 it merged with the Old Berkely Hunt and the South Oxfordshire to form the Vale of Aylesbury Hunt, due to the development of the New Towns and motorways etc.

Some brief accounts of meets in Little Gaddesden follow. Detail is taken from the diary of Jack Molyneux, Huntsman from 1922 to 1929.

Last day of season, 1922

Met at Bridgewater Arms, found in Ivinghoe Gorse, hounds ran through Combe Wood into Ringshall Copse, on to Hoo Wood and up to Little Gaddesden, then left-handed to Hudnall. After Hudnall they ran on to Home Farm and Ashridge Park. Then there came an awful storm but hounds hunted marvellously through a lot of deer and getting a good holloa on, the line was taken to a garden in

Ringshall where the fox was lost. This was a really good hunt of two hours full of excellent hound work. Found a fox again at Coldharbour and ran towards Berkhamsted, then back to Sallow Copse through the Park to Berkhamsted Common, back to Coldharbour and put him to ground at Toms Hill. - Time 1 hour and 38 minutes.

November 1st 1924
We found a fox in Ringshall Copse and killed him in the canal at Marsworth Locks after a brilliant 40 minutes with a 4 1/2 mile point. Hounds did not check until they reached the canal when one hound saw him in the water and it was all over.

1926: Another day in Ashridge
One Friday we ran into Ashridge Park one evening with a ripping scent and coming to the Park palings, I shouted to Mr Faulconer, a great sportsman, "Help me make a hole, sir", but he thought I meant with his horse when all I needed was a hole for the hounds. Anyway he rode straight at the palings which are unjumpable. Fortunately they were rotten and a whole length fell down and we got through.

I finish this brief account of country sports in Ashridge with another verse from "Ivinghoe Hill" which appears in the "Lays of the Hertfordshire Hunt" by George Robins:

Here, where the counties join hands in alliance,
Terrace on terrace and glade upon glade,
Ashridge looms up like a keep of the giants,
Buttressed with beech woods from Aldbury to Gade.
Northwards the vale stretches smiling and spacious,
Spurs of the Chilterns the far distance fill;
Never held dreamland a prospect more gracious:
Sunlight and shadow on Ivinghoe Hill.

Ringshall Cottages

Softness of the velvet
of deer's antlers
are the mossed roofs
of these old cottages,
huddled together
as if their closeness
buttressed them from harm.

Some tall,
some curiously small
but all arising,
as the woods around them,
garlanded, draped
by wild clematis
hung with ivy, by eglantine
woven together.

Concealed from unwanted
eyes, only smoke
pale as traveller's joy
curling from brick stepped
chimneys
rumours they are here...

Mary Blake

Village cricket

ASHRIDGE CRICKET CLUB

by Michael McCaul

The Reverend Charlton Lane died in November 1892. Many in the village felt his loss keenly, not least members of the Ashridge Cricket Club, of which he had been a keen supporter from the days of his curacy here in the 1880s. He worked closely with John Worall, the village schoolmaster, who had actually started the club in 1855, soon after his arrival here at the behest of Lady Marian Alford, to become the school's first head and subsequently the leader of so many strands of village life.

Lane had in fact played first-class cricket both at Oxford and for Surrey. Worall himself retired in 1894; his son-in-law, and successor at the School, 'Sammy'

Green, was secretary of the Cricket Club in the late 1890s, under the presidency of Lord Brownlow.

The Ashridge Cricket Club, however, was extremely fortunate that the new Rector, Rev F H Hodgson, was also a keen cricketer, albeit of moderate ability, and the reason why more is known about the Club's activities is that Hodgson was Editor of the newly founded Parish Magazine and included therein the Club's activities, including actual match card details. After the 1897 season Hodgson comments 'our successes were mainly due to the excellent all round play of Mr F Janes'. Fred Janes had a butcher's shop at Hudnall and, moving into the 20th century, it is worth noting that his son, Seth, still playing when the Club closed down in 1957, was a left-arm bowler who took hundreds of wickets in a long career. But in 1898, Hodgson accepted a living in Yorkshire and not only did the reports of the Ashridge Cricket Club dry up but the magazine itself 'folded' in 1900.

Hodgson's successor in 1900 was Dr H G Woods. He seems not to have been a cricketer but, in his annual 'report' for 1903, recorded that Mr Hogg had been appointed captain of the Cricket Club and Mr Peacock, Secretary of the Cricket and Football Clubs for 1904. No other record of Hogg has been found. He did not appear in the census of 1891 for Little Gaddesden.

In fact, Dr Wood's successor was Rev E Clark (1904-19) but he too recorded nothing about the Cricket Club, nor is there any written or anecdotal material available about the activities of the Club either before or immediately after the Great War (in which the village lost 22 men) but it is known that the Estate's Agent, Colonel W Wheatley, was supportive and, indeed, as far back as 1892 had levelled a strip in the village itself for use by boys who found the walk to and from the ground at Ashridge too much for them. The location of this strip is not known.

The Ashridge C Team in 1937

LEFT TO RIGHT
BACK ROW
Bill Marks (umpire), Steve Oakins, George Purple, Michael McCaul, Herbert Reasbeck, Geoffrey Cuthbertson

FRONT ROW
Bill Armstrong, Seth Janes, Arthur Clifton, John Oakins, Alec Austin, H.G.Stock, Jack Haines

The death in 1921 of Lord Brownlow had a profound effect on all aspects of village life and particularly after his Trustees gave instructions for the entire Ashridge Estate to be sold. But, somehow, the Cricket Club survived and although no records are available it is known to have continued to play opposite the 'Big House'. But about 1928, at the behest of the new owners, the Bonar Law Memorial Trust, the cricket ground was moved to a new site prepared some 300 yards away, which is the same as that currently used by the Ashridge Management College. An aerial photograph, taken about 1928, suggests that the cricket 'table' was then shared with a tennis court. This was the ground used by the Club up to 1950.

Jack Duncombe Snr and Phillip Collier are but two known to have played in the twenties. Actually, at the time, the Cricket Club was benefiting from the coaching given to boys at the Village School, including John Oakins, Alec Austin and Seth Janes, who were later to become stalwart members up to 1939. It also greatly benefited the Club in the thirties that the Accountant at Ashridge, Herbert Reasbeck, was a keen cricketer and rendered invaluable service to the Club as Secretary. He was able to ensure not only that the ground was well maintained but that the Club and its visitors could take tea in the Rose Garden restaurant; one or two teams brought supporters who were delighted to take tea and to see round the magnificent grounds. He also widened the scope of the fixtures list; fixtures were made with visitors to the College, and with clubs as far distant as Eversholt, on the Duke of Bedford's estate.

Practice was on Fridays, and village boys were encouraged to participate. Amongst those who played for the Club in the thirties were the incomparable Spencer Block (Cambridge and Surrey) and G B Cuthbertson (a Cambridge Blue and later Captain of Northants) and J C C Davidson, our local MP until created a viscount in 1937, and who lived at Ashridge. There was also Colonel A G Wykeham-Musgrave MC, a land agent who had come to live in the village and later became President of the Club.

In 1935, the Reverend C E Wager was appointed Rector. He was a keen and competitive cricketer who took over the captaincy from H G Stock in 1936. Wager possessed an exquisite 'late cut', a stroke he taught to some of the club's colts. He also bowled off-breaks and his appeals were made quietly but very firmly. Others who played for Ashridge in the middle thirties were 'Bill' Armstrong, both opening bat and fast bowler, Seth Janes, John Oakins, Alec Austin, who became Captain in 1938 and was a leg-break bowler, as well as Herbert Reasbeck. Later the team was reinforced by Steve Oakins, Jack Haynes, Dick Hitchman, Arthur Clifton and George Purple, as well as by the three colts, Bill Newman (who was killed serving in the RAF), Jack Duncombe, and the writer of this note. Not far behind in terms of age but of outstanding ability was Jack Baker. It may be recalled that in the 1939 season the effect of the Militia Act (George Purple was called up in July 1939) and the Territorial call-up (which involved Jack Haynes and Arthur Clifton) in August, left the Club barely able to find a team to take on Ivinghoe. It was therefore left to the 'colts' who scored a notable success there. This was the last match played by the Club before the War was declared on 3 September.

Memories of playing cricket at Ashridge include seeing Vicars Bell's trousers catching fire after being struck in the pocket while fielding at short leg; the ball had ignited a box of Swan Vestas. On another occasion a large swarm of bees swept around the ground at stump level. Their impending arrival had been detected by Bill Armstrong and everyone prostrated themselves just in time. Thirdly, and after an interval of some years, 'Sid' Batchelor, the village roadman, had returned in the mid-thirties to act as umpire. In one match (his last) he was struck in the back by a long throw-in while watching the crease. He was, in fact, standing on the wrong side of the crease and not facing the ball. It was a worrying incident (there was no insurance) and Sid's second retirement was much regretted.

Ashridge was not a high scoring ground. Not only was it large, but the outfield was slow and spongy. The Club felt it was breaking new ground when, at Eversholt, and thanks to a magnificent innings by Spencer Block, Ashridge scored 240 before tea; Eversholt replied with 210. Ivinghoe and Studham were amongst the keenest sides played by Ashridge. After another splendid knock by Spencer Block, who also had some success with the ball, Studham reported to the Press that 'Block beat Studham'!

The Club resumed its activities in 1947, when the first match played was against a still very strong Studham side. Our first team included Jack Duncombe Snr and Phillip Collier, who had first played in the twenties, as well as Bill Green, Tom Jackson and some pre-war members who had survived the War in many parts of the world. Bill Green played for the first time. The Club found it necessary to apply for a licence to provide 'economy' teas which were dispensed by Mrs S Oakins and Mrs M McCaul, who often found it necessary actually to carry the supplies up to Ashridge because there was no petrol. The Club found it necessary to share ground facilities with the Teachers' Training College, which had taken over the hospital accommodation. This arrangement proved much less than satisfactory; the student teachers who used the ground seemed neither to know much about pitch maintenance and management nor indeed to care. In 1948 the Club was glad to welcome back Christopher Bradby as well as to find room for Robert Whipp, a solicitor and an excellent batsman, who had come to live in the village for a time.

It was with considerable relief and anticipation that the Club heard of plans being made in 1948 in the village to take advantage of assistance offered by the National Playing Fields Association to establish a playing field in Church Road. The responsibility for preparing a 'table' was to be exclusively that of the Club and, although the site offered contained a noticeable depression where there had been a hedge, the necessary work was completed, thanks particularly to the efforts of John Oakins and Tom Jackson, in time for the 1950 season. New players included Ralph Parker, Bob Hunter, John Reasbeck and the somewhat unpredictable 'Jim' Cornes. Teas were served in the School Dining Hall (by permission of Vicars Bell) but changing facilities were primitive - in the garden shed!

The services of Commander Geoffrey Tandy were enlisted as umpire. Wearing a solar topee he was a formidable figure but impartial application of the Laws of Cricket, which he knew backwards, did not always endear him to players. But the Club was glad to avail itself of his services.

The Parish Council was persuaded to purchase a mower to keep the out field mowed (in preference to sheep!) and the Club settled down to enjoy six happy seasons on the new ground. But in 1957, following the retirement or departure of some senior players who had also provided the necessary administrative backbone, a lack of willingness of others to participate in administration (secretarial and ground maintenance) chores it was found necessary for the Club to close down after 102 years. Happily sufficient interest was forthcoming in 1962 to revive the Club under the name of Little Gaddesden Cricket Club. The successful activities of this club achieved in spite of many difficulties is a story for someone else to tell.

LITTLE GADDESDEN CRICKET CLUB

This was the successor to the Ashridge Cricket Club after an interval of five years. Derek Faulconer has been Chairman for most of its life. He founded the present Colts team also, in 1975, for coaching younger cricketers.

In their first match the Colts were all out for 3 runs, an achievement which they make no secret of. From that point the only direction could be up. Eight of the original members still play in the village team, including Ivan Veall who was Captain of Little Gaddesden Cricket Club in 1999. Derek's son, Patrick, took over as Captain in 2000

ABOVE:
Patrick Faulconer

BELOW:
Glenn Barrington and Tim Wooster

Little Gaddesden Football Club

1936 to 1986

by Alfred Sherringham

As you can see from the above dates, the Football Club has reached the fifty years of recorded existence. I am fully aware that older residents of the village will say that the Club began before that date but, unfortunately, I am guided by written records so, therefore, I can only refer to what is written down.

By 1936 it was decided that Little Gaddesden Football Club should enter into the 3rd Division of West Herts Football Association. The dressing rooms and pitch would be at the Bridgewater Arms Hotel. Unfortunately a problem, which was to occur many times, was that persons living outside the village were not allowed to play. This, of course, reduced the strength of the team's ability.

Time went on, finances being good - £6. 0s. 0d. being in hand at the end of the financial year for 1937. In 1938 the team was promoted to Division 2 of the West Herts FA. In 1939 a Grand Dance was held to bolster funds and a grand total of £3. 13s. 7d. was made and at the end of the financial year the balance was £4. 16s. 1½d. As we are all aware a far greater event occurred in 1939, which terminated the Club until 1945 and the ground was then at Ashridge. Again, the business of outsiders cropped up and it was considered that unless this attitude altered there would always be difficulty in raising a team.

1946 showed that money would have to be spent on nets for the goals, so garden netting was bought at 22 shillings a pair. Also this year, the Club joined forces with the Gaddesden Society, the ground was again moved - this time to behind Chapel Close, and the dressing rooms were in Mrs Shepherd's barns behind nos 60/61.

Mr Jopson offered to erect tin huts and a closet at Home Farm, without success. Attempts were made for First Aid lectures but failed through lack of interest. Members were insured for £4. 11s. 0d per year, benefit being £1 per week for a year.

In 1947 there were again problems in raising sufficient numbers for teams. Club finances were better in 1948 being £57. 8s .0d. Another problem arose - coupons were required for new kit and appeals were made to parishioners to help out in this respect.

The village playing field was beginning to take shape. The now familiar strip was decided on and, in 1951, the new pitch was available although one had to beware of sheep droppings and cow pats! 1952 proved eventful as the Club won the League Championship for the first time since 1929.

Problems arose again with dressing room accommodation but as the Club had donated £50 towards the erection of the new Village Hall, changing facilities were allowed in the Ladies and Gents Toilets, which proved embarrassing at times.

As time went on the Club managed to survive but lack of local members and scarcity of help were making it difficult for the faithful few. It was realised that outsiders must be allowed into the Club to comply with League commitments as in the 1959 season not one League match was won.

In 1974 the Club was able to donate £300 towards the erection of the new Sports Pavilion and Mr Albert Williams (Headmaster) offered the Club changing facilities in the School, which were gratefully received.

In 1976 the Sports Pavilion was completed which solved the changing problems and we were grateful to all concerned, especially Mr W Whitman, a then local parishioner and player, who did so much towards getting the building erected. The Club was now on a sound footing and with my good friend George Bunting, now sadly passed away, busy selling bingo tickets, the Club was also financially sound. 1981 was a further step forward as we were accepted into the West Herts County League, which meant higher commitments all round. The Committee unanimously decided at this time to have a shield for Clubman of the Year, which was presented in this year to Mr George Bunting in appreciation of all his good work for the Club.

So in 1986 the Club represented Little Gaddesden in Division 2 of the County League, Division 2 in the Reserves Section. The Club was indeed fortunate to have a sponsor, Mr Brian Burnell (Britone) of Rickmansworth, whose valued financial assistance was very much appreciated by all members of the Club. Without his help, with rocketing costs, the Club would have been hard pressed to carry on.

BELOW
George Bunting celebrates 50 years service with the football team, 1979.

RIGHT
The football team 1951 - 1952

TOP ROW (L-R):

Bob Hobbs, Tom Jackson, Harold Flitton, George Rogers, David Williams, Jeff Mantle, Michael McCaul, John Rogers, Harold Ward (Secretary).

FRONT ROW:
Brian Woodgate, Bill Green, Sid Moyse, Harry Flitton, Steve Oakins, Tim Sears.

Junior football

by Richard Tilley

Junior football is popular in the village. Thirty-five years ago, Alf Sherringham started a Saturday morning club to provide additional training for the children in the village school team. Even in those early days, younger children showed their enthusiasm to learn the game as well and came along with their dads to take part. The Saturday morning sessions attracted a few girls, as well as up to 20 boys.

Alf got us all involved, with the dads helping him train the children in passing, shooting and dribbling skills, and then joining in the practise matches that followed. There were some weeks when the number of dads turning up was getting so high, that the children were almost outnumbered! There were sufficient players to let us organise two games, separating the younger and smaller children from their older and larger brothers and sisters. Iain Horner, a former village school pupil, soon volunteered to help with the training of the elder group, for whom occasional friendly matches were organised against other local teams. This informal set-up gave many of us a great deal of enjoyment for several years.

However about 18 months ago, numbers started to drop as better facilities for junior level football were created at the sports centres or larger clubs in Berkhamsted and other towns. Some of the older players were keen to play regular matches in the growing youth leagues, which soon opened up to the younger children as well, when the Football Association launched its mini-soccer initiative, (7-a-side games for the under-11s). Berkhamsted and other sports centres organised more frequent courses with professional coaches, which proved very popular, especially with some of the younger children.

As numbers dropped at the Saturday morning club, we were forced to mix together children with a very wide age-span, which made it less enjoyable for both younger and older players alike. A chance meeting with another football club then opened our eyes to the real potential for providing facilities similar to those in the surrounding towns. We found that the small village of Ivinghoe was able to attract enough players to run several mini-soccer teams for the under-11s as well as some league football for older children.

With considerable help from several new volunteers, Little Gaddesden "Rangers" JFC was launched and registered with the Herts FA in May 1999. The new club is based on regular Sunday morning mini-soccer matches organised through the Bushey and West Herts Youth Leagues, with training sessions on Saturdays continuing as before, but clearly structured by age-group. New equipment and kit has been funded by the Leisure Department of Dacorum Borough Council, Watford Football Club, the Football Trust and a donation from the former Little Gaddesden Football Club, as well as contributions from the parents of our members.

The potential scale of the demand to

AND ON THE SUBJECT OF FOOTBALL

Mandy Haynes writes

I first visited the village in 1976 when my brother played in the Little Gaddesden football team and we were living in Hemel Hempstead. It was at the time when Alf Sherringham was managing them and characters like Paul Francis, Richard and Kenny Bunting and Billy Whitman were in the team. George Bunting was a regular supporter. I used to help Elsie Sherringham with the teas. Through this I made and remained good friends with Jackie Wilson.

I couldn't believe my luck when in 1996 we found a house we could afford in Hudnall with more than ample space for my "family". The family who live with me and Christian Ulf-Hansen are 5 Siberian Huskies: Lexi, Kia and Tammi who are 13, and Bear and Tyson who are 10 years old.

LEFT
Mandy Haynes with Huskies Kia and Tammi

Junior football in 1999

play mini-soccer in Little Gaddesden was revealed after coaches from the Watford Football In the Community scheme agreed to run a one-day training course in the village during the 1999 Easter holidays. 50 children (aged from 5 to 11) attended the course, and most of these have gone on to join the club. The 1999/2000 season has seen the launch of 4 mini-soccer teams (Under 7/8/9 and 11 age-groups).

This year we have also run occasional 11-a-side matches for an Under 13 team, including games against the dads who help with the training. Next year we hope to develop at least one regular 11-a-side league team for boys, and to encourage more girls to develop their football skills.

Given the clear enthusiasm expressed by children of all ages to play football, and the support from their parents, there is every prospect that Little Gaddesden Rangers teams will be taking part in West Hertfordshire leagues and tournaments for many years to come.

Ashridge Golf Club

by Peter Mann

Henry Cotton

To the west of Little Gaddesden village, set in the National Trust Ashridge Estate, lies the Ashridge Golf Club and 18-hole course.

The golf course was the brain-child of Thomas Place who, in the late 1920's, when the Brownlow Estate was broken up, acquired Ashridge House and part of Ashridge Park. Surrounding building plots were sold to fund the cost of construction.

The Architects who designed and supervised construction of the course were Sir Guy Campbell, C K Hutchison and N V Hotchkin. Many trees had to be cut down and the task of construction was given to James Hunter of Chester who took up residence in Woodyard Cottage, now the home of Antony Hopkins. A clubhouse was built and thatched with Norfolk reed.

In 1932 a syndicate, headed by the Earl of Rosebery, purchased the clubhouse and some land from Thomas Place, together with rights under a covenant with the National Trust which had earlier purchased part of Ashridge Park. Thus Ashridge Golf Club was formed.

Under the new management Ashridge Golf Club flourished. The inaugural

Rosebery Cup Competition was held in 1933 and remains one of the more important open events in the amateur calendar. The standing of the Club was enhanced by the engagement as Professional of Henry Cotton who by then had made his name as possibly the best British golfer, having won the British Open in 1934. Cotton established a teaching school at Ashridge, and when he won the Open again in 1937 at Carnoustie two of his assistants finished 7th and 18th – a remarkable achievement.

A special relationship was established in 1932 between Ashridge and the Officers of RAF Halton, whose Mess Members were allowed to play the course for an annual subscription from the Mess. During the Second World War the association became even closer and Air Vice-Marshall Norman MacEwan, AOC RAF Halton, was Club Captain for the years 1938-1945.

The club kept going through the War but some space in the clubhouse was allocated initially for bedrooms for staff from Ashridge House, then a wartime hospital. However, in May 1943 the clubhouse was burnt down by an arsonist and facilities were very limited until rebuilding was undertaken in 1948. In 1945 an Artisan Section was formed from the newly disbanded Home Guard.

ABOVE:
The old golf club in 1932 when it opened (burnt down in 1943)

BELOW:
Henry Cotton (putting) and A.J.Lacey on the first green, qualifying competition for the Daily Mail Tournament 1939

After the War the Club continued from strength to strength but it was not until 1960 that membership reached an adequate level. As finances improved investment was made in three bungalows for green staff and enlargement of clubhouse facilities. In 1982, the Jubilee Year, Ashridge was nominated as one of the Automobile Association's Top Fifty Golf Clubs in the United Kingdom.

In recent years substantial investment in new machinery together with good course management has brought the course up to a very high standard.

Mention must be made of the Ladies Section which is an

The clubhouse now

important part of the Club. Mrs Belinda Silver is at present Captain of the Hertfordshire Ladies and Mrs Shirley Aylwin has just retired from the prestigious appointment of President of the English Ladies' Golf Association.

Ashridge Golf Club enters the new millennium in great shape, with a playing membership of more than 540 and a substantial waiting list. A new Clubhouse is planned for early construction and will further enhance the excellent amenities.

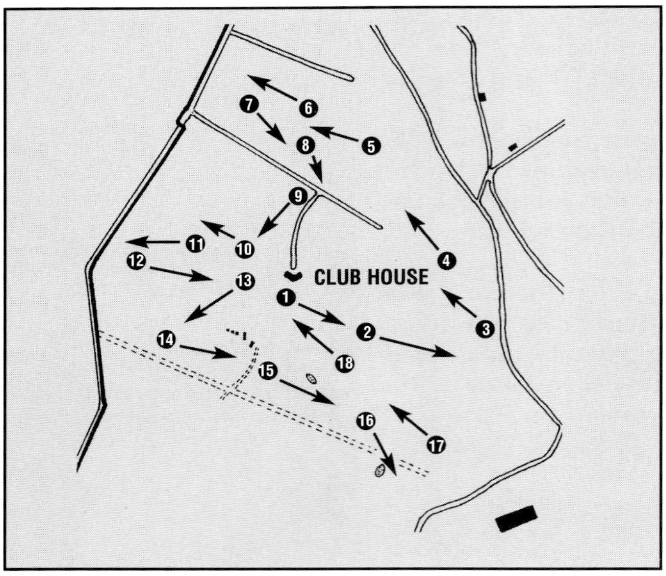

CAPTAINS

Captains of the Golf Club are elected for one year.
Past Captains who are living in the village in 1999 are: 1959 C. Baron, 1971 C.D. Garratt, 1973 S.Broughton, 1982 P.A. Mann, 1991 A.W. Fay

LADY CAPTAINS from Little Gaddesden

1962-3 Mrs Marjory Baron, 1974-5 Mrs Diana Rait Kerr, 1977-8 Mrs Shirley Aylwin, 1979-80 Mrs Pat Fraser-Beck, 1983-4 Mrs Jane Davis, 1988-9 Mrs Margaret Hopkins, 1996-7 Mrs Heidi James

ASHRIDGE GOLF COURSE

Names of holes

1. *Devil's Den*
2. *Golden Valley*
3. *The Rookery*
4. *Pook's Hill*
5. *Witchcraft Bottom*
6. *Highwayman's Hide*
7. *Ringshall*
8. *Knob's Crook*
9. *Cotton's*
10. *Pitstone*
11. *Thunderdell*
12. *Deer Leap*
13. *Queen Elizabeth's Drive*
14. *Old Park Lodge*
15. *Prince's Riding*
16. *Willow Pond*
17. *Hoo*
18. *Home*

Little Gaddesden Tennis Club

(REBORN)

by Jean How

During the early part of the 1970s a few enthusiastic tennis players namely me, Dorreen Barrington, Mike Stinton, Tessa Faulconer, Steve King and Nick Lloyd (Now Sir Nick Lloyd) began playing tennis on a Thursday evening on courts very kindly loaned to us for the evening. The long-suffering householders upon whose courts we played were the owners of 'Yew Tree Cottage', 'The Summer House', 'Gade House' in Hudnall Lane and 'Kilbracken'. Also we were allowed to use the courts at Ashridge Management College.

Thus inspired, and managing to obtain a great deal of local support, Dacorum Council and the Sports Council were approached by a committee with a view to obtaining a grant to enable us to have our own Village Tennis Club. We also received the approval of the Parish Council, upon whose land we were proposing to build the courts. A great deal of fund-raising was carried out and, finally, two courts were finished and played on in the later part of the 1970s.

In the 1980s, as the number of members, both Junior and Senior, increased, we once again approached Dacorum Council and the Sports Council for a further grant to enable us to build another court and, again with consent from the Parish Council, the third court was built.

With all three courts up and running, as it were, Thursday nights were allocated as club night for adult members only. The evenings were very successful and were always followed by a supper prepared and cooked by the members according to a rota scheme and were enjoyed by all who participated. The juniors had their own evening on a Wednesday until about 8 pm. Steven King, who lived at 'The Oak House' at the time, very kindly held coaching sessions for the juniors. He was later replaced by LTA coach Barbara Bean and then by Peter Bart. The ladies held friendly matches, played mostly on Tuesday mornings, against other local clubs such as Berkhamsted, Tring, Edlesborough and Harpenden; these were always followed by a lunch provided by the host club.

The men's section was also very well supported and ran a strong team in the Herts League. We were also fortunate enough to have friendly mixed doubles matches, usually held on a Saturday afternoon, with the tea once again provided by the ladies of the host clubs.

TOP LEFT:
Sue How and Alice Jones in 1985, with Chris Collins

TOP:
Alice Jones and Sarah Heard Spring 1983

ABOVE:
Caroline Heard and Kerry O'Donoghue in 1987

LEFT:
The tennis courts

During the early 1990s I, with coach Caroline Ward, started short tennis in the Village Hall for the very much younger members of the village. This was extremely popular, with a waiting list of young hopefuls waiting to join.

Various other activities which went on at the Club included Parent and Children competitions, usually played on Sundays, followed by a barbecue. Also the Club ran singles and doubles knockout competitions for both Seniors and Juniors during the summer months with the finals day usually being held in early September, followed by a prize-giving of the respective Cups and Shields for the winners and medals for the runners-up.

Winter was not forgotten as there was always a morning very near to Christmas when the ladies section held a mince pie and glühwein morning and we held a Christmas Party in the Pavilion every year for all members and their families. Additionally we prided ourselves on having a Senior Citizen section, which enabled our somewhat older but no less enthusiastic members to play as and when they were able, without incurring the price of a full membership.

It would be impossible to mention by name just how many people were involved initially in getting the Club up and running but to name a few who have sadly moved to pastures new: Colin and Annette Revell, Rod O'Donoghue and David Veall and, one still living here, Nick Webster. One can only hope that the Little Gaddesden Tennis Club continues to thrive in the next decade as it has in the past three.

The Bowls Club

by Barbara Mogg

The Bowls Club, 1999, with Keith Geater, keeper of the turf, centre

In 1980-81 a small group met at the Bridgewater Arms with Mr W Woods, proprietor, with a view to restart playing on the old British Legion Green at the rear of the public house. Permission was given. A notice was displayed at the Post Office requesting names of anyone interested in playing; approximately 25 people replied.

Work began on making the Green playable; it was not quite full length. The Club was known as The British Legion Bowls Club and a subscription to that organisation was paid by male members. Many happy games were played with other clubs and among ourselves for the next five years.

In 1983 permission was given for a new Green on the playing field in Church Road; work started in 1984 and play began on 17 May 1986. Since then we have grown to a membership of 70 plus, with our own pavilion with all facilities and storage and a fully-automatic watering system. This was achieved with grants and loans from Dacorum Borough Council, members' loans and fund-raising - and the Club is thriving.

Badminton Club

by Ann Kirkpatrick

Since about 1980 there has been a very active Badminton Club in the village and, for the last 16, I have been Secretary. For three years during that time we also had a Junior Badminton Group (from 6.30 to 8 pm). However, the Juniors 'grew up' and, at present, this is not needed.

We play most Wednesdays in the evening from 8 to 10 pm in the Village Hall and the members are all local residents. As other sports clubs in the village seem to have quite a lot of members from outside the village, the Badminton Club is lucky to survive with just local people.

We have also enjoyed organising and being involved with various fund-raising events in the village over the past few years when money was needed for repairs to the Village Hall.

Some of the original members still play but, when members leave for whatever reason, there always seem to be others to take their place. At present we are a lively bunch of 12 members, of mixed ages, who really enjoy the exercise and company each week. Long may it continue!

Swimming

Although I have no record of any swimming club, we have had a village swimming pool.

The Deer Leap Swimming Pool was constructed in the 1930's directly across the Ringshall Drive, thus cutting off Ringshall Lodge and the lodge gate from the rest of the drive which led down past Witchcraft Bottom. The Deer Leap Garage had been constructed about the same time, both pool and garage being under the same management.

The entrance to the pool led off the garage forecourt where the old lodge gates had been. The first owner was Leslie Bedford. Later the pool and garage became separate businesses, the pool being owned by John Constantine. A new entrance was made from the Little Gaddesden road. The pool, which was an open air one, but heated in later years, drew crowds from a wide area on hot weekends. Refreshments were sold (see page 198). Most of the adjoining field had to be used as a car park in later years. After the 1999 summer season the pool was closed and put up for sale.

Settled weather

Goldcrests whispering
in the conifers, swallows
clouding barn roofs,

so still, I almost
missed him, there against
the weathered gate,

silvered as old oak,
the same grain on mottled
wings, soft as thistledown,

head sugared by amber
pollen
basking in September
sunlight
a hawkmoth...

Mary Blake

16

Other social organisations in the village

The Gaddesden Society

This is the key society out of which many of the others evolved, and it is the publisher of the quarterly Gaddesden Diary. Instead of being covered in this chapter, it will be found in chapter 6 (the post-war chronological chapter) on page 74, with extracts from the Gaddesden Diary on pages 85, 90 and 95.

THE LITTLE GADDESDEN BRANCH OF THE

Royal British Legion

by Lt Col Michael Turner

One hundred and nineteen men from Little Gaddesden, Ringshall and Hudnall served in the Forces in the First World War. Their names are recorded in the document known as "the Scrap of Paper" which can be seen hanging in the Church of St Peter and St Paul, Little Gaddesden. Ninety-one men and women of the parish served in the Second World War. Twenty-nine members of the parish lost their lives in military service in the two world wars; none, thankfully, in the many conflicts since. The names of the fallen are inscribed on the War Memorial on the village green and on the War Memorial Tablet in the parish church.

The War Memorial is unusual and interesting. It was completed in 1921 to an Italian design described on page 30. Each year, on Remembrance Sunday in November, the parish remembers its fallen with a parade followed by a church service organised and led by the village branch of the Royal British Legion, which also cares for the memorial. It is a popular event, led by a local band, that attracts Royal British Legion delegations from beyond the parish, from Luton and from Berkhamsted.

The British Legion was founded in 1921 through the initiative of Field Marshal Earl Haig by bringing together the national organisations of ex-servicemen. A democratic, non-party political and non-sectarian organisation, it is pledged to keep alive the memory of those men and women who have fallen in the service of our country. Its social purpose is to promote the welfare, relieve hardship of and assist current and former members of our Armed Forces, their families and dependents who are in need, and especially the widows, widowers and children of the fallen. This charitable work is achieved thanks to donations from the general public made to the annual national Poppy Appeal and to the voluntary work done by Legion members and also many volunteer supporters within the community.

The Little Gaddesden Branch of the Royal British Legion was established in 1923 out of the Old Comrades Association. It was the seventh Legion branch to be established in the whole of the United Kingdom. Its catchment area now includes the villages and hamlets of Little and Great Gaddesden, Gaddesden Row, Water End, Dagnall, Studham, Ringshall, Nettleden and Frithsden. Little Gaddesden is proud that, as it comes to the millennium, its Branch is thriving with some 77 active members currently on its books.

It is also proud to have two pre-war territorials, Bill Corby and Ken Dickson, among its number. Colonel Bill Corby OBE, the Branch President, served in the London Scottish Territorial Battalion and with the 5th Scottish Battalion of the Parachute Regiment, also a TA unit, during the war. Ken Dickson, the current Secretary, served before and during the war in Royal Artillery heavy anti-aircraft units. One member, Jeff Hing, is the grandson of one of the 1923 founders, Joe Hing.

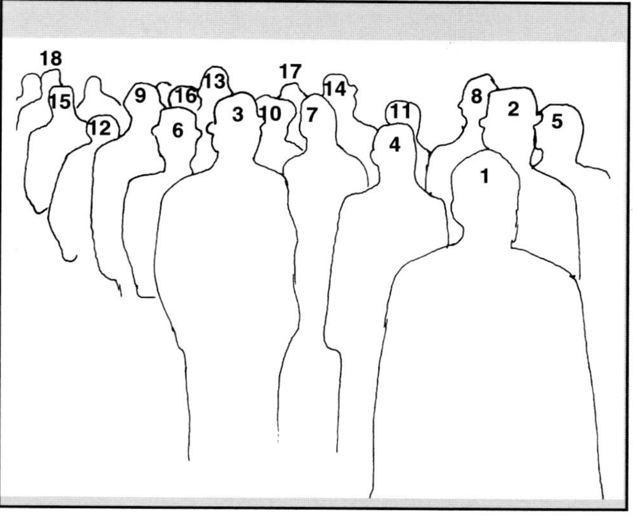

Veterans march to the service at Little Gaddesden Parish Church in 1978.

1. Gilbert Stone
2. Bill Corby
3. Peter Mann
4. Jack Pannell
5. Stan Austin
6. Jeremy Day
7. John Oakins
8. Cyril Buzzacott
9. Tony Wheatcroft.
10. Jim Foord-Kelcey
11. Ken Dickson
14. Gordon Rayment
15. Leslie Turner
18. Jim Fleckney

The Branch has had seven Gold Medals awarded since the Second World War. They went to Capt Oakley, W Wells and Joe Hing in 1956, to Stan Austin, the then Branch President, in 1967, to Bill Corby, the current President, in 1997, and to Bill Green, who was the Branch Standard Bearer for 30 years. The latest, awarded in March 2000, has gone to the Branch Secretary, Ken Dickson.

The Branch is a strong supporter of social good causes within the local community. For at least the last 20 years the Branch has spent an average of some £500 each year on good causes within the parish from funds it raises through charity events. Ex-Service men and women and their dependents and widows are the main beneficiaries, but the Branch additionally administers donations on behalf of Ashridge Management College at Christmas to a number of elderly parishioners who do not necessarily have any connection with the Services.

The Branch Poppy Appeal Organisers are at the centre of the annual fund-raising that enables the Legion to carry out its charitable function. They have included Jim Foord-Kelcey, Jeremy Day, Peter Mann and the current Organiser, Geoffrey Eccles OBE. The annual collections within the parish have gone up by more than inflation every year except one since 1946 and in 1999 it has exceeded three thousand pounds, a very creditable sum for a small community.

It has become customary that every year two Committee members, Ken Dickson and Geoffrey Eccles, visit each of the three village primary schools in the area. In each they lead a talk and discussion session with the pupils, covering such topics as the background of Remembrance Day, the significance of the poppy, the story of the unknown soldier and the nature and purpose of the Royal British Legion.

The origin of the Branch's investment funds is of some interest. In the early 1950s Mr Basil Phillips, a successful builder in the village, most generously donated a piece of land to the Branch for a British Legion Club. At the same time The Bridgewater Arms, then a Trust House Hotel, offered to place one of its rooms at the disposal of the Legion for its meetings, free and at any time. The Committee of the day duly seized the opportunity thus presented, accepted the offer from The Bridgewater Arms and sold the piece of land to the Hertfordshire County Council for £1,000 which it invested. The Police House now stands on

At the millennium, the Little Gaddesden branch committee comprised:

PRESIDENT
Col R A Corby OBE TD DL

CHAIRMAN
Lt Col M H Turner OBE

VICE CHAIRMAN
Mr D W Stevens TD

HON SECRETARY
Mr K A M Dickson

TREASURER
Mr P W Allen

SERVICE SECRETARY
Mr K Birks

POPPY APPEAL ORGANISER
Mr G Eccles OBE

MEMBERS
Air Cdr J B Mitchell CBE AFC
Mr M McCaul CMG
Mr G Thornhill
Mr G Stone
Mr R C Westmacott
Mr J Hing
Mr P W Woods (Standard Bearer)
Mr W T N Allen (Honorary Chaplain)

the site in Church Road originally meant for the Legion Club. The Bridgewater Arms became non-viable as a hotel soon afterwards and was sold off, the ground floor thankfully becoming the present Pub and Restaurant. The Legion now holds its meetings in the Committee Room of the Village Hall while its investment has flourished under the wise stewardship of successive Hon Treasurers, the latest being Peter Allen.

The Little Gaddesden Branch of the Royal British Legion has celebrated the Millennium by illuminating and rededicating the War Memorial on the Little Gaddesden Village Green. The rededication ceremony on 20th December 1999 was led by the Branch Chairman, Lt Col Mike Turner OBE, and prayers were said by the Honorary Chaplain, Trafford Allen. The purpose of the illumination, which will now be repeated each year, is to remind all who pass by of the sacrifice made by the 29 young village men whose names are on the memorial tablets and whose memory The Royal British Legion is pledged to keep alive. It also serves to reflect the close relationship of the ex-Service community, represented by the Branch, with the village community in which its members live and which has supported the Legion so generously over the years.

The Boy Scouts and Cubs

by the Editor

The early years of the Scout Troop are described in chronological sequence at pages 23 and 26, being part of a significant national phenomenon of that period.

Useful vocabulary: A Scout Group may contain units for different ages such as a Scout Troop and a Cub Pack or others not mentioned here. Age limits have varied over the years.

After the first world war we know that the Scout Group continued until at least 1922. It may have included a Wolf Cub Pack, as this section for boys aged 9 to 11 originated nationally in 1916. At some later date our Group went into abeyance until it was re-started in 1956 as a Wolf Cub Pack led by Marjorie Marshall and assisted by Mrs Moyse. Cubmasters, including lady Cubmasters (as they then were) have always had the title Akela, as they still do, (from Rudyard Kipling's Jungle Book). When Marjorie had to give up being Akela in 1960, the Rector, David Bickerton, took over for a while. The older boys were now ready for a Scout Troop which was started by Horace Rowe. About this time, Jim Wiggins, one of the National Trust forestry staff, was persuaded to help with the Cubs, and in 1963 he became Group Scoutmaster. This was one of those providential appointments in the village, on a par with Harry Temple's appointment in 1911. Soon after that a second-hand hut was obtained for the Group, and erected behind the village hall where it still stands. An old wheeled shepherd's hut, which stood in Cromer Close, was at some date taken to its present site beside the scout hut, where it is still used by the scouts though no longer mobile. There were other assistant leaders from time to time. In 1965 Jim Wiggins took over from Horace Rowe as Scoutmaster, as well as continuing as Group Scoutmaster.

John Oakins

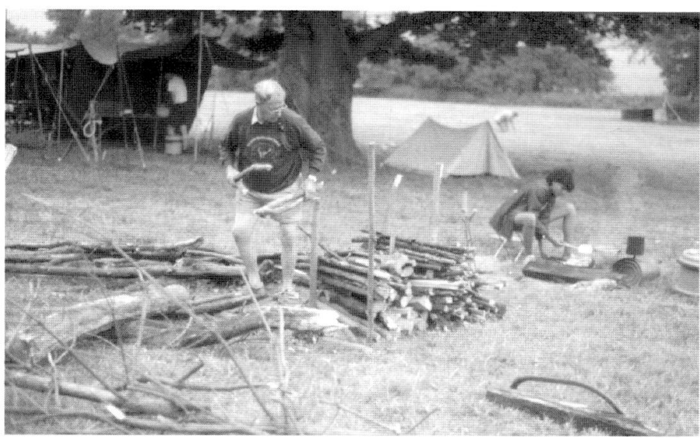

Jim remained actively involved in Scouting all his life, holding a Warrant as long as permitted by the rules on age limits, that is until he was 65, and long after that as an instructor, supporter, and fellow camper with the Troop or Pack. He was awarded the Medal of Merit by the Chief Scout in 1980

When he died early in the year 2000, his character was portrayed with realism in the extracts which follow:

EXTRACTS FROM THE ADDRESS AT JIM WIGGINS' FUNERAL, MARCH 2000

by Anthony Knott of the First Eastcote Scouts

I first met Jim about 35 years ago when as a young scout helper we organised a night wide game for the First Eastcote Scouts, which was based on the great train robbery. This was held on the Ashridge Estate, and as we wanted to stay overnight at a local scout headquarters, we were put in touch with Jim. On meeting him, it did not take long to realise that he was a special sort of man, as he was running the First Little Gaddesden as a Group Scout Leader, Scout Leader and Cub Leader more or less single handed. Obviously we invited his scouts to take part in the wide game, and from this one night came a long-standing connection between the two groups. He was over the moon, not for himself but for his cubs and scouts, for they now had the opportunity to join with us, on our camps, and using our resources and manpower which was not available to him. He came for his first scout camp with the first Eastcote, together with his son Ashley, in 1967. He continued camping with us until 1989.

TOP:
Jim Wiggins at his retirement

ABOVE
Jim Wiggins at camp with the Eastcote and Little Gaddesden Scouts in 1986. Souresh Banarse from Eastcote is on the right.

Jim was at home in the outdoors and loved nature. To walk through the woods with him was to discover the richness and wonder of God's world introduced gently by one who lived amidst it gratefully. To watch him work with the hand-tools in which he delighted was to share in the proper relationship of people with natural materials. He was a countryman who lived in harmony with plants, creatures and people, kindly, knowledgeable and tender within. Two of his most used expressions, as I recall, were "Well I never!" and "It's a rum old do". He never stopped finding things out and shared his knowledge with whoever he met, and he was always so interesting.

Scouting gave him a cause to which he was committed, a natural focus for his interests and an endless source of adventures. It was a clear and natural working out of his religious faith.

There was a large number of parents who were happy to know that Jim was helping their sons to learn what it is to be a good man by his influence on them in positive ways, physically, spiritually and mentally. He would only have to sit down for a breather in scout camp; it would not often be long before he had a few scouts sitting round him. He would either be entertaining them with one of his tales, or answering their questions. He often did not answer a question directly, but would make them stop and think and work it out for themselves. When a scout asked him what was the best wood for starting a fire, he replied, sucking on his pipe, "Well I always reckon that if a piece of wood's dead and got two ends that's good enough for me."

1986 to 1991

by John Leonhardt

When I started assisting the Little Gaddesden Troop in 1985, there were several other warranted assistants and helpers so Jim Wiggins was able to concentrate on leading the Cubs as Akela - though he was always called "Skip", the name he had acquired as Scout Leader. (Cub and Scout Masters had by now had their titles changed to Leaders, and Wolf Cubs were now called Cub Scouts). Jim was assisted by Chris Beddall, known as "Merlin", who after a year or two became the new Akela, and still is. Paul Swan from Dagnall, known as "Badger", was an instructor for many years. Boys from Dagnall regularly joined our Pack, as we were their nearest one, and went on into the Troop. Dave Cawdell, from Dagnall, was the Scout Leader, but he had to give up quite soon afterwards, leaving me as Scout Leader, which I was able to manage until 1991 when I also had to leave because of increased pressure of work. Edmund "Tim" Hambly was Group Scout Leader, but he left for the same reason in 1991, being replaced by Tim Cooper, who is still G.S.L. No one took my place as Scout Leader when I left.

Weekly Scout meetings were on Thursdays during this era.

As for the boys themselves, the records are not complete, but I'll mention a few names, first back-dating to the last Chief Scout's awards that I am aware of: Patrick Faulconer in 1980, Mark and Barry Stinton in 1982 and 1984, and Philip O'Connor of Dagnall in 1984.

The system of progress awards eventually got so complicated that you needed to be an accountant to work out who had qualified for them. Some of the scouts who were regular and useful members of the troop in its final years were Adrian Forster, David and Phillip Bunting, Tristram Hambly, Ian Knewstubb, Steven and Andrew Swan, Sam Ryall, Graham Cripps, Tim Osborn-Jones, Arran Millett, Peter Leonhardt, Willum Dover, Ian Fielder, Sam Fisher and Robert Wise.

Of these, Adrian, David and Tristram were the most qualified in the previous badge system, and Tim and Steven in the new system, but we didn't achieve any more Chief Scout Awards. We had a wonderful old white bell tent dated 1918 which we used to take to camp for stores or for a place to gather together in the evening or rain. Judging from its good condition it must have been in a good place of storage for at least 50 years before being put to use.

Phillip Bunting, Ian Knewstubb, Tristram Hambly and Steven Swan setting off on a hike from the Sussex camp in 1986

Activities from 1986 included summer camps at Uckfield 1986 (Sussex, with First Eastcote), Ardingly 1987 (Sussex: Herts County Scouts and Guides event), Ullswater 1988, Plush 1989 (Dorset, with First Eastcote), Marlow 1990 (Scout Boating centre); the Herts County Camp at Gilwell in 1990 with the Chief Scout, Garth Moore (while two of our number were on a hill training camp in Derbyshire); the West Herts Assault Competition; District Competitions of many kinds including cooking (which we won in 1988), annual raft races, patrol skills, camping competition, annual winter camping weekend and night hike, assault course, and swimming gala. In 1989 we had a Group village fair in which other Troops of the District competed with us in "soap box" races (home made pushed vehicles). Our own activities included sailing, a backwoodsman camp, pioneering constructions, wide games and camps, and the usual training. We had fire-lighting competitions with Potten End Girl Guides and we joined Potten End Scouts for their indoor assault course.

Regarding the 1987 camp at Ardingly, I wrote in the Gaddesden Diary:
"At our introduction to archery, Tim Osborn-Jones's shot of 150 metres, the longest shot of the week, must have been 130 metres beyond the target, which he wasn't aiming at. Graham Cripps held the record for burning his fingers the greatest number of times before learning which parts of a billy get hot. Chris Goodman showed the greatest improvement in fire-lighting. Steven Swan master-minded the best meal chosen and cooked by his patrol to win the Cordon Rose - but only just beat Tristram Hambly's patrol. Guy Foord-Kelcey was the first to complete a new progress award but Graham and Tim completed a more advanced one as they did a hike with an overnight camp stop on their own. Daniel Browne thought he had done the most washing up but this claim was constantly disputed. He volunteered to have wet sponges thrown at him for charity, thus raising some money for Guide Dogs and Lifeboats. Jude Bloor seemed to need sitting on the most but always came up smiling. Tristram Hambly's patrol won the Purple Duster for the most points in the camping competition."

Tim Hambly

The highlights of our final year, 1991, were a night wide game in fog on Ivinghoe Common with Potten End Scouts on Feb 1st, the District "Frosties" night incident hike and camping competition at Cosgrove on Feb 22nd-24th in which we came 6th out of 10 in the hike, and a weekend, Aug 30th-Sept 1st at Longridge Boating Centre, Marlow.

We tried to encourage the scouts to join other local Troops, there being very strong ones at that time at Potten End, Berkhamsted and Northchurch, with Venture Units for the older ones, but nobody did so for long. This was in contrast to the girls' movement, as the Brownies had for many years moved to the Potten End Company when ready to become Girl Guides. However, we still have the Cub Scouts, who have met on Tuesday evenings for as long as I've known them.

The Brownies

by Sue Godar

The fortunes of the 1st Little Gaddesden Brownie Pack have ebbed and flowed with the popularity of the Guide Association since its founding in 1908. The earliest recollections are those of Minnie Catchpole, now 79 years old who, in 1929, was a member of the pack that met in the crypt of Ashridge House under the captaincy of the Brownlow family's governess. She remembers walking down the brick path and following tracking signs on their evening nature walks, not unlike those we do today. She progressed to being a guide, meeting in the Scout hut near the old bridge opposite Robin Hood House. This unit was led by

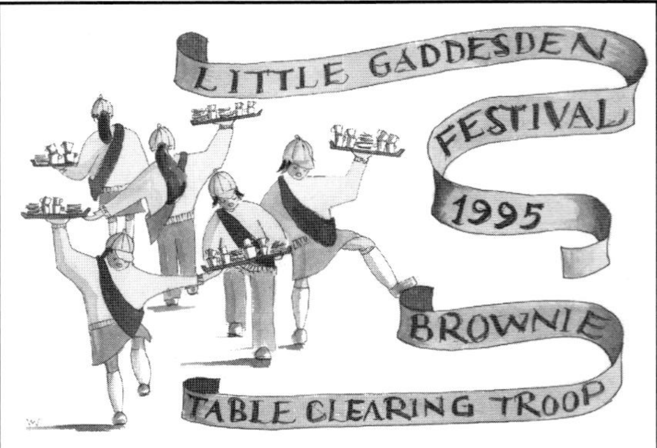

"Helpful Brownies" by Virginia Westmacott

Mrs Dorothy Bell and sadly folded when she became ill with tuberculosis.

During wartime the Brownie unit closed and was not reformed until 1955 as leisure activities recommenced. The unit met in the present Scout hut behind the Village Hall. The demographics of the village have affected the unit's continuity. As the number of children in the village fell in the late 1950's the pack was disbanded once again. At this time few families had second cars and so girls could not travel to meetings from outlying areas, as they do now, to swell pack numbers. The Pack has been run mostly by girls' mothers who have taken up the reins and become Guiders while their daughters were Brownies, then passing the leadership on as their own families grew up; and this has not changed. The aim has always been to offer opportunities for young girls.

The Brownies have always taken part in Village events, Church festivals, sports days and fetes. Happy, smiling, helpful girls joining in community life. The purpose of Brownies is to develop their personal and social skills in a safe, friendly environment amongst their peers. However, through the years the emphasis has changed. Whereas the movement began nurturing homely crafts, housekeeping skills and a love of nature, progress to more technical skills now offers badges in Computer Knowledge, Science Discovery and Downhill Skiing, as well as the more traditional badges. The Guide Association continues to strive to meet the needs of the young women of today.

THE ARTHRITIS AND RHEUMATISM SOCIETY

This society started in 1972 and was noted for its varied social events for raising funds for the Arthritis and Rheumatism Council. Norman and Bé Bailey made this their special interest. In 1998 the secretary, Joyce Huxtable, estimated that it had raised £25,000 in the last twelve years. She appealed in the Gaddesden Diary for new members, especially for the Committee, but without success. The society then closed.

Little Gaddesden Women's Institute

by Ann Williams

As the twentieth century draws to a close it is inevitably a time for reflection on events worldwide and closer to home that have shaped the way we live our lives today.

The two World Wars must stand as a turning point for women in this century; never before had they taken on the challenges that the wars presented to them and never again would their lives be the same. Working outside the home was, on the whole, a new concept for the majority of women and so changed attitudes and perceptions of 'the woman's place'. Of course there have always been working women but never on the scale that would evolve after the Second World War. Throughout the changing times and lives of women there has been one constant and that has been the WI. The largest number of members recorded in Little Gaddesden is 100 and, in 1999, the year of our 80th

Some menbers of the WI in 1930 in fancy hats

birthday, the membership stands at 49. The make-up of the membership is varied; there are professional career women, mothers at home with children and women who are retired, all with a variety of skills and interests which makes for a lively and thriving WI.

A YEAR IN THE LIFE OF LITTLE GADDESDEN WOMEN'S INSTITUTE

In February, to commemorate the Millennium, we planted 35 trees (purchased by our Institute members) at the Hilfield Reservoir, Watford. This was a County event organized by Hertfordshire WI and a very pleasant energetic morning, with plenty of digging, was enjoyed by all members who attended representing their own Institutes in Hertfordshire.

In the spring we entertained a group of senior citizens from Bicester (whose organizer was related to one of our members). After a mystery coach tour they arrived at Little Gaddesden Village Hall where we gave them afternoon tea and they met many of our members.

In May our Homecraft Group 7 Leader asked each Institute in the Group to make wall hangings and toys to be sent to Sri Lanka to help the street children who have no educational aids. Some very pleasant afternoons were spent in a member's house making the toys which were entered in the Herts Show, earning us gold, silver and bronze stars. They were then sent overseas. To pay for the materials used we held a very successful coffee morning.

In July we entertained, and provided tea for, a group from Age Concern in London. This has become an annual event and one which is enjoyed by both guests and members. To see a lovely village church and surrounding countryside is literally a 'breath of fresh air' for them all.

'Guess the weight of the Cake' was the attraction at our stall at the School Village Fête in July and our July Garden Meeting, held in a member's garden, was memorable with musical entertainment out of doors.

We also held a Workshop where some of our members learned the art of sugarcraft.

Our 80th Birthday Party in October proved to be a wonderful evening enjoyed by all present. To end the year our Carol Singers really excelled themselves and the local hospice was delighted by our three figure sum collection.

Every month a speaker is invited to our meeting in the Village Hall and a number of outings are organised throughout the year.

It is reassuring to know that as we head towards the 21st Century, the WI will be there to welcome, support and share all the good things it represents for the women of the future.

At the WI Diamond Jubilee in 1979 - L to R

BACK ROW:
Sally Peasnall, Jeanne Hope, Joan Greener, Phil Foord-Kelcey, Shirley Memory, Rene Rogers, Jean Stone, Phyllis Hucklesby, Barbara Mogg, Rose Marks, Miss Milsom.

THIRD ROW:
Jean Jones, Mrs Gillespie, Dot Nash, Ivy Cutler, Phyllis Price, Eve Ouseley, Marjorie Marshall, Win Oakins, Pat Creed, Unknown, Julie Leonhardt.

SECOND ROW:
Betty Rogers, Mrs Brooker Mary Tweed, Bertha Harvell, Ann Kirkpatrick, Val Janes, Jennie Waters, Chris Mawhood, Rosemary Jones, Mary Rogers, Eleri Edwards.

FRONT ROW:
Dorothy Bailey, Vi Hughes, Mrs Greener, Mrs Mayling, Gwen Johnstone, (President), Edie Thame, Edith Halsey, Phyllis Stone, Margaret Hopkins, Joan Humphreys.

80th Birthday Dinner, October 1999

From left to right:

Mrs Jean Curl (Hertfordshire County Chairman), Mrs Eve Ouseley (LG WI, who was also 80 in the same week), Mr Bob Ward (local resident and winner of the WI Cup for cookery at the Village Winter Show), Mrs Elizabeth Bradfield (past President), Mr Antony Hopkins (local musician and special guest), Mrs Ann Kirkpatrick (President), Mrs Phyl Mountfort and Mrs Jenny Graham (past Presidents).

A photograph of the WI in 2000 is featured in the colour section

The picture on the right shows the Youth Club and helpers making a presentation to Albert and Molly Williams when they left the village in 1988

CENTRE:
Andy Mogg (Youth Leader), Albert Williams (former Chairman), Molly Williams.

KNEELING:
Andrea Morris, Helen Morris, Phillippa Abraham, Tina Mooring, Debbie Shaw.

STANDING:
Miriam Shaw, Unknown, Unknown, Zoe Cripps, Brenda Ballad, Elizabeth Goodwin, Adrian Forster, Denise Halsey, Trafford Allen (Treasurer), Audrey Allen (Secretary), Phillip Bunting, Richard Abraham (Chairman), Graham Bunting, Doreen Gillespie, Diana Everall, Steve Ballad, Greg Sears, Mark Sears, George Cooper, David Ballad (who became Youth Leader a few years later).

Youth Clubs

There has been a Youth Club on and off over the years, sometimes with huge membership - over 100 in 1961. Canon Senar's book gives an account of its ups and downs from 1957 to 1981. It has existed since then, and many people have worked hard for it, but there is no youth club in 1999.

The Over Sixties club

by Rosemary Williams

In the Autumn of 1960 Mr Sid Batchelor approached the then Rector Mr David Bickerton to ask if a club could be formed for elderly people. The first Christmas supper was held on 15 December 1960.

Presidents have been: Mrs Wager, Dr Goddard, Lady del Tufo and currently Mrs R Williams.

Chairmen: Mrs Wager, The Rev D Bickerton, Canon Senar - currently Mr T Allen.

Secretaries: Mrs J Townsend, Mrs E Hollings, Mr H Reasbeck, Mrs P Price and currently Mrs B Thornhill

Treasurers: Mrs Banks, Mrs Bagnay, Mr H Reasbeck, Mrs Nightall and currently Mrs Eve Ouseley

The Jumble Sale in 1963 produced £65. In 1999 - £545. Membership does not seem to have varied much. There were 56 members in 1961 and about 60 now.

The original subscription was one shilling per year and 6d every month for tea. Now £1 a year and 20p for tea. The raffle tickets were 3d.

1962 January and February meetings were cancelled owing to weather conditions. The Bring and Buy sale each month was referred to as the Rummage Sale. Monthly meetings take place on the second Wednesday afternoons when slides are shown and speakers talk on various interesting subjects.

Visits are paid during summer months to places of interest; also to the pantomime or theatre. Local clubs entertain the Over Sixties. The VPA supper is a highlight of the year. Parties are held for the Birthday in May and at Christmas. Birthdays are remembered monthly; also a poem is prepared and read by a member. Our oldest members are Wilf Banks and Harold Bolton, both in their 90s.

PARENTS AND TODDLERS GROUP

This was started in 1975 by Gill Slade as the Mothers and Toddlers Group. The first meetings were fortnightly at the Bridgewater Arms, and then at the Village Hall. When Gill retired in 1979, the group was continued by a succession of other mothers.

Since summer 1998 the group has been run by Helene Hockings and the format of the meeting has remained pretty much the same. It is a friendly group which enables newcomers to the village to meet other parents and for their children to enjoy playing together. There is always a craft table set up with differing activities as well as other toys for the children to play with.

The meetings are still held fortnightly at the Village Hall between 10.30 and 12 noon.

THE GADDESDEN DISTRICT

Village Produce Association

as remembered by May Sears - September 1999

This was formed in April 1948 and the first Officers were Dr Rawdon Smith, Chairman; his wife was Secretary and Mr H Reasbeck was Treasurer. There were about 100 members in those days (who paid a subscription of 2/6d each family).

People are always asking me "Why not earlier than this?" as during the war years Miss Kathleen Talbot, of the Manor House, went all over the country encouraging people to 'Dig for Victory', later named 'Village Produce Associations' or 'Guilds', as in Staffordshire - where I am pleased to say there are more than 40 villages in that County still taking part today, thanks mainly to George Arnold, who is County Chairman and his wife, Phyllis, who supports him. Miss K Talbot went to Maer, Staffs. in 1941 and also started one in West Sussex at that time.

Little Gaddesden already had a flourishing Horticultural Society, started by Miss Talbot's father, the Hon Alfred Talbot of Little Gaddesden House. Flower and vegetable shows were held there, and at Ashridge in the stable area. I remember going with my father, Sid Batchelor, when he was showing there, about 1920. My husband, Tim Sears, when a boy, entered the Wild Flower Class. His entry was so large he arranged it in a bucket. He walked to the River Gade at Water End to collect bullrushes and other tall flowers and walking home again through the Park from Nettleden through the Golden Valley. Next morning he took the bucket of flowers to Ashridge in a wheelbarrow and it tipped over going up the hill, so he had to rearrange it when he arrived there. I am pleased to say he won First Prize.

Many years later, our shows were organised by a joint committee of British Legion, Women's Institute and VPA members in our Village Hall and a dance was held in the evening. Later, the VPA took over the organising of shows on their own, as the others dropped out, and gave up the dances (thank goodness - as we were tired out!)

There were only three VPAs in Hertfordshire, the others being Tewin, who were mainly wine makers, and Great Hormead, which was 30 miles away on the other side of the County. We used to meet about twice a year and hold quizzes, small shows and digging matches at Oaklands Horticulture College at St Albans. Not only our men took part, and won, ladies competed too. I remember Phyl Mountfort and Nellie Munden with prizes of stainless steel spades! Mrs Mercy Ede wrote to all the parishes in Herts telling them about the VPA but they didn't want to join us.

I was the Outings Organiser and the last time we went to the Spalding Bulb Fields and their Flower Festival, to see the decorated floats, the coach was parked in an empty field. When we came to leave I couldn't find our coach as the field was full of coaches. I don't remember who was with me, but we walked round until we were tired out, then waited at the entrance till our coach came round, with everyone else on board - I got teased and didn't take them there again.

We got more adventurous and went to Holland for four days with 'Clarksons' in the 1960s. We visited the Keukenhof Park, which was marvellous; we had never seen anything like it, with its lakes and trees and flowers, enormous greenhouses and a 'river' of blue hyacinths. Tim (always a joker) took off his jacket, borrowed a lawnmower from a gardener and had his picture taken there.

TOP PICTURE:
Tim Sears at Keukenhof

BELOW:
VPA members with their trophies in 1985, L to R:

Daniel Bunting, Alan Bunting, Gordon Welling, Richard Abraham, Jackie Hodgson, Toby Hodgson, Trafford Allen.

Mrs Win Mogg was Secretary for many years; she is 90 and came to our 50th anniversary last year.

I was first involved with the VPA by offering to deliver 'Village Life', the little green book which came from the National Federation with news from all the counties. I used to visit Mrs Nellie Mayling at Ringshall; she was VPA Area Representative there. Mrs Minnie Catchpole did from No 1 to Church Road. Mrs Marjorie Marshall has been Area Representative (without a break) from John O'Gaddesden House to Hudnall Corner since the 1950s.

Mrs Mary Dunham of Kaim End, Hudnall, was Area Representative for the first part of Hudnall and Mrs Brenda Corby of Kilbracken looked after the St Margarets /Covetous

Corner Area. Edna Welling was VPA Rep from Hudnall Lane to Pulridge Wood, including Home Farm and Cromer Close. I visited all these with VPA notices and show schedules, my transport was my bicycle.

We used to have a Daffodil show - the flowers were often flattened by snow the day before - a Rose show (you could never be sure when they would be at their best) and a Chrysanthemum show. Our Winter show (said to be the only one in Hertfordshire) and our Summer show too were and still are very popular. It is encouraging that more younger members are growing vegetables, fruit and flowers and also that the cookery, handicrafts and floral art classes in our shows are well supported.

Our VPA membership trebled when the Trading Store was opened beside the Village Hall on Sunday mornings, with lots of voluntary helpers. Three of the original members from 1948, Harry Smith, Tim Sears and Tom Bunting saw a VPA Store at Kesgrave Suffolk one Sunday when we were visiting for the day. They then asked Eddie Nightall and the committee if we could have one. It has gone on from strength to strength to this day. I hope the VPA lasts for another 50 years.

THE VILLAGE PRODUCE ASSOCIATION SONG

This is still sung as a round to the tune of Frère Jacques every year at the annual V.P.A. Harvest Supper. It dates from the days when many people kept a pig or two, and "Bowling for the live pig" was often a side-show at the village fête.

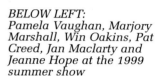

BELOW LEFT:
Pamela Vaughan, Marjory Marshall, Win Oakins, Pat Creed, Jan Maclarty and Jeanne Hope at the 1999 summer show

BELOW RIGHT:
Cup winners at the 1972 show: LEFT TO RIGHT: Nicola Carnegie, Diana Ashby with the Duncan Rose Bowl for flower arranging and Fiona Cullen

BOTTOM:
Ralph King ready for the 1999 show

Prime plump porkers
Prime plump porkers
Hens that lay
Every day
More and better veggies
More and better veggies
V.P.A.
V.P.A.

VPA UPDATE

by Ralph King

During the course of each year the VPA has always tried to span the age ranges with varying events. One of the highlights being the Children's Christmas Party. The joy on a young child's face when Father Christmas walks through the door and the excitement when his helper, Janet, calls out their name to collect a present is lovely to behold. Other events include the Over 60's Fish and Chip Supper, followed by an exciting game of bingo, the Harvest Supper where our Life Members are each presented with a red rose or carnation to signify their exalted office, and where we have enjoyed some wonderful entertainment. This has included some delightful choirs and on more than one occasion, Mick Wright giving his version of "Stories from the Country". There are Spring and Autumn Talks, occasional outings, and the Winter and Summer Shows. The VPA Store is run by volunteers each Sunday morning between 10.30 and 12.00 noon.

We consider it important to recognise the efforts of our supporters, past and present, and from time to time afford Life Membership status. The 1999/2000 list is proud to recognise the following as Life Members: Alec Andrews, Win

and Len Archer, Jane and Alan Bunting, Vera Bunting, Min Catchpole, Bertha and Len Harvell, Jeanne Hope, Marjorie Marshall, Win Mogg, Phyl and Vic Mountfort, Madge Nightall, Win Oakins, Eve Ouseley, Mary and Geoff Rogers, May Sears, Alf Sherringham, Pearl and Harry Smith, Janet and Mike Stinton, Sheila and Basil Thorne, Bob Ward, Mary and Mick Wright.

More poignantly in this Millennium year we have organised the Eddie and Madge Nightall seat, which is sited in front of Eddie's beloved store. The VPA *is* Eddie Nightall, as without his unstinting efforts, supported by Madge, with the Store as its focal point, the VPA would not be the association it is today.

POST-WAR YEARS IN CROMER CLOSE AND THE BIRTH OF A NEW BEAN

by May Sears

TOP
Geoff Rogers, Chairman at the 1999 Summer Show

ABOVE
1983 prizewinners, L to R: Rene Spencer, May Parker, Chris Dawson, Doug Ginn, Laura Bunting, Alan Bunting.

The war years came and my husband Tim joined the R.A.F. He qualified as a Flight Mechanic at Halton and worked on 72 Squadron's Spitfire Merlin engines at Biggin Hill. When he had leave he spent it working on the High Firs estate in Hemel Hempstead, with vegetable and flower gardens, orchard and greenhouses. He also kept chickens and ducks. While he was away I helped in the big house and looked after the poultry and greenhouses.

We moved back to Little Gaddesden in 1947. In 1949 the Cromer Close council estate was built and we moved into no 19 on 24th September. There were only concrete posts and wire to mark each person's ground and a lot of hard work was needed to make a garden and lawn at the back and a flower garden on the front. Tim planted hedges all round for a start. I don't remember what he planted first, but vegetables were his favourite, and he grew every kind. I have certificates that he won for first prize for a collection of vegetables from 1956 to 1966 at our village produce shows.

In 1974 and 1975 he won the Best Kept Garden in Area 2 (which included Berkhamsted and Potten End) organised by the Dacorum District Council. He hoped to win for the third time but it was cancelled because of drought in 1976. Of course we had fruit as well, four cordon pear trees which enclosed the lawn, loganberries growing along the wall of the house, a row of raspberries, a strawberry bed, blackberries, gooseberries, black and red currants and an apple tree at the bottom of the garden. When our granddaughter got married she wanted some white and cream sweet pea flowers, so Tim grew a row of each, and had them ready at the right time. He had a bed of roses in the front garden, and grew dahlias and many other varieties of flowers.

It was always his ambition to grow, or produce, a black seed runner bean, and he eventually managed to breed one, but he didn't know how to get it recognised or where to send it. He had to retire before he was 65 years with first a heart attack and later a stroke. He couldn't work in his garden so we asked to move to Bede Court, where he had seven happy years. He gave his black beans to all his friends and Geoff Rogers has kept them going for the past fourteen years. Tim, with the help of Michael Wright, named the black beans LOBENGULA, but it was four years later, 1996, when my friend and neighbour, Renee Daly, sent them to the Henry Doubleday Research Association, where they tested them and now have them in their seed bank. How pleased Tim would have been to know his V.P.A. friends are still growing and showing them in 1999

Tim sadly died in March 1992. We had been married 57 years. We had three lovely daughters, Jean, Jenny and Jacqui and they gave us six grandsons and one granddaughter. How proud he was of them all.

Tim's brother Fred joined the merchant navy when he was eighteen, and on his first voyage, to Alexandra, he died in an accident. When unloading the ship four crew members fell in the harbour. Fred was a very good swimmer, but he didn't survive. Sadly too, Ted Rogers, their foster brother, died in a prison camp during the second world war. As we had no boys the Sears name will die out.

OTHER GARDENS

In 1991 on the third weekend in June, 16 village gardens were open to the public to raise funds for church repairs. They are a good cross-section of the gardens in the main part of the village at that time - the sort that the owners would have been proud of, and the public curious enough to pay to see.

Farthings (Reginald and Sheila Coates): Herbaceous garden with garden room.
No.6/7 (Alfred and Barbara Cassell): Cottage garden, some trees and shrubs with flowers (plenty of roses), fruit and vegetables. Front garden retains old cottage garden layout.
No.13 (Min and Hilary Catchpole): Small cottage garden - previously a builder's yard.
No.18 (Owen and Rosemary Williams): One acre divided into sections with lawns, herbaceous and shrub borders; small orchard, trees and hedges; small kitchen garden and an outstanding old oak tree.
No.24 (Margaret Crawford): Gardening under difficulties: a small garden with five mature forest trees in it, one a big oak. Despite the shade it has an old-fashioned herbaceous border and some roses.
No.26 (Elinor Williams): Clever planning can make an almost rectangular plot interesting, with curved borders and unexpected corners. The trunk of a very old apple tree which died four years ago has been left and is now covered by the rare Kiftsgate rose. Collection of unusual and interesting shrubs.
Witchcraft Hill (Norman and Bé Bailey): Large garden in a woodland setting with lawns, herbaceous borders, paeonies, irises, roses, alpines and rhododendrons.
No.34 (Arthur and Marjorie Marshall) and **no.35** (Mr and Mrs Thornhill): Adjacent well-kept cottage gardens with vegetable patches.
1 Little Gaddesden House (Eddis and Dora Box): Garden in memory of a beautiful old ash tree lost in the 1990 gales: the space and the tree used to create rustic walks amongst a variety of herbaceous perennials, climbers and shrubs; pond, climbing roses, bedding plants and fuchsias.
2 Little Gaddesden House (Mike and Rita Sherring-Lucas): a five-year old garden started from scratch and established for a

Alan Bunting's prize Dahlias in 1999 at Cromer Close and Alan ready for the 1999 summer Show

flower arranger, with rockery, pond, herbaceous and annual beds and a magnificent oak tree.
3 Little Gaddesden House (Geoff and Marjorie Eccles): Mixed border, not yet fully established, in the dry conditions of a 14 ft high holly hedge.
1 Home Farm Cottages (Tommy and Annette Tucker): Garden under construction.
Shepherds Cottage (Mr and Mrs Ward): Attractive small walled garden with interesting plants
Home Farm House (Tim and Elizabeth Hambly): 3/4 acre natural garden, trees, shrubs, special roses, organically maintained for year-round interest.
15 Cromer Close: (Alan and Jane Bunting): Specialising in chrysanthemums, dahlias and prize-winning vegetables.

Rural Heritage Society

by Peter Grainger

In 1975, Little Gaddesden was threatened with a huge, speculative residential development right in the heart of the village. It was the last straw after a spate of planning applications which had caused such consternation that a number of villagers expressed anxiety about the fact that unsympathetic development was beginning to insinuate itself into the fabric of our environment.

A group of residents formed a steering committee and invited like-minded people to meet in the village hall on 14 March 1975. We were greatly encouraged to see the massive turn-out and the Rural Heritage Society was born.

Our aims were to support the planning authorities in their determination to maintain the rural character of villages such as ours to enable them to democratically represent our views. We wanted to promote high standards of planning and architecture and to preserve, protect and improve features of historic or public interest in the area. We were also charged with the responsibility for educating the public in the geography, history, natural history and architecture of Little Gaddesden.

This latter was a requirement of our being accepted for charitable status and was incorporated in the rules which were drafted in January, 1981. It is an awesome responsibility which we take as seriously as we can, considering we are all volunteers with other professional and social commitments.

Our activities include arranged guided walks around the area, with talks by notable local specialists in environmental matters. They achieve several aims. Firstly, they are educational, secondly, they keep our footpath network open and, thirdly, they are great fun. We have all learned to appreciate what our village has to offer since we have explored it in such great detail.

We publish a newsletter on a regular basis and invite contributions from anyone with an axe to grind or a gem of wisdom to impart and we have prepared a definitive footpath map, copies of which are available from the Secretary.

From Saxon days, when Little Gaddesden and the surrounding villages were separate manors, to the beginning of the twentieth century, development was

LITTLE GADDESDEN PRESERVATION SOCIETY

This organisation was founded in 1960 and wound up in 1969. Its aims were very similar to those of the later Rural Heritage Society (founded 1975), particularly in restricting new building in the village and preserving the rural landscape.One of the buildings it opposed was no.24 at the corner of Church Road.

THE CHORAL SOCIETY

This was formed by Miss K Talbot and was thriving in the 1920's and 1930's. Her friend Dorothy Erhart was closely involved. Brief accounts of it can be read in the articles by Barbara Cassell (page 80) and Antony Hopkins (page 50).

DANCE CLUBS

Eve Ouseley mentions how the Old Time Dance Club was started the week after she first settled here in 1949. Later on, a Country Dancing Club was run in the School Hall by Albert and Molly Williams. This was functioning in the 1970's to 80's. Both clubs have now ceased.

slow and unplanned. Bits were added here and there to meet the demands of increasing population. However, the newcomers had the foresight to retain open spaces and thus create a succession of ever-changing views. Views which create distant horizons, intermingled with some of the best examples of village architecture in England.

It is we, the present 'villagers' who are now responsible for handing down this heritage to the next generation. It is we who hold the future of our environment in our hands.

Today, with such an emphasis on Green issues it is even more important that we should all be aware of our surroundings and the actions we can take to preserve all that is best and discourage the swelling of the developer's wallet at the expense of the environment.

We are also, of course, the publishers of this book.

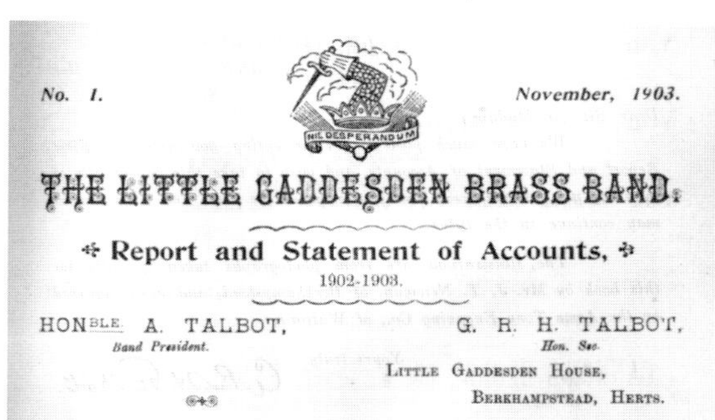
No. 1. November, 1903.

NIL DESPERANDUM

THE LITTLE GADDESDEN BRASS BAND.

Report and Statement of Accounts,

1902-1903.

HONBLE A. TALBOT, Band President.

G. R. H. TALBOT, Hon. Sec.

Little Gaddesden House, Berkhampstead, Herts.

ABOVE
The first accounts of the band in 1903

BELOW
The Little Gaddesden Brass Band in 1903:

BACK ROW:
S Johnson, T Johnson, F Cutler, F Pocock, J Wibden, E Hing, E Pinnock

MIDDLE ROW:
G Jay, W Warner, A Johnson, Samuel G Oakins, B Horn, H Wells, W Holland, H Fenn, T Scott.

FRONT ROW:
Stephen J Oakins, J Windmill, C H Ward, (Bandmaster), W Johnson, S G Rogers, E Whitman,
H Halsey (under bass drum)

Little Gaddesden Brass Band

The band was formed in 1902 by Humphrey Talbot, his father Alfred Talbot being president. The first annual report was in the form of a small but thick booklet with a photograph of the band, a list of members and an account of the funds. There are twenty-three members in the photograph, with their instruments. The booklet is filled with advertisements for shops and services in Berkhamsted and Hemel Hempstead. I have no knowledge of the subsequent history of the band, but from the composition of its membership it may have been badly disrupted by military call-up in the first world war.

In the village fêtes of 1945 to 1947 there was an undisclosed source of music: "Music All Day", said the posters. The dancing in the evening, however, was accompanied by outside dance orchestras.

The Music Club

by Alfred Cassell

The Music Club is one of the oldest in this country. We began in 1946 with recitals in private houses and in Ashridge College. After the Village Hall was built we used it as well. Nowadays we usually meet in private houses in or near the village. Over the years we have received much practical help and encouragement from our Patron, Antony Hopkins. Membership is open to all who ask, and we enthusiastically relieve them of a subscription to use towards the engagement of musicians.

Nowadays our membership varies between fifty and sixty and we are able to present five recitals each season. We specialise in young musicians, typically very soon after they have graduated from the Royal College of Music or the Royal Academy. Their standard is extraordinarily high and some go on to distinguished careers. We have heard many star performers including: the tenor, Alexander Young; the soprano, Ilse Wolff; the cellist, Sandy Baillie; the flamenco guitarist, Paco Pena; the pianist, Margaret Fingerhut and the harpist, Maria Korchinska. How many of the artists in our current programme will go on to fame and fortune? We listen to real music played by young virtuosi.

The Little Gaddesden Art club

by Virginia Westmacott

A 1945 poster

The Art Club was founded in 1945. It began as a group of like-minded friends and artists who wanted to improve their skills by painting together. Of the founder members, which included Mrs Winifred Patterson, her daughter Dorothea, Irene Foord-Kelcey, Dorothy Bell (Vicars Bell's wife), Mrs Wager and Mr Pipkin, only Dorothea Patterson remains. She tells me that the Club met every Saturday in the school hall where they had tuition from Mr Wynne Thomas and Mr Bernard Adams. Members also painted in the locality and in the woods of Ashridge. Information is sketchy as there appear to be no records before 1968.

Geoffrey Drewitt, whose mother taught at the school, was an early member of the Club. During the Second World War he painted a mural on the end wall of the school hall. (See photograph on page 167). This depicted life as it was then in the school with potato picking and a pig club and all aspects of rural life.

From the start a two/three day Summer exhibition was held; this was opened by local celebrities including Dorian Williams, Miss Erhart, Lady Davidson and Miss Emily Hahn. Records show that a smaller 'Christmas Present Exhibition' was held in November.

In 1969 a sort of 'Art in Action' was staged, with numerous skills being demonstrated, such as stone cutting, potting, lithography, spinning, screen printing, fashion and picture framing. From this year the annual subscription was set at 10 shillings a year. Preferably members were to be from Little Gaddesden and total membership was limited to 40. There were numerous painting days, which were popular, often including cheese and wine, outings and demonstrations.

In 1971 the top price paid was 20 guineas for 'Albert Bridge' painted by Ivor Hayes and bought by James Allason MP.

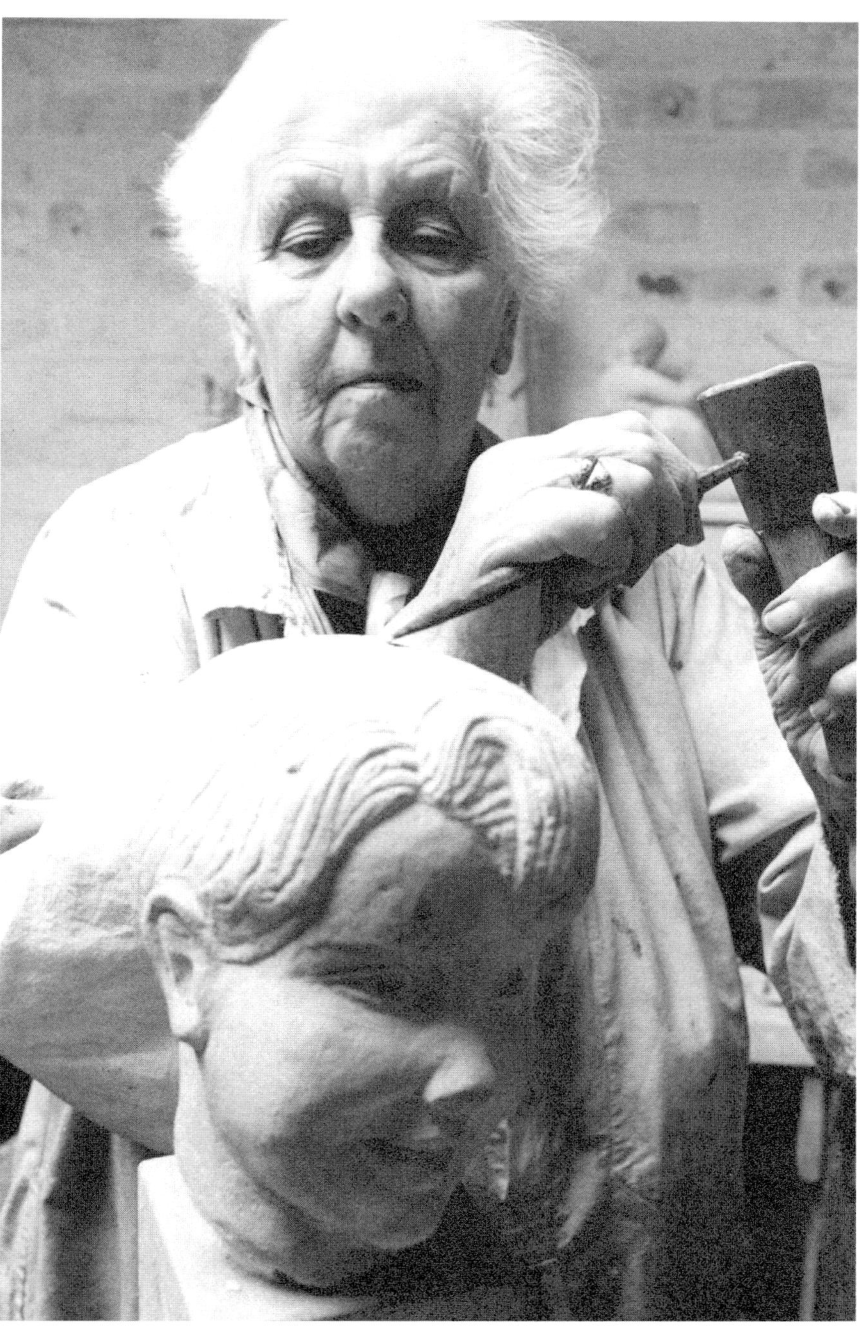

Irene Foord-Kelcey

In 1972 folios were allowed in the Summer Exhibition for the first time and Dorothea Patterson was invited to stage a show on the Stage. 27 pictures were sold. Tea/coffee and cake at the Exhibition cost 7 pence. The Bridgewater Arms invited members to hang pictures there for the first time and this continued for several years with a few pictures being sold. This year a New Year's Eve Arts Ball was held in the Village Hall. Tickets were 1 guinea and 120 people came. At the AGM, the Treasurer reported that there was only £56 in the bank, and expenses were ever rising, so he proposed the subscription be increased to £1 from the next year.

In 1973 the top price for a picture was £40 for 'Canal in May' by Olive Walker. Exhibition sales were rising and, in 1974, sales were £639. Mr Pipkin held an exhibition on the stage.

In 1975 sales were £754, with Gwen Webb showing on the stage. This year, for the first time, there was a size restriction on paintings.

The Club continued with various talks, criticisms, discussions and painting evenings and days. In 1977, sales were up to £923 and Brian Bennett sold two pictures for over £100.

The exhibition sales increased yearly. Christmas Parties continued to be held every year, venues were various and had, by now, settled in members' houses. The AGMs, which were being held in the Chairman's house, were also followed by a supper or BBQ. A link had been set up with the Stanhope Group of Painters through one of the members who taught there. They would come out to Ashridge and enjoy a day's painting with Club members. In 1976 sculpture was displayed on the stage at the Summer Exhibition and, in 1978, sales rose to £1,740. The membership remained at 50 with 'out of the village' applicants having to apply for membership. In 1979 sales rose to nearly £2,000 and in 1983 the cost of a cup of tea and a cake went up to 20p at the Summer Exhibition.

In 1993 a One-Day-Sale was introduced in November at which members could sell pictures previously exhibited as well as cards. In 1996 the Club contributed to new lighting in the Village Hall; this greatly enhanced the exhibitions, also two members made new sculpture stands. At the 1997 Summer Exhibition Jean Folkard exhibited on the stage. Also from 1997 to 1999, a small exhibition was held at the National Trust Visitors Centre in Ashridge. 10% of the proceeds went to the National Trust. In 1998 Rosemary Gardham was on the stage, since when we have had 'theme' displays there.

Now, in 1999, costs have soared and the membership is £5 and tea/coffee/ cake at the exhibitions costs 50p. There are 82 members. In order to maintain a high standard within the club, artists and sculptors from outside the village have been invited to join. Sales increase almost yearly, the 'top' year being 1991 with £9,000. This year £850 was paid for an oil painting, the highest price ever. We continue to hold 2 exhibitions a year, have demonstrations, expeditions to exhibitions, painting and drawing evenings and outdoor painting days. We hold two parties a year, New Year and after the AGM.

The objects and aims of the Club have not changed and are still for the promotion and furtherance of Drawing, Painting, Sculpture and Pottery within the parish of Little Gaddesden, although now rather more members come from outside the Parish.

ART CLUB EXHIBITORS, 1999

About half of the 82 members exhibited works in the June 1999 exhibition. Several of them are former residents of the village, and the following live here now:

Elise Erlick, Lilian Hayball, Heather Hodge, Jeanne Hope, Ken Hunt
John Leonhardt, Pat Martin, William Paterson, Loveday Saunders,
Virginia Westmacott.

Little Gaddesden Drama Club

by Patsy Blackmore

In 1947 a small group of people met in the Village School Hall to plan the performance of 'Yellow Sands' to be produced by Eleanor Wager, who was the wife of the Rector at that time. and this started what was known as the Gaddesden Society Drama Club. In those days only plays with a beginning, middle and an end, invariably happy, were performed. The village was not ready for the more serious, thought-provoking productions that were to follow.

Space was at a minimum. The theatre was in the school hall of the village, the stage erected on two courses of loose bricks and composed of platforms. The dressing room was the school kitchen, only accessible by a short run in the open air through weather fair and foul. It was truly a village club, performed by the village for the village. Facilities were incredibly basic, yet the standards that were set by producers, actors and set designers were very high and formed the heart of the club as it is today.

Dorothea Patterson and Irene Foord-Kelcey painted the marvellous sets which were expected in those days, very different today when so many productions are played with minimal scenery.

It has always been a family club, sometimes with grandparents, parents and grandchildren performing together. In all events there has been a bond of friendship that has brought help and concern for each other that has stretched beyond our productions. Members' children have been recruited as young actors, electricians, stage managers etc and have continued to support the Club even when grown-up and moved from the district.

In the 1950s the new Village Hall was opened and the society acquired a permanent stage and was able to widen its horizons. The Club had its own building at the rear of the Hall housing a large costume wardrobe, scene dock, props and committee room. A cat-walk was made to link the buildings.

There have been many great personalities over the years and the advent of David Wray in the 50s with his bold suggestion that the Club should stage Shakespeare's 'Twelfth Night' was a milestone in the Club's history. Never before had such a large-scale production been contemplated. Shakespeare was interspersed with plays such as 'The Love of Four Colonels', 'Rose without a Thorn', 'Arsenic and Old Lace' to name but a few. David (who not only directed, but also built and painted marvellous sets, designed and made costumes and armoury, etc) was always assisted by Enid Foxall, both of them giving great performances on stage too. They set even higher standards and their productions brought audiences from afar to Little Gaddesden.

Then Bill Oram joined the Club and an entirely new scene was staged. Pinter's 'Birthday Party', 'No Man's Lane', 'Old Times' made their mark as did 'Waiting for Godot' and 'The Crucible'. Melodramas and Music Halls were followed by musicals such as 'Oliver', 'The King and I', 'Wizard of Oz', 'Guys and Dolls', 'Lock up your Daughters' and 'A Funny Thing Happened on the way to the Forum'. The Gaddesden Revues, devised by me and produced with the help of Phyl Mountfort and Enid Foxall, have always been extremely popular and

BELOW
the cast from the 1992 production of Red Riding Hood:

Four on the left (L to R): Claire Fielder, Vivienne Turner, Anne Grant, Sue.

Five to the right of Sue: Meredith, not identified (make-up artist), Janet Godden, Maurice Godden, Peter Rogers.

Above Meredith: unidentified man,

Below Meredith: Andrew Mountfort.

Below the Goddens: Michael Swift.

Five in lower right: Maya Gabrielle, Sophie, Alice Leonhardt, Penny, Sally.

DRAMA CLUB PRODUCTIONS FROM 1949 TO 1999

1947	*Yellow Sands*
1949	*The Paragon*
1950	*Jupiter Laughs*
1951	*Miranda*
1952	*Bonaventure*
1953	*Blithe Spirit*
1953	*Lady Precious Stream*
1956	*The Shop at Sly Corner*
1956	*Down Came a Blackbird*
1957	*The Anniversary*
1958	*The Wishing Well*
1958	*Twelfth Night*
1959	*The Chalk Garden*
1960	*Ambrose Applejohn's Adventure*
1960	*The Merry Wives of Windsor*
1961	*The Love of Four Colonels*
1961	*Oh! What a Lovely War*
1962	*Three One Act Plays*
1962	*The Gaddesden Gaieties*
1963	*A Penny for a Song*
1963	*The Ghost Train*
1964	*Macbeth*

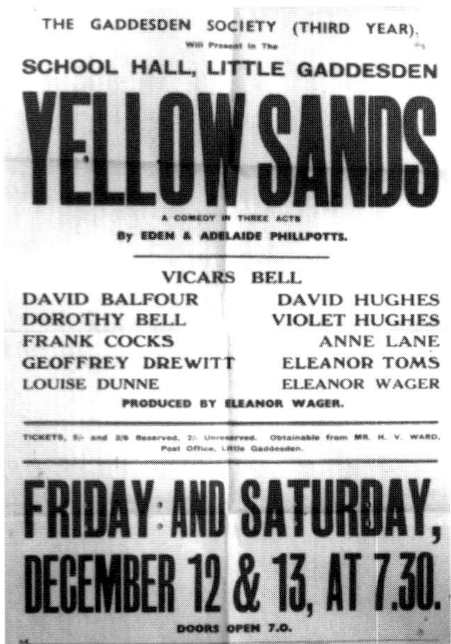

Gaddesden Revue 1999 celebrates our entry into the year 2000.

So many 'incidents' happen in Drama Clubs and ours is no exception. Scenery collapses, actors do not make entrances when they should, words are forgotten and one tries desperately to appear unfazed when, in actual fact, one wishes a trapdoor would open through which one could disappear. To recall one or two 'happenings', I remember well in 'Palladin', a pantomime, we had a stormy shipwreck on stage. Everyone had to stumble from side to side to depict the raging seas. Unfortunately dear George Catchpole (playing a portly bosun) stumbled too well and fell on top of me, completely winding me and rendering me speechless and I had to be dragged off the stage. Another production 'Summer of the Seventeenth Doll', with just a tiny hint of impropriety, suffered badly. Word went round the village that it was a naughty play and - whereas today it would probably fill the hall - back in the good old days we only had five people in the audience on the first night.

However, the major disaster must have been in the early 50s on the first night of 'Jupiter Laughs'. The play called for an explosion, so Ken Thorn, Stage Manager, went to Brocks for the appropriate explosive. Unfortunately he did not read the instructions carefully and it was let off inside the hall instead of outside. The result - the windows blew out, the set fell down and Enid Foxall had her tights burnt off and was thrown into the arms of Frank Cocks.

Sadly, in the middle of the 90s the Club's membership declined. People moved on, lost interest and too many faces from other districts appeared, audiences diminished and the Club ground to a halt. Our buildings were taken down, costumes, flats, props, etc were either given to other drama groups in the area or destroyed. A bad time. However, four years later we sprang into life again. This Club was too precious, with so many wonderful productions, creative personalities and happy memories, to let it disappear forever. 'Peter Pan' was staged in the winter of 1998 with many new and talented members joining the remaining faithful few.

It cost £50 to put on 'Yellow Sands' in 1947. I hold bills which show that timber cost £2.18.0d and paint 10 shillings. Royalties were £14.14.0d and tickets sales were £55.7.6d., expenditure £44.18.1d. How different the costs are today but not so different in the profit made, which so often now is helped by the bar.

My husband, Roy Blackmore, ran our first bar. His notes show whisky, 2/6d, gin and tonic 2/3d, keg beer 2/4d a pint, Chambertin 18 shillings and you could drink a bottle of Champagne for only 33 shillings.

How can we ever forget Doris Cocks on the piano, so patient and dependable, her husband Frank, Daisy Thorn (with an enormous fan club) still performing well into her 70s, Howard Pain and so many other people no longer with us but who made Little Gaddesden Drama Club so very special.

There has always been a nucleus of extremely hard-working and talented members at the heart of the Club, and today is no exception and, with their enthusiasm, the Drama Club will flourish in the new Millennium.

1964 *It's never too Late*
1965 *The Summer of the Seventeenth Doll*
1965 *1066 and All That*
1966 *A Question of Fact*
1966 *The Man who came to Dinner*
1967 *Candied Peel*
1967 *Maria Martin or Murder in the Red Barn*
1968 *Rose without a Thorn*
1968 *Arden of Faversham*
1969 *Blithe Spirit*
1969 *The Diary of Anne Frank*
1969 *Palladin*
1970 *The Marquise*
1970 *Home at Seven*
1971 *In the words of Confucius*
1971 *Dark of the Moon*
1972 *Separate Tables*
1972 *Oliver*
1973 *I'll leave it to You*
1973 *The King and I*
1974 *Anastasia*
1974 *Revue*
1975 *The Drunkard*
1976 *How the other half Loves*
1976 *Revue*
1977 *Ladies in Retirement*
1977 *A Peal of Bells*
1978 *A Man for all Seasons*
1978 *Revue*
1979 *Adventure Story*
1979 *A Funny Thing Happened on the way to the Forum*
1980 *The Birthday Party*
1981 *Much Ado About Nothing*
1981 *Gaddesden Gaieties*
1982 *Arsenic and Old Lace*
1982 *The Public Eye*
1983 *The Wizard of Oz*
1983 *Waiting for Godot*
1983 *The Winslow Boy*
1984 *Revue*
1984 *Pools Paradise*
1984 *The Crucible*
1985 *Lock up your Daughters*
1986 *Antigone*
1986 *Guys and Dolls*
1987 *The Philanthropist*
1987 *Old Times*
1987 *A Christmas Carol*
1988 *The Lady's not for Burning*
1988 *Female Parts*
1988 *Macbeth*
1989 *Revue*
1989 *Dick Whittington*
1990 *Sergeant Musgrave's Dance*
1990 *Smike*
1991 *A Family Affair*
1991 *Confusions*
1992 *Red Riding Hood*
1992 *Three one-act Plays*
1992 *Half a Sixpence*
1993 *Tom Sawyer*
1993 *Revue*
1993 *Harlequinade*
1994 *Annie*
1998 *Peter Pan*
1999 *Revue*

Pictured above - a poster from 1947

Buildings in the village

17

John O'Gaddesden's House

by Peter Allen with help from Margaret Crawford

John O'Gaddesden was born in 1280 and educated at Merton College, Oxford, where he qualified as a doctor. In his early life he wrote a well-known medical compendium 'Rosa Anglica' which was in use for over 200 years. Later on he was in the entourage of Edward the Third, as a court Physician and then that of Edward's eldest son, the Black Prince, and was most probably at the Battle of Crécy with him in 1346. John is referred to in Chaucer's 'Canterbury Tales' as one of the fifteen medical authorities studied by the Doctor of Physic.

A white timber-framed house existed in Little Gaddesden in the 14th Century but whether or not this was on the site of the present house is not known. However, a part of John O'Gaddesden's House probably dates from the 14th Century and possibly even from the 13th Century. It was substantially rebuilt in the 15th Century as a first floor mediaeval guild hall, or solar, with some modifications subsequently. It is not thought to have changed significantly by 1899, although its use had varied over the years. In the 19th Century it was described by the village school master, John Worrall, as a farm with an orchard. It was divided into two cottages in the 1880s and 1890s, with the Fenn family, who were straw plaiters, in one and the Rogers (James and Hannah - he was a scullion and his wife a dressmaker) in the other.

THE BEGINNING OF THE CENTURY - 1899 TO 1934

The house had been part of the Ashridge estate for many years and in 1899 was owned by the Brownlows. In 'A History of the County of Hertford', published in 1908, is a drawing of the house. At some stage a false ceiling was inserted in the solar and the four carved heads, which were attached to the lower beams, were removed.

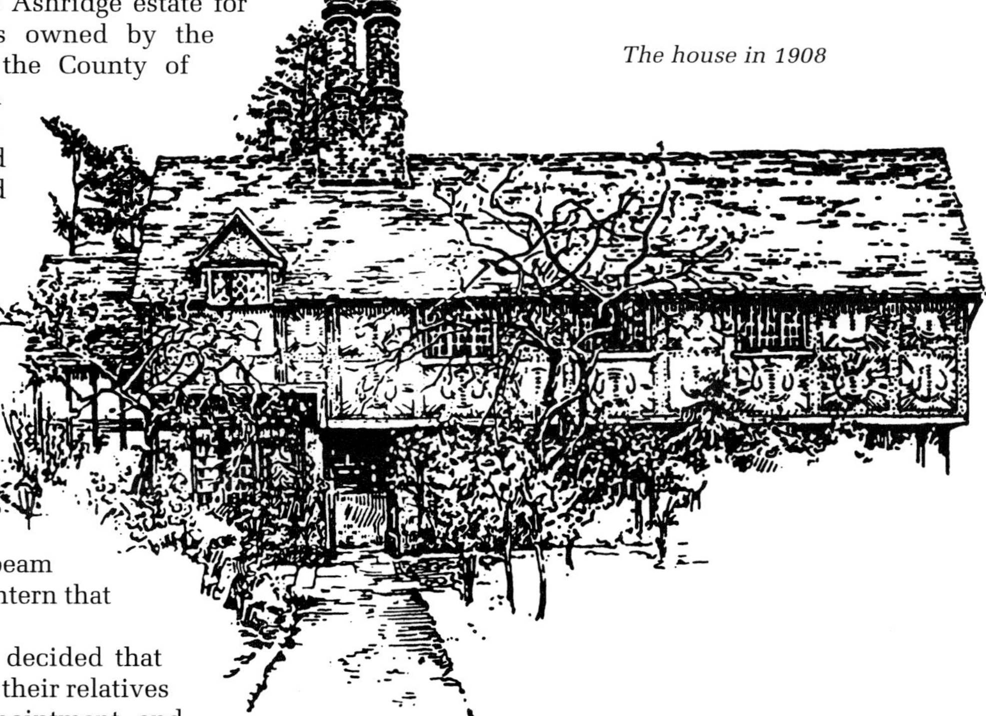

The house in 1908

During this period, the house was used as a village reading and meeting room and as a social club for the young men of the village, where they played billiards and also received some teaching. It is said that the charring on the main beam in the solar was caused by the lantern that hung over the billiard table.

In the 1920s the Brownlows decided that they needed the house for one of their relatives and thus, much to the disappointment and annoyance of the villagers, the house became a private residence. In 1932 the property was sold to Mr Edward Rawdon Smith and thus began an era of great change for the house.

THE RAWDON SMITH YEARS 1932 TO 1957

The house that Edward Rawdon Smith (ERS) bought in 1932 for £1,000 would have looked externally as in the 1908 drawing with a small piece of land surrounding it. Adjoining the property at the rear was the old Village Hall.

In 1933 ERS started to increase the land area by buying a strip between the house and the old Village Hall. The house was rented to Captain Richard Oakley for a few years but the Rawdon Smiths lived there during the Second World War. In 1950 ERS bought the land between the house and Church Road and the land at the rear which had become available due to an arsonist burning down the old Village Hall. He also acquired the two cottages on the Green numbered 31 and 32, now occupied by Nigel and Gill Frostick and their son Tom. This completed the expansion of the land.

It was during the late 1940s and early 1950s that ERS had the idea of significantly transforming the house into, in essence, what it is today. This was a labour of great love and ingenuity which involved adding two wings, consisting of parts of existing old houses from other parts of the country, to the main house. It took four years to find and dismantle the buildings, piece by piece, and find ancient door latches, nails, windows, glass, fire stacks, flooring, iron casements etc. It took eighteen months to construct the new wings.

The architect was Frank Jennings; the builder, F G Whitman of Hudnall and a local team of Richard Fountain of Ringshall as foreman, Steve Oakins, Arthur Clifton and Bill Green. Bill Green, who lives in Chapel Close and is now aged 87 years, remembers working on dismantling the buildings and rebuilding them here.

The main (south west) front wing was from a yeoman's house at Hawstead, Suffolk. This was originally a 15th Century open hall, with a great tie beam across the centre and a king post above it to the rafters. A first floor ceiling had been inserted in the 16th Century. In the bedroom of this wing is also a 16th Century fireplace which came from a north Essex house. The landing and new north west wing are William and Mary, about 1700, and came from Wrestlingworth Manor, Beds. This is the kitchen wing with bedrooms and bathroom above. Part of the main staircase came from Leex Priory in Essex, which was built in 1540. The remainder of the staircase is of oak in the 16th Century style. In addition, the carved wooden heads, which had been cut off earlier in the solar, were replaced by heads representing a priest, a lawyer, a doctor and a merchant. This work was carried out by Lawrence Turner, who also worked at Westminster Abbey. This work was finished by 1954, all in all a great project which transformed the house.

Edward Rawdon Smith only enjoyed the fruits of his labour for three years or so, dying in December 1957. His widow continued to live in the village at Glebe Cottage. When the house was auctioned the garden was described in the sale brochure as follows:

'Lawns shaded by trees and interspersed with flower beds and with masses of flowering shrubs and bulbs provide a delightful setting to the house. At the rear is the T-shaped walk between fruit trees arranged Espalier and Pergola fashion and there is a kitchen and soft fruit garden.'

THE PERIOD 1958 TO 1984

There were five owners during this period and further extensions and alterations were made. Dr Thomas and Nancy Parker bought the house and stayed for 12 years. Later, in memory of his wife, Dr Thomas donated to the Village Produce Association (VPA) the Nan Parker Rose Bowl prize for Dahlias. In recent years this has been won by Daniel Bunting eight times in succession. Daniel has helped us in the garden ever since we came here. Another prize which Dr Parker donated to the VPA was for the 'best fruit cake' baked by a man.

The house was next purchased by Bill and Betsy Warner. They were Americans whose main addition to the house was to install a central heating system, especially in the solar. Five years later George and Pamela Minden bought the house. It was George Minden who planned the garage extension and obtained old roofing tiles for it. But it was left to the next occupants to actually build it. The Mindens also put in the tennis court. Then the Brightmans moved in. Geoffrey Brightman was a local builder who built the present garage with two bedrooms and a bathroom above it. His wife, Paula, was a dancer and one of their children, Sarah, became famous as a dancer and singer. Sarah married Andrew Graham Stewart from the Manor House. Later, she went on to marry Andrew Lloyd Webber. In 1963, the house was bought by Michael and Marion Portlock.

THE PERIOD 1984 TO 1999

On 27 November 1984 the house was bought by Peter and Pat Allen and, fifteen years later, we are still here. We arrived with three daughters Samantha, Joanna and Annabel. Later Joanna married at the village church of St Peter and St Paul and the reception was held in our garden.

At the time of buying the house we were told that it was inhabited by a ghost, which caused great excitement amongst our daughters, especially our youngest who created wonderful stories about it. Otherwise we took little notice of this until one day Pat contacted a local builder. When she mentioned the name of the house he said straightaway that he had worked in the house 25 years previously and that there was a poltergeist in the solar, as their tools were constantly moved overnight without any apparent reason! However, we have yet to have the privilege of a visit.

The house was in need of some improvements and the garden had been left to its own devices. The major decision made was to open up the solar ceiling to its original form, thus showing off the timber framing to its best effect. We left the layout of the garden as it was but replanted the existing beds and planted some trees to replace those which had fallen over the years.

After a few years we planned an extension at

The solar of the original house, restored.

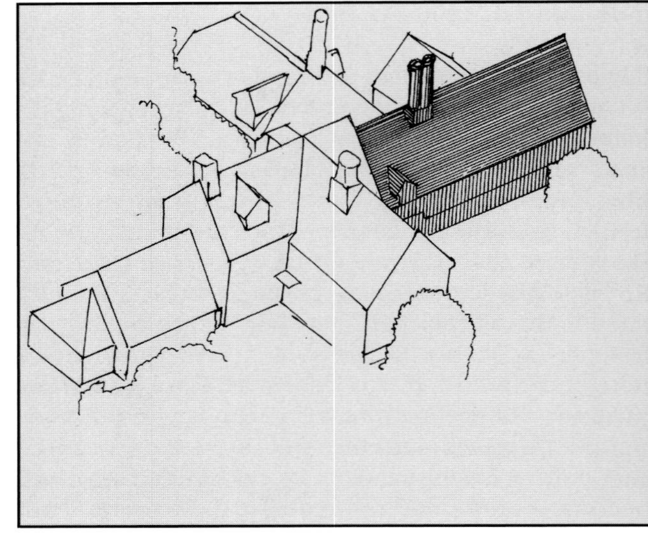

ABOVE
The house in 1999

RIGHT
The shaded area shows the original house as seen in the 1908 drawing on page 263

the north-west end of the house. As the house is registered Grade 2 this meant protracted discussions with the local planning authorities and English Heritage to ensure, not only that the plans were acceptable, but also that the appropriate materials were used. All was finally agreed and the addition fits in well with the existing house. The aerial view shows the house as it is now.

THE HOUSE NOW

We use the house differently from how it was used in the past - we use the 'library' as our study and family room, the panelled room, previously used as a sitting room, we have as our dining room and the previous dining room is now an inner hall. The solar is a great room for when the family are at home and for entertaining friends and it is always a delight to spend time in it. We celebrated Christmas this year with four generations of our family in John O'Gaddesden's House. The family feels very privileged to have spent so many years in a wonderful old house and we regard ourselves very much as 'trustees' and custodians for future generations.

The Manor House

by Roger Bolton

In the Spring of 1999 a Frenchwoman, in her sixties, walked tentatively up to the Manor House and knocked on the front door. Above the bay window, on her left, was a stone tablet with the date AD1576, and the door itself was of a very great age. Her name was Colette Camoin and some 44 years earlier, when she was just 19, she had spent a year in the village as a general help and companion to Dorothy Erhart and Kathleen Talbot, whose home it then was.

A few weeks later, on her return to Marseilles, she sent us some photographs of the two friends taken in 1956. One shows a white Rolls Royce parked in front of the house. Another, taken from the roof, shows the two old ladies in the garden with long shadows in front of them and, behind, the carefully trimmed yew hedges. There is one colour photograph, inscribed on the back: K.T. Salzburg 29.6.58. Miss Erhart told Colette it was taken on the last day of Miss Talbot's life. She has a wry smile on her face.

The Manor House - an etching by Dorothea Patterson

In her will Miss Talbot left the house and its contents to Dorothy Erhart who opened the Manor House to visitors, displaying her collection of musical instruments, furniture and paintings collected by the Talbot family. All are now gone. We have a leaflet for 'Manor House Music 1970', which advertises 6 concerts on Fridays from May to September. The last was given by Dorothy Erhart herself. She played Bach, Byrd and Bartok on the harpsichord. Single tickets were 10 shillings, light refreshment with wine was available afterwards, price 2 shillings. Miss Erhart died soon afterwards and her ashes were placed beneath a cherry tree to the north east of the nave of the parish church, next to those of her close friend Kathleen. So ended the Talbot connection with the Manor House.

There is another photograph of the Manor House, this time in Hemel Hempstead library, and it seems to date from around 1900. The front of the house is covered in ivy, a union jack flies jauntily from a flagpole on the roof, and more flags hang from several windows. Sitting proudly in front, a broad smile on his face, is the then occupant, Colonel Wheatley, Agent of the Ashridge Estate. The occasion is probably the Relief of Ladysmith or Mafeking in the Boer War. Colonel Wheatley had become Agent in 1882 and the house had been renovated for him in 1887 when he married his second wife, Miss Annette Cust. She was a cousin of Lord Brownlow, who owned Ashridge. Another cousin, the Dean of York, officiated at the wedding. The Colonel lived in the house for over forty years and had three daughters: Miss Pearl, Miss Pru and Miss Angel. Miss Angel worked as a nurse in Hemel Hempstead hospital but died young. Pearl was alive in the 1980's.

Before the renovation the main part of the Manor House had not been lived in for many years, having been damaged by fire and then used as an armoury. The Wheatleys had it refurbished and a Victorian extension built on the back. It was very convenient for the main estate works, which were behind the Red House, a hundred yards or so away. Colonel Wheatley had a brick cycle path made from the works to Ashridge House, and it is still visible today. He also had one of the earliest cars in the village, a 2-seater Napier, AR1, with yellow spoked wheels. Colonel and Mrs Wheatley lived on in the Manor House after the Brownlow Estate was broken up in the 1920's, and they both died in 1932. This was when Kathleen Talbot (the sister of Bridget Talbot who lived at Little Gaddesden House) bought the Manor House. As well as the musical enthusiasm already mentioned, Kathleen founded the Village Produce Societies of England and was national president. She never married.

On Dorothy Erhart's death the Manor House passed to the Graham Stewart family and eventually was divided up between the four sons. There followed a period which seemed to consist of rather wild rock and roll parties and Gothic horror movies....By the middle of the 1980's the Graham Stewarts began to sell parts of the Manor House complex. And by 1991 Andrew was the only member of the family remaining. His part of the Manor House comprised the main 1576 stone buildings, including the dining room with its magnificent painted Elizabethan fireplace and medieval screen taken from Ashridge monastery, and the Solar. Much of the stone, some of it bearing traces of wall paintings, had come from the medieval monastery. Andrew had married the daughter of a local builder, living at John O'Gaddesden's House, Sarah Brightman, then a member of Pan's People, the Top of the Pops dance group. She became an outstanding singer and later married Andrew Lloyd Webber.

When Andrew Graham Stewart decided to sell and move to Scotland, we (Roger and Julia Bolton) came to look at the house. There was no central heating, green mould was on some of the stonework, and fishing rods and gold records were on the walls. (Andrew had managed a successful German pop group, Tangerine Dream). When he moved he took with him the Tudor dining table which came originally from Ashridge, but left the 1576 portrait of Elizabeth I being arrested at Ashridge when a princess. It is painted on what was a door and will always hang on the dining room wall, whoever lives in the Manor House.

So on a wet grey December day in 1991 the Boltons moved in to the main part of the Manor House and joined the four other families in the complex. (The oldest part is actually the wattle and daub Manor Cottage, part of which is 15th century.) There has almost certainly been a hamlet on the site since Saxon times, and a Manor House since at least the Normans. We put in central heating, repaired the roof, and gently readjusted the Manor House to family life. For the first time for almost 100 years the sound of young children echoed in its stone corridors, not Pearl, Pru or Angel, but Olivia and Jessica. Jarman's ghost has remained in his coffin on the roof and since we had the faulty electricity repaired the lights no longer mysteriously flicker. One day we will try to excavate to find the missing north eastern wing, and perhaps a metal detector will discover some missing Tudor jewellery.

A few months ago I went to Hertford Public Records Office and looked at the original deeds of the house, which the builder, Sir Robert Dormer signed. (He lies buried in Wing church.) I hope that when we leave the Manor House, perhaps to rest in Little Gaddesden churchyard, another family will treasure it as we do and find the happiness we have enjoyed.

On dark evenings, sitting by the embers in the Elizabethan fireplace, I dream of those who warmed themselves here on winters' nights in the time of the Virgin Queen, whose portrait still looks down upon the living and the ghosts of the Manor House.

Little Gaddesden House

by Marjorie Eccles

Little Gaddesden House was built in 1859 for a dual purpose - as a private dwelling house for Lord Brownlow's land agent, and as an office for the Ashridge estate. It was used as such until 1880, when a new land agent, Colonel Wheatley, was appointed and expected to move in. However, when his wife saw it (she was a well-born lady with Brownlow connections) it was reported that she flatly refused to live in such an ugly house. Fortunately the Manor House was at that point available and, being obviously more to her taste, it was there she and her husband went to live, and where an office was built for him.

We shall never know precisely why Mrs Wheatley took against Little Gaddesden House. It was large, and handsome by Victorian standards, being brick built, with Bath stone mullions and facings around windows and doors, a score of tall, decorative chimneys, each having its own individual style of brickwork, and with gables surmounted by carved stone finials and roof tiles in two colours, laid in geometric patterns. It stood a hundred and fifty yards from the Nettleden Road, and was set in landscaped gardens and grounds, seventeen acres in all, and could boast an impressive view of Ashridge House and the Golden Valley. There were numerous rooms, spacious domestic quarters, kitchen gardens and glasshouses, and enough outbuildings with functions of different sorts to make life comfortable and self-sufficient for those who lived in the big house. There was also a range of magnificent stables.

Inside, the principal rooms had high ceilings, south and westerly aspects, and tall windows to let in plenty of light. The two main wings of the house were joined by a long hallway branching horizontally from an entrance porch, the estate offices being to the left and the private quarters to the right. The hall was floored with coloured encaustic tiles into which was set an iron grating allowing

Little Gaddesden House

BIOGRAPHICAL NOTE:
We came to Little Gaddesden from Solihull in the West Midlands when my husband's job meant that he was moved to Potters Bar. We searched for a house between there and London, the main requirement for me being (a) easy access to a tube station and (b) a good reference library. But one day we happened, by chance, on Little Gaddesden and Little Gaddesden House... the rest is history.

The quietness and unique atmosphere of Little Gaddesden House are especially valuable to me as a writer. Forget the tube station, forget the reference library even - there is always the internet after all, if I ever get round to it! But there is nowhere else like Little Gaddesden.

Marjory Eccles

heat to come through from hot water pipes beneath. The house was one of the first country houses to be lit by gas, generated from an acetylene plant in the grounds.

In 1880, it became occupied by the Honourable Alfred Talbot, a younger brother of Lady Brownlow, who evidently did not have Mrs Wheatley's aversion to it and was happy to live there and be near his sister at Ashridge House. Indeed, when he married two years later, he brought his bride, Emily de Grey, to the house, where later their four children were born. It was to be their home for the rest of their lives, and only ceased to be in possession of the Talbots on the death of Alfred's eldest daughter, Bridget, the last surviving member of the family.

From the date of Alfred Talbot's arrival at Little Gaddesden House it was used entirely as a dwelling house: the room formerly used as a clerks' room in the wing designed for the estate offices was turned into a schoolroom, and was also used for various village meetings, for putting on plays and occasionally as a rehearsal room for the village brass band, whose founder was Alfred Talbot.

Unfortunately, none of the family lived to a great age, except for Bridget Talbot herself, a redoubtable lady whose exploits have been recorded elsewhere in this book. For many years, until her death in 1971, she lived as the sole owner of this large house. She did, however, have a strong social conscience and when housing shortages in the village were at their worst after the war, she rented out parts of her home to various people, many of whom still recall the discomforts of sharing a house which was by then in some disrepair and not by any means equipped for multiple occupancy. Necessity, however, made even such damp and draughty accommodation acceptable.

After Miss Talbot died, the prohibitive cost of restoring the house to what it had once been prevented it from being converted to charitable uses, as she had reputedly wished. Instead, it was acquired by Mr Gordon Symondson, and later by Mr Michael Waterhouse of Chipperfield Homes, with the intention of dividing it into separate houses. Originally, the idea was to convert the main buildings into six individual dwellings and to build two detached houses on the site of the stables. The planning application was turned down and subsequently the decision was made to provide nine freehold dwellings in all, and to include parts of the stable buildings in the conversion.

These amended plans remain successful to this day, mainly due to the decision not to turn the property into flats, but to divide it vertically, so that each house is independent and retains an identity unique to itself. Original fireplaces and doors, splendid cornices, coffered ceilings and other features have been preserved. The estate office, with the big clerks' room which once contained a huge walk-in safe, together with the rooms above it, now forms a large, five-bedroomed house. The former entrance hall and the rooms behind it have become a charming, one-storey house which retains the old porch, an intriguing beamed roof, carved decorations on the door lintels and Victorian glass panels to the inner door, which incorporate features from the Brownlow coat of arms. The adjoining house, where once the long hallway opened out, houses the original main staircase, its height impressive except when paper-hanging, since one drop requires more than an entire roll of wallpaper!

Similarly, throughout the rest of the residence, accommodation such as the dining room, the large kitchen and parts of the stable block have been well-adapted for use as contemporary homes. Like most large Victorian houses, Little Gaddesden House was prodigal in the use of space, while being short on bathrooms and heating. But every inch of space has since been utilised and rearranged to provide the facilities required by modern-day living. One bath is in fact set into an alcove built into the unused three-chimney block of what is now the house next door; the former estate office strongroom provides the location for an oil-fired boiler.

Converting a house such as this was an ambitious project and as such not without its problems: not only did the brickwork and the intricate chimneys need to be completely repointed, and roof slates replaced, but also the soft stonework around windows and doors was crumbling and needed repair, there was dry rot, damp and woodworm everywhere, and leaky gulleys between the roof gables. The conversion did in fact take about three years to complete.

At the present time, in a less expansive era than the Victorian one, nearly 150 years since Little Gaddesden House was built, a residence that once accommodated a single household now provides comfortably spacious accommodation for nine. Around what were once the kitchen and stable yards, now turned into paved courtyards with plantings of shrubs, stand nine houses and garages, while behind each house stretches a large garden. Happily, this has all been achieved without substantially altering the way the original Little Gaddesden House was intended to appear when it was designed in 1859.

The old cottages at Ringshall

The Ringshall Cottages - etching by Dorothea Patterson

Canon Senar has written an excellent account of these cottages and their history in "Little Gaddesden and Ashridge". Here I am adding a few other points.

Firstly beware of the numbering in old documents. The present numbering starts at 3 and ends at 35. The one called number 3 was always the end one of the row.

Numbers 3 to 13 were recorded in 1891 as numbers 32 to 23, thus in reverse order, and one too few by present numbering. The gap for the old well and pump is between present numbers 4 and 5. This is the older row, dating from the 18th century.

Numbers 14 to 35 were recorded in 1891 as numbers 22 to 1, continuing the reverse order. Number 14 (old no.22) is Pear Tree House. This row was built in the early 19th century by the third Earl of Bridgewater (died 1823). Most of them are semi-detached.

Number 5 (immediately to the left of the pump) was Fountain's Stores until 1980 and can be read about in chapter 12. (Number 6 may have been the shop in the 19th century, but 5 and 6 are one house now anyway.)

Both rows of houses had meadows behind them, which have gradually been reduced by housing plots. The meadow behind numbers 14 to 35 used to be leased with number 30, as can be read in the smallholdings article on page 221 by Barbara Mogg.

Canon Senar has written almost a hall of fame of the more recent residents, but he has omitted no.17. Here is a little to make up for it: In 1891, William and Eliza Garrett and five children aged 5 to 17 lived there; William was a bricklayer.

Continuing, Ann Kirkpatrick, the present occupant, writes:

ABOVE
17 and 16 Ringshall in 1930 with the Timms family

BELOW
The pig, at the rear of one of the Ringshall cottages

Pre-1920 the Clifton family lived at number 17, having four children, one of whom was an excellent football player who eventually played for a Southampton club just before the second world war. The Timms family (no relation of the Timms of Pitstone Copse) lived here from 1928 when it was purchased by them for £1900. The Timms family left, and it was then purchased by Miss Evelyn Janes (who at that time lived with her parents at Hall Farm) and she was the owner until 1979. She was a very popular piano teacher for many years (see the article on the Andrews and Banks families, page 302) and always referred to her pupils as "my poopals". The cottage at present has been in the same ownership (myself and my late husband Keith) since 1979.

Some other historical notes:

Until 1968 there was only one tap to each pair of cottages.
If an Estate worker worked on a Sunday he didn't need to pay rent.
Dark green paint was supplied for use at every cottage (as the present owner found when the doorframes were stripped in 1980).
Every Christmas each Estate worker was given a pig to be fattened up, and most of the cottages had pig styes in their back 'barns' . (I think one still exists today.)
Harry Cutler (who lived at no.16 in the early 1930's) was a 'very good runner', so much so that when a doctor was needed locally he was immediately contacted to "fetch him from Dagnall post-haste".

Ann Kirkpatrick, like Howard Senar and Vicars Bell before her, has also found some of the Brownlows' tenancy rules intriguing.

Vicars Bell took a rather cynical view:

Where there is but one landowner there is but one employer. And if that employer is anxious to improve the lot and morals of his employees, it must be indeed difficult for him to avoid over-stepping the line which marks the confines of an individual's private life and concerns.

A cottage lease of this period well illustrates the danger.

The rent of the cottage and garden is £3 3s 0d per annum, and an allowance of one shilling in the pound is to be made 'if the tenant attends strictly to the rules'.

These rules are prefaced in this way:

'I have made the following regulations with the object of preserving the health of the Cottage Tenantry and for the encouragement of their cleanliness and good conduct.

Brownlow'

Rule 2 states that no lodger is to be taken in without written consent. Rule 3 reads: 'The Bed Room Windows unless in case of illness to be opened every morning from 8 o'clock until 12. The Agent or Estate Inspector to look over the whole of the premises as often as he or they may consider it necessary!

Clothing and Blanket Clubs, Choir Treats, School Treats, Harvest Homes, The Ladies' Glee Club, the Village Band, Concerts (complete with ballads sung by the Curate), the Bede Houses, blankets and red flannel, curtsies and the pulling of forelocks, the glass of port with the butler for those who attended evening service in the house chapel; Jubilee celebrations at Ashridge, with free meals, conjurors and acrobats, fireworks and 'suitable presents for all', with Lord and Lady Brownlow 'moving freely and graciously among their guests', the hearty cheers in response to the Rector's speech of thanks - how distant it all seems, how ridiculous - but how spacious and peaceful, in a world made safe for ever by the power, might, dominion and glory of an invincible Britain reigned over by an everlasting Queen. A Little Gaddesden where if 'a tenant attends strictly to the rules' he may be sure of care and protection as long as life lasts.

Those who remember the village in the last days of the Brownlows, or who came to live here shortly after the estate was sold, will remember the bewilderment and uncertainty, as of a child learning to walk, which beset the parish when the fatherly hand was withdrawn. But I doubt whether any, except perhaps the oldest of us, would choose to step back into those days beyond recall.

Thus wrote the village schoolmaster in 1949. As his pupils have since testified, his great gift was to make people think for themselves. He would not expect everyone to agree with everything he said. In 1949 he perhaps would not have foreseen how quickly even his own days would be beyond recall, but some of the Victorian traditions are still what we enjoy, even to the extent of getting the latest version of the good and the great to 'move freely and graciously' among us.

Canon Senar in his version lists all nine terms and conditions of Alfred Fountain's tenancy at no.5 Ringshall, but without comment. Some are what you might expect, but apart from those quoted above, two more stand out:

Every room to be lime-washed once a year, in May, at the expense of the tenant, the landlord delivering lime on the premises, on application. This would keep the interiors nice and light and may have hygienic qualities, but the white powder would rub off on your clothes if you leant on the walls.

All vegetable matter and refuse to be dug into the ground and not to accumulate in heaps or pits on any part of the premises. Well, no compost heaps in the garden then, but the desired effect was the same, even if a bit slower.

Ringshall Summer

Heat-heavy walking the meadow
high in cow parsley
in crackling dry grasses
to the cool of the wood
loud with the song of birds,

in the steep shade, no stream
but pools of sunshine
scattered as coins on dark earth.

Pale moons of elder
their blossoms enfolding hedges,
bowers puffed up as winter birds,
or a plump feather filled
patchwork quilt,
on an old brass bed...

Mary Blake

Denison House

This house is another instance of one old residence and its grounds being divided into many. It was called Marian Lodge when Lady Marian Alford rebuilt it in the 1850's, and when Mrs Helen Denison lived in it from the 1880's into the 20th century. She was a widow in 1891 when her household consisted of her daughter Katherine (aged 20), a governess, a butler, a cook/housekeeper, two lady's maids, a housemaid, an under-housemaid and a kitchen maid. These were nearly all 'in-comers', the exception being Tripp, the butler, born in Ringshall, and Martha Oakins, the under-housemaid from Dagnall. Miss Denison, her daughter and two of the servants were from London, the governess from Slough and the cook from Leicester.

As Canon Senar mentions in his book, the house was a centre for exquisite high-quality embroidery and weaving.

When Mr Cuthbertson lived here in the 1930's the house had been given Miss Denison's name. From 1940 to 1946 it was used as a war-time home for the Froebel School, as can be read on page 174. It was still one large residence at that time.

The division of the house into smaller residences, the conversion of the coach-house into a house, and the division of the grounds into plots for new houses all occurred in the second half of the century. In 1999 only the end nearest the road is called Denison House, the rest of the old house containing Denison Lodge, Marian Lodge (a re-birth of the old name for only a portion of the original), and Bannerdown 1 and 2. Eight detached houses, including the old Coach House, now occupy the grounds, the entire 13 dwellings making up what is now known as the Marian Lodge Estate.

The old pumping house

by Peter Grainger

The impressive entrance to the old pumping house in a state of neglect in the 1980s

The waterworks at Little Gaddesden were built in 1858 on land at the back of the Red House, off the Green, entirely at the expense of Lord and Lady Brownlow who owned Ashridge at the time. It replaced the previous rather primitive water supply from two ponds which frequently dried up. Until 1930 the pumps were still worked by the original steam engine.

Contracts for the building work were signed in September 1856 when Mr Paton of Watford undertook to sink a 275ft well for £1,180. Mr Joseph Harris built the engine house, boiler house and chimney for £473 and Messrs Easton and Amos provided the steam engine, boiler and pumps as well as the mains, for £4,737.

In the 1980s, The Rickmansworth and Uxbridge Valley Water Company, which was responsible at that time for providing water to West Herts, were given approval by Dacorum District Council, against the wishes of most of the village, to demolish this fine old building. It's replacement by a new structure, including a fluoridation plant, is still viewed by many villagers as an act of wanton vandalism.

The natural world

This is too big a subject to do justice to properly. You will find the detail varies a lot and there is nothing on the large and interesting subject of wild flowers.

Fortunately there are other sources of information on the natural world. There are natural history societies and county recording schemes for all three counties on our doorstep. Their records are subdivided to various levels of geographical area.

The first level is the County, which for stability of records is often referred to by the county boundaries as they were in 1859. These are now called the Watsonian Vice-counties. The civil parish of Little Gaddesden is therefore partly in Hertford, partly in Buckingham. Older records sometimes used parishes as sub-divisions.

The next level in modern use cuts right across county and parish boundaries, using the national grid reference system. There is firstly the 10km x 10km square, then the 2km x 2km square or tetrad, then the 1 km square, the smallest square shown on most ordnance survey maps. Our parish needs 2 of the first, 8 of the second or 22 of the last named squares (mostly just fragments of them).

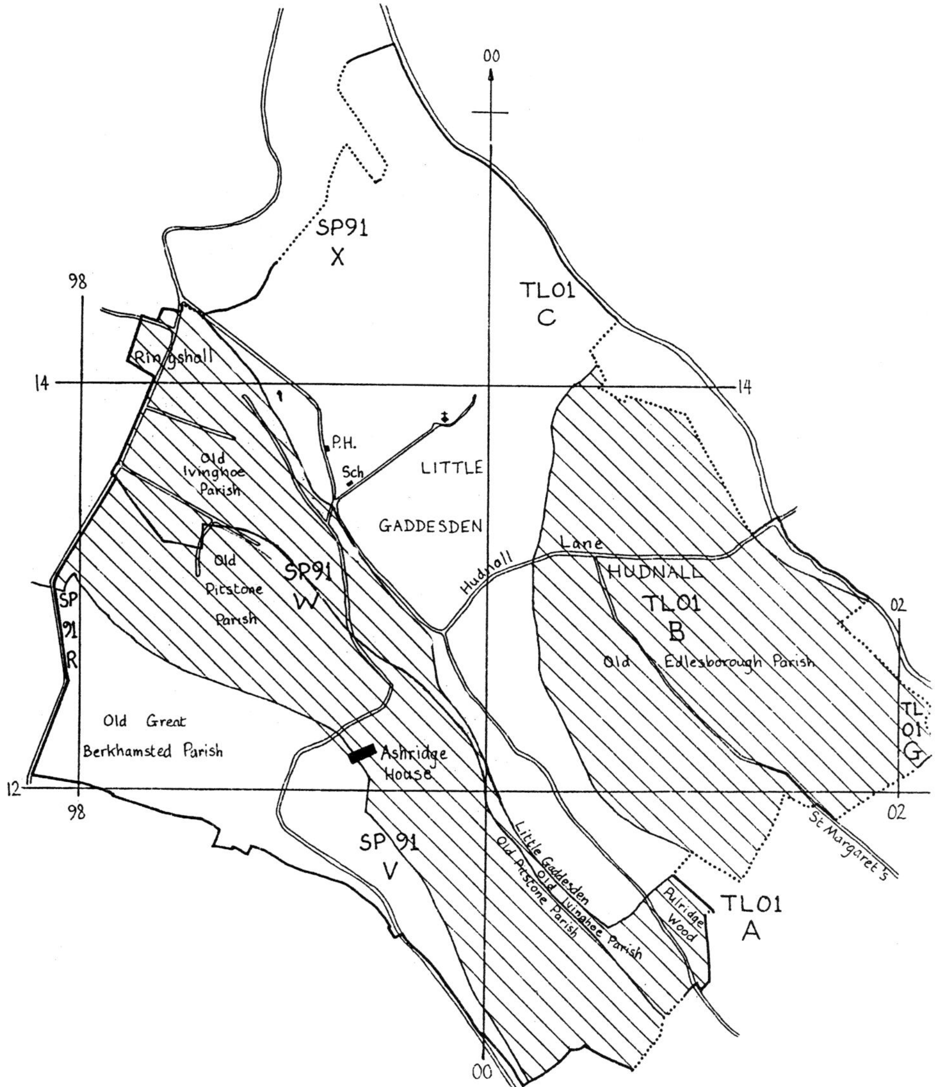

For natural history records, the shaded areas of the Parish are in the Watsonian vice-county of Buckingham and the rest is in Hertford.

The weather

Climatological records have been kept at Hudnall Park since 1978, only a few days having been missed each year. Here follow some of the 22-year summaries:

RAINFALL	1978 to 1999 in millimetres				
Month	Driest		Average	Wettest	
January	12.0	1997	73.0	141.5	1995
February	6.8	1993	48.2	118.8	1990
March	10.7	1997	58.7	130.6	1979
April	6.2	1984	59.5	142.8	1998
May	2.2	1990	56.3	128.4	1979
June	10.3	1996	65.3	136.2	1997
July	16.7	1984	50.2	104.3	1980
August	1.5	1995	53.1	118.3	1992
September	13.4	1996	63.3	120.9	1998
October	4.9	1978	74.0	192.8	1987
November	29.1	1978	64.7	135.3	1992
December	15.1	1991	78.1	169.8	1989
Whole Calendar Year	522.3	1996	744.5	926.3	1979

Earliest and latest dates for particular air temperatures, 1978 to 1999		
Temperature reached	Earliest date	Latest date
34.5C (94.1F)	August 3rd	Aug 3rd
33C	August 3rd	Aug 3rd
32.2C (90F)	July 22nd	Aug 3rd
30C	June 30th	Aug 12th
26.7C (80F)	May 23rd	Sept 11th
25C	May 4th	Oct 1st
21.1C (70F)	April 15th	Oct 13th
20C	March 17th	Oct 19th
15.6C (60F)	Feb 23rd	Nov 8th
15C	Feb 23rd	Nov 19th
13C	Feb 6th	Dec 28th

The temperature can reach 12C any day of the year.
The hottest day recorded was August 3rd 1990.
The coldest was 12th Jan 1987, below -7C all day

Driest 365-day run: Feb 12th 1996 to Feb 10th 1997: 458.9 mm
Wettest 365-day run: March 2nd 1998 to March 1st 1999: 966.6 mm

The rainfall varies so greatly from month to month and year to year that these averages are of no use at all in predicting the weather for any season.

December, the wettest month on average, was actually the driest month in the whole 27 month period from February 1987 to April 1989.

February has fewer days in which to attain its total rainfall, and if you scale it up to be equivalent to a 31-day month, its average is 52.9 mm, making July the true driest month. That's only on average, though. The only year in which July was actually the driest month was 1994, when it only just beat June by taking into account the fact that June has one less day.

STORMS

The two worst storms from 1978 to 1999 were in 1987 and 1990.

Thursday October 15th 1987: The morning was cloudy with sunny intervals. Rain started about 3 pm (BST) and poured continuously from then on and through the night, giving 32.9 mm total, that's 1.3 inches, a daily total that only occurs every few years, though it was the second time this month, 47 mm having been recorded on October 9th. Meanwhile the wind increased to a gale and on to at least storm force 10 locally during the night, blowing many trees down, and cutting off electric power lines. At Hudnall, however, the power was not cut until 6.50 am. It was restored $8\frac{1}{2}$ hours later. With daylight the winds died down and the clouds broke up to give sunny periods by the afternoon of the 16th. Further south the storm was worse, especially along the south coast where hurricane force 12 winds did much structural damage to buildings and flattened whole woods and orchards. London recorded its worst storm since records began. The storm was the end of a hurricane which had crossed the Atlantic and unexpectedly reached Biscay and turned north. There was severe damage in France also.

Ash tree on Hudnall Common,damaged by the storm of January 5th 1990.

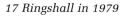

Thursday January 25th 1990: The day started with light rain and a force 5 breeze with a warm feel to it. The wind built up during the morning until it exceeded gale force. On this occasion there was only a litle rain, but the wind must have reached storm force 10 or 11 by the afternoon as it caused much more destruction in Hertfordshire than the 1987 storm, though less damage further south. The wind at this stage was blowing from the west. This was a daylight storm, when people were at work and children at school. One couldn't be sure about what to do for safety, as buildings were being damaged as well as trees, particularly roofs, chimneys and light weight panelling. Every road in the village was soon blocked by a fallen tree, and a huge oak at Water End fell onto a passing van, killing two men. Foresters were out with chain saws trying to open up the roads while trees around them were still in danger of falling, whipping round in a twisting motion while branches were being ripped off. Power lines came down, and at Hudnall this was at 3.30 pm. The wind died down gradually after dark. Power was restored at Hudnall after 23 hours, which was very good going. With the return of normality it was realised that far more trees were still standing than had blown down, a scene of destruction being easily created by a handful of spectacular big crashes and a litter of small branches everywhere. The 26th started with a light frost and a moderate breeze and became a fresh sunny day.

SNOW

From 1978 to 1999 snow fell more frequently in March than December. There is an account of severe snowy winter weather in 1928 and 1947 in the main school article, and in January 1963 in the account of the arrival of the Harts at Raglens. Here follow two more: one in 1958 and the other in winter 1981-82.

17 Ringshall in 1979

A snowy day

by Wendy Forster

This little story I'm going to tell happened way back in February 1958. I was only 15 years old at the time. I had just started work in my first job in a small hair-dressing shop in Old

MORE SNOW

by Carla Dover

In the very severe winter of 1981-82 there was a week of freezing conditions and heavy snowfall which caused snowdrifts to block the road through the village to Nettleden. No buses were able to get through, so many residents without cars were stranded. I could not open my back door because the snow was piled so high against it. All of our plumbing was frozen and I had to boil snow on the open fire for drinking water and cooking. This was before central heating was installed - an open fire was our only source of heat.

Editor's note: This was in Cromer Close. There were two weeks of snow and freezing in that winter to which this account could refer: December 8th to 14th 1981 and January 7th to 15th 1982. Roads were certainly blocked on December 11th - an unusually early date for deep snow. There were also drifts and deep snow on January 8th to 9th.

Hemel, called Betty Jeans.

On this particular day it had been snowing hard. I kept looking out of the shop window, knowing only too well it would be getting bad at Ringshall. Sure enough about 3 o'clock my best pal (Sue Cocks - Janet Stinton's sister) poppped her head round the door. (She worked just around the corner on the parade.) She said "Wen, we wont get home today. Mum has rung to say the buses have stopped running and I'm going home with a girl who lives locally." "Oh, I thought." My boss said that I had better go home with her to St. Albans. I didn't really fancy that so made an excuse about just going round to the bus stop and who should be there but Michael Sherringham. I relayed the story to him and he said "Oh, well, I'm going to walk"and so quickly I jumped in and said I would too. I went back to the shop to tell my boss but she had already gone.

So we set off. I wasn't dressed at all well for a seven mile walk in quite bad conditions. I had ankle boots and a long coat, scarf and bag. The snow was soon over the top of my silly boots. I tried to ring home at Piccotts End but no luck; the telephone wires were all down. We carried on walking; cars were abandoned in the old road of Piccotts End. The snow hung heavily over the hedges and made everywhere look so different. The wind was blowing and it was still snowing and I was getting cold.

We carried on to Water End. I must have looked a poor thing by now and we were just going to walk along the mile straight and a chap came along on a motor bike and sidecar. He stopped, looked at us both, and said to Michael "You had better get in the sidecar and your missis had better get on the back."

We were so pleased to get a lift even though the bike went everywhere skidding about. He took us as far as Nettleden where he lived. We then had to attempt Pulridge Hill - cars again were all marooned in the road. We had to walk along by the hedgerows. My legs by now were scratched, sore and chapped. We eventually got to the top of the hill and I just said "It's no good, I can't go any further." Anyway, with Mike's encouragement, we somehow kept going. We reached Cromer Close and our friends were just going to Youth Club. My mother must have been frantic with worry because it must have been 7.30 by now. We eventually reached the police house, Michael's home, and Mrs Sherringham took one look at me and said "You'd better get in the back, your lips are blue, and stay the night here. I was so pleased to be safe. I remember thinking I'm not going to work tomorrow. I didn't either.

For the next few days the only way to Hemel was via Berkhamsted. The bus was stuck in Hudnall Lane for a while. After a time the weather changed - the sun shone and the snow disappeared as quickly as it arrived!

Trees

It is told that a large number of trees were cut down for timber when the Brownlow estate was sold in the 1920's. Since then there has been a lot of planting, and natural regeneration as well. The old views of the Witchcraft Bottom area, before the timber felling began, show it as very open parkland, in which the cedars along Ringshall Drive stand out.

Nowadays many of those cedars remain, but there are no broad views because of the intervening trees, thickets and gardens. Hawthorns have grown up over wide areas, with self-sown oaks among them. The "new" houses have large gardens in which much of the space has been used for trees and shrubs, and the boundaries are often tall or thick hedges.

The articles on the National Trust (from page 192) include some information on forestry.

Three trees were marked for preservation when the estate was sold:

The Queen Beech: an outstandingly tall straight beech in Golden Valley. It blew down in 1928, however, and was found to be rotten inside.

The King Ash: a huge ash tree in Park Pulridge Wood: It was struck by lightning about the same time, at any rate before 1930, and did not survive. The tallest ash now is probably one in Witchcraft Bottom down hill from the house called The Croft.

Queen Victoria's Oak: Planted by Queen Victoria in the garden at Ashridge when she was still the very young princess of Kent: apparently in 1823 when she was only four years old. This tree did survive and still stands in excellent shape.

Some of the oldest trees in the parish are a group of Sweet Chestnuts about 400 metres north-west of the front of Ashridge House. The biggest girth in the group is about 7.1 metres (i.e. round the trunk at 4 feet above the ground ideally), or 2.25 metres diameter. That is about 7 feet 6 inches across: it is difficult to give an exact measurement to a huge fluted trunk which tapers. Three hundred years or more would be a reasonable guess for the age. Good chestnuts can be collected under these trees in season.

There are many fine big oaks of impressive spreading shape dotted about the parish, some in private gardens, such as the one behind no.18 Little Gaddesden, and others in the park and around the farms.

THE OAK AT BERKHAMPSTEAD LODGE

by Janet Stupples

The 394-year-old oak tree, standing dying in the garden of Berkhampstead Lodge in 1996, now forms the gilded pillars on the stage of Shakespear's Globe Theatre in London. At felling the circumference was 24 feet 9 inches around the trunk, which stood at 29 feet 6 inches before the first main branch, making it ideal for the purpose. Other timber from the tree has made replacement beams for the cottage, oak blocks, and the rest went for solid oak furniture.

The Queen beech prior to 1928

To those who abhor the felling of trees, please note that the others planted at about the same time along the edge of the old private drive to Ashridge House are all now standing dead and decaying as a contribution to the food chain. Not the way of my ancestors who have lived within 10 miles of my present home for over 250 years.

The trees on the Green

The Green, which here does not include the land on the far side of the road from the houses, consists of between 6 and 7 acres of grass, plus the area of the eight driveways which cross it. It is about 925 yards long or just over half a mile, and averages about 35 yards wide.

The trees on the Green were listed in a village school report dated to the period 1933-1937, (referred to below as c1935), and some comments were added. I listed the trees myself in 1981 and have updated the list from time to time up to 1999.

TOTAL NUMBER
c1935: "84", though the ones listed only add up to 81.
1981: 38. The stumps of two big trees were seen in the grass near the Adelaide Cross
1999: 35 but looks like 33 as three are growing from the same spot.

SPECIES
c1935: 10 or 11
1981: 9 or 10
1999: 11 or 12

CHERRY
c1935: 24. "Nearly all the cherry trees are by Hudnall Corner, and they look lovely when they are in bloom"
c 1946: A Wild Cherry tree was planted to represent each man who died in the War. That would be 6 or 7 trees.
1981:17. Only 3 of them were between the Adelaide Cross and Hudnall Corner. The 17 were spread fairly evenly along the whole green. They still look lovely in blossom. All are white flowered.
1997: 12. The five that had gone were: one in front of no.31 leaving a stump in the grass, with a self-sown Ash growing from its margin, one near Whitemeadows leaving a stump, one in front of no.40 which had been noted as a large tree, and two in front of Denison House wall, of which one has left a stump. Most of the surviving eleven were more or less like wild cherries with small fruit ripening "black" and sweet. The odd ones were a "white" cherry,

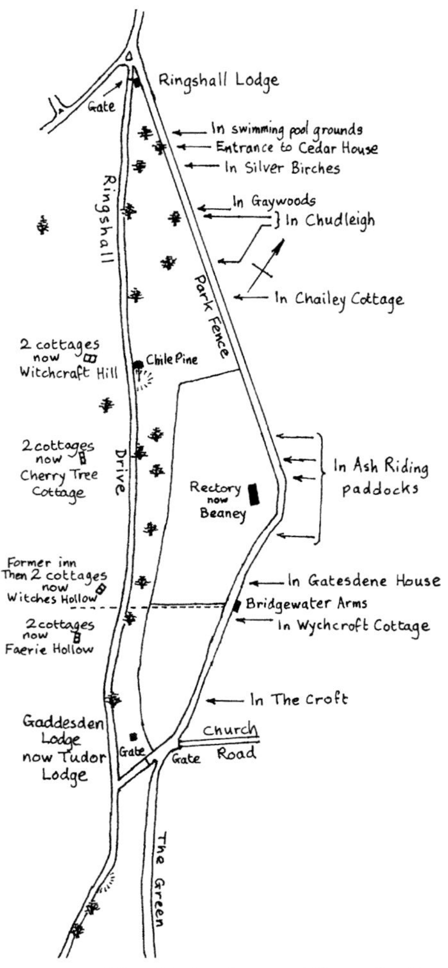

The Cedar trees of Ringshall Drive surviving in 1999 and the gardens in which they now stand.

BELOW LEFT:

A cedar tree on Ringshall Drive in 1930 with "Witches Hollow" in the background. The tree is still there.

BELOW RIGHT:
Cherries in blossom on the Green

rather insipid, between nos.40 & 42, and two sweet red ones in front of no.50 and the Manor House. The tallest ones, with typical wild cherry form, are one next to the war memorial, one in front of no.33 and one next to the drive to no.49. The last of these has an oak tree and a hazel bush growing right from the bottom of its trunk.
1999: 11. Another one in front of no.31 has gone leaving a stump. The red-fruited one by the Manor House has died back to a single weak branch. The biggest one, near no.49, was measured as 57 feet tall.

DAMSON
c1935: 9
1981-1999: None

VICTORIA PLUM
c1935: 1 by the village shop, no.42
1981-1999: None

OAK
c1935: 24
1981: 4, all big mature trees, survivors of the 1935 set.
1999: 4. The big one on the Manor House side of the Adelaide Cross had gone before 1997 leaving a stump in the grass. The one on the other side of the cross and the one beside the drive to no.45 are both fine. The big one in front of the war memorial may be a Durmast Oak, Quercus petraea. The others look more like the English Oak, Q. robur.
A new young one had appeared in 1997 growing from the base of the big cherry tree mentioned above, and is still growing well, though one-sided in this awkward position.

ABOVE:
Red Oak in front of no.35

BELOW:
Three old limes in front of the Red House

AMERICAN RED OAK
c1935: None
1981: 1. Two young ones had been recently planted but the one near Norwood Cottage gate was dead. The other was in front of no.35
1999: 1. It now looks well established.

BEECH
c1935: 6. “The beeches grow on the slope because they can get their roots down into the chalk”
1981-1999: None

ASH
c1935: 9
1981: 1. It is a fairly big one in front of no.37. It could be a survivor from 1935.
1999: 2. The extra one is the self-sown one found at the cherry stump mentioned above found in 1997. It is now growing well.

LIME
c1935: 3. “Some of the limes have been cut down but we are very

The Sweet Chestnut and the Horse Chestnut by no.39

lucky to have three fine specimens standing."
1981: 6. The "fine specimens" of 1935 are still standing, and they are huge. They are in front of the Red House.

The other three were young specimens, one in front of the paddock by the Manor House, one in front of no.54 and one in front of no.43.
1999: 6. Another young one had been planted in front of the paddock before 1998, but the previous one there had died. We measured one of the huge ones by the Red House and made it 91 feet tall, that's 28 metres. Most of these limes appear to be the hybrid European Lime, Tilia x europaea. The younger ones have a tendency towards the features of the Large-leaved Lime parent, particularly the one by no.43 which may be that species. The old ones tend more towards the Small-leaved Lime parent in their glabrous petioles and twigs and more flowers in the cluster.

WALNUT
c1935: 3
1981: 6. Two were mature trees, survivors of the 1935 set, in front of Denison House and no.49. A young one had also been planted in front of Denison House. A triangular group of three young ones had been planted in front of Whitemeadows.
1999: 6. Only one mature one remained, in front of no.49. It has very sparse foliage. The other had gone by 1997 and been replaced by a young one on about the same spot, which is still very small. The four young ones seen in 1981 are now well established.

SWEET CHESTNUT
c1935: 1
1981: 1. The same one. It is on the left of the drive to no.39, a fine big tree.
1999: 1. Still the same. Measured as 60 feet tall.

HORSE CHESTNUT
c1935: 1
1981: 1. The same one. It is near the Sweet Chestnut, a bit further up the drive, and matches it in size.
1999: 1. Still the same.

HAZEL
c1935: None
1981: None

1999: 1. First noticed in 1997 growing from the bottom of the big cherry tree mentioned above. Well established, producing nuts.

SWEET GUM (Liquidambar styraciflua)
c1935: None
1981: 1. The small rounded tree nearest to Hudnall Lane. This was planted in about 1965 to commemorate the Golden Jubilee of the Women's Institute.
1999: 1. Still there and not much bigger, though very healthy.

IRON TREE (Parrotia persica)
c1935: None
1981: None
1999: 1. Planted March 1999 by Francis Cory-Wright in front of no.47

Birds

by Pat Anstee

Our house, Beech Corner (at Hudnall), was one of those used by the British Trust for Ornithology for periodic bird censuses. The Trust was then based in Tring, and subsequently moved to Norfolk.

We took up residence in October 1987, and on Christmas Eve I answered the door to be greeted by a very large hairy man with an enormous bucket of peanuts, informing me that he was the birdman! There was mutual confusion, Chris Mead not being aware that the house had changed hands, but we

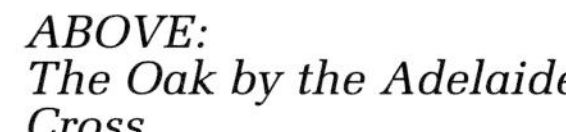

ABOVE:
The Oak by the Adelaide Cross

LEFT:
Sparrowhawks

RIGHT:
Lapwing

Tawny Owl

The photographs of birds and mammals on these pages are by Ernie Janes.

subsequently came to know him very well. I was assured it was a regular event for Chris and his team to put up nets, fill up nut feeders all round the garden, and subsequently count, weigh and ring the caught birds. This happened twice a year for some years, and the following is a typical count:

Dunnock	1
Goldcrest	2
Robin	1
Willow Tit	1
Blue Tit	67
Coal Tit	4
Great Tit	18
Nuthatch	4
Chaffinch	6
Greenfinch	6
TOTAL	110

MORE BIRDS

Editor's note: The next list is typical of the village gardens. Most would have a similar list, missing a few and adding others. Of the ten species in Pat Anstee's list above only the Willow Tit is missing here.

by Wallace Peters

PULRIDGE HOUSE EAST

The garden is immediately adjacent to fields from the northwest to the southeast and is only 100 metres from the edge of the Ashridge Forest to the southwest. Since 1979 we have observed the following species either in the garden, on the fences or flying above the house:

Ruddy Shelduck: A pair were seen sitting on the chimney for several hours in the early 1980's
Sparrowhawk: Fairly often hunting in the adjacent field or sitting on the fence
Pheasant: Occasional visitor to the garden, especially in winter
Wood Pigeon: Always nesting in the large oak tree
Collared Dove: Usually a pair feeding on the lawn and probably nesting in the laurel hedge
Green Woodpecker: A frequent visitor to the lawn and path to seek insects
Great Spotted Woodpecker: Very fond of nuts in the bird feeders
Skylark: Was flying in the adjacent field in 1979 and 1980 but has not been seen since.
House Martin: Nests here and on the next house every year
Pied Wagtail: Irregular visits, usually by single birds
Starling: Constant visitor and may nest in the garden
Jay: Irregular visitor
Magpie: A regular resident nesting in the oak and beech trees

Rook: Common, but has not nested here
Wren: A constant companion, nests here every year
Dunnock: Also a constant resident, breeds in the bushes
Goldcrest: Has visited the bird feeders
Spotted Flycatcher: Occasional visitor, nested here two years running
Robin: A constant resident, breeds in the bushes
Blackbird: Regularly breeds in hedges
Song Thrush: Here most years and nests in hedges or roses
Fieldfare: Regular visitor late autumn, sometimes in small flocks feeding on berries
Blue Tit: Nests here every year
Coal Tit: Nests here most years
Great Tit: Nests here every year
Long-tailed Tit: Has nested here twice, common visitor in summer
Nuthatch: Seen occasionally about ten years ago
Tree Creeper: Occasional visitor to old apple tree
House Sparrow: Was common in garden up to mid 1980's but not seen for some years
Chaffinch: Regular visitor and feeds on nuts every winter
Bullfinch: Occasional pair seen most years
Greenfinch: A regular resident and feeds during winter
Siskin: Seen on bird feeders one winter only
Goldfinch: Present most years and has nested in front wall Wisteria
Linnet: Nests in hedge most years
Yellowhammer: Present most years and probably nests in hedges here
Small green parrot, unknown species: One seen on chimney in about 1980.

A FEW MORE COMMENTS BY THE EDITOR

The Buzzard has started breeding at Hudnall in the last year or two.
The Cuckoo, which we expect to hear every spring, was, for the first time, not heard at all in 1999 in some parts of the village.
The Collared Dove only became a British bird in the 20th century, and is now common.
The Skylark is still seen in some parts of the village, but is much less common than in former times.
The Nightingale abundant in the mid 20th century in Ashridge is now seldom, if ever, heard.
The Song Thrush still sings regularly every spring and summer in the village, though the subject of a national decline.
The Tree Sparrow has become very rare in the last few years, and may have disappeared from the village.
The House Sparrow is still regularly seen in the village, though suffering an alarming disappearance from large areas of London in 1999.

The following birds, though not on the garden lists above, are actually regularly seen in the parish, either all the year round or in their appropriate season - I think I could safely say every year:

Heron, Mallard, Kestrel, Moorhen, Lapwing, Herring Gull, Common Gull, Black-headed Gull, Stock Dove, Turtle Dove (perhaps not in last few years), Little Owl, Tawny Owl, Swift, Swallow, Jackdaw (A flock live near the village centre all the

Maundy Eve. 1996

Full moon hanging low,
fat in black arms
red as the sun, glowing in
pipistrelle April dusk

under leafless branches,
antlers hold starlight,
deer move softly through
trees, air chill
as splintered ice,
enfolds the garden;

above the huddled cottages,
high to the north west
thistledown,
a dandelion clock
its slender stalk,
a comet's tail.

Mary Blake

In spring 1996 the comet Hyakutake made a few appearances. It had only a short period to appear in our skies while visible to the naked eye, and cloud was frequent at this time. When it could be seen it was quite striking.
In spring of the following year comet Hale-Bopp was seen by everybody for some weeks. It was small but beautiful and unmistakable with its two tails, one straight and one curved. - Ed

year round), Carrion Crow, Blackcap, Willow Warbler, Chiffchaff, Redwing, Mistle Thrush.

Other observers may well add a few more to this list of regulars, as well as many less frequent species.

Mammals

MISCELLANEOUS GLEANED INFORMATION AND PERSONAL OBSERVATION BY THE EDITOR

Hedgehog: Seems to be rare in this area. Not even found run over by cars.
Mole: Common.
Common Shrew: Common in live-traps, Hudnall.
Pygmy Shrew: Was common in live-traps, Hudnall, around 1980.
Bats: I haven't got the information that bat experts would be able to provide for the area. The bats around Hudnall Park look like Pipistrelles. Brown Long-eared Bats were recently identified in the churchyard.

Fallow Deer Fawn

Hedgehog

Fox: Always some around.
Stoat: Observed occasionally.
Weasel: Observed from time to time, and accidentally live-trapped at Hudnall Park twice since 1978.
Badger: Always some around.
Red Deer: Not seen here now. The herd kept in Ashridge Park were mostly rounded up in the 1920's and taken to Richmond Park, and the remainder were shot.
Sika Deer: Not seen here now. There used to be some in the Park in the Brownlow days.
Fallow Deer: Always some around. Confined to Ashridge Park in the Brownlow days but now unrestricted. A few hundred live in the neighbourhood of the National Trust Ashridge Estate. They have favourite areas in which they congregate, such as the field in front of Ashridge House, some areas which they avoid, such as the fenced parts of narrow roads, and they make casual use of everywhere else in the parish, especially at night. There are three main colour forms, the blackish, the off-white and the very attractive menil, which is bright brown dappled with cream spots.
Chinese Muntjac: Always some around, but they quickly bolt for cover when they know they are seen, and are usually solitary or just two.
Brown Hare: In the parish, but I have only seen them just outside the area.
Rabbit: Warrens of them are found throughout the parish in both woodland and open land. After the destruction of the majority of the population by myxomatosis in the early 1950's, there was a slow increase of resistant survivors. The disease is still seen to affect them in some areas, but the population is generally in good health.
Red Squirrel: Absent from the area for probably over 50 years now.
Grey Squirrel: Always some around. There has been a family of jet black Grey Squirrels at Ringshall since the late 1970's at least.
Dormouse: Rare.
Fat Dormouse: Always some around, noticed when they get into roof spaces and are heard dashing about.
Harvest Mouse: Rare or absent nowadays.
Wood Mouse (Long-tailed Field Mouse): Very common. Easily live-trapped.
House Mouse: Appears in houses and outhouses. Probably always somewhere about.
Brown Rat: Every so often a colony becomes a nuisance.
Bank Vole: Very common. Easily live-trapped.
Field Vole (So-called "Short-tailed Field Mouse"): Common. Live-trapped fairly often at Hudnall Park.

Common Dormouse

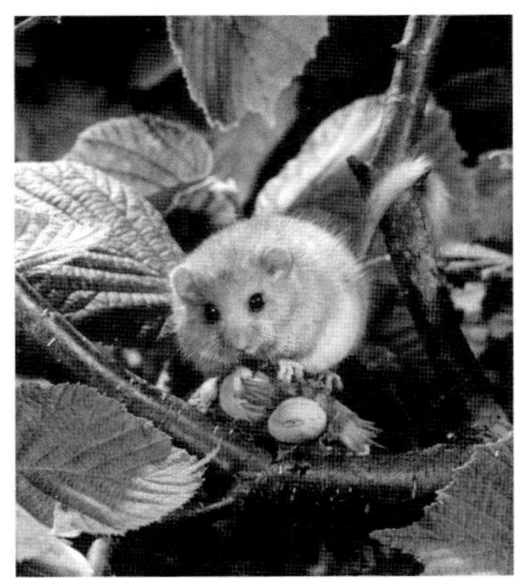

AMPHIBIANS
The Common Frog, Common Toad and Smooth Newt are all common.

REPTILES
Grass Snakes and Slow Worms are seen infrequently, but enough to assume a resident population.

Hoverflies

Professor Wallace Peters (whose profession is in both the entomology and parasitology of tropical medicine, and is a world expert on mosquitoes) has also made a list of the hoverflies caught in his garden, mainly from 1991 to 1998. Hoverflies are of no medical significance and do not bite or sting, but are interesting "mimics" of small wasps and bees, and are often seen on flowers. The list contains 45 species, and has been placed in the records of the National Hoverfly Survey. One is shown in the colour section)

Butterflies *(see colour pages for illustrations)*

In 1936, when Richard Bagshawe was 12 years old, he made a study of the butterflies on Hudnall Common. He identified 30 species by comparing them with a reference collection. He was living at Dagnallhill at the time. The nearest comparison I have is the list for Hudnall Park in recent years. Also Wallace Peters has sent me a list of those seen in his garden, Pulridge House East, near Cromer Cottages. Here the lists are set together for comparison:

Species	**Hudnall Common** 1936	**Hudnall Park** 1978 to 1999	**Pulridge House** 1979 to 1999
Small Skipper	Present	Regular in July	Seen
Essex Skipper	—	Identified in 1991,1992	Seen
Large Skipper	Scarce	Regular in July	—
Clouded Yellow	Rare	—	—
Brimstone	Common	Every year	Seen
Large White	Common	Every year	Seen
Small White	Common	Every year	Seen
Green-veined White	Present	Every year	Seen
Orange Tip	Common	Regular in May	Seen
Green Hairstreak	Rare	—	—
Purple Hairstreak	Rare	—	Seen once
Small Copper	Very common	Most years a few	Seen
Small Blue	Present	—	—
Brown Argus	Present	Once, August 1994	—
Common Blue	Very common	Every year a few	Seen
Chalkhill Blue	Common	—	—
Holly Blue	—	Most years a few	Seen
Red Admiral	Present	Every year	Seen
Painted Lady	Present	Most years	Seen
Small Tortoiseshell	Very common	Every year, esp. Sept	Seen
Peacock	Common	Every year, esp. Sept	Seen
Comma	Present	Most years a few	Seen
Pearl-bordered Fritillary	Present	—	—
Dark Green Fritillary	—	—	Seen once
Silver-washed Fritillary	Present	Once or twice, pre-1990	—
Speckled Wood	Present	Every year	Seen
Wall	Present	Last seen Aug. 1990	Seen
Marbled White	Present	Regular in July	Seen
Grayling	Present	—	—
Gatekeeper	Present	Regular in July	Seen
Meadow Brown	Very common	Commonest sp. July	Seen
Ringlet	Present	Regular in July	Seen
Small Heath	Present	1990 and 1999	—
TOTAL	30	25	23

The disappearance of the Chalkhill Blue and the Grayling are part of a national reduction in their range. The 30 species at Hudnall Common compares particularly favourably with the other two lists because it was made in a single year. Hudnall Common has not got such good butterfly habitats now, except for the verge of Hudnall Lane.

Maps

ECCLESIASTICAL PARISHES WITHIN THE CIVIL PARISH

SCALE OF MAIN MAPS

1: 27550
2.3 inches to the mile
36.3mm to the km

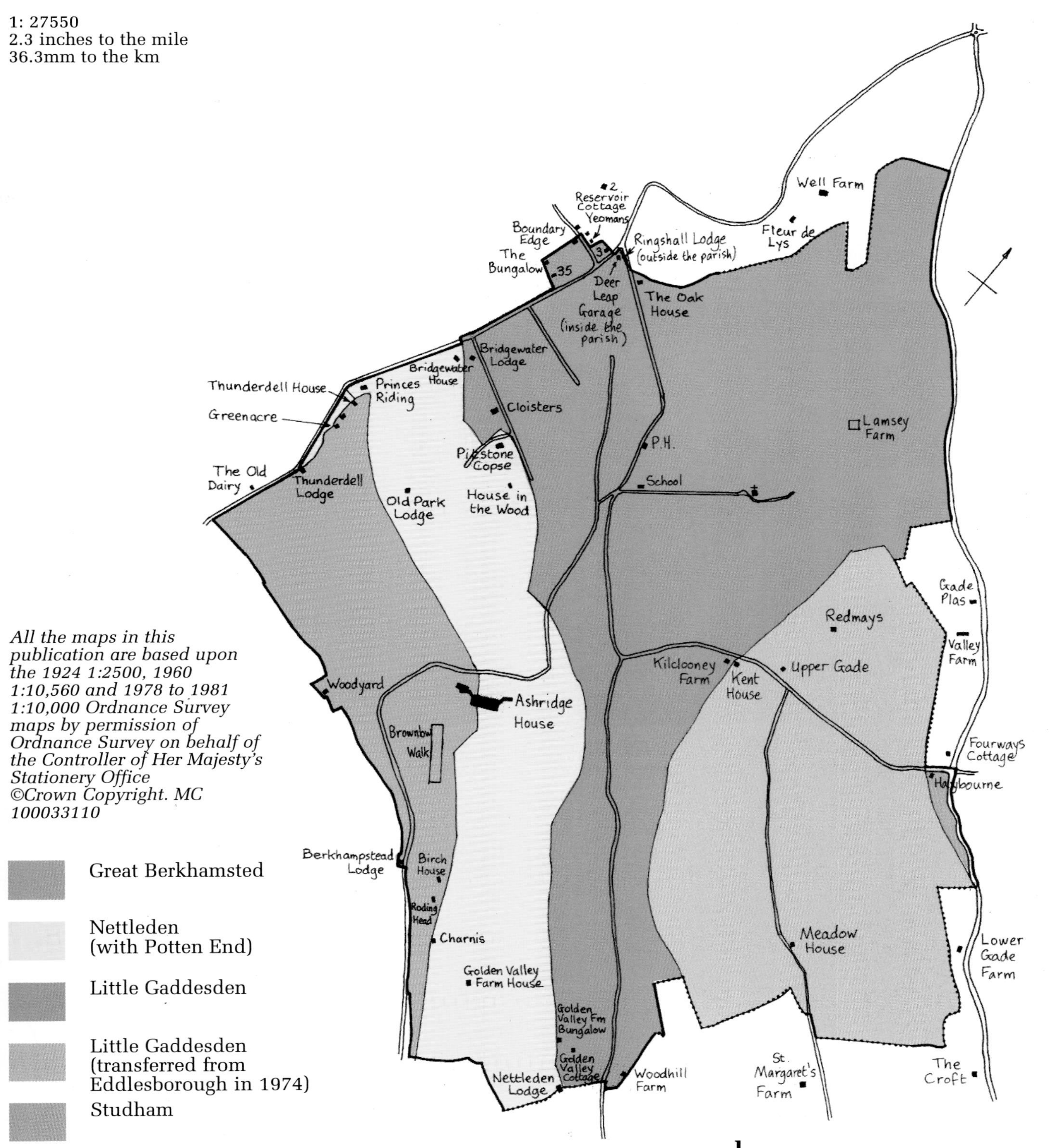

All the maps in this publication are based upon the 1924 1:2500, 1960 1:10,560 and 1978 to 1981 1:10,000 Ordnance Survey maps by permission of Ordnance Survey on behalf of the Controller of Her Majesty's Stationery Office ©Crown Copyright. MC 100033110

- Great Berkhamsted
- Nettleden (with Potten End)
- Little Gaddesden
- Little Gaddesden (transferred from Eddlesborough in 1974)
- Studham

Land use comparisons

The first Land Utilisation Survey of Britain was undertaken by L. Dudley Stamp of the London School of Economics in the early 1930s. He arranged for schools all over the country to submit the raw mapped data through county organisers. It was concerned with agricultural productivity in a few broad categories and only required 6 colours overprinted on black and white base maps. Subsequent surveys have been more ambitions and have varied the definitions of categories and allocation of colours. We have converted them all to a unified scheme as closely as possible.

More details about the key to the colours can be found overleaf on page lV.

Most of the farmland was surveyed by the children of the village school. They noticed that pasture was more frequently located on the plateau, and arable land on the slopes, and that this pattern continued across the valley into Studham. This, however, was rather a local phenomenon, and only a few miles away opposite examples could be found. It was also temporary, as the 1960 survey shows. The areas not covered by our school are added from Dudley Stamp's survey. Extra detail has been added from other maps and local information. The only post-Brownlow buildings shown are The Spinney, Ashridge Cottages, The Oak House and Kaim End.

1931

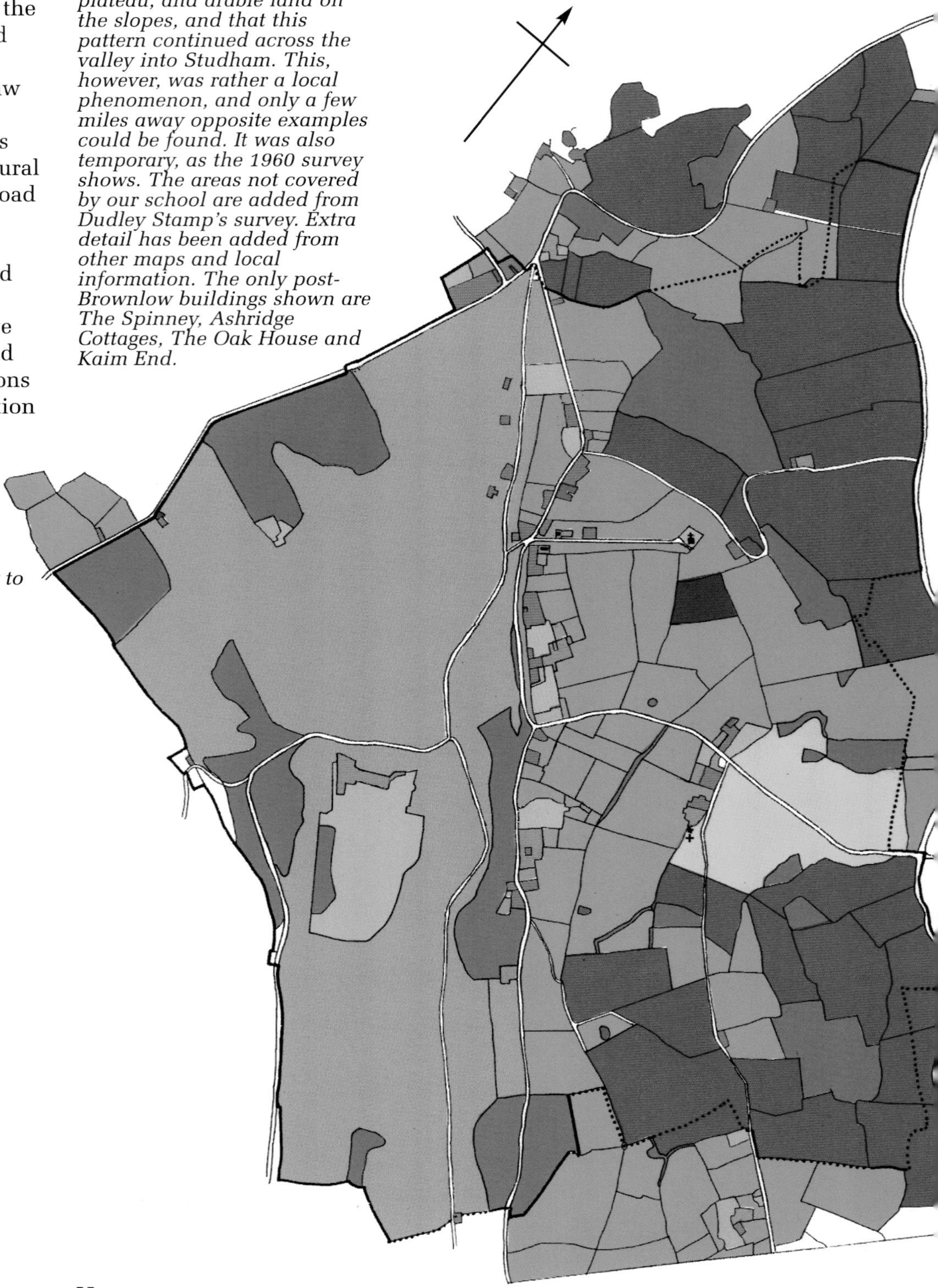

1960

This survey was organised by Alice Coleman of Kings College, London. Little Gaddesden, Ringshall and Ashridge were surveyed by Miss Ward of Berkhamsted Girls School; Hudnall by R. Hammond of Fryerns School, Basildon; Dagnall by Bennetts End School, Hemel Hempstead. We have added further details from aerial photographs and local information.

ARABLE LAND

Unnamed crop

Wheat

Barley

Oats

Oilseed rape

Linseed

Green fodder: Kale, Clover

Potatoes

HORTICULTURE

Orchards and glasshouses etc *(see page IV)*

OTHER VEGETATION

Agricultural grass

Tended or recreational

Parkland (1931 map only)

Rough open vegetation

Woodland and scrub

BUILDINGS WITH THEIR YARDS AND GARDENS

Private residential with one or two acres per residence

Denser residential or house plotted separately from its land

Commerce and industry

Other buildings

Utilities

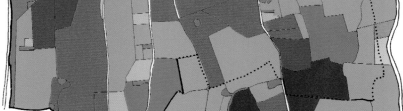

LAND USE *continued)*

ARABLE LAND

Unnamed crop

Wheat

Barley

Oats

Oilseed rape

Linseed

Green fodder: Kale, Clover

Potatoes

HORTICULTURE

Orchards and glasshouses (see note above)

OTHER VEGETATION

Agricultural grass

Tended or recreational

Parkland (1931 map only)

Rough open vegetation

Woodland and scrub

BUILDINGS WITH THEIR YARDS AND GARDENS

Private residential with one or two acres per residence

Denser residential or house plotted separately from its land

Commerce and industry

Other buildings

Utilities

The key shows Orchards and Glasshouses on the 1931 map and includes market gardens and nurseries on the 1960 and 1999 maps.

In 1931 rotational grass leys were plotted as arable land.

Parkland (grass with scattered trees) is only shown on the 1931 map.

Rough open vegetation includes grass, bracken and set-aside.

Light blue residential areas often include small paddocks or woodland.

Surveyed by the Editor with the help of aerial photographs and local information.

1999

MAIN FARMS AND GRAZING HOLDINGS, 1999
Excluding farm woodlands

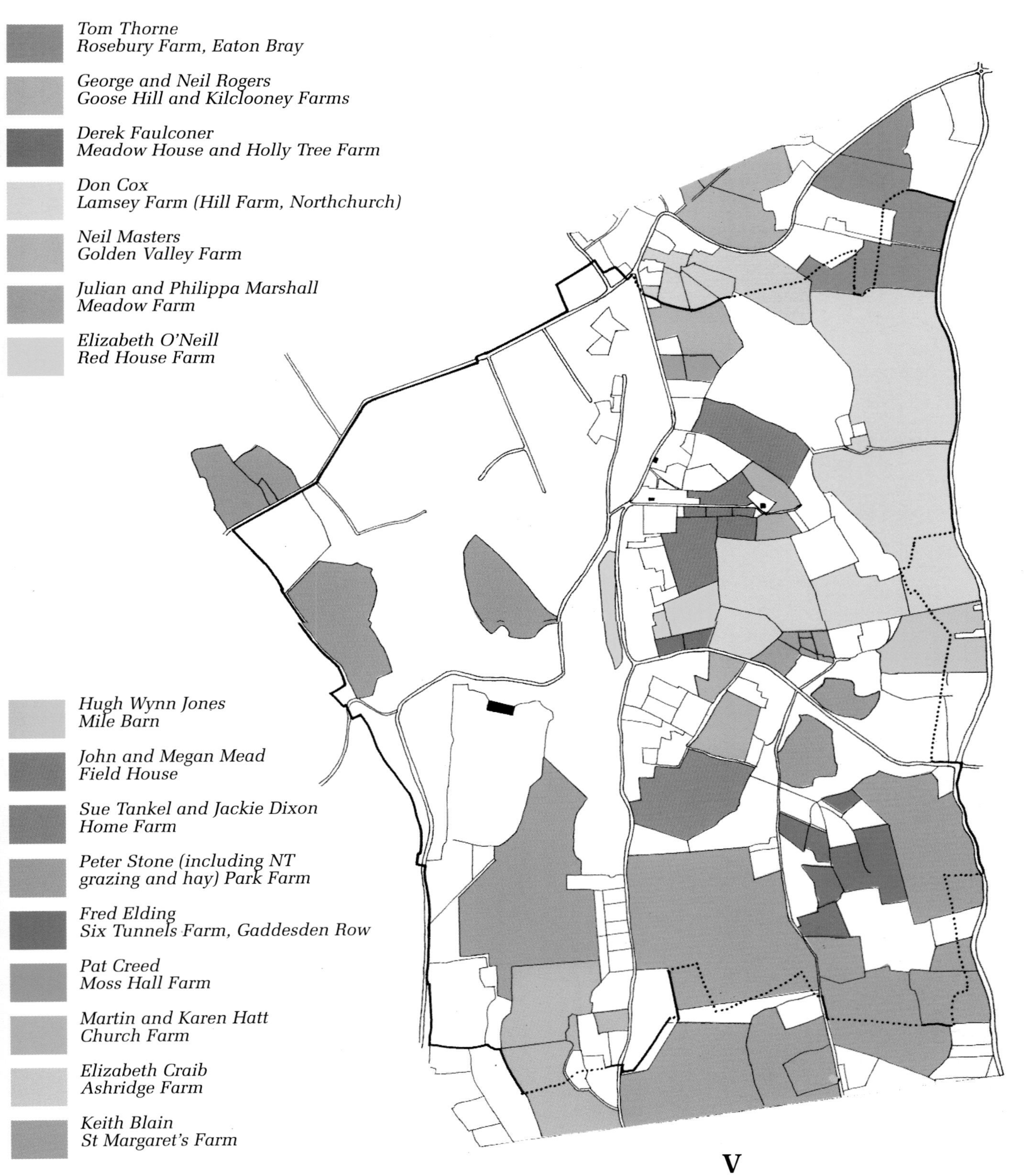
Tom Thorne
Rosebury Farm, Eaton Bray
George and Neil Rogers
Goose Hill and Kilclooney Farms
Derek Faulconer
Meadow House and Holly Tree Farm
Don Cox
Lamsey Farm (Hill Farm, Northchurch)
Neil Masters
Golden Valley Farm
Julian and Philippa Marshall
Meadow Farm
Elizabeth O'Neill
Red House Farm
Hugh Wynn Jones
Mile Barn
John and Megan Mead
Field House
Sue Tankel and Jackie Dixon
Home Farm
Peter Stone (including NT
grazing and hay) Park Farm
Fred Elding
Six Tunnels Farm, Gaddesden Row
Pat Creed
Moss Hall Farm
Martin and Karen Hatt
Church Farm
Elizabeth Craib
Ashridge Farm
Keith Blain
St Margaret's Farm

Field and Wood names in 1999

1. **Oakley Wood**
2. Goose Hill
3. **Levi Spring**
4. Dick's Hill (School field)
5. Small Top
6. Big Top
7. Near Triangle
8. Far Triangle
9. Sloping Field
10. Cadin (Big Bottom)
11. Gaddesden Field
12. **Hoo Wood**
13. Lamsey House Field
14. Hoo Field
15. Old Dairy Meadows
16. Four Acres
17. Six Acres
18. **Thunderdell Wood**
19. The Old Park
20. North Park
21. Over The Road
22. The Green
23. Applegarth Field
24. The Playing Field
25. The Strip
26. Church Meadow
27. Church Field
28. Home Field
29. Pond Field
30. The Paddock
31. **Badger Wood**
32. Mile Barn Field
33. Engine House Field
34. Mill Field
35. Stoneshill
36. Grey's Field (Fifteen Acre)
37. Nursery Field
38. Valley Farm
39. **Harding's Rookery**
40. **Cromer Wood**
41. By The House (Hatties)
42. The Apple Field
43. Hudnall Common
44. South Park
45. Birds Pickle
46. Little Russels Piece
47. Bungalow Field
48. Upper Tem Field
49. Steep or Lower Tem
50. **Whitfield Spring**
51. Fourways
52. Scoop Field
53. Park Field
54. Arden Hills
55. **Webb's Copse**
56. Mill Field
57. Essex
58. Marshalls
59. **Pulridge Wood**
60. Reddings
61. Great Nuns
62. The Nunnery
63. Wood Meadow
64. **Hill Wood**
65. Grossmiths
66. Wood Field
67. Mrs King's
68. New Grounds
69. Alford Arms 1
70. The Gallop
71. Macnally's

EARL BROWNLOW'S ESTATE COMPARED TO THE NATIONAL TRUST ESTATE

Reproduced by Paul Burdess from the original Ashridge Estate map

National Trust Estate 1999

Earl Brownlow's Estate 1883

Little Gaddesden Parish

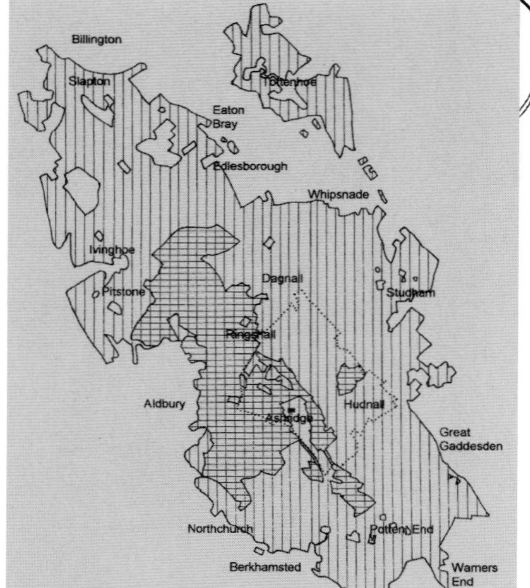

Public footpaths and bridleways

LITTLE GADDESDEN PARISH 1999

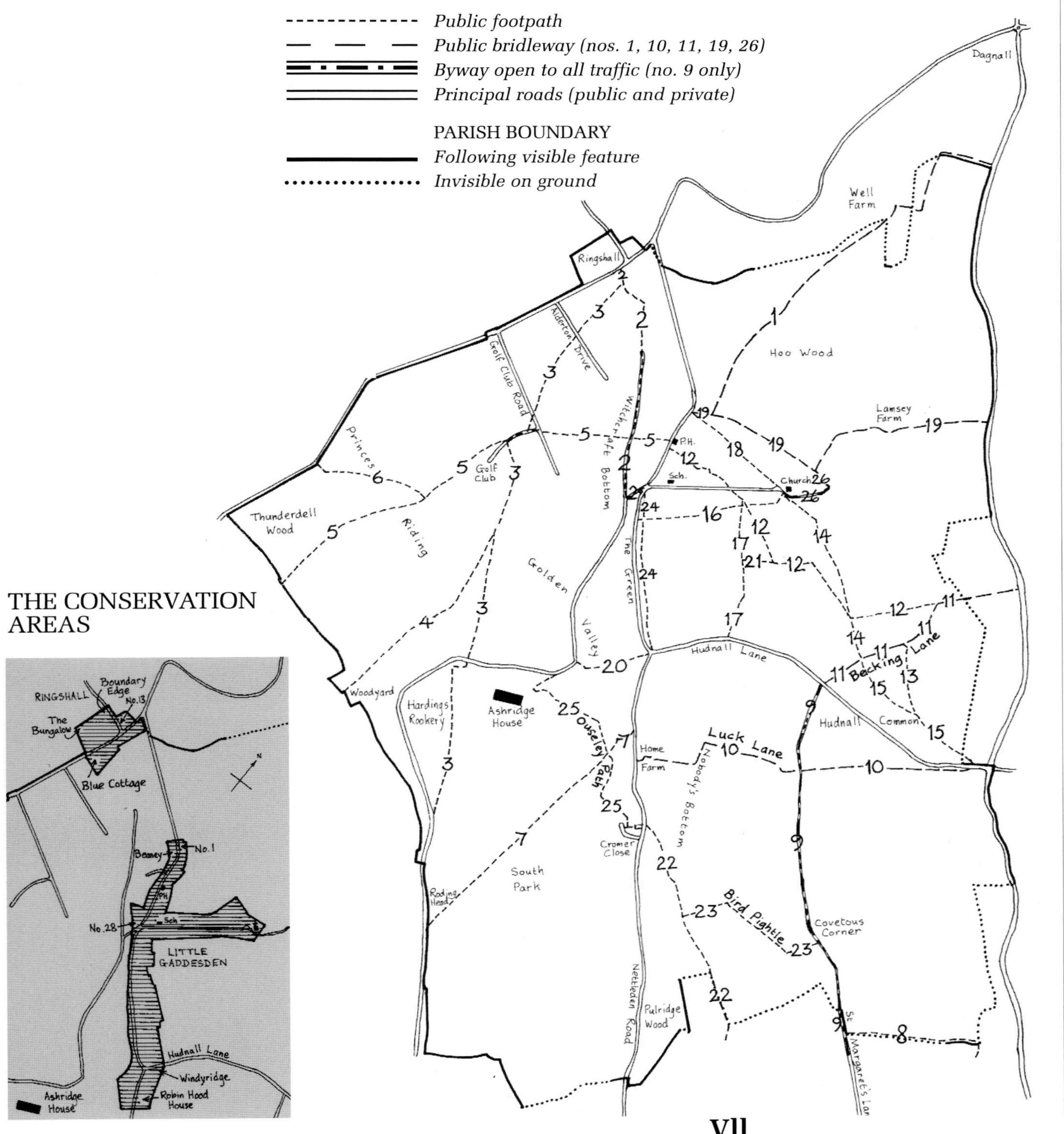

A miscellany of colour images

TOP LEFT:
A mode of transport reminiscent of a bygone era photographed at Home Farm in 2000

TOP RIGHT
A rider passes the entrance to Red House Farm, site of the former Brownlow Estate

CENTRE:
The old county boundary on Kilclooney Farm

BELOW:
A welcome sight after a Rural Heritage Society walk!

BOTTOM RIGHT:
A blaze of colour - Alan Bunting with his prize Dahlias in 1999

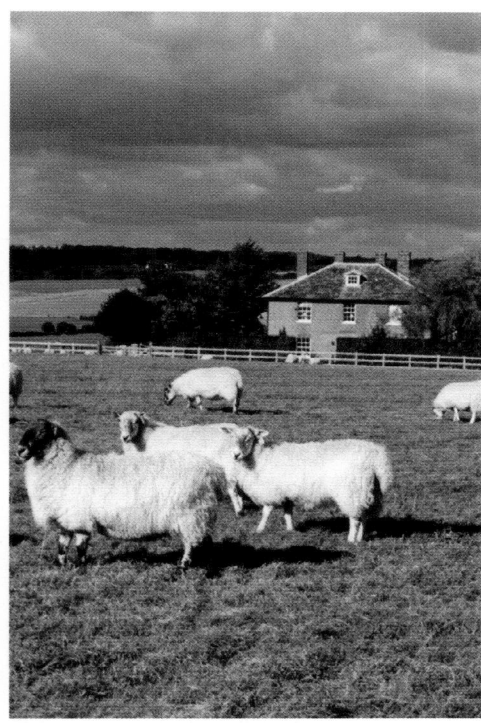

FAR LEFT:
Sheep at Church Farm, 1999

LEFT:
Megan Mead's Ponies, Church Road

BELOW:
Horses opposite the Green

RIGHT:
Covetous Corner, 1999

CENTRE:
Hot air balloons over Home Farm, 1988

BELOW:
Little Gaddesden Church with Church Farm sheep in the foreground

LEFT:
The view to Whipsnade across the valley and Lamsey Farm

CENTRE:
Painted Lady and Small Copper butterflies and a Hoverfly - Syrphus ribesii - photographed by Wallace Peters

BOTTOM RIGHT:
Another view of Little Gaddesden Church in May 2000

TOP:
Bales in Hugh Wynn Jones's field, behind Gade Plas

RIGHT:
Shiamala Comer's 'Dexter" cattle

BOTTOM:
Three counties seen from Ashridge Farm: The foreground and left background are in Buckinghamshire. Hertfordshire lies along the valley bottom and Bedfordshire is far right

LEFT:
Old Park - Park Farm

BELOW:
Hay baling in Russell's Piece at Hudnall Park, 1979

RIGHT:
The magnificent ceiling in the Drawing Room at Ashridge, created in the mid 1850s and cleaned in 1996. The room has been renamed 'Lady Marion Alford Room'

BELOW:
View of Ashridge House from the garden

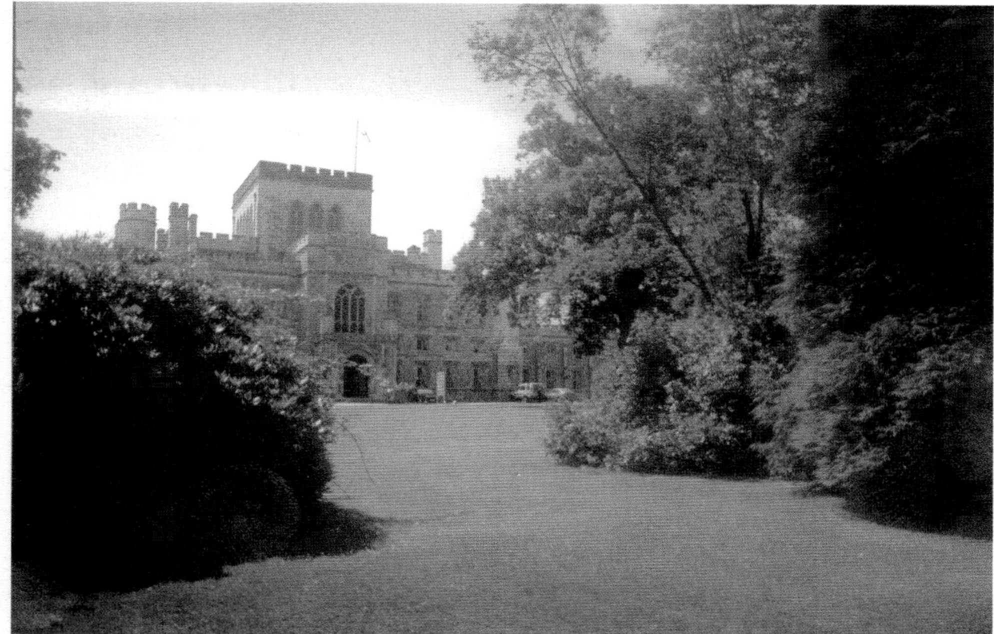

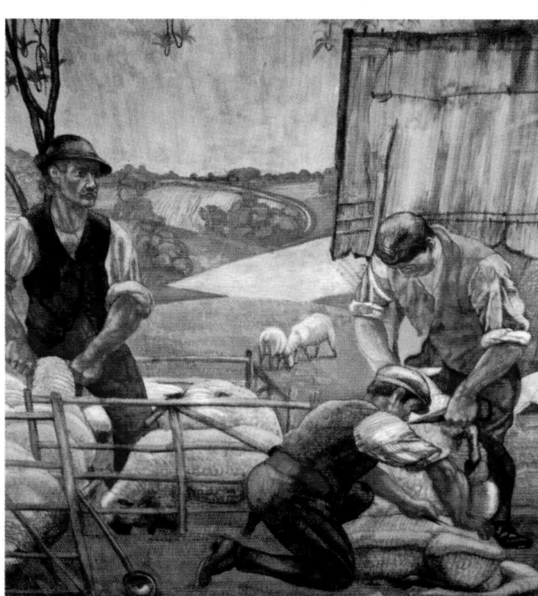

LEFT:
Ashridge House - the grand entrance

CENTRE LEFT:
Everywhere you look there are flowers

CENTRE RIGHT:
A fresco by Constance Lane and Dora Carrington painted in 1913 in the Servant's Hall, now the Learning Resource Centre

BOTTOM:
Ashridge woods

TOP LEFT:
October House, from the Little Gaddesden Village Quilt (far right) made in 1990 by local volunteers to a design by Virginia Westmacott. It won the section "Our green and pleasant land" in the National Patchwork competition

CENTRE:
The WI in 2000:

BACK ROW:
Chris Mawhood, Fiona Masters, Mo Grainger, Virginia Westmacott, Anne Isherwood, Janet Drinkwater

THIRD ROW:
Pauline Case, Peggy Heron, Sheila Dalton, Jean Jones, Rita Humphreys, Anne Wooster, Betty Rogers, Barbara Mogg

SECOND ROW:
Edith Cowlard, Bessie Gibson, Jeanne Hope, Chris Francis, Joan Burch, Daphne Geater, Phyl Mountfort, Eve Ouseley, Mary Rogers, Jan Maclarty, Shirley Reinecke

FRONT ROW:
Tess Faulconer, Sue Norton, Geraldine Berry, Blanche Ashman, Janet Davis, Anne Kirkpatrick (President), Marjorie Marshall, Mary Fletcher, Diana Rait Kerr, Mary Lishman

BOTTOM
'Aspiring Arches" The tapestry made for Ashridge for the millennium (see page 149)

A miscellany of village families

EDITOR'S INTRODUCTION

Do not look for any reason why people in this chapter are here, or why those who are not are not. Suffice it to say that there were still some pieces of paper in my files after all the other chapters and sections had been compiled, but before I finally said, "Enough!"

I have not left them to the final chapter because that privileged position has been reserved for those few families who have lived in the village for the whole century.

Here they are then, not selected for significance, nor a typical sample, but just a mixture of people who have lived in the village at some time in the last hundred years.

The Ashby family

Captain G.H. Ashby and his wife Diana came to the village in 1959 and were actively involved in its life. Diana was very keen on gardening and wild life generally, and used to run the plant stall at the village fête. In the VPA Show picture on page 253 she is the winner of the Cookery Cup and the Duncan Rose Bowl for Flower Arranging. She used to have a Pied Flycatcher nesting in her garden at Starswood, a rare bird for this area. The track of a Roman Road was predicted by Richard Bagshawe to pass through her garden, and she found an area particularly rich in flints which may have been its route. She left the village in 1982, her husband having died some years earlier.

Their son Nigel is a cabinet maker who worked at furniture restoration at a workshop at Hall Farm, home of the Cullen family, for 12 years. He also made miniature reproductions of furniture. (see page 99).

Richard Bagshawe

Richard is one of our local historians, although an engineer by profession. In this he was like his father, "Tom" Bagshawe (iron founder, engineer, antarctic geologist and founder of Luton Museum and Art Gallery). Richard lived for a time at "Hill Wood", Dagnall, which his father built.

From that base Richard explored Hudnall as a boy, (see chapter 18). Although obtaining an engineering degree at Cambridge and working for G.E.C. he also became a keen historian and joined the group calling themselves the Viatores who specialised in tracing Roman roads. Their inspiration was Ivan D. Margary, the expert in this field in Britain in the 1930's to his death in 1976, who had also established a numbering system for the roads. Richard has lived at Kent House in Hudnall Lane since 1951. Accordingly, we can now partly follow the routes of roads 169 along Gaddesden Row towards Eaton Bray; 169A (Roman development from Belgic route?) from Boxmoor, through Frithsden, via Woodyard and on to join the Icknield Way at Pitstone; and 169B (military?) running through St Margarets, across the fields between Hudnall and Little Gaddesden, and from Beaney up to Ringshall and on to Wards Hurst (hurst = look-out). The agger of this one, somewhat parallel to St Margaret's Lane, was distinctly visible in the 1950's, though almost impossible to see now.

Other local features which Richard has pointed out include the field marks of a possible mediaeval village in a meadow belonging to Meadow Farm, Hudnall.

The Bunting family

The Bunting family first appeared in Little Gaddesden in 1928, but their involvement in the practical side of village life makes you think there must always have been Buntings here.

William George "Shep" Bunting worked at Sandringham, and then in Middlesex, before coming here to work as shepherd at Home Farm, q.v. His wife was Martha, and his three sons were Stanley ("Nippy"), Thomas and George.

THE BYRNE FAMILY

Returning to the English countryside from Germany, Pat and Harry Byrne renamed their house Thornwood, after the first German village they had lived in. They then discovered that the first owners had called it Magumba on returning from East Africa and the second owners renamed it Kalkudah on returning from Sri Lanka. Pat and Harry are involved in Berkhamsted Baptist Church and have nine grandchildren who visit them.

Shep and Martha died in the 1950's and their three sons have all died now, though their widows outlived them: Stanley's wife Hannah died in 1998, George and Thomas's wives, Betty and Vera, were still alive in 1999, though Betty died early in 2000. Stanley and Hannah had two sons - Richard and Kenneth. Thomas and Vera had a son - Alban. George and Elizabeth had three sons - Alan, Tony and Peter. Thomas and Vera moved to Somerset in 1971.

Three families of Buntings still live in the village:
Kenneth and his wife Becky live at one of the Greenkeepers' Cottages on the golf course, with their daughter and son, Emma and Gary. Also on the golf course live Peter and his son David. Until recently his wife Janet and his other son Phillip were also here.

In Cromer Close lives Alan and his wife Jane. Of their five children, Charlotte, Laura, Andrew, Daniel and Graham, all but Daniel had moved away by 1999. Alan and Daniel have both kept sheep at times, and been successful exhibitors of garden flowers and produce at the VPA show. Alan was a prolific prize-winner for many years and has for years been the lightning-speed auctioneer selling off the unwanted produce at the end of every summer and winter show.

The Collier family

by Wayne Collier

My Great Grandad Stanley Albert Collier married my Great Nan Eve Putman and lived at Chapel Street in Berkhampstead and had four children, Percy, Stanley, Doreen and Dave and moved to Little Gaddesden House in a flat and then moved into 2 Chapel Close just before the second world war in 1937.

My Great Grandad was a painter and decorator at Ashridge College after the first world war and my Great Nan, who was from Fulham, born in 1903,worked at house cleaning and office cleaning at Van de Vierens staple factory in Hudnall Lane and she also took in people's washing. Great Grandad died in 1944 and would be over a hundred years old if he were still alive. Great Nan Eve died in 1978.

Their four children went to Little Gaddesden School and my Grandfather Stanley Collier has lived at 21 Cromer Close for 44 years with his wife Maura, formerly Maura Miles, who came from Southern Ireland in 1952 and got a live-in job as a house cleaner at Ashridge College where she met and married Stanley. Together they had five children, Christine, Clive, Jackie, Rosie and Steven. But before she married Stanley she had two other children, Michael and Breda who are half-members of our family. All her adult life she worked at Ashridge College till she died.

My father Clive married my mother, Penny Rye from Bovingdon and they had me, Wayne, now 11 and my brother Ryan, age 12, who have been to Little Gaddesden School. There are altogether 14 Granchildren and one Great Grandson. Me and my brother are the fourth generation of Colliers in the village which we are proud of, and have lived at 1 Chapel Close next door to where my Great Grandparents lived all those years ago.

Editor's note: Percy Collier, Stanley's brother, is the most well-known of this family as he is so often seen out on his bicycle delivering papers.

some more by Stanley Collier

My family moved into the village from Berkhamsted in 1934. We lived in Little Gaddesden House which was owned by Miss Bridget Talbot. Over the top of the garages there were flats and we had one of them. My mum and dad had to do work for Miss Talbot, my dad had the garden and mum house work.

My dad in the first world war was in India and Germany. He died in 1944 aged 48. My mum died some years later, both buried in the old church yard.

My wife, who came from Eire, and I were married for forty years. She died in 1995 aged 62, buried in the new part. I now live at 21 Cromer Close. I have lived in the village for 66 years.

The Cripps family

History compiled by Fiona Cripps

The first of this family to come to the village were Percy and Cecily Cripps, shortly after their marriage in 1929. Their first house was Yew Tree Cottage on the Green where their only child Gordon was born. Percy was the ninth of twelve children of John and Elizabeth Cripps of Frithsden, so even before 1929 their connection was very close to the village. Cecily came from Wales in 1921.

Their next home was Beaney Cottage where Cecily was housemaid and Percy was groom and chauffeur to Mr and Mrs Gibbs, who then built Acorn Cottage for them, a few doors away. In 1946 they moved to Well Farm Cottage where Percy was groom to George and Pat Strakosch, the horse breeders. In 1953 Gordon married his first wife Dot and moved to Studham Bury Farm. In 1955 Percy and Cecily moved into the wooden bungalow Fleur de Lys on the Well Farm Estate, and in 1959 Gordon came back there to live, with his daughter Linda who was born in 1958. In 1963 Nina Winterbottom came to work at Well Farm, and Gordon married her as his second wife in 1969. Also in 1969 Percy Cripps died.

So from 1969 the family at Fleur de Lys consisted of Cecily Cripps, Gordon and Nina Cripps, and Linda Cripps. To these were added Gordon and Nina's two children Zoe and Graham in 1971 and 1974.

Gordon was a carpenter in the building trade, but also became a cabinet maker of distinction. Nina kept goats and chickens: *there is a brief account under Fleur de Lys in the smallholdings chapter.*

Meanwhile Linda grew up and left. In 1996 Gordon and Nina left for Cornwall and in December 1999 Gordon's mother Cecily died, by which time she was the only resident left in Fleur de Lys.

In the next generation, Zoe had moved away from the village, married in 1998 and now lives in Dunstable.

One branch of the family remains with us: Graham Cripps and Fiona Ruggles moved into 6 Cromer Close in 1996 and they were married in 1997. After the wedding the bride and groom rode up to the village hall reception on a gleaming green tractor, the groom driving. Tractor driving and other farm work was Graham's job, but he now works at a local quarry. Fiona's daughter Hannah is now at the village school, and Graham and Fiona's son Harry should be starting there in 2000, following the footsteps of his father, his aunt and his grandfather.

THE CORY-WRIGHT FAMILY

The first of this family to appear in the village was Elsie Montague-Hall, youngest daughter of Sir Francis Cory-Wright, Baronet. She purchased the Denison House Estate in 1925. Her brother, Sir Arthur Cory-Wright, Bart., who was High Sheriff of Hertfordshire, rented it from his sister and he and his daughter Gwenda lived there until 1928.

Sir Arthur's son Ronald did not live in the village, but when he died his widow, Mrs Geraldyn Cory-Wright, née Villiers-Stuart, came to Little Gaddesden in 1938 with her son Francis, who is the only member of the family here now.

THE CUSDINS

Teddy and Peggy Cusdin bought 34 Ringshall in 1952, having stayed here regularly with James and Mrs Crooks of Meadow Farm, Ringshall, for many years before that. Their main home was in Devonshire Place, London, but they kept both homes in regular use until the 1990's when Peggy's failing health led to their choice of Ringshall as the better place for her care. She died in 1998. aged 88. Teddy's fame in the wider world is joined with that of James Crooks, a partnership of architect and surgeon working on modern hospital design with success at Great Ormonde Street and in Hong Kong, as Canon Senar has recorded. James Crooks died in 1980.
In Little Gaddesden Teddy co-operated with Canon Senar on such projects as the reconstruction of the probable layout of the 13th to 16th century monastery at Ashridge, and the architectural diagram of the parish church. Teddy's Christmas cards are treasured because each year he sends a new reproduction of one of his own meticulous architectural paintings, with his annual message printed from his own free-syle calligraphy. In 1999 he celebrated his 91st birthday.

The Cullen family

Robert Cullen worked for the Wellcome Foundation from 1959 until he retired in 1987. Mr and Mrs Robert Cullen arrived in Little Gaddesden in 1972 when his work was moved to Berkhamsted. They bought Meadow End in Hudnall Lane from General and Mrs Grant. Their daughter Fiona attended Little Gaddesden School and was the first pupil from there to go on to Tring School. Their two sons went to Berkhamsted Boys School. The family lived away from the village briefly from 1974 to 1976, returning to live at Hall Farm, Ringshall. *(The farm land at Hall Farm had already been sold separately. See under Ashridge Farm.)*

Wilfred (Jack) Duncombe

by his son Jack Duncombe

Wilfred Duncombe (invariably and hereinafter known as Jack) was born at Ivinghoe Aston in 1896. He descended from a long line of farming stock who had lived and worked in the Vale of Aylesbury.

At an early age Jack moved with his family to live at no.35 Little Gaddesden, one of the row of red-brick 'New Houses' built by Lady Marian Alford in 1869. From the age of 5, Jack attended Little Gaddesden School under the headmastership of Samuel (Sammy) Green. "Sammy" was a stern but fair disciplinarian. He made sure that his pupils were well versed in the "3 R's", became good citizens and were well prepared for the outside world of work.

At school every boy was assigned to a community task. The young Jack's task was to hold and maintain an oil lantern, the purpose of which was to illuminate the path to the Church on winter Sundays. In those days a wide asphalt path (long since overgrown) ran from the gateway adjacent to no.5 Little Gaddesden, across Bridgewater Field and beyond to the Church. The swing gate and adjacent fencing at the far edge of Bridgewater field were painted white to facilitate recognition. He had to hang the lantern on a bracket affixed to a pathside oak tree to light the path to church for the Rector and his parishioners. (The village Rectory was then the large house now known as "Beaney" the original entrance to which was opposite no.5.)

When boys left school "Sammy" Green helped them to find suitable employment and it was through him that Jack came to be apprenticed as a blacksmith/farrier on Earl Brownlow's Ashridge estate. Here he came under the influence of Tom Rance, a stern but wise taskmaster. Rance lived in an estate house in Studham and, together with many other estate workers he walked to and from Little Gaddesden across the fields.

The Ashridge estate workshops were located each side of a broad hardstanding at the top of the Red House drive. There was separate provision for blacksmiths/farriers, carpenters, wheelwrights, painters and carriage repairers.

As a young man Jack was the last secretary of the Reading and Recreation Room Committee. This facility had been established by Earl Brownlow in the long-room at John O'Gaddesden's House and provided recreation for the young men of the parish. Following the Earl's death, however, John O'Gaddesden's House was sold to a private buyer and this club had to be disbanded.

The blacksmith/farrier's workshop was responsible for maintaining the estate fences and gates, but its main task was the shoeing of the large number of working horses on the estate and farms.

It was the introduction of the steam-powered ploughing and cultivating system by Colonel Wheatley, Earl Brownlow's Agent, that made most of the working farm horses redundant. Under this system a pair of steam traction engines, each having a powered winding drum, were adapted to draw a multi-furrow plough and other cultivating or harvesting implements to and fro across a field by means of a wire hawser. Whereas a pair of horses drawing a single-furrow plough could only complete about one acre a day, the steam-powered system considerably increased productivity.

As the number of working horses was reduced, there was a marked reduction of the workload in the farriers' workshop. The end result was that Jack became redundant. Incidentally the steam-powered system was not without disadvantages. It was said that the deeply set multi-furrow ploughs turned up the clay subsoil on the Ashridge farms to the extent that fertility and therefore crop yield were adversely affected. This is perhaps one of the earliest cases in which the mechanisation of farming activity has made farm workers and ancillary personnel redundant. The ultimate result has been the vast depopulation of the countryside, particularly amongst the younger members of society.

At this juncture Jack was employed to service and maintain the steam engine and pumping equipment at the Ashridge Waterworks situated behind the Red House. Smoke from the steam engine exhausted through a tall brick chimney, which was a prominent feature of the Gaddesden skyline until 1936, when it was demolished. Hot water exhausted from the steam engine drained into the pond alongside the main road at the bottom of Red House drive. (This pond has been recently renovated.)

(Editor's note: See the article on water supplies, page 123. The reservoir used for cooling and recycling the water from the condenser was on the field side to the north-east of the engine house.)

When Jack married Alice Wheatcroft, who originated from Wakefield, Yorkshire West Riding, he was first offered the tenancy of Thunderdell Lodge (which his future wife firmly refused). He was eventually offered the tenancy of no.4, the end one of the "Towne Houses".

In his will Earl Brownlow had indicated a wish that his sitting tenants should be offered the freehold of their houses at a preferential rate. Accordingly, in 1928 Jack purchased no.4 for the sum of £160 (a considerable sum when village people having a capital of £100 were considered to be well off).

When the Ashridge estate was finally wound up, Jack had the opportunity to recover the equipment from the former blacksmith's shop, which would have otherwise been disposed of for scrap. This he installed in an out-building at no.4.

During the years of economic depression between the two world wars, the small, mainly milk producing farms grew only sufficient crops to feed their own animals. It was cheaper to import the high quality grain for human consumption from North America. The result was that there was insufficient traditional work to enable Jack to maintain a viable business. His work became a part time occupation and latterly a hobby.

In the years following the second world war, there were many examples of decorative ironwork forged by Jack. Sadly the forces of modernisation and natural decay have wrought their toll and none now remain.

In 1926 Jack enlisted as a Special Constable in the Hertfordshire Constabulary. This was the year of the General Strike throughout Britain, during which regular policemen were drafted to police strategic Government facilities and Special Constables were recruited to undertake their normal duties. He continued to serve as a special constable thereafter. In world war two, in particular, he assisted PC Tom Parker with the vastly increased workload generated by wartime activities and, in particular by the vast hospital established at Ashridge.

His most noteworthy wartime arrest was that of a youth who on successive nights in 1943 set fire to several farmyards, to the original Little Gaddesden Village Hall and to the original thatched Ashridge Golf Clubhouse. It was feared locally that the arson attacks were the work of saboteurs sympathetic to the German cause and vigilante patrols were mounted. It was SPC Jack Duncombe who caught the youth in setting fire to the house in which he was employed. It transpired that the youth was mentally deficient and in the event he was detained but no criminal charges were brought against him.

(Editor's note: George Rogers started the trail that led to the identification of the arsonist, when he had occasion to remember a youth running past the Deer Leap Garage, and later learnt that one of the fires had just been started. Someone had laughed "like a horse" as he ran by, and later the boy had asked who it was that laughed like a horse, and George realised that this was the boy he had seen running.)

THE FOORD-KELCEY FAMILY

Some explanation of the nicknames in this family might be helpful. Irene Foord-Kelcey who originally went from England to Canada came to Little Gaddesden as a widow in 1939. She was a sculptor, a leading member of the artistic group in the village (see page 258), and known to some as Foordsey. She had two sons who lived here, Alick and Reginald (known as Jim). Alick's son Nick married Vivien, who has written some articles for this publication. Nick and Viv went to live in South Africa for a while, returning to the village in 1983, and their children are Guy and Luke. Alick and Jim have both died. Jim's wife, Philippa (Phil) is also Ada. Jim and Phil's children Cherry (really Patricia), Sally and Toby do not live here any more.

The Geater family

Sam and May Geater came to work at Hudnall Farm in about 1935 where they lived first in one of the cottages. They had a daughter and son, Roma and Keith. They later moved to Cromer Close, and subsequently May moved to Bede Court. Keith and his wife Daphne live in Coronation Villas now, opposite the Bowling Green where Keith is a well known figure constantly seen tending the immaculate turf, and where both of them regularly play. Roma married Bill Green and they live in Chapel Close

The Hambly family

Edmund Hambly was known to us all as Tim. He and Elizabeth lived at Home Farm House (after it had become separated from the actual farm) where they brought up their children Loveday, Emma, and twins Tristram and Tamsin.

Edmund was an engineer of international reputation, but when he spoke to the Gaddesden Society about his special subject of the stability of bridges, tunnels, oil rigs and the tower of Pisa, he had the gift of making it both enjoyable and easy to follow, with his own models for demonstration. When asked which option he would consider the best investment: a channel tunnel or a channel bridge (at a time when the two possibilities were being seriously considered), he replied "Ships".

He was an international consultant on oil rigs, and was elected President of the Institution of Civil Engineers in 1994.

In the village he took on the task of Group Scout Leader. *(See Scouts article)* He died in 1995 of a heart attack, aged only 52, causing great shock in the village.

His family have now moved away, his son Tristram following in his father's footsteps as an engineer.

Raymond and Dorothy Hing's three pairs of twins.

TOP TO BOTTOM: Alan and Penny, Jeffrey and Trevor, Debbie and Robert.

The Hing family

information from Jeff and Frederick Hing

The origins of the Hing Family will be found under Meadow Farm, Ringshall, where they lived and farmed from 1893 to 1928 or 29.

Joseph and Sarah Hing had eight children between 1881 and 1895, all of whom got married, unlike most of the other large families of that period of which we have details, and we have a photograph of the whole eight with their parents which must have been taken about the 1930's. In order of age they were William, Jane, Edwin Edward (Teddy), Lewis, Minnie, Joseph, Frederick and Dorothy. Descendants continued to live in the village until about 1979.

Joseph Hing senior moved to no.9 Little Gaddesden. William married Edith Bradbrook and had two children, one of whom, another Frederick, is still living in Berkhamsted. Jane married Rubin Nash and had two daughters, one of whom, Gladys, married Stanley Austin. This couple lived at 54, Little Gaddesden.

Teddy married Daisy Glenholm and set up a garage in Berkhamsted.

Lewis and his wife Annie lived at 17 Little Gaddesden and their elder son Leonard will be found on the 1939-1945 roll of honour. Lewis ran a transport service from the Bridgewater Arms, while living in one of the cottages opposite. This used to be a horse-drawn wagonette, and was particularly used for getting to and from the station. Their second son was also named Lewis.

Herbert Andrews, known as Bert, who married Minnie Hing, will be found in the Andrews family tree, and elsewhere in the book as the manager of the Manor House nursery.

Joseph junior and his wife Rose lived at 2 Hudnall Lane. They had two children, Raymond and Joan. Raymond married Dorothy Webb. They lived at 26 Cromer Close and had three sets of twins, named in the photograph taken about 1957. One died young and the others grew up and left the village, Jeffrey now living in Berkhamsted and giving us this information.

The older Frederick Hing (1893 - 1959) and his wife Kate lived at 28 Ringshall. Kate ran a tea garden in front of this house. Dorothy Hing married Arthur Putman and their daughter was Iris. The last of the family to live in the village were Gladys Austin and Raymond Hing's wife Dorothy, both of whom left around 1979.

BELOW: Joseph and Sarah Hing with all eight children in the 1930s or 1940s.

Back row left to right:

Lewis Hing, Jane Nash née Hing, Joseph Hing, William James Hing, Minnie Andrews née Hing, Edward (Teddy) Hing.

Front Row:

Dorothy Putman née Hing, Joseph Hing, Sarah Hing née Ginger, Frederick Hing

The Hunn and Marshall families

Nicky Hunn is the daughter of Julian and Philippa Marshall of Meadow Farm, Hudnall, q.v. She married Simon Hunn in 1980. They moved into no.35 Little Gaddesden, and in about 1983 bought Gade Lodge, formerly known as Le Logis, where they now live. Their information is that it is an early 1930's Whitman house, though Madeleine Gilpin, who lived there in the 1940's, reckoned that her father had it built after the war had started. (See p 66).

Their children, Pippa and Lucy, are at Haresfoot School in 1999.

Simon comes from a Berkhamsted family. His grandfather was the manager of East's timber yard.

The King family

Ralph and Val King came to Little Gaddesden in 1989. Their four daughters and one son have all now moved on and are in work: Tamsin is the wife of Phillip Waters. They live at Pitstone and he is a chef at Ashridge and the son of Ronald and Jennie Waters. Ralph and Val's son Michael is at Warners End, and their other daughters, Sharon, Joanna and Lisa, are further afield.

In business life Ralph is an engineer specialising in air conditioning and electrical installation in large buildings such as Canary Wharf and hotels in foreign cities. In Little Gaddesden, however, he and his gardener Frank Peacock and Frank's son George can often be seen carrying out minor engineering works: a new car park for the church and new churchyard paths, with the same attention to detail as is needed to fit out a new hotel in Bahrain.

He is also an enthusiastic member of the VPA, in which he serves as secretary.

The Leonhardt family

by Julie Leonhardt

We moved to Hudnall Park from Watford in 1977 when John was appointed Warden there. Our children, Alice and Peter, were three and a half years and 6 weeks old respectively. We felt fortunate to live in such a beautiful place and the sight of all the bluebells on Hudnall Common and in the woods was amazing. Canon Senar visited and blessed our house. During our first winter we found that one disadvantage of living here was the frequency of power failures, including one lasting 36 hours when all the cooking had to be done on a small camping stove and all the heating from one open fire.

I was a full-time mother and, as for many in the village, this involved a great deal of chauffeuring. For the daily run to the village school rotas were arranged with Anne Pike and Carolyn Osborn-Jones. We also joined in many church and village activities. I helped to restart the Brownies, with Ann Webster as Brown Owl. John took over the Sunday School from Iris Clayton, and later the Scouts. Highlights of those years were the school Maypole Frolics, Sausage-and-Mash Supper and Christmas Bazaar, the Gaddesden Society Annual Sports, the Drama

JEANNE HOPE

Jeanne came from Berkhamsted to 5 Church Road in 1970 and retired from teaching at St Thomas More School in 1982. An enthusiastic member of the VPA and art club, well known for her simple style of paintings of imaginary children and farmyard animals, many of which she has sold.

THE HUTTON AND MORIARTY FAMILIES

Olive and Stanley Hutton moved to Little Gaddesden in April 1995, acquiring 2 Beaney Cottage (a 1920s Whitman house, known for a time as "Chittoe") from the MacFeeter family. In the 1960s they built a house in Northchurch, spent nearly 15 years abroad and later moved to Redbourn before coming here. Their family business in Harpenden provides marketing services to some of the worlds largest companies.

They were joined in March 1997 by their youngest daughter Jacqueline Moriarty and her daughter Sophie, born December 1995. Jacqueline runs the Little Gaddesden Pre-School Group. (see page 174).

Club productions and the V.P.A. Shows.

When the children were 11 they moved on to Hemel Hempstead School. I returned to nursing for a few years, and then to part-time work in the village shop.

We moved from the Lodge to 21 Little Gaddesden in 1995. This had been the police house, Alf Sherringham being an inhabitant, and the school house where Albert and Molly Williams lived, and we are still in contact with these predecessors. John passed this way back in 1954 when, on a two-day Scout hike, he and a friend camped at Duncombe Farm, and walked through Ashridge. Other links we have discovered to earlier days of the 20th century include two old friends in Wandsworth. One is Margaret Hofmann (née Cook), who spent many happy holidays here as a child in the 1930s with her cousin Eleanor Toms (now Hollings), daughter of Henry (the estate agent) and May Toms who lived at no.38. The other is Doris Vise, now aged 97, who enjoyed several courses at Ashridge when it was a college of citizenship. Going back further, my sister has a friend, June Tompkins, whom she first met in Malawi, who is descended from Adam Tompkins, a woodman who lived at no.22 or 23 in the 18th century. It is perhaps appropriate that John is editing this book. After 22 years in the village we now feel that we really belong!

George Catchpole laid church paths in about 1955-6 with a slight camber, side gutters and surface drains as Ralph King discovered in 1999 when it was neccessary to lay a new surface.

Standing - Ralph King, Frank Peacock, David Stevens. kneeling - George Peacock

The Maylings

George Mayling says that his family came here in 1904, but there were some earlier Maylings, one of whom is worth mentioning even if no known relation. This was "Keeper Mayling" who in Vicars Bell's account of the village used to tell ghost stories about the area around Hog Hall and Gallows Hill (the ridge adjoining Ivinghoe Beacon) and who died "a very old man, sixty years ago" - that's counting back from 1949 to about 1890. In 1891 there was a George Mayling, labourer, living at Hog Hall, but he was only 64. Hog Hall is about a mile outside our parish as the crow flies. There was also a Mayling family at "28" (i.e. no.8) Ringshall at that time, and William Mayling's name is on the War Memorial, died in 1916, aged 20.

To return to our own George Mayling, his father was Jack, and his mother Nellie Mayling was a nurse and midwife from before 1914. George was born about 1933 and worked at Church Farm in the school holidays and just after he left school, and then at Home Farm for 16 years, as a stockman with the cattle. He was therefore there when the pedigree Hereford herd was being built up, and up to the time when the stock was sold and the farm bought by Mr Palmer. George mentioned that Mr Palmer took his wife's surname, she being an heiress of the Palmers of "Huntley and Palmer", biscuit manufacturers.

MOCATTA

John and Naomi Mocatta live in Little Gaddesden now. John's mother's first cousin, Fred Green, built Chudleigh in 1926 and lived there until 1941 when he moved to Worcestershire.

NASH

Dot Nash was a Londoner who met her husband Lou, from Berkhamsted, in the forces. They came to Little Gasddesden in about 1953.

Wallace and Ruth Peters

Professor Wallace Peters, known to many as Peter Peters, and his wife Ruth, came to Little Gaddesden in 1979 from Liverpool. He was the Walter Myers Professor of Parasitology in the Liverpool School of Tropical Medicine for 13 years up to 1979, and then Professor of Medical Protozoology in the London

School of Hygiene and Tropical Medicine for the next 10 years until his retirement. Now an Emeritus Professor in the University of London, he heads a research group on malaria chemotherapy at the Northwick Park Institute for Medical Research in an honorary capacity.

They live at Pulridge House East where they have added an extension designed by Paul Burdess and built by George Catchpole, almost single-handed, which includes a studio used by Ruth for her art embroidery. When the church was undergoing major repairs in 1990 to 1991, Ruth embroidered a beautiful hanging depicting a cross in blue and gold which was used behind the temporary "altar" at all the services which were held in the school hall.

THE RAFFERTY FAMILY

From conversations with Gwen and Gillian Rafferty

Kathleen Rafferty came from Ireland to Little Gaddesden with her first husband, and she had a son Denis, born in 1932. Some time after her first husband died, she was married again, to Bob Hobbs from an old village family. Bob and Kathleen lived at no.35 on the Green. Denis married Gwen Pass, whom he met in York, in 1954, and in 1956 they moved into a bungalow of Bridget Talbot's in the grounds of Little Gaddesden House, where The Bothy now stands, so this may be the same bungalow that the Purple family lived in in the mid 1930's. In 1961 they moved to 20 Cromer Close where Gwen and her daughter Gillian still live now. They had two other children, Jacqueline and Ian, both of whom have moved away. Denis Rafferty died in 1996.

The Purple and Beddall families

George Thomas Purple, who gave his name as Reginald George Purple and was known as such, married Amy Willmore in 1916 and they first came to Little Gaddesden in 1926. They lived at Lamsey Farm Cottage until at least 1933, then at the old bothy at Little Gaddesden House (near where the new house "The Bothy" stands), and when the council estate in Hudnall Lane was built in 1936-38 they moved into what was then 10 Hudnall Lane, but is now 8 Chapel Close.

Reginald worked on various farms and did building work for F.G. Whitman. Their children were George, Arthur, Stan, Doris, Elsie and Alban, which gives us an excuse for a quotation from Vicars Bell's book "Little Gaddesden" - "In South Field near Lamsey, to the north of Church Farm, there was found in 1931 an axe head of beautiful workmanship. It was young George Purple who found it, and with it the only certain evidence that early man roamed these hills of Little Gaddesden." George was about 15 in 1931.

Doris now lives in Luton, and Elsie still lives at 8 Chapel Close. She worked for over 30 years at the Vanguard staple works in Hudnall Lane. Alban Purple, born in 1933, was named after Alban Stanbridge. (Tom and Vera Bunting also named their son Alban, but I have heard of no others.) Alban worked for George Rogers, and at Ashridge as a boiler boy, and for F.G. Whitman, and also at the staple factory. He married Mary Ryall who came from Ireland to do domestic work at Ashridge, and they had one daughter, Pauline.

Alban and Mary now live in Norfolk. Pauline married Chris Beddall who has worked for many years as a gardener at Ashridge House, and who has been the Cub Scout Leader since about 1987, and was Assistant for some years before that. Pauline, who has given us this account, is a hairdresser and does part-time domestic jobs. Their children are Amy and Martin. They lived at 2 Hudnall Lane from 1976 to 1999 and then moved to Tring.

The Simmons family

There used to be two cottages, numbered 24 and 25, at the corner of Church Road where no.24 now stands. These had disappeared before the 1891 census, and the ordnance survey 1897 map shows this corner as part of the field that led right down to the church. The corner was redeveloped when Thomas Simmons, building contractor, built the present house in 1962. He and his family were the first occupiers. He donated the edge of his plot to the parish to allow room for a pavement beside Church Road, and erected a notice board for the church at the corner just outside the fence. It was vandalised from time to time, and on the last occasion uprooted from its concrete base. This occurred some time in the 1970's. Margaret Crawford, who bought the property in 1965, removed the remains with the help of George Catchpole, churchwarden, and it has not been replaced. The concrete base and the post sockets can still be seen. Part of the grass corner, outside the garden fence, is still Margaret's property, the fence being placed where it is to allow a better view for traffic. The strip opposite, outside John O'Gaddesden's fence, is similarly part of the Allens' property.

The number 25 came to be adopted for the 1957 house between Norwood Cottage and number 33, thus adding to the confusing numbering system in this area.

The family of

Dr. L. Turner

and a typical Whitman house

by Michael Turner

Highfield, the end left house of the unfortunately named 'Grovells' private road, was built in 1954 by Mr F G Whitman. *(He called it Crovells - Ed.)* A three-bedroom house of small but pleasant rooms, it occupies one acre of land. It enjoys a good view of the village Church across the fields. The soil is heavy clay with flints, is murder to dig, but grows splendid roses. The first occupants were Mr Spittle, an engineer who worked for De Havillands at Hatfield, and his mother.

Dr Leslie Turner and his wife Nancy bought the house from the Spittles in 1960 having fallen in love with the village at first sight. Dr Turner, a consultant microbiologist, had returned from Malaya where he had worked for the Colonial Medical Service. From 1959 until his retirement in 1978 he worked for the Wellcome Laboratories of Tropical Medicine, the Public Health Laboratory Service and the WHO. He was awarded the MBE in 1946 for his services as a prisoner of war of the Japanese on the Burma-Siam railway and was responsible for much of the early work on Leptospirosis or Weill's Disease.

The Turners added a wing to the house with one room up and one down, and built an entrance porch.

Nancy died in 1995 and Leslie in 1998. They are buried in the same grave in Little Gaddesden churchyard.

The Turner's only son, Lieutenant Colonel Michael Turner, retired from the Army in 1998 and with his wife Maggie and daughter Kate moved into Highfield with his widower father. On his father's death later that year, Michael became the second generation of his family to own Highfield. He has been an infantry officer, helicopter pilot and logistician. He was awarded the OBE in 1991 in the Gulf War honours list, so joining his father in that Most Excellent Order. As Chairman of the Little Gaddesden Branch of the Royal British Legion he has written the article on that organisation on page 242.

His wife Maggie, who was an Air Traffic Control officer in the RAF before her marriage, qualified as a nurse in 1998 and now works in Hemel Hempstead

DIANA RAIT KERR

Diana Rait Kerr was the Curator of Archives for the MCC (Marylebone Cricket Club) at Lord's Cricket Ground, and joint author of the official history. When it was decided to admit women members to the MCC, she was made the first one. She has lived at Ringshall since the 1960s.

THE WATERS FAMILY

Ron came to Little Gaddesden as an evacuee. He is in the wartime picture with the school pig (page 164). He stayed with Philip and Ethel Collier (no relation of the other Colliers in chapter 19), and after leaving school went to work at Church Farm when Jim Whitman was managing it for the owner, Munro Cuthbertson.

Jennie Waters (formerly Jennie Sinclair) used to visit the village as a child, and also attended the school, though not as an evacuee. When she was 17 she came here to live with and look after her aunt Kathleen. Her uncle and aunt, Bob and Kathleen Willmore, lived at 9 Hudnall Lane. Bob Willmore worked for Jim Whitman's cousin Fred Whitman the builder. Bob was a cabinet maker, originally trained as a wheelwright, and did carpentry work on the buildings. Ron and Jennie Waters were married in 1965 and went to live at their present home, 6 Chapel Close. Jennie worked as cleaner at the village school from 1972 to 1999, and worked with Val Janes with the Pre-School Group also up to 1999. Ron and Jennie's son Phillip is a chef at Ashridge College, and married to Ralph King's daughter Tamsin.

Hospital. Their daughter Kate works in Berkhamsted. They have two cats of no identifiable breed, aged 17 and 14, who are the true owners of Highfield.

The Turners are building a conservatory onto the west side of the house and intend to grass over the large vegetable garden which has never successfully grown anything but weeds!

The Whitman family

See also the information on Hudnall Common Farm and Church Farm (chapter 14) and Frederick Whitman's buildings (page 47)

In the 1891 census, in Hudnall, Ringshall and Coldharbour there were 21 Whitmans recorded (none in Little Gaddesden proper): four heads of families, their four wives, and 13 unmarried Whitmans, of whom seven were girls aged from 9 to 22. A search through the subsequent parish registers may reveal which other village families some of these must have married into. We also know that Emma Oakins (aged 42 that year) and her sister Liz White were born Whitmans. Of the 19 of these who were born Whitman, 11 or 12 were born in Hudnall. The only decendants that I have been told about still living in the parish are those of Emma Oakins (see chapter 20).

Jim Whitman, who died in 1962, mentioned as the mid-twentieth century farm manager at Church Farm, was the son of Joe Whitman, so quite possibly the Joseph at no.3 Hudnall in 1891 and his wife Susan, then aged 26 and 33.

Frederick George Whitman, the twentieth century builder, although 3 or 4 years old in 1891, is not mentioned in the census, nor is his father George, who would have been 28 or 29. (There is another Fred, aged four, but he is recorded as the son of William (aged 26) and Belinda Whitman of Shepherd's Cottage, Coldharbour.)

Freda Morris of Aylesbury has provided information about her branch of the Whitman family, starting with her grandfather, the above-mentioned George Whitman, 1862 to 1911. He was both a builder and a farmer, and so was his son Frederick George Whitman (1887 to 1961), whose buildings are found everywhere in the village.

F.G.Whitman (Fred) and his wife Emily lived at Hudnall Common Farm from 1911. (At the time of his eldest daughter's wedding he was a Parish Councillor. - Ed)

by Freda Morris, daughter of Fred and Emily Whitman

At Hudnall we first got electricity and telephone in 1931. Our telephone number was 23. We first had our bathroom about this time. As children we were bathed in front of a lovely open fire. We took a lighted candle with us to bed; rooms were lit by lamps. Winters were much more severe: snow drifted and reached the top of farm buildings and Hudnall Lane would become blocked. Groceries were delivered and once a week we went by pony and trap to Berkhamsted dressed smartly and even wore gloves.

My grandfather and father had gone to Little Gaddesden School and so did we children: Lynda, Irene, Lena, Freda (myself) and George. (Lynda, Irene and Lena are all in the school photograph on page 154.) We walked to school in all weathers each way, taking a packed lunch with us. Miss Wright, the infant

teacher had the maypole early in May - we did love dancing and making pretty patterns on the pole with the ribbons.
I remember going to Aldbury Isolation Hospital when I had scarlet fever, and again when I had diphtheria. Books were burned and rooms fumigated. Mother paid 1d a week into a nurses' fund so that she would be able to have their help. Also 10s 6d for a doctor's visit.
The driver of our weekly bus would stop anywhere and even wait for passengers if necessary.

My children Jane, Brian and Susan Morris also went to Little Gaddesden School; Brian's children Andrea and Helen Morris went there (Brian's wife is Pam); and now Helen's son Tanis Parslow goes there, though they live in Hemel Hempstead. That's six generations of our family at the same school.

(Freda's sister Lena moved away in 1963 and her brother George in 1971.)

The Wooster Family

Arthur and Anne Wooster moved into Kingham's Meadow in June 1967 with their two small children (David aged 2 and Timmy aged 5 months). At that time Arthur was working as a director/cameraman in the documentary, sponsored and television film industry. His work included several Winter and Summer Olympic Games, Football World Cups and other sporting films. (He was a cameraman at the 1966 World Cup final at Wembley!) Around 1976 he became involved in the feature film industry working firstly as a cameraman for, amongst others, Robert Redford, Steve McQueen, John Schlessinger and, since 1980, as a Second Unit Director and Director of Photography. In this grade he has worked on 8 Bond films, as well as on productions for Richard Attenborough, Michael Apted, Andrew McLagen et al, and is now semi-retired with a boat in the Mediterranean which takes up much of his time. He received a BAFTA award in 1983 for 'services to the industry' and in 1994 the Royal Television Society honoured him with their Lighting Award for a Sharpe production. Anne also worked in the industry, initially as a freelance production manager and, for 8 years until she retired, as assistant to the producer in the same sports film company as David. She is also involved with many organisations in the village. Both children attended the village school, under Albert Williams, and went on to Halsey School in Hemel Hempstead. Amazingly they both joined the film industry - Tim on the camera side; he is now a camera operator and frequently works with his father - David on the production side; he has recently completed his first feature film as a producer. Arthur and Anne moved to Vine Cottage in 1993.

THE FAMILY OF OWEN WILLIAMS

by Rosemary Williams

In 1950 my husband and two sons came to live at 18/19 Little Gaddesden where I still live. It was a very different village, there was petrol rationing for one thing. We came because my husband, Owen, had spent many weekends at his father's cottage, Coppice Cottage in Ringshall and he loved the countryside as I did. Secondly Little Gaddesden is near London with easy access to the north of England. No Owen Williams would live south of the Thames! My father-in-law (also Owen) and husband were designing the M1 Motorway - the first 55 mile section was completed in 19 months and opened in 1959.

When they went to London they left their car in the front yard of the station with no parking fee. There were no objectons to motorways in those days. The M1 led on to Spaghetti Junction, also motorways in South Wales, all of easy access to Little Gaddesden.

Of my sons, one runs the firm in Birmingham, one lives in Australia, one at the moment temporarily with me and one near Wigginton, all engineers of one sort or another.

Families in residence for the whole of the 20th century

This chapter contains family trees all of which are structured as follows:

Bold face names have lived in Little Gaddesden

~denotes the approximate year

>denotes living in Little Gaddesden in December 1999

The Andrews family

INCLUDING JANES, DEAN, DREWITT, BANKS, CATCHPOLE AND GRIFFITHS

from information provided by various members

Thomas and Sarah Andrews were both born in Little Gaddesden. In 1891 they were living at no.37. Thomas was a tailor. Four of their children were there: Herbert, aged 14, was a general labourer, and Alice, Walter and Dora were still at school. Dora, aged 5, later became a teacher there herself, as Dora Drewitt, and lived at no.44. (See page 43 and 152). Her son, Geoffrey, painted the school murals shown on page 167.

Alice and three of the other children, Frances, Emily and Jane, all moved away to Hampshire eventually.

Their elder brother Leonard (born when they lived at no.6), was one of three gardeners living at "Ashridge Bothy" near Ashridge House in 1891. Aged 20, he was a garden journeyman. He went on to become garden foreman and married one of the Ashridge housemaids, Ada Cooksey, who had come from Potterne, Wiltshire. They went to live at no.32 on the Green and later no.13. This was where Min Catchpole was born (as Minnie Andrews) in 1921, making her probably the oldest resident in the village to be living still in the house where she was born.

Herbert married Minnie Hing. They lived at no.50 and had no children.

There are many references to the Andrews family elsewhere in this book. For Leonard (Len) and Herbert (Bert), and Len's sons Fred and Alec, see pages 199, 217 on the Bridgewater Farm and the Manor House nursery. In later years Alec worked at Mr Cheshire's butchers shop at Hudnall and was well known on the delivery round. Alec and his son Colin no longer live in the village, but Colin Andrews is one of our doctors (see page 120).

Annie Dean from Dagnall came to live at Hall Farm, Ringshall with her husband Walter Janes. Her sister, Minnie Dean, went to Dunstable when she married Albert Banks, but their son Wilfred used to cycle up to Ringshall with his friends to meet his cousins, the Janes sisters, and thus also met his future wife, Kathleen Andrews. Evelyn Janes was organist at Dagnall, and taught the piano to Minnie Andrews and cycled over to Dunstable to teach Wilfred. Although not a resident of Little Gaddesden until recently, Wilfred, now aged 90, has been closely connected with the village all his life and has been a church organist here for over 65 years. In the early years of his marriage he used to cycle over with Kathleen on a tandem for the church services. He eventually became the principal organist, sharing duty with Doris Cocks for many years, and still, in 1999, plays on most Sundays. He lived and worked in Dunstable, being a teleprinter engineer with the G.P.O. and working on the meteorological office machines. During the war his work took him to the teleprinters at the code-breaking establishment at Bletchley Park. Wilf and Kathleen came to stay at the Robin Hood House Residential Home in the 1990's, and Kathleen died in 1998.

Wilfred Banks at Little Gaddesden Church in 1999

George Catchpole came to Little Gaddesden in 1936 from Norfolk, first to thatch the house "Theccans", but then settled in Ringshall while working for Vauxhall in Luton. After war service he went into the building trade, starting with Fred Whitman, but later setting up on his own, and marrying Min Andrews. He became a churchwarden and a bell-ringer, followed in the latter

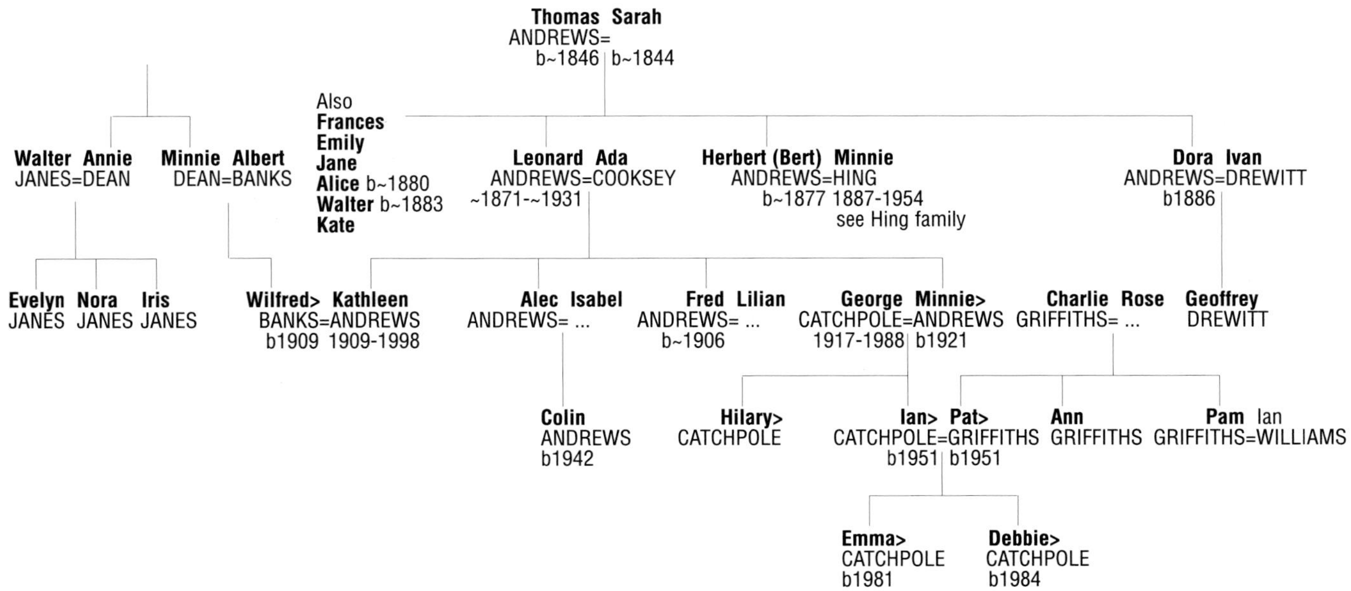

activity by his son and grand-daughter. (See page 139). See also pages 43, 84, 101, for recollections of the village school by three generations of this family, and page 136 re the Sword and Keys Society by Ian Catchpole.

Charlie and Rose Griffiths came to Little Gaddesden in 1958, Charlie as porter and driver to Ashridge College.

The Fountain family

INCLUDING COCKS AND STINTON

by Janet Stinton

The Fountain family were mentioned in the church records in 1687, while in 1891 there were three familes named Fountain in Ringshall including my great grandparents and their family at no.5, where my great grandmother Susan was the grocer. Alfred and Susan Fountain had twelve children between 1871 and 1893 all of whom were alive and many still living at no.5 in the year 1900. In 1910 Richard Fountain (child no.9) married Everelda Winter, and Doris, their only daughter, was born in 1911. Everelda became the shopkeeper at Fountain's Stores. Doris married Frank Cocks in 1939 and Janet was born in 1940 and Susan in 1941. Janet married Mike Stinton in 1964 and Mark was born in 1966 and Barry in 1968.

Being born in 1940, in my childhood all the gardens were full of fruit and vegetables and we kept chickens and pigs, so we were never short of fresh food. We also went gleaning and collecting rose hips, blackberries, raspberries, mushrooms, elderflowers and berries, and collected firewood in our home-made "truck". Everyone knew everyone and Mr Parker, later Mr Sherringham, were always around the village keeping us in order and were a very good deterrent to misbehaviour. I spent many happy hours at the Rectory nursery with Mrs Wager and went to the village school (often accompanied by Bob - the spaniel from the laundry) where Mrs Drewitt called me Doris because she had taught my mother. We lived with my grandparents and I certainly got my love of gardening from my grandfather.

My father Frank Cocks came to live in Ringshall in 1939 when he married my mother. He was away until 1945 during the war and came back to work at the post office when it was at no.15 Little Gaddesden before taking over Fountain's Stores with Doris. (See page 181 about the shop). He was a regular member of the church choir and either acted or sang in nearly every Drama Club production. He was a playing member of the Football Club, the Tennis Club and the Artisans Golf Club.

My mother Doris Cocks lived at no.5 until 1973 when she went to The Haven in Beacon Road, then to Bede Court and finally to Robin Hood House. When she left Little Gaddesden School she went to work at Sharlands in Berkhamsted - cycling there and back every day - where she was an excellent seamstress. She was the "second organist" at the church for many years. She was one of the "village pianists" and played both the piano and the piano-accordion at many social events. (She also played the violin.) She was a member of the Tennis Club, the Women's Institute, and pianist of the Drama Club.

When I got married in 1964 we moved to Houghton Regis because we could not afford anywhere in the village. Mike and myself, with Mark 6 and Barry 4 came back to live at no.5 in 1973 and lived with mum and dad until they moved to the Haven. Mark and Barry went to the village school - at least 5 generations at the school. Mike was one of the early members of the present tennis club and spent a lot of time coaching the youngsters and some not so young.

The family has been connected with the church for many generations, with many family members, such as my mother, being christened, confirmed, married and buried there, and there have been many of us in the choir.

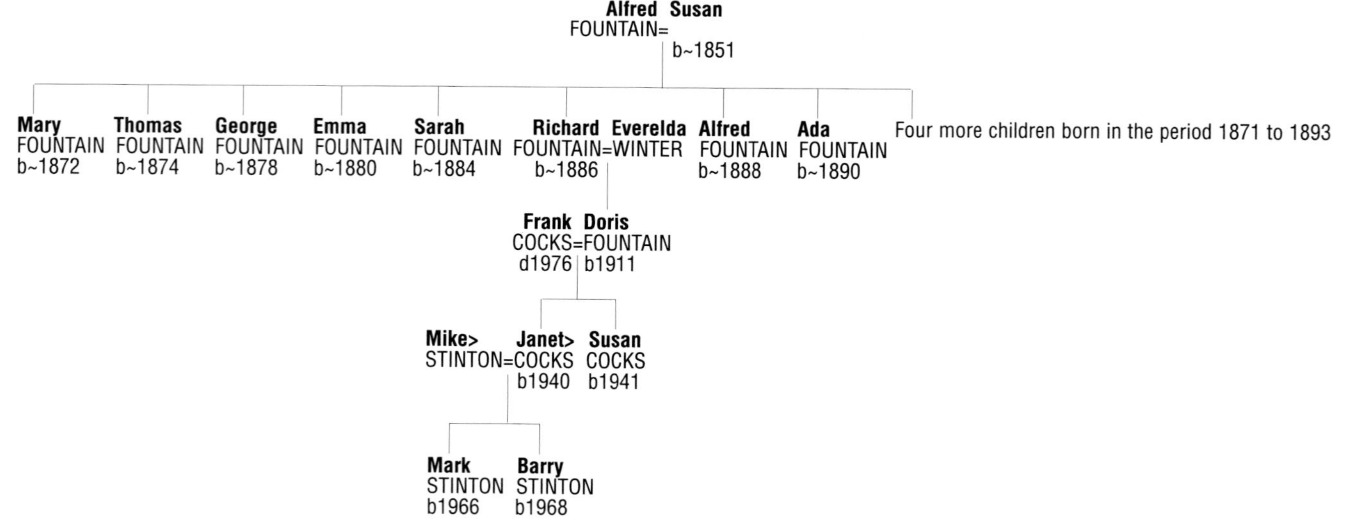

The families of Janes, Saunders, Stanbridge and Forster

from information from Geoff and Wendy Forster

The following notes should be read in conjunction with the family tree in order to understand them fully.

Wendy Forster has ancestors in both the Janes and Saunders families who lived in the village over a hundred years ago.

David and Ellen Saunders, who were born in Ringshall and Aldbury respectively, lived at 9 Ringshall where at least some of their 5 children were born. In 1891 David, aged 69, was a road labourer. (In the 1891 census, no.9 was recorded as no.27). Rather surprisingly they had a 12-year-old grandson born in Scotland living with them, called John Black, a "farm labourer" although so young. He would presumably be Adelaide Saunders's son.

John Saunders worked at Ashridge, and at the 1891 census was recorded as a gardener, and his birthplace Dagnall. He and his wife Caroline lived at 35 Ringshall where some of their 6 children were born, though the last died at birth. In 1891 (when no.35 was recorded as no.1), Caroline and their third child Francis had already died, leaving four children living with their father. His daughter Adelaide, aged 19, was their housekeeper. She was born at Whipsnade. (One or both Adelaides may have been "Adilaid") James, aged 13, was a farm labourer, who later joined the Guards. Rose and Ellen were still at school. Rose later moved to Harpenden. Ellen married her cousin Edward, who set up a haulage business at no.35, in which their son Alec also worked when he was old enough, but he died of tuberculosis when only 25. Alec's sister Edna married into the butchers' family, Janes. Edna is living in Berkhamsted at the present day.

Fred Janes (the elder one) was a butcher at Eaton Bray before he came to Hudnall and took over Edward Hoar's shop some time before 1900. Edward Hoar at Hudnall Farm was a dealer in livestock, but there was no mention of a butcher's shop in the 1891 census. On February 9th 1899 George Stanbridge paid Fred Janes a £4 18s meat bill. (There was another Janes family, Walter and Annie, at Hall Farm Ringshall around 1900, but I have not heard of any connection between these families. See page 302 under Andrews family.)

The butcher's shop was at no.9 Hudnall. Three of Fred Janes's sons worked there: Fred the younger, Seth and Ernest. Ernest went to work at a butcher's in Watford, but he died in 1925. Seth took over the lease of no.9 from his parents. The landlord was Leonard Card of Hemel Hempstead.

It was Seth who married Edna Saunders in 1942. Their first child, Wendy, was born at 9 Hudnall and the second, Ernest, at 35 Ringshall, Edna's old family home. In 1947, five years after his father died, Seth and Edna also moved to a butcher's shop in Watford. They returned to 35 Ringshall in 1954 just after Edna's mother died. The Hudnall butcher's shop was taken over by Mr Stringer. (See page 177).

Seth's sister Madge married Alban Stanbridge, but they left the village. They had three children. Alban's father, George, is mentioned frequently in this book, see mainly "Church Farm" and chapter 2.

Wendy Janes, now Forster, has written two items in this book, (see pages 199 and 277) and with her husband Geoff is the only member of these families still

John Saunders 1848 - 1934

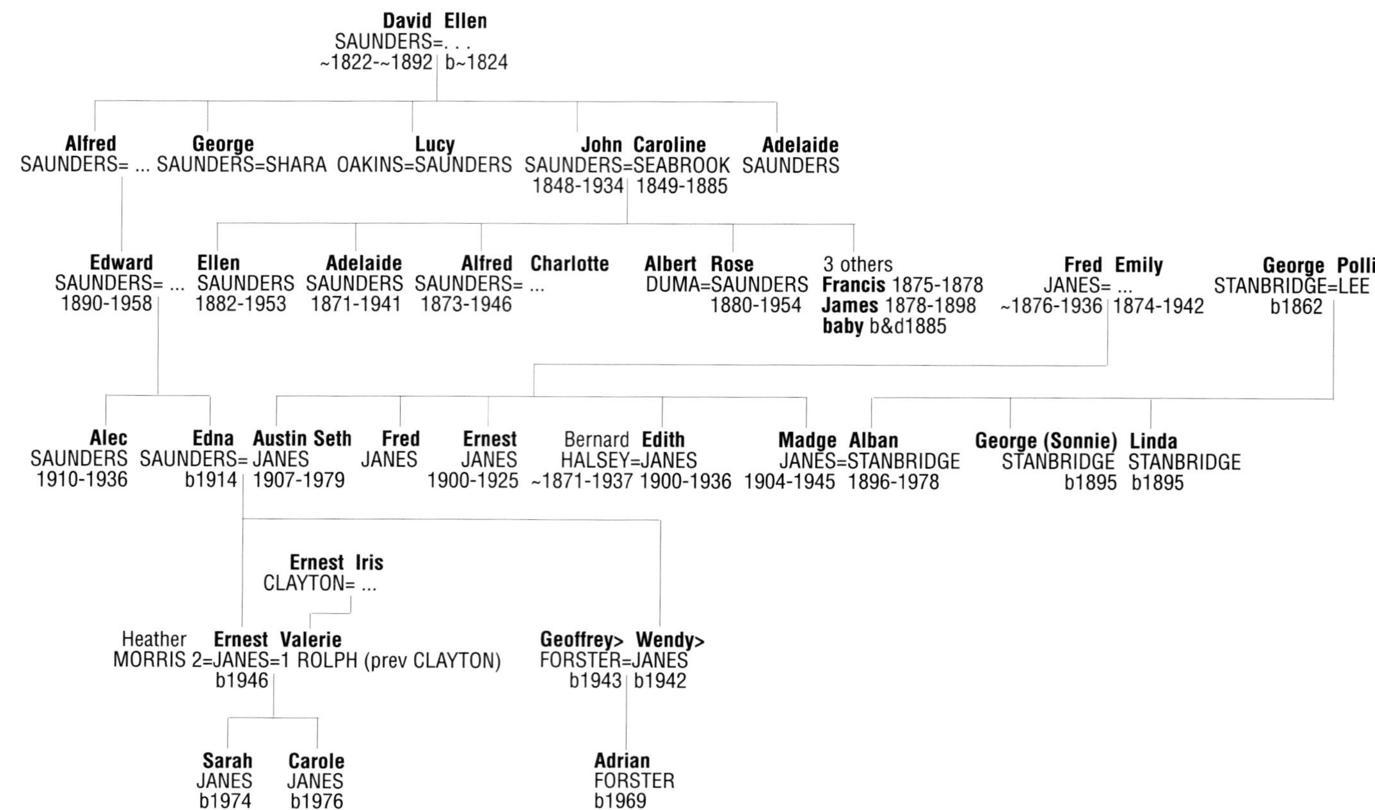

living in the village. She and Geoff lived at 10 Ringshall before moving to 3 Ringshall. Her brother Ernie, a professional photographer, has provided some of the wildlife photographs. He lived at 36 Little Gaddesden with his first wife, Valerie, who for many years ran the pre-school group in the village hall.

The Jones and Mogg families

by Barbara Mogg

The first part of the history of the Jones family in Little Gaddesden from1849 will be found in the section on smallholdings under 30 Ringshall. (Page 221). There follow here some details of those family members who continued in the village in other occupations.

Of George and Isabella Jones's five children, born in the 1890's to early 1900's, James and Harold left the village. Adelaide became a dressmaker. After her apprenticeship she was employed at Ashridge. She married Albert Batchelor. They had one son, Robert, and lived in Beacon Road. Robert built the house Smallmeadow. Kathleen trained as a teacher and during her studies became a

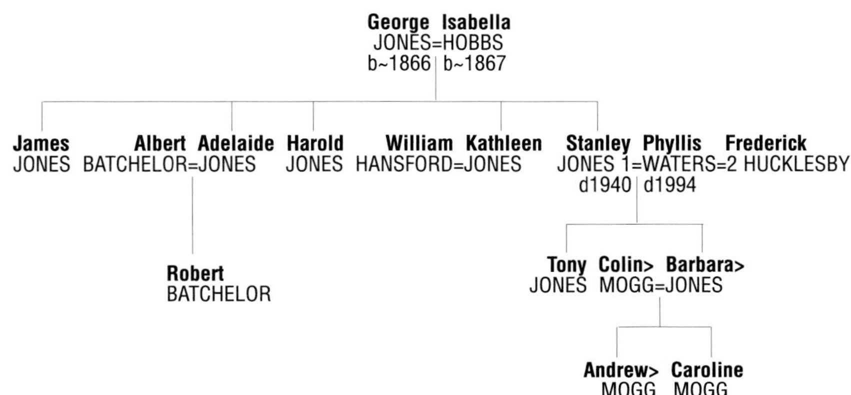

post woman employed by Robert Pratt (our village postmaster), her round including the village and Dagnall, 1916-1919. On qualifying she taught at the Council School in Berkhamsted. She married William Hansford and they lived at The Bungalow, Ringshall. She became Head Teacher of Dagnall School until her retirement in 1963. She had no children.

George and Isabella's other son was Stanley, my father, whose story is part of 30 Ringshall, so the continuation is from 1940 when he died, leaving my mother Phyllis and my brother Tony and me.

During the war we had evacuees, soldiers' wives, and people from London looking for relief from air raids, some of whom became life-long friends. I became a hairdresser in Berkhamsted. In 1953 I married Colin Mogg who had come to the village in the 1940's from Worcestershire. We were able to build a bungalow in the meadow, "Berrynarbor". We have two children, Andrew and Caroline. My brother left the village. Around 1963 no.30 Ringshall was sold and we built a second bungalow, Beechwood, for my mother who had re-married and was now Phyllis Hucklesby. Colin became self employed at this time as an electrical and plumbing engineer in the village and surrounding area until his retirement in 1994. Andrew became a telephone engineer with BT. He was also Youth Leader in the village during the 1980's. He also became self-employed, working with his father. In 1985 he was able to build a home, Wits End, Ringshall, thus making it possible to stay in the village and carry on the service. Caroline left the village. In 1994 my mother died and we now live at Beechwood, Ringshall. All members of our family attended Little Gaddesden School.

Emma Oakins and her daughter Edith Lilian (Lil) around 1890

The Oakins family

by Pat Creed (formerly Pat James)

Our family tree shows that the Oakins have lived between here, Great Gaddesden, Nettleden, Dagnall, Wardshurst and Ringshall since the end of the 1500's. Before that it is difficult to trace. My grandmother Emma's family, the Whitmans, seem to have been here from time immemorial. Our ancestors were labourers, farmers, wheelwrights, blacksmiths, hirers of agricultural equipment, lace makers, plaiters and many other occupations.

John T **Emma**
OAKINS=WHITMAN
~1840-1925 ~1849-1913

Liz
WHITE=WHITMAN

William OAKINS b1868 · **John** OAKINS b1869 · **Eliza** OAKINS b1871 · George **Ruth** SCUDDER=OAKINS 1876-1928 · **Stephen J** **Frances** OAKINS=SADD b1880 d~1970 · **Ernie** **Emmie Caroline** JAMES=OAKINS 1882-~1939 · **Samual G** **Ethel** OAKINS=LEE 1884-1917 · 4 more children · **Rosemary** b1872-d1894, **Hubert** b1874, **Elizabeth** b1885, **Edith Lilian** b1889

Thomas SCUDDER · Irene SCUDDER · **John** **Win>** OAKINS=BURCH 1910-1985 · William **Rosemary (Rose)>** MARKS=OAKINS b1913 · **Stephen** **Betsy** OAKINS=KING b1917 · **Douglas** **Pat>** CREED=JAMES d1975 · **Pelham** OAKINS b1912 · **Violet** OAKINS b1915 · **Samuel** OAKINS b1917

Gilbert **Pamela** VAUGHAN=OAKINS · **Jennifer** OAKINS · **John A** Wendy OAKINS=LEE · **Arnie>** **Lyn>** HYDE=OAKINS · **Ann** MARKS · **Peter>** MARKS · **Sandra** OAKINS · **Graham** OAKINS

Victoria> HYDE b1980 · **Robert>** HYDE b1982

The marriage of Ruth Oakins to George Scudder in 1910

Top row left to right: Stephen Oakins, Ethel and Sam Oakins, George and Ruth Scudder, George and Nance Dunn (née Oakins), Simmy Whitman (brother of Emma Oakins).

Bottom row left to right: John T Oakins, Lilian Oakins, Bob the dog, Caroline Oakins, Emma Oakins

It was in 1880 or 1881 that my grandfather John T. Oakins moved from Ringshall to no.1 Little Gaddesden as coachman to the Rector and my mother, Caroline, was the first to be born in the village. My grandmother died in 1913 and my mother had to walk to Edlesborough to register her death. Likewise, her younger sister Lil, who came home hurriedly because of her mother's illness, had to walk from Berkhamsted Station at midnight. My mother used to say her father was very strict. He was the Sexton and if children misbehaved in Church he would have them standing in front of the pews for the remainder of the service.

Eventually my grandfather moved to no.36 Little Gaddesden and, after his son Samuel was killed in 1917, his daughter-in-law. Ethel, kept house for him. He became Night Watchman at Ashridge and it was only after his daughters thought he was too old to work that he retired at 84.

Although I was born in London we spent much time in the village with my mother's family. My first outing was when my parents brought me at four weeks to Little Gaddesden to be christened. In those days Lewis Hing would meet you at Berkhamsted Station in his pony trap. As time went by it became an ancient motor car. I actually went to Little Gaddesden School for one day. They let me go the day of my grandfather's funeral in 1925.

My cousin Sam lived next to the Misses Munden's laundry, (they were at no.37), and used to deliver the laundry on Saturdays. Of course when we visited I would help. We always ended up at Pratt's shop, no.42, being served by Evelyn, and then we would sit in their porch gloating over our purchases. The shop included the Post Office where later my cousin Rose Oakins worked under the eagle eye of Miss Bevan. Miss Bevan later (at a very advanced age it seemed to me) became Mrs Cobb. She moved the Post Office to the front parlour of her house, no.15 Little Gaddesden, and later Harold Ward took over and stayed until he had the present Post Office built.

When Mrs Liberty at no.5 started her tea garden we would go for a penny glass of lemonade which we drank in great style in her garden.

Our highlights of the year were picnics at the Monument. I've photos of the big family parties we had there. I think the smallest children were carried part of the way but the distance didn't deter us. Another treat - usually on a Sunday afternoon - was going to the top of the Monument - cost 1d. Yet another treat was fossil hunting in the Park. I can remember running indoors when I was quite small because an aeroplane went over!

We loved going to Bert Andrews who kept the Manor House Nursery Gardens for our flowers, fruit and vegetables. It was also a reunion as he had been to school with my mother. Every afternoon at four o'clock we would collect the milk from Fred and Alec Andrews who farmed at the Bridgewater. Sometimes they would be a little late but we didn't mind as there were plenty of animals to see.

Although we lived in London we always had to go to Little Gaddesden for any celebrations so when, in 1935, George V had his Jubilee we naturally came to the village leaving London to its second class celebrations! I have photos taken with my box camera of the oldest inhabitant signing a message to the King, which we were informed would be taken by the King's Messenger. I imagined at least a knight in shining armour and was disappointed to find it was my Uncle Stephen, the local postman.

Whenever we visited my mother had to call on her relatives and the old ladies she knew. There was her Aunt Liz White who kept the Ringshall Laundry (Pear Tree House), Miss Saw also at Ringshall and numerous ladies who resided in the Bede Houses.

My mother died just before the 1939-45 war and although my father and I were bombed many times, it was only after we received a direct hit in 1944 that we came to the village to live. During the years 1939 to 1944 we were so grateful to my Aunt Fanny Oakins, who lived at no.11, for giving us a respite from the bombing for many weekends.

My cousin John and his wife Win lived next door (no.10). John was in the Army and out of the Country for some long time and Win filled her house with evacuees (as well as her own children) and also had their parents for weekends to give them a refuge from the London bombing.

My father, Ernie James, although born in Northampton, loved the village and was a founder member of the Over-60's and the VPA. He was also a keen bowler (when they played on the green at the Bridgewater) and as he had played first class cricket was always in demand for matches.

(See page 218 for details of Pat's flock of sheep.)

Stephen and Frances Oakins (centre) with their son John and his wife Win and one of their daughters, and their daughter Rose with her husband Bill Marks, 1939-1940

The Page family

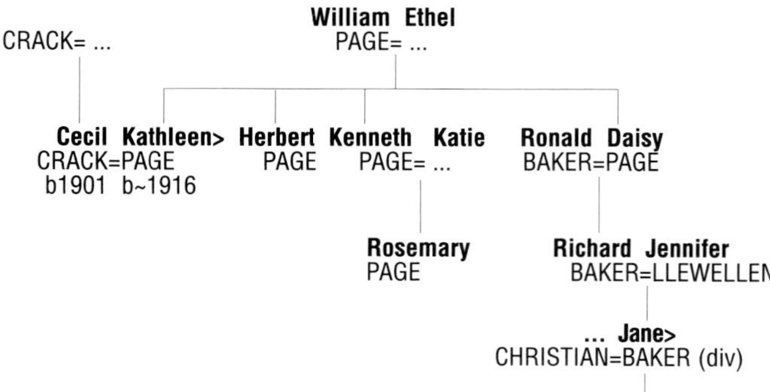

Information from Kathleen Crack and Jane Christian

William and Ethel Page came to Little Gaddesden in 1927, with four children: Kathleen, Herbert, Kenneth and Daisy. The family homes have been at Home Farm, Ashridge Park and Hudnall Lane. Kathleen married Cecil Crack who was born at 50 Little Gaddesden in 1901, and who had been the youngest boy to enroll in the Little Gaddesden Boy Scouts on the first day the Troop was formed in 1911. Cecil's father was a farm bailiff who used to ride on his horse to all the farms on the estate. Kathleen Crack is still living here, in Ashridge Cottages. She remembers:

"Miss Bridget Talbot would take some of the young people folk and country dancing; we had great fun dancing to a wind-up gramophone in the hall of her house, or on the lawn when it was fine."

Kenneth Page was an entomologist with Cooper's. He and his wife Katie had a daughter Rosemary. They moved to Berkhamsted in 1960. He retired in 1984 and died in 1986. Katie and her daughter now live in Spain.

Daisy Page married Ronald Baker and had a son Richard. Richard Baker married Jennifer Llewellen and had a daughter Jane. Richard and Jennifer also now live in Spain.

Jane Baker married, but divorced after five years, and is now Jane Christian, living in Cromer Close, where she has a daughter Daisy-Jane Lambert.

Nos. 5 and 6 Hudnall, where Heber and James Purton lived. This picture from the 1970s shows Kate Duncanson, the first owner of Hudnall Park.

The Purton and Liberty families

from a conversation with Mary Rogers (formerly Mary Purton)

Mary Rogers is the only known descendant of the Purton family still living in the village in 1999. Her grandfather, Heber Purton, was the brother of James Purton, the treasurer for forty years of the Hudnall Methodist Chapel. Mary remembers that the two brothers lived one in each of the two attached cottages, 5 and 6 Hudnall (now joined in one as "Hudnall House"). Back in 1891 Heber and his wife and their first two children, Ellen and Edwin, lived at Home Farm where he worked with horses. His wife Lizzie was formerly Lizzie Sams, and

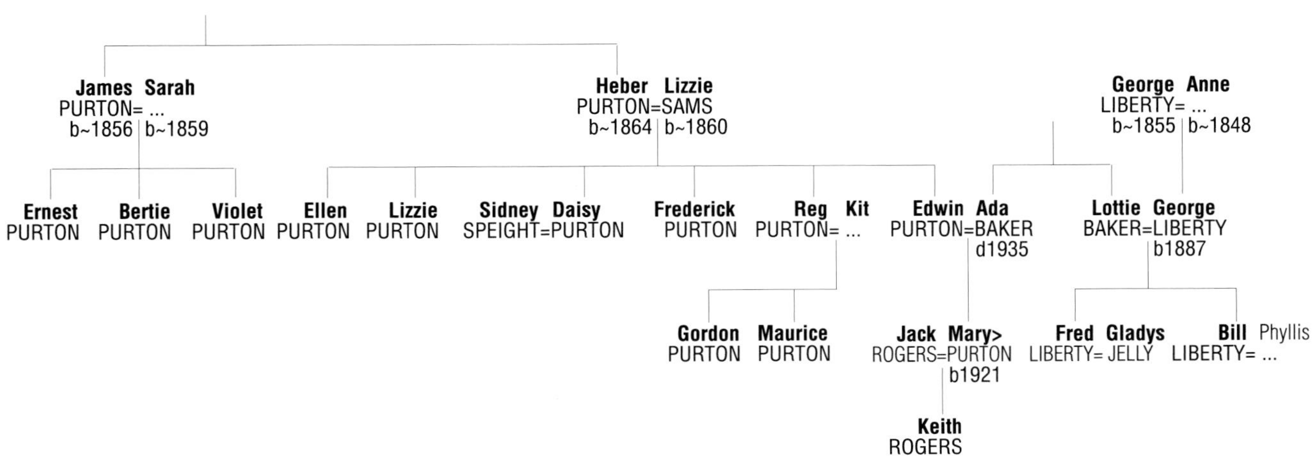

before her marriage had lived at Covetous Corner. Also in 1891 his brother James and his wife Sarah lived at no.8 Little Gaddesden with their first two children Ernest and Bertie. Mary could not recall the name of Heber and James's father, but he is buried at Nettleden. Heber and Lizzie had four more children, including Daisy, who married a soldier from Ashridge, Sidney Speight, and Reg, who went to live at 5 Chapel Close with his wife Kit.

Meanwhile a laundry-maid called Lottie Baker, who came from Grantham, was working for Lord and Lady Brownlow at Belton (which is near Grantham), and travelled with them to Ashridge in the course of her work. She met George Liberty, carpenter, who was born in 1887 at 8 Hudnall (Plum Tree Cottage), the son of George Liberty, forester, and Anne, his Durham-born wife. George junior and Lottie married and settled at 5 Little Gaddesden.

Lottie Liberty's tea garden there has been remembered on page 309. They brought up two sons in the village, Fred and Bill. Fred lived here for a while with his wife Gladys before they left the village, and Bill left when he married Phyllis.

Lottie' sister, Ada Baker, came down from Grantham on visits, and met Edwin Purton, another son of Heber and Lizzie. Edwin was a butcher. He married Ada just before the Great War, but after the war he was an invalid and went back with his wife to Grantham, and then worked on the railways at Nottingham. Edwin and Ada's daughter, Mary Purton, the source of these recollections, was 14 when her mother died in 1935, and she and her father returned to Little Gaddesden. They settled at no.1 Little Gaddesden which Heber had bought when the Ashridge estate was sold.

Mary married Jack Rogers, a Cornishman, and they had one son Keith who now lives in Surrey. Mary Rogers now lives in Cromer Close next door to the other Mary Rogers, who belongs to the next family in this chapter.

The Rogers and Orange families

See the family tree to clarify some of these notes.

Thomas Rogers and his wife lived at Well Farm in 1890 when their son Alfred was born, just outside our parish in Dagnall. He played the organ at Dagnall

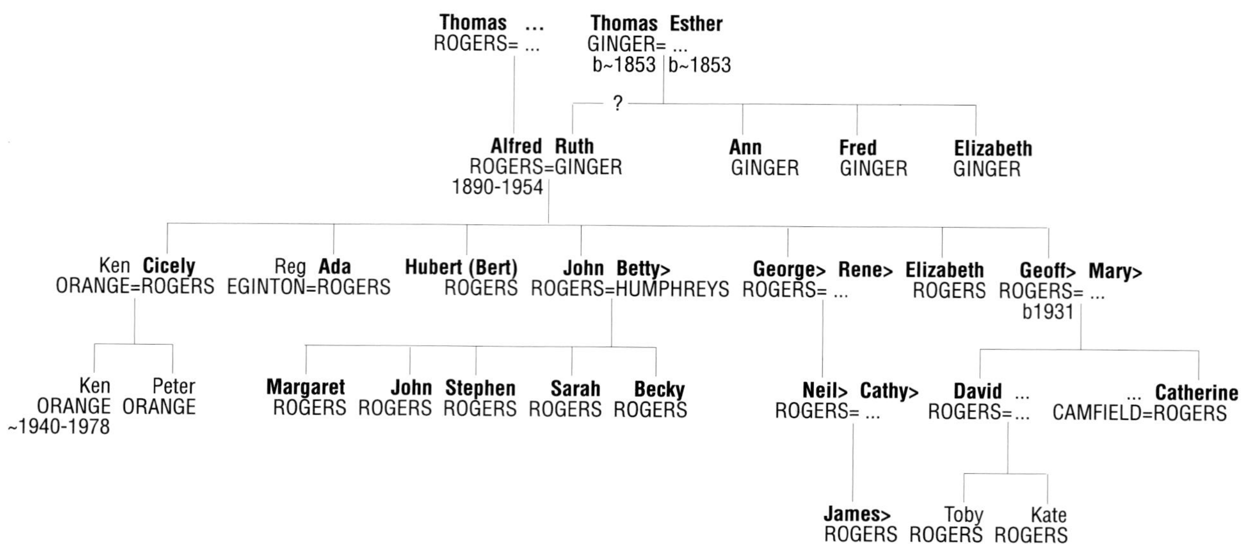

Church. Alfred grew up and married Ruth Ginger, one of an Eaton Bray family who had moved to 11 Ringshall. In 1891 the Ginger family at 11 Ringshall consisted of Thomas and Esther (the husband and wife) and children Ann, Fred and Elizabeth aged 16,11 and 9 respectively. Esther was born in Eaton Bray and her husband and children in Edlesborough. Another young Ginger, Hannah, aged 14 and born at Eaton Bray, was a living-in servant at no.14 Little Gaddesden. Ruth Ginger was therefore probably another child of Thomas and Esther, born after 1891.

Thomas Ginger was a labourer in the timber-yard and Esther was a straw-plaiter (one of only two left of what had in earlier times been a common occupation).

Alfred and Ruth lived at 3 Ringshall after their marriage, and there was a time when the family had 4 Ringshall also, and made a connecting door between them. Their three eldest children are in a Little Gaddesden school group photograph dated 1927. The eldest, Cicely, known as Cissie, married Ken Orange. One of their sons, also a Ken, was a cabinet maker, who died in 1978. The other, Peter Orange, is living in Dagnall.

Alfred and Ruth's second daughter, Ada, worked at the Ringshall laundry.

John Rogers married Betty, who has written about her experience here as a war-time evacuee. John worked at the butcher's shop in Hudnall and was working there for the last butcher, Mr Cheshire. Their five children have all left the village. John has died but Betty still lives in Chapel Close. Sarah Rogers, now Walters, has written about her schooldays, page 92.

George Rogers and his son Neil are farmers, and can be read about in the article on Goose Hill and Kilclooney Farms. Neil's wife Cathy is from Ireland. It is George who mows the village Green each year.

Geoff Rogers says "My grandfather and father were good hedge-layers and I have followed in their footsteps". Geoff has for many years been the chairman of the Village Produce Association, and Mary has been very actively involved in many societies including the VPA, Women's Institute and Drama Club. Geoff and his daughter Catherine have written their reminiscences (pages 61 and 91).

Their son David's children are at the village school. Mary and Geoff live in Cromer Close.

L to R:
Kneeling: Ray Hing, Bert Rogers,.
Sitting: John and George Rogers, in the 1930s.

The Talbot descendants

The information about this family will be found in Barbara Cassell's articles in the chronological section.

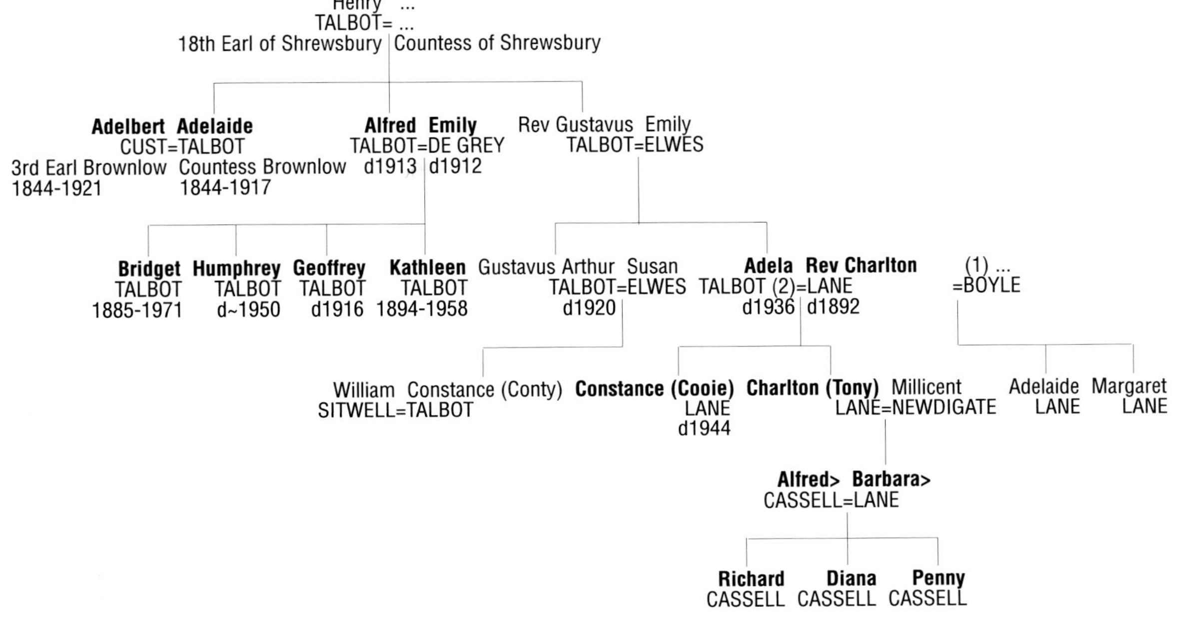

The cherry tree planted in Little Gaddesden churchyard in memory of the Talbots.

Reference

Woods and their owners

Badger Wood: The Mead family
Cromer Wood, most parts to south: The National Trust
Cromer Wood, part: Trafford Allen
Cromer Wood, part: other owners?
Hardings Rookery: The National Trust
Hill Wood, north-west part: Herts County Council
Hill Wood, greater part: Keith Blain
Hoo Wood: Richard Dunham
Hudnall Common Plantation: ?
Lady Grove: Now all enclosed in gardens of 3 houses
Levi Spring (outside the parish): Elizabeth Craib
Oakley Wood (outside the parish): George Rogers
Park Pulridge Wood, north part: Now enclosed in gardens of 5 houses
Park Pulridge Wood, remaining part: Neil Masters
Pitstone Park Copse, peripheral parts: Now enclosed in gardens of about 10 houses
Pitstone Park Copse, remaining parts: The National Trust
Pulridge Wood, north half: Keith Blain
Pulridge Wood, south half: Bob Mann
The Rookery, north part: The National Trust
The Rookery, south part: Ashridge College
Thunderdell Wood: The National Trust
Webb's Copse: The National Trust
Whitfield Spring: Herts County Council

The holders of archives

Not all of these archives have been referred to in compiling this book.

The holder of the archive is named first.

Ashridge College (Archivist in 1999 is Kay Sanecki): Historical records and books of all sorts.

The National Trust Ashridge Estate office, and regional office at Hughenden: Maps, photographs and other archives.

Wendy Forster and Ernest Janes: The Diaries of George Stanbridge, farmer of Church Farm Little Gaddesden (and formerly of Isle of Wight Farm, Kensworth). Hand written in thick exercise books 1891 to 1899, and in large diaries 1900 to 1916, mostly a good sized page for each day. Only the originals exist.

Hilary Catchpole: The Book of Little Gaddesden, compiled by the children of the Village School 1930-1937. Handwritten and illustrated on exercise paper, 150 pages, hand-bound into a leather-backed hard cover. Only the original exists.

Barbara Cassell: Album of Kathleen Talbot's productions of "The Masque of Comus" Mounted photographs, programmes, press reviews.

David Heard: Album of information about the servicemen commemorated on the village war memorial, including some photographs. The results of his own research.

Christine Francis: Scrap book of news cuttings about the village from about 1892 to 1985 compiled by Daisy Thorn. Mostly undated!

Hertfordshire County Record Office, Hertford: All the usual archives of such an office. Including: Little Gaddesden Scout Diary 1912 - 1922. Handwritten with pasted photographs and news cuttings, 54 pages. Photocopies (with poor copies of the pictures) are held by some current members of the scout group including Tim Cooper, Group Scout Leader.

Buckinghamshire County Record Office, Aylesbury: Archives relevant to those parts of the village which have been in Bucks, and parts of Ringshall which still are.

Secretary of the Parish Council (currently Eve Ouseley): Minutes and other documents.

Ken Dickson: Tape recordings of talks given by older residents to the school children, 1968-69.
+ Authorised copies of some of the census returns for more than a hundred years ago for the village. (All census returns over a hundred years old are held by the Public Record Office for public consultation.)
+ Various items resulting from his own research.

Lyn Hyde and John Leonhardt: Various other notes and records of the Cub Scout Pack and Scout Troop.

Sarah Gall: "Countess Brownlow". A story about "Billy", a fictitious London boy at the Countess Brownlow Home for Boys, by the late Sam Richards who really did stay there as a boy. Duplicated typescript, about 6 pages. Other copies must have been held or distributed by Sam Richards, Isle of Wight.

George Rogers: Map of Lord Brownlow's estate

Karoline O'Neill: Plan of the estate workshops at Red House.

John Wilson: "Ashridge Park": Development brochure for the sale of building plots on the estate, 1930. 50 pages liberally illustrated with photographs of the park and architectural drawings of suggested mansions. Plus 14-page Auction Particulars.

Alan Bunting: Auction books for the sale of the pedigree herds and flocks of Home Farm, 1960.

The Rural Heritage Society: Past copies of the RHS Newsletter.
+ Unedited handwritten and typed originals of many of the articles submitted for this book.

Editor of the Gaddesden Diary (currently Margaret Crawford): Past copies of the Gaddesden Diary

Mary Lishman: Old posters of the Gaddesden Society

Secretaries, Chairmen etc of various other societies, such as VPA, Art Club and Drama Group have their respective archives.

The Parish Church Officers: Registers of baptisms, marriages, funerals and burials.
+ Past copies of the Parish News and pre 1977 copies of Berkhamsted Deanery Magazine.

Little Gaddesden Village School Governors and Archivist, currently David Heard: All the usual school records, including historic head teachers' log books.
+ Album of annotated photographs covering the history of the school.

Peter Allen: John O'Gaddesden's House, Little Gaddesden, 1899 to 1999. By Peter Allen. Computer-printed text, 6 pages plus loose illustrations.

Hudnall Park Outdoor Centre: Meteorological records from 1977, collection of specialised local maps, records of local field observations in various studies, and sundry other collected books and documents of local interest.

Sarah Godar: Rurality in the Home Counties - Does Little Gaddesden in Hertfordshire still display traditional village characteristics today? By Sarah Godar, 1997. An academic study. Computer-printed with diagrams, maps and photographs, partly in colour, 60 pages. The Rural Heritage Society hold a good quality copy.

Bibliography

Richard BAGSHAWE "Roman Roads", pub. 1979 by Shire Publications in the Shire Archaeology Series. (Shows routes of two Roman roads through Little Gaddesden and photo of a milling stone found at Ringshall)

Vicars BELL "Little Gaddesden - The Story of an English Parish", pub. 1949 by Faber and Faber

Vicars BELL "Orlando and Rosalind" (A Play for Children), illustrated by Dorothea PATTERSON

Vicars BELL "To Meet Mr Ellis - Little Gaddesden in the Eighteenth Century"

Vicars BELL "That Night - a Play for the Nativity", pub. 1959 by Faber and Faber

Vicars BELL "The Dodo - The Story of a Village Schoolmaster", pub 1950 by Faber and Faber

Colin BOURNE (editor) "The Dunstable Methodist Circuit - One hundred and fifty years of witness 1843-1993", pub. 1993 by the Dunstable Methodist Circuit, ISBN 0 9520917 0 4

Douglas COULT "A Prospect of Ashridge", pub. 1980 by Phillimore & Co., ISBN 0 85033 360 1

Jack MOLYNEUX; edited by J. FAIRFAX-BLAKEBOROUGH "Thirty Years a Hunt Servant, being the Memoirs of Jack Molyneux", pub. 1935 by Hutchinson

Bernard FALK "The Bridgewater Millions", pub 1942

Doris FENN "The Ashridge Estate and Little Gaddesden 1915-1955 - A Personal History of Village Life", pub. 1996 by Mike Kearney DeskTop Publishing, Southampton.

Scott HASTIE and David SPAIN "A Hertfordshire Valley", pub 1996 by Alpine Press. (The subject is actually two valleys: Gade and Bulbourne, and has 14 pages and 41 pictures in the Little Gaddesden and Ashridge chapters.) ISBN 0-9528631-0-3

Dennis LITTLEBOY "On Being Evacuated", printed in the 1990's privately (A personal account of life as a Chiswick schoolboy in Little Gaddesden, written 50 years later.)

George U. ROBINS "Lays of the Hertfordshire Hunt and Other Poems", pub. 1916 by Arthur L. Humphreys

Kay SANECKI "Ashridge - a Living History", pub. 1996 by Phillimore & Co., ISBN 1-86077-020-7

The Revd Canon Howard SENAR "Little Gaddesden Parish Church (St Peter and St Paul)", 1980. (A guide booklet with architectural, furnishing and historical information.)

The Revd Canon Howard SENAR "Little Gaddesden and Ashridge", pub. 1983 by Phillimore & Co., ISBN 0 85033 460 8. (With photographs by Ernest JANES.)

The VIATORES (R.W. BAGSHAWE, D.B. BAKER, G.R. ELVEY, C.W.GREEN, D.E. JOHNSTON, C. MORRIS, E.V. PARROTT, and R.H. REID) "Roman Roads in the South-east Midlands" pub. 1964 by Gollancz

No named author "Ashridge Golf Club 1932-1982", pub. 1982 by Ashridge Golf Club

CURRENT PERIODICALS:
The Gaddesden Diary, published quarterly by the Gaddesden Society since 1955
Parish News, published monthly by the Parish Church since February 1977.
Rural Heritage Society Newsletter, published once or twice a year since 1975

Acknowledgements for pictures

p/b: provided by
t/b: taken by
o/f: originally from
d/b: drawn by:
pt/b: painted by
m/b: made by
Page number where picture is located, and positon:
T,B: top,bottom
L,R: left,right
C: centre
Roman Numerals: Colour section between pages 288 and 289

PICTURES HAVE BEEN PROVIDED BY THE FOLLOWING:

p/b Richard Abraham: 172T,250B
p/b Peter Allen: 263,265,266L
Ashridge College archives: 141 to 150 (except 143,146), ,XV.CR,XIV.T & B, XVI.B
p/b Wilfred Banks: 302
p/b Dorreen Barrington: 233B
Berkhamsted and District Local History Society: 77T
Permission of Berkhamsted Gazette: 242,245T,274
p/b Patsy Blackmore: 260
p/b Sarah Brattle: 11T,12B two,13 all, 15,79,124R
p/b Ron Brooks:187 both,189T
p/b Alan Bunting: 185,208 both,209TR & C,234L
d/b Paul Burdess: 172B
p/b Barbara Cassell: 20,80B,81 both
p/b Hilary Catchpole from school book: 123T & B,124
p/b Ian & Pat Catchpole: 84T,102
p/b Min Catchpole: 43
p/b Beryl Catesby: 47T
p/b Clive Collier: 107T
p/b Robert Corby: 228
p/b Margaret Crawford: 85
p/b Pat Creed: 218C & B,307
p/b Robert Cullen: 253CR
pt/bTeddy Cusdin: 143
p/b Nicola Darragh-Haddow: 239B
p/b Ken Dickson: 97,99L & C,137 both, 151T
p/b Jeffery Ede: 146,165
p/b Clive Fleckney: 57T,193B,195
p/b Gill Fleckney 182C & B
p/b Foord-Kelcey family: 259
p/b Geoffrey Forster: 180B,305
p/b Wendy Forster: 58,152B,178T,180T,277BL
p/b Froebel Foundation: 174
p/b Sarah Gall: 44 both
p/b Madeleine Gilpin: 66 both,67 both
p/b Sue Godar: 248T
p/b Golf Club: 236B,237 both
p/b Peter Grainger: 247
t/b Peter Grainger: 31,33,131,132,138,XV.T,XV.CL,XV.B
p/b Roy Haldane: 179T
p/b David Heard: 27,28,29,72 both
p/b Willy Hill: 88
p/b Jeff Hing: 80T,295 both
t/b Eric Holland: 77T
p/b Antony Hopkins: 49T,50 both
p/b Jean How: 124L,239TL,TR & C
p/b Dilys Hudson: 11B
p/b Lyn Hyde: 14B,25,34,36,77B,244,308,309
p/b Ernie Janes: 90,main cover
t/b Ernie Janes: 283BL & BR,284,286, 287 both
p/b Ann Kirkpatrick: 272T & C,277B
Hudnall Park archive: 310
p/b Betty Lait: 109,272B
p/b Alice Leonhardt: 261
t/b Peter Leonhardt: 114
p/b Mary Lishman: 41B, 74 both, 75 both,76,258B,262
p/b Mr Lowe: 178C & B,257
p/b Michael McCaul: 230
p/b Baroness McIntosh: 158
p/b Freda Morris: 47B,48,140TL
p/b Stuart Oswald: 107B
m/b Dorothea Patterson: 130,137B,267,271
t/b Wallace Peters: XI.BL (three)
p/b Jean Ponder: 64
t/b Geoff Price: 112T
p/b Marilyn Price: 188
p/b Geoff Rogers: 60
p/b George Rogers: 206TL & C,234R, 312
p/b Neil Rogers: 206BL
School archive: 84B,151 both,152C, 154,155,156,159B,160,161,162, 163 both, 164 both,167C & B, 169 both,171,184B
p/b May Sears: 12T,30,39 both,40T, 153,154,251,252T
p/b Felicity Senar: 133,134T
Sword & Keys Society. album: 136 both, 137T
VPA archive: 252B,254B
p/b Jane Walker: 177B
p/b Gail Webster: 71 all
p/b Virginia Westmacott: 258T,XVI.T
pt/b Virginia Westmacott: 14C,248T
p/b Rosemary Williams: 47C
p/b David Williamson: 139B
Brochure p/b John Wilson: 14T,40B,41T,42 both,49B,279,280BL
p/b John Wilson: 192C,BL,194W
Women's Institute archive: 179B,248B,249,250T,XVI.C
The remaining pictures were provided by, and mainly taken by, the editor.